S. WILLOUGHBY   433-7652

D1412620

An Introduction to Business Decision Making

Text and Cases

Third Edition

An Introduction to Business Decision Making

Text and Cases

Third Edition

John A. Humphrey, D.B.A.
Associate Professor of Business Administration
School of Business Administration
The University of Western Ontario

Michael R. Pearce, D.B.A.
Associate Professor of Business Administration
School of Business Administration
The University of Western Ontario

David G. Burgoyne, M.B.A.
Associate Professor of Business Administration
School of Business Administration
The University of Western Ontario

James A. Erskine, D.B.A.
Associate Professor of Business Administration
School of Business Administration
The University of Western Ontario

Richard H. Mimick, M.B.A.
Adjunct Professor of Business Administration
School of Business Administration
The University of Western Ontario

Ⓝ Methuen

Toronto   New York   London   Sydney   Auckland

Copyright © 1985 by Methuen Publications
A division of the Carswell Company Limited

All rights reserved. No part of this publication may be reproduced, stored in a retrieval system or transmitted in any form or
by any means, electronic, mechanical, photocopying, recording
or otherwise, without the prior written permission of Methuen
Publications, 2330 Midland Avenue, Agincourt, Ontario,
Canada, M1S 1P7.

Canadian Cataloguing in Publication Data

Main entry under title:

An Introduction to business decision making

First ed. by M.R. Pearce, D.G. Burgoyne and
J.A. Humphrey.
Includes bibliographical references.
ISBN 0-458-98990-8.

1. Business — Case studies.   2. Industrial
management — Canada — Case studies.   3. Business —
Decision making — Case studies.   I. Humphrey,
John A., 1937–   . II. Pearce, Michael R., 1946–
An introduction to business decision making.

HF5351.P42   1985   658.4′03   C84-099754-X

Printed and bound in Canada

1 2 3 4   85   89 88 87 86

CONTENTS

   * Note: Cases 18, 44, 54, 63, and 68 can be used in this section.

Case Contributors

R. Archibald	E. W. Lancaster
T. Bauer	M. R. Leenders
B. Behan	R. A. Lefebvre
G. Boydell	D. S. R. Leighton
B. S. Bruce	J. C. Lemmon
D. G. Burgoyne	A. J. Magrath
T. F. Cawsey	R. M. Malanchuk
S. N. Chakravorti	F. A. Mastrandrea
J. J. Dossett	J. McNee
D. Elgie	R. H. Mimick
J. A. Erskine	R. E. Oliver
B. Floyd	R. W. Orser
S. Foerster	D. A. Peach
G. R. Forsyth	M. R. Pearce
D. Francis	J. K. Pliniussen
J. Gandz	I. Rankin
T. L. Green	O. Richardson
M. G. Hagerman	C. D. Riegel
K. G. Hardy	D. M. Town
S. M. Head	H. Uren
G. R. Higgins	M. Vandenbosch
J. A. Humphrey	J. Walsh
D. G. Hyde	M. G. Webb
V. Jeffery	J. J. Wettlaufer
F. W. P. Jones	Government of Canada
T. C. Kinnear	Harper and Row Publishers
R. M. Knight	Richard D. Irwin Inc.

The cases presented in this book were prepared to provide a basis for discussion and were not designed as illustrations of either correct or incorrect handling of administrative problems. In some instances, people, places, and data have been disguised.

To: Lib
Michelle and David
Gerd
Heather
Claudia

PREFACE TO THE THIRD EDITION

A number of improvements have been made to the third edition of *An Introduction to Business Decision Making: Text and Cases*. These improvements reflect the many hours of dedicated teaching and case development by faculty using the second edition. In particular, the authors would like to thank the following:

Connie Badame	Dana Hyde
Gregory Barron	Frank Mastrandrea
Jeffrey Dossett	James McNee
Stephen Foerster	Jeffrey Murray
Chris Graham	Gregory Scott
Terry Green	David Town
Michael Guolla	Mary Ann Vandenbosch
Sonya Head	John Walsh
Gerald Higgins	

The above are the latest group of young people who have dedicated significant energy and enthusiasm to teaching the Business 020 course at the University of Western Ontario.

The authors would be remiss if they did not acknowledge the continuing support of Betty Freeborn, who for one decade has been the secretarial support for the Business 020 teaching faculty. In addition, the authors received competent, willing help from their own secretaries: Connie Irwin, Linda Minutillo, Betty Pennings, Pat Neatby, and Gerri Teal. Anna Currie, Jean Fish, and Ken Woytaz of the Word Processing Centre patiently typed, and retyped, the production copy of the teachers' manual.

The third edition has improved each text section, added twenty-five new cases, and revised six cases. All new cases are Canadian companies. A number of the new cases reflect the increasing involvement of women in the creation and development of businesses.

The authors have found working on an introductory business case book a challenging and worthwhile experience. We've always found young students eager to explore the challenge of making decisions in an uncertain world. We hope this revised edition will continue to engage their energies and enthusiasm for business decision making.

John A. Humphrey
Michael R. Pearce
David G. Burgoyne
James A. Erskine
Richard H. Mimick

London, Ontario, 1984

PREFACE TO THE SECOND EDITION

This book is designed for students embarking on their first case study course in management. Such a course (Business 020) has been offered at the School of Business Administration, The University of Western Ontario, for almost fifty years. This experience clearly indicates that a certain amount of textual materials combined with a selection of real management problems ("cases") provide the blend both students and faculty find most effective and exciting.

This is predominantly a casebook. It represents the culmination of a great deal of effort by many people. Most of their names are listed in the table of contents, but we would like to add a few comments of appreciation here.

First, this book is in the tradition established by its predecessors, *Canadian Business Administration*, published in 1957, and *Business Administration in Canada*, originally published in 1961. The pedagogical foundation laid by Professors W.A. Thompson, L.W. Sipherd, D.H. Thain, J.J. Wettlaufer, S.A. Martin, and M.R. Leenders is much in evidence and greatly appreciated.

Second, real management problems could not be presented as case studies without the full cooperation and participation of numerous managers. Their willingness to contribute time, information, and financial assistance has enabled us to offer a variety of contemporary problems to the student. We think this is essential to an informed understanding of how business operates today.

Third, many hours have been spent by our Business 020 faculty in the past few years to make this collection of material pedagogically effective. These faculty members have researched, written, tried, criticized, and rewritten materials in this book. Any attempt to acknowledge specific contributions to the textual materials would not fully recognize the team effort involved. Further, since Business 020 faculty are graduates of Western, their treatment of materials has been significantly influenced by their ongoing involvement with all the faculty of this school. Those involved in the process include Gary Boydell, Barry Bruce, Marilyn Campbell, Michael Conlin, John Craven, Robin Dow, Michael Hagerman, Rudi Kuhlman, Rick Lancaster, Ron Lefebvre, Chuck Lemmon, Bob Malanchuk, Rick Nesbitt, John Pliniussen, Dale Oliver, Rob Orser, Olga Richardson, Mark Webb, Steve Wilkinson, and Kevin Yousie.

Fourth, several other individuals have contributed meaningfully to this effort. Professors Al Mikalachki and David Peach helped us with the textual material. Cheryl Briglia, Linda Collins, Jean Fish, Betty Freeborn, Phyllis Jackson, Cathy Jillard, Judith Kerr, and Una Meyer have efficiently and willingly handled a heavy and hectic schedule in the preparation of the manuscript. Colonel Fraser Rowland, Professor Walter Thompson, and Professor Jack Wettlaufer have continued to provide a sterling example of concern for teaching an introductory course of high quality. Their leadership by example has inspired all of us. Dean C.B. Johnston and Associate Dean D.C. Shaw offered us every encouragement to complete this project.

We are indebted especially to the Associates' Plan for Excellence which has provided funds to support much of the school's case-writing activities. The Associates are a group of corporations and individuals that provide financial and other support to the school.

Finally, we are grateful for permission to reprint the "outside" cases. As noted in the table of contents, non-Western cases are included. We have found this outside material in problem solving complements our internally developed materials.

We appreciate the meaningful contributions of all these people but willingly take responsibility for any errors in this book.

We sincerely hope that this collection of text and cases will engage your attention, challenge your abilities, and improve your understanding of and skill in management decision making.

John A. Humphrey
Michael R. Pearce
David G. Burgoyne
James A. Erskine

London, Ontario, 1980

SECTION I
An Introduction to the Case Method

WHAT IS A CASE?

In this book, we use the term *case* to refer to a written description of an actual situation faced by a decision maker at some point in time. Although names, places, and other facts have sometimes been disguised at the request of the organizations involved, the cases in this book are real situations faced by real people. The objective of each case is to leave you at a decision point much like the one that the individual in the case actually confronted.

In each case situation, the decision maker was expected to analyze the situation, determine what problems and opportunities existed, generate and evaluate alternative courses of action, and recommend and implement a plan of action. The expectation is that you will go through this same process, except that you will not have the opportunity to actually implement action and see results.

A number of frustrations commonly plague decision makers as they grapple with problems: a shortage of good information on which to base decisions, a shortage of time in which to make decisions, uncertainty in how results will work out, and seldom any opportunity to reduce all of the uncertainty at a reasonable cost. You will experience these same frustrations because the cases give you the information the decision maker actually had, limit you with time pressures, and so on. In short, you will simulate the experience of decision making.

THE CASE METHOD

In fact, there is no one approach called the case method, but rather several variations on a theme. The general theme, however, is learning by doing rather than by listening. Class sessions are discussions, not lectures, with emphasis on developing skills in problem solving and decision making. A typical case discussion will involve students interacting with one another and with the instructor as everyone in the room works toward a solution of a particular problem being addressed. The student's role, then, is one of participation — active listening and talking. The instructor's role is to guide the discussion — to probe, question, and add some inputs.

Cases can be used in several ways. You will probably be asked to deal with cases in some or all of the following situations.

1. Individual preparation for a class discussion.
2. Small group discussion in preparation for a class discussion.
3. Class discussion.
4. Written report or in-class presentation of a case.
5. Written examination of your ability to handle a case.

Each of these situations is somewhat different and will require some variation in your approach. Your own instructor undoubtedly will have his or her own comments to add to the general comments we have written below for you about these different situations.

INDIVIDUAL PREPARATION FOR CLASS

Cases can be complicated and controversial. Your instructor may or may not assign specific questions for you to address as you prepare a case. When no questions are assigned, you must be ready in class to recommend what you would do as the decision maker and why. When questions are assigned, those questions should be considered as a means of assisting you in getting into the case and not as the limits of your preparation. Accordingly, each case should be regarded as a challenge to your ability to sort relevant from irrelevant information, to separate fact from opinion, to interpret information, to come to a reasoned course of action, and of course to communicate your thoughts persuasively during class discussions. Cases can also serve to communicate a good deal of descriptive information to you about a wide variety of institutions and business practices. Many cases are sufficiently complex to absorb all the preparation time you have available — and then some. Thus it is extremely important for you to develop skill in using your preparation time efficiently and effectively.

Much of your preparation time should be spent in interpreting information. In effect, the case presents facts and opinions. Your job is to become acquainted with those facts and opinions *and* to say what those facts and opinions mean when making decision choices.

The following steps are offered to help you in your individual case preparation.

1. Read the case once quickly to get an overview.
2. Skim the case exhibits, if there are any, just to see what is available.
3. Find out, frequently from the first few and last few paragraphs of the case, who the decision maker is; that is, the person you are supposed to be, what the immediate concern, problem, or issue appears to be, why this concern has arisen, and when the decision is to be made.
4. Read the case again more carefully. This time underline key information, make notes to yourself in the margin, and jot down ideas on a piece of paper as those ideas occur to you. At this stage you are trying to familiarize yourself as thoroughly as possible with the case information. Having done so, you are ready to begin your analysis.
5. Apply the problem-solving model which contains the following steps:
   a) What are the objectives of the organization? What does the organization do well? How do you know?
   b) What is the decision or the problem? How do you know? What is your evidence?
   c) What are the key relevant facts? Are these symptoms? Causes? What is your quantitative and qualitative size-up of strengths and weaknesses?
   d) What are the alternatives? Are they relevant to the problem at hand?
   e) What are the decision criteria?
   f) What is your analysis of the alternatives in view of the decision criteria? What are the pros and cons of each?

g) Which alternative or combination of alternatives do you recommend? Why?

h) What is your plan of action for implementation? Who, when, what, where, why, how?

i) What results do you expect? Why?

Watch out — the process of case preparation can be deceiving! Some students have thought they were on top of the situation without really doing much work. They read over cases rather casually once or twice, jot down a few ideas, go to class and listen to the discussion. As points come up they feel, "I touched on that" or "I would have reached the same conclusion if I had pushed the data a little further." When exam, report, or presentation time arrives and they are asked to do a case on their own, they find they are in serious difficulty. Such students spend all their time then trying to learn how to deal with a case, rather than dealing with the issues in the case for that testing occasion. This situation is not surprising since, in fact, this is the first case these students have really tried to do. They are in somewhat the same position as someone entered in a track event at an official track meet whose training consisted of watching others practise for a number of months.

SMALL GROUP PREPARATION FOR CLASS

Ideally, you will have an opportunity to discuss informally your preparation of a case with some of your classmates prior to the class. Many students find such study group sessions the most rewarding part of the case method experience. A good group session is a sharing situation in which you discover ideas you may have overlooked or not weighed heavily. Your colleagues will also benefit from your input.

The effectiveness of a small group case discussion can be increased substantially if you adhere seriously to the following guidelines.

1. Each individual must come to the group meeting with a thorough analysis of the case and understanding of any associated readings. The small group session is *not* the place to start preparing the case.

2. Each individual is expected to participate actively in the discussion. The small group discussion is an excellent place to check out your analysis before going into class.

3. It is not necessary to have a group leader in the sense of a decision maker. Everyone is responsible for making their own decisions based on what is said plus their own case analysis.

4. It is not necessary to have a recording secretary. Each individual is responsible for his or her own notes. It is important to be able to recognize a good idea when you hear one.

5. Consensus is normally not necessary. Everyone does not have to agree with everyone else.

6. Iron out individual disagreements after the small group discussion, especially if only one or two people are involved.

7. Set a time limit for discussion and stick to it. Effective small group case discussions can take less than thirty minutes.

Remember, two people can be a group. Spend some time with a friend over the phone or face to face reviewing your respective case analyses. You will feel better about your own preparation and be more confident in contributing to the class discussion.

CLASS DISCUSSION

In actual situations when managers address the issues represented in these cases, there are nearly always different views on interpretation of data and on what could and should be done. Therefore, you should expect that during a case discussion your classmates will express several different views. The essence of the case method is the process of stating points of view, defending positions, and listening actively so as to understand and constructively criticize the positions of others. Rarely will you leave the classroom unchanged in your position or perspective after discussing a case.

However, in spite of the common interest of all class members in resolving the case issues and in spite of the guidance of the instructor, sometimes class discussions will seem repetitious and unorganized. This is unavoidable and natural, especially during the early stages of a course. Over time, as a group develops its group decision-making ability, case discussions will be more orderly, efficient, and satisfying to all.

The need to be a skilful communicator arises repeatedly in management, and the case method presents an ideal opportunity to practise talking and listening skills. For some, talking in a group situation is difficult and threatening. Such individuals avoid talking in class even though they realize they are not getting full value out of the experience. If you are one of these individuals, the only way to overcome this problem is to jump in and begin. Make a habit of participating regularly in class. Do not wait until you have a major presentation to make where you will hold the floor for a lengthy period. Adding a key piece of information or questioning something can be done in a few sentences and may be the best way for you to begin active involvement. Your instructor and your classmates will be supportive of your efforts. Remember, the classroom is a place where we can learn from one another's mistakes as much as, or more than, from one another's correct solutions. The cost of making a mistake in class is minimal, relative to an actual situation. For others, listening is a poorly developed skill. Some individuals, in fact, do not listen: they simply wait for their turn to talk. The case method depends on the willing interaction of the students. Without that essential ingredient, the cases become interesting stories rather than opportunities to develop the ability to make and argue for management decisions.

Students, not surprisingly, are interested in learning "what actually happened" or what the instructor would do. Rarely will this be forthcoming. The learning is in the process and habit of making decisions, not in reviewing what others decided to do.

AFTER CLASS

After class take a few minutes to analyze your preparation in comparison to what happened in class. Was your preparation in the ball park or inadequate? Did you spend enough time preparing individually? Was your small group session effective? What can you do better next time? What generalizable lessons were learned? For example, while you may not be interested in remembering how the market for athletic shoes is segmented, you should be interested in remembering how to segment a market.

REPORTS, PRESENTATIONS, AND EXAMINATIONS

In a typical class discussion of a case, exactly what gets done is a function of the students — what preparation was done, who actively participated in the discussion, how one person related to the previous comments of another, and so on — and of the instructor — his or her pedagogical objectives and performance as a moderator and discussion traffic cop. Instructors view a case course as a sequence of problems that gradually foster the development of decision-making skills. With this longer time horizon, instructors often find it advisable to emphasize a specific analytical technique on one occasion, problem identification on another occasion, and so on. Thus it is possible that many class sessions are not complete, balanced developments of a case analysis and plan of action.

On the other hand, instructors frequently wish to provide opportunities for more complete, balanced treatment of cases. Sometimes instructors allow extra preparation time and ask for an oral presentation of a case by an individual or group. Sometimes instructors require students to prepare a written report to management on how they would handle a particular situation and why. And frequently case method courses have cases as examinations: students are given a case and asked to "do whatever analysis and make whatever recommendations you deem appropriate."

In reports, presentations, and examinations, instructors generally expect more complete, balanced arguments for a particular course of action. Such exercises are not intended to result in a diary of how a student or group looked at a case nor a rewritten version of the case. A report, presentation, or examination is supposed to be a concise, coherent exposition of what to do and why. In fact, a good report, presentation, or exam usually starts where most students leave off in their regular individual preparation for a case class. In short, think of a report, presentation, or examination as an organized, more fully developed (and perhaps rewritten) version of your regular class preparation notes.

You will find your audience — instructor, business executive, or whoever — has particular ideas about how a report, presentation, or examination should be organized. We urge you to find out as much as you can about format expectations, etc., before embarking on your task. In general, we counsel students to prepare such efforts with the following format: (a) executive summary (written last but appearing first); (b) statement of problem, opportunity, and objectives; (c) identification and analysis of alternatives; and (d) recommendations and implications.

SECTION II
An Introduction to Financial Statements

The purpose of this chapter is to introduce and explain financial statements, which give a picture of a company's operating results and its financial condition.
This chapter will discuss:

1. The balance sheet.
2. The income statement.
3. The statement of retained earnings.

All incorporated companies are obliged by law to provide annual financial statements to their shareholders. This information is usually presented in a firm's annual report. In addition to financial statements, these reports often contain a message from the president describing the corporation's past and planned activities including new product developments, plant expansion, and assessment of changes in market conditions.

The balance sheet, the income statement, and the statement of retained earnings provide the basic information which a business person, investor, lender, or shareholder needs to gauge the financial well-being of a company. Learning and understanding financial statements is not difficult.

This chapter will concentrate on the definition of the three financial statements. The "Introduction to Financial Management" chapter will focus on analyzing these statements and the statement of changes in financial position. Proper use of financial tools aids financial decision making. However, before analytical concepts can be used for decision making, there must be understanding of the basic financial vocabulary and the relationships between different statements and terms.

PART 1: THE BALANCE SHEET

The balance sheet presents the financial position of an enterprise as of a particular day, such as December 31, 1984. It is like a photograph of a firm's financial condition at a particular point in time.

The purpose of a balance sheet is to show what a company owns and what it owes. Assets represent economic benefits. The assets — what a company owns — are listed on the left side of the statement. The liabilities — what a company owes — are listed on the right side. The net worth (known as shareholders' equity for incorporated companies) — the difference between what a company owns and what it owes — is also listed on the right side. Both sides are always in balance.

Assets represent all the physical goods and things of value "owned" by the company. Assets include finished and unfinished inventory, land, building, equipment, cash, and money owed to the company from credit sales or money lent to others.

Liabilities consist of all debts or claims "owed" by the company, such as loans from the bank, and unpaid accounts due to suppliers.

Shareholders' equity (net worth) represents the interest, stake, or claim the owners have in the company. It is the owners' original investment plus (minus) the accumulation of all profits (losses) that have been retained in the firm since the company's inception.

Individuals can formulate personal balance sheets. What does it mean when Howard Hughes's net worth was estimated at several billion dollars? This amount is what is left when his liabilities (debts) are subtracted from his assets, physical holdings, cash, and any money owed to him.

Before studying a business balance sheet, try to formulate your own personal balance sheet. As a suggestion, first list your assets or things of value. After totalling your assets, list the credit claims against those assets. Such claims may be government loans to further your education or loans to purchase some of the assets you have listed previously. Subtract the total of the liabilities from your assets. The residual is your net worth, or equity. The net worth represents your claim as owner against the assets.

Another more complicated balance sheet is presented for XYZ Manufacturing Co. as of December 31, 1984 (Exhibit 1). Each of the XYZ accounts will be discussed in turn.

ASSETS

The size of the company is often measured in terms of its assets. Two major categories of assets are current assets and property, plant, and equipment (or fixed assets).

CURRENT ASSETS

Current assets include cash and items which in the normal course of business will be converted into cash within an operating cycle, usually a year from the date of the balance sheet. Each current asset item should be listed in order of liquidity (ease of conversion to cash). Current assets generally consist of cash, marketable securities, receivables, inventories, and prepayments (prepaid expenses).

Cash

Cash is the money that is on hand and the money on deposit in the bank.

    Cash $ 14 000

Marketable Securities

This asset represents investment of temporary cash surpluses in some form of short-term interest-earning instrument. Because these funds may be needed on short notice, it is usually considered wise to make investments that are readily convertible to cash and subject to minimum price fluctuations (such as certificates of deposit, commercial paper, and short-term government notes). The general practice is to show marketable securities at the lower of cost or market value. If market value differs from lower of cost or market, it is also shown, usually parenthetically.

    Marketable securities at cost
       (market value, $106 000) $ 102 000

Exhibit 1
XYZ Manufacturing Co. Ltd.
Balance Sheet
as of December 31, 1984

ASSETS
Current Assets:

Cash			$ 14 000
Marketable securities at cost			
(market value $106 000)			102 000
Accounts receivable		$252 000	
Less: allowance for doubtful accounts		12 000	
Net accounts receivable			240 000
Raw materials inventory		120 000	
Work in process inventory		74 000	
Finished goods inventory		130 000	
Total inventories			324 000
Prepayments			14 000
Total current assets			$ 694 000
Investment in subsidiary			40 000
Other investments (market value $15 000)			20 000
			—
Property, plant, and equipment:			
Land	$ 54 000		
Plant	$456 000		
Less: accumulated depreciation	168 500		
		287 500	
Machinery	$114 000		
Less: accumulated depreciation	43 200		
		70 800	
Office equipment	$ 12 000		
Less: accumulated depreciation	4 300		
		7 700	
Total property, plant, and equipment			420 000
Intangibles:			
Goodwill	$ 10 000		
Patents	64 000		
Organization expenses	6 000		
Total intangibles			80 000
TOTAL ASSETS			$1 254 000

Accounts Receivable

Accounts receivable are amounts owed to the company by customers who have purchased on credit and usually have thirty, sixty, or ninety days in which to pay. The total amount due from customers as shown in the balance sheet is $252 000. However, some customers fail to pay their bills. Therefore, a provision for doubtful accounts is estimated (based on previous experience), so that the net accounts receivable amount will represent the actual amount that is expected to be collected. The balance of $240 000 is thus shown as the net accounts receivable on the balance sheet.

Accounts receivable	$ 252 000
Less: allowance for doubtful accounts	12 000
Net accounts receivable	$ 240 000

Exhibit 1 (*continued*)

LIABILITIES

Current liabilities:

Notes payable (demand note)	$ 102 000
Accounts payable	120 000
Accrued expenses payable	38 600
Taxes payable	18 400
Current portion of long-term debt	25 000
Total current liabilities	$ 304 000

Long-term liabilities:

First mortgage bonds (10% interest, due 1989)	100 000
Debentures 12.5%; due 1994	300 000
Deferred taxes	40 000
TOTAL LIABILITIES	$ 744 000

SHAREHOLDERS' EQUITY

Capital stock:

Preferred shares, 5% cumulative, $100 par value each; authorized, issued, and outstanding 600 shares	$ 60 000	
Common shares, $5 par value each; authorized, issued, and outstanding 30 000	150 000	
Premium on stock	104 000	$ 314 000
Retained earnings		196 000

Total shareholders' equity	510 000
TOTAL LIABILITIES AND SHAREHOLDERS' EQUITY	$1 254 000

Inventory

Retailers' and wholesalers' inventories consist of the goods they have for sale to their customers. The functions these companies perform are to store, promote, sell, and distribute goods. The goods themselves are not changed in any major way from the time they are received to the time they are sold. The inventory is valued at its original cost or its present market value, whichever is lower.

A manufacturing company's inventory will consist of raw materials; work in process (subassemblies and partially completed products); and finished products manufactured but not yet sold. Finished and semifinished products are given a higher unit cost than the raw materials: the cost of labour content, the cost of energy consumed in production and other manufacturing costs are to be added to the raw material cost.

Inventory, like marketable securities above, is generally shown at the lower of cost or market value (also known as net realizable value).

Raw materials inventory	$ 120 000
Work in process inventory	74 000
Finished inventory	130 000
Total Inventories	$ 324 000

Prepayments (Prepaid Expenses)

At times, it is necessary or convenient to pay for items in advance. When the items are short-term, such as property or equipment rental and fire insurance, they are called prepaid expenses.

Although the payment is made at one time, the contract (in the case of rent) or the anticipated benefit or reward (in the case of insurance) is expected to last over a span of time. As the "value" is not fully received when the payment is made, the "unused" portion, or the benefit to come, is considered an asset of the company. For example, if two years of insurance are still unused on a five-year policy which originally cost $100, then $40 will be shown on the balance sheet as prepaid expense.

Prepaid Expenses	$ 14 000

To summarize, current assets include cash, marketable securities, accounts receivable, inventories, and prepaid expenses.

Total current assets	$ 694 000

Investment in Subsidiary

XYZ Manufacturing Co. Ltd. owns a small wholesale business that aids in the distribution of its manufactured products. Investments in subsidiary in this case represent a controlling interest, more than 50 percent, of the common stock. The common stock is not a tangible asset, and therefore not included with property, plant, and equipment. XYZ Manufacturing Co. Ltd. has no intention of selling its investment. As a consequence, the investment is listed in this separate category after current assets.

Investment in subsidiary	$ 40 000

Other Investments

XYZ Manufacturing Co. has invested in other business operations and processes. None of the investments represents a controlling interest in the project, and consequently they have been listed separately. Also, XYZ Manufacturing Co. has no intention of selling the investment. Consequently the other investment is listed in this separate category, separate from investment in subsidiary; marketable securities in current assets; and property, plant, and equipment. Other investments are listed at cost, *not* lower of cost or market, unless a decline in value is considered permanent.

Other investments (market value, $15 000)	$ 20 000

PROPERTY, PLANT, AND EQUIPMENT

Property, plant, and equipment (or fixed assets) are physical items which will last more than one year. They include those items not intended for resale which will be used in the operation of the company, such as land, buildings, machinery, equipment, furniture, automobiles, and trucks. All fixed assets, with the exception of land, are shown at their original cost, less accumulated depreciation. Land is not depreciated: only its original cost is shown. This presentation may be conservative: the original cost may well be lower than either present market value or replacement cost. For example, land which appears on the books as $54 000 may actually be worth $100 000. Fixed assets should be stated in order of "permanence," with land generally considered the most permanent.

Depreciation

Plant and equipment becomes useless over the years through wear or obsolescence. In order to allow for this loss of use, the asset is "written-down," or depreciated. These reductions are based on the *expected* useful life of the asset and estimated salvage value. The allowances for depreciation are usually accumulated separately so that the asset's original cost figure on the balance sheet is preserved. The accumulated depreciation amount then reflects that part of the original cost of the asset which has been depreciated and charged to the company as an expense. Thus, the net balance after accumulated depreciation (net book value) is not intended to reflect current or market value of an asset as of the balance sheet date, but rather the original cost less the accumulated depreciation to date.

There are a number of ways to calculate depreciation. The simplest is a straight line method whereby the cost of the fixed asset is allocated evenly over its useful life. For example, suppose a machine is bought for $100 000 and it has an estimated life of ten years, and zero salvage value. Its cost will be allocated at the rate of $10 000 each year. The accumulated depreciation would be $10 000 at the end of the first year; $20 000 at the end of the second year; $30 000 at the end of the third year, etc. By the end of the tenth year, the net book value of the machine would be zero. Other methods are also used; one, percentage declining balance, is a model for the calculation of depreciation for tax purposes.

The accumulated depreciation for each fixed asset is best shown separately, though usually only one total is shown for all the fixed assets.

Land		$ 54 000
Plant	$456 000	
Less: accumulated depreciation	168 500	
		$287 500
Machinery	$114 000	
Less: accumulated depreciation	43 200	
		$ 70 800
Office equipment	$ 12 000	
Less: accumulated depreciation	4 300	
		$ 7 700

If only totals are shown it would be:

Land		$ 54 000
Plant and equipment	$582 000	
Less: accumulated depreciation	216 000	366 000
Total property, plant and equipment		$420 000

Fixed assets, in summary, are the investments in property, plant, and equipment. As explained, they generally are expressed in terms of their cost diminished by the depreciation accumulated as of the date of the financial statement.

Total property, plant, and equipment	$420 000

Intangibles

Most of the company's assets can be seen and touched. There are, however, some items of value that are not tangible yet are customarily recorded as assets. For example, patents and franchise rights are intangible assets. The amounts listed for patents and franchise rights represent actual amounts paid. Some companies expense their research and development expenses as incurred. Others, such as XYZ Manufacturing Co., capitalize (set up as an asset) theirs.

Another item in intangibles is organization expenses. These expenses refer to the cost of the legal formation of the enterprise. In setting up a corporation, there are fees that are owed to the jurisdiction which grants the incorporation, plus legal fees which are associated with preparing the documentation for incorporation. Another intangible, "goodwill," is encountered only when companies change hands. When a company is purchased, establishing a price for it is difficult. Often a purchaser will pay more for a company than it seems "worth" on the balance sheet because he believes the loyalty of existing customers, or the company's reputation, etc., are worth a premium over the tangible assets. The purchaser's balance sheet for the company after it is purchased will include an amount called goodwill that reflects the premium paid. Over time, goodwill is amortized, which means it is written down, usually over forty years, similar to depreciation on a tangible fixed asset. One might expect to find listed under tangibles the value of trained, competent personnel, but the "human resources" of a company are not typically valued and reported on the balance sheet, primarily because there is no agreement on how to arrive at an appropriate value.

Intangibles:		
Goodwill	$	10 000
Patents		64 000
Organization expenses		6 000
Total intangibles	$	80 000

The total intangibles figure is net of amortization.

All the assets are added together

TOTAL ASSETS	$1 254 000

LIABILITIES

Liabilities refer to all the debts a company owes. They are categorized into current liabilities and long-term liabilities.

CURRENT LIABILITIES

Current liabilities reflect the amount of money the company owes and must pay within the coming year. Some of these debts include unpaid wages, bank and bond interest, legal fees, pension payments, and taxes. In addition, it is usual to include in current liabilities the portion of long-term debts due within the year.

Notes Payable

Companies often need additional cash to operate. Thus, money is borrowed from banks or other lenders, such as suppliers who sometimes request formal recognition of amounts owed them. In return, the borrower gives the lender a written promissory note, stating that borrowed funds will be returned within a year (plus any other agreed-upon arrangements, such as interest, etc.). These are called notes payable.

    Notes payable (demand note) $102 000

Accounts Payable

Funds owed by the company for goods and services provided on credit by its suppliers are accounts payable. The company usually has thirty, sixty, or ninety days in which to pay. Sometimes the suppliers offer a cash discount of, say, 2 percent, as an inducement to pay promptly.

    Accounts payable $120 000

Accrued Expenses Payable (Accruals)

In addition to its debt to suppliers and lenders, a company may owe for various goods not yet delivered in full or for services not yet fully performed. Examples are salaries and wages prior to payday, interest, fees to lawyers, architects, etc., for partially completed undertakings. Accrued expenses are expenses that have been incurred, but because of an incomplete transaction, they have not been recorded.

    Accrued expenses payable $ 38 600

Taxes Payable

If a corporation's tax bill is high enough, the corporation must pay its taxes monthly. The tax payments may be based either on the estimate of the current year's taxes owed or the previous year's taxes. The general practice is for corporations to choose the lower of the two bases to determine their monthly payment. Within three months of the end of its fiscal year, the final payment for the estimated taxes owed is due. As a consequence, taxes payable will have a balance in it as long as there is a difference between the base used for payment and the estimated tax liability that is determined when the company draws up its financial statements at the end of its fiscal year.

    Taxes payable $ 18 400

Current Portion of Long-Term Debt

Long-term debt contracts specify repayment terms. Of the long-term debts, the first mortgage bonds have a principal repayment of $25 000 due within one year. This portion of the long-term debt is added to current liabilities, or debts due within one year. The 12.5 percent debentures have no principal payments until 1990.

Current portion of long-term debt $ 25 000

To review, total current liabilities is the sum of all the debts that the company will have to pay within one year from the balance sheet date.

Total current liabilities $ 304 000

LONG-TERM LIABILITIES

Current liabilities were defined as debts due within one year. Long-term liabilities are debts due after one year from the date of the balance sheet. The principal portions of mortgages, bonds, and some loans are examples. The interest on these items may be payable quarterly, semi-annually, or annually. This year's or any previous year's interest, if not yet paid, would therefore be shown as an accrued expense payable, a current liability. Interest is charged against only those periods which have already passed. The interest that will be payable for the future may be known, but is not considered a debt until it has been incurred (but not paid). Therefore, future interest does not appear as a liability on the balance sheet.

First Mortgage Bonds

In the sample balance sheet, one long-term liability is the 10 percent first mortgage bonds due in 1989. The money was received by the company as a loan from the bondholders, who in turn were given a certificate called a bond as evidence of the loan. The bond is really a formal promissory note issued by the company, which agreed to repay the debt at maturity in 1989 and agreed also to pay interest at the rate of 10 percent per year. The term *first mortgage* is a safeguard initiated by the lenders. This means that if the company is unable to pay off the bonds in cash when they are due, the bondholders have a claim, or lien, before other creditors on the mortgaged assets. The mortgaged assets may be sold and the proceeds used to satisfy the debt.

First mortgage bonds
(10% interest, due 1989) $ 100 000

Debentures

The debentures (or bonds) are a certificate of debt. The security of the debenture is the general credit standing of the company. In other words, the debenture holders rank equally with the other general creditors, such as the trade creditors and non-secured creditors.

Debentures 12.5%, due 1994 $ 300 000

Deferred Taxes

Sometimes the accounting principles for the determination of net earnings set by the Canadian Institute of Chartered Accountants and the law for the determination of taxable income, as set by the government, are in conflict. As a consequence, the taxpayer, in establishing financial statements, may estimate one level of income tax payable; and when filing taxable income according to government regulations, set a different level of tax liability. The difference between the two amounts is put in this account.

It may be useful to give an illustration. Most of the cases with deferred tax credit arise because of the different rules for depreciation. For example, XYZ may have purchased new machinery in 1982 worth $20 000. XYZ's normal accounting practice would be to depreciate the $20 000 over its useful life, ten years. As a consequence, it would deduct from income for depreciation, $2000 per year. However, the government, in an attempt to encourage investment in new equipment, has permitted XYZ Manufacturing Co. to deduct at the rate of 50 percent per year, therefore, for the $20 000 machine XYZ Manufacturing Co. would deduct $10 000 in 1982 and $10 000 in 1983. This means that for both 1982 and 1983, for this asset alone, the taxable income as reported on XYZ's tax form would be $8000 less (i.e. $10 000 – $2000) than it reports on its financial statements. This would mean that its actual tax liability would be $1600 less than the tax liability shown on its financial statements (20% × $8000). In 1984, for this particular asset the situation will be reversed. For its financial statements, XYZ Manufacturing Co. will take depreciation of $2000; however, in reporting its taxable income to the government, it will have completely written off the machine by the end of 1983 and will get no further tax deduction. As a consequence, with this machine, the deferred tax credit will be reduced by $400 (20% of $2000).

Deferred taxes $ 40 000

Finally, all liabilities, current and long-term, are added and listed under the heading of total liabilities.

TOTAL LIABILITIES $ 744 000

SHAREHOLDERS' EQUITY

The total equity interest that all stockholders (owners of the company) have in a corporation is called shareholders' equity, or net worth. It is what is left after subtracting total liabilities from total assets. For corporations, equity is separated into two categories: capital stock and retained earnings, while the capital structure for proprietors and partnerships is somewhat different.

Capital Stock

The capital stock account reflects the owners' equity in the company. This account is treated differently depending on the company's form of ownership. (Forms of ownership will be discussed in more detail in the next chapter.) In a sole proprietorship, this will appear as a single account, which includes both invested capital and retained profits, for example:

Scott Meddick, capital	$ 50 000

In a partnership, the accounts will show the respective amounts of the partners' shares of the ownership equity, which also includes both invested capital and retained profits, for example:

Scott Meddick, capital	$ 50 000
Bill West, capital	30 000
Total capital	$ 80 000

In a public or private company, the shares of ownership are called capital stock. Anyone can purchase shares in a public firm, whereas the sale of a private company's shares is restricted. Shares are represented by stock certificates issued by the company to its shareholders.

The number of shares of capital stock which a company is authorized to issue and the par value, if any, of these shares is specified in the articles of incorporation. The company usually requests authorization of a larger number of shares than it will issue immediately. Thus, if more capital is needed in future years, the company will not have to change its charter by increasing the number of authorized shares. Outstanding shares represent the shares that are in the hands of shareholders. The term *par value* is the dollar value given to each share of stock on authorization. "No par value shares" have no such predeclared value, but may have a "stated value" similar to par value. Although par value still appears on balance sheets, it is no longer required to issue par value stocks. Companies federally incorporated are not allowed to issue par value stock, but most provinces permit a choice between par and no par stock.

A company often issues more than one kind of stock in order to appeal to as many investors as possible.

Preferred Shares

Preferred shares have preference over common shares. Normally, dividends are not declared on common shares until preferred shareholders have received their full dividend. If the company should be liquidated, preferred shareholders have first claim on remaining assets, after creditors (those to whom the company owes money as shown in the liabilities section) have been repaid. Dividends to preferred shareholders are normally limited to a stated percentage of share value and are not related to the level of profit. In the XYZ Manufacturing Co. example, the preferred stock is designated 5 percent cumulative, $100 par value each; this means that each share is entitled to $5 in dividends a year when declared by the board of directors. The word *cumulative* means that if in any year the dividend is not paid, it accumulates in favour of the preferred shareholders and must be paid to them before any dividends are distributed to common stock shareholders. In general, preferred shareholders do not have voting rights in the company, unless dividends are in arrears, i.e., have not been paid. Since there are many different kinds of preferred shares, the terms are specified on the balance sheet.

Preferred shares, 5% cumulative $100 par value
Each: authorized, issued, and outstanding
600 shares $ 60 000

Common Shares

Common shareholders control the company because the shareholders vote for a board of directors and vote on other management issues at shareholders' meetings. Common shares can be either par value or no par value. Dividends are not preset nor guaranteed. In prosperous times when company earnings are high, dividends may be high, and when earnings drop, so may dividends.

Common shares, $5 par value each:
Authorized, issued, and outstanding 30 000 shares $150 000

Premium on Stock

When a company sells shares, the buyers' investment is recorded under capital stock. However, shares may be sold for different prices at different times. To simplify the recording procedure, all shares sold are recorded first at the price of the first shares sold (original issue). When shares are sold at higher prices than the original issue, the difference is considered a premium. For example, if 10 000 common shares were sold at $5 each when the company was incorporated, this would have been recorded under capital stock as $50 000. If at a later date 20 000 additional common shares were issued and sold at $10.20 per share, then $20 000 \times \$5 = \$100 000$ would be added to capital stock. The additional capital $[20 000 \times (\$10.20–\$5) = 20 000 \times \$5.20 = \$104 000]$ would be recorded under premium on stock. (Underwriter's fees would normally be deducted, but for simplicity this detail is omitted here.)

Premium on stock $104 000
Note, total capital stock is $314 000

Retained Earnings

The second component of equity is retained earnings. This represents the accumulated total of after-tax profits and losses from operations over the life of the corporation that have been retained in the enterprise, i.e., not paid out in dividends. Profits add to the total and losses subtract from it. If a corporation has had more losses than profits, the amount in retained earnings will be negative (usually shown in brackets) and labelled "Retained Deficit." Any dividends paid are also subtracted from the running total through a statement of retained earnings which is discussed later in this chapter. XYZ Manufacturing Co., since it started, has retained a net total of $196 000 from its operations.

Retained earnings $196 000
Shareholders' equity accounts are then totalled.
TOTAL SHAREHOLDERS' EQUITY $510 000

All liabilities and shareholders' equity items are added together. This amount balances with the total assets.

TOTAL LIABILITIES AND SHAREHOLDERS' EQUITY $1 254 000

THE AUDITOR'S REPORT

The financial statements of a company are relied upon by management, shareholders, creditors, and potential investors. Shareholders and creditors place more credibility on statements prepared by independent auditors. Also, statutory regulations require an independent auditor for public corporations and for some private companies. Auditors report to the shareholders, not to the management, stating whether, in their opinion, the statements present fairly the financial position of the firm in accordance with generally accepted accounting principles and in a manner consistent with the previous year's report.

FOOTNOTES

Financial reports are condensed and formalized. Footnotes are used where explanation may be necessary, and to give additional relevant information, such as stock options, details of long-term debt, and the details of unconsolidated subsidiaries. It is essential to read footnotes in addition to the numbers in the balance sheet in order to appreciate fully the implications of the financial statements.

Before proceeding to the income statement, here is a summary of the important points to remember about the balance sheet.

FACTS TO REMEMBER ABOUT THE BALANCE SHEET

1. The balance sheet shows the financial picture as of a certain point in time.
2. The company name and date must also appear in the title.
3. Assets are on the left, liabilities and shareholders' equity are on the right. (Sometimes they are listed one after another on a page.)
4. Current assets are first, followed by fixed assets.
5. Current assets are listed in order of liquidity, from most liquid to least liquid.
6. Fixed assets are listed in order of permanence, from the most permanent to the least.
7. Current liabilities are first, followed by long-term liabilities.
8. Liabilities are listed in terms of due dates.
9. Shareholders' equity is capital stock + retained earnings.
10. Assets = Liabilities + Equity. A balance sheet always balances.

PART 2: THE INCOME STATEMENT

The income statement, also referred to as a profit and loss statement or statement of earnings, shows how much money the corporation made or lost during a particular period. While the balance sheet shows the financial position of a company at a given date, the income statement often is of greater interest to investors because it shows the record of the company's activities for an operating cycle, normally a year.

An income statement matches the revenue generated (usually from selling goods) against all the expenses incurred during the same period to generate these revenues. The difference is a net profit or loss for the period. The phrase "for the period" in the previous sentence is important. For example, if the period ended December 31 and a sale was made on December 30, it would be recorded as a revenue for the period even if the customer did not pay for the product until January. Similarly, expenses incurred but not yet paid, such as an employee's wage, are recorded for the appropriate period. Thus, the income statement does not relate to the actual movement of cash in a company, only to generating revenues and incurring expenses.

Examine the components and format of the income statement for the XYZ Manufacturing Co. Ltd. below, as Exhibit 2.

Exhibit 2
XYZ Manufacturing Co. Ltd.
Statement of Earnings
for the year ending December 31, 1984

Sales		$1 370 000
Less: Sales returns and allowances	$ 30 000	
Sales discounts	20 000	50 000
Net sales		$1 320 000
Cost of goods sold:		
Finished goods inventory, December 31, 1983	$ 115 000	
Cost of goods manufactured (Exhibit 3)	999 000	
Cost of goods available for sale	$1 114 000	
Less: finished goods inventory, December 31, 1984	130 000	
Cost of goods sold		984 000
Gross profit		$ 336 000
Operating expenses:		
General and administrative expenses	$ 66 000	
Selling expenses	102 000	
Depreciation expense	36 000	
Total operating expenses		204 000
Operating profit		$ 132 000
Plus: other income		6 000
Less: other expenses, interest		65 000
Net profit before tax		$ 73 000
Estimated income tax expense		14 600
Net earnings		$ 58 400

Net Sales

Net sales represent revenue earned by the company from its customers for goods sold or services rendered. When a company sells services rather than goods (e.g., a railroad, theatre, or dry cleaners), its net sales are usually called "operating revenues." The net sales item covers the amount received after taking into consideration the value of returned goods and the amount of discounts for quick payment. Remember, net sales refer to sales made during the period, not cash collected.

Sales		$1 370 000
Less: sales returns and allowances	$30 000	
Sales discounts	20 000	
		50 000
Net sales		$1 320 000

Cost of Goods Sold

A major expense associated with making sales is the cost to the company of the product itself, either to make it or to buy it. For a manufacturer such as XYZ Manufacturing Co. Ltd., included in the cost of goods sold are all costs associated directly with the transformation or production process: raw materials, direct labour, and factory overhead. A manufacturer transforms raw materials into a different final product. The process involves the acquisition of raw materials (the product of another manufacturer) and the placement of the raw materials into process. The process involves the effective combination of labour and machinery to transform the raw materials into the desired product.

In the statement of cost of goods manufactured, Exhibit 3, all the costs directly associated with the manufacturing process are included: raw materials costs, direct labour, and factory overhead items directly associated with the manufacturing process.

Exhibit 3
XYZ Manufacturing Co. Ltd.
Statement of Cost of Goods Manufactured
for the year ending December 31, 1984

Work in process inventory, December 31, 1983			$ 70 000
Raw materials used:			
Raw materials inventory, December 31, 1983		$125 000	
Raw material purchases		667 000	
Raw materials available		$792 000	
Less: raw materials inventory, December 31, 1984		120 000	
Raw materials used		$672 000	
Direct labour		120 000	
Factory overhead:			
Supervision	$30 000		
Indirect factory labour	85 000		
Power	25 000		
Heat and light	9 000		
Depreciation	28 000		
Other	34 000		
Total factory overhead		211 000	
Total manufacturing costs		1 003 000	
Total cost of goods in process, 1984		$1 073 000	
Less: work in process inventory, December 31, 1984		74 000	
Cost of goods manufactured		$ 999 000	

[handwritten annotation: 211 000 + 120 000 + 672 000 ; + 70 000]

In the statement of earnings, Exhibit 2, the cost of goods sold is made up of three components. The first step is to determine the cost of goods available for sale at the start of the period; the finished goods inventory, December 31, 1983, plus the cost of goods manufactured in 1984 (as per Exhibit 3). The final step in determining the cost of goods sold is to subtract from the goods available for sale the finished goods inventory as of December 31, 1984.

Cost of goods sold $ 984 000

In determining the cost of goods manufactured (Exhibit 3) there is a six-step process. For the first step, the raw materials used are determined by adding beginning raw materials inventory and raw material purchases during 1984; then subtracting the ending raw materials inventory as of December 31, 1984. For step two, add direct labour, $120 000, representing factory labour that is directly involved in the production of the goods. Step three adds the last component of the manufacturing process, a summary heading entitled "Factory Overhead." Included in the factory overhead are the costs listed: supervision (the salaries paid to supervisors and plant managers), indirect factory labour (the cost of maintenance and clean-up crews), power (the electricity used to run the machines), heat and light (the costs associated with only the factory facility), depreciation (the write-down of the useful life of the plant and equipment used directly in the production process) and other expenses (the cost of supplies for maintenance, incidental materials used in the manufacturing process too minor to be costed as raw materials, insurance on the plant and equipment, etc.). The sum of the factory overhead items included in the statement of cost of goods manufactured is $211 000. This means, in total (step four), XYZ Manufacturing Co. Ltd. incurred total manufacturing costs in 1984 of $1 003 000. The fifth step is to determine the "total cost of goods in process in 1984" by adding to "total manufacturing costs" the beginning work in process inventory (i.e., as of December 31, 1983). The final step is to determine the "cost of goods manufactured": from "the total cost of goods in process, 1984," deduct the ending work in process inventory (i.e., as of December 31, 1984) of $74 000.

Cost of Goods Sold, Nonmanufacturer

With nonmanufacturing enterprises, such as distributors and retailers, there is no transformation process. The economic function of the nonmanufacturer is to bring the goods to a convenient location for resale. Therefore for the nonmanufacturing company the cost of goods sold includes purchase cost and freight-in. Below, in Exhibit 4, is the cost of goods sold section for the wholesale subsidiary of XYZ Manufacturing Co. Ltd.

The cost of goods sold section is similar to that reported in Exhibit 2. Note, however, that the number of items listed to get net purchases is far less than required to list the cost of goods manufactured. As a consequence, the normal practice is to include the full details within the cost of goods sold for nonmanufacturing companies of all the activities associated with cost of goods sold. As a nonmanufacturer, the company does not transform or change the goods it sells. Therefore, there is only one type of inventory: finished goods. To the initial "finished goods inventory" (as of December 31, 1983), net purchases are added. Net purchases are determined as follows. The first step is to determine the delivered cost of purchases which is the purchase cost plus any freight-in. From the delivered cost of purchases, purchase returns, and allowances and purchase discounts (reductions for quick payment) are deducted. The sum of "net purchases" and beginning inventory gives "cost of goods available for sale." Finally, "cost of goods sold" is the result of deducting the ending inventory from "cost of goods available for sale."

Exhibit 4
XYZ Wholesale Subsidiary Company Ltd.
Statement of Cost of Goods Sold
for the year ending December 31, 1984

Cost of goods sold:		
Inventory, December 31, 1983		$ 50 000
Purchases	$330 000	
Freight-in	12 000	
Delivered cost of purchases	$342 000	
Less: Purchase discounts	$ 3 000	
Purchase returns and allowances	10 000	
Total deductions	13 000	
Net purchases		329 000
Cost of goods available for sale		$379 000
Less: inventory, December 31, 1984		48 000
Cost of goods sold		$331 000

Gross Profit

Gross profit (or gross margin) is determined by subtracting the "cost of goods sold" from "net sales." It represents the markup, or margin, the enterprise charges or earns on its product costs.

Gross profit $336 000

Operating Expenses

Operating expenses are generally categorized as "general and administrative," and "selling" expenses. The categories are usually separated, but this is not always necessary. Executive salaries, office payroll, office expenses, rent, electricity, and the like are the usual items included as general and administrative expenses. Selling expenses include sales people's salaries and commissions, as well as advertising, promotion, and travel costs.

Operating expenses
General and administrative $ 66 000
Selling 102 000

Depreciation Expense

As mentioned earlier, depreciation is the allocation of the cost of an asset over its useful life. The income statement, for a period of time, records all the costs associated with obtaining revenues. Expenditures, such as the acquisition of production equipment or trucks to deliver goods, if charged against the revenues generated during the first year of expenditure, though the asset had a few more years of use, would understate profits in the first year and overstate profits in subsequent years. As discussed in the section on accumulated depreciation on the balance sheet, the issue of understating or overstating is handled by spreading the purchase cost of the asset over several statement periods. The income statement records the amount of depreciation expense allocated to the income statement period. (It should be noted that depreciation applied to production-related fixed assets is recorded under manufacturing overhead whereas depreciation on all other fixed assets, such as office furniture, company cars, and so on, is recorded under operating expenses.)

Depreciation expense $ 36 000

Operating Profit

"Operating profit" represents the net gain from the enterprise's normal operating activities. It is calculated by subtracting "operating expenses" from "gross profit."

Operating profit $132 000

Other Income and Other Expenses

The company may have revenues that are not directly related to its primary business (such as interest earned on investments and sale of land or equipment). To include them under net sales would distort sales and make comparison of performance over several years unrealistic. Other expenses often include interest the company must pay on money it has borrowed. "Other income" and "other expenses" are usually reported after operating profit has been calculated.

Other income $ 6 000
Other expenses, interest   65 000

Net Profit Before Tax

"Net profit before tax" represents the company's determination of its income before estimation of its tax liability.

Net profit before tax $ 73 000

Estimated Income Tax Expense

Corporations earning profit must pay income tax which is calculated by applying a predetermined tax rate to the net profit before tax. If the net profit before tax is $73 000 and the tax rate is 20 percent, the estimated income tax would be $14 600.

Estimated income tax expense $ 14 600

Net Earnings

After all revenues (the plus factors) have been added and all expenses (the minus factors) subtracted, the residual is "net earnings." If expenses exceed revenues, the residual is a "net loss."

Net earnings $ 58 400

A SUMMARY OF FACTS TO REMEMBER ABOUT THE INCOME STATEMENT

1. The income statement covers a period of time. (The balance sheet shows the financial position of the enterprise at one point in time.)
2. Sales (revenues) made during a period are recorded. This does not necessarily mean that cash was collected.
3. Expenses incurred during the period to make these sales are recorded. This does not necessarily mean that cash was paid out.
4. The formal structure of an income statement is: sales first, then expenses, then net earnings (or loss).
5. Above all, remember an income statement matches expenses to revenues, for a specified period of time.

PART 3: THE STATEMENT OF RETAINED EARNINGS

Retained earnings represent the account that forms the connection between the balance sheet and the income statement. The retained earnings are the earnings remaining after dividends on preferred and common stock have been paid; that is, the earnings retained in the company. When an enterprise starts in business, it has no retained earnings, but as soon as it has any profits or losses, the retained earnings account is affected. (If losses are greater than earnings, the account is listed as "retained deficit.") For example, assume the following earnings were retained by XYZ Manufacturing Co. Ltd.

Net earnings for the year 1984		$ 58 400
Less: 1984 dividends paid		
on preferred shares	$ 3 000	
on common shares	15 000	
		18 000
1984 net increase in retained earnings		$40 400

The statement of retained earnings for XYZ Manufacturing Co. Ltd. would be as presented in Exhibit 5.

Exhibit 5
XYZ Manufacturing Co. Ltd.
Statement of Retained Earnings
for the year ended December 31, 1984

Retained earnings: December 31, 1983		$ 155 600
Net earnings for the year, 1984		58 400
		$ 214 000
Less: 1984 dividends paid on		
Preferred Shares	$ 3 000	
Common Shares	15 000	
		18 000
Retained earnings: December 31, 1984		$ 196 000

The statement of retained earnings is fairly straightforward. To the initial opening balance of retained earnings ($155 600 as of December 31, 1983) is added the net earnings for the year as determined from the statement of earnings, $58 400 for 1984. The resulting subtotal is $214 000. From this subtotal the total of dividends paid, $18 000 during 1984, is subtracted yielding the retained earnings as of December 31, 1984: $196 000.

Problems in Balance Sheet Construction

Problem 1
Stan Hardy Retail Florist

	Capital, S. Hardy	$9300
Equ.	Accumulated depreciation, store fixtures	4000
CL	Accounts payable	4100
Int.	Goodwill	2000
Equ.	Store fixtures, cost	7500
CA	Inventory	2500
CL	Bank loan (90-day note)	2200
CA	Cash	3700
CL	Accrued expenses payable	300
CA	Accounts receivable	4200

Assignment

Different accounts are listed above, in random order, for the florist business of Stan Hardy. The accounts are as of January 31, 1985.

1. Determine whether the account is a current asset, fixed asset, intangible asset, current liability, long-term liability or net worth account.
2. Prepare a balance sheet as of January 31, 1985 for the business.

Problem 2
Robinson Hardware Store Ltd.

FA	Land	$ 7 800
CA	Prepaid expenses	5 100
CL	Accrued expenses payable	4 200
CL	Notes payable, due in 90 days	15 000
LL	Long-term debt	20 500
FA	Accumulated depreciation, building, and equipment	22 900
CA	Marketable securities	1 700
CL	Accounts payable	29 500
CA	Accounts receivable	24 000
Eq.	Capital stock[1]	20 500
Int.	Organization expenses	1 000
FA	Buildings and equipment, cost	47 600
Eq.	Retained earnings	52 600
CL	Taxes payable	2 100
CA	Cash	7 300
CA	Inventory	72 800

Assignment

Different accounts as of January 31, 1985 are listed above in random order for Robinson Hardware Store Ltd.

1. Determine whether each account is a current asset, fixed asset, intangible asset, current liability, long-term liability, or equity item.
2. Prepare a formal balance sheet as of January 31, 1985, for Robinson Hardware Store Ltd.

[1]Authorized 2500 shares, $10 par value.

Problem 3
Best Furniture Manufacturer Ltd.

FA Accumulated depreciation, buildings✓	$ 27 200
Int Patents √	3 600
FA Building, cost✓	77 300
FA Accumulated depreciation, equipment ✓	62 600
CL Bank loan, short-term✓	69 700
SE Common stock[1] ✓	26 600
FA Equipment, cost ✓	104 800
CA Inventory✓	136 000
CL Accrued expenses payable ✓	7 400
CL Long-term debt, due within one year✓	4 000
CA Cash ✓	?
A other Inv Investment[2]✓	36 200
CA Prepaid expenses✓	4 100
CL Taxes payable✓	8 800
CA Marketable securities✓	5 600
FA Land √	10 500
LTL Mortgage, due in 1997 ✓	45 700
Int Goodwill ✓	7 300
Int Organization expenses √	1 500
CA Accounts receivable✓	134 700
Eq Preferred stock[3] ✓	23 700
Eq Retained earnings✓	158 400
CL Accounts payable✓	81 300
LTL Debentures, due 1990 ✓	20 000

Assignment

The above accounts are taken from the records of Best Furniture Manufacturer Ltd. as of December 31, 1984. Prepare a balance sheet for the company and determine the cash position.

[1]Authorized and issued 10 000 shares of no par value stock.
[2]Represents a 50 percent ownership in a major hardwood lumber supplier.
[3]Authorized 10 000, $10 par value shares.

Problems on Income Statements

Problem 1
Jones Department Store Ltd.
(in 000's of dollars)

✓Net sales	$3700
✓Cost of goods sold	2900
✓Other income	20
✓Selling expenses	480
✓Gross margin (profit)	800
✓Net operating profit	210
✓Administrative expenses	110
✓Other expenses	30

Assignment

Different income statement items for the Jones Department Store Ltd. are listed above in random order. All refer to the year ending December 31, 1984, and are in thousands of dollars. The tax rate is 45 percent.

1. Prepare a formal income statement for the period ending December 31, 1984, for the Jones Department Store Ltd.

Problem 2
J. T. Ross Retail Sales Co. Ltd.
(in 000's of dollars)

Gross profit	$217
Selling expenses	64
Ending inventory	190
General and administrative expenses	57
Net sales	850
Net profit before tax	96
Beginning inventory	157

Assignment

Different income statement items of J. T. Ross Retail Sales Co. Ltd. are listed above in random order for the three-month period ending April 30, 1984.

1. Prepare a formal income statement for the period ending April 30, 1984, for J. T. Ross Retail Sales Co. Ltd. Assume the income tax rate is 50 percent.

Note: To complete this exercise the following items will have to be calculated:
   (a) Cost of goods sold
   (b) Purchases
   (c) Net profit after tax

Problem 3
Adanac Textile Mills Ltd.
(in 000's of dollars)

Direct labour	$ 251
Goods in process, December 31, 1984	128
Sales discounts	9
Manufacturing overhead	193
Goods in process, December 31, 1983	130
Raw materials, December 31, 1984	163
Administrative expenses	98
Finished goods, December 31, 1983	74
Selling expense	49
General expense	85
Sales returns and allowances	11
Raw materials, December 31, 1983	166
Finished goods, December 31, 1984	73
Other expense, interest	28
Sales	1830
Indirect labour	33
Other expense, royalty	6
Material purchases	986
Other income	25

Assignment

Income statement items are listed above in random order. All are period accounts for the year ending December 31, 1984, except where noted. Assuming a tax rate of 40 percent, prepare a formal income statement and statement of cost of goods manufactured for Adanac Textile Mills Ltd. for the year ending December 31, 1984.

Problem 4
Canlan Pulp and Paper Ltd.
(in 000's of dollars)

Selling expenses	$ 126
Sales returns and allowances	11
Finished goods, December 31, 1983	151
Other revenue	71
Depreciation, manufacturing equipment	212
Indirect labour	330
Depreciation, office equipment	24
Direct labour	495
Sales discounts	15
Administrative expenses	235
Other manufacturing overhead	81
Net sales	3839
Goods in process, December 31, 1983	73
Gross profit	630
Estimated income tax expense	17
Raw materials, December 31, 1984	540
Raw materials used	2095
Cost of goods manufactured	3212
General expenses	157
Net earnings	29
Other expenses, interest	113
Raw materials, December 31, 1983	529
Net operating income	88

Assignment

Income statement items for Canlap Pulp and Paper Ltd. are listed above in random order. All are period accounts for the year ending December 31, 1984, except where noted. Prepare a formal income statement and statement of cost of goods manufactured for Canlan Pulp and Paper Ltd. To complete the assignment, sales, material purchases, ending goods in process and finished goods inventories, and cost of goods sold will have to be calculated.

Problems on the Relationship of the Income Statement and Balance Sheet

Problem 1
Cut Rate Stores Incorporated
(in 000's of dollars)

Inventory, June 30, 1984 B, I	$ 316
Accounts payable B	120
Gross profit I	357
Store fixtures, net B	60
Selling expenses I	142
Income tax expense I	5
Retained earnings, June 30, 1983 B	220
Cash B	20
General and administrative expenses I	180
Accrued expenses payable B	40
Long-term notes payable B	13
Accounts receivable B	135
Notes payable B	105
Inventory, June 30, 1983 I	285
Capital stock B	15
Sales I	1416
Depreciation expense I	15
Income tax payable B	3
Store fixtures B	75

Assignment

Different balance sheet and income statement accounts are listed above in random order. The balance sheet accounts are as of June 30, 1984, except where noted. The income statement amounts are for the year July 1, 1983 to June 30, 1984, in thousands of dollars.

1. Determine whether each account is a balance sheet or income statement item.
2. Prepare a formal income statement for Cut Rate Stores Incorporated for the year ending June 30, 1984.
3. Prepare a statement of retained earnings for the year ended June 30, 1984.
4. Prepare a formal balance sheet as of June 30, 1984, for Cut Rate Stores Incorporated.

860921

Problem 2
Garnier Wholesalers Incorporated
(in 000's of dollars)

Retained earnings, December 31, 1983 B	$ 190
Cash B	17
Retained earnings, December 31, 1984 B	216
Net sales I	1663
Accounts receivable B	159
Gross profit I	394
Capital stock B	45
Net profit before taxes I	35
Income tax expense I	9
Purchases I	1347
Long-term bank loan B	10
Prepaid expenses B	11
Depreciation expense I	20
Accumulated depreciation, December 31, 1983 B	140
Inventory, December 31, 1983 I	316
Accrued expenses payable B	13
Selling expenses I	168
Equipment, cost B	200
Notes payable — bank B	200
Inventory, December 31, 1984 I, B	394
Income taxes payable B	4
Cost of goods sold I	1269
Accounts payable B	133
General and administrative expenses I	171

Assignment

Different balance sheet and income statement accounts are listed above in random order in thousands of dollars. The balance sheet accounts are as of December 31, 1984, except where noted. The income statement amounts are for the year ending December 31, 1984.

1. Determine whether each account is a balance sheet or income statement item.
2. Prepare a formal income statement for the year ending December 31, 1984, for Garnier Wholesalers Incorporated.
3. Prepare a statement of retained earnings for the year ended December 31, 1984.
4. Prepare a formal balance sheet as of December 31, 1984, for Garnier Wholesalers Incorporated.

Problem 3
Lashbrook Commercial Printers Limited
(in 000's of dollars)

Equipment, cost	$204.3
Goodwill	15.6
Work in process inventory, December 31, 1983	22.2
Gross profit	188.1
Prepayments	4.2
Accounts payable	69.0
Raw materials used	254.3
Accumulated depreciation, building	41.2
Net profit before tax	63.8
Accumulated depreciation, equipment	92.8
Preferred stock	6.7
Investment in subsidiary (more than 50% ownership)	64.1
Estimated income tax expense	20.2
Selling expense	36.7
Finished goods inventory, December 31, 1983	19.2
Bank loan, due in 90 days	43.7
Raw materials inventory, December 31, 1983	25.7
Marketable securities	16.0
Long-term debt due within 1 year	4.3
Accounts receivable, net	132.5
General and administrative expenses[1]	99.3
Land	4.9
Material purchases	260.4
Taxes payable	10.7
Other income	21.4
Direct labour	140.0
Common stock	39.7
Building, cost	45.3
Other expenses, interest	9.7
Net long-term debt	93.8
Cost of goods manufactured	436.2
Net sales	617.6
Cash	?
Retained earnings	136.5
Accrued expenses payable	20.7
Factory overhead[1]	41.1
Premium on stock	7.9
Retained earnings, December 31, 1983	92.9

Assignment

Listed above in random order are balance sheet and income statement accounts as of December 31, 1984, except where otherwise noted, for Lashbrook Commercial Printers Limited (L.C.P.L.). Prepare an income statement, statement of cost of goods manufactured, and statement of retained earnings for L.C.P.L. for the year ending December 31, 1984, and a balance sheet as of December 31, 1984, using cash to balance assets and claims.

[1] Includes depreciation expenses.

Problem 4
Oakville Boat Manufacturing Limited
(in 000's of dollars)

Long-term bank loan	$ 40
Work-in-process inventory, December 31, 1982	44
Insurance expense — factory equipment	9
Net sales	1841
Net profit after tax	111
Factory heat, light, and power	23
Other expense, interest	34
Cost of goods available for sale	1368
Accounts receivable	179
Wages payable	91
Direct labour	540
Sales returns and discounts	97
Raw materials inventory, December 31, 1982	31
Goodwill	95
Prepaid expenses	17
Total manufacturing costs	1269
Accumulated depreciation: factory building and equipment, December 31, 1982	439
Factory supervision	112
Cost of goods sold	1289
Total cost of goods in process, 1983	1313
Organization expenses	4
Selling expenses	95
Total current liabilities	216
Retained earnings, December 31, 1983	334
Raw materials used	545
Bonds payable 1990	197
Factory building and equipment depreciation expense	40
Marketable securities	34
General and administrative expenses	151
Accounts payable	59
Cost of goods manufactured	1277
Taxes payable	33
Office space rental	110
Dividends paid on common stock, 1983	9
Raw materials purchases in 1983	542
Factory building and equipment (Cost)	939
Net operating profit	196
Investment in subsidiary	155
Other income	9
Accrued expenses payable	7
Preferred shares	143
Estimated income tax	60
Dividends paid on preferred shares, 1983	11
Cash	16
Bank loan due March 1984	?
Common stock	173

Assignment:

Listed above in random order are balance sheet and income statement accounts for the year ending, or as of December 31, 1983, except where otherwise noted for Oakville Boat Manufacturing Limited (OBML). Prepare a statement of cost of goods manufactured, an income statement, and a statement of retained earnings for the year ending December 31, 1983. Also, prepare a balance sheet as of December 31, 1983, using "Bank loan due March 1984" as the balancing figure.

SECTION III
An Introduction to Financial Management

The purpose of this chapter is to introduce the basic techniques used by financial managers and analysts to assess and project the financial performance and position of a business. An understanding of the basic financial statements from the previous chapter is essential to an understanding of this chapter. Several financial analysis tools will be discussed and their application to the financial management cases will be summarized. Financial analysis and management is not just number pushing; judgment must be exercised as to what numbers to look at and how to interpret them. Often, a "qualitative factor," something not expressed in numbers, is more important to the solution of a problem than all the numbers involved.

PART 1: FINANCIAL GOALS

There are five basic financial goals: profitability, stability, liquidity, efficiency, and growth. To survive, every business must meet each of these goals to some extent, though a business must determine for itself the relative emphasis to place on each of the five goals.

Profitability refers to the generation of revenues in excess of the expenses associated with obtaining it. This is the "bottom-line" test of how successful a firm's operators have been as shown at the bottom of the income statements.

Stability refers to a business's overall financial structure. For example, a businessman may wish to invest as little of his own money as possible in his firm and finance his operation mainly with debt. If the debt–equity mix is too far out of balance, the firm may go bankrupt should some of the creditors want their money back at an "inconvenient" time. Many of the spectacular financial disasters reported in the newspapers resulted from neglect of the stability goal of sound financial management.

Liquidity refers to a business's ability to meet short-term obligations. For example, a manager may wish to invest as much of his firm's cash in inventory and equipment as possible, but if he overdoes it and cannot pay his employees or creditors on time, he can be forced into bankruptcy.

Efficiency refers to the efficient use of assets. Efficient use of assets has an impact on profitability, stability, liquidity, and the ability of the enterprise to grow.

Growth refers to increasing in size or acquiring more of something. A businesswoman may assess her financial performance by calculating, for example, how much sales or assets have increased this year over last year. While there are many widely held concerns about growth in general (for example, the zero population growth movement) business people and investors remain very interested in financial growth.

There are no clear-cut guidelines on how much or how little financial performance is adequate or on how to trade off performance on one financial goal in favour of another. For example, 10 percent sales growth may be terrible for a firm in one industry but excellent for a firm in another. Similarly, a high level of liquidity may be preferable to growth for a firm at one time and detrimental for the same firm at another.

Financial analysis and projections are used to assess achievement of financial goals. The financial statements of LMN Retail Co. Ltd. will be used to illustrate the development of the Statement of Changes in Financial Position and the financial ratios. Exhibit 1 presents the income statements of LMN Retail Co. Ltd. for 1982, 1983, and 1984; Exhibit 2, the balance sheets as of January 31, 1982, 1983, and 1984.

Exhibit 1
LMN Retail Co. Ltd.
Income Statement
For the Years Ending January 31
(in 000's of dollars)

	1982		1983		1984	
Sales		$875		$849		$1 086
Cost of goods sold:						
Beginning inventory	$152		$153		$ 168	
Purchases	678		662		874	
Cost of goods available for sale	$830		$815		$1 042	
Less: Ending inventory	153		168		200	
Cost of goods sold		677		647		842
Gross profit		$198		$202		$ 244
Operating expenses:						
General and administrative	$ 76		$ 81		$ 95	
Selling	76		84		113	
Depreciation	15		15		14	
Total operating expenses		167		180		222
Net operating profit		$ 31		$ 22		$ 22
Other expenses — interest		3		2		2
Net profit before tax		$ 28		$ 20		$ 20
Estimated income tax		7		5		5
Net earnings		$ 21		$ 15		$ 15

In addition to discussing the Statement of Changes in Financial Position and financial ratio analysis, this chapter will illustrate an elementary process for developing projected financial statements. It will also examine the forms of business organization, credit evaluation, and sources of short-term and intermediate-term financing for small and medium-sized businesses.

PART 2: THE STATEMENT OF CHANGES IN FINANCIAL POSITION[1]

The statement of changes in financial position shows changes between two balance sheets. Over time, as shown in the LMN example, a company will have several balance sheets or "statements of financial position." There are a number of ways to analyze a set of balance sheets; one is by the statement of changes in financial position. Examine the 1982 and 1983 balance sheets of LMN Retail Co. Ltd. The changes in balance sheet accounts are as follows:

---

[1]Only the Statement of Changes in Financial Position on a cash basis will be presented.

	(in 000's of dollars)
Cash, an increase of	$10
Net accounts receivable, a decrease of	8
Inventory, an increase of	15
Fixed assets, a decrease of	15
Accounts payable, a decrease of	4
Notes payable — bank, a decrease of	2
Taxes payable, a decrease of	4
Accrued expenses, an increase of	7
Long-term liabilities, a decrease of	10
Common stock, no change	
Retained earnings, an increase of	15

Exhibit 2
LMN Retail Co. Ltd.
Balance Sheet
as of January 31
(in 000's of dollars)

	1982	1983	1984
ASSETS			
Current assets			
Cash	$ 2	$ 12	$ 6
Net accounts receivable	80	72	80
Inventory	153	168	200
Total current assets	$235	$252	$286
Fixed assets, net	49	34	32
TOTAL ASSETS	$284	$286	$318
LIABILITIES			
Current liabilities			
Accounts payable	$ 68	$ 64	$ 71
Notes payable — bank	28	26	40
Taxes payable	6	2	2
Accrued expenses	5	12	8
Total current liabilities	$107	$104	$121
Long-term liabilities	30	20	20
TOTAL LIABILITIES	$137	$124	$141
EQUITY			
Common stock	$ 15	$ 15	$ 15
Retained earnings	132	147	162
Total equity	147	162	177
TOTAL LIABILITIES AND EQUITY	$284	$286	$318

This procedure shows what has happened in each account, but does not give much insight into the way these changes relate to one another to result in a change in total assets of $2000 (or a change in total liabilities and equity of $2000).

Some of these changes represent money coming into the company. For example, the reduction of accounts receivable represents an incremental cash collection of

$8000. In other words, the reduction through collection of accounts receivable is a source of cash to the LMN Retail Co. Ltd. Similarly, the reduction of fixed assets, either through sale or depreciation, has an incremental impact on cash (i.e., it is a source of cash).

An increase in a creditor's claim represents the postponement of a cash payment; therefore it is also a source of cash. For example, the $7000 increase of accrued expenses is a source of cash. The last source of cash is retained earnings, which represents the increase in the cash position created by the postponement of dividends. Total sources of cash for the year ending January 31, 1983, for the LMN Retail Co. Ltd. are:

Sources	*(in 000's of dollars)*
Net accounts receivable	$ 8
Fixed assets, net	15
Accrued expenses	7
Earnings retained in business	15
Total sources	$45

Inspection of the income statements, Exhibit 1, reveals that in the 1983 fiscal year, LMN Retail Co. Ltd. charged $15 000 of depreciation expenses. The reduction of fixed assets was caused by the depreciation written off of $15 000, not by any sale of fixed assets. If LMN Retail Co. Ltd. were on a cash basis (i.e., all sales were for cash and all expenses paid as incurred), the impact of the operations in the fiscal year would have been to increase cash $30 000 — the net earnings plus depreciation. The cash was used when the fixed asset was purchased. Depreciation is a non-cash allocation of the original expenditure.

Some of the changes represent cash outflows or uses of money. The investment in inventory increased by $15 000. This represents a reduction in the cash position of LMN Retail Co. Ltd. to purchase the additional items. Similarly, a reduction in a creditor's claim represents a cash outflow or use of cash. For example, the decrease of accounts payable by $4000, notes payable, bank, by $2000, taxes payable by $4000 and long-term liabilities by $10 000 are uses of cash. In summary, for the fiscal year ending January 31, 1983, the uses of cash by LMH Retail Co. Ltd. were:

Uses	*(in 000's of dollars)*
Inventory	$15
Accounts payable	4
Notes payable, bank	2
Taxes payable	4
Long-term liabilities	10
Total uses	$35

For the 1983 fiscal year, the sources of cash for the LMN Retail Co. Ltd. were $10 000 greater than the uses of cash. In other words, the firm had a net cash inflow of $10 000 as represented by the increase in the cash account. Exhibit 3 presents the statement of changes in financial position of LMN Retail Co. Ltd. for the year ending January 31, 1983.

Exhibit 3
LMN Retail Co. Ltd.
Statement of Changes in Financial Position
for the Year Ending January 31, 1983
(in 000's of dollars)

Sources of cash:		
Net accounts receivable	$ 8	
Fixed assets, net	15	
Accrued expenses	7	
Retained earnings	15	
Total sources		$45
Uses of cash:		
Inventory	$15	
Accounts payable	4	
Notes payable, bank	2	
Taxes payable	4	
Long-term liabilities	10	
Total uses		35
Net cash increase		$10
Cash, January 31, 1982		2
Cash, January 31, 1983		$12

In summary, sources of cash are decreases in assets, increases in liabilities, and increases in equity. Conversely, uses of cash are increases in assets, decreases in liabilities and decreases in equity. For the sake of clarification it might be useful to take the viewpoint of an owner of a small enterprise at his cash register. The collection of a sale immediately increases the cash. If customers wish to pay their bills by credit card rather than cash, the impact on the retailer is the forgone cash collection and the increase in accounts receivable. If the retailer subsequently sells the accounts receivable to a bank, his or her cash position will increase and accounts receivable will decrease. In contrast, if a supplier on delivery of goods demands immediate payment, the owner must reach into the cash register to make payment. However, if the supplier does not wish payment immediately, the impact is the postponement of a payment and the preservation of or incremental impact on cash. Subsequently, when the account payable is paid, there will be a use of cash.

As an analytical tool, statements of changes in financial position can be prepared for any period the analyst desires, providing balance sheets are available. Exhibit 4 presents the statement of changes in financial position for the LMN Retail Co. Ltd. for a two-year period ending January 31, 1984.

In analyzing the statements, *first* identify the major changes (Exhibit 4), which are as follows:

Sources	*(in 000's of dollars)*
Retained earnings (profits)	$30
Fixed assets decrease	17
Bank loan increase	12
Uses	
Inventory increase	$47
Payment of long-term debt	10

Exhibit 4
LMN Retail Co. Ltd.
Statement of Changes in Financial Position
for Two Years
Ending January 31, 1984
(in 000's of dollars)

Sources of cash:	
Fixed assets	$17
Accounts payable	3
Notes payable — bank	12
Accrued expenses	3
Retained earnings	30
Total sources	$65
Uses of cash:	
Inventory	$47
Taxes payable	4
Long-term liabilities	10
Total uses	61
Net cash increase	$ 4
Cash, January 31, 1982	2
Cash, January 31, 1984	$ 6

The analyst cannot tell whether the profits were used to increase inventory or whether the bank loan was used to pay off the long-term debt. Instead, a general flow of cash can be observed. Also, without more information, the decrease in fixed assets can be a result either of depreciation or the sale of fixed assets. On this point, the income statement records that the total depreciation expense for 1983 and 1984 was $29 000 ($15 000 + $14 000). If the only change in fixed assets had been an increase in accumulated depreciation on the balance sheet, the decrease in fixed assets would have been $29 000, not $17 000. It appears LMN bought $12 000 worth of fixed assets. In other words, reported changes in financial position would be more accurate if a $29 000 source (increase in accumulated depreciation) and a $12 000 use (increase in cost of fixed assets) were shown. Such as:

Source of cash:	
Depreciation	$29
Uses of cash:	
Fixed assets	$12

The second step in analysis is to interpret the desirability of these major changes. Essentially, LMN management has used cash generated from operations (profits and depreciation) to (a) invest in inventory, (b) buy more fixed assets, and (c) pay off some of the long-term debt. Because cash from operations was not sufficient for this purpose, LMN management has, in effect, substituted short-term debt (bank loan) for long-term debt (the $10 000 paid off). Were all of these moves appropriate? It depends. For example, it appears that LMN's sales are now beginning to grow (see Exhibit 1). It is possible that the inventory increase was in anticipation of growth; or it is possible that it made the growth feasible by making a larger variety or quantity of goods available for sale. The relative amount of inventory will be examined in the next section of this chapter to see whether LMN management increased it too much. Because the terms of the long-term debt are not known, it is impossible to comment on the appropriateness of retiring some of the debt. Ordinarily, more information would be available to make better judgments about the desirability of changes. The LMN example is only an illustration of the analytical approach.

The statement of changes in financial position is a valuable tool, but clearly it is limited in its uses. For example, the analyst is not able to determine in the LMN example whether the increase in inventory was excessive or not relative to the increase in sales for LMN. Ratio analysis is required to complement the statement of changes in financial position.

PART 3: FINANCIAL RATIO ANALYSIS

As changes occur in the size of a company's various accounts, it is difficult to analyze what is happening by casual inspection of several income statements and balance sheets. If only one or two accounts changed and the rest stayed the same, it would be a relatively straightforward task to identify and interpret such developments. However, most of the accounts usually fluctuate. This makes the reasons for the fluctuations hard to determine.

An approach developed to assist in identifying and interpreting changes in financial performance and condition is called ratio analysis. A ratio is simply a fraction: it has two parts, a numerator (the top) and a denominator (the bottom). Using the LMN example, there are endless possible ratios that could be calculated by taking various numbers on the income statements and balance sheets and making up fractions. Most of the calculations would be meaningless. However, financial analysts have agreed upon a common set of fifteen to twenty ratios that are useful in assessing financial performance and financial position. Exhibit 5 presents several ratios for the LMN Retail Co. Ltd. The following are some observations of Exhibit 5:

1. The ratios are grouped into five categories; the headings refer to the five financial goals. In other words, the ratios help analyze the company's progress toward each of these financial objectives.
2. The ratios do not look like fractions! Each fraction has been simplified as much as possible.
3. Some ratios are percentages; others are in days; others are in the form of proportions, etc. The differences are the result of the various numbers used in the fractions.

4. Each ratio has been calculated for three years in order to compare ratios over time and to identify changes in them. A single ratio does not provide much insight as to the direction in which a firm is heading.

Exhibit 5
LMN Retail Co. Ltd.
Ratio Analysis
for the Years Ending January 31

	1982	1983	1984
	%	%	%
Profitability:			
(i) Vertical analysis[1]			
Sales	100.0	100.0	100.0
Costs of goods sold	77.4	76.2	77.5
Gross profit	22.6	23.8	22.5
Operating expenses:			
General and administrative	8.7	9.5	8.7
Selling	8.7	9.9	10.4
Depreciation	1.7	1.8	1.3
Subtotal	19.1	21.2	20.4
Net operating income	3.5	2.6	2.0
Other expenses	0.3	0.2	0.2
Net profit before tax	3.2	2.4	1.8
Estimated income tax	0.8	0.6	0.5
Net earnings	2.4	1.8	1.4
(ii) Return on investment[2]	15.4%	9.7%	8.8%
Stability:			
Net worth to total assets	51.8%	56.6%	55.7%
Interest coverage	10.3 times	11.0 times	11.0 times
Liquidity:			
Current ratio	2.2/1	2.4/1	2.4/1
Acid test	0.8/1	0.8/1	0.7/1
Working capital	$128,000	$148,000	$165,000
Efficiency:			
Age of receivables[3]	33.4 days	31.0 days	26.9 days
Inventory in days cost of goods sold[3]	82.5 days	94.8 days	86.7 days
Age of payables in days purchases[3]	36.6 days	35.3 days	29.7 days
Fixed assets/sales	0.096	0.040	0.029
Growth:[4]			
Sales		(3.0%)	27.9%
Profits, after tax		(28.6%)	—
Assets		0.7%	11.2%
Equity		10.2%	9.3%

[1]Detail may not add to totals because of rounding.
[2]Assumes 1981 equity was 1982 equity less 1982 net income after tax, i.e., $126,000.
[3]A 365-day year was used.
[4]Brackets indicate negative amounts.

Interpretation of Ratios

Interpretation of ratios will be discussed before outlining how to calculate each ratio. As an example, the net profit/sales ratio is made up of two numbers from the income statement, net profit after tax and net sales. The objective is to gain an indication of the change in profit relative to the change in sales. From LMN's income statements, Exhibit 1, net profit after tax declined from $21 000 to $15 000 and then remained at $15 000. Also, because sales declined from 1982 to 1983, some decrease in profits could be expected. Did profits decline more or less than sales? That is a hard question to answer without preparing the net profit/sales ratio. If both profits and sales had declined together to the same extent, the relationship between them would have remained the same; that is, the ratio of net profit to sales would be constant. From the ratios in Exhibit 5, the analyst can see that the relationship has changed: formerly profits were 2.4 percent of sales; now they are 1.8 percent of sales. In short, profits declined more than sales. From 1983 to 1984 sales increased but the ratio of net profit to sales deteriorated. Was this decline in the profitability ratio good or bad? If LMN's objective is to make as much profit as possible, this decline was bad, but this conclusion might be premature. First, because other firms in LMN's industry might have fared even worse, LMN might be doing very well in that respect. It would be useful to look at a set of industry ratios to check this possibility. Second, maybe LMN was intentionally trading off profitability for some other financial goal, such as growth, in which case the decline in profitability might be an expected consequence. To address this possibility, other ratios must be inspected and the goals of management must be investigated.

Ratios are indicators of change. They simplify relationships between numbers but net profit/sales has shown us that LMN's profitability on one dimension has declined. The ratio does not tell us whether that was good or bad or even why the decline occurred. Clearly, a ratio can change if the numerator changes, the denominator changes or both change. In order to understand the trend of net profit/sales from 2.4 percent to 1.8 percent to 1.4 percent, the cause of that change must be found. Why did profits change? Why did sales change? In short, a close look at the components of the ratio is required.

Ratios are similar to traffic lights: red, yellow, and green. Changes in the ratios (such as the net profits/sales example) signal whether the analyst should "stop" (take a close look at something), "be prepared to stop" (a problem may be developing), or "go" (so far, so good). In short, ratios are *indicators* of problems (or success) that can be monitored relatively easily.

Calculation of Ratios

It is suggested that in the following examples the student insert the data from the financial statements (Exhibits 1 and 2) of LMN Retail Co. Ltd. to verify the calculations in Exhibit 5.

Profitability

Vertical analysis is the restatement of the income statement in percentages, using net sales for the year as the base, i.e., 100 percent. The term *vertical* arises from the fact that percentages are calculated on a vertical axis, in contrast to growth ratios, such as sales growth, which make a horizontal comparison across several years of statements. The purpose of the analysis is to eliminate the impact of absolute dollar sales on expense amounts.

For example:

$$\text{Cost of goods sold to sales} = \frac{\$ \text{ Cost of goods sold}}{\$ \text{ Net sales}} \times 100 = ? \%$$

This ratio indicates the amount spent to provide the products sold; its complement is as follows:

$$\text{Gross profit to sales} = \frac{\$ \text{ Gross profit}}{\$ \text{ Net sales}} \times 100 = ? \%$$

This ratio measures the percentage of each sales dollar left to pay operating expenses and contribute to profits after paying for cost of goods sold. An increasing gross profit to sales ratio trend may be the result of a reduction in cost of goods sold (better cost control in a manufacturing firm, more astute buying in a retailing firm, etc.) or the result of an increase in selling prices or both. The opposite is true of a declining trend in gross profit to sales. Because cost of goods sold is usually the major expense associated with obtaining sales revenue, financial managers pay close attention to changes in this ratio. For manufacturing concerns, percentages should be calculated for each component of the cost of goods sold.

The next area of study is the level of operating expenses:

$$\text{Operating expenses to sales} = \frac{\$ \text{ Operating expenses}}{\$ \text{ Net sales}} \times 100 = ? \%$$

and the residual after deducting operating expenses from gross profit is

$$\text{Net operating income} = \frac{\$ \text{ Net operating income}}{\$ \text{ Net sales}} \times 100 = ? \%$$

The net operating income ratio indicates what percentage of each sales dollar is left after meeting operating expenses. For LMN Retail Co. Ltd., despite no change in the net operating profit in dollars from 1983 to 1984, the net operating profit percentage is down. Reviewing the operating expense ratios and cost of goods ratio, the factor creating the downward trend is the cost of goods sold. Despite the decrease in operating expense ratios between 1983 and 1984, the analyst may wish to investigate the substantial increase in selling expense ratios for the same period. A possible explanation may be that LMN management, after suffering a decline in sales in 1983, decided to expand sales volume through price cuts and increased promotion expenses. Other explanations are feasible. The analyst uses the ratios to decipher management's intent and measure their capabilities.

$$\text{Return on investment} = \frac{\$ \text{ Net profit, usually after tax, before dividends}}{\$ \text{ Average year's equity}} \times 100 = ? \%$$

$$\text{Average year's equity} = \frac{\text{Last year's ending equity} + \text{this year's ending equity}}{2}$$

Because there are several ways to calculate return on investment (ROI), care should be exercised in using this ratio. There are other methods of calculating these components that are equally good. The important thing is to be consistent and to label what method was used. The previous year's equity is found in the previous year's balance sheet.

ROI is a way of measuring how much money was made from operations relative to the shareholders' investment. (A company's equity section includes the original investment of the shareholders plus the profits retained in the company.) For the LMN shareholders, ROI has been declining from 15.4 percent in 1982 to 8.8 percent in 1983.

To assess ROI, look both at the trend (it is downward for LMN) and at alternative investment returns shareholders might make. For example, if a shareholder is comparing LMN to government bonds, he would have to assess the relative returns (returns have been higher for LMN) with the relative risks (risk is much lower with government bonds). If the ROI is the same or less for LMN stock versus government bonds over time, prudent shareholders will invest their money in the lower-risk bonds.

Stability Ratios

$$\text{Net worth to total assets} = \frac{\$ \text{ Total net worth (i.e. Equity)}}{\$ \text{ Total assets}} \times 100 = ? \%$$

$$\text{Debt to total assets} = \frac{\$ \text{ Total liabilities}}{\$ \text{ Total assets}} \times 100 = ? \%$$

Net worth to total assets (%) + Debt to total assets (%) = 100%

The net worth to total assets ratio, expressed as a percentage, indicates the amount of assets which were financed by the owners either through capital stock or reinvested profits (retained earnings). In general, the higher the ratio, the more interested prospective lenders will be in advancing funds. If the ratio is too low, the owners' investment may be so low that irresponsibility is encouraged. Also, creditors may have inadequate protection. There are no general rules for evaluating the size of this ratio: look for trends and seek comparative industry data to assess the appropriateness of the ratio. An unfavourable trend may forebode difficulty in raising additional money should it be required.

The debt to total assets ratio is another way of expressing the same thing. Because total liabilities plus equity equal total assets, the net worth and debt ratios equal 100 percent. For example, in 1982, LMN's net worth to total assets ratios was 51.8 percent, its debt ratio was 48.2 percent.

$$\underline{\text{Interest coverage}} = \frac{\text{Period net profit before interest and taxes}}{\text{Interest expense}} = ? \text{ times}$$

The interest coverage calculation indicates how many times the company's profit could pay the interest on the debt it owes. A high coverage ratio indicates minimal risk for lenders, and a favourable probability of increasing present loans. Before-tax profit is used because income taxes are calculated after deducting interest expenses. Thus, the ability to pay interest expenses is not affected by income taxes. If a company cannot cover the interest payments from its profit, it will have to delve into its cash and other assets. Failure to meet debt obligations can cause bankruptcy. An unfavourable trend or comparison with the industry average may also give the company a poor credit rating, impairing its ability to obtain additional debt. This ratio can be altered to include any fixed charges or obligations the company may incur to make this ratio more inclusive and indicative of potential problems in meeting long-term obligations.

Liquidity Ratios

There are a number of ways to assess liquidity for a company. Liquidity is the capability of a company to meet its short-term obligations. Ratio analysis is used to indicate whether liquidity problems appear to exist and whether more complex analysis is warranted.

$$\text{Current ratio} = \frac{\text{Total current assets}}{\text{Total current liabilities}} = ?/1$$

The current ratio is a measure of a company's short-term liquidity. It reflects the relative balance between short-term assets and short-term liabilities. In the LMN example the 1982 current ratio is 2.2/1 (also expressed as 2.2:1), which can be interpreted as $2.20 in current assets for every $1.00 in current liabilities. The rationale for using this ratio is that a company must meet its short-term obligations with short-term assets. As long as the company has more current assets than current liabilities, there is a margin of safety in case it becomes necessary to pay off some or all of the current liabilities. Every industry has found a different level of current ratio to be appropriate. There are no firm guidelines as to the "right" current ratio for a company.

The current ratio can be too high as well as too low. If too much money is kept in cash or inventory, for example, that money may not be being put to work as effectively as it could be. Enterprises usually earn more from investment in improvements than the interest earned from marketable securities.

$$\text{Acid test ratio} = \frac{\text{Cash + marketable securities + accounts receivable}}{\text{Current liabilities}} = ?/1$$

The acid test ratio (ATR) is a tougher test of liquidity than the current ratio. Usually, the main difference between the two calculations is the amount of money invested in inventory. Because inventory is often the least liquid current asset (the most difficult to convert into cash in a hurry), its inclusion in a liquidity ratio may overstate a company's immediate liquidity. For example, a distillery with an inventory of one-year-old whisky cannot readily convert its inventory into cash when the whisky requires five years of aging before it can be sold. There is no firm standard of an appropriate ATR.

$$\text{Working capital} = \text{Current assets} - \text{Current liabilities} = \$ \, ?$$

The working capital expressed in dollars (not as a percentage) is another way to assess liquidity. The rationale is that after the enterprise has enough current assets available to cover its current liabilities, the money left over — working capital — is available to "work with." Again there are no standards, but most managers appear to think "more is better."

Efficiency Ratios

Efficiency ratios adjust asset investments for volume levels. For current assets, "interval" ratios are used and for fixed assets, a percentage based on sales is used.

There are three common "interval" ratios: the age of receivables, inventory in day's cost of goods sold, and the age of payables. The intent in each case is to relate the position of the asset with the undertaking of an operating activity. Accounts receivable are generated by credit sales. Inventories are future expected sales at cost, and therefore are related to cost of goods sold. Accounts payable are credit purchases.[1]

$$\text{Age of accounts receivable} = \frac{\$ \, \text{Accounts receivable}}{\$ \, \text{Average daily sales}} = ? \, \text{days}$$

$$\text{Average daily sales} = \frac{\text{Total period sales}}{\text{Number of days in period}} = \$ \, ?/\text{day}$$

The average daily sales term in the denominator of the age of accounts receivable is the total sales for the period, divided by the number of days in the period. For example, the average daily sales for LMN Retail Co. Ltd. in 1983 would be calculated as follows:

$$\frac{\$ \, 875\,000}{365} = \$ \, 2\,397/\text{day}$$

Age of accounts receivable, expressed in days, shows the average number of days' sales that remain uncollected. In other words, on January 31, 1982 LMN had 33.4 average days' worth of sales for which money had not been received. In 1983 and 1984, sales and receivables changed for LMN. Management was able to reduce the amount of money invested in receivables, relative to sales level, from about thirty-three days to thirty-one days to twenty-seven days. An inspection of the balance sheet (Exhibit 2) may not have yielded the extent of this improvement in the receivables position.

Another way to think of the age of receivables is in terms of the length of time a company must wait, on average, after making a sale to collect its money. If the LMN Retail Co. Ltd. had credit terms of "due in ten days," an age of receivables of thirty days indicates poor credit management. The opposite would be true if its terms were "due in sixty days." The longer the age of receivables, the more money it takes to

---

[1]For those who have calculators and wish to set up the determination of these activity ratios quickly, the calculation can be handled by first dividing the numerator specified above by the denominator specified above, and then multiplying the resulting fraction by 365.

operate the firm because the company's customers have use of the company's money between the time goods are delivered and the time they are paid for. On the other hand, credit terms and procedures that are too stringent may drive customers away.

$$\text{Inventory in day's cost of goods sold} = \frac{\$ \text{ Ending inventory}}{\$ \text{ Average daily cost of goods sold}} = \text{? days}$$

$$\$ \text{ Average daily cost of goods sold} = \frac{\text{Period cost of goods sold}}{\text{Number of days in period}} = \$ \text{?/day}$$

Normally, management plans its inventory to meet sales expectations. The analyst does not have the management's expectation. Consequently, the most recent cost of goods sold is substituted for the sales estimate. Because inventory is valued at cost, cost of goods sold (or number of units sold times unit cost) is used for the calculation, not sales (i.e., number of units sold times selling price).

The inventory interval measure, expressed in days, indicates how fast merchandise moves through the business — from the date received to the date sold. For example, even though LMN substantially increased its investment in inventory between 1983 and 1984, the flow of inventory to sales improved.

A trend toward longer interval measures may indicate that the company is carrying excessive inventory for its sales level or that its inventory is becoming obsolete. Higher inventory levels represent larger amounts of money a company has tied up. Reducing inventory will not only release money which may be used more productively elsewhere, but usually it will also cut down on storage costs, obsolescence, etc. However, firms can lose business by not having inventory (known as "stock-outs") when the customer requests goods. Most companies try to balance the costs of running out of inventory and the costs of keeping large stock levels.

Another ratio for examining inventory is "inventory turnover." This ratio measures the number of times inventory turned over, that is, was sold. Inventory turnover is calculated by dividing cost of goods sold by the ending inventory:

$$\text{Inventory turnover} = \frac{\$ \text{ Cost of goods sold}}{\text{Ending inventory}} = \text{? times}$$

The results for LMN Retail Co. Ltd. by year are: 4.4 times in 1982, 3.9 times in 1983 and 4.2 times in 1984. The faster goods move through the business, the higher will be the turnover ratio.

$$\text{Age of accounts payable} = \frac{\$ \text{ Accounts payable}}{\$ \text{ Average daily purchases}} = \text{? days}$$

$$\$ \text{ Average daily purchases} = \frac{\text{Total period purchases}}{\text{Number of days in period}} = \$ \text{?/day}$$

Age of payables, expressed in days, shows how long the company takes to pay for what it buys on credit. Compared with industry figures and the terms of credit offered by the company's suppliers, this ratio indicates whether the company is depending too much on its trade credit. If the age of payables is excessive, creditors may demand repayment immediately, causing cash problems for the company, or may stop supplying the company until it pays for its previous purchases. Even though stretching the age of payables generates funds for a firm, a bad credit reputation can be developed which may cost the company dearly in the long term.

Good management of payables can save a company money. Many suppliers offer terms such as "1/10, net 30," which means a 1 percent discount if the invoice is paid within ten days, and the total bill must be paid within thirty days. The savings possible by paying 1 percent less within ten days work out to an annual interest rate of about 18 percent. Because bank loan rates are usually less than 18 percent, borrowing to take advantage of such discounts can increase profits.

If the age of payables is very low in comparison with industry practice, it may indicate the company is forgoing a potential source of cash.

$$\text{Fixed assets as a percent of sales} = \frac{\text{Fixed assets, net}}{\text{sales}} = ? \% \text{ or } \$ \text{ per sales dollar}$$

The ratio represents the investment in fixed assets per dollar of sale. LMN Retail has made increasingly efficient use of fixed assets given the decline in the ratio from 0.056 in 1982 to 0.029 in 1983.

Growth Ratios

Growth ratios are easy to calculate and can be done for any financial item. Usually, four growth rates are calculated before any more intensive growth analysis is made. Growth can be calculated over *any* period of time, one week or one decade. The Exhibit 5 ratios for LMN are for one-year periods. Growth is expressed as a percentage change from one point in time to another using the first point in time as a base.

$$\text{Sales growth} = \frac{\text{Year 2 sales} - \text{Year 1 sales}}{\text{Year 1 sales}} \times 100 = ? \%$$

$$\text{Profit growth} = \frac{\text{Year 2 profits} - \text{Year 1 profits}}{\text{Year 1 profits}} \times 100 = ? \%$$

Profit growth may be calculated before or after tax. In either case the approach used should be acknowledged.

$$\text{Asset growth} = \frac{\text{Year 2 total assets} - \text{Year 1 total assets}}{\text{Year 1 total assets}} \times 100 = ? \%$$

$$\text{Equity growth} = \frac{\text{Year 2 equity} - \text{Year 1 equity}}{\text{Year 1 equity}} \times 100 = ? \%$$

Other ratios

There are many other ratios that are useful in certain circumstances. Here are three ratios investors often use to assess investment performance:

$$\text{Stock yield} = \frac{\text{Annual dividend per share}}{\text{Current market price per share}} \times 100$$

$$\text{Price earnings ratio} = \frac{\text{Current market price per common share}}{\text{Earnings per common share}}$$

$$\text{Earnings per common share} = \frac{\text{Net profit after tax less preferred dividends}}{\text{Number of issued common shares}}$$

PART 4: PROJECTED FINANCIAL STATEMENTS

Every financial statement reviewed so far reflects past performance or position but, in order to plan future operations, anticipation of future performance or position is required. Statements prepared in anticipation of the future are called projected or pro forma statements. There are three basic reasons for preparing projected statements:

1. To forecast financial performance or position (e.g., what will profit likely be next year?);
2. To examine the interrelationship of financial policies with changes in marketing and production policies (e.g., if sales double, how much more money will be required in inventory investment?); and
3. To forecast cash needs, debt needs, capacity to expand operations, etc. (e.g., how big will the bank loan have to be six months from now?).

The financial statements can be projected if enough information is available to prepare meaningful estimates of future performance and position. *However, a projected statement is only as good as the estimates, assumptions and judgments that went into its preparation.* Three basic types of information can be used to prepare projected statements:

1. Managers' estimates (e.g., a sales forecast);
2. Past financial relationships (e.g., financial ratios of previous years); and
3. Assumptions as to what might occur.

It is important to explain the source of every number on a projected statement, usually with footnotes which outline the basis of the calculations. For example, a footnote for an inventory estimate may be as follows:

> Inventory calculated on the basis of thirty-five days average daily cost of goods sold. The age of inventory during the previous five years ranged between thirty and forty days.

There are two basic types of projected statements. One is a projection based on the assumption management will continue to follow past financial policies. The objective of this approach is to show what would happen if this were so. Proponents of change in financial policy often use this technique to show impending disaster unless changes are made. The other type of projection is based on a suggested set of changes. The objective of this approach is to show the impact on likely future performance and position if these changes were followed. Often these two approaches are mixed in practice.

Need for a Balancing Figure

For both the projected balance sheet and the projected income statement, a balancing figure is needed. Seldom can each account on each statement be projected in such a way as to make the statement "work out." For example, it is common when projecting a balance sheet to leave either "cash" or "bank loan payable" to the end and then insert a number that makes the balance sheet balance. For the income statement, the account often used to offset other estimates is purchases in the cost of goods sold section. No two projected statements are likely to be identical: individuals tend to use different assumptions about the future and, consequently, to have different balancing figures.

Projected Income Statement

Always begin a set of projected statements with the income statement, then the balance sheet and, finally, if desired, the statement of changes in financial position. Inventory, receivables, and payables are based on the income statement. Also, it is pointless to estimate the change in retained earnings on the balance sheet before attempting to project net profit on the income statement.

The following procedure should be used:

1. Estimating a new sales volume is the first and most important step. Use managers' estimates and/or past growth trends as guidelines.
2. Use the relationships among income statements accounts on past statements as calculated in the profitability ratio analysis to estimate cost of goods sold, gross profit, and operating expenses. Modify these for new information or for a developing trend.
3. The extent of detail in the operating expenses section depends on the quality of the information available and the objectives in preparing the projected income statement.
4. Sometimes it is appropriate to do more than one projected income statement. For example, if sales volume estimates vary significantly, statements based on a high, reasonable, or low projected sales volume may prove useful.

Perhaps it would be useful to develop a projected income statement. Exhibit 6 outlines a projected income statement for 1985 for LMN Retail Co. Ltd. Included in the exhibit is the basis of the estimate. Please note that the first step is estimating sales. The general manager of LMN Retail Co. Ltd., given his promotion plans, the economic potential in his region, and inflation rates, expected a 20 percent growth rate in sales from 1984. In reviewing the cost of goods sold from his ratio analysis, the general manager believed that he could maintain the 1984 performance; that is, cost of goods sold would be 77.5 percent of sales. The complement, gross profit, would be 22.5 percent of sales. The general manager, in reviewing his control of expenditures in the past year, felt that he could maintain general and administrative expenses at 8.7 percent of sales, and he intended to spend a fraction less on promotion, making a total of 10 percent of sales on selling expenses. Because the equipment and store fixtures would be maintained at the same level, the general manager expected no change in the depreciation charges in 1985. With regard to other expenses, such as interest, he was uncertain about how much to set aside, but decided to allow 0.3 percent of sales, which was in line with past trends. The taxes were given to him by his accountant.

The determination of the income statement, given the assumptions, is nothing more than an arithmetic exercise. The key judgment is whether the analyst agrees with the assumptions and their implications. Students should review the assumptions outlined in Exhibit 6 with the financial ratios to be found in Exhibit 5 and reach their own conclusions on the reasonableness of the projected income statement.

Projected Balance Sheet

Preparing a projected balance sheet is usually more difficult than preparing a projected income statement. The main reason for this is that there is no one key account, similar to sales on the income statement, that helps determine many others on the balance sheet. Generally, each balance sheet account must be calculated separately. Here are a few guidelines:

1. Begin by deciding what the balancing account will be (usually cash or bank loan payable).
2. Fill in all the accounts that probably remain the same (e.g., land will be the same if none will be bought or sold).
3. Fill in the accounts already calculated. For example, retained earnings will change

Exhibit 6
LMN Retail Co. Ltd.
Projected Income Statement
for the year ended January 31, 1985
(in 000's of dollars)

Item	Basis of Estimate	Amount
Sales	20% growth from 1984[1]	$ 1 303
Cost of goods sold	77.5% of sales[2]	1 010
Gross profit	22.5% of sales	$ 293
		—
Operating Expenses		
General and		
administrative	8.7% of sales[1]	$ 113
Selling	10% of sales[1]	130
Depreciation	same as 1984[1]	14
Subtotal		257
Net operating income		$ 36
Other expenses	0.3% of sales[1]	4
Net profit, before tax		$ 32
Taxes	25% of net profit before tax[3]	8
Net earnings		$ 24

[1]Manager's estimate.
[2]Last year's, best estimate.
[3]Supplied by accountant.

in accordance with the estimated profit (from the projected income statement) and in accordance with any plans for dividend payments.

4. Estimate the other accounts. Usually, a good way to begin is by using averages or trends of previous years' ratios and then adjusting these as needed. For example, suppose the estimated sales for next year were $36 500 and, based on previous patterns, the age of accounts receivable was expected to be thirty days. All but one component of the formula used to calculate age of accounts receivable, $ accounts receivable total, is known. Solve the formula to get an estimate of this missing number.

$$\text{Age of accounts receivable} = \frac{\text{Accounts receivable}}{\frac{\text{Sales}}{365}}$$

$$\text{Therefore 30 days} = \frac{\text{Accounts receivable}}{\frac{\$36\,500}{365\ \text{day}}}$$

$$\text{Accounts receivable} = 30\ \text{days} \times \$100/\text{day}$$
$$= \$3\,000$$

Therefore, estimated accounts receivable is $3 000. A similar process using the appropriate formula and estimates can be used to estimate ending inventory and accounts payable.

5. After filling in all but the balancing figure, calculate it.

Exhibit 7 presents a projected balance sheet as of January 31, 1985, based on stated assumptions, for LMN Retail Co. Ltd. In this projection, the general manager decided to maintain a minimum cash balance of $6000 and to use the bank loan as the plug. The manager reviewed the ratio analysis and determined the assumptions as set out. With regard to fixed assets, the general manager planned to invest $14 000 in new equipment during the year thereby incurring no net change in the fixed assets account. To help finance his fixed asset acquisitions, the manager planned to engage in new financing to maintain his long-term liabilities at $20 000. Again, note the key role that judgment has in the development of an appropriate assumption. The determination of the amounts for the accompanying balance sheet accounts is a matter of arithmetic calculation. The student should verify the calculations, noting that the calculations have been rounded to the closest $1000. In determining what the bank loan, that is, the plug figure, should be, the student should use the balance sheet truism that assets must equal the sum of liabilities and equity. In the initial extensions, the assets total $394 000, equity totals $201 000. This means that total liabilities must equal $193 000. From the $193 000, first the long-term liabilities of $20 000 must be deducted, giving total current liabilities of $173 000. From this total of $173 000, the $97 000 in current liabilities, which include accounts payable, taxes payable and accrued expenses, must be deducted. This means that the only other current liability available, notes payable — bank, must provide the residual amount of $76 000 in order for the balance sheet to balance.

In this case the interpretation of the balancing figure was fairly straightforward. However, if you assume that the cash was used as the balancing figure and the bank loan was set at $40 000, what would be the resulting balance showing in the account? You would first determine the liabilities, the sum of current liabilities accounts payable, $87 000; bank loan, $40 000; taxes payable, $2 000; accrued expenses, $8 000; yielding total current liabilities of $137 000. To this would be added the long-term liabilities of $20 000 and the total equity of $201 000 giving a total of $358 000. This, then, would be the total for total assets from which would be subtracted net fixed assets of $32 000 to get total current assets of $326 000. However, the current asset section would already include assets worth $356 000, the sum of net accounts receivable and inventory. To balance, cash would have to equal *negative* $30 000. Negative cash is a bank overdraft, so an additional loan of $30 000 is necessary to be added to the $40 000 provided for.

Exhibit 7
LMN Retail Co. Ltd.
Projected Balance Sheet
as of January 31, 1985
(in 000's of dollars)

Item	Basis of Estimate	Amount
ASSETS		
Current assets		
Cash	minimum equal 1984 level[4]	$ 6
Net accounts receivable	30 days sales[1]	107
Inventory	90 days cost of goods sold[1]	249
Total current assets		$ 362
Fixed assets, net	no change[4]	32
TOTAL ASSETS		$ 394
LIABILITIES		
Current liabilities		
Accounts payable	30 days purchases[2]	$ 87
Bank loan	plug	76
Taxes payable	no change[3]	2
Accrued expenses	no change[3]	8
Total current liabilities		$ 173
Long-term liabilities	no change[4]	20
TOTAL LIABILITIES		$ 193
		—
EQUITY		
Capital stock	no change[4]	$ 15
Retained earnings	1984 plus 1985 net earnings	186
TOTAL EQUITY		201
TOTAL LIABILITIES AND EQUITY		$ 394

[1]Midrange estimate from ratios.
[2]Note projected purchases equal cost of goods sold plus (minus) any increase (decrease) in inventory, 30 days is target of manager.
[3]Last year's, best estimate.
[4]Manager's estimate.

In another illustration, you may find that if you use a bank loan as a plug, it may be negative; let's say negative $30 000. How do you interpret this? This is similar to saying that instead of the enterprise owing the bank $30 000, the bank owes the company $30 000; in other words, the company has a deposit of $30 000.

Projected Statement of Changes in Financial Position

This statement is rarely prepared, but not because it is difficult. After preparing a projected income statement and balance sheet, most analysts do not find much cause to do a projected statement of changes in financial position. It is easy to construct one after one or more projected balance sheets have been completed. Follow the same procedures that are outlined for historical statements of changes in financial position.

Comments on Projected Statements

In the above example, the general manager should review the projected statements in terms of whether they make sense and what conclusions can be made. One obvious thing that shows up immediately is that, if he is successful in gaining the $76 000 bank loan, there is a high probability that the provision he has made in his projected income statement for interest of $4000 will be insufficient. A second concern would be that his plans call for a doubling of the current bank loan. Finally, though the return on equity is over 12 percent, a substantial increase from the 1984 levels can only be accomplished with a substantial increase in the bank's commitment in the business and may not compensate for the risk undertaken.

One thing to remember is that no projected statement is "right." The analysis can, and often should, continue to try new possibilities to see "what would happen if..." This is often referred to as a sensitivity analysis.

PART 5: SENSITIVITY ANALYSIS

Sensitivity analysis serves to test key assumptions made in the projected statements. This analysis will indicate which assumptions significantly affect the results of projected statements, and hence need to be monitored most carefully after a decision is made.

The following guidelines can be used to perform sensitivity analysis:

1. choose the assumption(s) you plan to vary. These may be internal factors which the company controls or external factors which the company does not control;
2. revise your assumption(s) making other reasonable assumption(s);
3. recalculate the appropriate accounts for the projected statements;
4. reconstruct the projected statements with the new assumption(s) and determine the affect on key accounts (required financing, net income); and
5. use this additional information to supplement your original conclusions.

Consider the projected balance sheets, as of January 31, 1985, for the LMN Retail Co. Ltd. Sensitivity analysis, using "what if" questions, allows the manager to explore the results of altering financial, marketing, and/or production policies. For example:

"What will happen to the bank loan if credit policy is tightened/relaxed?" The results of this analysis can be summarized as follows:

Assumption *Age of Accounts* *Receivable*	*Amount* *(000's)*	*Change* *In Plug[3]* *($000's)*	*Bank Loan* *Jan. 31, 1985* *(000's)*
30 days	107[1]	—	76
45 days	161[2]	+ 54	130
60 days	214	+107	183
15 days	54	− 53	23

[1]See Exhibit 7, original estimate.

[2]Accounts receivable = 45 days × $\dfrac{\$1303}{365 \text{ days}}$

     = 45 days × $3.57/day

     = $161

[3]Change in Plug = Change in Asset assumption from original estimate

     = New estimate — original asset estimate

For example: $54 = $161 − $107

The above sensitivity analysis shows that if LMN management relaxes its credit policy from thirty days sales to sixty days sales, the required bank loan for the company as of January 31, 1985, will be $183 000, an increase of $107 000. Notice that the increase in the bank loan equals the increase in accounts receivable. A similar format could be used to determine how variations in inventory policy and accounts payable policy would affect the required bank loan.

However, the impact on the loan varies with whether the analyst is changing a revenue or expenses assumption, or an asset or liability assumption. An increase in revenue will increase net earnings which will add to the cash position or subtract from the bank loan. Expenses have the reverse effect: a reduction in net earnings yielding a reduction in cash or an increase in the bank loan. Increases in assets lead to reductions in cash or increases in the bank loan. Increases in liabilities yield increases in cash or reductions in bank loans.

PART 6: FORMS OF OWNERSHIP

There are three major legal forms of ownership: sole proprietorship, the partnership and the limited company. It is important to note which form of ownership is involved because the different characteristics of each will have implications for the operation of the firm. The following section explains the various forms of ownership, their advantages, and their disadvantages.

Sole Proprietorship

A sole proprietorship is a business owned and usually operated by a single individual. Its major characteristic is that the owner and the business are one and the same. In other words, the revenues, expenses, assets and liabilities of the sole proprietorship are also the revenues, expenses, assets and liabilities of the owner. A sole proprietorship is also referred to as the proprietorship, single proprietorship, individual proprietorship, and individual enterprise.

A sole proprietorship is the oldest and most common form of ownership. Some examples include small retail stores, doctors' and lawyers' practices and restaurants.

Advantages

A sole proprietorship is the easiest form of business to organize. The only legal requirements for starting such a business are a municipal licence to operate a business and a registration licence to ensure that two firms do not use the same name. The organization costs for these licences are minimal.

A sole proprietorship can be dissolved as easily as it can be started. A sole proprietorship can terminate on the death of the owner, when a creditor files for bankruptcy, or when the owner ceases doing business.

A sole proprietorship offers the owner freedom and flexibility in making decisions. Major policies can be changed according to the owner's wishes because the firm does not operate under a rigid charter. Because there are no others to consult, the owner has absolute control over the use of the company's resources.

Disadvantages

As mentioned earlier, the financial condition of the firm is the same as the financial condition of the owner. Because of this situation, the owner is legally liable for all debts of the company. If the assets of the firm cannot cover all the liabilities, the sole proprietor must pay these debts from his or her own pocket. Some proprietors try to protect themselves by selling assets such as their houses and automobiles to their spouses.

A sole proprietorship, dependent on its size and provision for succession, may have difficulty in obtaining capital because lenders are leery of giving money to only one person who is pledged to repay. As a result, the sole proprietor often has to rely on friends, relatives, and government agencies for funds or loan guarantees.

A proprietorship has a limited life, being terminated on the death, bankruptcy, insanity, imprisonment, retirement, or whim of the owner.

A proprietorship, dependent on its size and provision for succession, may experience difficulties in attracting new employees because there are few opportunities for advancement, minimal fringe benefits, and little employment security.

Partnerships

A partnership is an unincorporated enterprise owned by two or more individuals. A partnership agreement, oral or written, expresses the rights and obligations of each partner. For example, one partner may have the financial resources to start the business while the other partner may possess the management skills to operate the firm. There are three types of partnerships: general partnerships, limited partnerships, and joint ventures. The most common form is the general partnership, often used by lawyers, doctors, dentists, and chartered accountants.

Advantages

Partnerships, like sole proprietorships, are easy to start up. Registration details vary by province, but usually entail obtaining a licence and registering the company name. Partners' interests can be protected by formulation of an "Agreement of Partnership." This agreement specifies all the details of the partnership.

Complementary management skills are a major advantage of partnerships. Consequently partnerships are a stronger entity and can attract new employees more easily than proprietorships.

The stronger entity also makes it easier for partnerships to raise additional capital. Lenders are often more willing to advance money to partnerships than to proprietorships because all of the partners are subject to unlimited financial liability.

Disadvantages

The major disadvantage of partnerships is that partners, like sole proprietors, are legally liable for all debts of the firm. In partnerships, the unlimited liability is both joint and personal. This means that the partners together are responsible for all the firm's liabilities. If one of the partners cannot meet his or her share of the debts, the other partner(s) must pay all debts.

Partners are also legally responsible for actions of other partners. Many partnerships include in their agreements stipulations as to what decisions — financial or otherwise — can be made without the consent of all partners. Even with this agreement, however, partners are still liable for actions under the firm's name. In these cases, a suit can be brought against a partner's actions that were not in accord with the agreement.

Partnerships are not as easy to dissolve as sole proprietorships. Partnerships terminate on the death of any one partner or when one of the partners breaks the partnership agreement or gives his or her notice to leave. It is often difficult for firms to find new partners to buy an interest. As a result, partners often take out term insurance on the lives of other partners to purchase the interest of a deceased partner, and sale prices are pre-set.

Limited Companies

Limited companies, unlike proprietorships or partnerships, are created by law and are separate from the people who own and manage them. Limited companies are also referred to as corporations. In limited companies, ownership is represented by shares of stock. The owners, at an annual meeting, elect a board of directors which has the responsibility of appointing company officers and setting the enterprise's objectives.

Advantages

Limited companies are the least risky from an owner's point of view. Shareholders of corporations can only lose the amount of money they have invested in company stock. If an incorporated business goes bankrupt, owners do not have to meet the liabilities with their own personal holdings unless they, as individuals, have guaranteed the debts of the corporation.

Corporations can raise larger amounts of capital than proprietorships or partnerships through the addition of new investors or through better borrowing power.

Limited companies do not end with the death of owners. A limited company can terminate only by bankruptcy, expiry of its charter, or a majority vote of its shareholders. With this continued life and the greater growth possibilities, limited companies usually can attract more diversified managerial talent.

Disadvantages

It is more expensive and complicated to establish corporations than proprietorships or partnerships. A charter, which requires the services of a lawyer, must be obtained through provincial governments or the federal government. In addition to legal costs, a firm is charged incorporation fees for its charter by the authorizing government.

Limited companies are subject to federal and provincial income taxes. Dividends to shareholders are also taxed on an individual basis. Thus, limited companies are taxed twice: on the profits they earn and on the dividends which come out of the profits. In proprietorships and partnerships earnings are only taxed once — as the personal income of the individuals involved.

With diverse ownerships, corporations do not enjoy the secrecy that proprietorships and partnerships have. A company must send each shareholder an annual report detailing the financial condition of the firm.

PART 7: CREDIT

When customers can purchase goods or services without paying cash immediately, they are buying "on credit." Credit is a major factor in today's business environment for both the seller and the buyer. Consumers use credit cards; firms purchase from suppliers on credit; banks lend short-term money to help companies or individuals. Attractive credit terms can increase sales by keeping present customers and attracting new ones.

Credit is riskier and more expensive than cash operations. The decision to offer credit means the credit-granting company must also be ready to accept the risk that some customers will not pay their debts. Credit management attempts to differentiate good risk customers from poor risk ones. Credit managers look at four characteristics to differentiate these firms. These are called the "four Cs of Credit": business conditions, character, capacity to repay, and collateral. The principles of credit analysis apply to bank loans, applications for charge accounts, and numerous other instances where credit is involved.

Business Conditions

Current or pending legislation (which could drastically affect the operation of a firm), economic conditions (such as seasonal and cyclical sales patterns, growth and profit potential, etc.), social trends (such as changes in market and in customer buying behaviour) and technological changes (such as innovations) are important indicators of a firm's likely potential success within an industry. Credit officers and bankers look at a firm in the context of its industry to determine, "What does the firm have to do in order to operate successfully? Is this possible for this firm?"

Character

An important consideration is the character of the borrower. Past credit records are good indications of a firm's (or individual's) chances and inclinations for paying liabilities. The marketing, production, and financial expertise of the management are critical to the success of a corporation. "Character" involves not only "trustworthiness" of the borrower, but also the capacity to achieve operating goals.

Capacity to Repay

Projected statements provide useful information about possible future financial performance and position. As stated earlier, in Part 3, ratio analysis helps the analyst make conclusions about a company's past financial policies and present position. Projected statements, as discussed in Part 4, take the analyst beyond the present to predict the potential money needs of the company and the time when repayment may be possible. Depending on the risk the lender is willing to accept, the ratios and projections may indicate the need for securing a loan against the possibility of default or bankruptcy. Restrictions on future borrowing or further capital investment may be found necessary, too. These methods of protection help ensure the lender of a higher likelihood of repayment.

Collateral

Lenders often seek protection in the event of a default (the credit loan is not repaid in full or in the time specified). This protection is usually in the form of collateral, which refers to assets pledged against the loan. For example, a company may offer its accounts receivable as collateral for a short-term loan, or an individual may offer a car as collateral for a vacation loan. The amount of collateral sought and the willingness to accept certain assets as collateral varies according to the lender and the loan situation. The realizable value of collateral varies with the selling and collecting skills of the lender, the state of the economy, and the saleability of the asset.

The above are guides to intelligent credit analysis. Every credit situation requires judgment, not just mathematical computation.

Credit Analysis

It might be useful at this juncture to use LMN Retail Co. Ltd.'s request for additional bank financing of $36 000, bringing their total to $76 000, as an example for credit analysis.

The bank manager, on receiving the projected statements outlined in Exhibits 6 and 7, would see almost immediately that there was insufficient provision for interest in other expenses. If the banker's current prime rate was 10 percent and was applied to a $76 000 loan, it would mean minimum interest of about $8000 per year. Adjusting earnings or net profit before tax for these figures would have a substantial impact. For example, if interest was believed to be $8000, this means that the net profit before tax would be $28 000 and the expected income liability would be $7000, leaving $21 000 as net earnings. This not only reduces the retained earnings in the projected balance sheet by $3000, but also implies increasing the bank loan by $3000. The net return to the owners of LMN Retail would also be reduced. At least for this one year, the company needs an additional bank loan. If the sales trend continues, by 1986 the company will need still more money. On its first calculation, the bank might not be concerned in 1985, given that its major collateral would be net accounts receivable of $107 000. Most times, banks are reluctant to take retail inventory as collateral because of the chance of possible fraud in a quick resale.

There may be some unencumbered collateral value in the fixed assets, but this is unlikely, given the fact that there is $20 000 in long-term liabilities, probably with a prior claim against these assets. As a consequence, the collateral position to support a $76 000 loan may be regarded by a commercial bank (ignoring retail inventory) as weak. If the commercial bank decides to place some reliance on inventory, it may be

Exhibit 8
Annualized Returns as of December 31
for Selected Investments
(in percentages)

Year	3-month Government of Canada Treasury Bill[1]	Bond Yield Average, 10 years and over Govt. of Canada[1]	Chartered Bank 90-day deposit receipts[1]	Chartered Bank Prime Business Loan Rate[1]	Toronto Stock Exchange Index[2]
1964	3.82	5.03	4.25	5.75	25.2
1965	4.54	5.40	4.88	6.00	6.6
1966	4.96	5.76	5.13	6.00	(6.9)
1967	5.95	6.54	5.75	6.50	17.9
1968	6.24	7.30	6.50	6.75	22.5
1969	7.81	8.33	7.50	8.50	(0.9)
1970	4.44	6.99	5.80	7.50	(3.8)
1971	3.21	6.55	4.62	6.00	7.8
1972	3.65	7.12	5.13	6.00	27.1
1973	6.35	7.70	8.50	9.50	(0.1)
1974	7.12	8.77	9.75	11.00	(25.8)
1975	8.64	9.49	9.46	9.75	19.8
1976	8.14	8.47	8.20	9.25	11.0
1977	7.17	8.77	7.24	8.25	9.7
1978	10.46	9.68	10.40	11.50	29.1
1979	13.66	11.32	13.84	15.00	42.5
1980	17.01	12.67	17.35	18.25	28.8
1981	14.41	15.27	15.70	17.25	(9.4)
1982	9.80	11.69	9.18	12.50	4.2
1983	9.71	12.02	8.50	11.00	33.6

[1]Source: Bank of Canada
[2]Source: Toronto Stock Exchange

$$\text{Yield} = \text{Dividends} + \frac{(TSE_t - TSE_{t-1})}{TSE_{t-1}}$$

t = any year

Note: brackets denote losses.

willing to lend more. The bank, in reviewing the projected balance sheet, Exhibit 7, would likely suggest that LMN Retail Co. should be looking to its suppliers for more credit. The bank is limited in its net margin, which is the difference between its normal lending rate and what it must pay for funds. (See Exhibit 8 outlining returns in bank prime lending rates, deposit rate, etc.) Supplier creditors, when they supply goods, generally are investing substantially less than the dollar amount reported as accounts payable. In a number of cases, the supplier may only invest 75 cents out of pocket for each dollar of his sale. This means that the supplier, if he collects the sale, would yield contribution to fixed costs and profit of 25 cents on the dollar for each 75 cents invested, a return of 33.33 percent.[1] Given the high returns for the supplier and the likely marginality of this account for the bank, the bank may set a lower credit line determined almost entirely by the collateral position of the net accounts receivable. If the bank agreed to invest up to 75 percent of accounts receivable, this would mean that the bank would be willing to lend approximately $80 000.

The owners should carefully inspect the projected statements, too. Note that their returns are marginal, in comparison with the stock market returns listed in Exhibit 8. The stock market is a diversified portfolio of securities encompassing all types of industries. It would seem that LMN Retail, which is subject to the vicissitudes of economic forces in one locality, should, if it is going to compensate itself for the risk undertaken, be demanding a higher return on its equity investment than the average. The owners might ask what things can be done to improve returns. Improving the returns can be done in two general ways, improving the profits, or by reducing the investment required to produce those profits. The information and background of LMN Retail Co. Ltd. operations is too sketchy to make other than the above general comments. The cases that follow should enable the student to undertake a more thorough analysis of the risk and return trade-offs from the viewpoint of both the owner and the credit supplier or the lender.

PART 8: SOURCES AND TYPES OF FINANCING

There are several sources of financing. The costs, availability, and conditions must be analyzed for each source in order to obtain the right "fit" for the firm. Financing sources can be categorized into three maturities: short-term, medium-term, and long-term. The cost of financing varies directly with the investor's perception of the risk of financing. Exhibit 9 outlines the 1978 financing sources of two different classifications of Canadian corporations.

Short-Term Financing

Enterprises can obtain short-term financing from trade creditors, chartered banks, finance companies, factor companies, and the short-term money market. Short-term financing is usually for a period of less than one year.

Trade credit refers to purchasing goods or services from suppliers on credit. It appears on the balance sheet as accounts payable. The buyer is allowed a period of

---

[1]Contribution is explained in greater detail in the marketing management section.

time, usually thirty or sixty days, in which to pay for the goods or services that have been received. To encourage prompt payments of credit sales, sellers often offer a discount from the invoiced amount if payment is made within ten days of billing. If the purchaser cannot pay the account within the given period, the creditor will often charge an interest penalty.

The Canadian chartered banks are another important source of short-term financing. Demand loans with a "line of credit" are the most common type of credit given by banks. A line of credit means the bank can arrange for an individual or a company to borrow up to an agreed sum over a certain period of time. This helps companies with seasonal products who may experience cash shortages in the off-season. The borrower is charged a rate of interest for demand notes and a fee for a line of credit. However, a bank can demand repayment of these demand loans at any time.

Finance companies, such as HFC and AVCO, also lend money but usually charge higher rates of interest than chartered banks because of higher costs of money and the generally higher risks they undertake.

Another method of short-term financing is "factoring." Instead of pledging accounts receivable for a bank loan, a borrowing company will sell the accounts receivable to a "factoring" company. Thus, except for paying the factoring company a fee, the firm does not have to concern itself with collecting the accounts or the risk of a bad debt. Customer's payments go to the factoring company rather than the seller.

Exhibit 9
Financing Sources, Last Quarter 1978
For Canadian Corporations
(total liabilities and equity = 100%)

	Corporations with $10 million or more in assets	Corporations with less than $10 million in assets
	%	%
Short-term loans		
Chartered banks	3.8	12.2
Other	3.1	6.9
Trade accounts payable	15.8	22.4
Other current liabilities	1.1	2.2
Long-term debt due in one year	0.9	1.1
Total current liabilities	24.7	44.8
	—	—
Long-term debt		
Bonds, debentures	12.2	1.1
Other	11.2	19.6
Less: Current position	(0.9)	(1.1)
Net	22.5	19.6
Other liabilities	7.6	1.8
Equity	45.2	33.8
Total	100.0	100.0

Source: Statistics Canada

Medium-Term Financing

Medium-term financing is for a period of over one year but not longer than ten years. Firms often require medium-term financing for growth, either for additional working capital or for new assets such as plant expansion, equipment, or machinery. Medium-term financing in the form of term loans can be obtained from chartered banks, private sources, or the Federal Business Development Bank. Interest rates are generally higher for these longer-term loans.

The most common source of this financing is through the chartered or commercial banks. Banks usually permit loans of this nature to remain unpaid for reasonable periods of time provided the company has pledged the required collateral, the interest payments are made on time, and the amount of the loan is reduced in an orderly fashion.

Finance companies, mortgage companies, insurance companies, and trust companies are other sources for medium-term financing. Collateral, as with banks, usually is required. If financing is required for equipment purchases, often the equipment supplier will provide partial financing.

Medium-term financing also can be obtained through the Federal Business Development Bank, previously known as the Industrial Development Bank (IDB). It lends money to companies which have good chances of success but cannot obtain financing from other sources.

Long-Term Financing

Long-term financing takes place over a period of ten years or longer. The major sources of long-term financing are from equity and long-term debt financing. Equity financing refers to the original money invested by common and preferred shareholders plus new issues of stock as well as all profits retained in the business. This money is seldom repaid. Individuals, investment companies and pension plans are the major purchasers of preferred and common stocks.

Long-term debt financing refers to bonds or debentures issued by the lender. Insurance companies, trust companies, mortgage loan companies and pension plans are the major purchasers of long-term debt issues. Fixed interest rates are levied and must be paid with repayments of principal at specified times.

Leasing is used increasingly in Canada. As a financial source, leasing is a surrogate for medium-term and long-term debt. A financial lease is an arrangement whereby the lessee acquires the use of an asset over its useful life. In return, the lessee promises to pay specified amounts, which are sufficient to cover the principal and interest objectives of the lessor. Normally, the lessor looks solely to the contract with the lessee to meet his financial objectives. Leasing is used in situations where the tax shelters associated with ownership are worth more to the lessor than the lessee.

Generally, long-term interest rates are higher than medium- and short-term rates, though market conditions will influence this relationship. Interest rates increase with the length of loans, because of the premium demanded for forgoing liquidity, plus the increased instability of security prices.

PART 9: SUMMARY

The financial analysis and management of an enterprise are complex tasks. This chapter has presented only an elementary framework. In order to be used successfully in the following exercises and cases, the framework requires more than just calculations; judgment is also needed.

The overall objective of the financial manager is to determine the expected return on investment and evaluate the risk incurred to earn the return. Projected results are required to determine the expected return. Quantitative analysis (statement of changes in financial position, ratio analysis, projections, and collateral appraisal) plus evaluation of qualitative factors (character and business conditions) are employed to assess the risk.

Finance Exercises

Exercise 1
ABC Distribution Co. Ltd.
(Statement of Changes in Financial Position)

Assignment

From the balance sheets of ABC Distribution Co. Ltd., prepare a Statement of Changes in Financial Position for:

(a) one year ending November 30, 1979
(b) one year ending November 30, 1980
(c) two years ending November 30, 1981

ABC Distribution Co. Ltd.
BALANCE SHEETS
As of November 30
($000's)

	1979	1980	Change	1981
ASSETS				
Cash	$ 6	$ 20	+16	$ 8
Accounts receivable	1 910	2 266	+ 956 u	3 220
Inventories	2 360	2 524	u	4 730
Total current assets	$4 276	$4 810		$ 7 958
Other investments	300	276	↓ S	356
Net fixed assets	886	1 080	u	2 588
Land	146	156	u	462
Other assets	38	12	S	8
TOTAL ASSETS	$5 646	$6 334		$11 372
LIABILITIES				
Working capital loan	$1 344	$ 756	u	$ 2 126
Accounts payable	456	876	S	1 928
Taxes payable	164	476	S	368
Other current liabilities	156	228	S	126
Total current liabilities	$2 120	$2 336		$4 548
Term bank loan (16%)	—	—		2 100
Mortgages payable	376	282	u	234
Total liabilities	$2 496	$2 618		$ 6 882
	—	—		—
SHAREHOLDERS' EQUITY				
Common stock	$2 192	$2 192		$ 2 192
Retained earnings	958	1 524	S	2 298
Total shareholders' equity	3 150	3 716		4 490
TOTAL LIABILITIES AND SHAREHOLDERS' EQUITY	$5 646	$6 334		$11 372

Exercise 2
ABC Distribution Co. Ltd.
(Calculation of Ratios)

Assignment

Listed below are the income statements of the ABC Distribution Co. Ltd. and a ratio sheet. Calculate the missing ratios and evaluate the company's performance.

ABC Distribution Co. Ltd.
INCOME STATEMENTS
For Years Ended November 30
(000's)

	1979	1980	1981
Net sales	$9 718	$11 772	$16 312
Cost of sales	7 142	8 246	11 260
Gross profit	$2 576	$3 526	$ 5 052
Less: Bad debt expense	$ 132	10	54
General & administrative expense	368	414	506
Interest expense	124	110	206
Salaries	1 388	1 640	2 210
Selling expense	376	444	660
Depreciation	132	132	208
Subtotal	2 520	2 750	3 844
Operating profit	$ 56	$ 776	1 208
Other income	198	276	222
Profit before tax	$ 254	$1 052	$1 430
Income taxes	124	486	656
Net profit	$ 130	$ 566	$ 774

ABC Distribution Co. Ltd.[1]

Ratio Sheet
for Selected Dates and Periods
(365-day year)

	1979	1980	1981
PROFITABILITY			
(a) Vertical analysis			
Sales	100.0%	—	—
Cost of goods sold	—	70.0%	—
Gross profit	—	—	31.0%
Less: Bad debts	1.4%	—	—
General & admin. exp.	—	3.5%	—
Interest	—	—	1.3%
Salaries	14.3%	—	—
Selling	—	3.8%	—
Depreciation	—	—	1.3%
Operating profit	0.6%	—	—
Other income	—	2.3%	—
Profit before tax	—	—	8.8%
(b) Return on average equity	—	16.5%	—
STABILITY			
Net worth to total assets	55.8%	—	—
Interest coverage	—	10.6 times	—
LIQUIDITY			
Current ratio	2.02:1	—	—
Acid test ratio	—	0.98:1	—
Working capital ($000)	—	—	3410
EFFICIENCY			
Age of receivables	71.7 days	—	—
Inventory in days of goods sold	—	111.7 days	—
Age of payables[3]	—	—	52.3 days[2]
Fixed assets/sales	—	0.92	—

GROWTH	1979-80	1980-81
Sales	21.1%	—
Net profit	—	36.7%
Total assets	12.2%	—
Equity	—	20.8%

[1]ABC Distribution Co. Ltd. is Carson Lumber Company Limited.
[2]Assumes purchases are $13 466 000 for 1981; i.e. cost of goods sold plus ending inventory less beginning inventory.
[3]In order to calculate the 1979 age of payables, assume beginning inventory = ending inventory.

Exercise 3
DEF Co. Ltd.
(Projected Statements)

1. Sales projection	$250 000
2. Gross profit	20% of sales
3. Last year's ending inventory	$100 000
4. This year's age of ending inventory	90 days
5. Other operating expenses	8% of sales
6. Income tax	20% of profits
7. Accounts payable	30 days
8. Accounts receivable	20 days
9. Taxes payable	25% of year's taxes
10. Land — at cost	$10 000
11. Building and fixtures — at cost	$30 000
12. Accumulated depreciation — building and fixtures as of end of last year	$ 7 000
13. Depreciation expense for year	$ 2 000
14. Capital stock	$40 000
15. Retained earnings (last year)	$25 000
16. Salary expense	$14 000

Assignment

A. The above data has been supplied to you by the general manager of DEF Co. Ltd., a retailing firm.

1. Prepare a projected income statement for the next year.
2. Prepare a projected balance sheet for the next year.

Use a 365 day interval measure.

B. The sales manager disagrees with the general manager's sales projection. He believes sales will be $400 000. Do another set of projections using the sales manager's sales estimates. Does this difference of opinion make much difference in DEF's projected financial performance and position next year?

1

Carson Lumber Company Limited

In March 1982, Mr. Michael Carr, the new vice-president of the Eastern Ontario Region of the National Bank of Canada, was reviewing the file of the Carson Lumber Company, one of the region's biggest borrowers. The following day, Mr. George Carson and Mr. Frank McMillan, the president and controller respectively of the Carson Lumber Company, would present their request to the bank's loan committee for a loan of up to $5.4 million. The loan committee, consisting of Mr. Carr, the central credit manager and the assistant central credit manager, would then make a recommendation to the bank's board of directors. This recommendation would be the basis of the bank's decision on Carson Lumber's request.

PRE-1978

The Carson Lumber Company was founded in the 1870s by the Carson family to market the lumber on their land. After the original lumber stands near Cornwall, Ontario, had been depleted, the wholesale lumber business was continued and slowly expanded. In 1950, Carson Lumber owned four small lumber yards in the Cornwall area, each operating as a separate company.

In 1959, Mr. J. H. Carson became president and amalgamated the four companies into Carson Lumber Company. The company acquired six more lumber yards north and west of Cornwall, Ontario, but further growth was limited by Mr. J. H. Carson's belief that growth should only be financed by internally generated funds. For nearly one hundred years, Carson Lumber had been dealing with the Cornwall branch of the Eastern Bank, and in 1978 borrowed approximately $700 000 on a seasonal basis each year to finance an inventory build-up needed to offset the seasonal sales. From April to November, 77 percent of the sales occurred evenly, while 23 percent were evenly distributed from December to March. The company's sales were between $5.0 million and $7.0 million in the 1970s, 90 percent wholesale to local residential contractors. Exhibit 1 presents profit before tax from 1971 to 1981.

In 1978, Mr. J. H. Carson realized that, because of his health, he would not be able to continue managing the company. His son, Mr. George Carson, agreed to take over as president. Mr. George Carson had taken over the business for the summer of 1976 when his father became ill. After his father returned, Mr. George Carson assumed the advertising and budgeting responsibilities for the company.

1979 AND 1980

Mr. George Carson had a postgraduate degree in business administration and several years' teaching experience. When he became president of the company, Carson Lumber had been primarily a wholesale business, subject to the volatility of the demand for housing. The new president felt that, with minimal changes in inventory and yard operations, the company could take advantage of the growing retail market for building products and thereby stabilize its operations.

He approached the company's banker, the Cornwall branch manager of the Eastern Bank, with a request for a loan to finance these changes in the company. However, the Eastern Bank branch manager would support only a seasonal loan to finance inventory and refused to pass the loan application on to his superiors.

Consequently, Mr. George Carson approached the National Bank of Canada with his plans and needs. The National Bank of Canada granted an initial working capital loan in 1979 of $1 344 000, taking accounts receivable and inventory as collateral. The National Bank asked that it be provided with quarterly financial statements and monthly reports of inventory, sales, and receivables.

Mr. George Carson reorganized the company's eleven branches into three regions. The Northern Region served an urban market and consisted of three yards just outside the city of Ottawa. Four lumber yards in the Cornwall area made up the Eastern Region and five lumber yards near Kingston formed the Western Region. The Eastern Region was a rural market and the Western Region was partially a resort and partially an urban area. In an attempt to minimize inventory levels, one branch in each region operated as a depot. A fleet of trucks kept frequent and regular schedules between the lumber yards and the depot to provide rapid delivery to the customer.

Each region was made the responsibility of an area supervisor who had worked for many years in the company's lumber yards. A management committee, consisting of the president, controller, and area supervisors, met monthly to discuss operational strategy. The committee set budgets for each branch every four months. Exhibits 2 and 3 outline the financial statements from 1979 to 1981.

1981 PROJECTIONS

Exhibit 4 outlines the projected capital expenditures for 1981 and 1982. The projected 1981 capital expenditures of $900 000 were primarily for improvements in the company's showrooms and display areas. Depreciation and profit were expected to cover these capital expenditures. A sales increase of $3.2 million was anticipated for 1981 based on the opinions of contractors, yard managers, and business publications on the outlook for the economy and the housing market. Operating profit was expected to be $1 460 000, assuming a gross margin of 30 percent and expenses of $3.04 million. To finance an increase of $1 260 000 in receivables and inventory, a total working capital loan of $1 800 000 was requested and granted by the National Bank.

1981 ACTUAL

After spending six months studying the potential of the Ottawa market and discussing the revised capital budget with the bank, Carson Lumber opened a discount home centre in September 1981. The bank granted a term loan of $2.1 million.

The home centre was aimed at the retail market. The concept enabled the consumer to purchase in one store all types of building and household products such as tiles, wallpaper, carpet, lumber, plumbing supplies, and lighting fixtures. Each item in the store had two prices clearly marked so that the customer only paid for the service received. The regular price was the price at which the item could be charged and delivered. The discount price applied if the customer wished to pay cash and take the goods away. A third price was also charged if the customer wished to pay cash and have the purchase delivered. The new store's sales in its first two months of operations were $1 140 000.

Sales in 1981 were $1 340 000 greater than projected, and capital expenditures were $1 800 000 above budget. In addition to granting the term loan, the National Bank increased the company's working capital loan to $2.12 million.

1982 PROJECTIONS

For 1982, Mr. George Carson projected a 65 percent increase in sales to $27.0 million and an operating profit of 8 percent of sales. To finance inventory and receivables of up to $12.0 million, a working capital loan of up to $5.4 million in June and July was requested.

THE NATIONAL BANK

As he reviewed the file, Mr. Carr looked for anything which suggested that the bank should take steps to increase its protection of the loan. He particularly noted the increase in profits since 1978 and his predecessor's confidence in the management ability of Carson Lumber. However, he closely examined the 1982 projections, questioning their accuracy. It was obvious that, because 65 percent of Carson Lumber's sales were to contractors, the company was still dependent on the housing market. Total housing starts in Canada were 178 000 in 1981 and in January–February 1982 were 27 000, 10.9 percent less than the same period in 1981. Total housing starts in 1982 were expected to decline because of higher interest rates charged for mortgages. In February 1982, the price of residential building materials was 6.8 percent higher than February 1981. As he examined this information, Mr. Carr wondered whether he should recommend an increase in Carson Lumber's working capital loan, and, if so, by how much and under what terms as to collateral and maturity.

Exhibit 1
Carson Lumber Company Limited
Profit Before Tax
($000's)

1971	(72)
1972	20
1973	6
1974	220
1975	256
1976	268
1977	322
1978	510
1979	254
1980	1052
1981	1430

Exhibit 2
Carson Lumber Company Limited
Income Statements
For years Ended November 30
(000's)

	1979	1980	1981
Net sales	$9 718	$11 772	$16 312
Cost of sales	7 142	8 246	11 260
Gross profit	$2 576	$ 3 526	$ 5 052
Less: Bad debt expense	132	10	54
General & admin. exp.	368	414	506
Interest expense	124	110	206
Salaries	1 388	1 640	2 210
Selling expense	376	444	660
Depreciation	132	132	208
Subtotal	2 520	2 750	3 844
Operating profit	$ 56	$ 776	$ 1 208
Other income	198	276	222
Profit before taxes	$ 254	$ 1 052	$ 1 430
Income taxes	124	486	656
Net profit	$ 130	$ 566	$ 774

Exhibit 3
Carson Lumber Company Limited
Balance Sheets
As of November 30
($000's)

	1979	1980	1981
ASSETS			
Cash	$ 6	$ 20	$ 8
Accounts receivable[1]	1910	2266	3220
Inventories[1]	2360	2524	4730
Total current assets	$4276	$4810	$7958
Other investments	300	276	356
Net fixed assets	886	1080	2588
Land	146	156	462
Other assets	38	12	8
TOTAL ASSETS	$5646	$6334	$11 372
LIABILITIES			
Working capital loan	$1344	$ 756	$ 2126
Accounts payable	456	876	1928
Taxes payable	164	476	368
Other current liabilities	156	228	126
Total current liabilities	$2120	$2336	$ 4548
Term bank loan (16%)[2]	—	—	2100
Mortgages payable[3]	376	282	234
Total liabilities	$2496	$2618	$ 6882
SHAREHOLDERS' EQUITY			
Common stock	$2192	$2192	$ 2192
Retained earnings	958	1524	2298
Total shareholders' equity	3150	3716	4490
TOTAL LIABILITIES AND SHAREHOLDERS' EQUITY	$5646	$6334	$11 372

[1] Accounts receivable and inventories were pledged as security to the National Bank of Canada.

[2] The 1981 term bank loan was secured by a demand debenture, in the amount of $3 500 000, which provided a fixed and floating charge over the company's assets, together with an assignment of fire insurance over the fixed assets subject to prior encumbrances. The loan was repayable in six semi-annual instalments of $70 000 each commencing November 30, 1982, six semi-annual instalments of $105 000 commencing November 30, 1985, and $124 050 semi-annual instalments thereafter. The debenture also contained restrictions on capital expenditures, payment of dividends, redemption of capital stock, and certain other restrictions.

[3] Mortgages payable 12 percent, repayable in annual instalments of $30 000, plus interest on June 30 of each year, secured by mortgages on certain properties.

Exhibit 4
Carson Lumber Company Limited
Capital Expenditures
1981 and 1982
(000's)

	1981		1982
	Projected	Actual	Projected
Showroom renovations	$ 70	$ 160	$ 80
Showroom expansion for two lumber yards	160	140	—
New showrooms for two lumber yards	520	850	200
Land for new yard in Northern Region	50	50	—
Land for new yard in Western Region	—	—	30
New vehicles	100	700	240
New retail outlet in Ottawa	—	800	—
Total	$900	$2700	$550

2

Confederation Sporting Goods Ltd.

In early May 1980, Gail Edwards,[1] assistant credit manager, was receiving the credit application of Bowhill Sports Stores Ltd. The sales manager had just called her and asked for her decision on the request of Mr. Bowhill to ship $15 000-worth of merchandise to him, to be paid over an eighteen-month period, with all replacement orders to be treated as normal credit sales.

In 1980, Confederation Sporting Goods Ltd. was one of the major manufacturers and distributors of sports equipment in Canada. The company's line included hockey, baseball, football, soccer, basketball, and other team sport equipment. The company, in addition to its manufacturing activities in Canada, contracted with foreign suppliers. At the last executive meeting the president, while pointing out the progress of the company, related that the out-of-pocket costs, or variable costs associated with producing the company's line, had steadily declined, and were now 70 percent of sales. He expected that the new facilities and production techniques planned would further reduce the cash paid directly to generate a dollar of sale. In closing his address to the executives, the president stated that if the aggressive selling activities were maintained and the expected production efficiencies realized, Confederation would have its best year on record, achieving the objective of a net profit return on sales of 5 percent.[2]

In April 1980, Scott Bowhill had called the sales manager, Ian MacKay, to inquire whether Confederation would be willing to help finance a new undertaking. Ian MacKay, an acquaintance of Mr. Bowhill, replied that while he, of course, was interested in increasing Confederation's sales, any deal would be subject to review and approval by Confederation's credit department. With new accounts, the credit department was empowered to arrange longer terms and grant extended normal terms, where the return justified the risk undertaken. The practice of extended and special billing was prevalent throughout the industry.

Gail Edwards was given the assignment of evaluating Mr. Bowhill's credit request. In preparation for the assessment, she obtained the latest credit report on Bowhill Sports Stores Ltd. The credit report outlined that the company had been in business for two years in West City. The credit agency had been unable to get financial data on the company: Mr. Bowhill refused to comply with the credit agency's request for such information. The agency reported, however, that the company did have a bank loan. Payments in the initial year were reported by other suppliers as slow. The payment record in the second year of operation had worsened.

After receiving the credit agency's report on Bowhill Sports Stores, Gail Edwards discussed the prospective request with Ian MacKay. The sales manager said that he had known Mr. Bowhill for a number of years. Mr. Bowhill had been a very successful sales rep with a competing sports goods manufacturer, Best Equipment Inc. In fact, several years previously, Ian MacKay had tried unsuccessfully to hire him. Mr.

---

[1]All persons in this case have been disguised.

[2]The difference between 5 percent profit and 30 percent after direct out-of-pocket costs are expenditures that are made irrespective of sales levels achieved.

Bowhill, prior to undertaking sales activities, had been in Best's public relations department. Formerly he had been a professional football player, and in the off-season promoted the use of Best's equipment by participating in sports clinics. Unfortunately, early in his football career, Mr. Bowhill suffered an injury that terminated his participation in professional sports. With the sudden end of his professional sports career, Mr. Bowhill sought a sales position with Best Equipment, and in a matter of a few years he had become one of Best's leading salespeople. Given his success in selling and his desire to be independent, Mr. Bowhill decided to start a sporting retail/wholesale business in 1978.

At Ian MacKay's urging, Gail Edwards arranged a meeting with Mr. Bowhill during a trip that had been arranged for her through western Canada to review other accounts and sales activities. On approaching the store, Gail Edwards noted that the taxicab driver had some difficulty in finding the location of Bowhill's store and that when they arrived, all of the four parking spaces in front of the store were full and the front window was covered with signs, "Sale, 50% Off." As she arrived, Mr. Bowhill was there to greet her. He apologized for the fact that he could not meet her at the airport, but explained that he was needed to help organize the forthcoming sale. Inside, the store seemed spacious and well organized. Several salespeople were busy pricing goods or talking to the customers in the store. Mr. Bowhill laughed as he noted Gail Edwards inspecting his premises. He stated that this was the start of his dream to own a chain of sports stores.

After entering his office, a small cubicle set at the back of the store, Mr. Bowhill discussed his business and the opportunity he now had. He mentioned that he had started his store with the intention of becoming a price discount leader in West City. He stated that his previous experience had taught him that if a good product was delivered on time, at a good price, sales would grow easily. Consequently, he established a retail/wholesale sports business with a dual concept: a discount operation for the general public and a focus on team equipment orders for the amateur sports associations in the region, that is, a wholesale operation. Best Equipment had agreed to stock a substantial portion of his inventory with the understanding that within two years his payables would be normal.

As Mr. Bowhill handed the company's financial statements to Gail Edwards, he said, "Now look at the results, not the hopes." Referring to the income statement (Exhibit 1), Mr. Bowhill pointed out that he had been successful in gaining a healthy sales volume; however, profits had not been what he had originally hoped for. In reviewing the two years of hard work, Mr. Bowhill said that he might have chosen the wrong location. He had chosen his current site because of the low rent. The current location provided spacious facilities (about 186 m²) and allowed him to keep his overhead at a minimum but in doing so made direct contact between his business and prospective retail customers difficult. He said that in the last year promotion expenses had been increased in an attempt to overcome the disadvantage of the location. But the retail promotion had been only marginally successful. The wholesale business had been successful from opening day. Before he started his own business, Mr. Bowhill had called on the contacts he had made in the sports clinics. He discovered that with price cuts and delivery, he was able to gain significant penetration in the West City and regional wholesale market. However, the competition had responded, and he expected that significant wholesale sales increases, at profitable levels, would be impossible to achieve.

While Mr. Bowhill had accepted his profit situation, he was disturbed by the financial position of the company as presented in Exhibit 2. He said that the company's cash position was such that he could not meet his original commitment to Best Equipment. In fact, they had called a few days earlier to say they were going to cut Bowhill off, unless he made immediate payment of 50 percent of their bill. In order to do this, Mr. Bowhill was preparing a sale.

Mr. Bowhill then became more intense as he outlined his plans for turning the operation into a success. He had been approached by the owner of a shopping mall, due for completion in early July, who was interested in obtaining a sports shop to round out the mall shopping activities. The mall owner was a personal friend of Mr. Bowhill and was impressed by the volume of business he had generated in a short time. The mall had a 93 m² outlet available for rent. If Mr. Bowhill agreed to move his retail business there, the mall owner would grant him a lease at $109.00 per square metre annually or 7 percent of gross sales, whichever was greater. The new store would feature both individual and team sports equipment and accessories. The mall was being constructed in the fastest growing segment of West City, and would be the major shopping centre for a section of the city with twenty thousand people. The surrounding neighbourhood comprised single-family residential, detached, semi-detached, and attached units, plus high-rise apartments.

Mr. Bowhill viewed the sales opportunity as excellent despite loss of his wholesale business. In fact, he expected to generate a sales volume 20 percent higher than the current rate at a substantially higher gross margin. The increase in retail sales and the addition of higher margin products to his sales mix would yield on average, he hoped, a gross margin of 45 percent. Mr. Bowhill mentioned that he had been wrong before but that he believed sales would be no lower than 80 percent of his current level and a minimum gross margin of 35 percent would be achieved.

If his venture proved successful, Mr. Bowhill continued, the mall owner was planning to open similar malls in other sections of the city and in western Canada.

Mr. Bowhill's problem was a lack of cash to stock the new store. He suspected that he would have little inventory or cash left, once the current sales campaign had eliminated the inventory at his present location. The expenses associated with the move were minimal. The rent was paid monthly since the conclusion of the lease agreement in March 1980. Many of the current store fixtures could be used in the new store, with only $4 000 of new fixtures being required. The mall operator had agreed to finance the leasehold improvements required to convert the space to a sports shop. Financing the inventory would be difficult. All monies and assets that Mr. Bowhill had were pledged to liquidate his current business, to provide a minimal opening cash balance in July and to purchase the additional store fixtures. Exhibits 3, 4, and 5 present the projected two-month results and projected balance sheet as of July 1, 1980.

Mr. Bowhill added that he had contacted Best Equipment about a financial arrangement similar to the one two years previously. Best declined, and continued its efforts to collect past due accounts. Consequently, Mr. Bowhill contacted Confederation's sales manager, Ian MacKay, about financing some of the original stock and future replacements for the new store. Mr. Bowhill estimated that his initial requirements for a line of credit with Confederation would be $15 000. This would be equal to three months' sales. Mr. Bowhill would make a note payable to Confederation for the $15 000 and start payments at the rate of $1 000 per month, three months after the store opened and goods were received. He stated a number of other suppliers had indicated their willingness to supply goods on a similar basis. All other shipments after the initial sale would be on normal credit terms of net thirty days. While walking Gail Edwards to her cab, Mr. Bowhill thanked her for her interest in his business and said that he would call Ian MacKay at the end of April to find out Confederation's decision.

Exhibit 1
Bowhill Sports Stores Ltd.
Income Statements for the Years
Ending March 31
(in 000's of dollars)

	1979	1980
Sales	$278	$305
	—	—
Cost of goods sold:		
Beginning inventory	$—	$ 68
Purchases	253	210
Goods available for sale	$253	$278
Less: ending inventory	68	77
Cost of goods sold	185	201
Gross profit	$ 93	$104
	—	—
Operating expenses:		
Salaries and wages	$ 45	$ 49
Rent	12	12
Selling and administrative	26	33
Interest	3	2
Total	86	96
Net profit before tax	$ 7	$ 8
Estimated income tax	2	2
Net earnings	$ 5	$ 6

Exhibit 2
Bowhill Sports Stores Ltd.
Balance Sheets as of March 31
(in 000's of dollars)

	1979	1980
ASSETS		
Current assets		
Cash	$ 1	$ 3
Accounts receivable	16	16
Inventory	68	77
Total current assets	$ 85	$ 96
Fixed assets		
Store fixtures, net	18	16
TOTAL ASSETS	$103	$112
LIABILITIES		
Current Liabilities		
Bank loan	$ 23	$ 18
Note payable — Best Equipment	25	25
Accounts payable	37	47
Taxes payable	2	—
Total current liabilities	$ 87	$ 90
Long-term note due — S. Bowhill[1]	10	10
TOTAL LIABILITIES	$ 97	$100
	—	—
EQUITY		
Capital stock	$ 1	$ 1
Retained earnings	5	11
Total equity	6	12
TOTAL LIABILITIES AND EQUITY	$103	$112

[1]Subordinated to bank loan and note payable.

Exhibit 3
Bowhill Sport Stores Ltd.
Projected Income Statement
For Two Months Ending May 31, 1980
(in 000's of dollars)

	Basis of Estimate	
Sales	Bowhill's estimate, sale of inventory at cost	$ 77
Cost of goods sold:		
Beginning inventory	Exhibit 2	$ 77
Purchases	No purchases during liquidation	0
Cost of goods available for sale		$ 77
Less:		
Ending inventory	Bowhill's assumption, all inventory sold	0
Cost of goods sold		77
Gross profit		$ 0
Operating expenses	Annual operating expenses, Exhibit 1, for two months, ($96/12) times 2	16
Net deficit		($ 16)

Prepared by S. Bowhill.

Exhibit 4
Bowhill Sports Stores Ltd.
Projected Balance Sheet
As of May 31, 1980
(in 000's of dollars)

Basis of Estimate

ASSETS		
Cash	Plug	$ 8
Store fixtures	No change	16
TOTAL ASSETS		**$24**
LIABILITIES		
Bank loan	No change	$ 18
Notes payable	Paid off	0
Accounts payable	Paid off	0
Long term note		
due S. Bowhill	No change	10
TOTAL LIABILITIES		**$ 28**
EQUITY		
Capital stock	No change	$ 1
Deficit	Retained earnings less	
	Exhibit 3 net deficit	(5)
TOTAL EQUITY		**(4)**
TOTAL LIABILITIES AND EQUITY		**$ 24**

Prepared by S. Bowhill.

Exhibit 5
Bowhill Sports Stores Ltd.
Projected Balance Sheet
As of July 1, 1980
(in 000's of dollars)

	Basis of Estimate	
ASSETS		
Cash	Plug	$ 4
Store fixtures	Additional investment of $4	20
TOTAL ASSETS		$ 24
LIABILITIES		
Bank loan	No change	$ 18
Long term note due S. Bowhill	No change	10
TOTAL LIABILITIES		$ 28
EQUITY		
Capital stock	No change	$ 1
Deficit	No change	(5)
TOTAL EQUITY		$ (4)
TOTAL LIABILITIES AND EQUITY		$ 24

Prepared by S. Bowhill.

3

Fletcher Industrial Supply

In June 1973, Mr. Fletcher was working out the financial details of a tentative plan to build an extension onto his warehouse. He was concerned as to what source of funds he should use in order to raise the $10 000 required for construction costs.

THE COMPANY

Fletcher Industrial Supply was a distributor of machine tools, maintenance parts, and related equipment in Barrie, Ontario. Eighty-eight kilometres north of Toronto and situated on Lake Simcoe, Barrie was the largest and fastest growing industrial centre in the Georgian Bay region of Ontario. In 1972 the city had an estimated population of 34 500. In addition it served the surrounding farming communities and summer cottage trade. The customers of Fletcher Industrial Supply were mostly industrial maintenance departments, but there was also some high margin retail business, principally from farmers in the surrounding area.

Mr. Fletcher purchased the business from its previous owner in February 1970. By this time he had already gained wide experience in a series of jobs. He had worked for a variety of different companies, including one of his current Toronto-based competitors. During those years, however, a persistent ambition to operate his own business dominated him. His first personal venture was a retail hardware store in Peterborough, which he sold when he acquired the Barrie Industrial Supply distributorship.

Mr. Fletcher felt pleased with the progress his company had made in the three years since he had purchased it. He had enjoyed considerable success in building up sales. In June 1973, monthly sales volume averaged over $20 000. (Exhibit 1 gives income statements for the past three years.) Mr. Fletcher was also proud of the company's reputation for dependability and integrity. He believed his success was due largely to the personalized service and engineering advice he offered his customers. He also realized that an important factor in attracting new customers and building lasting customer relationships was his success in obtaining exclusive rights to handle the products of some of the better manufacturers. Maintaining good supplier relations with those manufacturers who granted him exclusives was a key element to future success.

COMPETITION

Until late 1972, Mr. Fletcher had been the only distributor of machine tools and parts who was situated in Barrie. Competition had come from salespeople operating from out-of-town warehouses. In the fall of 1972 another distributor started up an operation in Barrie. Mr. Fletcher believed, however, that the new competitor would not conflict directly with more than a small part of his business because of the exclusive distribution rights he held and his specialized products. This new distributor also did not as yet have the reputation for dependable service that Fletcher enjoyed.

THE FUTURE

Although market information was limited, Mr. Fletcher thought that he had about 35 percent of the machine tool and equipment market in Barrie and the surrounding region. Given the existing market potential, he felt that he could not expect to increase his sales beyond $400 000 without expanding his geographical market area. For the next two years he projected probable sales to be $273 000 for the year ending January 31, 1974, and $322 000 to January 31, 1975. He felt sales could fall as low as $261 700 and $297 000 for fiscal years 1974 and 1975 respectively, or go as high as $300 000 and $350 000.

THE PROBLEM

In June 1973, one of Mr. Fletcher's major concerns was the cramped space in his warehouse. With his present facilities he felt he could not handle any significant increases in inventory on hand. In order to maintain his high standard of service and delivery, he wanted to add a warehouse extension as soon as possible. At the same time one of his top priorities was to reduce the age of his accounts payable to sixty days before the end of the fiscal year. If he failed to do so he feared that he would put some of his exclusive distribution agreements in jeopardy. First, Mr. Fletcher wanted to determine the amount of money he needed to carry out his plans, and then to decide which source of funds to use. Several options were available. Mr. Fletcher's preference would be to borrow either from the bank or from a private lender. He did, however, have another alternative, namely selling some of his interest in the company to a friend. He could do this either by forming a partnership or by incorporating and selling shares. At the time of his decision, Mr. Fletcher was hesitant to use equity financing. He felt he would not get as much now for a share in the company as he could expect in a year when his hard work had paid off in increased profits. He was also wondering about the company's capability to generate its own funds.

Exhibit 1
Fletcher Industrial Supply
Comparative Statement of Profit and Loss
for the Year Ended January 31

	1971		1972		1973	
Sales (net)		$93·011		$159 992		$206 682
Cost of sales						
Inventory, opening	$22 651		$ 30 898		$ 34 208	
Purchases	72 666		$120 486		160 939	
	$95 317		$151 384		$195 147	
Inventory, closing	30 898	64 419	34 208	117 176	47 463	147 684
Gross margin		$28 592		$ 42 816		$ 58 998
Expenses						
Wages and commissions	$10 987		$ 14 555		$ 19 176	
Rent[1]	1 943		2 220		1 110	
Interest expense	2 723		2 922		3 375	
Provision for doubtful accounts	671		—		—	
General selling expenses	2 910		2 756		2 386	
General administrative expenses	7 643		10 472		13 285	
Depreciation	—	26 877	1 030	33 955	2 436	41 768
Net profit		$ 1 715		$ 8 861		$ 17 230
Drawings		$ 7 375		$ 10 836		$ 11 441

[1]With the purchase of the land and building, rent expense had now been eliminated.

Exhibit 2
Fletcher Industrial Supply
Comparative Balance Sheets as of January 31

	1971	1972	1973
ASSETS			
Current Assets			
Cash	$ 8 606	$ 1 751	$ 142
Accounts receivable, net	12 850	20 167	33 869
Inventory	30 898	34 208	47 463
Prepaid interest and rent	302	302	174
Total current assets	$52 656	$56 428	$ 81 648
Fixed assets			
Automobiles	$ 3 435	$ 3 435	$ 4 785
Land	—	—	6 088
Building	—	—	12 294
Equipment	—	—	399
	$ 3 435	$ 3 435	$ 23 566
Less: accumulated depreciation	—	1 030	3 466
Total fixed assets	3 435	2 405	20 100
Other assets			
Goodwill	3 000	3 000	3 000
Deferred charges	657	385	275
TOTAL ASSETS	$59 748	$62 218	$105 023
LIABILITIES			
Current liabilities			
Accounts payable	$18 464	$29 074	$ 50 250
Employee deductions payable	165	237	268
Sales tax payable	445	948	1 937
Accrued interest and salaries payable	969	—	1 380
Total current liabilities	$20 043	$30 259	$ 53 835
Long-term liabilities			
Bank loan[1]	$12 690	$10 170	$ 7 650
GMAC payable[2]	3 024	1 773	521
O'Connor payable[3]	19 651	17 651	17 651
Mortgage payable[4]	—	—	17 212
Total long-term liabilities	35 365	29 594	43 034
TOTAL LIABILITIES	$55 408	$59 853	$ 96 869
CAPITAL[5]			
Personal capital	4 340	2 365	8 154
TOTAL LIABILITIES AND CAPITAL	$59 748	$62 218	$105 023

[1]$15 000 was borrowed in 1970. Principal repayments — $210/month, interest — $58/month.

[2]Balance owing on a truck bought in 1970. It was totally repaid in April 1973.

[3]Loan from previous owner of the business, secured by inventory, incurred in February 1970 as part of the purchase agreement. Principal repayments of $1000 due in January 1971 and 1972, with repayments of $2000 due every succeeding January. Interest of 8.75 percent to be paid half-yearly on the balance of principal owing, in January and June.

[4]Mortgage loan made in August 1972 when Mr. Fletcher purchased the property and building. Five-year mortgage for $17 500 at 9 percent. Combined interest and principal repayments of $176 were due each month.

[5]Fletcher originally contributed $10 000.

Exhibit 3
Fletcher Industrial Supply
Long-Term Debt Interest and
Principal Payments for
Selected Fiscal Years
Ending January 31

Fiscal Year	Opening Balance	Interest Payment	Principal Payment	Ending Balance
1. Bank Loan				
January 31, 1974	7 650	696	2 520	5 130
January 31, 1975	5 130	696	2 520	2 610
January 31, 1976	2 610	696	2 610	0
2. GMAC Payable				
January 31, 1974	521	20	521	0
3. O'Connor Payable				
January 31, 1974	17 651	1 544	4 000[1]	13 651
January 31, 1975	13 651	1 194	2 000	11 651
4. 9% Mortgage Payable				
January 31, 1974	17 212	1 496	616	16 596
January 31, 1975	16 596	1 440	672	15 924
January 31, 1976	15 924	1 378	734	15 190

[1]The $2000 principal payment due January 31, 1973 was not paid and will have to be added to the January 31, 1974 payment.

4

Gardiner Wholesalers Incorporated (A)

In early February, 1983, Kathy Wilson, assistant credit manager of Gardiner Wholesalers Inc., sat at her desk reviewing the financial information she had gathered on two of her company's accounts — S.D. Taylor Jewellers Ltd. and Elegance Jewellers Inc. Gardiner Wholesalers Inc., a jewellery wholesaler located in Southwestern Ontario, had for many years followed a policy of thoroughly assessing the credit standing of each of its accounts about one month after Christmas. The assessment, which would be used to determine whether changes in credit policy were necessary, had to be submitted to both the credit manager and the sales manager in one week. Ms. Wilson wondered what comments and recommendations concerning the two accounts should be put in her report.

The retail jewellery trade was largely composed of national chain stores such as Birk's, People's, and Mappins and smaller independent jewellers like S.D. Taylor Jewellers Ltd. and Elegance Jewellers Inc. Most retail jewellers carried both jewellery lines, such as gold and diamond rings, and giftware items, such as silverplated items and crystal. Most jewellery chains purchased jewellery pieces from jewellery manufacturers, and mounted the finished products in-house. Independent jewellers were supplied by wholesalers, like Gardiner Wholesalers Inc., who received the jewellery and giftware from such manufacturers as Jolyn Jewellery Inc., the French Jewellery Co. of Canada Ltd., Royal Doulton, and Belfleur Crystal. The wholesalers distributed products to regional department stores, small regional jewellery chains and independent jewellery stores. An independent jeweller would be supplied by at least five jewellery wholesalers.

Jewellery store sales were lowest during the summer months and peaked during the Christmas season. The smaller, often family-owned, independent jewellers were much more affected by the seasonal pattern of jewellery sales than were the national chain-store operations. As a result, the independent jewellers relied heavily on their suppliers for financial support in the form of extended credit, in order to remain competitive with national chain stores. The competition among suppliers for the retail jewellery trade made credit terms and retailer financing necessary wholesale features. Factors that influenced the consumer purchase decision were style, selection, quality, and customer credit. In 1982, layaway sales accounted for 25 percent of all retail jewellery store sales. Layaway sales were necessary in the jewellery business because people often balked at making large cash expenditures for luxury items. The layaway sales technique was also a powerful tool in influencing customers to purchase more expensive items.

S.D. Taylor Jewellers Ltd., located in London, Ontario, had been purchasing jewellery products from Gardiner Wholesalers for the last twenty-five years. The store handled a complete line of jewellery and giftware items. Peak periods of sales were traditionally Christmas, Valentine's Day, Mother's Day, and graduation time. Seventy percent of S.D. Taylor's sales were cash, and 30 percent were on ninety-day installment plans. Installment terms called for a ten percent deposit, and there were no interest charges or carrying costs on the remainder of payments made within ninety days.

S.D. Taylor Jewellers Ltd. had been established in 1953 as a sole proprietorship and was incorporated in 1958. The couple who owned and operated the business were noted for their friendliness and were well respected in the local business community. Mr. Taylor was a member of the Southwestern Ontario Jewellers' Association and had attended numerous courses offered by the Gemological Institute of America. On reviewing the company's file, Ms. Wilson found that payments on account had, for the most part, been prompt.

Elegance Jewellers Inc. was a comparatively new customer of Gardiner Wholesalers Inc., having switched suppliers in early 1981. No reason for the change was given in the files. Elegance Jewellers Inc. was owned by a small group of businessmen who had interests in four other unrelated businesses. The company owned and operated two small-sized jewellery stores, both located in Sarnia, Ontario. The Elegance Jewellery Stores carried mostly jewellery lines, and very little giftware. Most of Elegance Jewellers' sales were for cash. Installment plans were available and called for a 20 percent deposit plus a 1 percent per month carrying charge on the outstanding balance. Comments in the file indicated that Elegance Jewellers' account had been satisfactory through 1982.

Both accounts were sold on standard terms of 1/10, net thirty, and the terms were extended to net ninety during the fall. The sales manager felt that the extension of a fairly liberal credit policy to Gardiner Wholesalers' customers was necessary to remain competitive in a tough market.

Prior to starting her report, Ms. Wilson investigated some pieces of economic information. She was aware that the Canadian economy was doing very poorly and that consumer spending was down in 1982. The Statistics Canada report on retail jewellery store sales confirmed her belief that 1982 had been a poor year (see Exhibit 1). Ms. Wilson also had some 1981 financial information on the jewellery industry published by Dun and Bradstreet. She found that, on average, the age of receivables was 21 days; the current ratio was 1.8:1; the age of inventory was 230 days; and net worth was 44 percent of total assets. Although these statistics were from 1981, Ms. Wilson felt that they were still reasonable today. With that information in mind, Ms. Wilson leafed through the company files, Exhibits 2 through 7, and prepared to write her report.

Exhibit 1
Annual Sales Growth of Jewellery Stores in Ontario

Year	Independent Stores	All Stores[1]
1982	1.2%	1.5%
1981	10.5	7.3
1980	6.3	8.3
1979	7.3	8.9
1978	25.4	21.3
1977	7.8	5.9

[1]Includes chain stores.
 Source: Statistics Canada Catalogue 63-005, *Retail Trade*.

Exhibit 2
Elegance Jewellers Incorporated
Income Statements
for years ended June 30, 1981, 1982

	1981	1982
Sales	$860 765	$991 402
Cost of sales	387 000	472 800
Gross profit	$473 765	$518 602
Operating expenses:		
Selling & administrative	$292 058	$357 103
Depreciation	22 295	26 868
Total operating expenses	314 353	383 971
Operating profit	$159 412	$134 631
Unusual income (loss)	(5 250)	(5 850)
	$154 162	$128 781
Less: interest expense	17 388	76 040
Net profit before tax	$136 774	$ 52 741
Income taxes	34 193	13 184
Net earnings	$102 581	$ 39 557
Dividends paid	$ 17 500	$ 25 000

Exhibit 3
Elegance Jewellers Incorporated
Balance Sheets
as at June 30, 1981 and 1982

Current Assets		1981		1982
Cash		$ 580		$ 638
Accounts receivable		4 613		21 612
Inventory		574 097		577 718
Prepaid expenses		2 667		2 975
Total current assets		$581 957		$ 602 943
Loans to employees		13 175		12 837
Investment in subsidiary		—		343 120
Other investments		8 805		8 992
Fixed Assets				
Land		$12 758		$ 12 758
Buildings	$187 018		$220 535	
Furniture & fixtures	30 938		54 255	
	$217 956		$274 790	
Less: accumulated depreciation	83 637		110 505	
Net		134 319		164 285
Total fixed assets		147 077		177 043
TOTAL ASSETS		$751 014		$1 144 935
Current Liabilities				
Working capital loan		$ 66 475		$ 5 210
Accounts payable		189 887		111 870
Income taxes payable		61 830		1 235
LTD due within one year		4 967		—
Total current liabilities		$323 159		$ 118 315
Bank loan (due Dec. 31, 1983)		—		209 208
Long-term notes payable		76 410		451 410
Total liabilities		$399 569		$778 933
Equity				
Common stock		$ 55 000		$ 55 000
Retained earnings		296 445		311 002
Total equity		$351 445		$ 366 002
TOTAL LIABILITIES AND EQUITY		$751 014		$1 144 935

Exhibit 4
S.D. Taylor Jewellers Ltd.
Income Statements
for years ended June 30

		1981		1982
Sales		$1 029 651		$1 162 488
Cost of sales		484 176		566 894
Gross profit		$ 545 475		$ 595 594
Operating expenses:				
Salaries & benefits	$185 167		$215 360	
Overheads	61 709		73 487	
Advertising	36 997		46 320	
Supplies	34 978		41 750	
Depreciation	17 529		19 712	
Bad debt	2 064		3 467	
Other miscellaneous	40 226		46 690	
Total operating expenses		378 670		446 786
Operating profit		$166 805		$148 808
Plus: other income		16 424		18 700
		$183 229		$167 508
Less: interest expense		18 484		26 837
Net profit before tax		$164 745		$140 671
Income taxes		41 146		35 168
Net earnings		$123 599		$105 503
Dividends paid		$ 49 500		$ 42 000

Exhibit 5
S.D. Taylor Jewellers Ltd.
Statement of Retained Earnings
for the years ended June 30

		1981		1982
Beginning retained earnings		$326 067		$400 166
Net earnings for the year		123 599		105 503
		$449 666		$505 669
Less: dividends		49 500		42 000
Ending retained earnings		$400 166		$463 669

Exhibit 6
S.D. Taylor Jewellers Ltd.
Balance Sheets
as at June 30

Current Assets		1981		1982
Cash		$ 4860		$ 4983
Accounts receivable		52640		63267
Inventories		442756		538337
Prepaid expenses		8308		11628
Total current assets		$508564		$618215
Loans to employees		14151		14145
Investment in subsidiary		60355		39616
Other investments		8715		9093
Fixed assets				
Land		$ 14913		$ 14913
Buildings & fixtures	$221017		$256317	
Less: accumulated depreciation	140076		159788	
Net		80941		96529
Total fixed assets		95854		111442
TOTAL ASSETS		$687639		$792511
Current Liabilities				
Working capital loan		$ 15110		$ 34733
Notes payable (bank)		106142		164429
Accounts payable		91512		92430
Income taxes payable		42064		10709
Total current liabilities		$254828		$302301
Long-term debt		12209		6105
Total liabilities		$267037		$308406
Equity				
Capital stock		$ 20436		$ 20436
Retained earnings		400166		463669
Total equity		$420602		$484105
TOTAL LIABILITIES AND EQUITY		$687639		$792511

Exhibit 7
Gardiner Wholesalers Incorporated
Aging of Accounts Receivable as of December 31, 1983

Due From	Prior	Sept.	Oct.	Nov.	Dec.	Totals
S.D. Taylor Jewellers Ltd.		$15423	$2426	$ 9366	$ 2732	$29947
Elegance Jewellers Inc.	$1320	16916	3554	15073	31601	68464

5

Gardiner Wholesalers Incorporated (B)

Two days had passed since Kathy Wilson, assistant credit manager for Gardiner Wholesalers Inc., had begun her report[1] on two of the company's accounts — S.D. Taylor Jewellers Ltd. and Elegance Jewellers Inc. Her analysis of the past financial performance of the two companies was complete, and Ms. Wilson felt she was ready to make some recommendations. However, lunch with Jim Ferraro changed her mind. Mr. Ferraro was the assistant manager in charge of loans at a downtown bank, and a personal friend of Ms. Wilson. He suggested that a credit appraisal report should include projected statements so that the future financing needs of the two jewellery retailers could be estimated. This additional information would then help Ms. Wilson to determine if these accounts would need to extend their payables in order to finance operations.

The next day, Ms. Wilson proceeded to have a meeting with Laurine Breen and Bert Haase, the managers of the two Elegance Jewellery Stores. Mr. Haase discussed operations for the past few months, describing them as "a little slow." He mentioned that because of the slowdown in sales volume, Elegance Jewellers had reduced prices on some items which "squeezed our margins a little more." Mrs. Breen added that the company was dropping its 1 percent per month carrying charge on layaway sales "in order to stimulate sales." Mr. Haase thought that the overall sales growth for the fiscal year would be between 5 and 10 percent, and that even though operating expenses had increased substantially last year, this year they would probably be about the same percentage of sales as last year. Mr. Haase also thought that age of inventory would be reduced because of closer scrutiny of inventory levels in the past few months, and that expenditures for renovations to the building were expected to equal depreciation expenses, so that the net book value would remain the same. Mrs. Breen concluded the meeting with a remark which she hoped Ms. Wilson would acknowledge in her report, "I hope you noticed that we've been paying our accounts more quickly than last year!"

In a meeting with Mr. Stan Taylor, manager and owner of S.D. Taylor Jewellers Ltd., Ms. Wilson again discussed recent retail performance. Mr. Taylor said that he experienced a "negligible" reduction in margins. He felt the expected sales growth for the coming year would be between 5 and 10 percent with operating expenses expected to be the same percentage of sales as last year. Mr. Taylor had no plans for changes in the credit policy of his company. Mr. Taylor noted that S.D. Taylor Jewellers Ltd. had been paying its accounts at comparatively the same rate as last year, and that he had been watching age of inventory levels more carefully. Mr. Taylor also told Ms. Wilson that the increase in buildings and fixtures was expected to equal depreciation, so the net book value would remain the same.

With this additional information from the two retailers in mind, Ms. Wilson set out to complete her report.

---

[1]For details on the nature of this report see "Gardiner Wholesalers Incorporated (A)."

6

Kingston Millwork Limited

In mid-1977, Mr. John Davies, president and owner of Kingston Millwork Limited in Kingston, Ontario, was considering moving his operations to new facilities. The company was operating at capacity, sales were increasing every year, and Mr. Davies believed that it was time to decide whether the move was a logical step for his company.

COMPANY BACKGROUND

Kingston Millwork Limited opened for business in 1961. Since that time it had matured to the position of one of southern Ontario's leading wooden office furniture specialists. As the company expanded Mr. Davies had been forced to rent a second and third building. The buildings were very old and located in an old industrial section of the city. The structure was a wooden frame on a concrete foundation.

According to Mr. Davies, the reasons for his success, in order of importance, were quality, low overhead, reputation, price, delivery, and knowledge of the capabilities of his employees. Because of the emphasis on quality, Mr. Davies insisted on purchasing top-grade material. By 1977 sales had grown to over $600 000. Exhibits 1 and 2 present Kingston's financial statements.

THE FURNITURE INDUSTRY

In 1977 total domestic sales of Canadian furniture manufacturers reached $1.477 billion.[1] Over the past few years the average annual growth rate had been in the 10 percent range with future sales projected to be $1.8 billion by 1980.[2] Ontario accounted for approximately 60 percent of Canada's total furniture production.

The Canadian furniture industry began long before Confederation. Over the years many changes took place, and the traditional small, family-owned wood shop became a thing of the past. Recent trends indicated numerous acquisitions of these small family businesses by large industrial concerns which were attracted to the furniture industry's good returns, ease of entry, and growing market. With these acquisitions came a high degree of specialization of products and materials along with increased pressures to obtain maximum efficiency. Professional managers of the larger corporations introduced cost controls, improved production technology, and purchased specialized production machinery.

The American industry changed in the same way as its Canadian counterpart; however, the U.S. had larger companies with larger volumes and often lower costs. Bruce McPherson, chairman of the Ontario Furniture Manufacturers Association, explained that:

> One has only to compare the average wage settlements of about 7% in the Carolinas over the past two years to the average of some 19% in Ontario and Quebec to find an area disparity much in the imports' favour.[3]

---

[1] Statistics Canada, #61-207.
[2] Maclean-Hunter Research Bureau: *Canada's Furniture Market*, 1977 Edition, S.I.C. 2510.
[3] *The Globe and Mail*, January 13, 1976.

Growth in the Canadian furniture industry was fostered by a 20 percent tariff[1] on imported furniture. A Canadian company was subject to only a 5 percent excise tax[2] on furniture exported to the United States. The office furniture segment was 46 percent of the total Canadian furniture industry in 1976, but was expected to increase to 57 percent by 1990. Other industry data are provided in Exhibit 4 and Exhibit 5.

Mr. Davies and some of his American customers believed that one major reason for the continued success of the Canadian furniture industry was the difference in the value of the Canadian and American currency.

Although American manufacturers had lower costs, Canadian manufacturers exporting to the United States had the benefit of the difference in the American and Canadian dollar exchange rate. Primarily because of this exchange difference, Canadian furniture companies selling to the United States remained competitive with American manufacturers.

TRIMAC INTERNATIONAL

Mr. Davies' largest customer, Trimac International, placed a considerable amount of pressure on the office furniture company, attempting to force it to expand. This client accounted for 67 percent of Kingston's total company sales. Trimac told Mr. Davies that "Kingston could grow as we grow, provided a few changes are made."

Trimac International designed finance company branch offices coast to coast. Every branch of one finance company was identical, to create a consistent image and to lower construction costs. Trimac was the only company in North America which catered to finance companies on a national scale and had furnished new offices or refurnished old offices for AVCO, Associates, Budget Plan, AETNA, Finance America, General Finance and Laurentide. Over the period of a weekend, Trimac painted the office and installed counters, carpets, furniture, partitions, and paintings. Their own offices were located in Georgia; California; Michigan; London, England; and Kingston, Ontario, where the company was founded.

Kingston Millwork had been associated with Trimac for many years. Trimac designed a product, Kingston manufactured it in a knocked-down form, and Trimac then assembled the product at the customer's premises. On occasion, Trimac granted Kingston advances in times of cash shortages. The management also allowed Mr. Davies to raise prices even after annual contracts had been signed.

Trimac's primary concerns were price, delivery, quality/consistency, and reliability, in that order. Their customers did not expect the furniture to last much more than six or seven years, at which time styles would change and the furniture would be old, warranting replacement. With little regional competition and virtually no national competition, Trimac had expanded rapidly in recent years. In the past, Kingston's deliveries had been late even though Trimac usually placed their orders two months in advance. As a result, changes in inventory management and scheduling, both handled solely by Mr. Davies, were required if good relations with Trimac were to continue.

A large majority of Trimac's sales were in the United States. With the monetary exchange difference sales had boomed in the U.S., and Kingston and other Canadian suppliers expanded as Trimac grew. The pressure on Kingston to expand was

---

[1] McGoldrick's Canadian Custom and Excise tariffs.
[2] *1978 Custom House Guide*, 116 Annual Edition.

heightened by the fact that Trimac had recently had some of its orders completed by woodworking firms in Toronto.

FINANCES

Exhibits 1 and 2 outline the financial statements for the past three years. For comparison purposes additional industry information is provided in Exhibit 3. Sales and profits had recently increased a great deal. Mr. Davies believed that the reason for this was his company's role in the growth of Trimac International. Some of the information in the financial statements were rough estimates since the statements were unaudited. The bank had extended a $50 000 line of credit to Kingston Millwork Limited with the president's personal guarantee. Due to past success and good bank relations, Mr. Davies believed that there would be no problem in extending his line of credit further if required.

ALTERNATIVES

Kingston Millwork Limited was faced with the decision of whether or not to expand. A major determinant in the decision was the reaction of Trimac International.

If the present capacity situation continued, Kingston risked losing part of the Trimac account. Costs in the furniture industry were increasing at a faster rate in Canada than in the United States which was Trimac's major market. To maintain past profit margins, Mr. Davies believed that he might have to decrease quality and/or increase production. The present facilities could not accommodate increased volume and the president felt that if quality were reduced the Trimac account would be lost.

Trimac management confirmed these fears and stated that they would always give Kingston Millwork Limited some business if prices and delivery dates were competitive. However, if the capacity situation remained unchanged, no additional large orders to Kingston would be considered and existing orders would decrease in 1978, with a further decline in 1979. This would leave Kingston with estimated total company sales of $500 000 in 1978 and $450 000 in 1979. Gross profit would probably decline to 20 percent of sales.

THE MOVE

If Mr. Davies' company did expand, Trimac inferred that they could increase sales to Kingston by as much as $150 000 in 1978. Mr. Davies estimated that the combined effect of additional Trimac orders with orders presently being turned away could give the company total sales of $815 000 in 1978, and $950 000 in 1979. These sales figures were feasible only if a larger building was found. Unfortunately, Trimac would not guarantee in writing the increased sales figures.

The president believed that a new 1860 m² cement block building would suit his needs. Moving expenses would be $10 000 and new machines worth another $10 000 would be required if Kingston did move. The new equipment would be depreciated over ten years. Mr. Davies believed that with improved efficiency arising from a new facility, gross profit margins would be approximately 27 percent. The present lease had four years remaining but could be cancelled on two months' notice without penalty.

If Kingston did move into a new building, Mr. Davies would have to decide whether to buy or lease. If he leased the building, the rate would be $16.13 per year per square metre and the rate would be indexed annually for inflation. The lease contract would be for a minimum of five years with Kingston responsible for all taxes, insurance, and utilities expenses. The same 1860 m² building would cost $275 000 to purchase and would be depreciated over twenty years. To determine the cost of financing a new building, Mr. Davies approached a mortgage company. Following is a summary of the data he collected.

Mortgage Table

Date	Annual Interest Payments	Annual Principal Payments	Annual Total Payment	Balance Owed (on February 28)
1978	$30 100	$2 200	$32 300	$272 800
1979	$29 900	$2 400	$32 300	$270 400

Although bank relations had been excellent, Mr. Davies wondered what effect the move to a new building would have on his $50 000 line of credit.

With the combined risks of the Canadian/American currency exchange increasing American competition and pressure from Trimac International for expansion, Mr. Davies was wondering if he should move. To remain competitive and profitable the president believed that a solution was required before the end of the month.

Exhibit 1
Kingston Millwork Limited
Income Statements for
the Year Ending February 28

	1975	1976	1977
Sales	$420 122	$466 703	$613 250
Cost of goods sold:			
Opening inventory	$ 47 216	$ 46 715	$ 28 803
Material used	120 670	127 090	212 802
Wages	180 270	197 128	241 378
Manufacturing overhead	29 263	30 543	34 583
Less: closing inventory	46 715	28 803	55 947
Cost of goods sold	330 704	372 673	461 619
Gross profit	$ 89 418	$ 94 030	$151 631
Expenses			
Rent	$ 9 596	$ 9 825	$ 19 034
Management salary	28 045	21 772	29 553
Depreciation	8 257	6 612	12 946
Automotive	4 369	5 081	5 291
Repairs	1 996	1 214	2 928
Other expenses[1]	22 090	21 532	30 837
Total expenses	74 353	66 036	100 589
Profit before tax	$ 15 065	$ 27 994	$ 51 042
Income tax	3 302	6 101	7 969
Net profit after tax	$ 11 763	$ 21 893	$ 43 073

[1]Consists of 21 small accounts

Exhibit 2
Kingston Millwork Limited
Balance Sheets
as of February 28

	1975	1976	1977
Current Assets			
Cash	$ 1500	$ 1675	$ 2200
Accounts receivable (net)	51405	71040	115913
Income tax overpaid	675	—	—
inventory	46715	28803	55947
Prepaid expense	202	224	980
Advance to shareholder	7075	8477	—
Total Current Assets	$101572	$110219	$175040
Fixed Assets (net)			
Leasehold improvements	$ 6352	$ 5716	$ 5347
Machine & equipment	15242	13412	31845
Office equipment	238	190	152
Auto equipment	8592	6014	10160
Total Fixed Assets	30424	25332	47504
Other Assets			
Incorporation expense	$ 560	$ 560	$ 560
Goodwill	5600	5600	5600
Subtotal	6160	6160	6160
TOTAL ASSETS	$144156	$141711	$228704
Current Liabilities			
Accounts payable	$ 19162	$ 19806	$ 51810
Accrued liabilities	18099	12058	12053
Shareholder loan	—	—	2187
Taxes payable	—	3256	498
Bank loan	24820	2623	13435
Deferred income taxes	—	—	1680
Total Liabilities	$ 62081	$ 37743	$ 81663
Equity			
Preferred stock	$ 11200	$ 11200	$ 11200
Common stock	1123	1123	1123
Retained earnings	69752	91645	134718
Total Equity	82075	103968	147041
TOTAL LIABILITIES AND EQUITY	$144156	$141711	$228704

Exhibit 3
Kingston Millwork Limited
Financial Ratios

	Canadian Office Furniture Industry Ratios[1]			Kingston Millwork Limited Ratios		
Profitability	1975	1976	1977	1975	1976	1977
Sales	100%	100%	100%	100%	100%	100%
Cost of goods sold	75.5	77.3	71.6	78.7	79.9	75.3
Gross profit	24.5	22.7	28.4	21.3	20.1	24.7
Operating expenses	16.7	18.1	20.0	17.7	14.1	16.4
Net profit before tax	7.8	4.6	8.4	3.6	6.0	8.3
Taxes	3.1	1.8	3.5	.8	1.3	1.3
Net profit after tax	4.7	2.8	4.9	2.8	4.7	7.0
Return on investment	21.7%	12.9%	22.3%	15.5%	23.5%	34.3%
Liquidity						
Current ratio	1.67	1.59	1.80	1.73	2.92	2.14
Acid test	.86	.89	1.03	.85	1.93	1.45
Working capital ($000's)	—	—	—	45.5	72.5	93.4
Age of accounts receivable (days)	63.9	65.3	71.5	44.0	54.8	68.0
Inventory in days C.G.S. (days)	50.4	48.2	69.0	50.9	27.8	43.6
Age of accounts payable (days)[2]	79.9	74.1	77.4	57.2	56.1	87.6
Stability						
Net worth/Total assets	44.8%	41.9%	47.9%	56.9%	73.4%	64.3%
Growth (percentages)						
Sales	14.2	14.9	17.7	0.2	11.1	31.4
Net profit	1.4	(31.0)	104.1	(27.8)	86.1	96.7
Total assets	7.5	15.6	11.7	(10.2)	(1.7)	61.4
Equity	29.2	13.6	27.9	17.3	26.7	41.4

[1]Compiled from Statistics Canada Information, #61-207.
[2]Based on materials used.

Exhibit 4
Canadian Office Furniture Industry Data
(in millions of dollars)

Year	Sales	Total Imports	Imports from U.S.A.	Total Exports	Exports to U.S.A.
1970	$ 89.2	$ 5.5	$ 4.9	$10.4	$ 9.7
1971	88.6	4.9	4.2	9.5	9.1
1972	107.9	5.9	5.2	11.5	10.7
1973	123.8	7.8	6.9	18.5	17.4
1974	165.2	12.0	10.9	18.2	17.0
1975	180.9	12.0	11.0	14.3	12.7
1976	188.6	11.7	10.8	21.7	19.9
1977	209.1	12.6	11.2	33.5	31.2
1978[2]	218.7	—	—	51.0	47.1

Canadian/American Exchange Rates[1]
(Canadian $ in U.S. Funds)

1958	101.90	1969	92.56
1959	102.51	1970	92.69
1960	104.83	1971	99.42
1961	101.04	1972	99.54
1962	95.12	1973	100.69
1963	92.24	1974	102.79
1964	92.00	1975	100.09
1965	92.42	1976	100.97
1966	92.37	1977	97.05
1967	91.94	1978[2]	88.23
1968	91.27	1979[2]	80.45

[1]Taken the end of February of each year.
[2]Estimated figures by Maclean-Hunter Research Bureau.
Note: in 1976, U.S. total office furniture sales were $1.35 billion.

Exhibit 5
Kingston Millwork Limited
The Relationship Between Export Office
Furniture Sales and Exchange Ratios[1]

Year	A Percentage Export Sales to Total Sales	B Percentage Export Sales to the U.S. to Total Sales	C Cdn/Amn Exchange Rates
1970	11.7%	10.9%	92.69
1971	10.7	10.3	99.42
1972	10.7	9.9	99.54
1973	14.9	14.1	100.69
1974	11.0	10.3	102.79
1975	7.9	7.0	100.09
1976	11.5	10.6	100.97
1977	16.0	14.9	97.05
1978	23.3	21.5	88.23

[1]From Exhibit 3 of the case.

Exhibit 5 (continued)
Kingston Millwork Limited

The Relationship Between Export Office
Furniture Sales and Exchange Ratios

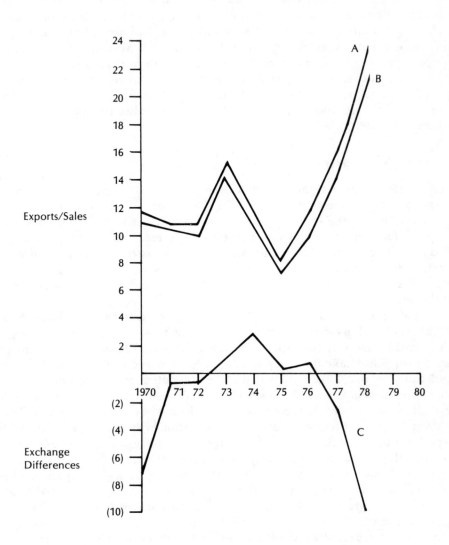

Legend

A   Percentage of Export Sales to Total Sales

B   Percentage of Export Sales to the U.S. to Total Sales

C   Difference in Canadian-American Exchange Rates

7

Lakeshore Fabricators Co. Ltd.

On September 12, 1973, Mr. C.W. Middleton, manager of the Belleville, Ontario, branch of the National Bank of Canada, was reviewing his file on Lakeshore Fabricators Co. Ltd. Andrew Blake, president of Lakeshore, had just called to arrange a meeting to discuss an additional loan of $125 000 to finance working capital required by the most recent expansion proposal. Lakeshore's loan from the bank had grown rapidly over the past years and was now well beyond the authorization level of a branch bank. Following his analysis, Mr. Middleton was required to submit a report to the regional office in Toronto and copies would be forwarded to the commercial loan department of Head Office.

COMPANY BACKGROUND

In 1967, Mr. Blake, after spending nearly twenty years as an executive in the textile industry, formed his own company, Lakeshore Fabricators Co. Ltd. The company was primarily involved in the texturizing of synthetic fibres using the Taslan process, whereby different synthetic fibres were fed at varying speeds into an air jet. The air jet blended and stretched the fibres, resulting in a textured effect similar to wool yarn. Originally developed by Du Pont, the Taslan process created a demand for the textured fibres by weavers[1] and manufacturers for upholstery in the automotive and furniture industries.

Mr. Blake began operations in 1967 with ten employees and a few used machines of limited capacity. Financing for the operation came from some personal savings, a bank loan and advances from prospective customers. For the first two years, Mr. Blake struggled to establish Lakeshore. Suppliers assisted by extending their credit terms on the understanding that Lakeshore would make every attempt to return to the forty-five-day terms as soon as possible. Since then, the company had enjoyed considerable success, increasing sales by 30 percent in each of the last two years (Exhibit 1). Sales projections for the near future indicated an acceleration in the rate of growth. Profits during this period had been adequate but had not grown at the same rate as sales. In the future, Mr. Blake expected profitability to improve significantly.

At the beginning of each fiscal year, Mr. Blake projected sales and capital requirements and arranged the necessary credit with the bank. However, sales growth continually had been greater than anticipated and the bank had agreed to increase Lakeshore's credit levels.

To cope with the rapid growth of Lakeshore, Mr. Blake hired Roy Tatum, an old friend, to supervise the production of the fibres. As the company grew, Mr. Tatum took on more responsibility within the company. At present, he held the title of Vice-President of Sales and shared a small, cluttered office with Mr. Blake.

---

[1] These organizations were generally large producers of varied types of woven materials who sold their products to other manufacturing concerns for use in their own production process.

The management style of the company was quite informal. Decisions regarding policy were often negotiated between Mr. Blake and Mr. Tatum as problems arose. Decisions regarding pricing, purchase, and/or delivery or orders were sometimes made between the two men while the interested party waited on the telephone. Although both men carried full workloads in the sales, purchasing, and administrative activities of the company, they were not above taking wrench in hand when production delays occurred due to machine breakdown.

RECENT COMPANY DEVELOPMENTS

In 1972, Mr. Blake began an expansion program designed to increase production of fibre by the Taslan process from 35 000 kg per month to 70 000 kg per month. This expansion would require significant capital outlay because the last quoted price on one 24-position machine was approximately $18 000 and, in addition, each machine required an air compressor. Compressors were valued at approximately $8000 each.

Mr. Blake had successfully offset a significant amount of the cost of the Taslan expansion by purchasing used machines in good condition. However, because the only manufacturer of the new machines had recently gone out of business, the actual rate of expansion of this line was restricted by the uncertainty of a continued supply of used equipment.

As well, Mr. Blake had added the "Knit de Knit" line to produce a yarn which was used in the manufacture of double knit garments. This line was successful but put additional strain on Lakeshore's capital position. Each new spinning head cost approximately $1500 and by the end of 1973 Mr. Blake expected to have forty heads in operation. Mr. Blake and Mr. Tatum had drastically reduced the capital cost of the line by engineering and modifying spinning machines to make them suitable for the "Knit de Knit" line. Even so, Mr. Blake had been forced to lease some air compressors because he could not raise sufficient funds internally or externally to purchase all the equipment he desired.

In addition to the capital equipment program, Lakeshore Fabricators had purchased the land and building from which the company operated early in 1972. Although the company leased only one-quarter of the building, Mr. Blake thought that the purchase of a site in an industrial mall close to the business section of the city would be a sound investment. He maintained that it would ensure Lakeshore's ability to expand and industrial land would appreciate in value. The purchase, which cost $375 000 in total, had been financed largely by the Industrial Development Bank and Montreal Trust.

As a result of this expansion program, the capital structure of Lakeshore Fabricators was altered significantly (Exhibit 2). The company had borrowed $57 000 from the National Bank of Canada to purchase equipment and had negotiated a $100 000 line of credit for working capital requirements. At the end of 1973, $49 000 of the line of credit was outstanding. Lakeshore expected to repay the bank term loan of $47 000 at the rate of $1500 per month. The company also owed $120 000 to the I.D.B. and $251 000 to Montreal Trust, both of which were secured by mortgages on the building. The principal of the I.D.B. loan was repayable in ten instalments of $12 000. Annual principal payments of $11 000 would be made to Montreal Trust. Principal payments, by fiscal year, are summarized in Exhibit 3.

THE EXPANSION PROPOSAL

Mr. Blake's most recent proposal called for an additional line of credit of $125 000 for working capital to allow Lakeshore Fabricators to produce and market false twist yarns from polyester fibres. The market for false twist polyester yarns was estimated by textile industry sources to be about 35 million kilograms per year in Canada.

Mr. Blake had negotiated the purchase of the most advanced machines available from an English company. The British government would provide the financing for the $275 000 deal. The contract terms were 10 percent down on the machines at the time of ordering, 10 percent on arrival of the machines (expected to be January 1974) and the remainder to be paid over 36 months, with an annual rate of 8 percent interest charged on the outstanding balance. Monthly principal would be $6111.

The new machines would run continuously and allow Lakeshore to produce about 750 000 kg of false twist yarn per year. Although the operation of the new machines did not require substantial supervision, Mr. Blake proposed to hire a plant manager who would take on all production responsibilities of the day-to-day polyester production. The new man would also supervise the 110 production workers currently employed by Lakeshore on the other product lines.

The major suppliers of polyester fibre were Du Pont and Celanese and these companies were also the main producers of false twist yarn. Mr. Blake had approached both of the potential polyester fibre suppliers to gauge their reaction to his entering the false twist yarn market as a competitor.

Du Pont had indicated that they would like to see Lakeshore become a licensee of Du Pont whereby Lakeshore would produce for and sell to them at a negotiated volume and margin. Celanese had indicated that they would supply Lakeshore with polyester fibre and Lakeshore could produce at whatever volume and price they could negotiate with users of false twist fibres.

Although the Du Pont offer was attractive in that there was a degree of guarantee against the cyclical nature of the industry, Mr. Blake had decided to take the Celanese offer because of its potential for higher profits.

Under the proposed expansion, the new line would come on stream early in 1974. Mr. Blake had already made contracts with certain accounts which would, if confirmed, take all the false twist fibres Lakeshore could produce. As part of the expansion, Lakeshore would take up one-quarter more of the building to house new equipment and offices. Arrangements were currently being made with the present tenants and Mr. Blake did not foresee any difficulty.

Mr. Blake expected total company sales to be about $3.125 million for the year ending April 30, 1974. There would be no appreciable increase in sales from the polyester false twist yarn until the next fiscal year. He felt that there would be no significant change in the overall profitability of Lakeshore in the year ending April 30, 1974. He foresaw sales of $6.25 million in 1975, with the polyester false twist yarn line accounting for about $2.5 million of total sales. Purchases were expected to be $1.82 million in 1974 and $3.38 million in 1975. It was anticipated that the addition of the false twist yarn line together with improved operating procedures in the Taslan and "Knit de Knit" lines would increase the overall gross profit margin to 25 percent in 1975. Mr. Blake also expected that selling, general, and administrative expenses would remain constant as a percentage of sales. Other income would decrease to about half the 1974 figure since Lakeshore would be taking up more of the premises in 1975 and consequently receiving less rental income.

Exhibit 1
Lakeshore Fabricators Co. Ltd.
Profit and Loss Statement
for Years Ending April 30
(in 000's of dollars)

	1970	1971	1972	1973
Sales[1]	$881	$1 028	$1 359	$1 935
Cost of goods sold[2]	705	829	1 091	1 582
Gross profit	$176	$ 199	$ 268	$ 353
Selling expenses	$ 58	$ 77	$ 105	$ 165
General and administrative expenses	38	47	54	73
Total operating expenses	96	124	159	238
Operating profit	$ 80	$ 75	$ 109	$ 115
Less: other expenses[3]	14	20	65	105
Plus: other income[4]	12	8	17	38
Net income before taxes	$ 78	$ 63	$ 61	$ 48
Provision for income tax[5]	30	21	15	12
Net income	$ 48	$ 42	$ 46	$ 36

[1]Lakeshore was started in 1967. Sales and profits for the years 1967 through 1969 were as follows:

	(000's)		
	1967	1968	1969
Sales	$465	$806	$1 009
Profits (after tax)	$ 34	$ 48	$ 34

[2]Cost of goods manufactured included direct and indirect labour, depreciation, and overhead as well as purchases plus freight-in. Purchases for the years 1970-73 inclusive were:

		(000's)		
1970	1971		1972	1973
$539	$611		$853	$1128

[3]Other expenses included interest incurred to service investments made by Lakeshore. Other expenses for 1972 and 1973 included respective losses of $11 250 and $41 250 on a retail fabric outlet undertaken by the company. The venture had been terminated but would account for a further loss of approximately $27 500 in 1974.

[4]Other income included interest and investment income but consisted principally in rental income from the company property.

[5]The income tax rate was expected to be about 20 percent on income up to $50 000 and 40 percent on income above this level.

Exhibit 2
Lakeshore Fabricators Co. Ltd.
Balance Sheet as of April 30
(in 000's of dollars)

	1970	1971	1972	1973
ASSETS				
Current assets				
Cash	$ 24	$ 17	$ 50	$ 16
Certificates of deposit	13	13	13	55
Accounts receivable	79	109	139	217
Returnable bobbins[1]	1	—	4	1
Inventory	150	154	227	220
Prepaids	4	3	12	8
Deposit on machines	—	—	—	28
Total current assets	$271	$296	$ 445	$ 545
Fixed assets				
Land	—	—	$ 63	$ 63
Building (net of depreciation)[2]	—	—	321	305
Machinery and equipment (net)[2]	116	109	149	157
Total fixed assets	116	109	533	525
Other assets				
Securities	$ 8	$ 8	$ 8	$ 5
Kingsway Textiles[3]	—	65	33	33
Swiss Yarns	—	—	—	—
Other	—	—	1	1
Total	8	73	42	39
TOTAL ASSETS	$395	$478	$1 020	$1 109

[1]Purchases of raw material yarn included the winding core or bobbin which was returnable to the supplier for credit.

[2]The building was depreciated at the rate of 5 percent per year. The machinery and equipment were depreciated at an annual rate of 15 percent.

[3]Kingsway Textiles was an operation similar to Lakeshore Fabricators, located in Durham, North Carolina. Kingsway was started by Mr. Blake and some American associates in 1969 and appeared to be stabilizing after a period of rapid growth. Sales were expected to be over $15 million at year end. Mr. Blake personally held an interest in this company. Additionally, Lakeshore Fabricators Co. Ltd., owned an interest in the American company. Together, Mr. Blake and Lakeshore held about 40 percent of the outstanding shares of Kingsway Textiles.

Exhibit 2 (continued)
Lakeshore Fabricators Co. Ltd.
Balance Sheet as of April 30
Liabilities and Shareholders' Equity
(in 000's of dollars)

	1970	1971	1972	1973
LIABILITIES				
Current liabilities				
Working capital loan	$ 14	$ 33	$ 39	$ 49
Accounts payable	144	125	210	269
Royalty payable[4]	5	10	24	34
Accrued expenses	5	20	12	18
Miscellaneous liabilities	18	4	16	—
Total current liabilities	$186	$192	$ 301	$ 370
Long-term liabilities				
Bank term loan[5]	$ 13	$ 50	$ 49	$ 47
Mortgages payable				
I.D.B. 10.5%	—	—	122	120
Montreal Trust 7%	—	—	262	251
Deferred taxes	9	7	11	10
Total long-term liabilities	22	57	444	428
TOTAL LIABILITIES	$208	$249	$ 745	$ 798
Shareholders' equity				
Capital stock	$ 23	$ 23	$ 23	$ 23
Retained earnings	164	206	252	288
Total shareholders' equity	$187	$229	$ 275	$ 311
TOTAL LIABILITIES AND SHAREHOLDERS' EQUITY	$395	$478	$1 020	$1 109

[4]The Taslan process was patented by Du Pont and texturizers were required to pay a royalty for use of the process. The royalty amounted to approximately 3¢/kg per month.

[5]This bank loan had been negotiated for purchase of equipment. A lien against all the machinery and equipment owned by Lakeshore provided security for the loan.

Exhibit 3
Lakeshore Fabricators Co. Ltd.
Projected Debt Principal Payments
By Fiscal Year Ending April 30

Debt	1974	1975	1976	1977
Bank term loan	18 000	18 000	11 000	0
I.D.B. 10.5% mortgage	12 000	12 000	12 000	12 000
Montreal Trust	11 000	11 000	11 000	11 000
New equipment loan	24 444	73 332	73 332	48 892

8
Maple Leaf Hardware Ltd.

On May 29, 1981, Stuart Foreman, assistant manager of the London, Ontario, branch of the Central Canadian Bank, was reviewing information he had received from Maple Leaf Hardware Ltd. Robert Patrick, President and Manager of Maple Leaf Hardware Ltd., had requested an increase in his line of credit with the bank to cover seasonal working capital needs. Mr. Foreman, who had just received a transfer and promotion to the London branch, realized he would have to evaluate this request carefully.

COMPANY BACKGROUND

Mr. Patrick.was thirty-two. His father had owned his own hardware store in the Maritimes, where Robert had worked since the age of sixteen. In 1973, Mr. Patrick accepted a job offer from a large retail department chain. Two years later he was transferred to London, Ontario, and eventually became manager of one of the branch stores. In 1978, he decided to leave the department chain in order to open his own retail hardware business. With a personal investment of $60 000 and $40 000 from a friend, Mr. Les Harrison, Mr. Patrick incorporated the company on September 1, 1978. Mr. Patrick was able to arrange a long-term loan of $120 000 and a line of credit of $30 000 with the Central Canadian Bank through Mr. Terry Woods (Mr. Foreman's predecessor, who had recently left the bank). After a detailed analysis, Mr. Patrick located his business on Maple Leaf Street in a growing area of the city. The nearest hardware store was located several kilometres away. Sales increased steadily during the first few years, and in 1980, Maple Leaf Hardware Ltd. realized its first profit.

THE INDUSTRY

There were over twenty stores in London in the retail hardware business, including independently owned, chain, and department stores. Hardware stores offered a wide variety of goods including tools, appliances, adhesives, cleaners, and, in some cases, sporting goods and toys. The major determinant of a hardware store's success was its location: it was important to have a large area from which to draw customers. This was especially true for independent stores.

Hardware sales were traditionally highest around Christmas. January to April were slow months, while sales were much stronger from May to August. Because of this seasonality, and since a company had to order inventory well in advance, a hardware store's greatest need for working capital financing usually occurred in February or March. The strongest cash position was in December. The difference between the best and worst monthly cash position for a store the size of Maple Leaf Hardware Ltd. was typically in the $40 000 to $60 000 range.

In difficult economic times, with increasing inflation and interest rates, many industries were hit hard financially; however, this was not the case with the hardware industry. During economic recessions, consumers' emphasis shifted from purchasing new goods to repairing and rebuilding old goods. This resulted in increased "do-it-yourself" purchases from hardware stores.

PRESENT SITUATION

Mr. Patrick presented his proposal for an increase in the short-term line of credit from $50 000 (the line of credit which had been granted last year) to $80 000. Mr. Patrick included in his report specific information which Mr. Foreman had requested, including financial statements for the years the company had been in operation (see Exhibits 1 and 2). Exhibit 3 provides financial ratios for the company and also includes available industry information. Mr. Patrick stated that sales for the year ending December 31, 1981, were expected to be close to $850 000. A further increase in sales of 10 to 20 percent was anticipated in 1982. There were no anticipated purchases of fixed assets in the next few years. Mr. Patrick planned to pay a common stock dividend of $10 000 each year starting on December 31, 1981. The monthly rent was expected to increase by $1 200 in September with the signing of a new two-year lease. Mr. Patrick was planning to introduce a new inventory control system which he hoped would eventually reduce the age of inventory to the industry average of the past few years; however, he was not sure if he would be able to accomplish this within the next year.

Mr. Foreman set out to decide whether or not to increase the size of the line of credit for Maple Leaf Hardware Ltd. He noted in his file that on one occasion in the past the company had been slow in sending financial data the bank had requested, but when Mr. Foreman mentioned the incident, Mr. Patrick dismissed it as a misunderstanding with Mr. Woods. In further conversation, Mr. Foreman learned that Mr. Patrick and Mr. Harrison (who owned 40 percent of the common shares) had recently had some disagreements as to how Mr. Patrick should be running the business. According to Mr. Patrick: "Les and I go way back. We've had our differences throughout the years, but things always get straightened out. I'm the major shareholder in this business, and I know how to run a hardware store profitably. I think sometimes Les forgets that."

Since this was Mr. Foreman's first evaluation of a loan request in his new position, he wanted to proceed cautiously and perform a thorough analysis. He realized he would have to present his decision within the week.

Exhibit 1
Maple Leaf Hardware Ltd.
Income Statements
(in 000's of dollars)

	4 months to Dec. 31, 1978	Year ended Dec. 31, 1979	Year ended Dec. 31, 1980
Sales	$200	$609	$709
Cost of goods sold	135	406	468
Gross profit	$ 65	$203	$241
	—	—	—
Operating expenses			
Wages[1]	$ 26	$ 86	$ 91
Rent	18	57	60
Property Tax	3	10	12
Utilities	2	7	8
Depreciation	3	9	9
Advertising	3	11	12
Other	15	15	9
Total operating expenses	70	195	201
Operating profit	($ 5)	$ 8	$ 40
Less: other expenses, interest	6	18	16
Net profit before tax	($ 11)	($ 10)	$ 24
Income tax	—	—	1[2]
Net profit after tax	($ 11)	($ 10)	$ 23

[1]Includes manager's salary of $12 000 in 1979 and $15 000 in 1980.

[2]Tax laws allow the company to offset the $24 000 profit of 1980 with the combined $21 000 loss of the last two years. Thus in 1980, the company only pays tax on the $3 000 difference, at the rate of 25%.

Exhibit 2
Maple Leaf Hardware Ltd.
Balance Sheets
as of December 31
(in 000's of dollars)

	1978	1979	1980
ASSETS			
Current Assets			
Cash	$ 17	$ 6	$ 5
Accounts receivable	10	15	16
Inventory	147	160	208
Total Current Assets	$174	$181	$229
Fixed Assets			
Leasehold improvements (net)	$ 39	$ 36	$ 33
Fixtures (net)	48	42	36
Total Fixed Assets	87	78	69
TOTAL ASSETS	$261	$259	$298
LIABILITIES			
Current Liabilities			
Accounts payable	$ 55	$ 62	$ 85
Bank loan	—	9	10
Current portion of long-term debt	8	8	8
Total Current Liabilities	$ 63	$ 79	$103
Long-term debt[1]	109	101	93
TOTAL LIABILITIES	$172	$180	$196
EQUITY			
Common Stock			
R. Patrick	$ 60	$ 60	$ 60
L. Harrison	40	40	40
Retained earnings	(11)	(21)	2
TOTAL EQUITY	89	79	102
TOTAL LIABILITIES AND EQUITY	$261	$259	$298

[1]Principal repayments of $667 were due each month. The interest rate was 15 percent. The loan was secured by personal assets of the owners.

Exhibit 3
Maple Leaf Hardware Ltd.
Financial Ratios

	Canadian Hardware Stores Industry Ratios[1]		Maple Leaf Hardware Ltd. Ratios		
	1978	1979	1978	1979	1980
Profitability					
Sales	100%	100%	100%	100%	100%
Cost of goods sold	68.9	67.8	67.5	66.7	66.0
Gross profit	31.1	32.2	32.5	33.3	34.0
Expenses					
Wages			13.0	14.1	12.8
Rent			9.0	9.4	8.5
Property tax			1.5	1.6	1.7
Utilities			1.0	1.1	1.1
Depreciation			1.5	1.5	1.3
Advertising			1.5	1.8	1.7
Other			7.5	2.5	1.3
Interest			3.0	3.0	2.3
Total Expenses	27.2	27.8	38.0	35.0	30.6
Net profit before tax	3.8	4.3	(5.5)	(1.6)	3.4
Income tax	1.1	1.2	—		0.1
Net profit after tax	2.7	3.1	(5.5)	(1.6)	3.2
Return on Investment	14.9%	18.7%	(34.8%)[4]	(11.9%)	25.4%
Liquidity					
Current ratio	1.87	1.86	2.76	2.29	2.22
Acid test	.53	.46	.43	.27	.20
Working capital ($000's)	64	73	111	102	126
Efficiency					
Age of accounts receivable (days)[3]	26.0	21.7	6.1	9.0	8.2
Inventory in days[3] C.G.S.	137.4	142.5	132.8	143.8	162.2
Age of accounts payable[2] (days)[3]	48.1	44.1	23.8[5]	54.0	60.1
Stability					
Net worth/Total assets	37.5%	36.3%	34.1%	30.5%	34.2%

Growth (percentages)	1978-1979	1979-1980
Sales	20.8	16.4
Net profit	41.2	—
Total assets	19.4	15.1
Equity	15.7	29.1

[1]Compiled from Statistics Canada Information #61-207. Industry Information for 1980 was not yet available.
[2]Assuming purchases = cost of goods sold plus ending inventory less beginning inventory.
[3]365-day year used, except in 1978, when 122-day period used.
[4]Annualized.
[5]Assuming beginning inventory was zero.

9

Pioneer School Furniture Co. Ltd.

Gerry Wig, manager of the downtown branch of the Dominion of Canada Bank in London, Ontario, had to make a decision regarding a loan proposal in time for a meeting Monday morning. It was now late Friday afternoon. Mr. Schmidt, president of Pioneer School Furniture and a long-standing customer of the bank, had visited Mr. Wig the previous week with a plan for an expansion of Pioneer's facilities. Mr. Schmidt needed money for working capital and for the construction of the plant addition. He had gone to a mortgage company, which had agreed to lend him the money needed for the plant addition. He was asking Mr. Wig to increase Pioneer's line of credit to cover his increasing need for working capital. Mr. Wig knew as he reviewed the Pioneer file that he would have to evaluate the proposal as objectively as possible, especially in view of a recent memo received from the bank's head office (Exhibit 1).

COMPANY HISTORY

Mr. Schmidt was fifty-two years of age. He and his wife had immigrated to Canada from Europe in 1948. For several months he worked in Montreal as a labourer, then moved to London in response to an advertisement for trained machinists. Since Mr. Schmidt had both excellent qualifications and experience he was given a position in the newly formed school and institutional furniture division of a large Canadian metal-fabricating company.

The division grew rapidly, enjoying the benefits of the expansionary postwar economy. Mr. Schmidt advanced within the company on the basis of his own skill and determined nature. Eventually he was made plant superintendent of the division, and his responsibilities included meeting production requirements, maintaining plant efficiency through a system of standards, and supervising a staff of over one hundred workers, most of whom were highly trained. Mr. Schmidt was expected to select, train, and supervise foremen. As well, he participated in the industrial relations procedures in the plant. As plant superintendent he earned a reputation for his product knowledge, his ability to solve problems, and the exacting standards he set for himself. These attributes resulted in Mr. Schmidt's increasing participation in the design of new products and the capital budgeting for the plant.

Late in 1966, Mr. Schmidt's company merged with another large company and he learned that the new management had decided to phase out the metal furniture division. But he wanted to remain in the school furniture industry, and the company's decision prompted him to enter into business for himself.

In 1967, Mr. Schmidt began operating Pioneer School Furniture Co. Ltd. The company's financing was provided primarily by Mr. Schmidt's own savings and a bank loan secured by his personal assets. The first years were extremely difficult ones. Mr. Schmidt worked long hours with little help and with limited facilities. During this period he withdrew only $2000 to $3000 a year from the company for the support of his family. Gradually, however, the company began to grow, producing a quality product at a price which made Pioneer highly competitive. Mr. Schmidt maintained that high product quality and guaranteed service combined with a fair price would be a successful combination for the school furniture market.

Producing school furniture exclusively in the years 1967-1970 created certain problems for Pioneer. It was necessary to bid for contracts in January and February for delivery in September. Most school boards purchased significant quantities of furniture by tender only once a year. Consequently, this required skilful bidding, as contracts missed due to noncompetitive bids could not be easily replaced. Nor could contract estimates be adjusted to offset rising costs. This tender system also necessitated the production of virtually all of the required furniture over the summer period for delivery in the fall. In addition, school boards and government agencies, who were Pioneer's principal clients, were traditionally slow in settling their accounts. In most instances these customers took from 60 to 120 days after delivery to complete payment.

In 1971, Mr. Schmidt purchased the A & B Co. Ltd. in order partially to offset the seasonal production problems of Pioneer. A & B was a small, specialized operation which produced a high-quality line of metal office furniture. A drafting table which A & B had manufactured and marketed as a licensee was redesigned by Mr. Schmidt and became a very profitable product for Pioneer School Furniture.

In 1972, the company moved from its rented quarters in an old building to a more modern plant in an industrial area of the city. At that time, Mr. Schmidt's lawyer and accountant advised him that for estate and tax management purposes, Pioneer School Furniture should not purchase the new building. They advised Mr. Schmidt to form a second company called H. Schmidt Ltd. which would buy the plant and then rent it to Pioneer School Furniture. Acting on behalf of H. Schmidt Ltd., Mr. Schmidt convinced the Dominion Bank to loan it $137 000 to finance the building. The loan was secured by a mortgage on the property. Pioneer paid a monthly rental for the use of the facility. The rent had been established by an appraiser at fair market value.

INDUSTRY SITUATION

Until the 1950s and early 1960s most school furniture was made from wood. However, during the 1960s the sharp increase in the cost of wood and labour resulted in significant price increases. School boards, in an attempt to comply with budget constraints, began to buy furniture made from combinations of metal and plastic. The trend toward metal furniture provided an opportunity for new and existing metal-fabricating companies to expand their sales by entering the school furniture market. In these early years competition was intense, but the market for metal furniture expanded sufficiently to allow most companies to earn adequate profits.

Toward the end of the 1960s, the education system faced continued pressure to reduce costs in view of levelling student enrolment. Pressure was felt among the suppliers to the education industry as competition for contracts increased. Some manufacturers of metal school furniture, particularly those with other related product lines or those which were divisions of large established companies, began to cut prices. Industry participants viewed this as a move to force small and inefficient operators out of the industry. The price-cutting policy intensified through 1970, 1971, and 1972. Pioneer School Furniture was able to compete in these years due to its low overhead, company reputation, and contacts already developed by Mr. Schmidt through his years in the industry. In 1973, with the sharp increase in material costs and continued price competition, the outlook looked bleak for industry participants. From the dozen or more Ontario manufacturers who had been in the industry in 1966, only six major competitors remained. Midway through 1973, a year which promised to be difficult for Pioneer, three major manufacturers announced their withdrawal from the market. Each of these Ontario-based operations was a division of a large company and each cited inadequate returns as the major reason for quitting the school furniture industry.

EXPANSION PROPOSAL

Mr. Schmidt assessed this turn of events in 1973 as an opportunity for the makers of school furniture to pass increased raw material costs, previously absorbed by the manufacturers, on to the school boards. There was also the chance for enterprising companies to increase their market share significantly.

In order to compete during the recent lean years, Pioneer had been forced to restrict capital expansion. Lack of plant facilities now posed a severe impediment to any expansion plans. Even at present levels of production, raw materials and finished goods were stacked in the aisles on the production floor. The blocked aisles restricted the workers' ability to perform their jobs, limited productive capacity, and increased costs.

In early 1973, Mr. Schmidt purchased from Global Manufacturers the manufacturing rights to a new line of metal shelving for school and institutional use. This product's earnings potential, based upon market response to date, was limited by the lack of plant capacity. Mr. Schmidt wished to build a 651 m² addition to the present plant, which would increase the plant area by approximately one-third and provide ample storage for Pioneer product and for raw material. Mr. Schmidt, acting on behalf of H. Schmidt Ltd., had asked the bank to give him additional funds to finance the addition to the plant. The bank changed its lending policies and wished to withdraw from that area of financing so they suggested that H. Schmidt Ltd. approach a mortgage company for the money. Mr. Schmidt negotiated with a mortgage company, which agreed to provide the $103 000 needed to finance the plant extension. In addition, the mortgage company agreed to take over the existing mortgage currently held by the bank on the original plant. The mortgage company had agreed that the mortgage on the property, including the plant and the addition, would provide adequate security. The cost of the addition would be reflected in increased rent charged to Pioneer by H. Schmidt Ltd. This arrangement with the mortgage company pleased the bank since it relieved the bank of its mortgage commitment, which was consistent with its expressed desire to withdraw from that area of financing.

In presenting his request for the bank to extend Pioneer's current line of credit beyond $225 000 to handle the expected increase in working capital needs, Mr. Schmidt had indicated that effective immediately, prices on existing products would be raised on an average by 5 percent. The price increase would reflect the higher cost of materials and labour. Most school board representatives to whom he had spoken did not object to price increases reflecting increased costs. These individuals had indicated that they were more concerned that quality and service remain the same. Mr. Schmidt felt that the price increase would do much to improve his profitability (Exhibits 2, 3, and 4).

Mr. Schmidt projected Pioneer's future total sales volume to increase by 25 percent in 1974 in addition to the price increase and by a further 20 percent in 1975 if the expansion could be financed. Purchases were expected to be 75 percent of cost of goods sold. He also felt that working capital requirements would increase in direct proportion to sales increases but that expenses would remain constant as a percentage of the new dollar sales figure. Income taxes were expected to rise to a 40 percent rate. With regard to capacity, Mr. Schmidt projected that current equipment would be adequate to handle the proposed increases in sales and that any further capital expansion could be put off until late in 1975.

Exhibit 1

MEMO: DOMINION BANK OF CANADA
FROM: VICE-PRES. COMMERCIAL SERVICES, AUG. 16, 1973.
TO: BRANCH MANAGERS

In view of the recent forecasts by our economists on the movement of interest rates, the shortage of raw materials, the tightening of the money supply and the general business outlook for the upcoming quarter, I would like to remind all managers that in periods of economic uncertainty our standards for quality and risk factor should be weighed even more heavily in investigating alternative commercial placements.

The growth of loans outstanding at the branch level should not exceed 2 percent. Similarly, as loans are repaid every effort should be made to place available funds with the proposals offering the highest return and least risk.

Exhibit 2
Pioneer School Furniture Co. Ltd.
Income Statements
for the Years Ending September 30

	1970	1971	1972	1973
Sales[1]	$1 264 426	$1 083 965	$1 058 659	$1 564 389
Cost of goods sold[2]	969 185	863 659	844 256	1 278 314
Gross profit	$ 295 241	$ 220 306	$ 214 403	$ 286 075
Operating expenses				
Office salaries	$ 29 497	$ 30 900	$ 33 216	$ 50 054
Freight	33 690	30 450	28 652	43 924
Advertisement	4 770	7 047	9 141	10 465
Telephone	3 681	3 941	5 242	7 066
Car & truck	20 820	20 000	19 839	26 357
Office	2 562	2 936	2 139	4 246
Fees & dues	710	229	284	1 503
Legal	1 925	2 247	3 436	3 884
Interest	3 798	2 819	6 472	13 801
General	967	782	715	743
Sales commission	39 445	33 228	31 759	46 931
Depreciation	6 401	12 675	9 560	23 810
Management bonuses	99 325	25 208	—	—
Total expenses	247 591	172 462	150 455	232 784
Net operating profit	$ 47 650	$ 47 844	$ 63 948	$ 53 291
Less: extraordinary expenses[3]	—	—	16 320	—
Earnings before income tax	$ 47 650	$ 47 844	$ 47 628	$ 53 291
Provisions for income tax	11 694	10 555	11 540	12 666
Earnings after tax	$ 35 956	$ 37 289	$ 36 088	$ 40 625

[1]Pioneer was incorporated in 1967. Sales and profits for the years 1967 through 1969 were as follows:

	1967	1968	1969
Sales	$320 022	$686 793	$856 429
Profit (after tax)	$ 2 052	$ 21 256	$ 28 851

[2]Cost of goods included raw materials, rent, direct labour, indirect labour, depreciation, and plant overhead. Purchases of materials for the years 1970-73 respectively were

	1970	1971	1972	1973
	$730 056	$428 244	$764 747	$908 089

[3]In 1972, Pioneer experienced nonrecurring expenses as part of its relocation to a new plant site.

Exhibit 3
Pioneer School Furniture Co. Ltd.
Balance Sheet
as of September 30

	1970	1971	1972	1973
ASSETS				
Current assets				
Cash	$ 1549	$ 1111	$ 275	$ 384
Accounts receivable	298 560	247 111	241 135	297 654
Inventory	62 500	108 827	114 262	211 920
Prepaid expenses	2 371	2 603	4 300	3 804
Total current assets	$364 980	$359 652	$359 972	$513 762
Fixed assets				
Equipment	$ 52 202	$ 66 913	$118 801	$156 150
Vehicles	23 069	23 069	37 535	41 571
Tooling[1]	—	—	—	40 473
Subtotal	$ 75 271	$ 89 982	$156 336	$238 194
Less: accumulated depreciation	34 075	46 750	56 310	80 120
Total fixed assets	41 196	43 232	100 026	158 074
Other assets				
Due from H. Schmidt Ltd.[2]	—	—	50 249	23 775
Patents	274	274	274	274
Goodwill	13 700	13 700	13 700	13 700
Incorporation expenses	274	274	274	274
TOTAL ASSETS	$420 424	$417 132	$524 495	$709 859
LIABILITIES				
Current liabilities				
Bank loan	$ 52 060	$ 82 200	$116 450	$219 200
Accounts payable	116 809	74 229	145 302	169 510
Wages payable	125 882	58 088	42 869	35 241
Notes payable A & B Co.	—	—	—	2 364
Taxes payable	5 214	204	—	262
Total current liabilities	$299 965	$214 721	$304 621	$426 577
Long-term liabilities				
Lien notes payable[3]	$ —	$ 9 459	$ 23 577	$ 17 406
Due to shareholders[4]	18 502	41 882	23 227	16 940
Notes payable A & B Co.	—	11 824	2 364	—
Notes payable Global Co.	—	—	—	36 867
Deferred income tax	—	—	2 118	2 856
Total long-term liabilities	18 502	63 165	51 286	74 069
Total liabilities	$318 467	$277 886	$355 907	$500 646
SHAREHOLDERS' EQUITY				
Authorized				
2600, 6% nonvoting redeemable preferred, par value $10.				
10 000 common no par value				
Issued				
Preferred[5]	$ 13 700	$ 13 700	—	—
Common	141	141	$ 141	$ 141
Retained earnings[6]	88 116	125 405	168 447	209 072
Total Equity	101 957	139 246	168 588	209 213
TOTAL LIABILITIES AND SHAREHOLDERS' EQUITY	$420 424	$417 132	$524 495	$709 859

---

[1]In previous years tooling had been expensed in the year purchased. Changes in the tax act required that tooling be capitalized and

Exhibit 4
Pioneer School Furniture Co. Ltd.
Sales and Manufacturing Cost Breakdown
by Product Line in 1973
(in 000's of dollars and percentages)

	School Furniture	A & B Products	Global Shelving	Custom Work	Total
Sales — $	$1 127	$178	$152	$107	$1 564
Manufacturing Costs — $					
— Material	$ 653	$ 73	$ 64	$ 50	$ 840
— Labour	118	32	33	17	200
— Overhead	133	39	46	20	238
Subtotal	904	144	143	87	1 278
Gross Profit — $	$ 223	$ 34	$ 9	$ 20	$ 286
Sales — %	100.0	100.0	100.0	100.0	100.0
Manufacturing Costs — %					
— Material	57.9	41.0	42.1	46.7	53.7
— Labour	10.5	18.0	21.7	15.9	12.8
— Overhead	11.8	21.9	30.3	18.7	15.2
Subtotal	80.2	80.9	94.1	81.3	81.7
Gross Profit — %	19.8	19.1	5.9	18.7	18.3

depreciated. Mr. Schmidt felt purchases of tooling would remain at the 1973 level for the next two years. Mr. Schmidt intended to depreciate all tooling at the rate of 30 percent per year on a declining basis.

[2]Pioneer had lent H. Schmidt Ltd. approximately $50 000 in 1971 to be used for improvements on the plant. The amount was to be repaid over two years.

[3]Purchases of tooling and equipment were financed through suppliers and finance companies using lien instruments. Mr. Schmidt felt that the lien notes payable would remain relatively constant over the next two years.

[4]For tax purposes this money was considered to be distributed to the shareholders (principally Mr. Schmidt). However, to accommodate Pioneer's working capital requirements, the account was set up as a liability.

[5]The preferred shares were retired for tax purposes in 1971.

[6]Retained earnings were readjusted for tax purposes in 1972.

10

The Prominent London Lawyer

Hugh Fraser smiled ruefully as he put down the telephone after receiving the sign painter's quotation. This occasion had been five years in the making; it was May 1981, and Hugh was finally qualified to "hang out his shingle." It seemed ironic that during those five long years — three at law school, one spent articling, and one involved with attending the bar admission course — no one had ever mentioned that the "shingle" itself would set you back almost $300.

Hugh intended to open his own law office on June 1, and was gathering the necessary data to put together a presentation requesting bank financing. This process was opening his eyes to the fact that there was a lot about establishing and operating a law office which hadn't been put in the textbooks or lectures of his academic career!

THE INDUSTRY

Hugh was well aware that almost any year in the past hundred would have provided a better reception for a young lawyer going out on his own. Recent research by two Waterloo lawyers had formalized the depressing trends which all practising attorneys were only too well aware of: too many lawyers, too little work, and bargain basement pricing. According to the researchers, one lawyer per every 1,500 people was an acceptable ratio. The table below shows that this ratio had been spiralling downward at an increasing rate in Ontario. Over the 1960–1981 period illustrated in the table, the population of the province had increased 41 percent while the number of lawyers had jumped 181 percent.

Year	Ratio of Lawyers: Population Ontario
1960	1:1142
1965	1:1143
1970	1:1043
1975	1: 817
1980	1: 599
1981	1: 574

Source: Gazette; Vol. XV#4: Dec. 1981; The Law Society of Upper Canada

Hugh knew that as a result of the proliferation of lawyers, which was even more intense in London than in other areas of the province, price cutting was occurring. Comparison shopping — a new phenomenon in the legal business — was becoming the norm, especially in real estate and family law matters. The lawyers' work often carried a lower dollar price tag than it would have several years before, despite inflationary times.

Not surprisingly, the industry trends just described were affecting lawyers' paycheques. The research done by the Waterloo lawyers polled lawyers who had been in practice three to eight years. The majority earned a taxable income of less than

$25 000 per year, and many did not surpass $20 000 in 1980. Of his classmates who had landed jobs practising law in the London area, the highest gross salary which Hugh had heard of was $18 000. Some had been taken on "in association" with firms and would be earning a percentage of their billings rather than a fixed salary. Others "in association" kept all of their own billings but paid a fixed overhead monthly.

HUGH FRASER: BACKGROUND AND OBJECTIVES

The relatively poor salaries offered by law firms, and the insecurity of positions with them, had reinforced Hugh's decision to open his own office. He felt that if he was going to put a great deal of effort into building a practice, he would prefer it to be his own. As well, one of his strongest motivations in attending law school had been the prospect of "being his own boss."

Hugh had initially graduated from university in 1974, with a degree in geography. He had worked for the government as a real estate appraiser for the next two years. It was a dissatisfaction with the life of a civil servant, and an urge to find a more challenging profession, which led him to enter law school in 1976.

Hugh had initially thought that he might relocate upon being called to the Bar but, by this time, he was very well settled in London. His wife had a reasonably good job paying nearly $20 000 per year, and had just had a baby. The family owned a modest home in the city, but had less than $5 000 equity in the property. Their other assets were not substantial and Hugh felt that, apart from their emotional attachment to the city, they really could not afford to move without dropping their standard of living. He was, therefore, committed to opening his practice in London and had spent the past couple of weeks gathering information on the costs involved.

THE LAW OFFICE

Choice of a location had been one of the most difficult decisions which Hugh had faced. He finally decided on the upper floor of a house on a busy street in East London; the main floor of the house was occupied by three doctors. The office was one of the most moderately priced which Hugh had seen, at $250 per month inclusive of utilities. It was bright and had some turn-of-the-century charm. Moreover, Hugh felt that it would help him to build his clientele of small businesses, as it was unpretentious and located among many small, family-owned shops and cottage industries. Hugh's eventual goal was to specialize in small business, though, at the outset, he certainly did not intend to turn anyone away!

The office was actually a suite of three rooms, consisting of Hugh's office, a reception area, and a coffee and storage room. He planned to furnish the rooms with oak office furniture of 1920 vintage, as he thought that this would be cheaper and more in keeping with the building. He planned to restrict equipment purchases to a minimum and to depend on part-time staff initially. The only piece of advice which an MBA friend had proferred was: "Keep your costs variable." He intended to follow it.

FINANCIAL CONSIDERATIONS

Hugh had $5 500 of personal capital which he intended to invest in his business. Beyond this, all financing would have to come from bank credit or, more optimistically, from operations.

Hugh was very unsure of what to expect in revenue for his first year of operations. When he asked other lawyers for their experience, the parallel between their profession and that of fishermen became evident. There was no hesitation to swap stories, but Hugh suspected that he was hearing more about the clients who got away than the ones who were caught. He eventually decided that 390 billable hours for the year, at a rate of $40 per hour, was realistic. The Law Society had indicated that 1,200 billable hours per annum was the most which any lawyer could expect.

Hugh was aware that there would be a lag between billing and payment for the accounts which he did collect. He estimated an average wait of ninety days. He did not anticipate that he would have any accounts payable outstanding at the end of a normal month due to the nature of his business. Approximately $500 would be kept in his cash account, representing about twelve days of operating expenses.

In law, many expenses were incurred on behalf of clients and subsequently charged out to them directly. For example, long distance telephone calls made to incorporate a company were billed to the lawyer, who then passed these costs on to his client. Billable costs cannot be marked up by lawyers. In making his financial projections, Hugh ignored these costs and concentrated on the expenses which he knew he would have to pay regardless of his level of business.

In order to practise law, Hugh was required to pay the Law Society $1 220 annually for fees and insurance. The insurance, which was $5 000 deductible, covered him for errors or omissions made in his practice. The Law Society also required an annual audit of trust accounts and traditionally conducted surprise audits of the books of a law office. Hugh had, therefore, budgeted $500 for accounting fees and planned to spend $300 on a legal accounting system. The accounting system, which was basically a set of ledgers, would be considered as "office supplies," and treated as an expense in his first year of operation.

A further restriction of the Law Society prevented lawyers from advertising and permitted them one sign with letters a maximum of six inches high. It was this sign which Hugh had discovered would cost $300. In light of his inability to advertise, Hugh felt that he should take advantage of the fact that the Law Society allowed starting practices to publish an announcement of their opening. An ad in the Free Press for this purpose would be $150; he also planned for an opening party, to cost $200. In addition, he set aside $600 per year as an expense account for promotional purposes.

Hugh planned to rent a typewriter for $30 per month. His anticipated furniture and equipment purchases, to be depreciated by 10 percent of the original price per annum, were:

Air conditioner	$500
Library	500
2 desks	500
6 chairs	400
3 filing cabinets	450
Bookcases	300
Stationery cabinet	100
Art	200

The office contents would be insured at an annual cost of $100. For accounting purposes, Hugh's sign would be included in the category "furniture and equipment," and depreciated accordingly.

In the course of the year, Hugh anticipated spending $400 on stationery, $250 on office supplies, $75 on kitchen supplies, and $360 for postage. All of these would be treated as expenses on his income statement. His average monthly phone bill, according to Bell Canada, would be $45 plus long distance charges. He could foresee $40 monthly in long distance calls which could not be billed to clients. Finally, Hugh felt that it would be important to attend some of the continuing education courses offered over the course of the year by the Law Society. He budgeted for four courses, at an average cost of $150 each. These fees would be yet another of his operating expenses.

Hugh had weighed the pros and cons of hiring a trained legal secretary and decided that, in the beginning, he would be better advised to secure a part-time typist. He felt that this would be considerably cheaper at $5/hour, and that he would have time to train the individual. For his first year, he estimated a $5300 expenditure for a part-time secretary to work half days.

The final issue which Hugh had to address before he could complete his projections was the matter of how much money he personally would require in his first year. He would be paid through drawings, since his practice was not legally permitted to incorporate. The most conservative estimate which he thought his family could get by on was $1000/month. That seemed very low, considering that his house mortgage alone was nearly $500 monthly, but he knew that the banker would measure his commitment to his business partly by the size of his draw. He was also very concerned with keeping his bank borrowing at a minimum.

Hugh was anxious to put together all of the information which he had gathered, in order to determine the amount of the bank loan which he would need. He had two classmates who were also starting out in London, and they had mentioned that the bankers they had visited were being more selective about their professional lending than they had been in the past. Hugh wondered what, if anything, he should put in his bank presentation to supplement his financial projections and gain a more favourable response from the banks.

11
Sprucelawn Farms

"When is the closing date on the deal?" asked Michael Ireland.

"March 31st, 1980; that's a week from tomorrow, but I really need an answer from you before that, in case things don't work out here and I have to look for money somewhere else," answered Sjef de Meyer (pronounced Chef).

"I'll get back to you day after tomorrow, then," Mr. Ireland proposed. The two men shook hands and Mr. de Meyer left for his farm. Michael Ireland, manager of a London, Ontario, branch of a large Canadian bank, knew he was cutting the time short to make a decision on Sjef de Meyer's loan request. Sjef was planning to buy a 40-hectare[1] farm for $250 000 in order to expand his operations. He was requesting a loan of $175 000 to help finance the purchase.

Rising interest rates had caused problems for some farmers and Mr. Ireland was aware of the bad publicity banks had been getting for their role in farmers' difficulties. He was anxious to make the right decision in this situation.

BACKGROUND INFORMATION

In 1953, at the age of 27, Sjef de Meyer came to Canada. He brought very little with him apart from his grade seven education and a keen desire to succeed. He felt the opportunity to farm would be much better in Canada than in his native Holland.

Sjef started out farming land owned by a convent in London, and his wife Anna cleaned houses for wealthy families in the area. Sjef and his family stayed at the convent until 1966, when they bought and moved to Sprucelawn, a 55-hectare farm just east of the city, in Middlesex County. It was around this time that Sjef began growing some crops under contract to large canning companies such as Green Giant.

By 1980, Sprucelawn farms had expanded to include 166 hectares, spread over four farms in the vicinity. In addition, Sjef rented about 40 hectares of land. The purchase of "the Carroll farm" would increase the total hectares owned to 205. The crops grown on the farms included sweet corn, green peas, grain corn, and wheat.

In 1976, Sjef started into a new aspect of business. He installed a grain-drying system. This system was used to reduce the moisture content in grains such as grain corn and wheat. This enabled them to be stored without spoilage. The capacity of the dryer was greater than he required for his own crops, so Mr. de Meyer also dried corn for many neighbouring farmers.

Farming had changed dramatically since Sjef's younger days. When he left Holland, tractors were not used at all, and now he owned six of them, including two large air-conditioned ones with enclosed cabs. The complexity of fertilizers, pesticides, and insecticides had also escalated markedly. To keep up with the changes, Sjef periodically attended short courses at the Ridgetown College of Agricultural Technology.

---

[1] 1 acre = .405 hectares
1 ton = .9072 tonnes

Mr. de Meyer was quite involved in the community. He had been a township councillor for six years and was now on the Planning Board of the township. He was also a member of the Parish Council Advisory Board at his church. For the next few years, he would be involved with the planning of the 1982 International Plowing Match, which was to be hosted by Middlesex County. He was also a member of the Ontario Vegetable Growers' Marketing Board.

Sjef and Anna had four children, aged 18 to 24. One of their sons, who was currently in university, had expressed a definite interest in farming. Their other son, who was just finishing high school, was also considering that possibility, though not as strongly. This explained, in part, Sjef's desire to purchase the Carroll farm. If both sons were to farm, more acreage would be needed. Sjef and Anna were happy that their sons were considering a future in agriculture. They felt that the lifestyle was almost ideal. Sjef liked being his own boss and making his own decisions. Winter provided him with a fair amount of free time, and he and his wife usually made a point of taking a holiday at this time of year. In fact, they had recently returned from a Caribbean cruise.

Ever since his purchase of the original Sprucelawn farm, Sjef had done his banking at the London East branch of the bank. He had always repaid his loans, and frequently took advantage of low-interest government loans for farmers, but Mr. Ireland recalled that Sjef was also frequently overdrawn.

THE FARMING INDUSTRY

Mr. Ireland knew that farming was a sensitive area for banks. While a bank foreclosing on a farmer's loan generally created bad publicity, there was also a feeling among many consumers that farmers were usually quite well off. The opinion of farmers, with respect to that attitude, was expressed by the bumper sticker Mr. Ireland had seen recently: "Next time you gripe about the farmer, don't talk with your mouth full!"

Farming was a risk-filled industry. Concentrating on the cash crop segment of the industry, one of the major risks was the drastic fluctuations that could occur in crop prices from year to year. Over the past twenty years, price fluctuations for some crops had been monitored and minimized by various marketing boards and associations. For example, the Ontario Vegetable Growers Marketing Board established set prices each year for the sale of certain crops such as sweet corn, green peas, and tomatoes. Thus, for Sjef, price fluctuations were not a serious concern for his sweet corn and peas. Wheat prices were also generally quite stable. Grain corn,[1] however, could sell for $4.15/bushel one year and $2.00/bushel the next. The price of corn was determined by many factors. Droughts or bumper crops in other parts of the world could affect the local price of corn. The U.S. restrictions imposed on trade with Russia as a result of Russian interference in Afghanistan caused corn prices to drop in North America because of the reduced market size for the North American crop.

Another risk for farmers was the effect of the weather on crop production. In recent years, crop insurance had reduced the risk of bad crops. Some farmers, however, disliked crop insurance because they felt farming wasn't really farming any more if you could buy protection against the weather. Sjef agreed with this view, but believed

---

[1]Used for livestock feed, flour and cereals, oils, syrup, etc.

that unless you were well established, you were probably better off buying insurance.

Seasonality, which was especially marked for cash crop farmers, resulted in heavy financing requirements at certain times of the year. It also made it difficult to obtain hired help. Seasonal work was not very popular, and, contrary to what many people believed, not "just anyone" was good enough to be a hired hand.

Mr. Ireland, having moved to London recently from a large urban centre, had learned much about farming from his rural clients. He was aware that 1980 was presenting farmers with a new problem — rapidly rising interest rates. Exhibit 1 shows the changes in the Bank of Canada's lending rate over the previous year. High interest rates made it extremely difficult for young farmers to start up. The investment required in both land and equipment was substantial. Growing interest payments made it very difficult to earn enough, after financing charges, to make farming worthwhile. As a result, some rationalization had occurred. Fewer farmers were operating larger farms. While the example of the young farmer most clearly illustrated the difficulties created by high interest rates, Mr. Ireland realized that high interest rates made farming less attractive for others as well. Exhibit 2 shows some rough calculations Mr. Ireland had done concerning the interest rate impact on farming. These calculations suggested to him that in times of high interest rates, most farmers would probably be better off selling their land and collecting interest on that money. But farmers, Mr. Ireland had also learned, usually liked their work. If they could earn enough by farming, they would likely continue to farm even though it might not be as financially rewarding as selling out.

THE CARROLL FARM

Sjef de Meyer felt the purchase of the Carroll farm would be worthwhile for several reasons. He wished to help build a future for his sons. He had also accumulated a fair bit of cash (see financial statements in Exhibits 3, 4, and 5) and was anxious to invest it wisely. (It was currently invested in marketable securities.) He felt land was a secure investment and, just as importantly, an investment he understood. The farm was in an excellent location with respect to his existing land holdings, and the quality of the land was very good.

PLANS FOR 1980

Although Sjef de Meyer had never prepared projected statements himself, he had little difficulty in supplying Mr. Ireland with the necessary information. He broke down his plans as follows:

1. *Sweet Corn*: Sjef expected a contract of about 69 hectares[1] from Green Giant. This meant that Green Giant would supply seed and chemicals for the crop, and at the end of the season would harvest and purchase the entire crop. The selling price for the corn had been established at 73.60 per tonne and Mr. de Meyer's average yield for Green Giant was 16.1 tonnes/hectare. (Mr. de Meyer proudly pointed out that

---

[1] Farmers have no say in the size of their contracts from year to year, but if they get along well with contractors, the size does not vary much from year to year.

this was the highest average yield for farmers at Green Giant's London plant.) Of course, this year's yield could vary from the average.

2. *Green Peas*: Sjef estimated that he would receive a 32.5 hectares contract, and the selling price had been fixed by the marketing board at $358/tonne. Mr. de Meyer said that the yield would vary between 3.6 and 5.8 tonnes/hectare.

3. *Wheat*: Sjef planned to grow 24.3 hectares of wheat. He anticipated a selling price of $4.25/bushel and expected a yield of between 148 and 173 bushels per hectare.

4. *Grain Corn*: Sjef had set aside about 110 hectares for grain corn. This crop was the most difficult one for which to anticipate a selling price, but Sjef thought $3.75/bushel was a realistic expectation. The yield for grain corn usually varied between 270 and 307 bushels per hectare.

5. *Corn Drying and Resale*: Since Sjef had put in his grain drying system, he found himself drying corn for neighbouring farmers. This earned him some income and he expected a 5 percent increase in volume in the next year. In addition, he had taken to buying corn from his neighbours and reselling it later, he hoped at a profit. This was a risky venture and involved anticipating future corn prices but, to date, Mr. de Meyer had been successful.

In terms of anticipated machinery and equipment purchases, when Mr. Ireland summarized Sjef's plans he found that new purchases would approximately equal depreciation charges. Seed, fertilizer, and chemical purchases would be approximately $47 000 according to Mr. de Meyer.[1] The $250 000 for the farm would be allocated $200 000 to land and $50 000 to buildings.

The uncertainty surrounding final results for the year, despite Sjef de Meyer's clear-cut plans, emphasized for Mr. Ireland the risk involved in farming. He knew his decision on the loan request must be carefully thought out.

---

[1] In addition, Mr. de Meyer predicted that corn purchases for the next year would amount to $17 500. Therefore, *total* purchases for 1980 would be $47 000 + 17 500 = *$64 500.*

Exhibit 1
Sprucelawn Farms
Bank of Canada Interest Rates
March 1979–March 1980

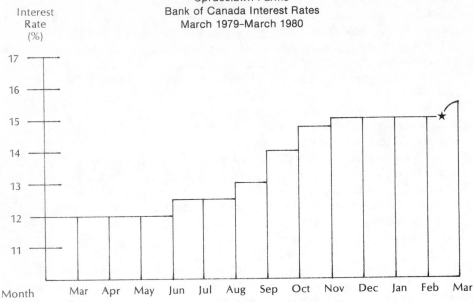

*On March 13, 1980, the Bank of Canada began setting the bank rate each week.
Taken from Bank of Canada Annual Reports of the Governor to the Minister of Finance, 1979 and 1980.

Exhibit 2
Sprucelawn Farms
Effect of Interest Rates on Farmers

Grain Corn

If you were a farmer growing grain corn:

Anticipated selling price per bushel[1]	$ 3.75
Average yield per hectare[2]	272 bushels
Sales per hectare 272 × 3.75	$1020
Cost per hectare[2]	445
Profit per hectare	$ 575

Selling Out:
Farm land near the city sells for $5000/hectare. If you sold your land and banked the money, you would earn 15 percent interest. The interest per hectare you would earn in a year is $5000 × .15 = $750.00.

Crop Budgeting Aid — Ontario Ministry of Agriculture and Food.

Exhibit 3
Sprucelawn Farms
Income Statements for Years Ending December 31

Income:	1977	1978	1979
Grain & sweet corn	$129 360	$172 360	$168 490
Wheat	3 710	3 845	13 110
Peas	10 775	15 500	34 960
Corn drying & resale	12 420	2 950	15 815
Total income	$156 265	$194 655	$232 375
	—	—	—
Cost of goods sold			
Beginning inventory	$ 57 650	$ 94 300	$ 89 700
Custom work[1]	5 540	6 340	5 840
Land rent	7 265	5 165	6 850
Fuel	8 660	7 720	14 640
Labour	1 810	3 650	3 720
Corn purchases[2]	27 930	69 850	34 700
Seed, fertilizer & chemicals	26 200	23 060	49 600
Depreciation	24 430	20 840	31 760
Repairs & maintenance	6 710	10 625	10 370
Less: ending inventory	94 300	89 700	132 500
	71 895	151 850	114 680
Gross profit	$ 84 370	$ 42 805	$117 695
	—	—	—
Operating expenses			
Insurance	$ 1 340	$ 3 510	$ 1 015
Property tax	1 690	3 050	4 025
Interest & bank charges	13 250	5 860	5 480
Miscellaneous	1 790	2 035	835
Total operating expenses	18 070	14 455	11 355
Operating profit	$ 66 300	$ 28 350	$106 340
Plus: other income[3]	3 315	2 400	2 400
Net profit	$ 69 615	$ 30 750	$108 740
Drawings	$ 30 790	$ 31 060	$ 60 840

[1]Planting, harvesting etc. done by outside workers such as Green Giant.
[2]These are purchases of grain corn intended for resale at a later date.
[3]Income received from renting out house on another farm.

Exhibit 4
Sprucelawn Farms
Balance Sheets as of December 31

	1977	1978	1979
ASSETS			
Current assets			
Cash	$ 0	$ 0	$ 2330
Marketable securities[1]	148 000	145 000	135 000
Accounts receivable[2]			7 000
Inventory	94 300	89 700	132 500
Total current assets	$242 300	$234 700	$276 830
	—	—	—
Fixed assets			
Land	$122 650	$122 650	$122 650
	—		—
Buildings, cost	$ 68 150	$ 68 150	$ 68 150
Less: accumulated dep'n	39 155	40 605	41 980
Buildings net[3]	28 995	27 545	26 170
	—	—	—
Machinery & equipment, cost	$164 880	$176 370	$235 290
Less: accumulated dep'n	97 870	118 710	149 090
Machinery & equipment, net[4]	67 010	57 660	86 200
Total fixed assets	218 655	207 855	235 020
TOTAL ASSETS	$460 955	$442 555	$511 850
LIABILITIES			
Current liabilities			
Bank overdraft	$ 20 920	$ 4 980	$ 0
Accounts payable	2 100	1 500	5 000
Current portion of long term debt[5]	19 950	8 545	4 600
Demand loan—bank	3 500	23 000	54 410
Total current liabilities	$ 46 470	$ 38 025	$ 64 010
	—	—	—
Long-term liabilities			
Farm improvement loan	$ 17 760	$ 11 060	$ 9 060
Mortgages — Junior Farm	30 850	29 750	28 650
— Broome Farm	21 000	20 000	19 000
Tile loans	1 345	500	
Total long-term liabilities	70 955	61 310	56 710
TOTAL LIABILITIES	$117 425	$ 99 335	$120 720
	—	—	
CAPITAL			
Opening balance	$304 705	$343 530	$343 220
Plus: net income	69 615	30 750	108 750
Less: drawings	30 790	31 060	60 840
Closing balance	343 530	343 220	391 130
TOTAL LIABILITIES AND CAPITAL	$460 955	$442 555	$511 850

[1]Includes term deposits, Canada Savings Bonds, and Registered Retirement Savings Plan.
[2]Awaiting partial payment for wheat, sweet corn crops.
[3]Buildings depreciated at 5% of the net balance.
[4]The average depreciation on machinery + equipment was 27% of the net balance.
[5]In 1977 the final mortgage payment ($14 900) on 3rd farm was paid off. In 1979 the final instalment of the tile loan ($500) was paid. Farm Improvement Loan: Repayment of $2000/year required. Junior Farm Mortgage: Mortgage on original farm—payment of $1100 per year required. Broome Farm Mortgage: Mortgage on 4th farm. Payment of $1000 required yearly.

Exhibit 5
Sprucelawn Farms
Ratio Sheet

	1977	1978	1979
Profitability			
Vertical Analysis			
Revenue — corn	83%	89%	72%
— wheat	2	2	6
— peas	7	8	15
— corn drying & resale	8	1	7
Total Revenue	100%	100%	100%
Cost of Goods Sold	46	78[2]	49
Gross Profit	54	22	51
	—	—	—
Operating Expenses			
Insurance	1	2	1
Property tax	1	2	2
Interest and bank charges	8	3	2
Miscellaneous	1	1	—
	11	7	5
Operating profit	42	15	46
Other income	2	1	1
Net profit	44%	16%	47%
Drawings as % of net profit	44%	101%	56%
Return on Investment	21%	9%	30%
Liquidity			
Current ratio	5.2x	6.2x	4.3x
Acid test ratio	3.2x	3.8x	2.3x
Working capital	$195 830	$196 675	$212 820
Efficiency			
Age of receivables	—	—	11 days
Inventory in days c.g.s.	479 days	216 days	422 days
Age of payables[1]	14 days	6 days	22 days
Fixed assets per sales dollar	$1.40	$1.07	$1.01
Stability			
Net worth/Total assets	75%	78%	76%
Interest coverage	6.3x	6.2x	20.8x
Growth			

		77-78	78-79
Revenue		25%	19%
Profits		(56)	254
Assets		(4)	16
Equity		—	14%

[1]Based on purchases of corn, seed, fertilizer, and chemicals.

[2]In reviewing the 1978 ratios Sjef explained that "1978 was one helluva weird year." For example, the 1978 aberration in the Cost of Goods Sold section is explained by irregular corn purchases.

12

The Village Variety Store

In the fall of 1984, John McGee inherited $120 000 from his father's estate. John, forty-two years old, had been a wholesale company sales representative for fourteen years. Now, with his home paid off, he wished to satisfy a lifelong ambition to run his own business. With the help of his longtime friend Tony Marshman, John sought out many small retail business opportunities in southwestern Ontario. Early in 1985, Tony received a call from a London, Ontario, realtor who informed him that the establishment of a variety store — The Village Variety Store — in Stratton, Ontario, was for sale. Stratton was a community of approximately 12 000 people located some forty-eight kilometres northwest of London. The Village Variety Store was established in 1934 as a general store by David Goldback. In 1956, when Mr. Goldback died, his son Larry took over and changed it to a variety store. The store was located at the main intersection of Stratton.

John had a professional appraisal made of the business. In addition, he and Tony went over all the past business records of the firm and made personal appraisals of its value as a going concern. With these figures, John negotiated a sale price of $150 000 for the business, including equipment and inventory. The settlement was arranged for March 1, 1985, with Mr. Goldback taking a note, due 1990, for $50 000, and cash of $100 000.

All the time John was looking for a good buying opportunity, Tony continually stated that he wished to work for him. "John, I think this store could turn into a small gold mine. Goldback has been resting on his reputation and hasn't taken nearly the advantage of that location or the type of products that will move there. With some reshuffling of shelf space and a little work, sales could be increased by 50 percent by the end of the year. I only wish I could help you with the money end." John realized that Tony had had difficulties making ends meet. With two children in university and a recent home purchase, Tony had not saved money, though both he and his wife were working. In spite of this, John realized that without Tony's assistance and expertise, he would not have considered buying the variety store alone.

Tony Marshman, age forty-four, was the son of a tailor and had worked in his father's store after finishing high school until he married at the age of twenty-two. Then Tony moved to Toronto where he joined a major department store. He served with this store as a salesman, department manager, and assistant accountant. After twelve years, Tony found Toronto very expensive and moved to London, where he was assistant store manager in a grocery chain. After six years in the same position, Tony realized that the company had no plans for advancing him. Thus, when John McGee approached him for help, he was more than eager to become involved.

John discussed the purchase of the variety store with David Stone, his lawyer. Mr. Stone explained over the telephone that there were a number of possible ways to establish the new business. He followed his telephone conversation with the following letter.

David M. Stone, LL.B.
Barrister and Solicitor
London, Ontario
January 22, 1985

Mr. John McGee
Box 188
Stratton, Ontario

Dear John:

This letter is a follow-up of our conversation on the telephone last week. As I mentioned at that time, there are three ways to establish ownership in The Village Variety Store. Most smaller stores are operated as proprietorships. Under this form of ownership, you would own the store and have entire control over its operation. From a legal standpoint, your only requirements are to obtain a vendor's permit and establish yourself with the retail sales tax people. The simplicity of establishing a proprietorship must be weighed against the risk. You are liable not only to the extent of your investment in the business, but also your personal assets are liable if you cannot meet your debts from assets of the business. When you leave the business, it is legally dissolved. The profits from operations can either be retained by you or distributed to other employees. Any distribution does not constitute a partnership unless the parties agree to share both profits and losses.

If you chose to form a partnership, you and your partner(s) continue to have unlimited personal liability. The tax act states that each activity of the partnership will be viewed as being carried on by the partnership as if it were a separate person resident in Canada. Income and taxable capital gains amounts, as calculated for the partnership, are shared by the partners in the manner agreed on by them and each partner declares his share of *the taxable proceeds*. A legal partnership agreement is required to define the initial investment and the division of income. Any partnership is dissolved when any partner dies or any change is to be made in the partnership agreement.

Your third alternative would be to form a limited company. The most significant difference between the sole proprietorship and the partnership on the one hand and the corporation on the other is that in law the company is regarded as an entity, with an existence of its own quite separate from that of the people who own it. Property acquired by the corporation does not belong to the shareholders of the corporation, but to the corporation itself. The corporation may, subject to certain restrictions, contract with its owners as would a separate person. It may also sue or be sued — just like a person. However, unlike a person, it has indefinite life until terminated by bankruptcy or voluntary dissolution. Its whole character depends on the grant of life which it receives from the government and upon such legislation and law as may have developed in the jurisdiction where it is chartered.

To incorporate a company in Canada, an application must be made to the government department designated by the provincial legislature or the Canadian Parliament to have jurisdiction in such matters. The petition sets out the proposed name of the corporation (which must not conflict with an existing name), the purposes and objects which it is intended that the company shall pursue, the amount of capital to be authorized, the number of directors and the names of the provincial (temporary) directors. Assuming that the application is found to be in order, a charter will be issued in the form of "Letters Patent" (provincial — articles of incorporation). The company is deemed to exist from the date of its charter.

The word "corporation" most often takes the place of "company" in the company's name and under Dominion company law. In the law of some provinces, the word "limited" or "incorporated" must be added. Changes in the company's charter may be obtained by application to the authority granting the charter, which upon approval, will incorporate the changes by the grant of "Supplementary Letters Patent" (provincially — articles of amendment).

Through the right to vote at the annual meeting and special meetings, the shareholders exercise their right as owners to control the destiny of the corporation. Here, they elect their representatives, the directors, who guide and control the business operations of the company through its officers. The matters upon which the stockholders must be consulted are found in the law of the jurisdiction of the incorporations (federal or provincial) and in the charter.

Under the usual methods of voting, each common shareholder has one vote for each voting share owned. Under this system, one or more shareholders controlling one share more than half of the total number of voting shares can carry every question and elect every director on the board. The result is rule by those holding a majority of the voting stock and not necessarily by the majority in number of shareholders.

Profits from the company accrue to the shareholder(s). Profits must be paid out in the form of dividends or retained to finance future growth. The allocation of the profits is the responsibility of the directors elected by the shareholders.

Total cost of incorporation for a business such as yours would be approximately $1500, which includes all registration costs.

I trust this letter will help you in establishing your business.

Sincerely,

David Stone, LL.B.

John was concerned about the tax implications of his new operation. After a thorough examination of the past operations of The Village Variety Store, John and Tony determined that it could reasonably expect a profit of $100 000 before any wage payments. It would take two full-time people to operate the store since it was to be open fourteen hours a day, seven days a week. To ascertain better the financial implications of the business, John contacted the Toronto chartered accountant firm of Wiley and Company. Jim Wiley, the senior partner of the company, sent him the following letter explaining the relative tax considerations of each of the forms of ownership John was considering.

Wiley and Company
Chartered Accountants
February 10, 1985

Mr. John McGee
Box 188
Stratton, Ontario

Dear Mr. McGee:

In regard to your inquiry concerning the effect of current Canadian tax laws upon expected income of $100 000 before taxes or salaries, I will outline the tax considerations which apply to your new business.

Under a proprietorship or partnership, all earnings are treated as personal income and taxed accordingly. The proprietorship income is distributed at the discretion of the proprietor while the partnership income is divided by a prearranged formula established in the initial partnership agreement.

To determine taxable income for an individual taxpayer, the income from employment, business, investments, and capital gain must be determined. If the business is unincorporated, the net income of the enterprise will be taxable in the owner(s) hands as business income. If the business is incorporated, the employees/owners will probably receive wages (employment income) and dividends (property income). The business of the corporation will be taxed in the hands of the corporation at the rates quoted below. A couple of points should be noted. You are allowed to deduct from employment earnings only 3 percent of gross employment income, up to a maximum of $500, whereas with business and property income, all reasonable expenses incurred to earn business and property revenues may be deducted to determine net income. On your tax form, "total income" is the sum of the net incomes from employment, business, and property. To calculate "taxable income," Canada Pension Plan contributions (maximum $338.90 for employed taxpayers, $676.80 for self-employed), registered retirement savings plan contributions and personal exemptions are deducted from "total income."

To calculate "basic federal tax," apply the applicable rate as outlined in Exhibit 1 and deduct the "federal dividend tax credit," defined below. Your "federal tax payable" is the "basic federal tax" less a federal tax reduction of $200. Provincial taxes are a percent of the "basic federal tax." Exhibit 1 outlines the percent of "basic federal tax" used by the various provinces.

If you decide to form a corporation, the corporation is taxed as a separate entity. In determining the corporation's taxable income, you are allowed to deduct reasonable salary payments for services rendered by employee/shareholders. The federal corporate tax rate is 15 percent on the first $200 000 of taxable income and 36 percent on the excess. Each province also taxes corporate taxable income. The provincial rates are outlined in Exhibit 1.

With regard to capital withdrawals, there is no tax on drawings from a proprietorship or partnership because the income has already been taxed. However, there is a 12.5 percent dividend distribution tax payable by the corporation for dividends distributed by corporations subject to the 15 percent corporate tax rate. The dividends are also subject to tax in the hands of the shareholders.

The taxation of dividends is complex: first the taxable amount of dividends is not the dividend received, but the dollar receipt plus one-half of the receipt. This additional one-half is called a tax credit and is partially used to reduce your federal tax liability. The federal tax credit is 68 percent of the tax credit. An example may aid your understanding: if your federal personal tax rate was 30 percent and you received a dividend of $300 from a taxable Canadian corporation, the taxable amount of the dividend would be $450; $300, plus one-half of $300, i.e. $150 (the tax credit). Your gross federal tax liability would be $135, 30 percent of $450. However, your basic federal tax liability would be less because you would deduct $102, 68 percent of the tax credit ($150), from the gross federal tax liability. The consequence is a basic federal tax of $33 ($135 – $102). Your provincial tax then is calculated in the normal manner as a percent of the basic federal tax or, in Ontario, 48 percent of $33, i.e., $15.84. Note that dividends received from a Canadian corporation controlled by you are not eligible for the special interest and dividend exemption of $1000.

If I can be of further assistance, please call.

Sincerely,

J.W. Wiley

For 1984, John found that he would have total personal exemptions of $3960, while Tony Marshman would have total exemptions of $9520. He was considering the following alternatives:

1. An individual proprietorship under which he would pay Tony Marshman a salary of $36 000 per year and the remainder would go to himself.
2. A partnership in which he and Tony Marshman would share all profits and losses on the basis of 60 percent for himself and 40 percent for Tony.
3. A corporation in which the common stock was owned by himself. The corporation would pay Tony Marshman a salary of $36 000 per year and himself a salary of $30 000 a year. The remainder would be retained in the business.

John believed he needed $20 000 after taxes to support himself. Any amounts that remained would be reinvested in the business to aid its development.

Exhibit 1
The Village Variety Store

I. Individual Federal and Provincial Tax Rates
(a) Federal Income Tax — 1984

Taxable income

Over (Column 1)	Not over	Tax on Column 1	Percentage on excess
—	$ 1 238	—	6
$ 1 238	2 476	$ 74	16
2 476	4 952	272	17
4 952	7 428	693	18
7 428	12 380	1 139	19
12 380	17 332	2 080	20
17 332	22 284	3 070	23
22 284	34 664	4 209	25
34 664	59 424	7 304	30
59 424		14 732	34

(b) Provincial Income Tax — 1984

	% of basic federal tax
Newfoundland	60
Prince Edward Island	52.5
Nova Scotia	56.5
New Brunswick	58.0
Quebec	N.A.[1]
Ontario	48.0[2]
Manitoba	54[3]
Saskatchewan	51[4]
Alberta	43.5
British Columbia	44[5]

[1]Quebec collects its own tax on a different tax schedule.
[2]For 1984, there is a 5 percent surtax on provincial tax greater than $110.80.
[3]20 percent surtax of provincial tax on taxable income in excess of $25 000.
[4]12 percent surtax of provincial tax on taxable income in excess of $4 000.
[5]10 percent surtax of provincial tax greater than $3 500, plus surtax of 4 percent of provincial tax, including 10 percent surtax.

II. Provincial Corporate Income Tax — 1984

	Rate on First $200 000	Rate on Excess
	%	%
British Columbia	8	16
Alberta	5	11
Saskatchewan	10	16
Manitoba	10	16
Ontario	0	15
Quebec	3	11.5
Nova Scotia	10	15
New Brunswick	10	15
Newfoundland	16	10
Prince Edward Island	10	10
Northwest Territories	10	10

SECTION IV

An Introduction to Management of Human Resources

INTRODUCTION

We are all human resource managers. We are family members, belong to clubs, attend classes, live with other people, have jobs, and are therefore always managing relationships with people. Whether we are a sales representative or the company president, we are always accomplishing tasks through the efforts of others. The study of human resources management, the interaction of people with and within an organization, is therefore a very important one.

Since managers accomplish tasks through the efforts of others, all managers are both functional (sales manager, production manager, etc.) *and* human resources managers. An understanding of the management of human resources will enable managers to better analyze "people" problems, develop solutions to these problems, and improve their ability to predict and therefore better handle future problems.

This chapter introduces some basic concepts of human resources management — the interaction of people with and within an organization — beginning with a basic human resource problem-solving approach. We then discuss the people part of the organization — individual, interpersonal, and group behaviour. The structure and goals of organizations are then examined and the formal responsibilities of the human resources manager discussed. Discussion of the interaction of people with and within an organization, describing successful organizations, leadership, and management of change follows. Lastly, we will discuss future challenges in human resources management.

HUMAN RESOURCE PROBLEM-SOLVING APPROACH — AN OVERVIEW

A combination of managerial experience and psychological research has provided us with a general approach to human resource problem solving.

1. Begin by identifying the problem clearly. What is the behavioural performance that is not as desired? How often has it happened? How severe a problem is it? Is it a symptom of more serious problems? Is the problem defined properly: not too narrowly and not too broadly? How much time have you got to remedy the problem?
2. Next, try to understand what caused the problem. What factors in the individual, the task, the organization, and the environment outside the organization contributed to undesirable performance? Your job is not to describe the behaviour or the situation, but to explain why it occurred. By doing this, you can identify ways to alter the behaviour toward more desirable outcomes. In effect, you go through two steps:
   (a) What caused the observed behaviour?
   (b) What new "causes" will result in the desired behaviour?

3. There are generally three factors which the manager may be able to alter in order to obtain new behaviour: the nature of the task (job to be performed), the conditions of work (a very broad catchall) and the people involved (e.g., replacement of personnel). As manager, you must decide (a) whether (and to what extent) any of these can be altered (those factors which cannot be changed become constraints to be considered) and (b) which of the possible changes gives the most "leverage" on the problem of a reasonable "cost" (money, time, impact on others, etc). Some solutions may be short-term and some may be long-term. Does the solution you propose fit the real problem? For example, dismissing a complaining employee may be short-term if the task and work conditions are such that all replacements will complain as well.

4. All of the analytical tools do not work all of the time. You must be selective in the tools you use and flexible in your method of use. The analytical models tend to represent situations as black and white. In fact, human resource problems are most often grey. Further, many of the models lead aspiring managers to think behaviour can be easily explained with a single "cause" or two. In fact, behaviour is nearly always the result of multiple causes, interacting with one another.

5. Recommendations for action can be evaluated in much the same way as managers assess financial, marketing, or production proposals. We have found that a pictorial "decision tree" is often useful with human resource problems. Suppose you have an employee who is a poor performer and a complainer too. Your options might be as follows:

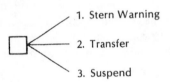

(Notice we use a ☐ to indicate a "decision point" for you)

As a manager, as you weigh these options, you are concerned with what will happen *if* you follow any one of these courses of action. You can diagram that too as a set of "consequences":

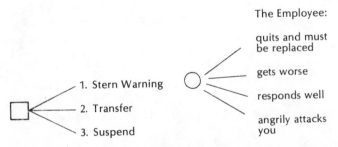

(Notice we use an O to indicate a consequence point — after your action, these are the events you think could happen)

After outlining the alternatives there are two tasks: first, to decide what consequences are possible for each alternative, and second, to decide which consequences are most likely. The first task is based on your understanding of the individual involved. If you can figure out why he/she acted as he/she did in the past, you have a reasonable (not perfect) way to predict what might happen in the future given various sorts of stimulation. The second task involves pushing a bit further. If you had to place bets on that employee's behaviour, what is the behaviour that is most likely to occur?

You may do this for all of the alternatives you feel can reasonably be expected. Clearly, the trick is to confine this approach to a plausible set of options based on the value of your analysis of past behaviour. The better your analysis, the easier this "decision tree" approach becomes.

Such analysis is useful only if extended to the stage when the problem is resolved and the "dust has settled." For example, it may involve a rather "bushy" tree:

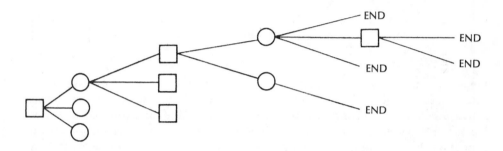

Here, after facing a set of consequences (reactions by individuals and groups involved), another set of decisions must be faced, and so on. Diagram until you reach what we call "end" on our diagram.

6. Make a decision based upon your best alternative. It will never be a "perfect" decision; however, it will be the alternative with the best possible outcome, given the situation.

7. Action recommendations, both short- and long-term, must be specific in terms of what to do, who is to do it, when, where, and how. Naturally, a complete job will include provisions for monitoring behavioural outcomes to see if they are as expected and as desired.

8. The final step will be the development of a contingency plan if performance does not meet expectations. A contingency plan is, in effect, another plan of action based on the assumption that your original action creates behaviour which you felt was less likely to occur.

PEOPLE

PART 1: UNDERSTANDING INDIVIDUAL BEHAVIOUR

The function of all managers is to ensure results by developing the work environment so that employees will be motivated to achieve the enterprise's goals. To motivate people, we must first understand the individual's behaviour.[1]

Leavitt's Cause/Motivation/Behaviour Model

A useful starting place in understanding individuals was offered by H. J. Leavitt in the text *Managerial Psychology* (1958). He stated that behavioural analysis may begin with three basic assumptions:

1. All behaviour is caused (by conditions or situations outside the individual).
2. All behaviour is motivated (by forces which are internal to the individual).
3. All behaviour is goal directed (toward that which will neutralize the prior cause and motivation).

These assumptions are illustrated in this model:

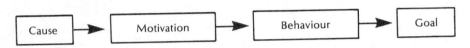

Behaviour, as represented in this model, is the overt, or observable, response to an external stimulus (cause) and to internal needs (motivation). Behaviour may consist of activities, expressed feelings, expressed expectations and/or expressed perceptions. Because behaviour is observable, there is a temptation to make judgments about people on this basis alone. The model forces us to consider the cause(s), underlying motivation and goal(s) sought. By so doing, we should be able to make better judgments about individual behaviour and, where necessary, take more appropriate action to deal with it.

All Behaviour is Caused

The individual operates in an environment which conditions certain beliefs, values, customs, factual information, etc., which, in turn, cause or stimulate certain behaviours. Moreover, these *external* forces are always coloured by the individual's perception of them. Thus, in looking at causes for behaviour, we must be careful to consider external causes in terms of how the individual perceived them if we are to deal with the behaviour that resulted.

All Behaviour Is Motivated

According to Webster's dictionary, a motive is "something (as a need or desire) that causes a person to act" and further it "implies an emotion or desire operating on the will and causing it to act." Our understanding of human behaviour is dependent upon an understanding of the underlying wants, needs, or desires that drive an individual to action.

---

[1]The principles used to develop a training program are beyond the scope of this note — and this book.

All Behaviour Is Goal Directed

An individual's actions are goal directed in the sense that they are aimed toward the satisfaction of aroused needs. Pinpointing what an individual's goals are can be very difficult. One may attempt to draw conclusions on the basis of observed behaviour, the apparent need level, the work situation, and so on. Seldom will people tell you explicitly what they are after. The more specifically you are able to identify a person's goals, the more likely you will be able to understand and deal with specific behaviour patterns of that individual. For example, "prosperity" is too vague a goal to offer much useful insight into behaviour, whereas "an income level of at least $40 000 per year" is more likely to be useful goal information.

Sometimes we have difficulty understanding how some particular behaviour could possibly be goal directed. It seems counterproductive to goal achievement, sometimes even "neurotic." By adding to our model we can explain much of that kind of behaviour, and take into account those occasions when attempts to attain a goal were blocked by some obstacle or barrier. Such situations result in what is called "frustration" and is behaviour that does not neatly fit the previous model. An expanded model appears as follows:

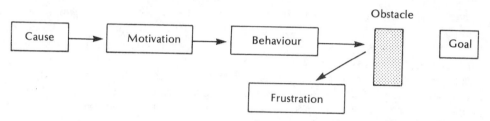

Before moving to a discussion of the forms of behaviour that are a consequence of frustration,[1] it is useful to differentiate between the types of obstacles. Obstacles may be either overt (external, physical) or covert (internal, psychological). The most difficult obstacles to surmount are covert obstacles because their solution often demands an altering of one's self-concept.

All of us are faced with a multitude of obstacles, real or imagined, as we go through life. Most often, when faced with an obstacle, we are able to adopt a problem-solving form of behaviour. Sometimes it is simply a matter of substituting an alternative, and more realistic, goal. Other times we need only try harder. Or it may require that we change our perception of the problem, such as discovering that the door wasn't stuck, it was locked. In these and other ways, we are able to face up to most obstacles presented to us and surmount them with a minimum of frustration. This is called "coping behaviour."

While as reasonable, "well-adjusted" people we are often able to approach our problems in this manner, frustration sometimes triggers "defence mechanisms" in an individual. These mechanisms serve to protect the "self" but often do so at the price of distorting reality or causing more problems than existed at the outset. There are many such mechanisms but they may, for simplification, be categorized into the following

---

[1]This analytical approach was significantly influenced by lecture notes provided by Professor A. Mikalachki, School of Business Administration, The University of Western Ontario.

three types: aggression, withdrawal, and fixation. The particular form of reaction which an individual adopts depends upon his/her personality, the situation and how he/she perceives the barrier.

Aggression is forceful, attacking behaviour, either constructively self-assertive and self-protective, or destructively hostile to others or to oneself.[1] The physical form of this mechanism is more readily recognizable but it is not the only form. In fact, "education and training have taught most adults in most situations to channel their aggressive impulses into non-violent forms." The non-violent forms are more subtle: rumour spreading, ostracism from a work group, work slowdowns, and so on.

Sometimes a person finds it inadvisable or impossible to attack the real source of frustration (especially if it is oneself); therefore one picks on an innocent person or object. This form of aggression, known as displacement, is exemplified by the individual who cannot retaliate when the boss has proven to be a source of frustration and therefore goes home and makes life miserable for his/her family.

Withdrawal refers to physical or mental retreat as a means of avoiding an obstacle. Physical withdrawal may involve resignation from a job, while mental withdrawal may involve fantasy or even a nervous breakdown.

Fixation refers to a continuation of the particular behaviour that has already proven inappropriate to goal attainment. Unlike aggression and withdrawal, fixation behaviour increases rather than decreases tension in the individual. As an example, suppose a foreman is trying to improve the quality of production, but the workers are angry with company disciplinary procedures and are deliberately reducing quality as a means of protest. The foreman has tried threats of disciplinary action to improve quality, but this has only aggravated the situation. Continued, even escalated threats by the foreman of disciplinary action (when this action will not result in achieving the foreman's goal) would constitute fixated behaviour.

An individual, when faced with an obstacle preventing attainment of a desired goal, may assume a coping or a problem-solving approach. Should such an approach prove impossible, as it often does when the obstacle is covert, the individual may resort to defensive behaviour as described above. Recognition of the symptoms of defensive behaviour can help us deal with problems related to individual behaviour. Sometimes it is possible to remove such barriers; at other times the solution can only lie in helping the individual surmount the obstacle by forcing him or her to face up to the situation and alter that aspect of his or her behaviour, motivation, or goals that is creating the problems.

Leavitt's Cause/Motivation/Behaviour theory recognizes that all human behaviour is caused, motivated and goal directed. The use of this model helps us to deal more effectively with individuals, provided we take the time and effort to identify each of these aspects of the behavioural situation.

Maslow's Hierarchy of Needs

The psychologist and behavioural scientist Abraham H. Maslow studied the underlying wants and needs that drive people. As a result of his studies, he postulated

---

[1] *Webster's New World Dictionary, Second College Edition* (Toronto: Nelson, Foster and Scott, 1970).

that there is a definite rank order priority or "hierarchy of needs." Schematically, Maslow's hierarchy appears as follows:

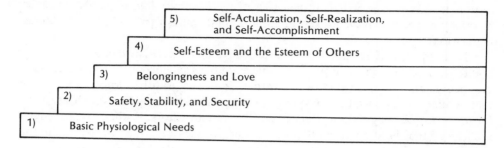

1. Man's first priority, according to Maslow, is the need to survive and thus to satisfy basic physiological needs. The physiological needs include the need for food, water, shelter, clothing, and sex. Only after these needs have been reasonably satisfied do other needs motivate the individual.
2. Maslow suggested that, given reasonable satisfaction of the physiological needs, man next becomes aware of the need for safety and security. These needs are reflected in man's desire for job tenure, an orderly society, insurance, and protection. In a sense, man's safety and security needs are satisfied in part by an assurance that his physiological needs will continue to be met.
3. Once the necessities for continued existence have been reasonably met and there is reasonable assurance that they will continue to be, the three "higher" needs are activated. The need for belongingness and love, or the social needs, refer to man's need for affection and the desire for association with others. Such needs are satisfied by membership in formal or informal groups, satisfactory marital and family relationships, and so on.
4. The esteem, or ego, needs include the drive for social approval and self-respect. Gratification of these needs contributes to a feeling of self-confidence, worth, and capabilities.
5. Finally, the highest need level, according to Maslow, is that of self-actualization. Self-actualization refers to man's desire for self-fulfilment and achievement. It encompasses not only the ability to accomplish but also the need for actual achievement of some significance in one's life. Self-actualization is a very personal thing in the sense that satisfaction is internally generated. External plaudits are not sought by individuals operating at this need level and, if received, are superfluous. It is a complicated concept and it appears few of us are primarily motivated by this need level.

The hierarchical arrangement of needs in the model stems from Maslow's central assumption that "higher" needs may not be activated until "lower" needs have been *reasonably* satisfied. Needs that cannot be activated, or aroused, do not result in motivation. Thus, before we can hope to gain cooperation from people by way of stimuli designed to arouse higher level needs (such as self-esteem), we must ensure that lower needs (such as job security) have been reasonably satisfied. There is not much merit, for example, in a professor's attempting to entice a student to devote more time to his/her studies with the expectation of a higher grade if, in order to do so, it means that the student must give up a part-time job, which is supporting the student's education. In this case, the esteem needs cannot be aroused until the student has some reasonable assurance that he/she will continue to satisfy the physiological needs. Maslow's hierarchy of needs may be looked upon as a "first things first" approach to human motivation.

Next, Maslow asserted that people are motivated by unsatisfied needs, in the sense that these needs have been aroused, but have not been satisfied. Conversely, he stated that people are not motivated by needs that have been gratified. Maslow contended that in our society, since the physiological and security needs are reasonably satisfied for most people, they cannot be used as effective motivators. Rather, it is the higher need levels that hold potential for motivation. Regrettably, most of our traditional reward/punishment systems are geared to the lower, not higher, need levels. The successful manager of human resources is one who, in recognizing the existence of higher need levels, is able to exercise the necessary creativity to assure that the pursuit of these needs is not frustrated, but rather is associated with desired work behaviour.

Herzberg's Hygiene/Motivators Theory

Yet another approach to motivation was provided by Frederick Herzberg. Concerned with the role that work and working conditions[1] play in the lives of people, Herzberg conducted research directed toward determining the factors that lead to employees' satisfaction.

On the basis of the data that were gathered, Herzberg concluded that there were two significantly different classes of factors affecting job satisfaction. The first class, which he termed "hygiene" or "maintenance" factors, make up a continuum ranging from job dissatisfaction to no job dissatisfaction.

JOB
DISSATISFACTION •————————————• NO JOB
DISSATISFACTION

Hygiene factors include the following:
- Company policy and administration
- Supervision
- Working conditions
- Interpersonal relations
- Salary
- Status
- Job security
- Personal life

Herzberg contended that these factors do not serve to promote job satisfaction but, if deficient, they can lead to job dissatisfaction. In other words, the provision of good working conditions, competitive salaries, and job security only serves to reduce dissatisfaction. Provision of such factors does not result in satisfaction.

---

[1]Working conditions generally refer to all aspects of the work situation, both physical (such as the type of facilities) and emotional (such as atmosphere or mood). In short, it is the work environment.

The second class of factors Herzberg termed "motivators" because his findings suggested that these are effective in creating job satisfaction that *may* lead to greater performance and productivity. Included in this class are such factors as:

- Achievement
- Recognition
- Responsibility
- Advancement
- Opportunity for growth

Motivators make up a continuum ranging from no job satisfaction to job satisfaction.

NO JOB   JOB
SATISFACTION   SATISFACTION

The motivators are concerned with the work itself rather than its surrounding physical, administrative, or social environment. Motivation, therefore, evolves from the sense of achievement, recognition, opportunities for advancement and growth and the responsibility inherent in the job itself. All of the other factors serve only to "clean up" the environment and prevent dissatisfaction.

Hygienic factors prevent dissatisfaction and pain by providing a good work environment. Motivation factors enable growth and movement toward some degree of self-actualization. While he emphasizes the importance of the latter in terms of motivation, Herzberg is not deemphasizing the importance of hygienic factors in successful management. These factors constitute an essential base on which to build. If management neglects to provide such a base, employees will become dissatisfied with their jobs and antagonistic toward the organization. Motivation, of course, is not possible in such an environment. Herzberg does try to impress on management, however, that provision of a comfortable workplace, competitive salaries, and other such hygienic factors will not, in themselves, result in motivation or increased effort.

In order to better understand individual behaviour it is helpful to examine the individual's frame of reference or "personal system." A personal system is the manner in which a person sees him/her self and perceives what is good or poor behaviour. According to Allan R. Cohen et al.,[1] the personal system is influenced by four factors: goals, competencies, beliefs, and values.

Each person has goals which he/she tries to achieve to satisfy needs. Different people have different goals: the task of a manager is to ensure compatibility between the goals of the individual and the goals of the organization. This becomes difficult because it is usually difficult to know or determine people's goals.

An individual's competencies, including skills, expertise, and knowledge, highly influence the attainment of goals. Perceptions of one's own and others' competencies may be different. For example, an employee may believe he/she has done a good job only to be told by a supervisor that he/she performed inadequately. This may affect the individual's behaviour and could result in problems for all concerned.

Beliefs, the individual's ideas about the environment and how it operates, are either confirmed or denied by various situations. People like to have their beliefs

---

[1]Allan R. Cohen et al., *Effective Behaviour in Organizations*, rev. ed. (Homewood: Richard D. Irwin Inc., 1980).

confirmed, to make them feel "right." Denial can lead to frustration and resentment, and negatively affects behaviour.

Values, or the "core" that is really important and basic to the individual, exert a strong influence on behaviour, as they are in effect the foundation of an individual's character. These are highly important matters to individuals, and, though some values may change over time, the "core" tends to be kept. Honesty, standing up for your rights, doing your best, and never cheating are examples of values. As personal values serve as the most important factors affecting the personal system, conflicts arising out of values are among the most difficult to resolve.

The Self-Concept

The self-concept is the individual's unique way of organizing his/her personal system; the way the individual views him/herself. Theorists have separated the self-concept into two distinct parts: "I" and "me." The "I" is the personal view the individual takes of him/herself; the "me" is the way a person believes he/she appears to others.

One way to determine a person's self-concept is by examining his/her behaviour. For example, someone who decides to become an accountant may be very methodical and orderly, and likes to work with numbers. People strive to maintain their self-concepts by behaving in ways that reinforce this image of themselves; it is from this observable behaviour that we can get a picture of the self-concept of the individual.

Another notion in self-concept theory is the concept of "other," or how an individual views other people (how John perceives Mary). An individual's "concept of other" may also usually be determined by observing his/her behaviour toward other people.

In summary, understanding the individual behaviour of people, their wants and needs, personal systems, and self concepts, is essential to good human resource management. As managers, however, we will also be managing the behaviour and interaction of two or more people. The next section will aid in furthering the understanding of interpersonal behaviour.

PART 2: UNDERSTANDING INTERPERSONAL BEHAVIOUR

Wherever two people work together, the outcome depends on the relationship between them and on how they get along. In addition to managing individual behaviour, managers must also manage the interaction of the individuals, or their interpersonal behaviour. Since individuals interact by communicating with each other, we now discuss the difficulties involved in communication.

Communication between people involves an exchange of the content of what is being discussed, feelings about the content, and feelings about the other person. For example, building on the self-theory discussed previously, the content of what John says will be modified by Mary's self-concept (which includes what Mary thinks of John). The content will also be affected by John's feelings about the content. The message sent by John may therefore not be the same message received by Mary.

The potential barriers to communication are numerous. In addition to people's perception of each other, communication problems may be caused by language, as words are imprecise and take multiple meanings. The use of body language, facial expressions, and voice intonations can also pose barriers to communication, and the emotions of the people involved can cause communication difficulties. However small, these difficulties can build into a major source of interpersonal conflict.

One way to improve the process of communication is by effective listening. Effective listening requires listening for the feelings as well as the content expressed, accepting and supporting the other person's message, and testing for understanding to ensure that the communication has been properly received.

Another way to improve communication is by offering effective feedback to the individual's message. Feedback is not telling others what is wrong with them: it is offering your perceptions in a nonjudgmental way, to help the other person. Offer your feedback, do not try to impose it, and offer it as "your thoughts," not "the truth." As your action may be contributing to the other person's behaviour, you should be open to receiving feedback yourself.

The quality of communication between two people is crucial to their effective interaction. By improving communication, being aware of barriers, listening effectively, and offering feedback, managers can better manage the interpersonal behaviour of individuals.

PART 3: UNDERSTANDING GROUP BEHAVIOUR

A group is a number of people together, acting as one unit. As membership in a group can often change individual behaviour, the behaviour of group members is often different from the behaviour one might expect of the individuals. Groups thus make the management of human resources much more complex.

To effectively manage groups, managers must understand why individuals join groups.

Think about some of the groups to which you belong or have belonged. Think further why you joined the groups. Your first thoughts will no doubt centre on the benefits you acquired, or expected to acquire, from membership in the group. People join groups because they see membership as yielding benefits that are in their self-interest to acquire. The following are some examples of these benefits.

1. *Fellowship* Membership in a group may provide an individual with a sense of belonging. Abraham Maslow rated social needs as being very high on the average individual's priorities. Thus, one possible benefit derived from membership in a group is satisfaction of social needs.
2. *Protection* Of even higher priority is the recognition that banding together to present a united front against common enemies has been essential to the survival of humanity. Similarly, membership in a group is sometimes essential to an individual's survival in the modern industrial setting such as an office or factory. The group protects its members by closing ranks to speak up for those who find themselves in trouble with management, by covering up for mistakes made by members, or even by doing the work for members who are having a bad day.
3. *Prestige* Some groups hold a reputation which makes membership attractive to an individual. In becoming a member of a prestigious group, the individual inherits some of that prestige.

4. *Effect Change*   Presenting a united front often allows people to change conditions that they find undesirable. Unions, for example, are often able to increase wage rates or improve working conditions because the members act in unison. In these instances people recognize that a united group stands a much greater chance of achieving a desired goal than do individuals operating independently.

5. *Assistance with a Task*   Often an individual requires the assistance or advice of others in accomplishing a task. Isolating him or herself from neighbours at home or from fellow employees in the workplace can place the individual in dire straits when the task requires skills or strength beyond his or her capacity.

6. *Communication*   In the industrial setting the informal organization provides a communications network. This network, known as the grapevine, keeps members informed of what is going on. Moreover, it generally does so more quickly than do the formal channels of communications. Membership in the informal organization, then, is often essential to keeping informed of developments in the formal organization.

Many factors affect the togetherness, or cohesion of a group. A group that is close-knit and unified will often have positive effects. Group togetherness is enhanced by common group values and goals, such as "keen" students working hard together on a report toward a good mark, or employees going on strike for better wages and benefits. Cohesiveness is also enhanced by a set group task, such as a report or meeting on production quotas. Group norms, or standards of behaviour set by the group, also affect cohesion by ensuring that all group members conform. For example, trade unions are able to maintain group solidarity during a strike by forming picket lines. Members are attracted to cohesive groups, and behaviour of the cohesive group is quite coordinated.

The important point to remember is that when you are dealing with a cohesive group, you must be careful: find out what the focus of cohesion is before attempting to change behaviour — otherwise your efforts may backfire.

Highly cohesive groups can be very productive if the focus of the group is on the task. If, however, the group is overly socially oriented, productivity may suffer. For example, a student work group whose focus is on preparing a good report may be more productive than a group motivated by purely social activities. Groups with low cohesiveness are not as effective, as their behaviour is not as coordinated and members are not as attracted to the group. Such groups ultimately fragment or dissolve entirely. The "ideal" is to have the proper blend between the task and social orientation.

Many factors thus affect the behaviour of groups. With an understanding of these factors, managers are more likely to succeed in effective management of groups and of the individuals in the groups.

THE ORGANIZATION

PART 1: GOALS AND STRUCTURE

The organization of any human endeavour is a complex task. There are four major components in effectively organizing human activities: one, the careful delineation and communication of goals or targets; two, the assignment of the goals and tasks to an organizational structure; three, the provision of effective authority, control, and resources to members of the organization to accomplish the tasks assigned; and four, the development of a monitoring program to ensure successful completion of the task.

In setting goals, an enterprise first must set its general objectives. People in the organization must be able to understand and identify with company goals. People aware of their contribution toward the goals will be more committed to those goals and thus perform more productively. While a general philosophical statement is helpful, unless it can be interpreted in terms of specific targets to be accomplished it will lose significant meaning. This is true in any form of human endeavour. For example, a student may have a general educational objective. However, unless the student has carefully plotted what he/she is going to achieve in the first year, looked at the requirements for the second year and the ensuing years, and developed some detailed plan or set of targets to aim at each year, the probability of achieving the general objective is substantially reduced. Furthermore, in setting targets, the goals should be attainable, otherwise the probability of achieving them will be greatly reduced and the most likely outcome will be frustration for the person concerned.

Design of the organization's structure does not mean simply drawing up an organizational chart with boxes and arrows. Instead it means deciding what tasks must be performed, how to group similar tasks together, how to set up appropriate organizational units to handle these task groupings, how to staff the organizational units with "specialists" and how to find ways (and people) to achieve cooperation and collaboration among the separate units. Designing an effective organizational structure requires consideration of job functions, the number of individuals a manager can control, communication networks, authority and responsibility networks, and trade-offs between centralization and decentralization.

It is not sufficient to assign tasks and hire sufficient human resources to meet them. People assigned for the jobs must be given sufficient *authority and control* to accomplish their tasks. Care should be taken to minimize situations where a subordinate may be subject to the authority of several superiors. Lack of "unity of command" may lead to organizational conflict as several managers attempt to achieve different tasks with the same resource. The converse of this argument is that often managers can be put in a position where they have a great amount of responsibility, but do not have the real (or perceived) authority to accomplish their tasks. This can be a major source of stress for the manager and can lead to a number of outcomes, such as physical ailments, unusual behaviour or resignation.

Authority is difficult to define, but basically managerial authority means that the manager has the right to make decisions within well-set parameters and believes that his or her superiors will support the decisions as long as reasonable judgment was used within the scope of the defined responsibility.

A *monitoring program* includes a variety of operating mechanisms: the reward/punishment system, the communication system and the development system. Each of these can be broken down into components. (The control system, for example, comprises performance evaluation, feedback methods, etc.) The important questions however are whether these mechanisms:

1. are internally consistent, that is, work together to reinforce the organizational structure and achieve goals;

2. are consistent with the organizational task, the people involved, environment, etc., in order to realize organizational goals.

In summary, a manager must be able to understand the nature of the organization: what it is, how it works, and what factors influence what actions in order to guide the resources under his or her control to achieve the objectives of the enterprise.

PART 2: RESPONSIBILITIES OF THE HUMAN RESOURCES MANAGER

The Human Resources Department in an organization has formal responsibilities for the following:

- Recruiting and selecting competent employees
- Orienting (training, etc.) new employees
- Motivating the poor performer (and improving productivity in general)
- Deciding on appropriate compensation schemes
- Handling promotions, transfers and dismissals
- Dealing with complaining workers (and "conflicts" in general)
- Delegating responsibility
- Dealing with rule infractions, absenteeism, turnover, etc.
- Conducting performance appraisals
- Retirement, pensions and benefit planning.

These tasks assist in accomplishing the organizational goals previously described. In order to hire the appropriate personnel, a job description of the task to be done and the skills required to complete the task are the first step. The job description should flow from the enterprise's objectives and its operating targets. From the delineation of the job description, the second step for the human resource manager should be to specify the types of persons suited for the task in terms of the personality characteristics and technical skills required.

The third step is the development of recruitment sources. Recruits may be developed from appeals to the general public through newspaper advertisements, from recruiting at high schools, technical schools and universities, or from employment agencies. Unless the enterprise has done a good job in outlining the task to be done and the required skills and characteristics for the job, it will be difficult to develop recruiting efforts that will gain sufficiently qualified applicants.

The fourth step in the process is selection for hiring. Some of the common techniques used are application forms and resumes to gain some comprehension of the applicant's personal background, character references to verify key elements in the application form, and, finally, interviews and aptitude tests to evaluate personality, as well as communication and other skills. The final selection is an attempt to make the best match between the applicant's skills and disposition and the job requirements.

Once the individual has been selected and hired, the next step is the provision of sufficient training that will allow the new employees to perform their tasks efficiently and effectively. Corporations or enterprises can describe their tasks and set personal specifications, but are very fortunate if they can find the ideal individual who can be productive immediately. Often there are unique tasks within their organizational structure that require training for a new employee. A training program should be motivating and interesting to recently hired employees and provide them with sufficient background to handle their new jobs.

The human resource function also establishes and monitors performance reviews to ensure employees are meeting job requirements and to identify and encourage people with potential for advancement.

Individuals not meeting minimum job requirements may have to be dehired. Due care must be taken in dehiring to ensure the individual has been properly matched to the job, trained, and reviewed. The impact of dehiring on other individuals and groups within the organization needs to be considered and the reasons for dehiring may need to be communicated.

Pensions and other retirement concerns are also part of the formal responsibilities of the human resources department. Many organizations are now also assisting employees with planning for their retirement years.

In summary, the manager of the human resources department has a number of vitally important tasks to accomplish. One of the most important assets of any company is its people, and the human resources area is responsible for interacting with other functional areas to ensure the proper treatment of this asset in line with overall organizational objectives.

HUMAN RESOURCES MANAGEMENT

We have so far discussed the two key components of human resources management: people, and the organization. Human resources management is the combination of the two, the interaction of people with and within the organization. We will first describe what "excellent" companies do to successfully manage their human resources. We will then discuss the manager/leader's role, and ways to overcome difficulties in managing changes in the interaction. Future challenges in human resources management will then be outlined.

A characteristic common to all of the "excellent" companies identified by Peters and Waterman in their book *In Search of Excellence*[1] was the high value accorded to the companies' human resources. These "excellent" companies considered their people to be their most valuable assets. As a result, these organizations had a real people orientation, and treated each individual with respect. The results of the study indicated that companies with such high regard for human resources were rewarded with higher productivity and profits.

PART 1: THE JOB OF A MANAGER

The job of a manager is a very demanding one, consisting of many activities related to the interaction of the people and the organization. In "The Nature of Managerial Work," Henry Mintzberg broadly described the three major activities of a manager: relationship building, information gathering, and decision making.

Relationship building is an important part of the manager's job. Because he/she has been assigned a managerial position, the manager is automatically expected to

---

[1]Thomas J. Peters and Robert H. Waterman, *In Search of Excellence* (New York: Harper & Row, 1982).

form relationships in many directions: with subordinates, peers, and superiors. As managers accomplish tasks through the efforts of other people, a manager must be good at building relationships with these people.

These relationships are necessary to enable the manager to gather information needed for making decisions. While much of the information managers need can be found in written reports, some of the most important information is acquired from other people. Thus, the manager's skill at building relationships with those people is needed to assist in the gathering of information.

This information is in turn needed for the decision making process. Managers are required to make many decisions within the organization, from settling disputes to setting budgets. The success of these decisions depends on the information and relationships available to the manager. Thus the manager must be good at building relationships, acquiring information, and making decisions.

A manager is responsible for meeting the organization's objectives. Since a manager accomplishes tasks through the efforts of other people, one of the manager's most important tasks is to ensure that those people understand, and can identify with, the organizational objectives. It has often been demonstrated that if people identify with the objectives, and are aware of the importance of their contribution to meeting those objectives, they will perform more productively. The manager needs to ensure that the goals of the people are congruent with the goals of the organization, so that the people are committed and will work toward achieving these organizational goals.

PART 2: LEADERSHIP

We use the term "leadership" to describe the way a successful, effective manager chooses, either explicitly or implicitly, to lead other people. It is difficult to precisely define the characteristics of a leader. However, many of them are related to the manager's job of relationship building, information gathering, and decision making as described above. For example, leaders are willing to make decisions and accept the consequences. They also have the ability to influence other people's behaviour, to use interpersonal relationships to accomplish tasks, and to exercise initiative. Leaders also have energy and self-confidence and a willingness to tolerate stress, frustration, and risks.

Those are general characteristics of good leaders. However, the specific requirements for effective leadership will depend on two factors: the manager's leadership style, and the particular situation.

PART 3: LEADERSHIP STYLE

McGregor's Theory X and Theory Y

One factor affecting the manager's leadership style is his/her beliefs about the people being led. Douglas McGregor[1] described two distinctly different sets of managerial beliefs. A "Theory X" manager assumes that people dislike work, will avoid it if possible, and need to be coerced, controlled, and directed to accomplish work. This set

[1]Douglas McGregor, *The Human Side of Enterprise* (New York: McGraw-Hill Book Company, 1960).

of beliefs also assumes that people prefer to be directed, wish to avoid responsibility, and are motivated by money, threats, and security.

A "Theory Y" manager believes that people enjoy work to which they are committed, and are able to exercise self-control and self-direction. He/she believes that people will not only accept but seek responsibility, and are motivated by achievement of objectives.

No one set of beliefs is valid for all situations. There will always be people who operate best in a "Theory X" environment, and those who do best in a "Theory Y" setting. Managers must be careful about the assumptions they make about people. Treating people in certain ways may bring out the expected behaviour, and the assumptions will become self-fulfilling prophecies.

Managerial Grid — Blake and Mouton

Robert Blake and Jane Mouton[1] have identified several styles of leadership. Each style is a combination of varying degrees of concern for two managerial functions: concern for production, and concern for people.

The style with highest concern for people and lowest concern for production is labelled "country club management." The opposite style is a very "task-oriented" management style, with the lowest concern for people and the highest concern for production. Low concern for both people and production was termed an "impoverished" style. The managerial grid implies that a "team" style, with high concern for both people and production, is the most desirable and effective.

PART 4: SITUATIONAL LEADERSHIP

The Hersey and Blanchard Model

While the Blake/Mouton model appears to suggest an optimum leadership style, research has clearly shown that there is not one "best" style of leadership for all occasions. An effective leadership style will depend on the particular situation. Paul Hersey and Kenneth Blanchard[2] have shown that the style of situational leadership will depend upon (i) the amount of guidance and direction (task behaviour) a leader gives; (ii) the amount of support and encouragement (relationship behaviour) given; and (iii) on the readiness and responsibility (maturity) that followers exhibit in performing the task at hand.

The appropriate leadership style for each level of maturity is the right combination of support and direction. For example, high direction/low support is appropriate with people unable and unwilling to accept responsibility, if they are to accomplish the task. Low direction/high support is appropriate if people are unable but willing to perform the task.

Regardless of the maturity level of an individual or group, change may occur. The leader should therefore be constantly aware of the maturity levels of the followers in order to make appropriate style changes as necessary.

[1]Robert R. Blake and Jane S. Mouton, *The Managerial Grid* (Houston, Texas: Gulf Publishing, 1964).
[2]Paul Hersey and Kenneth Blanchard, *Management of Organizational Behaviour: Utilizing Human Resources* (Englewood Cliffs, N.J.: Prentice-Hall, Inc., 1982).

The requirements for effective leadership, then, depend on the leadership style of the manager, and on the particular situation. The leader's beliefs about the followers and his/her concern for production and people will influence his/her choice of leadership style. The leader must adjust this style, depending on the amount of support and direction needed, and on the maturity of the followers. The leadership style will thus be altered to reflect the particular situation.

PART 5: MANAGEMENT OF CHANGE

All enterprises are changing continually, and one of the manager's most important and most difficult tasks will be the management of change. Assuming we are able to identify problems and formulate desirable solutions, how do we implement changes when we "know" people tend to resist change in general?

First, we must be able to anticipate such resistance. Resistance occurs most often when change is unexpected or undesired. Why does resistance occur? For several reasons, including:

- Change may be perceived as a threat to economic security.
- Change introduces uncertainty and inconvenience.
- Individuals usually feel a sense of loss when required to give up familiar ways.
- Change may be perceived as a threat to the competence or status of individuals.
- Change often entails a shift in personal relationships.
- Change may be unexplained and/or unanticipated.

Second, we must be able to formulate ways to deal with change management. There are some general ways to reduce resistance. These include:

1. Tell those involved the reasons for change.
2. Involve those affected in the design of the change process.
3. Be especially sensitive to their needs for reassurance and recognition during the transition stage.
4. Provide help in learning new tasks and new roles and establishing new relationships.
5. Be more available for discussions, questions, etc., than usual.
6. Encourage them to talk about the change, the "old days" and their feelings of frustration, anxiety and concern.
7. Be sensitive to the need for patience and clarification. The change process may cause "shock" temporarily, so restatement of information may be necessary before an employee fully comprehends it.
8. Be enthusiastic and hopeful by demonstrating frequently and constructively that the transitional problems can be overcome.

Notice that resistance to change itself can be understood by using our frustration model discussed previously. The manager must be able to define the obstacle before effective action can be taken.

Seldom, if ever, is it wise to impose change by "decree," expecting that such power will accomplish the required changes. People and organizations need time and help in order to adjust to change. As a manager, you will find that deciding how to implement changes, no matter what their size, is just as important as deciding what to change.

PART 6: FUTURE CHALLENGES

The coming years will pose many new challenges to all managers. We must be aware of the changes in the environment around us to take advantage of the problems and opportunities of these challenges. For example, the values of people are rapidly changing. There is a greatly increased emphasis on involvement in the workplace, reflected in quality of working life and profit-sharing programs. There is also an increased emphasis on the value of leisure time.

The demographics, or makeup, of the population is also changing. The average age of the North American population is on the rise, and the number of young people is dropping as the birth rate declines. The composition of the work force is also changing, reflecting the increasing number of minorities employed.

Increasing numbers of women are entering or reentering the work force, thus increasing the number of dual-career families.

The impact of technology on the workplace is potentially the most challenging issue to face modern society. As new technologies are developed and implemented, more and more people will be displaced from jobs and require retraining, and the job composition of the market place will change.

Finally, repatriation of the Canadian constitution, with its entrenched Bill of Rights, underscores the changes in the human resources environment by establishing protection of certain basic rights and freedoms, such as equality rights, language rights, and fundamental freedoms.

These are but a few of the challenges facing managers in the 1980s. If managers remain aware of these challenges posed by the environment, they will be able to take a proactive stance to facing these challenges. They will then be better able to contribute effectively to the management of the organization.

CONCLUSION

The purpose of this chapter is to provide you with some generally recognized "tools" with which you may approach human resources problems. Our treatment has by no means been exhaustive, as you will discover when you read more about "human relations," "managerial psychology," "personnel administration" and the like. It is extremely important for you to realize that the mechanical use of these tools of analysis will not make you a good manager of people. What we cannot provide for you is a set of values, an orientation with which you put these tools and human resources problems into perspective. Only with this set of values can you tailor your decision-making skills and analytical tools to the circumstances in which you find yourself. Effective management of human resources, in the final analysis, is a creative approach to people and circumstances. Creativity in leadership means thoughtful action by a concerned person who has an understanding of the whole situation.

As managers, we will be responsible for meeting organizational objectives through the accomplishments of other people. Effective management of these people and their interaction with and within the organization is therefore essential for attainment of the objectives. Although the organization sets its objectives and goals, it is only by establishing the appropriate environment in the organization, through good human resources management, that the organization can effectively gain the support of individuals to achieve its objectives.

13

Ajax Distributors

In April 1984, the sales manager of Ajax Distributors, Ltd. received a letter from his field supervisor urging that consideration be given to the rehiring of a former employee of the company, Mr. Rod Adams, who had left the company three years earlier.

COMPANY HISTORY

Ajax Distributors was organized in 1936 to act as wholesaler and exclusive agent for products used in concrete construction. The main product distributed by the company was material used for hardening concrete. In conjunction with this, the company distributed iron rods and mesh, wire, light structural steel, and other allied products. The chief customers were industrial concerns, building supply outlets, and construction companies. During the past ten years the company had been transformed under new and progressive management, and a number of valuable agencies and rights had been secured from United States and European firms.

Basically, Ajax Distributors was a sales organization with warehousing as a key function. Since it was necessary to develop the market for the new product lines, a group of well-trained, energetic salespeople was required. In 1984 these salespeople were considered well paid: on a salary and commission plan, the average salesperson drew $20 000, with top salespeople earning slightly over $30 000. While a successful salesperson was appreciated, the company executives at this time were also looking for potential management ability, since they planned to expand the general office sales department and to open new branch offices. In 1981, there were fourteen such branch offices in Canada with plans for an additional twelve to fifteen to be opened within five years. Five had been opened by 1984. At each branch warehouse, the manager was in charge of one to ten salespeople, depending upon the size and potential of the area served, as well as responsible for the warehouse staff.

The head office of the firm was in Hamilton, Ontario, where the sales manager and his field supervisor were located.

EXPANSION PROGRAM

The company's policy was to promote from within but, when this was not possible, salespeople were recruited from placement agencies, competitors, colleges, allied businesses, etc. In view of the expansion program the sales manager was instructed to step up his efforts to get good people. He realized that this could not be done entirely at a central location since salespeople sent out to the branches would not be completely acceptable to the branch managers who wanted a hand in choosing those who worked for them. Also, such a policy would, in effect, confine the company's source and contacts for new people to one geographic area. To help the branch managers hire intelligently, specifications were prepared for the type of salesperson they thought might later become part of management. The specifications were compiled by a committee that studied some of the star salespeople and analyzed the job to be done.

The branch manager held two interviews with candidates (where possible, someone else from the branch was also present), then made a specific recommendation and forwarded the application to the sales manager for a final decision.

ROD ADAMS

During the course of recruiting in 1981, the Hamilton branch manager, whose office was in the head office of the company, drew to the sales manager's attention an interesting application submitted by a Mr. Rod Adams. This application (Exhibit 1) indicated that Adams was thirty-seven years of age, was married and had two children. He had the minimum educational requirements that the company desired, Grade 13. He had no previous selling experience but had been with the Hamilton Police Department for a number of years, where he had moved ahead and was well regarded by his superiors and the men with whom he worked. Mr. Adams pointed out in his application that he had gained wide experience in the field of public relations while employed with the Police Department, where he had handled all types of people, from irate employers whose men he had had to arrest, to the offenders themselves. The branch manager had secured former job information by contacting the Police Department. Rod Adams also submitted the names of a bank manager and a minister as character references and they had replied favourably.

Rod Adams had resided in Hamilton for fourteen years but stated he was willing to go elsewhere for the company. The credit reports showed that he had a good equity in his home and owned his car. He had a reasonable amount of life insurance and was believed to have a savings account that was increasing at a slow but steady rate.

The sales manager and the branch manager decided to hire him on the basis of his favourable impression on several people at head office. They thought he would do very well in their business because he was "a big, likeable chap." The general manager had questioned the decision since his previous positions showed "lack of initiative." Nevertheless, he was willing to accept the opinion of the sales manager and the branch manager.

TRAINING PERIOD

Rod Adam's training record was most satisfactory. He began the training program which the company had established for salespeople at a starting salary of $1200 per month. This program involved one month in the office learning policies and procedures, two weeks in a warehouse becoming familiar with the products and the warehousing system and four weeks in sales training which included travelling with other salespeople and a branch manager, and a formal selling course involving lectures, role-playing, etc., that was put on by a sales training organization.

The branch manager in Hamilton in charge of Rod Adams during his training became well acquainted with his wife and family. He discovered that the couple were keenly interested in the welfare of their elder son, a third-year high school student, who planned to enter the medical profession. The family physician was already very interested in the boy and promised to help with his education in terms of getting enrolled in university and financially, if necessary.

At the end of the training period, Adams was given a good sales post at the company's Thunder Bay, Ontario, branch which served approximately 150 customers. The branch sales volume had average $1 000 000 over the past three years and it was felt that the sales potential in this territory was increasing rapidly. Upon completion of the training period, salespeople began selling on a basic salary of $900 per month, plus a car and an expense account, and the opportunity to earn an additional $600 to $800 per month on commissions. The basic salary was increased to $950 per month after one year, to $1000 after the third year, and so on in accordance with a sliding scale.

Adams seemed very enthusiastic about this move, but mentioned that he was very ambitious and wanted to advance to a larger branch and eventually to the head office. He was told that if his record was good, he might expect a move in three years, depending on conditions and his progress.

While in Thunder Bay completing his preparatory training with the older salesman he was replacing, Adams seemed worried about whether he could handle the job, how much money he would make, and particularly whether the older salesman felt he might be able to get back to western Ontario. This anxiety reached the point where Adams was not sleeping at nights and seemed physically ill during certain periods of the day. He finally asked permission of the Thunder Bay manager to call the sales manager. He agreed since he felt that it might be the way to get Adams straightened out. The sales manager talked with Adams and reassured him he was experiencing the bewilderment common to some new salespeople. Finally, Adams asked flatly to be brought back to Hamilton and be given a territory there, since he felt he needed more training. Since he was due to return to Hamilton on the weekend, he was urged to discuss the matter then. He did so, and at this point the real source of trouble was revealed: Mr. Adams's wife did not want to go to Thunder Bay.

The sales manager, who was forty-eight years old, could think of similar instances that had taken place, and it had been his experience that in the majority of these cases it was just a matter of getting used to the new location. He recalled one recent case in which a salesman had objected strongly to a move to another northern Ontario location but within two years had become so well established among new friends and business acquaintances that he did not want to leave.

The sales manager suggested Mrs. Adams go to Thunder Bay at the company's expense to look over the situation. Mrs. Adams made the journey, but stayed less than twenty-four hours. Adams then wrote the sales manager and explained that he felt the real trouble was that his wife thought leaving Hamilton might affect the future of their boy, who would be entering the premedical course in two years. The Hamilton branch manager, who had been taking a close interest in Mr. and Mrs. Adams, pointed out to them that this would be just as possible from Thunder Bay, but they remained unconvinced.

ADAMS'S RESIGNATION

Adams seemed not only disappointed but embarrassed, since he had stated on his application that he would be willing to go anywhere the company wished to send him. His only suggestion, however, was that he be given a territory in Hamilton or its vicinity. Adams felt that he could do a good job there and be contented, and that eventually his wife might decide that they could move elsewhere. He reluctantly stated that he would be forced to tender his resignation if this were not possible.

Rod Adams had made several friends within the head office, and serious consideration was given to his case, which, like all other matters involving a policy decision, was discussed at a general executive committee meeting. The sales manager, arguing against accepting Adams's conditions, stated that there were many other salespeople's spouses who would like to choose where the salespeople were employed. His experience while building the business had been that salespeople who stayed on in one place got into a comfortable rut, and were not suitable for advancement. He felt quite strongly that an employee should be willing to go wherever the company wished to send him or her. He also raised the question about Adams's sincerity, since in his application for employment he had specifically agreed to go wherever the company sent him. The company had gone to considerable expense to train him, and while accepting this training and the offer to have his wife visit Thunder Bay, Adams must have had some indication that he would eventually be unable to accept the conditions of such a move.

The field supervisor, whose opinions were held in high regard by all members of the executive, argued the other side of the case. He said that he had come to know Rod Adams and his family well and was confident that Adams had been sincere but that the move did impose some special hardships on his family. In his view, the sales staff could be strengthened by such men as Rod Adams even if they remained in one location.

In spite of his satisfactory record in training and other obvious attributes, it was finally decided that Rod Adams's resignation must be accepted, although the decision was reached most reluctantly by only a small majority of the executive committee.

Subsequently, Mr. Adams secured a job with a firm selling hospital supplies and was given a territory near Ottawa, where he lived in a small apartment. Mrs. Adams and the children remained in Hamilton. He was promised that as soon as an opportunity opened up closer to Hamilton he would be transferred, but three years later, no other had opened up, nor had he been promoted, though his record had been an excellent one. As Ajax Distributors was continuing to expand and having difficulty in finding suitable salespeople, the Hamilton branch manager, with whom Adams had kept in contact, decided to sound out Adams's feelings with regard to his present position. Mr. Adams stated that he was about to resign the hospital supply job since his wife was still adamant over the Hamilton location, and the situation at home was becoming strained. His son was now attending the local university and hoped to be admitted to the medical school when his science courses were completed.

Although no basic changes had occurred in the company's personnel requirements regarding staff mobility during the three-year interval, the Hamilton branch manager urged the sales manager to hire Adams in Hamilton and recommended that later, when conditions at his home had changed, he might be moved elsewhere.

Date April 17, 1981

NAME — Rod Adams   HOME TELEPHONE NO. 477-4386

PRESENT ADDRESS — 424 Elm Avenue   HOW LONG HAVE YOU LIVED

Hamilton, Ontario   THERE? 14 years

PREVIOUS ADDRESS — 217 William St.   HOW LONG DID YOU LIVE

Hamilton, Ontario   THERE? 5 years

POSITION APPLIED FOR? Salesman   EARNINGS EXPECTED (as discussed)

Personal

DATE OF BIRTH — Sept. 12, 1944   SINGLE MARRIED x SEPARATED

WIDOWED DIVORCED

HEIGHT — 183 centimetres, MASS — 95 kilograms   NO. OF CHILDREN — 2 AGES 10 & 15

NATIONALITY OR COUNTRY OF ALLEGIANCE — Canadian

NO. OF OTHER DEPENDENTS — 0   NAME AND ADDRESS OF

BIRTHPLACE — Acton, Ontario   NEAREST RELATIVE — Mrs. C. R. Adams

(Town & Province)   Acton, Ontario

DO YOU OWN YOUR HOME? x RENT?

WOULD YOU BE WILLING TO WORK ANYWHERE IN CANADA? YES x NO

DO YOU OWN FURNITURE? YES x NO

IS YOUR WIFE EMPLOYED? NO x YES PART TIME   YES FULL TIME

DO YOU CARRY LIFE INSURANCE? NO x   YES

WHAT PHYSICAL DEFECTS DO YOU HAVE?   None

DATE LAST MEDICAL — Feb., 1980

DO YOU WEAR GLASSES? NO   x   YES, ONLY FOR READING   YES, ALL THE TIME

Education

Type of School	Name and Address of School	Courses Majored in	Check last yr. Completed	Graduate Give Degrs.	Last Year attended
Public	Acton P. School		5 6 7 8 x	Yes x No	1958
High S.	Acton High		1 2 3 4 5 x	Yes x No	1963
College	N/A		1 2 3 4 5		

COLLEGE STANDING?   HONOURS PASS

EXTRACURRICULAR ACTIVITIES IN H.S.? — Football, baseball, student assembly

WHAT OFFICES DID YOU HOLD IN THESE GROUPS?

EXTRACURRICULAR ACTIVITIES IN COLLEGE?   OFFICES HELD?

Work History

List positions held commencing with the most recent	Time Employed	Nature of Work	Starting Salary	Salary at Leaving	Reasons for Leaving
1. Hamilton Police Department	June/73	Police Constable	$525/mo.	$1650/mo.	Present employer
2. Hamilton Fabrication	Apr./67 May/73	Labourer	$450/mo.	$ 525/mo.	More appealing work with Police Force
3. Acton Cooperative	June/63 Apr./67	Attending customers and some delivery	$225/mo.	$ 375/mo.	Sought work with more opportunity to get ahead

MAY WE REFER TO ABOVE EMPLOYERS?   YES ☒   NO ☐

HAVE YOU EVER BEEN REFUSED BOND?   YES ☐   NO ☒

HAVE YOU ANY RELATIVES IN OUR EMPLOY?   YES ☐   NO ☒

REFERENCES (Not employers or relatives) ADDRESS   POSITION

1. Rev. A. S. Bessinger, Acton United Church   Minister

2. Mr. R. A. Turner, Hamilton   Bank Manager

3. Sgt. Blossenz, Police Department, Hamilton   Sgt.

WHY DO YOU WISH TO WORK FOR THE AJAX DISTRIBUTORS LTD.?

I like meeting people. Have handled all kinds of groups in police work. Have heard Ajax is progressive and I want to get ahead.

WHEN CAN YOU START WORK IF EMPLOYED? — 2 weeks notice.

14

A Salary Dispute

JoAnn Burns and Nancy Carr were bank tellers at the Goderich Branch of the Ontario Bank. (See Exhibit 1 for the organization chart.) Burns, the more senior of the employees, had been with the organization for more than twenty years, while Carr had several years' experience. Burns's position in the organization was that of head teller. Although her formal job description did not indicate it, she handled from sixty to eighty thousand dollars cash per day. She was also responsible for all incoming and outgoing money parcels in the branch. Consequently, she had a high degree of responsibility and was normally quite a complacent individual. Her day-to-day work was adequately done from a customer relations point of view and she had produced well on various deposit campaigns in the past. (See Exhibit 2 for backgrounds of the employees.)

Carr, on the other hand, was a very outgoing individual with an attractive appearance and personality. She was considered highly productive and a good company employee. According to John White, the assistant manager (credit), her productivity and selling capabilities appeared to entitle her to a higher salary than Burns. (See Exhibit 3, Staff Report Worksheet.) Her job was to run the cash. She assumed no responsibilities equal in degree to Burns's. She worked well with the rest of the staff.

Unfortunately, one day after work Burns discovered that Carr was making considerably more money than she. This upset her and an argument took place over the matter. The argument, in turn, upset Carr and she told Burns, "It is none of your damn business," and later, "I'm not going to apologize for the way I'm speaking to you." Both employees left the office upset over the argument.

That evening Burns phoned John White. She was crying and very distressed over the whole incident. Prior to this Burns and Carr had appeared friendly and had had no trouble getting along.

The next morning while opening the mail John White said to Bill Fox, the accountant trainee of the branch, "We're going to straighten this thing out this morning. If JoAnn is going to behave this way, she can get the hell out of the branch. We don't need that kind of behaviour in this office."

As Bob French, the manager, would not be returning from a trip for several days, White knew he had to make a decision. He was especially concerned about the tension that was spreading though the whole office because of the incident. He wondered how to solve the problem.

Exhibit 1
A Salary Dispute
An Organizational Chart

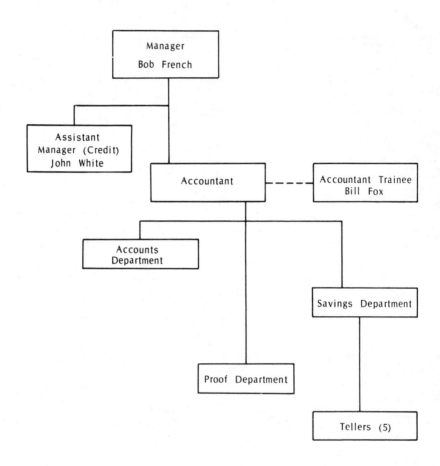

Exhibit 2
A Salary Dispute
Background of Employees

	Nancy Hawkins	Nancy Carr	JoAnn Burns	Clara Williamson	Betsy James	Sylvia Purne
Length of service in years	1/2	3	23	N/A	3	2
Salary approximately/year	$8000	$9600	$9000	—	$8800	$8400
Attitude toward Nancy Carr	+		—	Neutral	+	+
Attitude toward JoAnn Burns	Neutral	—		+	—	—

Exhibit 3
A Salary Dispute
Staff Report — Worksheet

NOT TO BE RETAINED AFTER REPORT IS COMPLETED

APPRAISAL OF PERFORMANCE — REFER TO PERSONNEL MANUAL

	EXCELLENT	VERY GOOD	GOOD	IMPROV REQUIRED	NOT ACCEPTABLE	NOT APPLICABLE	REMARKS		EXCELLENT	VERY GOOD	GOOD	IMPROV REQUIRED	NOT ACCEPTABLE	NOT APPLICABLE	REMARKS
ACCEPTANCE OF RESPONSIBILITY								ORAL EXPRESSION							
ACCURACY								ORGANIZATION							
ATTITUDE								PERSONAL NEATNESS							
CAPACITY								STAFF RELATIONS							
CUSTOMER RELATIONS								STAFF SUPERVISION							
INITIATIVE								STAFF TRAINING							
JUDGEMENT								SUCCESS IN SOLICITING BUSINESS							
KNOWLEDGE OF DUTIES								WRITTEN EXPRESSION							
MENTAL ALERTNESS								OVERALL PERFORMANCE _____							

ASSESSMENT OF POTENTIAL — REFER TO PERSONNEL MANUAL

1 PROMOTABLE
- [ ] 1 AS SOON AS THERE IS A SUITABLE OPENING
- [ ] 2 WITHIN A YEAR OR TWO
- [ ] 3 LIKELY TO QUALIFY FOR FURTHER PROMOTION TIME UNCERTAIN
- [ ] 4 LATERAL TRANSFER
- [ ] 5 NOT LIKELY TO QUALIFY FOR FURTHER PROMOTION

2 DOMINANT STRENGTHS
A.
B.
C.

3 AREAS FOR IMPROVEMENT | NOW | FUTURE
A.
B.
C.

4 IF THE EMPLOYEE HAS ANY SKILLS OR APTITUDES WHICH COULD BE USED MORE EFFECTIVELY BY THE BANK PLEASE SPECIFY UNDER COMMENTS SECTION

5 ASSIGNMENT PREFERENCES
A.
B.

6 IF THERE ARE ANY CIRCUMSTANCES WHICH RESTRICT THE MOBILITY OF THE EMPLOYEE IN ANY WAY PLEASE INDICATE AND SPECIFY UNDER COMMENTS SECTION YES [ ] NO [ ]

7 INDICATE AND EXPLAIN UNDER COMMENTS SECTION IF DURING THE NEXT TWELVE MONTHS THE EMPLOYEE WOULD BE RELUCTANT TO ACCEPT THE DEMANDS INHERENT IN HIGHER LEVEL POSITIONS

RELUCTANT TO ACCEPT YES NO
A. MORE RESPONSIBILITY [ ] [ ]
B. TRAVEL [ ] [ ]
C. GREATER SOCIAL DEMANDS [ ] [ ]

8 IF THE EMPLOYEE IS INTERESTED IN AN ASSIGNMENT IN ANOTHER COUNTRY PLEASE INDICATE YES [ ] NO [ ]

9 IF THE EMPLOYEE IS INTERESTED IN AN ASSIGNMENT IN ANOTHER DISTRICT PLEASE INDICATE YES [ ] NO [ ]

10 GEOGRAPHIC PREFERENCES
A.
B.
C.

11 COMMUNITY SIZE PREFERENCE
- [ ] 1 NO PREFERENCE
- [ ] 2 LARGE (OVER 100,000)
- [ ] 3 MEDIUM (10,000 – 100,000)
- [ ] 4 SMALL (UNDER 10,000)

12 PARTICIPATION IN WORTHWHILE COMMUNITY ACTIVITIES?
- [ ] ACTIVE
- [ ] MODERATE
- [ ] LIMITED

13 COURSES COMPLETED BY THE EMPLOYEE WITHIN THE LAST THREE YEARS

COURSE NAME	DURATION		COURSE NAME	DURATION
A.		D.		
B.		E.		
C.		F.		

COMMENTS (ELABORATE ON QUESTIONS 1 TO 3 AND 5 AND IN ALL OTHER CASES WHERE APPLICABLE CONTINUE ON REVERSE IF NECESSARY)

15

Collins Company Ltd. (A)

Two years ago, Mr. J. Robertson became the manager of the Collins Company Ltd., a large clothing store in Prairie City. Mr. Robertson took over from Mr. B. Collins and his wife, who had founded the store some thirty years earlier. Mr. Robertson felt that there was room for improvement in the way in which Collins had merchandised its garments. He realized that Collins had been profitable in the past solely because it was one of a small number of clothing stores in the Prairie City area. With a new fifty-five-store shopping mall planned for directly across the street from Collins, Mr. Robertson believed he must improve the store's performance in order to compete. He felt a change in the store's image, from one of catering to elderly people to a modern, fashionable store which would attract a more fashionable crowd, would be beneficial. Also, Mr. Robertson was concerned about the poor sales performance of his staff, particularly the staff in the Ladies' Wear Department.

BACKGROUND

Mr. Robertson came to Collins with twenty-six years of experience in the retail clothing industry. He had been with a national department store chain for twenty-four years, ten years as a merchandise manager, and later with a regional department store for two years, as general merchandise manager.

Mr. and Mrs. B. Collins had founded their small shop some thirty years ago, and from a very meagre beginning had built up the store's reputation over the years.

Presently, the store was divided into four departments: Children's Wear, Men's Wear, Sportswear (ladies' sports and casual outfits) and Ladies' Wear (dresses, coats, wedding gowns, etc.). Each department (except Men's Wear) was staffed by two saleswomen and a department head. In Men's Wear, there were two salesmen and a department head. Because the manager of the store had always acted as the department head for Men's Wear, Mr. Robertson now acted in this capacity. There were also three part-time women employees who moved from one department to another depending upon the number of customers in the store at any one time.

Within each department, the sales staff were responsible for such things as changing and maintaining the different displays (a single display was usually changed once a week and was never allowed to be left for more than two weeks); making sure all garments were properly hung in the racks; watching for any damage to the clothes on display (i.e., missing buttons, torn hemlines, etc); maintaining the cleanliness of the department and, most important, aiding the customers as they came into the store and writing up sales. The department head was responsible for many of the same duties as the sales staff as well as some administrative duties, such as the selection of the garments for his/her department; taking inventory counts; recording the sales performance of the different makes and styles of the garments; counting and balancing the cash at the end of the day; leading the sales (i.e., have the largest sales tally) in the department; and generating enthusiasm and performance among the other staff.

After starting at Collins, Mr. Robertson believed the Children's Wear and the Men's Wear Departments were functioning well. However, in the Ladies' Wear Department, Mr. Robertson felt the staff should be given more direction in buying garments and designing displays.

THE LADIES' WEAR DEPARTMENT

Performance in the Ladies' Wear Department was disappointing. From a stock of approximately 300 short dresses, 400 long dresses, 150 wedding gowns and 400 coats, the department was often selling only one item a day. Mr. Robertson believed that the quality (style and dollar value) of the merchandise had to be improved. He thought that the key to better performance would be to improve the choices Mrs. Corser (the department head) made in her buying (see Exhibit 1 for Mrs. Corser's background). He subscribed to various fashion magazines to show her the latest styles, took her to several fashion shows in Toronto, and urged her to experiment and buy more expensive and more stylish goods. Mrs. Corser's selection remained unchanged as did sales. Finally, Mr. Robertson began to do some of the buying himself in order to refresh the racks with more attractive merchandise. Mrs. Corser refused to sell Mr. Robertson's selections and put them in obscure places at the back of the racks. Mr. Robertson told Mrs. Corser that he was disturbed by her poor sales performance and by her selection of dresses. He told her that she must improve, for it was specifically her department that was the store's biggest problem. Mr. Robertson said he was intent on solving that problem.

A month later, when Mr. Robertson was calling in his staff for their spring raises, Mrs. Corser informed him that she was no longer interested in aiding in the selection of any merchandise except the wedding gowns. Mr. Robertson replied that this decision was acceptable to him, but that he therefore would have to withhold Mrs. Corser's raise. Mrs. Corser agreed.

THE FOLLOWING YEAR

As soon as Mr. Robertson took over the buying, sales began to increase. At least five to ten items were being sold daily. Mr. Robertson was pleased. He thought perhaps his many discussions with Mrs. Corser were finally paying off and that she had, in turn, concentrated on improving her sales performance. Mr. Robertson therefore personally told Mrs. Corser and her staff that he was pleased with their performance in increasing sales.

However, as time went on, Mr. Robertson observed that Mrs. Corser and her staff hesitated to approach customers and employ aggressive sales techniques. His impression was that they sat on stools behind the counter chatting most of the day when Mr. Robertson was not in sight. He concluded sales improved solely because the merchandise had improved, not because of any efforts by the staff. The customers were virtually serving themselves. Mr. Robertson removed the stools from behind the counter but performance remained unchanged and the saleswomen spent more time on coffee breaks. Mr. Robertson told the staff that they should be more helpful to the customers. He suggested that this helpfulness would lead to better sales. They pointed out that sales were up and said that they deserved the credit for this increase.

About the time he removed the stools, Mr. Robertson discovered that Mrs. Corser was doing her personal shopping at a competitor's store even though she received a 15 percent discount at Collins. Mrs. Corser had also chosen to make her daughter's wedding dress rather than purchase it from Collins.

A NEW TECHNIQUE

At about the same time, Mr. Robertson visited a number of competitors and attended a trade show for retail clothing merchants. From these sources, Mr. Robertson learned a new technique for displaying garments within a department. This new technique was called "colour blocking." The basic principle was that instead of hanging garments by size or style, the garments should first be grouped into a colour block and then hung on racks according to size and style. Many people who had experimented with this technique were pleased with the visual appeal it presented to the customer. This technique made extra work in terms of set-up and maintenance of the display, but resulted in a great improvement in the presentation of the merchandise. Mr. Robertson decided to try this technique in the Ladies' Wear Department; however, the introduction of colour blocking was met with much disapproval by Mrs. Corser and her assistant, Mrs. Hajnik. (See Exhibit 1 for Mrs. Hajnik's background.) They explained that this technique made it difficult for the customers to find their size. Mr. Robertson still felt that it was worth a try and suggested that they experiment with colour blocking first, and see how it worked out. Then, he concluded, they would decide whether or not to implement it on a permanent basis.

Mr. Robertson, at the same time he introduced the new colour-blocking technique, added a new saleswoman to Ladies' Wear and transferred Miss Varnel to Ladies' Wear from Children's Wear. Sales increases were recorded for all of the members in the Ladies' Wear Department and the new saleswoman had the best record of all. Soon Ladies' Wear was selling more than any other department. Mr. Robertson also transferred his seventeen-year-old daughter into Ladies' Wear. His daughter's sales accounted for 50 percent of a day's sales. Both of these new saleswomen were part-time staff and wished to remain as such. The colour-blocking experiment seemed to be working out satisfactorily. Several customers mentioned to Mr. Robertson that they strongly approved of the new look in the department. Since sales were rising, Mr. Robertson found no need to revert to the old set-up.

Later, Mr. Robertson discovered under the counter a notebook in which customers and staff had been writing about the problems with colour blocking. Mr. Robertson was most disturbed by this discovery but made no comment. He noted that only three customers had signed the book, and that the rest of the comments were from staff members.

Despite the increase in sales, Mr. Robertson was still disappointed with the situation because Mrs. Corser and Mrs. Hajnik continued to oppose the changes in their department and had not participated in the sales increase. They laughed at many of the new styles and would not show them to customers.

Relations between Mr. Robertson and Mrs. Corser continued to deteriorate, Recently, Mr. Robertson had been told that Mrs. Corser suggested to customers that they wait to buy the items after they went on sale. Given this latest incident, Mr. Robertson was concerned about what action he should take about Mrs. Corser.

Exhibit 1
Collins Company Ltd.

Personal Background
of Selected Collins' Personnel

Mrs. Corser
- Was in her early fifties
- Worked at Collins since she was in her late teens
- Quit when she got married and raised her family but had returned to Collins and had worked there for the past twelve years
- Performance had always been poor
- Had become department head because all of the other experienced people had left

Mrs. Hajnik
- Was second in command to Mrs. Corser
- Was in her late forties
- Had worked at Collins for the past five years
- Also had relatively poor performance when compared to other full-time staff and some of the part-time staff

16
Durand Company

The Durand Company was a Canadian company which manufactured consumer products. A tense situation had developed between Mr. Robert Grier, general manager of a Durand subsidiary and Mr. Jim Hickey, the recently appointed assistant general manager.

The products of Mr. Grier's subsidiary were sold to the consumer through large retail chains and specialty shops. Bob welcomed the variety provided by a few of the products which had limited industrial application. With close to $2 million in sales, the subsidiary represented about 14 percent of the total company sales. Bob felt this proved he was a master salesman. Even though his regional salespeople were good, he felt he provided the driving force. He made sure he saw them frequently and got out into the field to visit the major accounts. Bob believed contacts should be maintained in the field. Besides, he enjoyed travelling.

At fifty-two years of age Bob Grier could say he had come up the hard selling route. He had an English-Scottish background and had lived all of his younger life in a large western Canadian city. His father had represented a major Canadian company through western Canada. Bob often smiled when reminiscing about boyhood scrapes but never admitted to serious trouble. He completed high school and felt that was enough education to make his way. One thing for sure, he could outtalk and outsell anyone.

During the war, Bob had not been in the armed forces. He stayed in his job, had enjoyed travelling and selling in western Canada and soon developed a reputation for being a "character." Perhaps he was a bit loud in a group, but then most people would ignore any social transgressions because he was amusing.

It certainly proved quite a day six years before when the president of Durand Company picked Bob to be a product director in head office. Bob knew most of the people there and felt sure he could "do the job better than most of those galoots in that head office." Within six months, his products were grouped in a subsidiary company and he became the general manager. Bob soon found he was much more comfortable and confident while selling, but the management responsibilities left him feeling uncertain and anxious. His blustering, swearing manner alienated some people at head office but everyone still classified him as a character and he could usually talk any sensitive people out of being disturbed. Besides, as he often said, "Who were these idiots who worried about a little cutting of corners to get things done?"

After five years of good growth, the subsidiary acquired another division of Durand to provide a better product mix. Bob's products had a low net profit-to-sales position, while the other division had higher net and complementary products. Jim Hickey had been product director of the merged division and then became assistant general manager of the subsidiary. The president of Durand felt the changes would result in a more efficient operation.

Jim Hickey was prepared to work with Mr. Grier even though Bob had a reputation for losing assistants within short periods of time. However, it was a good promotion and considered to be equivalent to a divisional director's position in the parent company (a divisional director reported directly to the president). Jim felt it would be good experience because indications were that the future growth of the Durand Company could be substantial. In addition, Bob was basically a likeable person and was reputed to approach management aggressively on behalf of people who worked for him.

From the beginning, Bob Grier insisted that Jim should have his own private office and indicated that he would arrange this as soon as possible. Temporarily Jim had a desk in the general office but was separated into a private work area. It was rather noisy but quite satisfactory.

Within a short time Jim realized that Bob Grier's dealings with executives were rather hectic. Often there was much shouting and many accusations emerging from Grier's office. Very little seemed to be accomplished during certain meetings.

An uncomfortable pattern began to develop when product, research, advertising, and financial people started clearing many matters with Jim rather than with Mr. Grier. One day the vice-president for manufacturing, Kevin MacLeod, came to see Mr. Grier.

MacLeod:	Jim, Bob Grier is not in his office. Is he out of town?
Hickey:	Yes, he's out West.
MacLeod:	Good. Then I can clear this with you and that will avoid the normal arguments.
Hickey:	I've only been in this area a short time so I am not sure what you mean, but what is the problem?
MacLeod:	Will you make a decision on this production quantity you want on these new products? I've got to get this settled or you won't get what you want in time for your campaign.
Hickey:	Sure. We want 50 000 of the A model and 35 000 of the B model. I made the forecast so I'm sure of these quantities.
MacLeod:	Thanks, Jim! That was a lot less trouble than I expected. Bob is a good man but he can create the atmosphere of an "ulcer factory." However, he really is the man who can sell refrigerators to Eskimos.

Bob Grier returned from his western trip on the following Monday, and about mid-morning came storming out of his private office to exclaim in a loud manner:

Grier:	You stupid idiot! What are you doing, telling MacLeod to produce these quantities of A and B? You better improve your memory, boy! We decided on 40 000 of A and 25 000 of B. Get the papers and come on in. Every time I go away, things get fouled up!

A few minutes later, Jim entered Grier's office with the forecast sheets.

Hickey:	Bob, here are the forecast sheets. We decided, on the basis of a better Ontario potential, that we could increase the quantities. Here are your initials on my memo.
Grier:	Guess you're right. Sorry, Jim, but I hate administrative problems.
Hickey:	I appreciate your saying that, but I wish you'd confine your shouting to this office. This is the fourth time this type of thing has happened and it

is rather embarrassing. Everybody outside hears your accusations but nobody hears any apology.

Grier: Oh, don't be so damn sensitive! We only need to be concerned with keeping this subsidiary humming! What do you care what they think? Most of them are only clerks anyway. Boy, you college kids sure are sensitive!

Jim Hickey was brought up in a medium-sized Ontario city. His parents helped him develop an independent spirit. However, the chance to work in teams came in athletics and summers spent at a boys' camp. He liked school and entered university. This was interrupted by two years in army service which allowed Jim to travel and helped develop his leadership understanding, as well as an ability to cooperate to get a job done. He returned to complete his university degree. Before coming to Durand, Jim had worked as a field sales representative with two large companies. For five years he gained some valuable selling experience.

Before being transferred to the subsidiary company, Jim had worked over a year with Mr. William Hendricks, one of the best divisional directors at Durand. With Mr. Hendricks, Jim had developed a good understanding of most people in the company and a competence in his job. It seemed to be excellent training for operating a division of his own. Bill Hendricks appeared to be able to get the maximum of cooperation and spirit from everyone with whom he was associated.

The move to Bob Grier's area was rather sudden, but was welcomed since Jim had been groomed for more challenge. At first Bob Grier seemed to promote the idea of turning as much work as possible over to Jim. He mentioned several times that, although Jim had come to him an "inherited way," the subsidiary "needed a man with your training."

The incidents described above seemed to paint a different picture. One or two other incidents brought the situation to a crisis. The following exchange took place in Grier's office.

Grier: How come you O.K.'d that advertisement which appeared in *Weekend Magazine* last week? I thought I told you that everything in that campaign was to be cleared through me first.

Hickey: Well, it had reached the deadline. All the details had been reviewed by you. Furthermore, I was sure from our discussion that was what you wanted.

Grier: Just because you got some advanced ad training with Hendricks downstairs, it doesn't make you an expert. The rule is you check things with the boss up here. If you spent a little more time following instructions rather than trying to run your own show, things might improve around here. Didn't that army service teach you anything about following orders?

Hickey: Was there something wrong with the ad? The president said it was one of the best company ads he'd seen in some time.

Grier: Never mind about the president. You work for me!

For a while things seemed to improve. Sales were going well and Jim did what he could to improve his relationship with Bob Grier by putting some extra work on special projects that he knew interested the general manager. Even the president had been making complimentary remarks about the subsidiary's success. The situation looked better until the hectic summer preparations for fall business.

In late July, Bob Grier phoned the office even though he was on a golfing holiday.

Grier:	What are you doing in there, Hickey? I hear you're now revising the routes of my Ontario sales representative.
Hickey:	Bob, you were away so I couldn't check with you. Our analysis showed that Henry should redirect his efforts toward certain accounts to achieve optimum results. Calls on certain companies have been too costly for their potential so we just revised his schedule a bit. You and I had a general discussion about this before your holidays. After the analysis it did seem obvious what had to be done.
Grier:	I knew I'd have this sort of trouble with you. All you Hendricks alumni seem to want to run your own company. Everyone he hires seems to turn out this way. Can't you wait for orders?
Hickey:	There's no need to shout, Bob. I get the message. We should have a chat about things in general as soon as you return.

That afternoon Jim talked with his close friend Maurice Masson, who was a special assistant to the president. Jim mentioned that he was preparing to resign since he found it impossible to work with Bob Grier any longer. Transfer seemed impossible since four major divisions of the company all appeared to have competent directors.

Maurice informed Jim that there were some opportunities coming up in the creation of two new divisions and of a new position as sales manager of large national accounts. The latter position of sales manager was sales work with accounts such as Eaton's, Simpsons, Woodwards, and the like, with considerable responsibility but few management duties. The presidential assistant assured Jim that when the new divisions were created, they could grow to become large operations.

In addition, Maurice pressed the point that hasty action now might be regretted later. Also, the company had been looking at the entire subsidiary situation as to whether it should be separate from the main company. As though to support his case further, Maurice added that lasting eight months with Bob Grier was longer than any other assistant had managed.

However, Jim was not to be mollified. He felt things had gone too far and it was impossible to tell how much longer it would take the company to decide on any new divisions. Although he liked Durand and its people, Jim had had one or two good offers from outside the company that could be pursued.

The next morning, Maurice briefed the president. The president concluded by saying, "Something has to be done. I hate losing people as good as Jim Hickey. Bob Grier manages to increase sales in that subsidiary but he seems to be causing personnel problems. It's about time we made some positive moves. What do you think we should do, Maurice?"

17
Hovey and Beard Co.

PART 1

The Hovey and Beard Co. manufactured wooden toys of various kinds: animals, pull toys, and the like. One part of the manufacturing process involved spraying paint on the partially assembled toys. This operation was staffed entirely by women.

The toys were cut, sanded, and partially assembled in the wood room. Then they were dipped into shellac, and afterwards painted. The toys were predominantly two-coloured: a few were made in more than two colours. Each colour required an additional trip through the paint room.

For a number of years, these toys had been produced entirely by hand. However, to meet tremendously increased demand, the painting operation had recently been re-engineered so that eight women who did the painting sat in a line by an endless chain of hooks. These hooks moved continuously past the line of women and into a long horizontal oven. Each woman sat at her own painting booth, specially designed to carry away fumes and to backstop excess paint. The woman would take a toy from the tray beside her, position it in a jig inside the painting cubicle, spray on the colour according to a pattern, then release the toy and hang it on the hook passing by. The rate at which the hooks moved had been calculated by the engineers so that each woman, when fully trained, would be able to hang a painted toy on each hook before it passed beyond her reach.

The women working in the paint room were on a group bonus plan. Since the operation was new to them, they were receiving a learning bonus that decreased by regular amounts each month. The learning bonus was scheduled to vanish in six months, by which time it was expected that they would be on their own — that is, able to meet the standard and to earn a group bonus when they exceeded it.

PART 2

By the second month of the training period, trouble had developed. The women learned more slowly than had been anticipated, and it began to look as though their production would stabilize far below expectation level. Many of the hooks were going by empty. The women complained that they were going by too fast, and that the time-study man had set the rates incorrectly. A few women quit and had to be replaced, which further aggravated the learning problems. The team spirit which the management had expected to develop automatically through the group bonus was not in evidence except as an expression of what the engineers called "resistance." One woman whom the group regarded as its leader (and management regarded as the ringleader) was outspoken in making the various complaints of the group to the foreman: the job was a messy one, the hooks moved too fast, the incentive pay was not being correctly calculated, and it was too hot working so close to the drying oven.

"Group Dynamics and Intergroup Relations" by George Strauss and Alex Bavelas (under the title "The Hovey and Beard Case") from *Money and Motivation* edited by William F. Whyte. Copyright © 1955 by Harper & Row, Publishers, Inc. Reprinted by permission of the publishers.

18
Jack McGraw

For three months Jack McGraw had been president of the Central Hamilton Chapter of Squires International, a men's voluntary community service club. During that time he had become increasingly concerned about the problems facing the chapter, and questioned his own effectiveness as chief executive in handling those problems.

NORTH YORK CHAPTER EXPERIENCE

There were local chapters of Squires International throughout Canada and the United States. While many of these chapters were becoming involved in community service projects in general, most of the organization's effort was directed toward youth work. The chapters organized team sports, provided recreational facilities, and planned events such as hockey tournaments and bicycle rallies. The money for these activities was provided through the chapters' various fund-raising projects such as bingo, raffles, dances, and exhibitions. Many of the chapters had received commendation from local governments and police forces for their efforts in combating and reducing juvenile delinquency.

Before joining the Central Hamilton Chapter, Jack had been a member of the North York Chapter for five years. During two of those years, he had served as vice-president in charge of external activities. Chairmen in charge of such activities as community service, fund raising and youth work were responsible to him. His counterpart was a vice-president in charge of internal activities who worked with chairmen involved in membership, finance, and program activities. The organization was typical of all Squires International chapters. Jack had gained a great deal of personal satisfaction from his association with the North York Chapter, and he was anxious to join a chapter in Hamilton when he was transferred there by his company.

The North York Chapter was a highly successful club in spite of a very weak beginning. In retrospect, members attributed its success to a single member, Roy Wizowski. Roy had joined the chapter during its second year, and the following year was elected president. He recognized that this triumph was a dubious honour since he had run unopposed. Nevertheless, he treated the post with utmost respect. Roy was described by members as a tireless, enthusiastic individual who could easily instil his own enthusiasm in others. The chapter's fortunes were reversed with Roy's pet project: the establishment of a hockey league in North York. The hockey league required an arena and thus the chapter found itself suddenly committed to two large projects.

Some members thought Wizowski was striving too high, but he soon had fund-raising projects under way as well as a high-powered membership drive. Jack was among the men introduced to the club during that drive. He had been hesitant about joining the club because at twenty-two he was considerably younger than the majority of members who ranged in age from late twenties through early forties. Roy was insistent that the chapter *needed* Jack, his help would be invaluable in dealing with young people. Jack, like all members of the chapter, learned that it was impossible to say "no" to Roy Wizowski. Even after his term of office Roy remained the driving force behind the success of the group.

ESTABLISHMENT OF CENTRAL HAMILTON CHAPTER

Jack was employed as a manager of the Hamilton branch of a national chain of department stores. After his transfer to the city, he attended meetings of various local chapters of Squires International. All of these were long-established clubs. Each had its pet project around which most of its efforts were centred. None seemed anxious to branch into anything new. For some, this attitude predicted disaster as established members became apathetic and the club had difficulty in attracting new members.

At one of these meetings Jack met the district coordinator of Squires International who described a new chapter that was being organized. This chapter, to be chartered as the Central Hamilton Chapter, was a new concept in Squires clubs. First, the club would be made up predominantly of younger men between twenty and thirty years of age. More important, there was a fundamental difference in the group's emphasis. It was to deal with problems, such as drug abuse, which were common to all areas of the city. At the same time, the district coordinator hoped that the members would establish organized recreation for young people in the previously neglected core area of the city. Jack was excited by what he heard and agreed to attend an organizational meeting.

Jack joined the Central Hamilton Chapter and was elected vice-president in charge of internal activities. The president of the club was a young lawyer and the external activities vice-president was an insurance salesman. Both appeared to share Jack's enthusiasm for the new club.

The membership of the club numbered forty-five on charter night early in October; everyone seemed very enthusiastic. Included in the group were twelve university and community college students, four high school teachers, two social workers, eight salesmen, three private businessmen, and two lawyers. A notable plus, the members felt, was the inclusion of two city aldermen in the chapter. Jack was the only member who had prior experience as a Squire, but help was promised from the sponsoring chapter.

During the months immediately before and after the charter was received, a large number of social events were held. Other Hamilton chapters invited the men to their meetings to welcome them as new Squires. The Central Hamilton Squires themselves organized several parties for the men and their wives. Both Jack and his wife were impressed with the conviviality and enthusiasm of the group.

The social gatherings resulted in the initiation of a few projects. One weekend about eight of the members and their families took a group of children from a local orphanage on a camping trip. Most of the members volunteered to supervise boys' basketball and floor hockey games in a church basement in the core area. One of the social workers had initiated a "help" program for reformed drug abusers. Two raffles held before Christmas provided the funds for these projects and others. The club seemed to be off to a successful start.

After Christmas, however, there were some foreboding signs. Attendance at the twice-monthly dinner meetings fell off. Some members would wait until after dinner to arrive, claiming that they could not afford the meal. Similarly, the club had difficulty in collecting membership dues. In March, the group was forced to locate its meeting in a less attractive setting because attendance had not been sufficient to meet the minimum cover charge for the room. The excess had been taken from the dues kitty, but the kitty was dwindling. Meanwhile all efforts at fund raising had ceased, thus limiting community service projects.

In April the president-elect was badly injured in an automobile accident that forced him to remain in hospital for an extended period of time. During the third week he phoned the president of the chapter to notify him of his resignation from the club. He said that he would have a great deal of work to catch up on when released from the hospital and would not be able to spare any time.

As a result, Jack was named president-elect. He welcomed the opportunity since he was still very optimistic about the club's future.

THE RECREATION CENTRE

In May, Phil Whalen, a member of the chapter, came forward with a proposal from his uncle, Mr. Henry Jenkins. Mr. Jenkins owned an abandoned factory in the core area of the city. He had planned to tear the building down and sell the property, but now offered the Squires the use of the building as a recreation centre if they would agree to pay the taxes on it. Alternatively, he would sell them the property for $10 000, which represented one-half its appraised value, *if* they agreed to use it for youth work.

Jack and other members of the executive visited the site the following day. They were impressed by the size of the building and by the opportunities it presented. It was located in the older section of the city, an area with few recreational facilities. The high concentration of juvenile crime in the area had often been attributed to the lack of organized recreational activities. Jack saw this as the answer to the club's problems, likening it to Roy Wizowski's hockey league.

Jack's enthusiasm seemed to carry over to the other members of the club. The next meeting of the Squires was held at the factory. Attendance was almost 100 percent. The members toured the factory, each making suggestions on how to utilize the rooms and commenting on the work that had to be done. They agreed unanimously to take over the building and convert it into a neighbourhood community centre.

Almost immediately, teams of the club's members started tearing down interior walls, sweeping, washing, repairing and painting. This early industry, however, did not continue. By late June there was little indication of progress. Often the work teams spent more time playing basketball at the rear of the building than they did working. Oddly enough these men blamed the lack of progress on others who were not coming out as often. There had been a very big clash between two members who argued over who was "in charge of the building." Jack was able to settle the disagreement, but the friction had already broken the spirit of a few members. The summer broke up many of the work teams as members left for vacation. In mid-July the president of the chapter announced that he would be out of town until September. He suggested that Jack take over as president immediately instead of waiting until September. Jack agreed. He and a few other dedicated members continued to work at the factory a couple of nights a week, but their enthusiasm, too, was waning.

FUND-RAISING PROBLEMS

Meanwhile, in their excitement over the factory, the members had forgotten about fund raising. Plans which the fund-raising chairman had put forth were rejected with little discussion. Jack saw that the members were reticent about it. He had hoped their enthusiasm for the opportunities presented by the factory would carry over to fund raising. Some members were frank and admitted that they didn't like to ask anyone for money, even if the cause was right. Jack suspected that most members felt this way.

In August, Jack received the first municipal tax bill for the factory property. It was payable within ten days and an emergency meeting was called. The members voted to borrow the money from the bank; each signed a promissory note for a portion of the loan. They discussed possible fund-raising projects and agreed that "something" had to be done, but no one agreed on a specific course of action

One night after Jack and three members had finished some work at the factory, the subject of fund raising came up again. The four decided to run a raffle and to have tickets printed without the approval of the group as a whole. Once the tickets were printed, they felt the members would feel obliged to sell them.

Details of the raffle were explained and the books distributed at the next dinner meeting. No one expressed any opposition to the raffle or dissatisfaction with the way it had come about. Jack emphasized that it was important that the group sell the tickets since the bank would soon be asking for repayment of the loan. The members agreed to *try* to sell the tickets. Tickets were delivered personally to the large number of members not at the meeting that night.

Jack took over much of the responsibility for this fund-raising project. Each week he phoned or visited each of the members to encourage them to sell the tickets and to get a tally on the number sold to date. On each occasion he warned that the failure of this project would result in loss of the factory. Many of the members said the tickets were too difficult to sell.

By October, Jack knew that the raffle was not going to be a success. In fact, a tally taken at a meeting showed the club would actually *lose* money when the draw took place. The members present agreed to try to sell more tickets so that the club would at least break even. The fund-raising chairman did not think this was enough. He said there was no sense in going through all this effort simply to break even. Furthermore, he felt that because he had been able to sell more than his quota others should do the same. The discussion became an argument and many harsh statements were shouted in anger. Jack calmed everyone down and the meeting ended with no further incidents. Afterwards the fund-raising chairman apologized to Jack, but resigned from the club. He said that he had better things to do with his time than sit on a sinking ship.

OTHER PROBLEMS

It was not the first resignation he had received, and Jack had learned not to try to convince anyone to stay. In fact, membership had fallen to twenty-eight in spite of the introduction of five new members. Jack hated to lose the men who resigned, who were hard workers, but efforts to convince them not to quit were unsuccessful. Losing members was not unusual, but recruits were expected at least to balance the outflow.

The small number of newcomers was partially due to the lack of a recruiting effort by the individual members. Where members had brought prospective members to meetings, the membership chairman had failed to follow up with a letter inviting them to join. This simple procedure had proven a valuable tool for other Squires chapters in recruiting new members, yet it wasn't being done in the Central Hamilton Chapter.

Jack wondered if the fund-raising chairman had been accurate in describing the chapter as a "sinking ship." The club's difficulties were not limited to fund raising; dues collection, meeting attendance and membership were also problem areas. The chapter's program chairman had been remiss in his duties too, and the club had not had a guest speaker at many meetings.

The chairmen in charge of community service and youth work were both energetic and had initiated some worthwhile projects. Unfortunately, they often worked alone because they were tired of begging people to come out to help. Jack felt that once members were exposed to the worthwhile kinds of projects these men had instigated they would want to help. He knew it was necessary to push the members into projects but considered it up to the individual chairmen to provide this push even if it was a hard, frustrating job.

Fred Mathers, publicity chairman, also presented a problem for Jack. Fred was the fourth person to take over this position and the first who had managed to get the biweekly news bulletin out on time. Under earlier chairmen it often did not get out at all. Fred's bulletins were thorough, imaginative, and interesting. Unfortunately, Fred tended to get carried away with his enthusiasm for producing an entertaining bulletin. Some of the language and cartoons had proved offensive to some members and definitely to the president of Squires International, who received copies of all chapters' bulletins. He reminded Jack that the bulletin was sent to the members' homes so that the whole family could read it. Jack agreed but did not know how to approach Fred. He feared that his criticism might dull Fred's interest. Thus, Jack found that even the bright spots in the organization presented difficulties for him.

To compound his troubles, Jack's workload at the department store was expected to be heavy due to an upcoming store-wide sale. This would leave him with little time to do Squires work. Furthermore, his wife had been urging him to resign from the club because it took up so much of his time and paid off only in frustration for him. Initially, Jack had promised himself that he would give the club a full year as president during which he would try his utmost to make it a success. Now, after only three months, he wondered if he shouldn't give up the presidency to someone who might handle it better.

19

La Femme Fashion Boutiques (B)

"Our first boutique is scheduled to open in eight weeks," said Dean Marshall, "so we have a relatively short time to hire a manager. Since she will control our major source of revenue, which is the sale of products, as well as the fact that we will spend a little less than $2300 to train her, it is extremely important that we select the right person for the position."

Dean went on to say, "We have put all of our own money into the company, so we are forced to draw some salary. We are also obligated to make monthly payments on the money we borrowed. Since the company is incurring operating expenses and expected revenues are uncertain, it is crucial at this stage of our corporate development that we do not make any decision which could jeopardize our present or future working capital position."

After graduating from university, Dean Marshall and Vince McClain incorporated Marshall and McClain Ltd. Their initial capital was approximately $100 000, over two-thirds of which was borrowed and personally guaranteed. They purchased from a Chicago company the Ontario franchise for La Femme Cosmetic Boutiques. The contract they signed allowed them complete freedom to adapt the concept to suit the Canadian market.

McClain and Marshall demanded this type of contract because they were not satisfied with the American design for the interior of the boutique and had decided to change its general atmosphere to give it a very modern, intimate, and personalized image. In addition to these changes, they also wanted to expand the product line to fit the new atmosphere. They would search for, screen, and select new products that would appeal to their defined major target market — women from fifteen to thirty-five years of age. The product line would include high-fashion clothing as well as jewellery and other accessories. In other words, the original concept of cosmetic boutique was completely changed to one of a fashion boutique.

During the first three months of incorporation, Vince had contacted various suppliers of merchandise and put together a complete product mix. Dean found a location in a large mall suitable for their first boutique with floor space of approximately 96 m^2 (12 m by 8 m, roughly comparable to the size of an average classroom).

The mall was situated in North Toronto near a major expressway and was adequately serviced by public transportation. The surrounding market area was almost entirely residential with a population of 425 000. The mall had eighty-five stores, two of which were major department stores. All of the services usually provided by a mall to ensure customer convenience and satisfaction were available. This was the type of location that was planned for all future boutiques.

Vince commented concerning the type of person required for the job. "Because of the product and service we are offering to our consumer group, I feel we must hire a manager with whom our customers can identify. Age and physical appearance are therefore very important. Such a person will be expected to dress according to the current fashions and know how to wear and match her clothes and cosmetics for best effects.

"We intend to give the woman we hire almost complete freedom and flexibility in the operation of the boutique. However, she will not be directly involved in the purchasing of merchandise for the product line. Dean and I will concentrate our efforts in this area as well as the overall expansion of the company, so we will not have time available to become involved in the day-to-day managing of each boutique."

Part of the manager's responsibilities would include hiring, training, and supervising additional part-time sales personnel. Since the boutique was required to be open from 10 00 to 22 00, six days a week, it was estimated that two temporary saleswomen would be necessary.

Part-time saleswomen could expect to earn $3.45 an hour. They would be required to work during the busy times at the mall, which included Wednesday, Thursday, and Friday evenings and all day Saturday. The manager was also expected to be at the boutique during these hours.

One part-time saleswoman could be left alone at the boutique during slow periods at the mall. Such periods were usually Monday, Tuesday, and Wednesday mornings and Saturday evenings.

The manager would keep up-to-date on style changes and colour combinations for various types of clothing by reading modern fashion magazines and attending major local fashion shows. She would also do most of the selling in the boutique. In addition, the manager would be responsible for keeping a very simple bookkeeping system, paying all bills under seventy-five dollars, compiling weekly sales reports, balancing the cash account, paying the part-time saleswomen, and making daily cash deposits at a nearby bank. Since cooperative promotion and sales were customary among location owners in large mall complexes, the manager would work in conjunction with other store managers in the mall to promote the sale of La Femme products.

Regarding the manager's salary, Dean commented, "Initially we cannot afford to pay whomever we hire a great deal of money. We plan to pay her a basic salary of $200 a week, which is comparable to an average secretary's salary. This will be supplemented by a 4 percent commission on net sales, and we expect the average daily sales volume to reach $420 once the store is established. We will also, of course, have to pay the employer's portion of various compulsory fringe benefits. In addition to monetary remuneration, she will spend two weeks in Washington, D.C., at our expense where she will receive excellent training at a leading fashion school in the various aspects of coordinating styles, colours, and accessories to complement the physical appearance and personality of the customer."

Since Dean and Vince had developed a new and unproven approach to merchandising this type of product and service, they realized it would be difficult to predict accurately the future success of their company. Because of their limited financial resources, they estimated they had sufficient working capital to last only eight to ten months if their target market did not accept the products and services offered in the boutique. Therefore, it was imperative to get the boutique open, keep overhead low, and generate as much revenue as possible.

An advertisement briefly describing the job and the requirements of the position was placed in the job opportunities section of a daily Toronto newspaper (Exhibit 1).

All replies were by letter. Exhibit 2 contains three letters typical of those received. Vince and Dean planned personally to interview the better applicants. Not only did they have to decide which applicant was best suited for this particular manager's position, but they also wanted to develop their selection and hiring process since their objective was to open three more boutiques during the first year of operation and this would mean hiring three new managers.

Exhibit 1
La Femme Fashion Boutiques (B)
Newspaper Advertisement

Actual Size of Advertisement

The advertisement as it appeared in the job opportunity section of a daily Toronto newspaper.

POSITION AVAILABLE

POSITION	Manager of a women's fashion boutique in a centrally located, large shopping mall.
THE JOB	Selling very modern, high-fashion women's clothing and accessory items. Managing the operation of the boutique.
REQUIREMENTS	Attractive, well groomed, sales ability and experience necessary, management experience desired. Willing to accept responsibility and use own judgment.

Reply giving brief personal history to:
La Femme Fashion Boutiques,
c/o Marshall and McClain Ltd.,
P.O. Box 201, Station B,
Toronto, Ontario.

Exhibit 2

220 Holt Road,
Etobicoke, Ontario.
June 13, 1984

La Femme Fashion Boutiques,
c/o Marshall and McClain Ltd.,
P.O. Box 201, Station B,
Toronto, Ontario.

Dear Sirs:

I would like to apply for the position as offered in your recent advertisement. I am thirty-three years old, married and do not have any children.

I have worked in the Toronto area for the past three years as a consultant for Helena Rubenstein. My duties include visiting retail outlets, showing the buyers our new products and explaining the aspects of our products to the salesgirls. I am also responsible for setting up displays for our products.

Before working at my present position, I was a saleslady for a women's sporting goods store in Montreal. I was in the clothing section and for three years received a great deal of sales experience.

Prior to this position, I was a secretary for a large law firm in Toronto. I had general secretarial duties as well as responsibilities for collection of accounts receivable. I also acted as receptionist.

I have my senior matriculation as well as a diploma from a secretarial school. I have also taken two modelling courses from a large and reputable modelling school.

My personal interests are painting, modelling, tennis and reading. My husband is a salesman for a large company that manufactures air conditioners.

If I received the position you are offering, I would have to give two weeks' notice to my present employer. I would like the opportunity to discuss the job further.

Sincerely,

Edith Martin

1201 Langsdown Crescent,
Scarborough, Ontario.
June 11, 1984

La Femme Fashion Boutiques,
c/o Marshall and McClain Ltd.
P.O. Box 201, Station B,
Toronto, Ontario.

Dear Sirs:

I was really happy to see your ad in the paper. I have been looking for a job like this for a while now.

My name is Laura McDermott. I'm forty years old but a very modern thinker. I'm married and have three children. Two are in public school and one is in high school. My husband also has a good job.

I'm not working now. The canning company I had a position with had a lay-off and I got layed off. That was a few months ago but I was going to quit anyhow. Before that job, I worked for four years as a hairdresser. I really enjoyed that sort of thing but then I got pregnant again.

Before I worked for Helen's Beauty Shop, I worked for Eaton's selling. I got a lot of experience selling and I liked it. They are after me to come back but I would sooner have your job. I like to work with people and sell things. Eaton's said I was a good saleslady.

I read fashion magazines all the time and I make a lot of my own clothes. I go to Eaton's fashion shows all the time and the K-Mart near our home asked me to wear some of their clothes in a fashion show two weeks ago but I couldn't make it.

I know I can sell and my experience has helped me to know how to manage. I will be looking forward to hearing from you. Give me a call at 722-9600. I am usually home everyday but Wednesday afternoon.

Sincerely,

Laura McDermott

1240 Riverside Drive,
Apt. 1402,
Toronto, Ontario
June 8, 1984

La Femme Fashion Boutiques,
c/o Marshall and McClain Ltd.
P.O. Box 201, Station B,
Toronto, Ontario.

Dear Sirs:

I am replying in regard to your recent advertisement concerning the position of manager of your fashion boutique. I will attempt to relate my personal background and general experience.

I am twenty-nine years old. I have been divorced for two years and do not have any children. I am currently employed as a saleslady for Diest Fashions. I have worked for this company for 1-1/2 years. During this period of time, I have been responsible for supervising three salesgirls.

Previous to this position, I was employed for five years by Fayette's Modelling School where I was an instructor. I terminated my employment here because I was offered a managerial position with Diest.

I have a Grade 13 education with sales and modelling experience during the summer. The sales experience was with a large merchandising chain in the women's clothing department.

The reason for my willingness to terminate my present employment is due to the fact that I am presently one of three supervisors and I do not see any chance for immediate advancement and increase in responsibilities. Remuneration is not a prime objective but there must be the possibility for future growth and development.

I have attempted to briefly outline my past history. If you would like to discuss it further, I would appreciate the opportunity to meet with you at a mutually convenient time.

Yours truly,

Patricia Lemieux

20
Maintrel Ltd. (A)

On August 21, Mark Rogers returned to his office at 18 00. He found his friend Joe Kelt, supervisor of the mechanical group, waiting for him. (See Exhibit 1 for a partial organization chart.)

"Hi Joe! I don't see you here at night very often."

"No," replied Joe, "but I heard I would probably find you here after your dinner so I stopped off to see you."

"Oh, I just wanted to clear my desk of all this paper," said Mark. "During the day I'm quite busy just keeping the jobs moving. I never get enough time to clear up the paperwork within normal hours. So I come back here for a couple of hours, twice a week, to do this."

"Why do you have to be so very busy with details, Mark? Can't your people do things by themselves?" Joe asked.

"Well, yes, and no. You see, Joe, this company can't seem to find the number of experienced engineering designers we need, so we have to depend on an inflow of new graduates. These people are intelligent and self-motivated, but they don't have very much experience. So I try my best to help. And, Joe, except one, all of my people are doing well. I don't think I will have to come in at night again after, say, about two months. They will all be in good shape by then."

Joe: Mark, I know you don't like beating around the bush, so I will come right to the point. I want to tell you something before you hear it from rumours and gossip. But, please, don't lose your cool after hearing what I have to say. Your report on the Calgary Project caused quite a stir. In fact, Bert Phillips called a meeting for 15 30 this afternoon to discuss the report.

Mark: Well! I wasn't asked to attend.

Joe: No, but don't forget that Bert is the project manager, and he explained to the rest of us that he didn't think you should be there, but he neglected to say why. Anyway, the report literally got thrown out of the window. Except for two of us, the majority decided to ignore the report.

Mark: Well, it's Bert's problem now. I did my part. Jack Manning asked me to review the Calgary Project, with emphasis on engineering design. He wanted me to find out if everything was all right. And I think I did just that. Bert's approach to the project boils down to "Well, it's the client's money, so what the hell." I don't agree with that. You know, this company had been out in the cold for a few years with Felicity Ltd. They never got over the engineering and financial mess our company got them into when we put in their first automatic labelling machine in Regina. Jack knew this, and when we got our second chance we underbid everybody to the extent that we almost didn't get away with the shirts on our backs. But we got what we wanted. We managed that project so well from both technical and management points of view that Felicity now feels that we proved our worth and gave us the Calgary Project on a cost-reimbursable-plus basis.

Do you think we should screw it all up now? Oh, well, I've done my share, and my responsibility ended with the report.

Next morning, Thursday, at 08 00, Mark Rogers was in Jack Manning's office. He had in his pocket two letters of resignation: one giving the company one month's notice, and the other requesting to be released at 17 00, Friday.

Manning: And how's Mark today?

Mark: O.K. Well . . . I have to talk to you for a few minutes, Jack.

Manning: Give me a couple of minutes will you, Mark. I will be right back.

Mark placed the second letter down on Jack's desk. Manning glanced through the letter and shouted, "I won't have it. I knew it. I knew I was going to have trouble today. No, I won't accept it."

He tore up Rogers's resignation and threw it into the trash can.

Manning: You go back to your office and settle down. It's not going to happen. I won't accept it.

Mark: Well, what's that going to do? If you don't accept it, I just have to keep going higher and higher until I reach the president's door. Then where are you going to be? The cat is really going to be out of the bag then. Think about it.

Rogers went back to his office.

In his office, Mr. Manning sat and pondered.

One year ago, Mark Rogers came to Canada from England. He came to Maintrel Ltd. as a freelance mechanical designer through an employment agency. He seemed like a loner to most of the supervisors he worked with. But within the first month of his employment, everybody concerned agreed that he was one of the best designers they had ever had. He never seemed too talkative, never wasted his own or anybody's time, and in fact whenever a job was given to him, he never needed to discuss any problem with his supervisors. Mark Rogers was an engineer with about seven years' experience in design and two further years' experience in project management. With this information, and personal knowledge of his capability, Manning offered him a substantial salary, more than Rogers was earning as a freelancer, if he would join Maintrel full time. When he explained that the position was permanent with unlimited potential for advancement, Rogers took the job.

Manning noticed a change in Rogers's attitude within about two months after he started with Maintrel. In fact, he became a sort of father confessor-cum-adviser to most of his coworkers. It was apparently never too troublesome to him to lend a hand to less experienced men with problems, even when he was most heavily loaded with work himself. He was not regarded as a bosom pal by everybody, but he was thought of as a man one could go to for help, if needed.

Seven months later one of the three engineering supervisors quit the company for a better job. An immediate replacement to fill the vacancy could not be found because of a general shortage of experienced talent in the industry. Manning decided then to use Rogers as a temporary replacement in this position. When he asked Rogers if he would like to try the job out, Mark accepted it without any outward show of emotion, but Manning had a feeling that Rogers was pleased.

During the next six months Rogers functioned in that position quite successfully. Manning thought. In fact, quite a few of the designers came to see Manning, especially to tell him how well they liked working with Rogers, and requested that they not be transferred to any other group. They indicated that their daily work-problems did not seem like problems at all. They were mostly young designers, and probably liked working with a young supervisor, Manning thought. These events led Manning seriously to consider offering Rogers the position permanently. At about this time the company's manager of construction requested Manning to consider a Mr. Hugh Horton for the position Rogers was holding temporarily. The interdepartmental relationship between the engineering and construction departments had always been in a state of hostility. Manning felt that the construction manager's request was well worth considering, since "a favour done is a favour returned." Furthermore, Horton's supervisory ability seemed to be outstanding and he appeared well qualified in all respects, including the fact that he had spent a couple of years in engineering design at the start of his career. He was reasonably young, and commanded high praise from the construction manager, who more than hinted that he would like to see Horton advance. Upon considerable deliberation, Manning decided to offer Horton the position, and acted upon it.

He realized that Rogers could be upset on hearing this news, but decided to promise Rogers the next vacancy that occurred. He called Rogers into his office and informed him of the changes. He carefully noted Rogers's reaction to this news and felt relieved when Rogers left his office, laughingly saying, "Well, it was pretty good while it lasted, but don't worry about it, the job was a temporary one to me anyway."

About a month after Horton took over the group a major contract was awarded to Maintrel by a very large diversified company, Felicity Ltd. Some years ago Maintrel had a project to design and construct an automatic product-labelling unit for Felicity Ltd., and because of certain organizational problems within Maintrel, coupled with lack of experienced supervisory staff, Maintrel failed to satify its client. This resulted in Felicity's declaring it would not consider giving Maintrel any further business. Maintrel management was concerned about this problem, and decided to "buy" a project under public tender by bidding deliberately low, so that Maintrel could get a chance to restore a good relationship with Felicity. In fact, this course of action proved successful, since Maintrel's board of directors issued a definite directive to all related departmental heads that the talent employed in this particular project must be the best Maintrel could offer. The client was so pleased with the marked quality of work that some time later Felicity awarded a further contract to Maintrel, which not only ran into several millions of dollars, but also was at no financial risk to Maintrel as it was on a cost-plus basis. This was known as the Calgary Project.

About three-quarters of the way through the engineering stage of this contract, Manning became concerned about any potential foul-up of the project, similar to that experienced by the company before. He wanted a thorough and independent analysis of his department's handling of the job before it went to the client, so that any problems uncovered could be erased at source. Since Mark Rogers had been involved in the last successful contract with Felicity Ltd., and was not associated with the current contract, Manning decided he was the most suitable man for the job.

After spending three whole weeks independently investigating all design feasibilities associated with the project, Rogers produced a report which was highly critical of the design features of some very crucial parts of the project. Manning passed it on to Bert Phillips, project manager, expressly warning him of the possible consequences that might follow should the contents of the report prove to be correct. A meeting was called on that day to discuss the report, and by a majority vote, coupled with assurances from Phillips that the project was going well, they decided to ignore the report.

At this time, Manning personally felt that Mark Rogers was correct in his assessment of the state of the project, but he felt Phillips, as project manager, must be given a free hand to decide upon his own affairs. But now, with Mark Rogers's letter of resignation in the trash can, he felt a little uncomfortable. He collected the pieces carefully and taped them together. He felt worse now than he felt when he first looked at it, and he pondered his problem.

Exhibit 1
Maintrel Ltd. (A)
Partial Organization Structure

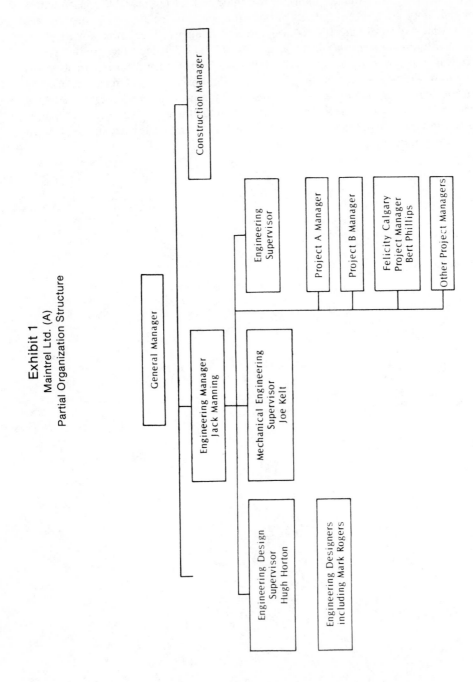

21
Ottawa Valley Food Products Ltd.

In his fourteen years as plant manager for Ottawa Valley Food Products Limited, Ralph Jennings felt he had not faced a more difficult management decision than he did on February 13. Earlier that day, he had fired his personal secretary, Mary Gregory, for refusing to pick up the Valentine gift he had selected the day before for his wife.

Ottawa Valley Food Products Limited (OVFP) was a small company located in Arnprior, Ontario, about 65 kilometres southwest of Ottawa. The company manufactured nine varieties of specialty snack crackers sold primarily in national grocery store chains. Over one hundred production workers and eighteen management and support staff were employed by OVFP.

Ralph Jennings had worked for OVFP for thirty-one years, beginning as a production line worker at the age of twenty-three. Although he had not obtained a college or university degree, he was very well respected by his superiors and his peers for his plant management expertise. In fact, many OVFP employees felt much of the company's current success could be attributed to Ralph Jennings's never-ending dedication to operating "the most efficient production process in the entire Ottawa Valley."

Mr. Jennings's high expectations of his employees were exceeded only by those he placed upon himself. It was not uncommon to find him working at his cluttered desk past 8 o'clock at night or on a Saturday or Sunday afternoon.

At fifty-four years of age with over thirty years of company service, Ralph Jennings was eligible for early retirement in one year. However, when approached by the personnel department about the subject, Ralph had laughed and said he was too busy to consider retirement.

Mary Gregory, twenty-three, had been hired by OVFP January 16 after completing the last semester of a two-year Secretarial Studies program at an Ottawa community college. A description of the program's core courses appears as Exhibit 1. Mary had graduated fourth in her class of 104 students.

Having moved from Arnprior to Ottawa for her college program, Mary was extremely pleased when an opening for a secretary became available in her home town at OVFP. She had responded to a newspaper ad along with seven other applicants. After several interviews, the personnel department awarded Mary the position of personal secretary to Ralph Jennings. Mary's desire to become a "professional" secretary had finally become a reality.

Upon returning from lunch with a customer's purchasing agent, Ralph sat with his chair facing the window and tried to recount the events leading up to Mary's dismissal earlier that day.

When Miss Arnold had been required to retire as a result of deteriorating eyesight after ten years as his personal secretary, Ralph was bitterly disappointed. Miss Arnold was fifty-eight years old when she retired. As a team, Ralph and Miss Arnold had worked extremely well together and had become very close friends. When required, Miss Arnold had always been willing to work overtime, often without pay, even if it meant breaking a previous personal commitment. Ralph recalled that somehow she had known when things were building up on him and she would go out of her way to eliminate any unnecessary distractions from his work . . . including taking part of her lunch hour to run various errands for him.

Why then, wondered Ralph, had Mary reacted so strongly to his request to take *company* time to pick up a Valentine gift for his wife? She had simply snapped, "no bloody way" and had stomped out of his office. It wasn't as if he asked her all the time to run special errands for him. Didn't she realize that he was a senior manager in the company and his time was better spent on pressing company problems? Ralph remembered making the same type of request of Miss Arnold many times and never experiencing any problems whatsoever. Is it not a personal secretary's responsibility to help improve the efficiency and effectiveness of her boss, Ralph mused?

While he was generally satisfied with Mary's performance to date, Ralph recalled that she had exhibited this type of behavior several times since joining the company and each time it had become more disruptive.

The first incident occurred on Mary's first day on the job. Ralph recalled he had asked Mary to bring him a coffee while he read the production reports from the previous day. This was a morning routine he had practised for almost ten years! Mary had said she was quite busy and unable to get him his coffee. However, Ralph knew that he had purposefully given Mary a light workload to complete considering that it was her first day. With a busy day ahead, Ralph let the incident go by without further comment or thought.

The second incident was related, but more disruptive and serious in nature. For several months, OVFP had been trying to secure an order from a national chain that had not been carrying OVFP's cracker products. A meeting with Ralph had been requested by the chain store's purchasing agent, in order to confirm OVFP's ability to produce and ship sufficient quantities of product on a long-term basis.

On the day of the meeting, Ralph had ushered the purchasing agent into his office and asked Mary to prepare and bring coffee for both men. Within hearing range of the purchasing agent, Mary had refused. She had explained that she was not hired as a coffee maker. Ralph had remained calm and was forced to prepare the coffee himself. Ralph recalled how humiliated he had felt during the rest of the meeting. Ralph managed to regain his confidence and composure and was able to negotiate a successful contract. When the meeting ended, Ralph called Mary into his office and demanded an explanation. Ralph remembered Mary only repeated her previous comment, "I wasn't hired as a coffee maker and that's that!"

Staring out the window, Ralph was convinced he had worked too hard for too long to gain his current level of authority and respect and he wasn't about to hand over control to a "green" college kid! He would simply find someone more like Miss Arnold to fill Mary's position.

With these thoughts in his mind, Ralph once again felt justified in his decision to dismiss Mary and he returned to the pile of papers on his desk.

At exactly 2:30 that afternoon Ralph heard a knock at his door. Karen Russell, a highly respected, well-liked secretary, entered his office. Without comment, Karen presented to Mr. Jennings a one-page note and left immediately. The note explained that all nine remaining secretaries had left their respective posts in support of Mary Gregory and were congregated in the employees' lounge.

Stunned, Ralph read over the note three times before its message became clear. Either he backed down and reversed his decision to dismiss Mary by 3 o'clock that afternoon, or all ten secretaries, including Mary, would travel to an Ottawa radio station to publicize their grievance. Apparently, the producer of the radio station's 6 o'clock newscast had promised to air the secretaries' complaint if it was not resolved by showtime.

Bewildered, Ralph checked the time on his watch — a watch he had received for thirty years of distinguished service to OVFP Ltd. It was 2:42 p.m. With less than twenty minutes in which to make a decision, Ralph wondered what action, if any he should take.

Exhibit 1
Secretarial Studies Program

Core courses include:

1) Word Processing I, II
2) Records Management
3) Office and Administrative Functions I, II
4) Written Communication
5) Introductory Business Administration
6) Introductory Economics
7) Office Environment Planning
8) Human Relations in the Organization

22
Pollockk Emergency Vehicle Sales Ltd.

On June 1, a meeting had been held between Peter Dekker, production foreman; Jim Devanie, fibreglass mould maker; and Dan Patterson, general manager; to make final arrangements for the new fibreglass headliner, required for a new class of ambulance, the SBS74. It was agreed that Jim would have the new mould completed and the first headliner ready for installation by July 31. After a conversation with the first SBS74 customer, Dan decided a few changes should be made in the headliner. The customer felt that having a storage cupboard in the headliner would be useful. On June 15, Dan instructed Jim to make several design changes. Two days later, Peter noticed the changes and instructed Jim to change the work back to the original specifications. To carry out Peter's instructions, Jim would drop a week behind schedule unless he worked a considerable amount of overtime. This was not the first time that Jim had been forced to work weekends because of a mix-up between Peter and Dan. Outraged, Jim demanded that Peter find out who was boss or he was quitting that afternoon.

The Ambulance Division was engaged in custom designing and building ambulances. The basic process involved the modification and conversion of existing vehicles. Production orders would be received from the customer by Peter. He would estimate completion dates and schedule the completion of the preliminary vehicle work. Wood and fibreglass products would be brought directly to the vehicle for installation on schedule. Preliminary work usually took one day and the entire production five days, once the wood and fibreglass parts were available. A lead time of two weeks was required for the wood and fibreglass shops.

Peter Dekker was forty years old. Prior to joining Pollockk's he was employed as a foreman for a local furniture plant. Having five children, Peter had been forced to moonlight as a cab driver. The increased wage at Pollockk's enabled him to give up the cab job. Within a year after joining Pollockk's, Peter had started work on a new five-bedroom house. Peter believed that it was best to treat his men as friends. He was always reluctant to assert authority. If a man was slacking off, Peter would assign the work to someone else rather than discipline the worker.

The general manager, Dan Patterson, previously had been the sole owner of the Ambulance Division for twenty-seven years. Stiff competition and a need for future capital forced Dan to merge with Pollockk's. Prior to going into business, Dan had spent five years as an officer in the navy. Exhibit 1 shows the organizational structure before and after the merger.

Jim Devanie was forty-five years old. He had been in the mould-making trade for twenty-two years. Previously, Jim had worked for a large mobile home manufacturer as head of the fibreglass department, where he had been in charge of new mould preparations and repairs to the old ones. Fabricating moulds was a painstaking task which required a great deal of experience. Jim was highly regarded by the mobile home manufacturer's management. He said that he quit there to come to Pollockk's because the pressures of having more than one boss hindered his workmanship.

Jim was periodically absent because of a drinking problem. His attendance was very irregular, but when he was on the job he did excellent work. Under most circumstances management wouldn't have kept him on, but his skills were such that he was worth the trouble. Jim took great pride in his moulds. He made it quite clear to Peter that he wanted to know who his boss was and that he would only report to that one boss.

Peter was unsure what to do. He felt that Jim was just blowing off steam, but a confrontation with Dan might be necessary.

Exhibit 1
Pollockk Emergency Vehicle Sales Limited
Organizational Structure of Ambulance Manufacturing Division

BEFORE MERGER

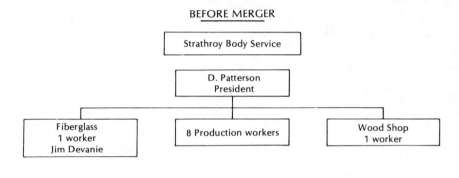

AFTER MERGER

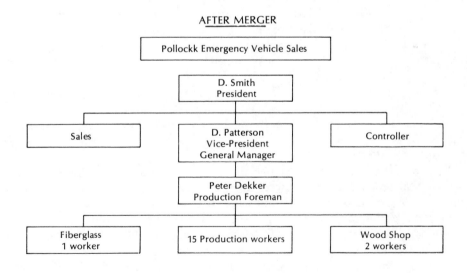

23
Queon Textile Mills Ltd.

Allan Bulmer, general foreman of the Queenstown plant of Queon Textile, had just received a call from Mrs. Floyd Woods concerning the disciplinary action taken against her husband during the night shift.

Allan Bulmer was fifty-two years old. He was born and raised in Queenstown and had known the Woodses for as long as he could remember. Mr. Bulmer had been with Queon Textile for over twenty-eight years, having joined them as an unskilled worker. His willingness to undertake difficult assignments had led to further opportunities in the Queenstown mill. Mr. Bulmer had done almost every job there was in the Queenstown plant, and was promoted to assistant foreman, then foreman, and finally general foreman. As general foreman, Mr. Bulmer reported to the plant superintendent and was responsible for the scheduling of men and machinery. Under his direct supervision, he had seven operating foremen and one foreman responsible for maintenance.

Floyd Woods was fifty-five. He was born in Queenstown and had joined Queon Textile twenty-five years ago. He joined the company as a skilled tradesman, assigned to the Repair and Maintenance Department. Mr. Woods's skills were highly regarded in the Queenstown mill, and he had proven to be its most able maintenance man. Several times, Mr. Woods had been offered a promotion to assistant foreman but had declined. Three years ago, however, the opening of assistant foreman was posted on the employees' bulletin board before being offered to Mr. Woods. Immediately after the notice was posted, Mr. Woods went to the personnel manager and asked why the job had not been offered to him first. The personnel manager replied that, given his continual refusals, he had assumed he was not interested in the job. Mr. Woods responded that he could do the job and that he was the best man in the department. After further discussion, Mr. Woods applied for, was offered, and accepted the position of assistant foreman.

Mr. Woods undertook the assignment with relish. The foreman of maintenance, Gerry Clarke, was a man Mr. Woods had trained several years before, and he was glad to have him as his assistant. Mr. Woods was given the task of managing the night shift maintenance schedule, which was a change because previously he had worked the prime shift from 08 00 to 16 00.

For several months after the change, things seemed to go well, and Mr. Clarke was satisfied. Maintenance schedules were kept, and the work done was of acceptable quality. However, some eighteen months after Mr. Woods's appointment as assistant foreman, the performance of the night shift work crew began to deteriorate. Consequently, Mr. Clarke approached Mr. Woods about the problem. Mr. Woods said he had not realized that the work was sloppy, and that he would talk to his crew that night. The talk between Clarke and Woods seemed to have some effect. The quality of work returned to its past level.

Several weeks before, Mr. Woods had shown up for the night shift intoxicated. When this was discovered, a warning was given and Mr. Woods was sent home. Thereafter, it was not obvious that Mr. Woods was drinking, though his speech and movements became awkward as the night shift passed. Concurrently, the level of performance of the night shift maintenance group again deteriorated. Several of the night shift workers complained to Mr. Clarke about Mr. Woods.

In response to the complaints, Mr. Clarke returned to the plant in the middle of the night shift and found Mr. Woods asleep. Mr. Clarke awakened Mr. Woods with difficulty and told him he was suspended. An argument followed which ended with Mr. Clarke stating that Mr. Woods's days as an assistant foreman were over, and about all Mr. Woods was good for was pushing a broom, "if he could ever find the right end of the handle." Mr. Clarke, with the help of a few night shift workers, was able to get Mr. Woods into a taxicab and on his way home.

The next morning, Mrs. Woods called Mr. Bulmer and asked him to rescind Mr. Clarke's decision to demote her husband. Mrs. Woods stated that she was concerned about any change in Mr. Woods's status that would affect him and make his situation worse. Upon questioning, Mrs. Woods admitted that her husband did have a drink or two before going to work, but "nothing that would cause any problems." In concluding her call Mrs. Woods stated she could not understand how the company could treat a loyal employee this way.

24
Royal Hardware Co. Ltd.

John Kurtis decided it was time for action. His company was in the midst of an internal reorganization, but Ernie Lamb, one of his oldest and dearest friends, was impeding the completion of the reorganization. Every day, John Kurtis received more and more complaints concerning Ernie's lack of cooperation, especially towards Stan Burns, the new production supervisor.

COMPANY BACKGROUND

Royal Hardware was located in Hartsville, population 84 000: situated eighty kilometres from a major industrial and commercial area. Forty years ago, Royal was formed through the purchase of a business by the Kurtis family. The main function of the business was the manufacturing and wholesaling of doorknobs, shelving, and miscellaneous hardware items. In the years that followed, Royal was able to identify a profitable market segment, which it successfully exploited. Consequently, Royal's growth had been quite rapid in the past decade.

CURRENT PRODUCTION LINES

At the time of reorganization, a buyer could choose from 520 hardware items, some with up to ten colour and material variations. Royal was widely known in the industry for its custom work, whereby it would copy any competitor's product or make a product to the customer's specifications. Royal's production strategy could be summarized by the quote: "We will produce anything, and in any amount, as long as we have an order for it."

The company assembled and manufactured most of its own parts. In contrast, the competition was more dependent on suppliers for unassembled parts.

A small part of the firm's business also involved the distribution of a line of small consumer appliances. Another division of Royal manufactured gaskets for industrial use.

Royal faced severe competition in the hardware field. The hardware line was not expected to grow as rapidly as in the past. However, the company, in Mr. Kurtis's opinion, could still remain competitive by developing better operating information and controls. John Kurtis believed the need for Royal to reorganize was crucial.

PRODUCTION

Production was carried out on two floors of the Royal plant. On the lower level, forty-one people were employed in the control of inventory, shipping and receiving, stamping, degreasing, plating, and painting. Sixteen people were employed on the second floor, working on design, component manufacturing, and assembly. One elevator was the main means of moving goods between the two floors and had become a bottleneck in the production flow.

John Kurtis stated that he wanted a reorganization of the production and support activities to insure efficient and effective production. Currently, there were no formal organization and scheduling, inventory, purchasing, sales, and production procedures. Consequently, there were many inefficiencies, such as: one, salespeople sometimes brought in orders for immediate delivery of discontinued lines; two, inventories became obsolete — $192 000 had been written off the previous year; three, there were many complaints by production workers of the poor quality of parts which led to constant adjustments of assembly tasks; four, employees spent too much time searching for parts; and five, because deadlines had not been met, parts for orders were not available, and consequently Royal had high work in process inventories.

John Kurtis had appointed Stan Burns as production supervisor and had given him the task of developing a formal production system for Royal. In addition, John Kurtis had asked Ernie Lamb, who had the background knowledge of Royal's operation, to help coordinate the various activities required for the reorganization.

RAW MATERIALS HANDLING

In the past, the raw materials inventory was handled by the lead hands in each department and coordinated through the plant's superintendent. Now, Stan Burns, Ernie Lamb, and Will Hilton were assigned to coordinate the three classifications of raw materials: glass, sheet materials, and miscellaneous. Ernie Lamb also was supposed to aid Will Hilton in developing a material requisition system, but as Mr. Hilton commented, "Ernie says he is always too busy in the plant (where Stan's supposed to have control) to help me out. This is the same story everyone else gets too. The employees and old customers keep asking for Ernie, and that doesn't help either."

PERSONNEL

In the Hartsville plant and head office, Royal employed seventy-two people. Fifty-seven were hourly rated production workers, eight were salaried office staff, and seven were members of the management team. (Personal data for the management team are outlined in Exhibit 1.) In general, worker–management relations were satisfactory. The workers were divided into two segments, older and younger. Their feelings about the reorganization and the new appointments could be summarized as follows:

Older Worker: "Stan's been trying hard to get things running the way he thinks they should, by using all his new ideas, but Ernie's the only one here who knows how this place really works. We make this place run and Ernie knows that."

Younger Worker: "It's good at last to have someone at the controls who's got some new ideas in his head. You've got to change with the times — Stan can, but Ernie's been here too long."

Ernie Lamb took great pride in the fact that he had worked his way up, and that he had "helped them make the place what it is." Recently, Ernie Lamb had been honoured at a special banquet by the workers in celebration of his golden anniversary with Royal. When he was plant manager, Ernie had been very popular with the workers. It was not uncommon for him to socialize with them off the job. Ernie Lamb commented on his old job as follows: "I've gained the workers' respect and they've got mine. You need that around here. If you don't have confidence in each other, the problems that pop up will never get solved. Now they've got me in another part of the plant, and I'm supposed to be tied to a desk writing down all that I know. My place is on the floor! That's what I'm good at, and the workers need me there too!"

There was no formal personnel department. Salaried staff were hired by John Kurtis and Keith Holland, while hourly workers were hired by Stan Burns and Keith Holland. The last union contract brought Royal up to, and slightly above, the standards of other Hartsville plants.

The union contract had no mandatory retirement age, and thus many of the workers were over sixty years old. The average age of the employees was forty-four years. There was a four-to-one ratio of women to men in the plant. Key plant jobs were held by senior employees and there were no back-up personnel to replace them if they left or were absent. At present, Stan Burns was looking for three additional workers to train in specialized work. This step was being taken to ensure that production bottle-necks were not caused by absenteeism, and that additional capacity would be available for rush periods.

Royal had a very low turnover of workers, which the employees attributed to: a wage which was characterized as being "good" or "acceptable," the relative infre-quency of layoffs in the plant, and the fact that the jobs were neither too difficult nor too demanding.

Stan Burns believed that the workers, especially the older ones, felt that there was no reason to do above-average work, since there was no pay or incentive for doing so. While management wanted to develop an incentive program, one could not be intro-duced until proper work standards had been established. Management, at one point, did try to introduce a piecework plan, but the workers rejected the offer due primarily to an inadequate inventory system which would have meant that they would spend a lot of time searching for parts.

Despite the lack of an incentive plan, the employees gave the following reasons for the good morale: (1) they were happy with the new contract and higher wages; (2) some new equipment had made jobs easier; (3) more women were recently hired, therefore the seniority and security of workers increased, and (4) the new management changes had shown that the company cared, and was not "old-fashioned" as it had been before.

Management was on a bonus plan, which provided a bonus related to overall profits and individual performance. Since many believed the new internal reorganiza-tion would increase Royal's efficiency, Royal's executives felt that their bonus would be augmented once the change had been completed.

MANAGEMENT ORGANIZATION

Royal had never developed a formal organization structure. There was much confu-sion over the lines of authority and communication. The confusion was greatest among the new members of the management team: Stan Burns, Will Hilton, and Keith Holland.

Prior to the reorganization, Ernie Lamb had been responsible for inventory, production, scheduling, and shipping, as well as general plant upkeep. Overall, Ernie Lamb had to make sure that the plant could produce what was demanded by the sales force and to get the products out to meet delivery deadlines. With reorganization, two new positions — scheduling and controlling — were created, and the old position of plant supervisor was eliminated and changed to production supervisor. The scheduling and control funons were given to Will Hilton and Keith Holland, respectively. Stan Burns was appointed to the new position of production supervisor.

Ernie's job as plant manager had now been redefined; he was assigned the following tasks in the office: to compare all labour standards against actual standards and to perform the analysis appropriate for recommending change to Ned Learner, the costing coordinator; to work directly with the designer, Stew Morris, and Ned Learner in developing accurate material lists for costing purposes; to work with Keith Holland and Will Hilton in the development of a materials requisition system for purchasing; and to be available to Stan in an advisory capacity relating to production problems on which Stan needed assistance.

However, Ernie had not been carrying out these tasks. He was aware of the inventory and purchasing problems, but as he said, "I can't see the relevance of this job. I'm a people person, not a paper person."

In relation to Stan Burns, Ernie Lamb said, "Stan will have to learn it as I learned it . . . he will have to make his own decisions." Ernie Lamb was still the main focus of plant communications. The employees still went to Ernie Lamb, not Stan Burns, for advice and help. The consequences of this situation could be illustrated by the following comments:

Ernie: "What's the use of going to Stan, when he doesn't have the answer?"

Stan: "How can I get experience when people still go to Ernie?"

Ernie: "I can't concentrate on my new job since daily problems take up too much time."

Will Hilton, Stan Burns and Ned Learner all felt that Ernie Lamb could be of great help to them, if he would apply his knowledge to establishing standards and proper purchasing and inventory systems instead of handling day-to-day problems. Ernie had indicated an interest in retiring within two years, but there had been questions raised about his value to the company if his behaviour continued to emphasize short-term activities.

DILEMMA

All management agreed that the dilemma of poor operating control was due to lack of planned coordination between all functions of production. However, Royal was now actively trying to solve these problems, but before they could be solved, John Kurtis had to do something about his management personnel problems which seemed to centre around Ernie Lamb.

Exhibit 1
Royal Hardware Co. Ltd.
Background on the Company Operations
Management Personnel Data

STAN BURNS

Position:	Production Supervisor
Age:	43
Years with company:	1
Background:	Design and Metal Works Foreman
Responsibilities:	Maintain and improve production, handle personnel function for plant
Education:	Engineering diploma from U.K.

WILL HILTON

Position:	Production Co-ordinator (Scheduling)
Age:	37
Years with company:	2
Background:	Production planning supervisor in clothing industry
Responsibilities:	Scheduling, inventory control, purchasing for some parts
Education:	Grade 12 and production planning courses

KEITH HOLLAND

Position:	Controller
Age:	34
Years with company:	1.5
Background:	Sales management and office administration in drug industry
Responsibilities:	Office management, development and operation of control systems
Education:	Attended university for three and one-half years, R.I.A.

NED LEARNER

Position:	Costing Coordinator
Age:	47
Years with company:	21
Background:	Costing and standards development, maintaining and updating material and labour standards, costing and production
Education:	Grade 12

ERNIE LAMB

Position:[1]	Plant Manager
Age:	68
Years with company:	50
Background:	Has worked his way up in plant
Responsibilities:	Developing purchasing control, pricing, updating standards, establishing information flows
Education:	Grade 10

GORD PULDING

Position:	Vice-President and Sales Manager
Age:	69
Years with company:	30
Background:	Selling and administration
Responsibilities:	Development and sales territories, account administration, sales force management, pricing
Education:	Attended university for three years

JOHN KURTIS

Position:	President and majority shareholder
Age:	53
Years with company:	31
Background:	Commissioned officer in the RCAF, purchasing of some parts, personnel administration and public relations

[1]Ernie Lamb was employed for ten years with the original company that the Kurtis family bought.

25
Stockmall Industries

"John, I feel like resigning," Paul DeMarco said, "even if I have been here only three months and just moved my family to this town."

John Wilson, who had been the President of Stockmall Industries for eighteen months, replied, "Surely there is some way you and Churchill can work this problem out." "I doubt it," said DeMarco as he left Wilson's office.

Mr. DeMarco, who had received his Registered Industrial Accountant (RIA) professional designation five years ago, and an MBA degree last year, had recently been hired by Mr. Wilson for the position of Controller. Mr. DeMarco, aged 30, had previously worked for Mr. Wilson at another firm. Both were now employed by Stockmall Industries, a light manufacturing and assembly subsidiary of a British company in London, England. Stockmall Industries was located in a small town of about 10 000 people in a Maritime province.

Mr. Alec Churchill, the financial director, was 66 years old, and had emigrated to Canada from England thirty-five years ago. After working for a bank for a few years he joined one of the bank's customers — Stockmall Industries — as the financial manager. His younger brother, Sir Arthur Churchill, had become a well known industrialist in England. Seventeen years ago, at Alec's recommendation, Sir Arthur's mini-conglomerate purchased controlling interest of Stockmall Industries. The original founder, Jonas Stockmall, remained as president until Mr. Wilson joined the company. Mr. Stockmall and both Churchill brothers agreed on Mr. Wilson's selection. Alec Churchill did not want the job, as he was getting on in years and wanted to cut back on his workload, though he had no immediate plans for retirement.

Although now retired, Mr. Stockmall remained on the Canadian Board of Directors, and he and Mr. Churchill had become the best of friends. In addition to Mr. Stockmall, Mr. Wilson, and Mr. Alec Churchill, the Board consisted of the following:

Mrs. Helen Irving — sister of Mr. Stockmall and current city councilwoman.
Mr. Patrick Miller — a young business attorney, appointed by Mr. Wilson.

At the time Mr. Wilson became president, Canada was in a recession, and all efforts were spent trying to maintain sales and keep costs under control. Stockmall Industries weathered the recession well, and Sir Arthur was most pleased with Mr. Wilson's performance. As the recession eased, Mr. Wilson made plans for the establishment of a proper cost control and reporting system, and hired Mr. DeMarco as controller. Although no formal job descriptions were in existence, the plan was to have Mr. Alec Churchill continue with duties of the treasurer: cash management, bank relations, credit and collections, etc. Mr. DeMarco was to handle the control functions: reports, financial statement preparation, etc.

Mr. Churchill had hired three assistants in the past, but none had lasted more than a couple of months. Five clerks worked in the finance and accounting department. Formally, the Controller (Mr. DeMarco) would report to the finance director (Mr. Churchill), but Mr. Wilson had been clear about the fact that he wanted Mr. DeMarco to report to *him* on the cost control systems being developed. Although there would certainly be areas where Messrs. Churchill and DeMarco's functions would overlap, it was clear that Mr. DeMarco was not to be Mr. Churchill's assistant. If required, however, each would fill in for the other in the other's absence.

Mr. DeMarco had moved his wife and two young children about 500 miles (800 kilometres) to join Stockmall Industries. The DeMarcos were young, energetic, and personable. They were immediately welcomed and accepted into the community, joining some civic clubs and attending many social functions. They enjoyed their new home and hoped to stay for some time.

At the office, Mr. DeMarco's friendly style made him a hit with the financial staff and with other executives (i.e., sales and production). The sales director informed Mr. Wilson that he had overheard one finance clerk tell another that "it sure is nice having someone who actually explains things to you, instead of being impatient like Churchill."

Mr. DeMarco felt that he and Mr. Churchill were not getting along especially well. Mr. DeMarco believed that Mr. Churchill was forever "looking over my shoulder." In addition, Mr. Churchill continually asked him for advice regarding treasury duties. He didn't think Mr. Churchill was that competent and had only risen to his current position because of his brother and Mr. Stockmall's friendship.

Mr. Wilson was somewhat perplexed. He knew and liked Mr. DeMarco, and believed he was extremely competent. The new cost control system was coming along much faster than even Mr. Wilson had expected. Mr. DeMarco had brought some of the latest management techniques to Stockmall and in the future Mr. Wilson could see a number of challenging problems to which Mr. DeMarco could be assigned.

Messrs. Churchill and DeMarco had recently had a couple of heated disagreements, and Mr. Wilson had decided to call the two men together to try to resolve the situation. At the meeting, Mr. Churchill said that he did not like Mr. DeMarco's "cocky" attitude and he believed "this kid is trying to undermine my position." DeMarco denied the accusation, but stated that he could "easily handle both jobs." Both men left the meeting upset, with no resolution of the problem in sight.

Word of the conflict between the two had been brought to Mr. Stockmall's and Mrs. Irving's attention by Mr. Churchill. It also leaked into the community as Mr. DeMarco was asked about it at a civic club meeting by Stockmall's local bank manager.

Shortly before the meeting, Mr. Wilson and Mr. Churchill had travelled on business to London, England. No mention of the situation was made to Sir Arthur during any company discussions. Mr. Churchill stayed in London for an additional two weeks to visit his family, and returned to find the office working well, and up to date on all financial and accounting matters. Neither man spoke to the other, except to say hello. Mr. Churchill could see, however, that things had gone well in his absence.

Within a week, the two men had clashed again, this time over the reporting of cost data to be used in the projected financial statements for the next year. These statements were prepared by DeMarco, and were to be presented to the bank manager by Churchill as part of an application for an increase in the company's line of credit. With the two men still at odds with each other, and the presentation scheduled for the next day, Mr. Wilson wondered what to do to resolve the situation.

SECTION V
An Introduction to Industrial Relations

Since the early 1880s, organized labour has played an increasingly important part in the Canadian economy. The union movement has grown to the point where more than one in every four Canadian workers is a union member, and where approximately 40 percent of the country's nonagricultural workers are members of unions. Much of what we think about organized labour and collective bargaining comes to us through the media, and we tend to think that strikes, violence, and militancy are the major characteristics of unions and collective bargaining situations. As in almost all things, though, the media tend to report the exception rather than the rule with regard to industrial relations. In truth, well over 90 percent of all contract negotiations end in a settlement rather than a strike, and under collective bargaining, most disputes between employers and their unionized employees are handled in an orderly and peaceful way by arbitration during the term of a collective agreement.

Regardless of what one's opinions of unions are, the fact remains that in Canada, public policy says that employees have a basic right to form or join unions, and that if they choose to do so, the employer must bargain with them over wages, hours, and other conditions of employment. Thus, virtually all employers face one of two possible situations: either the presence of a union in the workplace or the potential presence of a union in the workplace.

Consequently, managers need an understanding of our industrial relations system, including an understanding of organized labour and its origins, structure, and functions. Managers need also to know something of the legal framework within which collective bargaining occurs, as well as the actual mechanics of the collective bargaining process. This chapter will present such an overview of Canadian industrial relations under the following headings: (1) A Brief History of Canadian Industrial Relations; (2) Union Organizing and Certification; (3) The Union–Management Relationship; (4) Dispute-Handling Mechanisms; and (5) The Contemporary Canadian Labour Movement.

A BRIEF HISTORY OF CANADIAN INDUSTRIAL RELATIONS

Three basic "freedoms" underlie the labour relations systems in Canada. They are: (1) employees should be free to organize; (2) representatives of employees should be able to engage employers in bargaining; and (3) employees and employers should be free to invoke meaningful sanctions in support of their positions: employees to withdraw services, that is to strike, and employers to close their doors, that is to lock out or to take a strike. One hundred and fifty years ago, all three of these component freedoms did not exist. The history of Canadian industrial relations, then, is really the story of the development of employee organizations and the development of these three "freedoms."

Preparation of this chapter was significantly influenced by Professor David Peach, a co-author of *The Practice of Industrial Relations*, Revised Edition (Toronto: McGraw-Hill Ryerson, 1985).

Union organization in Canada began in the early 1800s. During the first half of that century the union movement came under two direct influences: domination by skilled trade organizations and the impact of British and European tradesmen. The majority of early union activities centred on the skilled trades: the earliest organizing activity occurred among tradesmen in Saint John, N.B., in 1812. Many tradesmen in Canada were immigrants, and they brought with them the traditions of the older British and European labour movements. Although this connection rapidly diminished during the second half of the nineteenth century, it put an international focus on the Canadian labour movement. Today this international orientation is one of the major aspects of industrial relations in Canada.

Organization by crafts and trades dominated the movement until the 1930s and 1940s. The change to "industrial" organization is the subject of much of what follows in this section.

Early organization was encumbered by two legal concepts which had been inherited through British common law. The Masters and Servants Act discouraged, under penalty of imprisonment, a worker's moving from one job to another. Such action was liable to charges of breach of contract. Also, the Criminal Conspiracy Doctrine maintained that it was a criminal activity for workers to combine to seek collective rewards. These two legal constraints were used repeatedly in the early 1800s to discourage labour organization.

The first major turning point in Canadian labour history occurred in 1872. The initial impetus for the changes that followed was a strike in April by Toronto printers, members of the Typographical Society. The issue was singular: the printers wanted their working day reduced from ten to nine hours. The employers, led by George Brown, rejected their demands and the strike ensued. In Canada's first real demonstration of labour solidarity, the Toronto Trades Assembly, which represented twenty-four unions in the city, showed its support for the printers in a mass rally on April 15. Brown then secured the arrest of the leaders of all affiliated unions under the conspiracy doctrine. The men were arrested, tried and convicted on April 17. News of this resulted in another mass meeting calling for political action. Action came in the form of the Trade Union Act of 1872, which said that, henceforth, combining to bargain collectively would not be considered criminal conspiracy.

The impetus behind the Trade Union Act is interesting. Similar legislation recognizing labour's right to organize had been passed in England in 1871. However, the immediate reasoning behind the Canadian legislation was more political than historical. John A. Macdonald, the Conservative prime minister, secured passage of the act on April 18 in order to embarrass his political opponent, the Liberal George Brown. Regardless, the legislation resulted in victory for the striking workers; their work day was reduced to nine hours. By the end of the year, many major industries, including the railroads, had adopted the nine-hour work day.

While the act theoretically opened the way for labour to organize actively, such was not the case for many years, primarily because of the passage in the same year of the Criminal Law Amendment Act which provided penalties for violence or intimidation during strikes and also established that a union–management contract was not legally binding. Therefore, although the conspiracy doctrine was theoretically dead, union organization was still considered in practice to fall into the criminal conspiracy realm and was treated as such until the mid-1900s. It was not until 1943 that Ontario finally did away with the conspiracy doctrine.

Out of the success of the printers' strike, Canada's first union combination was formed. In May 1872, union members from Toronto, Brantford, and Montreal met to discuss common problems. The result was the formation of the Canadian Labour Union (CLU) in September. However, despite the successes of 1872, the labour movement did not grow significantly; by World War I, less than 10 percent of Canadian workers were organized.

In the period leading up to 1918 the labour movement became increasingly dominated by American unions. In 1886, the Knights of Labor, an industrial organization originally founded in Chicago, combined with a number of Canadian craft unions to form the Trades and Labour Congress (TLC). In addition to the international aspect of this merger, it also represented the first time a merger had combined industrial and craft unions, which led to further trouble in the labour movement.

Under pressure from the American Federation of Labour (AFL), a predominantly craft union combination, the TLC in 1902 expelled the Knights from its ranks because they competed in the U.S. with AFL affiliates. Further, at its 1902 convention the TLC elected as its president a paid officer of the international union. Thus, Canada's largest union organization clearly opted for U.S. domination and organization along craft or trade lines.

Following World War I, the 1918 TLC convention demanded a shift toward industrial organization and greater Canadian control. Western delegates who had spearheaded the demand for change met in March 1919 and formed the One Big Union (OBU). They resolved to cut their affiliation with international organizations and to organize along industrial lines.

Concurrent with this development was the Winnipeg General Strike. Workers, dissatisfied with their economic lot in light of their contribution to the war effort, demanded an eight-hour day, double pay for overtime, and recognition of the newly formed Metal Trades Council. With 35 000 workers on strike, the city of Winnipeg was paralyzed, support spread throughout the labour movement across Canada, and as a result all three levels of government joined to end the disruption. When Winnipeg policemen and firemen joined the strike, the Royal Canadian Mounted Police, supported by "irregulars," entered the city. One month after the strike began, its leaders were arrested and in the riot which resulted during a protest rally, two demonstrators were killed, thirty were injured, and over one hundred persons were arrested. Winnipeg was placed under military control. Forty-one days after it started, the General Strike was broken.

Little was gained from the strike. Some concessions were made concerning the length of the working week. However, the image of radicalism it fostered tainted the union movement for years to come and led to the deterioration of the OBU; by 1921 it had ceased to be a major force.

In 1938, U.S. domination of the labour movement was again confirmed when the AFL-controlled TLC expelled members affiliated with the newly formed Committee for Industrial Organization (CIO). The CIO was an AFL competitor, formed from dissident unions including the United Auto Workers (UAW)) and the United Mine Workers. As had been the case in 1902 when the Knights of Labor posed a threat to the AFL, so the CIO in its three-year history did the same. However, the expelled CIO unions combined in 1940 to form the Canadian Congress of Labour (CCL) which, because of its drive to organize along industrial lines, continued to grow at a faster rate than the predominantly craft-oriented TLC.

By the end of World War II, the AFL had softened its line on industrial organization and the two U.S. organizations and their Canadian counterparts staged bitter fights for members throughout the late 1940s. Because their efforts were proving to be counterproductive, the AFL and CIO merged in 1955 to form the AFL-CIO; in 1956, the TLC and CCL followed suit, merging to form the Canadian Labour Congress (CLC).

Legislative developments during the first half of this century focused primarily on dispute-settling measures and federal–provincial jurisdiction. The Conciliation Act of 1900 allowed the minister of labour to supply mediators to disputing parties if they requested such help. In 1903 the Railway Labour Disputes Act provided for compulsory mediation and arbitration for disputes involving railway workers. The arbitrator's recommendations, however, were nonbinding and the act provided no constraint on strikes or lockouts. The inadequacies of both the 1900 and the 1903 legislation were compensated for in 1906 with the Conciliation and Labour Act which was revised in 1907 and called the Industrial Disputes Investigation Act (IDI). The act called for compulsory conciliation of disputes and prohibited any activity beyond that of conciliation until the dispute had been fully investigated. Further, conciliation boards were given power to make recommendations concerning the outcome of the dispute. The act, however, failed to provide penalties for employers who actively fought against union-organizing drives. Regardless, the IDI remains as one of the keystone pieces of industrial relations legislation in Canada.

The jurisdiction of federal legislation was challenged in 1925 with the case of the *Toronto Electric Commission* v. *Snider*. The courts ruled that the IDI applied only to enumerated industries of a national nature. With the exception of Prince Edward Island, all provinces then either passed enabling legislation to make the IDI applicable or passed their own IDI-type legislation. As a result of the Snider case, the provinces have become the principal makers and enforcers of labour law in Canada.

This means that there are eleven different sets of labour laws in Canada, one for each of the provinces, and one for the federal jurisdiction. Consequently, it is somewhat difficult to generalize about labour legislation in Canada. The rules of the game vary from jurisdiction to jurisdiction, and for a full knowledge of those rules in any particular circumstance, the laws of the appropriate province or of the federal government must be consulted.

Beginning in 1940, the government of Canada (under the War Measures Act and via orders-in-council) introduced a series of labour relations regulations. These regulations guaranteed the freedom of workers to organize themselves into unions not dominated by employers, compelled employers to engage in collective bargaining with these organizations and provided for the use of strikes or lockouts after conciliation procedures were exhausted. Following the end of World War II and the dismantling of the wartime controls program, these provisions found their way into all of the provincial labour relations acts as well as that of the federal government.

These legislative guarantees opened the way for the massive growth of the labour movement in Canada in the postwar period and for a considerable amount of labour unrest caused in part by the years of sacrifice required during the war. A strike by Ford Motor Company workers in 1945 demanded, among other things, that their plant become a "union shop"; that is, employees had to be union members. In a precedent-setting decision, Justice Ivan Rand suggested and got agreement to a compromise which is now known as the Rand Formula. Under this arrangement, workers represented by a union must pay dues to their local, but they do not have to become members of the union.

This decision further advanced union security and has played an important part in the growth of organized labour in Canada since 1945.

The passage in 1967 of the Public Service Staff Relations Act was significant because it recognized that federal government employees had the right to organize and bargain in the same manner as private sector employees. The unionization of public employees at all levels — municipal, provincial, and federal — has represented the latest major growth in union ranks. Unionization of white-collar workers has occurred, but so far has not been as widespread as had been projected in the 1960s.

More recent developments will be discussed later in this chapter.

UNION ORGANIZATION AND CERTIFICATION

The labour relations acts of all Canadian jurisdictions provide for a labour relations board to administer that legislation. One of the duties given to labour relations boards is to determine whether employees indeed desire to be represented by a union and which particular union is desired, and also what particular grouping of employees is appropriate for bargaining purposes.

The process of organization begins when either a group of disgruntled employees seek out a large established union and ask its help, or when a field worker from a union contacts an employee of a nonunion shop and persuades him or her to help in an organizing drive.

After determining whether organization of the employees is feasible, the organizers invariably set about to sign up a majority of employees in the organization. This is done by having workers sign a card that indicates they wish to be represented by the union in question. The organizer's objective is to work as quickly and quietly as possible in order to avoid possible management retaliation. At times, though, organizing campaigns are quite open. Organizing activity is protected by the various labour relations acts, that is, employers are not permitted to discriminate against workers seeking union representation. However, it is obvious that such discrimination can occur and organizing campaigns are often conducted in secret to minimize this possibility.

The labour legislation in each of the Canadian jurisdictions differs slightly on the percentage of the proposed bargaining unit that the union is required to sign up before it can approach the labour relations board to request certification. In general, the organizers will attempt to sign up a majority of employees in the proposed bargaining unit before approaching the board. When it has achieved the required number of signed cards, the union then files an application with the labour relations board. It submits the cards as evidence of employee interest in being represented by the union, and also states which employees it seeks to include in the bargaining unit.

The board then notifies the employer that an application for certification has been made. The employer is asked to comment on the application and must conspicuously post a copy for all to see. At the same time, the employer must provide the board with a list of employees in the proposed bargaining unit along with specimen signatures so that the board can verify the sign-up cards.

The board then has a hearing on the application. In the hearing, the board will attempt to get enough information to do four things: (1) Determine the appropriateness of the unit. In general, the bargaining unit is generally agreed upon by the union and the company. If the bargaining unit cannot be agreed to by the parties, the board will itself decide on what is appropriate. General guidelines for assessing appropriateness are as follows: (a) Is the unit distinguishable by geography, skill, or craft? (b) Has the unit ever been agreed upon previously? (c) Is there a "community of interest among members of the unit"? (d) Are the typical lines of advancement/demotion found in the unit? (e) Is the proposed unit typical? (2) Determine number and percentage of employees indicating a desire for membership. (3) Entertain objections to certification from outside parties (e.g., competing unions). (4) Indicate subsequent action. The subsequent action taken by the board may be either an order for automatic certification, denial of certification, or an order for a representative vote on the question among employees under the auspices of the board. Usually, unions are certified automatically; that is, without an election being held to determine employees' desires in regard to certification, with the board relying on signed membership cards as sufficient evidence of this. In general, if the board is satisfied that a majority of employees in a bargaining unit wish to be represented by a union, they will certify that union without an election being held.

Once the union is certified as the bargaining agent for the employees in question, the board will then order the employer to bargain with that union with the object of achieving an agreement covering wages, hours, and other conditions of employment. It is then illegal for the employer to bargain with any other organization or with individual employees over the terms and conditions of employment. The union is certified as the *exclusive bargaining agent* for that group of employees.

THE UNION–MANAGEMENT RELATIONSHIP

Once certification has occurred, union, and management are free to develop whatever contract provisions they believe to be appropriate, and to develop a working relationship with each other. (In some jurisdictions, the board has the power to impose a first agreement if the parties cannot come to an agreement on it, but even where this power exists, it is rarely invoked by the board.) Thus, we find that a clear understanding of industrial relations requires some way of thinking about the union–management relationship. Traditionally, the relationship has been one of union challenge and management response. Considering the varied stances unions can adopt in their challenge and the equally varied stance management can adopt for its response, we find a model useful for studying the relationship. The varying types of relationships can be shown on what has been called the spectrum of union–management relations. Any particular union–management relationship will fall somewhere in this spectrum.[1]

---

[1]Benjamin Selekman et al., *Problems in Labor Relations*, 3rd ed. (New York: McGraw-Hill, 1965), pp. 1-11.

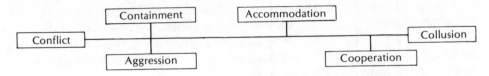

Conflict Relationship

Both parties are highly militant and communication or cooperation is nonexistent. The evolution of labour law has all but eliminated this particular posture.

Containment–Aggression Relationship

Both parties working under this relationship, while acting within the legal letter of their collective agreement, actively work to increase their degree of power. This stance is characterized by a sense of militancy and little cooperation or communication.

Accommodation Relationship

Both parties work within the bounds of their collective agreement while actively seeking to increase mutual trust. This posture is characterized by a degree of cooperation and communication above and beyond that demanded by the agreement. It is productive because it lessens the chance of disruptions and strikes.

Cooperative Relationship

Management considers labour as full partners in the business and the relationship is characterized by a very high degree of cooperation and communication, profit sharing, and participative management.

Collusive Relationship

Union acts in concert with management to the detriment of the membership. For example, a union fearing a raid might agree with management that in return for a high wage settlement (which would protect the incumbent against the raid) it would not fight technological changes which would reduce the work force.

The point at which any union–management relationship falls on the spectrum is dictated by a series of internal and external influences. Internally, a union's stance toward management evolves from the following:

1. Its history and tradition
2. The nature of its leadership
3. The current union political scene
4. Its policies regarding the collective agreement

External influences cannot be controlled by either party and obviously a complete list would be lengthy. Some major influences are:

1. The specific characteristics of the industry (elasticity of demand, degree of union-ization, intensiveness of labour content, cyclicability of business)
2. The state of technology and the degree of automation in the production process
3. Legislation
4. Government policy and administration
5. The judiciary
6. Socioeconomic conditions

DISPUTE-HANDLING MECHANISMS

Under Canadian labour legislation, the use of strikes or lockouts in the settling of disputes is restricted. Two of the principal ways of handling disputes in industrial relations prior to or instead of the strike or lockout are conciliation and arbitration.

Conciliation

Conciliation, or as it is sometimes called, mediation, is the intervention by a third party into negotiations to help produce an agreement. In Canada, in the negotiation of a collective agreement, the parties are required to submit any disputes to a conciliation officer before a strike can legally occur. This means that one of the parties must request the services of a conciliator to help resolve any disputes. However, this is sometimes just a formality since conciliation officers have no power to enforce their suggestions for settlement; they cannot require that the parties settle on any particular terms. The success of conciliation, therefore, depends first upon the disputing parties having an honest desire for agreement, and second, upon the persuasiveness of the conciliation officer. Under some circumstances, the labour minister can invoke a second level of conciliation activity which results in a set of recommendations for settlement that are made public. While these recommendations, which are made by a conciliation commissioner or a conciliation board, sometimes provide the basis of a settlement, the parties are not required to accept the recommendations. Conciliation boards are rarely used, however.

Arbitration

Arbitration is the resolution of any industrial relations dispute by an impartial person or by a board. The decision of the board or the arbitrator is final and binding, though it can be appealed through the courts in certain instances.

Two forms of arbitration are found in Canadian labour relations. The most common type is *grievance* or *rights* arbitration; that is, disputes over the application or interpretation of a collective agreement. This type of arbitration is used for disputes which arise during the term of a collective agreement. Canadian law requires that all such disputes be submitted to final and binding arbitration. That is, strikes or lockouts are prohibited in connection with disputes arising during the term of a collective agreement.

The second, less common, form of arbitration, is called *interest* arbitration. Interest arbitration deals with impasses that occur during contract negotiation. Thus, rights arbitration involves questions of what the contract means, while interest arbitration involves questions of what the contract should contain. Interest arbitration is only compulsory in a few sectors of the economy, notably certain public sectors such as those involving police, fire, or hospital workers.

GRIEVANCE ARBITRATION PROCESS

Most disputes concerning the contract are settled before going to arbitration. Arbitration is the final step in the appeal process and as such is generally required only when a dispute relates to significant changes in policy on either party's side. Grievances of a routine nature are nearly always resolved by the foreman or personnel manager and union steward.

Before a dispute can be submitted to arbitration it must be first judged arbitratable. One general rule states that a dispute is arbitratable if it directly concerns the interpretation, application, administration, or violation of the contract. Thus an employee's complaint, in order to be submitted to arbitration, must directly relate to a specific violation of some term of the agreement.

Actual arbitration is usually carried out by boards of arbitration in Canada. Boards comprise three persons: one representative chosen by each of the two parties and a neutral chairperson. Rulings are based on majority votes. A single impartial arbitrator can also be appointed to hear a case.

Arbitration is quasi-judicial in nature, and, although informal, it is conducted according to general legal protocol (cross-examination, summation, etc.). Arbitration differs from judicial procedure significantly in its treatment of evidence. Hearsay evidence, allegations, circumstantial evidence and insinuations are generally admissible, though treated according to their merits. Further, arbitration is not subject to precedent to the same degree as are judicial proceedings, and appeal is not justified on the basis of precedent.

INTEREST ARBITRATION

Resorting to interest arbitration is growing. Already compulsory for areas of vital public concern (nurses, police, etc.), trends indicate a willingness on the part of other sectors of industry to submit to binding interest arbitration. Some countries, Australia for example, require an impasse in any collective bargaining process to be settled by arbitration.

Because individual party interests are at stake, interest arbitration is much more complex, and criteria for decision are ambiguous. It is less legalized and occasionally contradictory.

Some efforts have been made to establish standards for contract settlement; the most notable are those contained in the Public Service Staff Relations Act.

THE CONTEMPORARY CANADIAN LABOUR MOVEMENT

Industrial relations in Canada exhibit certain characteristics, many of which have come from its history and many of which are a result of the changing economic environment.

Size

Contrary to popular opinion, the majority of Canadian workers do not belong to unions. Overall, less than a third of the total work force was unionized in the early 1970s. Membership in various industries, however, varies dramatically. While 99.5 percent of agricultural workers are not unionized, 100 percent of workers in the brewing industry are unionized. With the exception of significant growth in public employee unions and some growth in white-collar unions, union growth has been relatively stable since the late 1950s.

Composition

There are over 400 separate unions in Canada with a total membership of over 3.5 million ranging in membership from fewer than ten members (for example, the International Association of Siderographers) up to huge international unions with membership in the hundreds of thousands. Twenty unions make up over 50 percent of total union membership. The four largest are the Canadian Union of Public Employees, National Union of Provincial Government Employees, the Public Service Alliance of Canada, and the United Steelworkers.

The majority of unions in Canada are affiliated with two federations of unions — the CLC and the Confédération des Syndicats Nationaux (CSN). The major difference between the two federations is that the CLC is national, comprising international, national, and independent unions across Canada. The CSN is a federation of Quebec unions only. One large union, the Teamsters, has no affiliation with either federation. Although neither federation has strong constitutional power, both are important in the development of interunion cooperation and the overall development and growth of the union movement. There are two other federations, the Canadian Federation of Labour, composed of unions in the construction trades, which split from the CLC, and the Confédération des Syndicats Démocratiques, a Quebec federation which split from the CSN.

Control and Leadership

One of the most significant developments in Canadian labour relations in recent years has been a decline in the domination of the labour movement by international unions; that is, unions based in the United States. In 1961, 72 percent of union members in Canada were members of international unions. Now that figure has dropped to less than 50 percent, which means that most Canadian union members are members of national unions; that is, unions operating only in Canada. These developments have occurred because of two factors, one of which is the growth of unionization in the public sector. In addition, a number of Canadian branches of international unions have split away to become fully autonomous. Historically, there has been little detectable difference between international unions operating in Canada and truly Canadian unions. However, the situations where national unions have become slightly more dominant is relatively recent and what changes may flow from this development really remain to be seen.

The historical domination of the Canadian labour movement by international unions has been controversial and has led to both positive and negative results. On the positive side, the labour movement has probably developed more rapidly in Canada through the greater resources and experience of the American-based unions. In addition, American affiliated unions have enjoyed greater bargaining power simply because of their connections. Finally, Canadian unions have gained some measure of respectability and acceptance from their affiliation with U.S. unions.

In terms of negative consequences, the most serious has been that policy and control of finances, to a large extent, have rested with headquarters outside of Canada. The strong ties between unions have resulted in calls for Canadian wage parity with equivalent American industries, parity which many claim we cannot afford. Greater rationalization of national unions has been retarded by the growth and dominance of international unions. And, according to many, the presence of international unions has resulted in the occasional infringement of Canadian economic sovereignty.

Power

The Canadian labour movement is parochial. The strength of the movement lies in its grass roots nature. The local is the main unit of power.

Even the enormous growth of some unions has failed to produce a significant centralization in any executive committee which any local would hesitate to challenge. Many tentative agreements have not been ratified by union membership, indicating the power usually lies with the members on such major issues as contract settlement.

Political Affiliation

The Canadian labour movement is conservative in comparison with the European movement. Both Canadian and American unions support and work for the continuation of the capitalist economy. Unions in both Canada and the United States support, to some degree, political parties financially and in other ways. In this sense, the Canadian movement is less politically active than the European labour movement. In Canada organized labour has been closely associated with the New Democratic Party.

Union Management

Union management is becoming more sophisticated. The giant unions now have support staffs of lawyers, economists, and administrators which match many large corporations. Increasingly, training of union administrators is being done professionally. A prime example is the CLC's labour relations school hosted by McGill University.

Unions' Role in Industry

A subtle but sure shift in the attitude of some major union leadership toward labour's part in the economy is evident. This shift encompasses a number of important areas. For instance, some major unions are now actively seeking significant changes in industrial work environments. In line with this concern for issues other than financial reward, unions are taking an active interest in the future of their respective industries.

WHAT A UNION MEANS TO HUMAN RESOURCE MANAGEMENT

So far in this chapter, we have described industrial relations, but unlike earlier chapters, we have not said much about making industrial relations *decisions*. We will conclude with a brief discussion of decision making.

We believe there are two ways to think about industrial relations decisions. First, there are a host of decisions that have to do with a union–management relationship, including:

1. Should we encourage or discourage union certification in our company?
2. What basic posture do we want to take with union leaders and members?
3. What bargaining strategies will we employ during contract negotiations?
4. Are we willing to take a strike?
5. To what extent will we back other members of management in disputes with union leaders and members? (This is especially a problem when we think such managers are in the wrong.)

Second, there is a set of decisions that have to do with overall personnel relationships, including:

1. How will we treat nonunionized employees as compared with our unionized employees on issues such as pay, seniority, promotion, dismissal, etc.?
2. How technical (or legal) do we want to be in interpreting contract provisions? For example, if an employee lets us down, will we "throw the book at him" or will we use some of the principles we've learned about human resources management?

There are both advantages and disadvantages to having a unionized work force. For example, it becomes difficult for a manager to be flexible in the treatment of employees when the union contract requires equalized treatment. This characteristic prevents manipulative managers from dividing and conquering their employees on such issues as compensation and termination. In fact, specified expectations of what employees must do and what management must do can make human resource management in a unionized firm much easier to achieve than in a nonunionized firm, provided the firm and the union are on good terms. On the other hand, legal rules and regulations for human resource management often make it difficult for management to recognize unequal performance, ability instead of seniority, and so on. We challenge you to prepare your own list of advantages and disadvantages of the unionized work force from both the management and employee points of view.

26

Hamilton Steel Products Ltd.[1]

Edgar Howe, the newly appointed assistant to the industrial relations manager, realized that he had less than a week to prepare a report for Don Perry, industrial relations manager of Hamilton Steel Products Ltd. The purpose of the report was to outline the alternative courses of action open to the company in settling an overtime dispute. The dispute involved a company tractor-trailer driver who had been stranded for five days in a snow-storm which had devastated the northeastern United States and Canada earlier in the winter.

COMPANY BACKGROUND

Hamilton Steel Products Ltd. was located in Hamilton, Ontario, and manufactured suspension and chassis parts for the automobile industry. The company had been in operation since 1935 and supplied Canadian and American automobile, truck, and bus manufacturers. Distribution of the products was by both rail and road. In addition to using common freight carriers, Hamilton Steel maintained a fleet of ten tractor-trailer trucks to handle the long-distance deliveries. These trucks were equipped with sleeper cabs to enable drivers to stop and sleep where and when it was convenient.

UNION AGREEMENTS

Hamilton Steel had a total staff of 522 people of whom 402 were hourly paid production workers represented by the Canadian Steelworkers Union. The average wage for these workers was $7.11/hour. The ten company truck drivers, employed to operate the tractor-trailer trucks, were represented by the Teamsters Union and were paid $8.02/hour plus expenses incurred while on duty. The company relationship with both unions was longstanding; however, in 1976 the Canadian Steelworkers had gone on strike over a new collective agreement and, in 1977, there had been a three-day wildcat walkout because of "heavy discipline." The workers returned to work when management obtained a cease and desist order from the Ontario Labour Relations Board.

The Hamilton Steel Products' Collective Agreement with the Teamsters Union was based on the Ontario General Freight Master Agreement. The drivers were paid for every ten out of eighteen hours they were away on a trip, plus an allowance per kilometre and expenses. The company paid the full cost of hotel accommodation when necessary, or $2.50 per night. In effect, a driver sleeping in the truck cab received $2.50 per night.

Overtime (time and one-half) was paid on the regular $8.02 after ten hours in any one shift. This time excluded meal periods, coffee breaks, and rest periods. Company practice, in unusual situations, was to continue paying the drivers on a normal basis, ten hours on, eight hours off, to prevent loss of earnings due to breakdowns and storms beyond their control (see Exhibit 1 for relevant sections of the Collective Agreement).

---

[1]Names and places have been disguised.

THE INCIDENT

On Thursday, January 26, one of the company's transport drivers, who had been with Hamilton Steel Products for more than sixteen years, was en route to Pittsburgh, Pennsylvania, when he became stranded in a severe snowstorm that closed all roads. The driver pulled off to the side of the highway, and went to sleep in the cab of the truck. The storm was still raging nine and a half hours later and showed no signs of letting up.

The driver awoke because the cab was cold. Apparently the engine had seized while he was asleep. The driver subsequently walked nearly half a kilometre along the highway to a motel and restaurant where, after telephoning the company in Hamilton to inform them of the situation, he attempted to book a motel room. The motel was full because of the severity of the storm. The driver spent the next forty-eight hours in the restaurant with other stranded travellers, sleeping at night on tables until rooms became available. By this time it was 2:00 p.m. on Saturday, January 29. The roads remained closed for several more days and, as a consequence, the driver spent three more nights in a motel room before continuing to Pittsburgh. During the entire five-day period, the driver checked his truck daily, as he was responsible for the equipment and cargo until delivered. After the storm, a second tractor unit was dispatched from Hamilton so that the driver could complete his delivery.

When the driver finished his trip and submitted his time sheet, he claimed over-time for the entire 57½-hour period during which he had been stranded but unable to get a motel room (see Exhibit 2). The driver claimed he had been on duty until he could find accommodation. The company did not request a statutory declaration (Exhibit 1) and reimbursed the driver for the meal and accommodation expenses as submitted, as well as for the time claimed before and after the 57½ hours he had been stranded. For the 57½-hour period, the company paid the driver on the basis of ten hours on, eight hours off formula. The difference between the driver's claim and the company's payment amounted to $382.95.

THE GRIEVANCE

The union filed a grievance report with the company's Labour Relations Department according to the terms of the Collective Agreement. In the event that the company and the union could not come to an agreement on a grievance, the union had the option of submitting it for arbitration. The cost of arbitrations in the past had averaged $3 000 and had been shared equally by the union and the company. The arbitration process itself often took longer than a year to complete.

The union was entitled to an answer within seven days, and Don Perry wanted the report on his desk before that time.

Exhibit 1
Hamilton Steel Products Ltd.
Relevant Sections of the Collective Agreement

Article 23
Section 23.2 (g) — Overtime

Any highway driver working a combination of hourly and distance rates shall be paid at the rate of time and one-half the regular rate of pay for all hours worked and distance driven after 10 (ten) hours in any one (1) shift on sixty (60) hours in anyone week. In conjunction with the foregoing, hours worked and distance driven shall include all hours and distance from the time the employee has reported for duty until he or she has punched out. Time not included will be specifically defined as follows:

(1) Meal Periods
(2) Coffee Breaks
(3) Rest Periods

Section 23.2 (r) — Time Payment

All time payments of highway drivers shall include way-freighting, terminal delays, breakdowns, completing of log forms, tach cards, or other unavoidable delays and shall be calculated at the prevailing wage rate of the driver's home terminal. It is agreed that a driver while performing work where a higher scale prevails, shall receive the prevailing drivers scale while performing work in that area. Any claim for pay must be accounted for by the highway driver on a form provided and approved by the Company's representative in charge. In the event of breakdowns or other allegedly unavoidable delays such as major snow storms occurring in areas without supervision, the Company may, at its discretion, require drivers to sign a statutory declaration having the same force and effect as a statement made under oath and by virtue of the Canada Evidence Act setting forth the causes to the best of their knowledge and belief for such breakdowns and/or delays.

Exhibit 2
Hamilton Steel Products Ltd.

	CLAIMED				PAID			
Thursday, Jan. 26	4:30 a.m. - 2:30 p.m.	10 hrs. at $ 8.02	= $ 80.20		4:30 a.m. - 2:30 p.m.	10 hrs. at $ 8.02	=	$ 80.20
	2:30 p.m. - midnight	9½ hrs. at 12.03	= 114.28		2:30 p.m. - 10:30 p.m.	8 hrs. off		0.00
					10:30 p.m.			
Friday, Jan. 27	12:01 a.m. - midnight	24 hrs. at 12.03	= 288.72		8:30 a.m.	10 hrs. at 8.02	=	80.20
					8:30 a.m. - 4.30 p.m.	8 hrs. off	=	0.00
					4:30 p.m.			
Saturday, Jan. 28	12:01 a.m. - 2:00 p.m.	14 hrs. at 12.03	= 168.42		2:30 a.m.	10 hrs. at 8.02	=	80.20
					2:30 a.m. - 10.30 a.m.	8 hrs. off	=	0.00
					10:30 a.m. - 8:30 p.m.	10 hrs. at 8.02	=	80.20
	2:00 p.m. - 10:00 p.m.	8 hrs. off	= 0.00		8:30 p.m.			
	10:00 p.m.							
Sunday, Jan. 29	8:00 a.m.	10 hrs. at 8.02	= 80.20		4.30 a.m.	8 hrs. off	=	0.00
	8:00 a.m. - 4:00 p.m.	8 hrs. off	= 0.00		4:30 a.m. - 2:30 p.m.	10 hrs. at 8.02	=	80.20
					2:30 p.m. - 10:30 p.m.	8 hrs. off	=	0.00
	4:00 p.m.				10:30 p.m.			
Monday, Jan. 30	2:00 a.m.	10 hrs. at 8.02	= 80.20		8:30 a.m.	10 hrs. at 8.02	=	80.20
	2:00 a.m. - 10:00 a.m.	8 hrs. off	= 0.00		8:30 a.m.- 4:30 p.m.	8 hrs. off	=	0.00
	10:00 a.m. - 8:00 p.m.	10 hrs at 8.02	= 80.20		4:30 p.m.			
	8:00 p.m.							
Tuesday, Jan. 31	4:00 a.m.	8 hrs. off	= 0.00		2:30 a.m.	10 hrs. at 8.02	=	80.20
	4:00 a.m. - 10:30 a.m.	6½ hrs. at 8.02	= 52.13		2:30 a.m. - 10:30 a.m.	8 hrs. off	=	0.00
			$944.35					**$561.40**

Sleeping Accommodations

	Paid	Claimed
Thursday, January 26	$2.50	$2.50
Friday, January 27	$2.50	2.50
Saturday, January 28	$18.72	18.72
Sunday, January 29	$18.72	18.72
Monday, January 30	$18.72	18.72
	$61.16	$61.16

27

International Equipment Co.[1]

On August 10, 1979, the general manager of International Equipment Co. received notice of application for certification of his office employees (see Exhibit 1). He was undecided whether he should permit the application to go through without contest by management, or try to influence his employees to reject the union.

The International Equipment Co. was a wholly owned subsidiary of the International Manufacturing Co., an American corporation, with its principal offices in Minneapolis, Minnesota, and with plants in various cities in the United States. There were two Canadian Manufacturing plants of International Equipment, located at Magog, Quebec, and Brampton, Ontario.

The products manufactured at the Brampton works included heavy-duty machinery controls, such as hydraulic systems. It was anticipated that other lines of manufacture would be undertaken in Canada on a scale similar to that in the United States. It was noted in this connection that while the Brampton plant presently occupied less than one hectare, the company had purchased approximately twenty-two hectares at Brampton for future expansion.

The parent company maintained an industrial and community relations division, which was created in 1957 for the purpose of coordinating the industrial relations policies at the various company plants and of maintaining a cordial relationship between the company and its employees and the community in which particular works were situated. Another purpose of the division was to keep the company informed of variations in factors affecting industrial relations and to anticipate and facilitate adjustments were the company deemed it advisable. This ability to survey wages and working conditions on a company-wide basis assisted in determining fair and reasonable working conditions in the particular plant concerned.

On August 2, 1979, there was a total of 246 employees at the Brampton plant, who were classified by type of work as follows:

Production and maintenance employees		180
Office employees		32
Supervisory and other		34
production	13	
office	21	

The production and maintenance employees were organized by the United Automobile Workers (UAW–AFL/CIO), which had been their certified representative since October 5, 1960. The current two-year agreement, which expired December 20, 1980, was the ninth between the company and the union. Since the Brampton plant had no industrial relations or personnel office or officers, these agreements had been negotiated by the plant manager with the help of the Magog and Minneapolis offices.

Even though the company had 246 employees, the general manager was reputed

---

[1]Names and places have been disguised.

to know every employee by first name. The relationship between the union and the company was said to be excellent. The union was obtaining satisfactory rates and benefits for its members. One of the consequences of this was that a production worker at a comparable level to an office worker and with comparable skill was earning a higher salary. The company recognized the need for a revised salary plan and was in the process of formulating a program which was slated for installation on September 1, 1979. The employees were unaware of this plan.

The office employees were all located in one large L-shaped room with rows of desks touching each other except for one aisle in the centre of the room. There was considerable non-work interaction among the office employees and they were regarded by management as a tightly knit group.

On August 10, 1979, the Brampton works received by mail a notice of certification of the office employees from the Ontario Labour Relations Board (see Exhibit 1). The union involved was the same one that was certified to represent the production and maintenance employees. The notice came as a complete surprise to management. Through initial inquiries the company learned that the majority of the eligible office employees had signed union cards. If certified, it would be the first office union to gain representation in the entire International Manufacturing organization. Upon receipt of the notice of certification the Minneapolis industrial relations office was contacted immediately and given full details of the situation. A labour relations specialist was sent to Brampton to deal with the matter first-hand.

The general manager assembled his management team to discuss the various courses of action. It was apparent that there was no general agreement. The comptroller was very disturbed. He visualized many problems in dealing with a union that involved all of the office and clerical workers with the exception of the general manager's secretary, the department heads and engineers.

"It will be impossible to keep anything confidential with my assistant, my secretary, and the telephone operators in the union. People will want to do only one job and no overtime. Our best policy is to fight this certification. If we tell the employees that they are really members of management, and that we have a new salary plan which can be installed immediately, I believe they will reject the union."

The engineering department manager agreed with the comptroller that there could be many problems, but he believed that it was too late to do anything about it.

"Apparently about 60 percent of the employees want the union and have signed membership cards. The Labour Relations Act states that we cannot interfere [Exhibit 2]. I think it would be better in the long run if we accept certification now. This will enable us to negotiate a better contract and help us develop a more satisfactory working relationship for the future."

The plant manager reported that relations with this particular union had been satisfactory at the shop level; however, he was of the opinion that it might be wise to ask the Labour Relations Board to conduct a vote by secret ballot to make certain that the employees had really signed cards without duress. Regardless of the board's action on the vote, the plant manager believed that the company should file a reply to the board listing management's idea of what jobs should be in the bargaining unit. He stated that it should be possible to exclude people who were performing managerial functions and also any persons handling confidential matters relating to industrial relations.

The head office labour official said, "The plant manager is correct. We must file exclusions immediately. However, the additional action is not clear at this moment. I suspect that salary inequities are a major part of the employees' dissatisfaction. Legally, management can announce and implement the plan immediately. The company can carry on business as usual. It can discipline, make improvements, talk to its employees individually or collectively, but it must carefully avoid any reference to the union; however, while management has the legal right to institute the salary plan, I can recall many instances where the union has successfully turned this kind of action into a union victory by stating that merely the threat of a union has brought rewards to the employees."

After listening to the various points of view, the general manager was still undecided about which course of action to follow. He realized that the notice (Exhibit 1) had to be posted immediately. It was possible also that a group of employees might have second thoughts, withdraw from the union, and intervene at the hearing on August 19.

Exhibit 1
THE LABOUR RELATIONS ACT
NOTICE TO EMPLOYEES OF FILING OF APPLICATION
BEFORE THE ONTARIO LABOUR RELATIONS BOARD

Between: International Union, United Automobile Aircraft and Agricultural Implement Workers of America, Affiliated with the American Federation of Labour and Congress of Industrial Organizations
Applicant,

— and —

International Equipment Co. Ltd., Brampton Works
Respondent.

TO THE EMPLOYEES OF

International Equipment Co. Ltd., Brampton Works

TAKE NOTICE that the applicant, International Union, United Automobile Aircraft and Agricultural Implement Workers of America, Affiliated with the American Federation of Labour and Congress of Industrial Organizations, on August 7, 1979, filed with the Ontario Labour Relations Board an application, a copy of which is attached, for certification as bargaining agent of the employees of International Equipment Co. Ltd., Brampton Works in a unit described as

All office and clerical workers of the respondent company, save and except engineers doing engineering work, private secretary to the manager, department heads and all those above the rank of department head.

AND TAKE NOTICE THAT any employee or group of employees, affected by the application and not desiring the applicant to be certified as the bargaining agent, whether or not that desire has been indicated in any other manner, may so inform the Board in writing not later than the 17th day of August, 1979.

AND TAKE NOTICE of the hearing of the application by the Board at its Board Room, 125 Harbour Street, Toronto, Ontario, on Monday, the 19th day of August, 1979, at 09 00.

AND FURTHER TAKE NOTICE THAT any employee, or group of employees, who has informed the Board in writing of their desire may attend and be heard at the hearing; and that upon failure to attend, the Board may dispose of the application without further notice and without considering their desire in writing filed with the Board.

The desire shall be signed by the employee or each member of a group of employees.

An employee, or group of employees, may attend and be heard at the hearing by a representative.

DATED this 7th day of August, 1979.

(A. M. Brunskill)
Registrar

(Note: Address all communications with respect to this application to
The Registrar
Ontario Labour Relations Board
125 Harbour Street
Toronto, Ontario)

Exhibit 2
Excerpts from the Labour Relations Act
Revised Statutes of Ontario, 1970
Chapter 232

UNFAIR PRACTICES

56. No employer or employers' organization and no person acting on behalf of an employer or an employers' organization shall participate in or interfere with the formation, selection or administration of a trade union or the representation of employees by a trade union or contribute financial or other support to a trade union, but nothing in this section shall be deemed to deprive an employer of his freedom to express his views so long as he does not use coercion, intimidation, threats, promises or undue influence. R.S.O. 1970, c. 232, s. 56.

57. No trade union and no person acting on behalf of a trade union shall participate in or interfere with the formation or administration of an employers' organization or contribute financial or other support to an employers' organization. R.S.O. 1970, c. 232, s. 57.

58. No employer, employers' organization or person acting on behalf of an employer or an employers' organization,

(a) shall refuse to employ or to continue to employ a person, or discriminate against a person in regard to employment or any term or condition of employment because the person was or is a member of a trade union or was or is exercising any other rights under this Act;

(b) Shall impose any condition in a contract of employment or propose the imposition of any condition in a contract of employment that seeks to restrain an employee or a person seeking employment from becoming a member of a trade union or exercising any other rights under this Act; or

(c) shall seek by threat of dismissal, or by any other kind of threat, or by the imposition of a pecuniary or other penalty, or by any other means to compel an employee to become or refrain from becoming or to continue to be or to cease to be a member or officer or representative of a trade union or to cease to exercise any other rights under this Act. R.S.O. 1970, c. 232, s. 58.

59. (1) No employer, employers' organization or person acting on behalf of an employer or an employers' organization shall, so long as a trade union continues to be entitled to represent the employees in the bargaining unit, bargain with or enter into a collective agreement with any person or another trade union or a council of trade unions on behalf of or purporting, designed or intended to be binding upon the employees in the bargaining unit or any of them.

(2) No trade union, council of trade unions or person acting on behalf of a trade union or council of trade unions shall, so long as another trade union continues to be entitled to represent the employees in a bargaining unit, bargain with or enter into a collective agreement with an employer or an employers' organization on behalf of or purporting, designed or intended to be binding upon the employees in the bargaining unit or any of them. R.S.O. 1970, c. 232, s. 59.

60. A trade union or council of trade unions, so long as it continues to be entitled to represent employees in a bargaining unit, shall not act in a manner that is arbitrary, discriminatory or in bad faith in the representation of any of the employees in the unit, whether or not members of the trade union or of any constituent union of the council of trade unions, as the case may be. R.S.O. 1970, c. 232, s. 60.

61. No person, trade union or employers' organization shall seek by intimidation or coercion to compel any person to become or refrain from becoming or to continue to be or to cease to be a member of a trade union or of an employers' organization or to refrain from exercising any other rights under this Act or from performing any obligations under this Act. R.S.O. 1970, c. 232, s. 61.

62. Nothing in this Act authorizes any person to attempt at this place at which an employee works to persuade him during his working hours to become or refrain from becoming or continue to be a member of a trade union. R.S.O. 1970, c. 232, s. 62.

28
Ladbroke Valve Co. Inc.[1]

The Ladbroke Valve Company manufactured two lines of valves, flanges, and spigots. One of these lines was sold to industrial users such as refineries and chemical works, the other to the dairy industry. Its office employees were members of the UAW, Local 9275. Although they were generally assigned to work either in the Industrial or Dairy divisions, they were all members of the same Local and there was one seniority schedule covering all unionized office employees.

John Jeremy was an estimator who worked on the Dairy line of products. He had been employed with Ladbroke for twenty-five years and had been one of the first employees to become a member of the UAW when it organized the office staff in 1963. He was a former president of the Local and had served in other Local offices for most of the last ten years.

In early 1983, sales of the Dairy line of products declined sharply and, as a result, there were only about twenty hours a week of estimating to be done. The company assigned additional estimating and scheduling duties on the Industrial product line to Mr. Jeremy. This resulted in a more junior employee, Mr. Wilson, being placed on temporary layoff. However, after about one month, the sales supervisor in the Industrial division complained that Mr. Jeremy was unable to cope with working on both the Dairy and Industrial products. He was returned to the job of estimating the Dairy products only and Mr. Wilson was recalled.

Mr. Jeremy was clearly underemployed in this job. The office manager, Frank Webster, decided to place Mr. Jeremy on a shortened work week; he would work (and be paid for) only twenty hours per week, though he would continue to receive full company benefits, including vacation entitlements, as if he were working full time. This would continue until sales picked up in the Dairy division and Mr. Jeremy could return to full-time estimating. In Mr. Webster's view, the company could do this since the Management's Rights clause of the collective agreement stated:

> The Union further recognizes the undisputed right of the Company to operate and manage its business in all respects in accordance with its responsibilities and commitments. The products to be manufactured, the schedule of production, the methods, processes, and means of manufacturing and office methods are exclusively the responsibility of the Company.

When advised that this would happen, Mr. Jeremy and his Union representative spoke with Mr. Webster. They pointed out that, according to Article 9 of the collective agreement, Mr. Jeremy had the right to displace (or "bump") a more junior employee who was doing a job that Jeremy was qualified for. There were several jobs in the production scheduling office which Jeremy was qualified for and which were filled by employees with much less seniority.

Article 9 of the Agreement said:

---

[1]Names and places have been disguised.

In the event of a reduction in the working force, employees will be laid off in inverse order of seniority provided there are available other employees able and willing to do the work of the employees to be laid off.

Mr. Webster spoke with the supervisor of the production scheduling office before responding to this request. The supervisor was opposed to allowing Mr. Jeremy to "bump" one of the production scheduling clerks. He pointed out that the four production scheduling clerks had full workloads and that the department was running very smoothly. Mr. Webster also realized that if Mr. Jeremy was allowed to displace one of those employees, he would not have time to do the twenty hours per week estimating on the Dairy line of products. Jeremy was the only qualified person who could do that estimating.

At a meeting that afternoon with Mr. Jeremy, the Union representative, and the industrial relations manager, Mr. Webster denied Mr. Jeremy's request. He also pointed out that no reduction in working force was taking place. Mr. Jeremy was not being laid off; he was only being placed temporarily on a short work week. There were still the same number of employees in the office. Therefore, the question of layoff and the "bumping" of less senior employees did not arise.

Neither Mr. Jeremy nor his Union representative were prepared to accept this decision and they indicated that a formal grievance would be filed. In the event that such a grievance was not resolved to its satisfaction, the Union could refer it to a neutral arbitrator who would render a decision which would be binding on the company and the Union.

29

Les Vignettes des Travailleurs

In early March 1984, Raymond Rossignol, the newly appointed Food and Beverage Manager for Place Ville Marie Restaurants in downtown Montreal, was reviewing the collective bargaining agreement between Place Ville Marie and the Confédération des Syndicats Nationaux. Three recent complaints from the union claimed unfair management practices were violating the "spirit" of the collective agreement. Raymond wanted to respond to the union in such a way as not to upset the balance of what he felt was a delicate labour relations situation.

PLACE VILLE MARIE

The Place Ville Marie restaurants were built in the early 1960s to provide sorely needed "quality" food services in the city's downtown area. The complex consisted of twelve food and beverage outlets located in the Place Ville Marie shopping mall beneath four major office buildings in Montreal's downtown core. The shopping mall was immediately accessible by passageways and escalators to train and subway stations and the twelve-hundred-room Queen Elizabeth Hotel. The restaurant facilities included a cafeteria, a fine dining restaurant, a steak house, a seafood restaurant, bars, and a catering and "coffee wagon" service. These food and beverage outlets employed almost three hundred people and had an annual payroll of over $3.2 million.

Ownership

The Place Ville Marie restaurants were owned by Canadian National (CN) Hotels, a Canada-wide chain of luxury hotels and other hospitality-related operations. When the complex was first opened in the early 1960s, Hilton Canada was retained on a management contract to manage these restaurants. The rationale for this was complicated, but had to do primarily with the fact that Hilton already managed the adjacent Queen Elizabeth Hotel for CN. Also, Hilton had a great deal of experience in operating the types of restaurant concepts that CN wanted to install in the Place Ville Marie complex. Recently, however, CN had reversed its philosophy concerning management contracts and had taken over, as of December 31, 1983, the operating management of both Place Ville Marie and the Queen Elizabeth.

Financial Performance

In the early years the Place Ville Marie restaurants were very successful in terms of sales volume, profitability, and reputation. At one point, sales exceeded $12 million per year. More recently, however, annual sales had declined to less than $8 million and the outlets had lost money for the last two years. In fact, 1983 losses approached $2 million. CN management attributed the decline in performance to several sources including high costs and outmoded food service concepts. Payroll costs for 1983 totalled 43 percent of sales,[1] and CN management believed that part of the reason for this high figure was due to union-mandated wage rates and work rules. Since many of the restaurants in competition with Place Ville Marie were not organized, CN management believed that they were paying 30–50 percent more for labour than many of their competitors.

Also, many of the successful new restaurants in the downtown area achieved high customer service levels with less labour-intensive concepts. This was accomplished through a variety of means, including limiting the number of menu items and restructuring the way service was delivered. In fact, one of the alternatives being considered as a solution for Place Ville Marie's poor performance was a restructuring of concepts, menus, and service.

Management

The Place Ville Marie restaurants and bars were incorporated into the management structure of the Queen Elizabeth. The facilities were organized under the food and beverage department of the hotel, and the Food and Beverage Manager for Place Ville Marie, Raymond Rossignol, reported to the Food and Beverage Manager of the Queen Elizabeth. Although both the hotel and Place Ville Marie restaurants shared numerous resources, they maintained separate collective bargaining contracts with the Confédération des Syndicats Nationaux (CSN).

Raymond Rossignol

Raymond Rossignol was only thirty years old, but had a strong background in food and beverage cost control. He had worked in both the Queen Elizabeth and Place Ville Marie during his four-year tenure and had assumed his present position in January 1984. Before this he had served as food and beverage controller, a beverage control supervisor, and a food and beverage supervisor.

CONFEDERATION DES SYNDICATS NATIONAUX

Confédération des Syndicats Nationaux (CSN) was a Canada-wide union which represented employees in a variety of industry settings, including social service agencies, hospitals, and, most recently, hotels. CSN was presently representing the employees of four hotels in Montreal.

CSN was relatively new to both the Queen Elizabeth and Place Ville Marie. Under Quebec labour law it was permissible for the employer to attempt to decertify the existing union or for another union to attempt to gain official representation status during the ninety-day period immediately preceding the expiration of a collective bargaining agreement. This ninety-day period was unofficially referred to as *mauradage* or loosely translated, "raiding period."

---

[1] *Foodservice & Hospitality* magazine's 1982 *Fact File* reported that the national average for total payroll costs as a percentage of sales for restaurants (excluding those located in hotels) ranged between 20 percent in some Western provinces to 32 percent in the Toronto area.

During the "raiding period" in 1982, CSN won the right to represent both Queen Elizabeth and Place Ville Marie employees from Local 31 of the Hotel Employees and Restaurant Employees International Union. This right was won after a hard-fought battle which included numerous recounts of votes and which resulted in a situation where rank-and-file employees were without a contract for almost two years.

However, as of December 8, 1982, CSN was the official bargaining agent for these employees. The contract was for a period of twenty-four months and some of the highlights included a 21 percent pay hike over two years (15 percent the first year and 6 percent the second), well-specified procedures for dealing with seniority and job posting, a detailed grievance procedure, and strong contract language concerning worker health and safety (See Exhibit 1). Additionally, CSN offered the employees control over local union affairs. As such, they enjoyed more autonomy than under the representation of Local 31.

CSN's Current Status

Although the present contract still had almost nine months to run, CN's labour relations specialists felt that CSN would soon be implementing strategies to cement its official status for another contract period. Rumours running through the employee ranks had it that CN might attempt to decertify CSN and that Local 31 would try to reestablish itself. Also, there was growing sentiment among the rank and file that future negotiations should concentrate on Place Ville Marie employees achieving parity with employees at the Queen Elizabeth.

Presently, wages at the Queen Elizabeth were almost 25 percent higher than for similar jobs at Place Ville Marie. In addition, Queen Elizabeth employees had their own cafeteria, where Place Ville Marie employees had to make do with a sectioned-off area in La Grand Place. Finally, there was a commonly held feeling that more public attention focused on the hotel. Thus, some employees did not like the idea of these facilities being recognized as separate bargaining units.

UNION COMPLAINTS

During the past week, Raymond had received three complaints from the local union president, a Place Ville Marie employee. While these complaints were informal and thus outside of the grievance procedure, their nature had implications for both management rights as well as union solidarity.

Electronic Cash Registers

The first complaint addressed a situation that resulted from the installation of electronic cash registers. In the latter part of February, CN management replaced the existing mechanical-type cash registers in six of the outlets (Hilton had installed new registers in the remaining units in 1982) with state-of-the-art electronic cash registers. Prior to the installation of the new machines, waiters and waitresses would present their guest checks to a cashier who would "ring up" each item, total the bill, take money from the serving person, and make change to be delivered to the customer.

The new equipment made the cashier's position redundant, since the operator was only required to press the button corresponding to menu items being ordered. The electronic cash registers automatically placed the order in the kitchen, recorded the sale as well as the payment, and instructed the operator as to the correct amount of change. Further, the new cash register recorded sales and transactions for each serving person. The result of this was that each waiter or waitress was issued a change fund and required to handle the cashiering function for the customers they served. Prior to the changeover, training in the use of the new equipment was given to waiters and waitresses. This training was accomplished over a four-day period in staggered shifts.

Since cashiers were no longer necessary, eight full-time cashier positions were abolished. Three positions were retained, however, in La Grande Place, a self-service cafeteria. Five of the incumbents in the abolished jobs were assigned new duties in different units and three were laid off.

CSN's grounds for complaint lay in the fact that waiters and waitresses were now doing the work of cashiers and that this was a violation of the spirit of the contract, since separate classifications and salary schedules existed for each job.

Coffee and Pastries

The second concern of the union was in many ways similar to the first. Place Ville Marie management had recently decided that pre-lunch mall traffic and people en route to their offices in the morning provided a potential source of business. In order to capitalize on this potential, management had set up a counter in La Grande Place to sell coffee, donuts, and other pastries. The counter was designed to face the mall hallway and as such had to be operated separately from the rest of the cafeteria. It was open Monday through Friday, 0700 to 1100, and had been performing adequately since its opening. A pastry and a cup of coffee sold for 85¢, and daily sales had been averaging $250.

The person operating the stand was classified as a pantry attendant and was paid $5.73 per hour. Her job required her to stock the stand, dispense the products, collect money, record the sale on the cash register, and make change. CSN argued that this was really two separate jobs and that a cashier should be employed as well.

Floor Catering and the Coffee Cart

The last complaint concerned a supervisor performing work which CSN believed rightly belonged to a union member.

Floor catering was organized as a separate department within the Place Ville Marie complex. Its primary function was to provide catered food and beverage service to the offices in the buildings connected to the mall and to operate mobile sandwich, coffee, and snack carts in these office buildings. The department operated three such carts daily (Monday through Friday) and performed in-office catering on an as-needed basis. On the average, the department catered between five and twenty-five special events a day. Combined 1983 sales for the coffee carts and floor catering approached $450,000. There were four full-time union employees and a salaried supervisor. Fluctuations in business were handled by using part-time "on call" personnel.

The recent complaint centred on the work activities of the supervisor, who had recently been promoted to this position from a union job. Since the heaviest amount of business occurred between 1130 and 1300, the department sometimes found itself understaffed during these peak periods. On days that were particularly busy, the supervisor would try to reduce some of the pressure on the staff by retrieving carts of soiled dishes and equipment from offices which had requested special catering. The previous supervisor had regularly helped in the same manner. The union argued that this constituted work that should be done by a union employee.

As Raymond contemplated his response to these three complaints, he felt that the tradeoffs would not be easy. On the one hand, he was reasonably sure that these incidents violated neither the spirit nor the specific provisions of the collective bargaining agreement. On the other hand, he did not want to do anything to unnecessarily upset management and labour relations at Place Ville Marie.

Exhibit 1
Les Vignettes des Travailleurs
Collective Bargaining Agreement Excerpts

ARTICLE 1 — PURPOSE OF THE AGREEMENT

1.01 The purposes of the present agreement are to maintain and to promote orderly labour relations between the parties and to facilitate an equitable settlement of problems which may arise between the Employer and the employees covered by this agreement.

ARTICLE 2 — RECOGNITION AND JURISDICTION

2.01 The Employer recognizes the Union as the sole representative of all the employees, as provided by the certification issued by the Minister of Labour, Manpower and Income Security on April 15th, 1982, as follows:

"All the employees, who are employees as defined in the Labour Code, working in the restaurants and bars of the Place Ville-Marie complex, including the Royal Bank building and the I.B.M. building, with the exception of office employees, maîtres d'hôtels and employees of the security department."

2.02 No special agreements to the contrary to the provisions foreseen in the present agreement and which are reached between an employee and the Employer are valid unless they are ratified by the Union.

2.03 *Jurisdiction of the agreement*

The present collective agreement applies to all employees mentioned in the certification issued to the Union.

2.04 The parties subscribe to the principle according to which as a general rule tasks normally done by a Union member are not given to supervisory personnel outside the bargaining unit.

In application of the above principle, the parties agree to maintain the practice in existence before the signing of the collective agreement.

ARTICLE 3 — MANAGEMENT RIGHTS

3.01 The Union recognizes that the Employer has the exclusive right to assure the efficiency and the profitability of his operations, to manage and operate his establishment and to conduct his business as he wishes, subject only to the restrictions imposed by Law or by the present agreement. The Employer maintains all rights and privileges which are not specifically abandoned or restricted by the present agreement.

3.02 The Employer pledges to exercise his management rights in a manner compatible with the present agreement. If this is not done, a grievance may be filed.

3.03 The Employer has the right to make, and to change from time to time, reasonable regulations which the employees must observe. These regulations must not come into contradiction with the provisions of this agreement. These regulations shall only take effect seventy-two (72) hours after they are posted by the Employer. A copy of this posting shall be remitted to the Union.

ARTICLE 4 — GENERAL PROVISIONS

ARTICLE 5 — DEFINITIONS

5.01 "Regular employee" shall mean an employee who has completed his trial period in conformity to the provisions of the of the present agreement and who is normally scheduled to work more than three (3) days a week or more than twenty-four (24) hours a week, even if he is scheduled for a shorter period from time to time.

5.02 "Part-time employee" shall mean an employee who has completed his trial period according to the provisions of the present agreement and who is normally scheduled regularly three (3) days or less a week or more than twenty-four (24) hours or less a week, even if he is scheduled to work for a longer period from time to time.

5.03 "Trial employee" means an employee who has not completed his trial period according to the provisions foreseen in the present agreement.

5.04 "Temporary employee" shall mean an employee who is not usually scheduled on a regular basis and who only reports to work on call from the Employer.

5.05 The provisions of the present agreement only apply to temporary employees when there is an explicit reference to that effect.

ARTICLE 6 — TECHNICAL AND TECHNOLOGICAL CHANGES

6.01 In the event that technocal or technological changes of a nature that mean significant changes in the nature of an employee's work, the Employer shall make an effort to enable the employees affected to adapt to the aforementioned changes, or if possible, to be re-assigned to other positions within the estab-lishment.

ARTICLE 7 — UNION REGULATIONS

ARTICLE 8 — UNION ACTIVITIES

ARTICLE 9 — PROCEDURE FOR THE SETTLE-MENT OF GRIEVANCES

9.01 A grievance shall be defined as any disagree-ment relative to the interpretation and/or the application of the collective agreement.

9.02 No grievance may be presented without first having been the subject of a discussion beforehand between the employee involved and his immediate superior. The latter may, if he desires, be accompanied by his union steward when there is a disagreement relative to the interpretation of the collective agree-ment.

9.03 Any grievances must be submitted in writing, by the employee concerned, accompanied, if he so desires, by the steward representing him, to the Personnel Manager, within fifteen (15) calendar days of the date on which the employee proves he was knowledgeable of it, in so far as the employee proves that it would have been impossible for him to have been knowledgeable of it earlier. The Personnel Manager shall give his response in writing within the seven (7) following calendar days.

9.04 If the Personnel Manager's decision is not given within the time limit foreseen or if it is not considered satisfactory by the Union, the latter may take the grievance to arbitration. To do so, it must advise the Personnel Manager within a time period not to exceed the dead-line for the step foreseen in article 9.03 by more than thirty (30) calendar days.

9.05 Upon receipt of this notice, the parties shall proceed with the choice of a single arbitrator. If no agreement is reached within fifteen (15) days, either party may call upon the Labour Department to have it choose an arbitrator in conformity to article 100 of the Labour Code.

9.06 If a group of employees taken collectively or if the Union as such feels it/they have been unfairly treated, the Union may file a collec-tive grievance or one of a general nature at the second step of the procedure for the settle-ment of grievances. The aforementioned grievance must be submitted in writing and bear the signature of a Union officer. It is agreed that this provision is not intended to sidestep the procedure of filing individual grievances.

9.07 Only regular employees and part-time em-ployees who have completed their trial periods may have recourse to the grievance and arbitration procedure to challenge their dismissal.

ARTICLE 10 — ARBITRATION

ARTICLE 11 — UNION REPRESENTATIVES

ARTICLE 12 — SENIORITY

12.01 The right to seniority is acquired as soon as an employee has completed thirty (30) days actually worked in the service of the Em-ployer. As soon as he has completed this trial period an employee's seniority is retroactive to the date of the last hiring.

12.02 A part-time employee's seniority is calculated on a proportional basis to the time worked starting with the date of the signing of the collective agreement.

12.03 In the event of equal seniority among two (2) or more employees, seniority shall be deter-mined according to the employee's number.

12.04 An employee loses his seniority and his job in the following cases:

a) voluntary resignation from his job;

b) dismissal for just and sufficient cause;

c) lay-off for a period equivalent to his con-tinuous service not to exceed nine (9) months.

d) Failure of a laid-off employee to inform the Employer of his intention to return to work except in the case of sickness or accident, within the seven (7) calendar days of receipt of the notice of return to work which is addressed to him at his last known address by registered mail.

12.05 Promotions outside the bargaining unit are not subject to the provisions of the present agreement and persons thus promoted shall continue to accumulate their seniority for a period of six (6) months starting with the date of their promotion.

If they return to the bargaining unit less than six (6) months after their promotion, they shall receive full credit for their seniority.

If they do not return within this seniority period, they lose all seniority.

ARTICLE 13 — VACANT POSITIONS, LAY-OFFS, RECALL

ARTICLE 14 — WAGES AND CLASSIFICATIONS

14.01 The wages are shown in Appendix "A" which is an integral part of the collective agreement.

14.02 If the Employer creates a classification not foreseen in the present text, he shall determine the rate after agreement with the Union. In the event of disagreement between the parties, the Union may have recourse to the grievance and arbitration procedure to have the applicable rate set.

14.03 Any employee absent on the day the pay is distributed and who expects to remain absent for at least four (4) days for reasons of sickness or accident and who wishes to receive his paycheque must communicate with the payroll department to agree on the procedure for remittance of the cheque, i.e. by mail or by any other method.

14.04 The following details must be shown on each employee's paycheque:

1. name;
2. date of pay period;
3. number of hours worked on regular time;
4. number of hours worked overtime;
5. number of hours paid on leaves;
6. gross amount of pay;
7. employee's number.

14.06 When an employee performs work in another classification, at the Employer's request:

a) He shall receive the wage rate for this other classification if this rate is higher than his regular rate, provided that he then performs more than two (2) consecutive hours of work in this classification;

b) he maintains his regular rate if this rate is higher than the salary rate in this other classification.

14.07 An employee transferred at his request or following a staff cut is paid according to the rate of the new classification he occupies.

ARTICLE 15 — HEALTH AND SAFETY

ARTICLE 16 — DISCIPLINARY ACTION

ARTICLE 17 — TOOLS AND CLOTHES

ARTICLE 18 — HOURS OF WORK, WEEKLY DAYS OFF

ARTICLE 19 — SOCIAL LEAVES

ARTICLE 20 — OVERTIME

Appendix A
Classifications and Salaries

CLASSIFICATIONS	December 8, 1982	December 8, 1983
Rotary chefs	6.75	7.16
Butcher chefs	6.60	7.00
Pastry chefs	6.75	7.16
Rotating helpers	6.02	6.38
Pastry helpers	6.02	6.38
Service barmen	6.05	6.41
Bartenders	4.72	5.00
Busboys/girls	4.72	5.00
Pantry attendants	5.41	5.73
Vegetable-cookware attendants	5.29	5.61
Head dishwasher	5.57	5.90
Dishwashers	5.18	5.49
Night cleaners	5.18	5.49
Public location attendants	5.18	5.49
Coffee attendants (caterer)	5.29	5.61
Hostesses	5.29	5.61
Cashiers	5.29	5.61
Storeroom attendants	5.24	5.55
Captains	4.37	4.63
Waiters (waitresses)	3.97	4.21
Barmen on tips	4.77	5.06

Notwithstanding the rates set above, it is understood that employees in the employ of P.V.M. as of the signing of the agreement shall receive a minimum pay increase of 15% in relation to their basic pay as of December 7, 1982; on December 8, 1983, they shall receive a minimum increase of 6% in relation to their basic salary as of December 7, 1983.

Hiring Rate

The hiring rate for the term of the present agreement shall be the rate for the job or classification reduced by ten per cent (10%). As soon as an employee has completed his trial period, he receives the rate for the classification.

30
Primo Electric Co. Ltd.[1]

In May 1980, Local 54 of the United Electrical, Radio and Machine Workers of America (UE) and Primo Electric Co. Ltd. met with a board of arbitration to settle Grievance No. 230, which read as follows:

> The unjust discharge of Richard Stevens, a layout person and boring mill operator, based upon company reasons of refusing to obey orders, poor work record, and using abusive language to a foreman.

The Primo Electric Co. had several plants in a large city in western Ontario which turned out a wide variety of products from major appliances, such as stoves and refrigerators, to heavy electrical apparatus, such as motors and generators. The incident causing the grievance took place in Department D-1 of the Power Products Division of the company's plant No. 1. The work performed in this department was generally of a machining nature, utilizing various types of machines to process material for use throughout all three plants. The grievor had worked in this department first as a boring mill operator and later, since August 1973, as a layout person.

Richard J. Stevens, age twenty-eight, the grievor, was an extremely active union steward in Local 54. He had worked for the company since September 1972, and had been appointed union steward in April 1978. For eleven months after his date of hiring, he had been a vertical boring mill operator, and from then until August 1979, he had been employed as a second-class layout person.[2] On company work histories, his attendance, application, and skill were reported as good. However, his general deportment was described as poor; he was a chronic complainer. In his foreman's opinion, Stevens was a very aggressive union steward who was often inclined to be quite unreasonable in his dealings with management.

Two unfavourable incidents stood out on Stevens's record. One involved a charge of obstructing police in a picket line disturbance. This had occurred in October 1978 when Stevens and two other Primo employees had been absent from work without leave because they were serving on a picket line which the UE had thrown up around another local company. The company laid them off for a period of three days. The layoff was later interpreted by a board of arbitration to have been an unjustified suspension.

In addition to the layoff which Stevens received in October 1978, he received a suspension in December 1978 for leaving his work station without permission. This was in connection with a complaint by a number of employees regarding the scheduling of alternate work days over Christmas. On this occasion, Stevens refused to return to his work station when told to do so. As a result, he was suspended for four days, but a board of arbitration subsequently reduced the suspension to one day.

Because of a work shortage in Department D-1 in August 1979, the foreman,

---

[1]Names and places have been disguised.
[2]Working from blueprints, this person outlines the various cuts on work pieces to guide operators who are doing the machining.

Donald Jackson, deemed it necessary to transfer Stevens back to a vertical boring mill. Stevens had asked to be allowed to exercise his plant-wide seniority to bump[1] onto a layout job in another department, but Jackson required him to exercise his departmental seniority first as provided in the Collective Agreement.

Donald Jackson was the general foreman in Department D-1 and had worked for the company for twenty-nine years; eleven years as a supervisor and nine years as a supervisor in Department D-1. He was a rough-and-ready sort of man who sometimes caused strained relations with his employees.

Jackson contended that even a month after Stevens had bumped onto the boring mill he was not doing a satisfactory job nor making a real effort to raise his performance. The major point of annoyance was Steven's continual moving back and forth between his layout table and the boring mill to obtain tools from the former location. Stevens refused to take his personal tools to his new work station on the grounds that there was not a satisfactory place in which to lock them at the boring mill.

Jackson considered this to be nonsense as other operators had stored their tools at the boring mill without difficulties. Both the foreman and subforeman repeatedly told Stevens to move his tools to his new work station, but Stevens continually refused and began stating that he was promised a new tool cabinet which would be built by the carpenter shop.

It was the opinion of some management people that Stevens's real reason for resenting the boring mill job was that it did not allow him to move around in the department on union business. The layout job had facilitated his contact with the workers as he had to show each one how materials were to be machined. It was known that a cabinet at his layout table contained union documents and files relating to departmental time studies.

Supervision also surmised that Stevens's appointment as a union steward had given him an exalted opinion of his own importance and the feeling that his duties as a steward were more important than his work for the company. It also seemed apparent that Stevens felt his position gave him a degree of immunity from any effective supervision by his superiors.

On October 12, 1979, at approximately 1530, an incident occurred which ultimately resulted in Stevens's dismissal by the company. Jackson's account of the episode was as follows:

"I went to the grievor while he was at the layout table and asked him what he was doing there. He replied that he came up to get some tools. I again told him to get all his tools up to the boring mill and I was not going to tell him again. He said there was not room at the boring mill and I told him there was plenty of room. At this point he became annoyed and as we started back to the boring mill he said, 'Jackson, you're an s.o.b.; you want to hang your cross with those other bastards in labour relations.' I told him to watch his language or be fired. To this, he retorted, 'You damned s.o.b., fire me if you want to — I don't care — I know that's what you want to do.' He persisted in his abusive language and I finally told him to pack up his tools and be out by seventeen hundred hours, and not to report until I sent for him. I doubt whether anyone in the vicinity heard our conversation but at no time did I use abusive language."

---

[1]Bump — to displace another person with less seniority.

The following day, Stevens was telephoned and told to report to the employment office. A meeting was held between the supervisor of labour relations, the plant superintendent, and Mr. Jackson for the company, and Mr. Stevens and Mr. Robertson, the president of Local 54. The grievor was told by Mr. Jackson that he was being discharged for: (1) use of profane and abusive language and (2) repeated refusal to obey his supervisor's orders with respect to moving his tools.

The same day, Richard Stevens submitted his grievance (Exhibit 1). This grievance, No. 230, was processed through the various stages as provided for by Article XVI of the Collective Agreement.

Throughout the processing of this grievance, the company steadfastly maintained that Stevens had been justifiably discharged (Exhibit 2). Finally, on October 27, 1979, the union informed the company that it was posting the grievance for arbitration, and at the same time named its choice of representative for the board of arbitration.

The Chairman was appointed on May 16, 1980. During the six-month interval that had expired due to the time taken to obtain a suitable chairman for the board and to schedule a date for the hearing, Richard Stevens had applied for unemployment insurance. He had subsequently terminated it when he took another job with a local radio and television store. Stevens had received unemployment insurance after the Unemployment Insurance Commission court of referees heard his case and ruled that his discharge was unjust as the order to move his tools to the boring mill was an unreasonable one. This ruling was not accepted as union evidence by the board of arbitration.

At his hearing, and at the arbitration, Richard Stevens's account of his actions contradicted that of the foreman. It was Stevens's contention that he had an understanding with supervision that he did not need to move his tools until such time as space was provided for them at the boring mill. He claimed that the foreman of the carpenter shop had been to his work station to obtain measurements for the construction of a new tool cupboard. Stevens admitted that he had not spoken with the foreman but had been right beside him when plans for the new cupboard were discussed. Management stated that this new cupboard was to be used to store clamps used for work on a number of machines in Stevens's area, and that it would contain no space for tools as there was already a cupboard available for tools used by the boring mill operator.

Stevens also stated that he needed all his tools for the boring mill job and they were locked in drawers at the layout table. (Management steadfastly maintained that very few tools were needed for a boring mill as compared with layout table work.) The grievor maintained also that profanity was common in his conversations with Jackson and that a few words such as damn or hell might have been spoken in the particular altercation in question. A number of workers who had witnessed the altercation between the two men corroborated Stevens's statements, and one stated the exchange of words seemed only a normal argument.

Stevens's account of the October 12, 1979, episode differed considerably from that of Jackson. He said that, while at the layout table getting a tool he required for boring mill work, Jackson stormed in and bellowed: "Get those goddamned tools up to the place you work!" A heated discussion followed, which ended with the foreman telling him to go home at 17 00 and not return until called.

In addition to the grievor's reasons, the union listed a number of items of provocation which would justify a considerable resentment by the grievor against his foreman. These items were:

1. A previous five-day suspension of the grievor by the company (the agent of which was Mr. Jackson), which was later reduced to a one-day suspension by a board of arbitration (although the exercise of discipline was upheld as justified).[1]
2. A three-day suspension later cancelled by a board of arbitration. (Stevens and three others involved here.)
3. Mr. Jackson's placing of the grievor on the boring mill which the grievor found uncongenial, unpleasant, and dangerous, as well as a form of demotion. (No evidence of this.)
4. The boring mill in question was considered by the grievor to be the worst one in the plant. (Company evidence to the contrary.)
5. Mr. Jackson's broken promises to the grievor. (Denied by Jackson.)
6. Mr. Jackson's excessive watching and besetting the grievor at his work on the boring mill. (Denied by Jackson.)
7. Mr. Jackson's misleading the grievor about his intention to build a secure cupboard for the grievor's tools at his boring mill. (Company denied that any such cupboard was planned.)

---

[1]Company rebuttal in brackets.

Exhibit 1
Primo Electric Co. Ltd.
Grievance Report

Plant — East
Date — October 13, 1979
Name — Richard J. Stevens
Address — 108 East 13th Street
Department — D1 Operation — layout boring mill
Length of service — Seven years   Clock No. — 3707
Nature of grievance — I feel that I have been unjustly discharged. Request immediate reinstatement and full reimbursement for lost wages.

....
....
....
....
....

                                                        Richard J. Stevens

Copy for Foreman

Exhibit 2
Primo Electric Co. Ltd.

cc: D. Jackson
October 22, 1979
Business Agent, Local 54
United Electrical, Radio & Machine
Workers of America

Dear Sir:

Re; Grievance #230 — Third Stage
    Unjust Discharge — R. Stevens
    Department D-1

As pointed out at the third stage hearing, the grievor was discharged due to his refusal to obey orders of supervision, and his use of abusive language to his foreman. This action was taken after careful consideration of the grievor's previous record including warnings and suspension.

Evidence submitted by the Union at the third stage hearing in no way justifies any change in the Company's position.

This discharge, therefore, stands.

Yours truly,

Supervisor,
Labour Relations,
Industrial Relations Dept.

SECTION VI
An Introduction to Marketing Management

The purpose of this chapter is to provide you with an understanding of the fundamental concepts and techniques of marketing decision making. Although we will begin with a discussion of individual elements of a marketing program, our ultimate goal is the improvement of your ability to integrate these individual elements into a well-reasoned and practical marketing plan. Such a plan connects the organization's aims and abilities with the customers' needs and wants in the context of an environment. Several of these terms merit classification at the outset.

There have been innumerable definitions of marketing management — no individual phrasing has captured universal acceptance. Most contemporary definitions include the following notions:

1. Marketing management is purposeful — those engaged in it are attempting to accomplish organizational objectives such as dollar profit, share of market, political candidate's success, charity donation goals, etc. The most common goal is profit, but it is not the goal in all situations.

2. Marketing management is designed to satisfy the needs and/or wants of *constituencies*; for management to achieve organizational goals, some constituency (hereafter referred to as *customer group* or *consumer group*) must buy a product, service, or idea from the organization.

3. Marketing management involves trade-offs — an organization's resources (dollars, skills, location, costs) impose limits on how well it can meet the requirements of its customers. No organization can be all things to all people. Thus, marketing managers must decide upon a specific customer group to whom to cater (called *the market target*) and decide what, of the several alternative possibilities, it will offer to that group.

4. Marketing management is competitive — with rare exceptions, organizations must compete for the attention, initial patronage, and continued patronage of their customers. Sometimes the competition is very direct (one shaving cream versus another) and sometimes very indirect (the relative share of milk versus other beverages in individuals' daily fluid intake). Usually there is a spectrum of competitive offerings a manager must "better" to obtain and maintain customers' patronage.

5. Marketing decision making can be improved via a combination of experience and academic discipline; while only a few would maintain marketing management is a science, most knowledgeable individuals would agree that there are some conventional wisdom and "fundamental concepts."

The above five points are all essential to an understanding of what modern marketing management entails. Marketing does not equal selling, nor does it equal advertising. Marketing is an approach to improving the relationship between an organization and its existing (or sought-after) clientele. Most business observers can cite countless examples of successful marketers and unsuccessful ones. In our opinion unsuccessful marketers always make one or more of the following mistakes:

- They did not understand or ignored the first principle of marketing management, which is: "Know the characteristics of your clientele." They tried to *sell*, rather than *market* their product, service, or idea. Marketing begins with establishing the existence of a market and learning what the market wants. One can sometimes peddle products without knowing much about the market, but the chances of success, especially over time, are much slimmer. It is easier to determine what is wanted and then try to provide it in terms of the product, price, method of distribution, and so forth.
- They did analyze the characteristics of their clientele, but either did it poorly or did not use what information they had to design the best possible marketing program. This is an extremely common shortcoming that results from going through the motions of decision making rather than understanding the point of it all.
- They underestimated the competition. In short, if someone else offers a better package of benefits, in time, customers usually discover it.
- They were overly ambitious or optimistic. Many marketing failures are the direct result of marketers with big plans, little patience, and inadequate resources.
- They thought in terms of product characteristics and features (the seller's viewpoint) instead of product benefits and use (the buyer's viewpoint).

There are other reasons that may contribute to failure in the market place, but the point of this discussion is that the odds are against the marketer who ignores basic marketing principles.

If we define the critical task of a marketing manager as the determination of the most appropriate marketing program for the organization, several questions arise. First, what is a marketing program? Second, how do we formulate a marketing program? And, finally, how do we know whether it is the most appropriate? The remainder of this chapter is a discussion of these three questions.

MARKETING PROGRAM CHARACTERISTICS

A marketing program consists of a selection of activities that will be performed by or for the organization (hereafter referred to as the company) to attract the patronage of its target group of consumers and, in turn, to achieve its marketing objectives. The usual decisions to be made in establishing an integrated marketing program include:

- What product (or service) will be offered?
- At what price?
- Through what distribution channels?
- With what communications effort?

This list can be expanded by subdividing each of these questions; for example, communications includes advertising, personal selling, packaging, publicity, and sales promotion. In most situations, a marketing manager has some discretion as to what combinations of policies along these dimensions will constitute the marketing program. Hence, the ingredients of marketing programs may be mixed according to an enormous variety of recipes. One often hears of these variables referred to as the "marketing mix." The "trick" is to find the particular recipe that is consistent with customers' needs, corporate abilities, and environmental realities.

PRODUCT POLICY DECISIONS

Product policy decisions relate to the number, type, style, and quality of products or services to be offered as well as production quantities and schedules. Consumers buy total "packages of benefits" that have both physical and psychosocial dimensions. For example, a product may be characterized in terms of what it is or does (physical attributes) or in terms of how the consumer perceives it (benefits). To many adults, an expensive car is more than a mechanical means of conveyance. The same toothpaste may mean prevention of cavities to one consumer and enhancement of sex appeal to another. The basic question under the heading of product policy is: What package of benefits should we offer?

Many firms offer more than one individual product in a particular product category. Related products are referred to as a product line; related product lines are referred to as product groups. For example, an electrical goods firm may offer several lines including toasters, irons, and blenders and organize its marketing management under the heading of electric housewares group. Clearly, decisions such as *number* of product lines, *depth* of product line (number of sizes, colours) and *brand* names are also major product policy decisions.

Products may be classified by a variety of dimensions. Two common dimensions are product life duration and type of buyer. Using the former, products may be durable goods (automobiles and refrigerators) or nondurable goods (deodorants and food). Using the latter dimension, products may be consumer (breakfast cereals), industrial (tractor trailers) or government (military equipment). These two dimensions may also be combined. For example, breakfast cereals are classified as consumer nondurable products. Such classifications are often used to generalize experience with one product to another comparable product; for example, many of the principles of shampoo marketing are useful in deodorant marketing.

MARKETING COMMUNICATIONS POLICY DECISIONS

Marketing communications refers to those methods a marketer may use to inform and persuade consumers to buy a product or service. The methods include:

- Advertising — print (newspapers, magazines, billboards)
  — broadcast (radio, television)
- Sales promotion — coupons, premiums, contests, samples, direct mail, point-of-purchase displays
- Publicity — editorials, news articles, interview shows
- Personal selling — door-to-door, telephone
- Packaging — boxes, cans, bottles

Each of these methods may be used to (a) give information about the product and its availability; (b) influence attitudes as to the product's superiority; (c) cause action (purchase or repeat purchase). While each method of communication may be examined separately, it is important to recognize the similarities among them; hence the concept of the communications (or promotion) mix to refer to the right blend of the five methods into an overall communications strategy.

In each instance, the marketer must ask the following questions:

- What message will be most appropriate for the target audience to achieve the communications objectives (which may include awareness of the product, favourable attitudes toward the product, persuasion to try the product)?
- What methods of transmitting this message are most appropriate (reach the target at reasonable cost with high impact)?
- When should communications occur (scheduling)?
- How much money should be spent (budget)?
- How will results of the communications campaign be evaluated (effectiveness)?

If the marketer cannot answer each of the above questions specifically, any communications program implemented may be insufficient. An enormous amount of money is wasted on ill-conceived communications programs. A cost–benefit analysis, however rudimentary in form, is mandatory for effective communications decision making.

PRICING POLICY DECISIONS

The answer to "what price should be charged for Product A?" is seldom simple. In addition to legal considerations (which we will not discuss here), there are a number of issues to consider: (a) cost, price, volume relationships; (b) margins, and (c) overall price strategy.

First we must examine the relationship among cost, price, and volume. For example, suppose we knew a ballpoint pen could be produced at 75¢ per unit and that we had two choices: sell the pen at $1.50 per unit or at $3.00 per unit. Without some indication of the number of units that might be sold at each price level, a decision amounts to a guess. Suppose further that an experienced ballpoint pen salesperson estimated that on a monthly basis 1500 units could be sold at $1.50 and only 500 units at $3.00. What would the best decision be then? We would obtain more revenue per month at the lower price ($2250 versus $1500). At the same time, 1500 units would cost $1125 while 500 would cost $375. Profit per month at the lower price would be $1125 — the same as at the higher price. If profit is our goal, it does not matter which route we choose in this example. Clearly such calculations may become much more complicated:

- Production costs may vary with volume (suppose 1500 pens could be produced at 60¢ per unit instead).
- Marketing costs may vary with volume (suppose we had to hire more salespeople to handle higher volume).
- We may not have very good estimates of the sensitivity of consumers to different price levels and thus be forced to calculate a variety of possible outcomes (an optimistic and pessimistic forecast).

One technique developed to simplify such calculations is called break-even analysis. The purpose of break-even analysis is to determine the minimum acceptable relationship among cost, price, and volume to make a venture worthwhile. For example, returning to the pen, suppose we had the following information:

- Cost per unit — $.75
- Plant cost in order to produce — $5000 (per year)

- Salaries and other administrative expenses — $10 000
- Expected selling price per unit — $1.50
- Advertising expense planned — $2000

Suppose, further, management has decided it will not proceed unless enough pens are sold this year to cover all the costs. How many pens must we sell to at least break even?

The arithmetic in this example is not very difficult, so an answer may be achieved in a variety of ways. Here is a general approach to this type of problem:

- Separate costs into two categories, fixed and variable. Fixed costs do not change with volume (at least not over some range of volume), while variable costs change directly with volume.

Fixed costs:	
plant	$ 5 000
salaries	10 000
advertising	2 000
Total Fixed Costs	$17 000

Express variable cost on a per unit basis:
Variable cost: $.75/unit

Notice that sometimes this separation into categories requires judgment or is done according to some particular industry tradition:

- Calculate unit contribution.[1] Unit contribution refers to the difference between selling price per unit and variable cost per unit.

$$\text{(Selling price — cost)} = \text{contribution}$$
$$(\$1.50 — \$.75) = \$.75$$

- Calculate break-even unit volume.

$$\text{Break-even} = \frac{\text{total fixed costs}}{\text{unit contribution}}$$

$$\frac{\$17\,000}{\$.75} = 22\,667 \text{ pens}$$

Thus, we learn that given these cost figures, 22 667 pens must be sold per year to break even. Each pen that is sold contributes $.75 toward the $17 000 fixed costs. After 22 667 pens are sold, each additional pen would contribute $.75 toward profit. How many pens must be sold to achieve a profit of $1000? (24 000, or 22 667 to break even and 1333 to make the $1000 more). In short, to test profit targets, add the dollar amount of profit to the total fixed costs and divide by the contribution per unit. Remember, most businesses are seeking profit, not break-even.

Break-even analysis does not reveal how many we *will* sell, only how many we *must* sell to reach a certain relationship among cost, price, and volume. Using the pen

---

[1] An alternative approach is based on percentage. Calculate the contribution percentage
$$\left(\frac{\text{contribution}}{\text{selling price}} \times 100\right)$$
then divide total fixed costs by this percentage.
Number calculated is sales dollar volume required. To calculate units, divide total required sales dollars by selling price per unit.

example again, the experienced salesperson predicted a sales level of 1500 units per month (18 000 pens per year) at $1.50 selling price. If this is correct, not enough pens will be sold to reach break even. With this approach we may change any or all of the variables and calculate the results. In this way, we become more familiar with the relationships of cost, price, and volume and learn what factors will most influence our performance goals.

A second pricing consideration involves margins. Margin refers to the difference between cost price/unit and selling price/unit. Some people like to express margin as a percentage of selling price and others as a percentage of cost. For example, suppose an item cost the seller $1 and it sold for $2:

Margin as a percentage of selling price= $\dfrac{\$2.00 - \$1.00}{\$2.00}$ x 100 = 50%
   (Markon)

Margin as a percentage of cost = $\dfrac{\$2.00 - \$1.00}{\$1.00}$ x 100 = 100%
   (Markup)

This difference in approach can be confusing when it is not specified which method is being used. When in doubt we suggest you use the margin-as-a-percentage-of-selling-price method. You may encounter the term markdown, especially in the context of items on sale. Markdown is the reduction in selling price. Markdown can be expressed several ways, but the public usually thinks of it as a percentage of selling price. For example, if an item which ordinarily sold for $2 was marked down to $1.80, the markdown is 10 percent:

$$\dfrac{\$2.00 - \$1.80}{\$2.00} \text{ x } 100 = 10\%$$

Each business has "customary" margin levels and ways of expressing those margins. We urge you to be flexible about this, and to be careful to discover what method of margin calculation is being used in any particular situation.

Finally, in addition to the above considerations, companies usually have overall strategies regarding price. Some believe in low price–high volume (called penetration strategy; for example, McDonald's hamburgers) while others believe in high price–low volume (called skimming strategy; for instance, Joy perfume). Some companies like to set the price for a product category (price leader), while others like to imitate (price follower).

DISTRIBUTION POLICY DECISIONS

In most instances, a marketer may change prices frequently and with little difficulty. Changes in methods of distribution are much more difficult to implement. All marketers have to decide how their goods will physically reach the ultimate customers, be they householders, industrial users, or government. The major decision is whether to perform the tasks involved oneself, or pay someone else to help out. Distribution involves skills often quite different from manufacturing, and a great variety of middle parties has developed to perform specialized distribution tasks. Often, such specialized middle parties can reach customers more effectively and more efficiently than manufacturers could directly. Some common channels (distribution routes) are as follows:

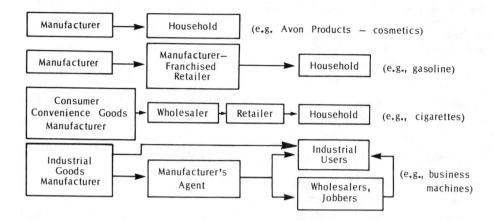

Sometimes there are no reasonable alternative channels to consider. For example, liquor can be sold for home consumption only through the government retail network in Ontario. At times, however, there are a variety of options to consider that involve issue such as:

- Who performs what tasks (e.g., stocks the retail shelves, does warranty work)?
- Who bears what costs (e.g., has to hold the finished inventory)?
- Who makes decisions on selling methods, advertising, amount of stock to carry, etc.?
- Who gets what share of the final sales dollar?

To complicate matters, distributive institutions are changing constantly in character. Some of the relatively new retail types include catalogue showrooms, off-price malls, warehouse outlets, and electronic shopping and ordering. As channels change, opportunities for improved distribution methods are presented to alert marketers.

One generalized way to categorize types of distribution was developed many years ago. Products and outlets are classified as either "convenience," "shopping," or "specialty." Convenience goods are those which the consumer wants readily available. Such items are bought usually at the nearest outlet. Cigarettes are a convenience item. Shopping goods are those which cause the consumer to compare prices and other features in different outlets. The usual examples are automobiles and home appliances. Specialty goods are those for which the consumer will go far out of his or her way. For example, one may be willing to drive across town to buy a certain kind of stereo receiver. Convenience goods generally require mass distribution (many outlets), shopping goods selective distribution (not so many outlets, but well-situated ones), and specialty goods exclusive distribution (one or very few dealers in any particular region).

MARKETING PROGRAM FORMULATION

The preceding brief discussion of the elements of a marketing program and the need to fit these elements into a coherent package should make it clear that marketing decision making generally is a challenging task requiring information and judgment. In this section we will examine the types of information, both internal and external to the firm, most useful to program formulation, including:

- Customer analysis
- Competitive analysis
- Environmental analysis
- Corporate capabilities analysis

In addition, we will make a few comments about judgment and the use of marketing research to improve decision making.

CUSTOMER ANALYSIS AND TRADE ANALYSIS

Many students of marketing quickly latch onto the fact that a customer analysis is essential to marketing decision making, go through the motions of such an analysis, and then proceed to make decisions without much use of the analysis. The only point of a customer analysis is to enable you to make better decisions on the characteristics of your marketing program. Any analysis that does not contribute to improved decisions may be interesting but is definitely useless to us in this context.

Experience has shown that there are six simple questions which will serve well as an outline for customer analysis:

- Who are existing and potential customers?
- What do these customers want?
- How do these customers make buying decisions?
- Where do these customers shop?
- When do these customers shop?
- Why do they behave as they do?

Answers to these questions serve to guide marketing program formulation. For example, some of the implications are as follows:

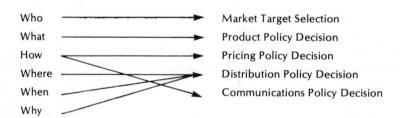

The usefulness of the analysis is greater than can be simply diagrammed here. Further, the answers to these questions frequently overlap with one another. The point is not to fill out a checklist, but rather to make sure you understand your customers and use that understanding to make better choices among decision alternatives.

Who

Except in the case of a very large volume buyer (large industrial concern, government agency), it is seldom worthwhile to examine each individual customer or buyer in detail. Each will have different characteristics: age, sex, income, lifestyle, attitudes, needs, and wants. It is important, however, to see if there exist groups of customers with similar characteristics. Such groups of customers are called *market segments.* The principle of market segmentation is to find groups of customers that are similar within groups and different across groups. There are many dimensions that may be used to segment a market and the choice of which dimensions to employ depends on the specific situation. Perhaps age and income are most important for distinguishing among high-potential and low-potential users of perfume, while amount of consumption may be important for distinguishing among types of breakfast cereal customers. Sometimes the most useful dimensions are demographic (age, sex, income, stage in life cycle), sometimes psychological (status, peer group pressure, self-image) and sometimes a combination of both, known as psychographic (lifestyle).

The major reason for examining a market for segments is that it is difficult to be all things to all people. We use segmentation to select a target audience to whom we will cater in particular. In this way, we tailor our marketing program to the segment or segments we believe will be most responsive to us. If a segment is described in ways that do not allow us to reach it, then the segmentation method is useless. For example, one might say "blue-eyed, left-handed Anglicans who were born in July represent our best market for Product A," but in this absurd instance, how would we use this information?

Another outcome of this analysis is an estimate of the size of the relevant market. For example, there is obviously an important difference between "all Canadian malt beverage drinkers" and "Ontario males under thirty who drink a case or more of ale per week." A 5 percent share of market of the former is clearly different in size for a company from a 5 percent share of the latter. In short, is the segment big enough to justify the marketer's efforts?

What

In order to design an appealing marketing program, we must have some idea of what our target market wants. People buy packages of benefits that include product characteristics, price, service promises, status feelings, delivery convenience, etc. To use one famous example, "People buy ¼-inch holes, not a ¼-inch drill." What characteristics of the package of benefits are most important to customers? A solid understanding of the desired package of benefits tells us what product features to offer, what to say in our advertising, how much the customer might pay, and so on.

How

The question "How do customers buy?" may seem simple, yet the implications of more than superficial answers are far-reaching. Do consumers compare features and prices, do they respond to advertisements or to the advice of friends, do they buy on impulse or only on a carefully preplanned basis, do they want credit or prefer cash? Do customers buy cars the same way they buy cigarettes?

We attempt to find out how the customer buys in order to see what, if anything, we can do to predispose the customer to our offering. If customers want to compare deals, perhaps we will locate close to our competition so the customer will include us in the set of stores considered. For example, clothing and automobile outlets are usually found in groups. If the customer seeks a great deal of product information, we may hire knowledgeable salespeople and keep product literature at the point of purchase. For example, better household furnishing stores employ expert salespeople to assist customers in demystifying the differences among furniture.

Two other concepts are useful in answering the "how" question. First there is a need to understand the different roles that individuals can assume in the buying process. There can be significant distinctions between those who actually use the product (consumer), those who make the purchase (buyer), those who make the key decisions (decision makers), and those who have an influence on the decision (influencer). In some situations only one person may be involved, but in other cases there can be two, three, or more. For years, cereal marketers have operated on the principle that, for many brands, although the mother makes the decision on what will be bought and usually actually buys the cereal (and must be reassured there is some food value in it), it is usually the child who influences which brand will be selected (and must be convinced one brand is better than another). Second, there appears to be a generalized process customers go through at varying speeds in making a purchase which may be simplified as follows:

- Awareness of the product
- Knowledge of the product's characteristics
- Favourable attitudes toward the product
- Purchase
- Post-purchase experience and feelings
- Repeat purchase

If these steps are necessary before a sale (or repeat sale) is made, we should be interested in ensuring that customers do move through the process. Do they know about the product and where to get it? Will advertising or personal selling influence their attitudes toward the product? Application of this process model helps us understand why the customer buys (or does not buy) our product and, thus, what we might do to improve our market performance.

Where

Where do potential buyers shop or want to shop? We have seen recently a trend toward convenient, one-stop shopping. Shopping malls with easy parking facilities have prospered based on this "need." Location is also critical for the industrial purchaser, as it has implications for costs and delivery time. A wholesaler who carries a full line of industrial goods may be preferred over more limited wholesalers by an industrial purchasing agent.

The location of a product or service often has a crucial effect on its image. There would probably be a negative effect on the potential consumer of expensive Paris fashions if they suddenly became available at a discount department store. Similarly, where do customers expect to find certain products? Despite the trend toward "scrambled retailing" (stores carrying all kinds of unrelated products), customers expect to find hardware items in certain stores and not in others, and so on. Having the right product in the wrong location can be disastrous for any marketer.

When

When do potential customers buy? Daily? Weekly? Monthly? Yearly? Seasonally? Morning? Afternoon? Evening? Holidays? Currently, many downtown merchants believe they have been adversely affected by the fact that with the exception of one or two nights a week, their hours are basically 10 00 until 18 00, whereas shopping malls are often open until 21 00 or 22 00 every night. As more and more women pursue full-time careers, dramatic changes are occurring in purchasing time for many products, such as groceries.

The customer life-cycle dimensions are also critical here. For example, marriage involves a whole new buying process, from the engagement ring to the retirement home. Companies also have different purchase needs as they grow and develop. It is important for us to be aware of these changing needs and purchase patterns in order to plan production and distribution activities. Sometimes special incentives can alter when customers buy (e.g., the pre-season sale), but usually it is the marketer who must adapt to the customer's pattern of behaviour.

Why

The more we know about a customer, the better able we are to gain that customer's business. It is one thing to know that women between the ages of forty-five and sixty with reasonably high income prefer our product and buy it in department stores; it is another to know why. For example, DuBarry cosmetics discovered that its customers had aged with the company (and both were dying), that they preferred a cosmetician's help in purchase selection, that price was an indicator of quality to its patrons, that the company had an old-fashioned image, and that skin treatment was their major concern. DuBarry suddenly realized it was not reaching the large group of young, fashion-conscious single women who preferred self-service outlets and sex-oriented advertising, had more limited budgets, and wanted colour and style more than creams and lotions. Subsequently the company drastically revamped its marketing program. For a long time, management knew what was happening to sales and profits, but they did not look at the customer to find out why. Asking "why do customers act as they do?" does not mean psychoanalyzing our clientele, but rather trying to understand better the way they see their needs, circumstances, and the market place.

Trade Analysis

As mentioned previously, most products are offered through a distribution network. As manufacturers look at the flow of their products from factory to ultimate consumer, they think of all the intermediaries as "the trade." Retailers, wholesalers, and other members of the trade are the manufacturer's customers, and one another's customers. Therefore, the same principles of customer analysis mentioned above apply equally to understanding why a product is or is not attractive to members of the trade. For example, why should a food retailer be interested in carrying yet another breakfast cereal or household cleaner? Without trade support, that breakfast cereal or household cleaner may be a total marketing failure. Astute marketers understand and cater to the needs of customers — whether those customers are housewives, corporation purchasing agents, governments, or retailers.

Summary

The development of significant customer and trade analysis is seldom an easy task. Some statistical evidence is often available, but frequently judgments must be based on experience, educated guesses, and observation. Marketing writer Philip Kotler put it this way: "Customers are neither so simple that they do not require study nor so complex that there are no rewards from study."

COMPETITIVE ANALYSIS

A comprehensive and continuing study of our competition is obviously important. We may and should study our competition in the same depth as we study our target market. A successful marketing program both satisfies the needs and wants of a target audience and does so better than the marketing program of the competitors. The following questions usually assist in an analysis of the competition:

1. Who are relevant competitors, both direct and indirect?
2. Are they now after the same target market? Could they be after the same target market in the future?
3. What are their marketing programs (product, price, distribution, communication) and how successful have they been?
4. What competitive stance are they likely to take either in anticipation of or reaction to your own marketing program?
5. How strong are the competitors? In a head-to-head battle, who would likely win? What implications does this assessment have for your own marketing strategy?

One way of characterizing competition in product categories is referred to as the *product life cycle*. It refers to the pattern all products seem to follow at varying speeds from birth (introduction) through adolescence (growth) through adulthood (maturity) to death (decline and withdrawal). In general, the concept is diagrammed as follows:

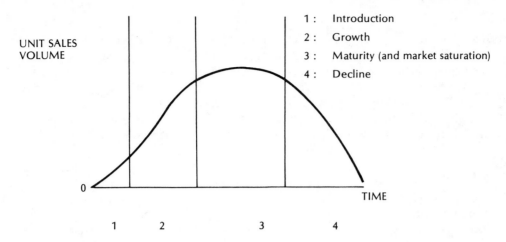

This curve can be prepared for an individual product or service, a product line, or even a product category. It varies in shape across product types. For example, the product life cycle for pet rocks was very peaked (fast up, fast down) whereas the product life cycle for commercial airplanes is usually quite flat (long product life). This concept is important for several reasons:

- The overall shape gives us clues to an approximate time horizon. For example, short product life means we must recoup and exceed our investment in a short time period. This usually means high initial prices and more aggressive marketing. For example, consider fashion and fad items. What will the product life be for this year's most popular clothing style?
- The current or anticipated position of a product in its cycle gives us clues to the likely marketing activities of our competitors. For example, price cutting is frequently very prevalent as unit sales begin to slip in the decline stage.

The product life cycle is clearer in retrospect than in prospect for most products; however, by examining the history of comparable products and how other marketers behaved at various points in time, we may derive considerable insight as to an appropriate marketing program to combat competition.

ENVIRONMENTAL ANALYSIS

The external environment (here meaning the context in which the firm or organization operates) presents a host of dynamic, largely uncontrollable problems and opportunities for marketers. Some of the most important areas to monitor are as follows:

- Political
- Economic
- Social
- Technological

In brief, we must analyze other aspects of the market situation in addition to the customer and the competition.

Political

Recent ground swells of consumer discontent with marketing practices and institutions (referred to as *consumerism*) have produced a raft of new regulations and restrictions at all political levels that marketers must now consider in the formulation of marketing programs. Legislation has resulted in restraints on advertising, merchandising, pricing, labelling, interest rate, etc. Further, we have seen government become directly involved as a marketer, as with Petro-Canada. The trend toward more government involvement in marketing seems inexorable and irreversible.

Economic

As a marketing decision maker, you should also evaluate the current economic situation and try to predict its future direction. How will a recession affect the sale of your products? Inflation? Wage and price controls? Does the value of the dollar affect overseas sales or the supplies which are brought in from other countries? Are there any economic indicators (housing starts, GNP, for example), which will aid in forecasting the problems or opportunities the economy might bring to bear on your plans?

Social

Studies have shown that consumers are changing drastically. Most of the buying power is now in the hands of the younger part of the population. Some of their characteristics include:

- Transience (home and job)
- Fewer children and at a later age
- Husband and wife both work
- Increasing interest in leisure-time activities
- Alternative lifestyles

Perhaps the greatest single social trend affecting marketing is the aging of the "baby boom" generation. How will such changes affect the demand for our product or service? Will marketing programs need to be changed to achieve greater impact?

Technological

The unprecedented acceleration in the rate of technological development in the twentieth century has shortened product life cycles, accelerated changes in distribution, moved more information to more people faster, and so on. What will be the impact of the much-heralded "cashless" market place? Marketing has become faster paced, more complex, more interesting, more expensive, and more risky.

Summary

An analysis of the environment reveals both opportunities and problems. Makers of small economy cars saw and exploited the opportunity to capture a large share of the automobile market. Inflation has altered the promotion strategies of large super-market chains to an emphasis on "deep discount prices!" Consumer activists and political reformers have dramatically reduced marketing freedom in autos, toys, drugs, food, etc. Sometimes these environmental factors can be influenced by marketers, but more often marketers are influenced by these factors.

CORPORATE CAPABILITIES ANALYSIS

Analysis of customers, trade, competition, and the environment enables you to deter-mine what your company *might* do to realize marketing objectives. Analysis of your finances, people, equipment, R & D, and other corporate resources enables you to determine what your company *can* do to realize marketing objectives. What resources are needed? What are now available? What are potentially available and at what cost? Can the existing distribution network handle the new product? Can new salespeople be found and trained in time? Can production provide the product in time and in sufficient quantity? Will finance provide the funds to finance inventory and accounts receivable increases? The list of important questions is lengthier than this, but perhaps the point is clear.

MARKETING RESEARCH

Information may be classified as follows: that which we have and is useful; that which we have and is useless; that which we want and can get at a reasonable cost; that which we want and cannot get at a reasonable cost.

All marketing decision makers operate in a situation that is less than perfect; that is, we do not have all of the useful and necessary information at hand. Sometimes, it is worthwhile to seek more information; at other times, it is futile. There are several ways to collect information: sales reports, trade magazines, government statistics, telephone and mail surveys, interviews, observation of competitors, and so on. The management of this information collection, analysis, and dissemination is usually called *marketing research.*

Marketing research is a service function — it exists to make better marketing decisions. Marketing research activities should only be undertaken if there will be a direct payoff in improved marketing program decisions. As a decision maker seeking research information, you should be able to state:

- What specific information is wanted
- How that information will result in better decisions

Marketing research may involve learning more about customers or about competitors. For example, marketers frequently test their new products, test new advertising cam-paigns, experiment with price levels. There are a host of data collection methods and analytical techniques. You must be careful never to lose sight of the basic purpose of marketing research — some techniques and some research are seductive, but inappro-priate for the problem at hand.

THE APPROPRIATE MARKETING PROGRAM

It is important that you develop your own approach to marketing decision making which, through experience, proves most helpful. Even though we can analyze a problem thoroughly, seeking logical approaches and the best marketing program, the test comes in the market place. You can tell if your program is successful by monitoring several performance criteria, such as the following:

- Dollar sales
- Unit sales volume
- Share of market
- Sales growth rate
- Profitability (several measures including return on investment)
- Number of customers who have heard of the product
- Number of repeat customers

The following diagram may help you remember the points made in this chapter.

The marketing management process involves completing a thorough customer and trade analysis, competitive analysis, environmental analysis, and corporate capability analysis before commitment to a particular marketing program. Decisions on the appropriate mix of product, price, distribution, and communications are developed through a research and information system that scans the external factors that are the key determinants of appropriate strategies.

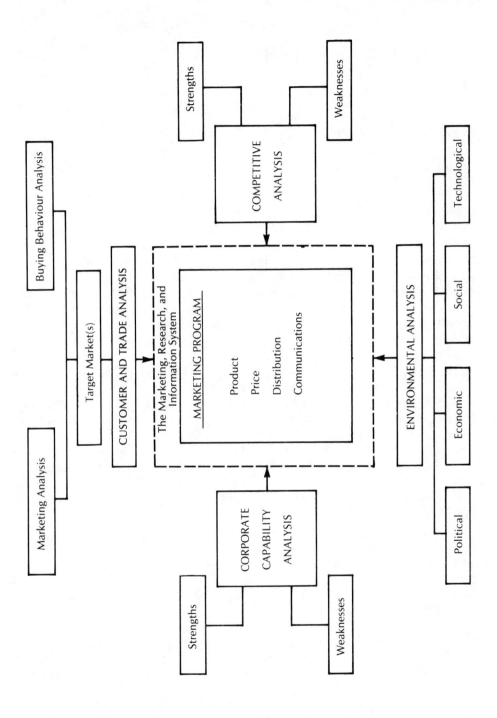

Marketing Arithmetic Exercises

1. A ballpoint pen manufacturer had the following information:

Plastic tubes: top and tip	$.06/pen
Ink	.01/pen
Direct labour	.01/pen
Selling price	.20/pen
Advertising	$ 40 000
Managerial and secretarial salaries	$100 000
Salespeople's commissions	10% of selling price
Factory overhead	$60 000

   Total ballpoint pen market is 10 million pens
   Calculate:
   (a) Unit contribution
   (b) Break-even volume in units
   (c) Share of total market required to break even
   (d) Total profit of the company if 3 million pens are sold.

2. Sylviane Longet was considering making crafts during the winter months. In previous winters, she had done sewing for local individuals, earning a profit last year of $2000. She could work from her townhouse, which had an extra bedroom and most of the basement free (about one-third of her floor space). She felt this much space would be needed for the scale of operations she was considering. Currently she paid $500 per month in rent and $115 in utilities costs. Her accountant had told her that the business should write off the space used and utilities costs incurred proportionately as an expense and that this situation would have no impact on her personal taxes one way or another.

   She was considering hiring two friends to help her. She wasn't sure whether to pay them an hourly rate of $4.50 guaranteeing a full ten hours a week for the period or to pay them on the basis of items produced. If the latter, she was willing to split the gross margin on a basis of 50 percent for the worker and 50 percent for herself.

   Sylvaine was intrigued by the growing interest in her area in small needlework and other related crafts. After talking to a relative in another city who was already doing what Sylviane proposed, she decided she could sell all the crafts she could make. Her relative suggested a product line and price levels. Further, she advised Sylviane to plan in terms of "average items." The going price for an average item was $9.50. Sylviane calculated after several hours experience that the average item could be made in forty-five minutes once a person got organized to make several. Some items would take more or less time, but Sylviane planned to set her prices according to time taken. The average item would involve $2.00 worth of materials. Sylviane calculated she could devote ten hours a week to the project for twenty-six weeks and that her friends could each do the same.

   a) How many average items could the team produce in the season?
   b) If they sell all they make, will Sylviane make more money or less than she did the previous year sewing? (Calculate based on paying her friends an hourly rate and also paying a piece rate.)
   c) Should Sylviane proceed? Why or why not?

d) If Sylviane could get equivalent quality help at $3.50 per hour, how much more money would she make?

e) Sylviane could rent a small office space of the same size as the space she would use in her townhouse for twenty weeks at a total cost of $750, including insurance and utilities. Would this be a better idea for her economically?

3. Richard Miller was preparing a new product analysis for Brand A. He had decided Brand A would sell at $10 at retail, based on his market research. Retailers customarily expected a 40 percent margin and wholesalers a 20 percent margin (both expressed as a percentage of their selling price). Brand A's variable costs were $2/unit and estimated total fixed costs were $28 000. At an anticipated sales volume of 9000 units, would Richard's Brand A make a profit?

4. Jane Murray was wondering whether to increase her advertising expenditures or hire more salespeople. Her overall sales last quarter were $750 000 and her cost of goods sold $500 000. She currently had five salespeople who cost her $250 000 in compensation and expenses per year. Her advertising budget was $240 000 on an annual basis. Her other fixed costs she calculated to be approximately $500 000 annually. Jane had recently been experimenting with increased expenditures in sales effort and advertising. A three-month test using a temporary additional salesperson at regular rates had resulted in additional sales revenues of $75 000. A one-month test in one city using a 20 percent increase in advertising resulted in increased sales revenue of 10 percent. Jane knew these tests were not all that conclusive, but wondered how she might spend her $600 000 planned marketing budget next year based on them.

5. For a summer job, Joe wanted to work independently. Acme Vacuum Company had agreed to hire him to sell their products on a door-to-door basis. The company estimated that Joe's variable costs per actual sale would amount to approximately 60 percent of the sales price of the cleaners. Joe's fixed costs for the summer, including room, board, and spending money, would amount to $2 500. Joe figured that he needed $4 500 to finance his second year at university comfortably. The Acme Company estimated that a keen salesperson could sell $15 000 worth of vacuum cleaners in a four-month period. Joe knew that he could return to his old summer job in a factory. Although his salary would be assured at this factory job, Joe would be able to save only $3 500 for his schooling.

   Which job should Joe take?

6. Management of Michelle's Lingerie were considering several packaging and pricing alternatives for their style 4D5. 4D5 was currently packaged in individual units and was offered in white or pastel colours. Last year, Michelle's sold 72 702 dozen white and 27 975 dozen coloured 4D5, contributing $97 421 and $33 570 respectively to general overhead and profit. 4D5 had been selling for the past year to retail accounts at $12.60 per dozen, for a suggested retail price of $2.50 each. Several retail customers had indicated that they thought Michelle's should double pack 4D5, so management had explored the costing situation. It was estimated that double packing would save about $.50 per dozen. Management had decided that if they went to a double pack, they would only offer white so packaged at the outset. Four suggestions had been made, but the Merchandise Manager wanted to examine the impli-

cations for Michelle's contribution and volume as well as the implications for retailers' margins. Which of the following suggestions do you favour?

		Wholesale	Retail
A	White	$12.15	2/$4.75
	Colours	$12.60	$2.50
B	White	$12.10	2/$4.95
	Colours	$12.10	$2.50
C	White	$12.35	2/$5.25
	Colours	$12.35	$2.60
D	White—1	$12.60	$2.50
	White—2	$12.10	2/$4.95
	Colours	$12.60	$2.50

31

Canada Packers—Flakes of Ham

In September 1978, Bill Clark, a brand manager for Canada Packers Limited, was preparing his recommendation for the introduction of a canned flaked ham into the Canadian market. One year earlier, this type of product had been successfully introduced in the United States. In March, a Canadian competitor had entered a flaked ham product in the Canadian market. Although it was too soon to evaluate its success, Mr. Clark had acquired their pricing structure and some product samples. With this information Mr. Clark began to reevaluate the potential market and the return on investment. One of the major investment decisions would be the advertising and promotional spending. Mr. Clark had just received the Engineering Department's request for funds for equipment to produce the new flakes of ham line. As there was a three-month lead time for equipment, he knew a decision on whether or not to proceed had to be made soon.

COMPANY BACKGROUND

Canada Packers Limited comprised seven major operating divisions organized by product lines. The largest operating division of the company was the Packinghouse Division, which accounted for 30 percent of the domestic industry's meat packing production, and was the largest individual producer of fresh meat in Canada. The Packinghouse Division was divided into Fresh Meats (which included the Food Service Division), Processed Meats and Grocery Products. Each of these three sections had its own management group and sales force.

GROCERY PRODUCTS OPERATIONS

Grocery Products Operations was responsible for the production and marketing of shelf stable products sold through grocery stores. Canned meats was the largest and most profitable product line. Other products included, cheese, nut products, refined oil products, pet foods, and toilet soaps.

Each product was assigned to a brand manager, who developed brand strategy, advertising, sales promotion, pricing, packaging, product reformulation, and new products. The brand manager was also responsible for profitability, and had to develop and meet annual volume and profit projections that satisfied company objectives.

THE CANNED MEAT MARKET

The canned meat market comprised products such as canned hams, luncheon meats, and meat spreads. The canned meat market was declining from 3 to 6 percent annually.

Canned meats usually were purchased by the female head-of-household. Users of canned meats acknowledged convenience, longevity, versatility, and ease of preparation as the product's key benefits. Nonusers tended to dislike the flavour.

Canned luncheon meats were made with lower quality cuts of pork, and 79 percent of the usage was for sandwiches. In comparison, canned hams used high-quality ingredients and were considered acceptable for entertaining or for emergency meals. Seventy-three percent of canned ham primary usage was as a main course, while 27 percent of sliced canned ham was used in sandwiches.

THE COMPETITION

Canada Packers' principal competitors in the canned meat industry were Swifts and Burns. Both firms tended to sell at a discount price, in some cases off-setting the difference in price with less expensive ingredients. Canada Packers marketed premium quality products under its Maple Leaf trademark and supported its reputation for quality with advertising. Canada Packers was the dominant company in the industry, with a 1977 market share of 60 percent for hams and picnic hams, and 48 percent for luncheon meats.

THE U.S. EXPERIENCE

Canada Packers executives were concerned that the declining canned ham and luncheon meat market would have a negative long-term impact on profitability, and were investigating other canned meat alternatives. In 1976, the George A. Hormel Company in the United States had test marketed a new product which Canada Packers management believed represented an opportunity for the Canadian market.

Hormel was the meat leader in the canned meat category and one of the United States' major food processing companies. Hormel Canned Ham and Spam Luncheon Meat were brands with dominant share positions and strong consumer franchises supported by advertising and promotion spending.

Hormel had developed a unique ham product that, like salmon and tuna, could be broken into flakes with a fork. The product was designed to capture part of the large and growing salmon and tuna market. Research had shown that consumers perceived canned salmon and tuna as high quality and versatile. Hormel's Tender Chunk Ham was made of 95 percent lean ham — a very high quality ham containing only 5 percent fat. It was positioned against salmon and tuna, with emphasis on the product's versatility. Hormel's Tender Chunk Ham was introduced in a 6¾ ounce tin and retailed at $.89 U.S. ($1.00 Canadian at that time).

Hormel tested the product in nine major metropolitan markets before launching the product nationally in 1977. In its launch year, Tender Chunk received moderate advertising weight equivalent to a national Canadian campaign of $200 000. The advertising headline was "Does everything tuna does except swim." That year, Tender Chunk ham received a 4.0 percent share of the salmon and tuna market. In 1978, Hormel continued to spend at the same advertising weight, and by September their share had grown to 7.1 percent with further share growth projected for the calendar year.

Exhibit 1 provides retail price comparisons of the leading salmon, tuna, and canned meat products. Exhibit 2 compares the sizes of the U.S. and Canadian canned ham, salmon, and tuna markets.

THE CANADIAN EXPERIENCE

In late March 1978, one of Canada Packers' Canadian competitors launched nationally with a 60 percent lean ham product. The product was packed in a 6¾ ounce tin and sold to the retailer at $18.00 for a twenty-four-tin case. The introductory retail selling price was $0.99 per tin. The product was supported with deals of $1.50 off each case and trade terms of 4 percent off selling price with no advertising or coupon programs.

Canada Packers executives began to monitor the results of the competitive launch with Hormel's performance in the U.S.:

Launch Year Results

| | Volume (000 lbs) | | | | Per Capita Sales |
	Months 1 & 2	Months 3 & 4	Months 5 & 6	Cumulative 6 Months	Cumulative 6 Months
Hormel	1950.0	3460.0	4110.0	9520.0	0.043
Canadian competitor	10.7	55.6	42.3	108.6	0.005

Reliable sources indicated that a second Canadian competitor was about to launch a similar flaked ham product in the near future.

THE CURRENT SITUATION

Mr. Clark realized that he had to determine whether the Canadian market could support two flaked ham products before he could recommend the launch of Maple Leaf Flakes of Ham. Before calculating a potential market share for Flakes of Ham, he believed that he had to determine the market size. Assumptions of market size would be influenced by the decision to position Flakes against ham, salmon, or tuna users.

Canada Packers had just completed consumer testing of its final product formulation of Maple Leaf Flakes of Ham. According to the test results, Maple Leaf Flakes of Ham was equal in quality to Hormel's Tender Chunk Ham. Excerpts from the research are shown in Exhibit 3.

Mr. Clark had to determine whether the high-quality Maple Leaf Flakes of Ham should be sold at parity or at a premium to the competition. Mr. Clark knew a premium price could potentially depress volume, but he felt that Maple Leaf Flakes of Ham might require a retail price of $1.29 to $1.39 per 6¾ ounce tin to be profitable. The research and production managers had verified the costs for the flaked ham product as outlined in Exhibit 4. These costs were believed to be $0.11 per tin higher than the competition. Retail margins on wholesale cost were expected to be equal with the competition at 20 percent of the selling price to consumers.

In addition to the production costs, there were standard industry discounts given to the trade volume incentives and feature pricing. Canada Packers' Volume Incentive Program and Cooperative Advertising allowances with the trade amounted to 4 percent of selling price. At least four times a year, Canada Packers offered price-reducing allowances to the trade in order to reduce retail prices for the consumer. These deals were 8 percent of the selling price, and usually 60 percent of the annual volume was sold on deal. Lower priced competitive brands tended to deal more frequently and at 10 percent of the selling price, and usually sold 80 percent of their annual volume on deal.

Mr. Clark believed that couponing and sampling programs in the first year of a launch were necessary to generate trial. An estimated couponing and sampling budget for the launch year of a new product would be $750 000. In succeeding years, an annual budget for consumer promotions would average $250 000.

Mr. Clark also believed that Maple Leaf Flakes of Ham would require some advertising support. He had four options for advertising spending.

1. Historically in competitive markets such as toilet soap, a budget of $750 000 was required in the first year for high awareness and trial levels. A budget of $450 000 was sufficient to sustain awareness in succeeding years.
2. Moderate spending of $450 000 would achieve a strong share of voice (percent of ad expenditures) in the salmon and tuna market. Salmon and tuna advertising budgets are outlined in Exhibit 5.
3. With a low advertising budget equivalent to $200 000 in Canada, Hormel had successfully built share and volume of Tender Chunk Ham in the United States.
4. Although no advertising at all would reduce share and market potential, it would allow Canada Packers to price more competitively.

Mr. Clark realized that his recommended marketing strategy would have to meet company objectives for new products. Although Canada Packers' management would accept losses in the first year, a product was expected to have a cumulative break-even profit by the end of the third year and have a return on investment of 15 percent in the third year. Beyond advertising and sales promotion, investment for Flakes of Ham would consist of $300 000 for equipment and 10 percent of sales to cover inventory and receivables.

Exhibit 1
Canada Packers
Suggested Retail Prices for Canned Hams/Picnics/Tuna/Salmon

PRODUCT	Size oz.	Cost per ounce ($)	($)
Canned Hams			
Maple Leaf Canned Ham	16.00	2.89	0.180
Burns Canned Ham	16.00	2.70	0.169
Swifts Canned Ham	16.00	2.65	0.165
Canned Picnics			
Maple Leaf Canned Picnic	16.00	2.45	0.153
Burns Canned Picnic	16.00	2.38	0.149
Tuna			
Clover Leaf — Chunk	6.50	.84	0.129
Star Kist — Chunk	6.50	.84	0.129
By the Sea Flakes	6.00	.97	0.162
Salmon			
Gold Seal — Cohoe	7.75	1.33	0.172
Gold Seal — Sockeye	7.75	1.51	0.195
Clover Leaf — Sockeye	7.75	1.51	0.195

Exhibit 2
Canada Packers
Selected Canned Meat Markets in the United States and Canada
(000 pounds)

	U.S.A. 1976	Canada 1976
Hams and picnics	113 240	10 500
Tuna	484 768	27 159
Salmon	63 438	28 268
Total Salmon and Tuna	542 207	55 428

Population ratio: U.S.A. to Canada 10:1

Canadian population in 1976: 22 million

Exhibit 3

Canada Packers
Excerpts of Canada Packers Flaked Ham Study

1. Which canned meat products did you use in the past month?

	Total
	(102)
	%
Canned Ham	45
Canned Luncheon Meat	45
Canned Salmon	87
Canned Tuna	83

2. How many tins of tuna and salmon do you use in an average month?

	Salmon	Tuna
	%	%
One or less	12	19
Two	23	23
Three or four	36	26
Five or more	16	15
Don't use	13	17

3. Having sampled the Flakes of Ham, would you buy the product?

	Total Pretrial	Total Post-trial
	%	%
Definitely buy	29	52
Probably buy	48	39
Might or might not buy	18	8
Probably not buy	5	
Definitely not buy	—	1
Weighted average	7.3	8.4

4. On a scale of 1 to 10, ranging from the average price of tune (1) to the average price of salmon (10) what would you pay for Flakes of Ham?

	Scale		Results (%)
Average Price of Tuna	1		6
	2		2
	3		12
	4	Average	9
	6	5.8	10
	7		16
	8		18
	9		7
Average Price of Salmon	10		4

Exhibit 4
Canada Packers
Flakes of Ham Cost Analysis

Costs	Cost Per Tin*	
	Maple Leaf Flakes of Ham	Competitor
Cost of product	$0.6600	$0.5318
Freight and delivery	$0.0200	$0.0200
Selling and other head office expenses	$0.0775	$0.0400

*There are 6¾ ounces per tin, and 16 ounces in one pound.

Exhibit 5
Canada Packers
Promotional Budgets for Selected Canned Meat Products

Brand	Expenditures* 1976 ($000)
Maple Leaf canned hams	325
Swift canned hams	42
Total canned hams	367
Tuna	
By the Sea	52
Clover Leaf	109
Gold Seal	7
Total tuna	168
Salmon	
Clover Leaf	60
Gold Seal	100
Total Salmon	160
Total Clover Leaf	169
Total Gold Seal	170
GRAND TOTAL	695

*Source: Elliot Research Corporation and industry sources.

32
Duncan Automotive Limited

In early December 1982, Mr. F.P. Duncan, associate dealer of the Dominion Tire Store in Brandon, Manitoba, was considering the purchase of toy tow trucks in preparation for Christmas. The tow truck was a well-designed, durable toy that operated on two 1.5 volt dry cells. The truck, without batteries, had retailed for $9.95 the previous year in his store and in the local department store. A local discount store had sold the trucks "on special" the week before Christmas for $8.95. Batteries varied in retail price according to their length of life and brand name, but Mr. Duncan estimated that on average a consumer spent $2 per truck for batteries.

Duncan Automotive was located in the downtown section of the city. The product line in Duncan's store ranged from mufflers, tires, spark plugs, and car radios to hockey sticks, toys, hammers, saws, piping, small appliances, and sporting goods.

Duncan's total sales in 1981 amounted to $2 000 000 with profit after tax amounting to 3 percent of sales. He stocked toys heavily only at Christmas. In 1980 he sold $75 000 worth of toys, virtually all in the months of November and December.

During the recent visit to the Dominion Tire Winnipeg regional warehouse in September, Mr. Duncan noticed a stock of four hundred toy trucks left over from 1981. He found that the line had not moved as well as expected, and since each truck had been imprinted with the Dominion insignia they could not be returned to the manufacturer. The warehouse manager stated that they had sold only 350 toy trucks the previous year and did not intend to reorder any more. They hoped to move the stock in bulk and offered the complete stock to Mr. Duncan at $3.25 per unit, or half the stock at $4 per unit. Mr. Duncan asked for a day to think it over.

On his return to Brandon, he stopped in at the local department store and saw that they were offering the same truck, without the insignia, at $9.95. When he returned to his store, he looked up his records and found that last year he had ordered and sold fifty trucks in the two and a half months before Christmas. His cost had been $6 per truck. He decided he would not buy any trucks unless he was reasonably confident that he would at least double the total gross profit he made last year on the sale of the trucks.

As he thought about likely price levels, Mr. Duncan reasoned he could sell fifty trucks at $9.95, seventy-five trucks at $8.95 and one hundred trucks at $7.95, all without any advertising support. Based on other toys he had carried, he felt that about $250 advertising support would increase sales by fifty trucks, and that about $350 advertising would increase sales by one hundred trucks. Mr. Duncan's son, who was second in command at the store, disagreed with Mr. Duncan's estimates. "Last year we left money on the table on toys because we did not take a big enough risk by having inventory right up to the end," he said to his father. "I think we can sell 100 trucks at $8.95 without advertising support. I would prefer to sell them at $8.49. We would sell 150 trucks easily without advertising and at least 200 if we spent about $200 on advertising."

Mr. Duncan did not envisage any other costs unless he was stuck with trucks at the end of the Christmas buying season. As a general rule, he figured it cost him 20 percent of cost to carry Christmas seasonal items from one year to the next. With these thoughts in mind, Mr. Duncan wondered whether he should buy the toy tow trucks for the upcoming Christmas season.

33
Garrett Truck Co. Ltd.

Mr. Barton, manager of the London branch of Garrett Truck Co. Ltd., had decided to hire an extra salesperson. He believed the three salespeople he currently employed were doing a good job, but felt they were not able to give intensive enough coverage to their areas and, as a result, the potential of the district was not being fully exploited. In adding a fourth salesperson, however, Mr. Barton was faced with the decision of how to redefine sales areas and/or sales duties for the four. (Exhibit 1 shows the existing geographic divisions of the sales district.)

The Garrett Truck Co. manufactured and sold heavy-duty diesel trucks and parts as well as providing maintenance and repair service. The product line was limited to larger units (tractor only) in the price range of $27 000 to $53 000 with an average selling price of $35 000. This was somewhat higher than the industry average for comparable sized units and, in the company's view, was maintained through the high quality of the trucks and the level of personal service and attention accorded each customer. In the year ending September 1980, the London branch sold 107 new and 64 used trucks which, with parts and service, made up a sales total of $5 541 000 (see Exhibit 2). Garrett trucks were sold throughout Canada to large and small fleet operators as well as one-unit operators; however, the London branch traditionally generated 90 percent of its sales from very small fleet operators that were located in nonurban areas and used trucks for local and long-distance runs to haul a wide range of items including grain, cattle, sand and gravel, lumber, petroleum products, and freight. They tended to utilize the local servicing facilities in London provided by Garrett.

The city of London itself was not a large market for Garrett trucks, mainly due to the relatively small amount of heavy industry. In 1980, thirty-three new and twenty-one used trucks were sold to customers located within the city limits.

The London branch of Garrett Trucks had enjoyed little success selling to the major freight carriers and other major fleet operators such as oil companies, ready-mix cement firms and large manufacturers. One reason always put forward was that many of the large operations had their headquarters in Toronto and Montreal, and truck purchase decisions were made there. Another often suggested reason was that the "Big Three" auto manufacturers, with 50 percent of their total Canadian manufacturing capacity in Mr. Barton's sales area, had captured a large part of the major freight carrier business in the district, since deliveries of raw materials and supplies to their plants represented significant volumes for truckers.

The normal selling process was initiated by a Garrett salesperson calling on a potential customer. As most new truck buyers were fairly knowledgeable about the performance characteristics of different trucks, they generally did not need to view the truck itself, but bought according to quotes given on their required specifications. In only perhaps 25 percent of sales, a customer wanted to see a truck before buying it. The salesperson's prime task then was to sell a buyer on the value of Garrett's higher-than-average quality and price. Maintenance and repair services were provided in a number of ways. The largest number of major overhauls were done at the London branch. However, two service dealers, one in Sarnia about 96 km to the west, and one in Windsor abut 192 km to the southwest, had franchise rights to repair Garrett trucks in their area. The London branch also had a small service truck to dispatch for minor work on trucks that could not be brought to the main depot. A small number of customers had maintenance contracts with Garrett whereby for a certain fee, assessed either per hour or per kilometre, the trucks were overhauled on a set preventative maintenance schedule.

When Mr. Barton was transferred to the London branch, which had one salesperson in 1977, he almost immediately added another salesperson. In the fall of 1979, he added a third person and simply subdivided the two existing territories to create the third territory. His decision to hire a fourth salesperson in the fall of 1980, however, involved a more complex situation, and Mr. Barton was currently considering three alternatives:

1. Divide the district into four territories as evenly as possible to give each salesperson approximately equal potential sales. The new territory would include a westerly portion of territory #1, an eastern part of territory #2, and the southern part of territory #3.
3. Divide the territories, excluding the London city market, three ways, and make one salesperson the used truck manager plus sales responsibility for the city of London.
3. Leave the three territories basically unchanged geographically but assign one person the exclusive responsibility for fleet sales for the entire district.

Trade-ins were a necessary, integral part of new truck sales. Over the past three years, used trucks had accounted for just over 40 percent of all units sold by the London branch. At an average selling price of $8 900, this represented over $500 000 in 1980, and yet the price barely covered the used truck department's out-of-pocket expenses (repairs, commissions) incurred plus the trade-in price. An additional factor was that used trucks were being carried in inventory for an average of one and a half months, which required a considerable amount of funds. In contrast, new truck contributions for the London branch were significant and well above the corporate average.

Mr. Barton personally had been acting as the manager for both new and used truck sales, and all the salespeople had been selling both new and used trucks. With the growth of the branch, Mr. Barton felt he needed to reduce some of his commitments and for this reason had considered establishing the position of used truck manager. In addition to relieving some of his own responsibilities and giving one of his salespeople some management experience, it would also give focus to the selling of used trucks. Under this approach, all salespeople would continue to sell used trucks at the present commission rates. However, they would need to have the deals approved by the used truck manager, who would receive an overriding commission of 1 percent on all used truck sales, plus the normal salesperson's commission on any personal sales. This manager would also be responsible for the profitability of the used truck department, and thus would have authority over the price at which Garrett would accept trade-ins, the extent of repairs to be made, and the selling price to be charged. This meant that, on any new truck sale involving a trade-in, the used truck manager would have to test and inspect the old truck and advise what Garrett deemed to be an acceptable trade-in value. In addition to the foregoing, the used truck manager would be responsible for new truck sales in the city of London.

"Fleet sales" had never been high in the London branch. Mr. Barton's definition of a fleet customer was any company that operated twenty or more trucks. Although quite often these were the products of a single manufacturer, this was by no means always the case. Mr. Barton estimated that there were fifty such potential customers spread over the total district. These figures did not include those companies which bought their trucks through a Toronto- or Montreal-based head office, nor those companies which were committed to buying from one of the Big Three manufacturers. The territory estimates reflected Mr. Barton's best estimate of real market potential based on truck registration data and his knowledge of the market. The number of trucks purchased by these companies annually would amount to about 25 percent of their fleet size, some as replacements and some as additions. Of the fleet customers, six operated in the order of 150 trucks, ten operated around 50, and the remainder operated, on the average, about 25 trucks. Only 10 percent of the London branch's 1979 sales were to fleet customers, but by mid-1980 fleet sales had already exceeded that level. Mr. Barton felt that the London branch should be able to get at least 10 percent of the available fleet market. Since he felt they had 20 percent of the single-unit owner market, he was convinced that it would be difficult, but it was both possible and necessary to increase the branch's penetration of the fleet market segment. One salesperson with primary responsibility for this activity might be the answer.

One of the problems was that fleet customers, not surprisingly, expected larger discounts than the ordinary customer. The necessary discounts would probably exceed 27 percent. This could have considerable effect on a salesperson's potential commission earnings, and Mr. Barton accepted that he might have to adjust the base salary to compensate.

One of Mr. Barton's concerns was the reaction of his existing salespeople to any changes in their territories. These salespeople, with their expertise, experience, and personal ties with the customers, were the backbone of the branch's operations. They earned $400 per month base salary plus commissions for an average total of $35 000 per year. The structure of commission payments is given in Exhibit 3, and a typical month's sales by one person are shown in Exhibit 4.

Fred, the salesman in the southwest region (Territory 2), was thirty-six years old and had sold Garrett trucks for two years. Before joining the company, he owned his own small trucking operation. Fred was not a high-pressure salesperson, but sold on the basis of personal knowledge of trucks and truck driving and his understanding of the needs of small truckers. Mr. Barton characterized him as a hard-working salesperson with little ambition for, or interest in, a management position.

Allan, also thirty-six, had the London city and east region (Territory 1). He joined Garrett Truck in 1976 prior to the time that Mr. Barton was made branch manager. Previously an insurance salesperson, Al had a charming personality and a polished style, but at times was considered a little "pushy" by some customers and prospects. He had no previous experience with trucks before joining Garrett, yet with what Mr. Barton considered to be at best average effort, he was the branch's highest paid salesperson.

Harvey, twenty-eight years old, became the third salesperson in the branch in the fall of 1979, and had the northwest region, an area not well covered previously (Territory 3). He initially joined Garrett as an apprentice mechanic and after achieving his Class A standing, rose to service foreman at the London branch before entering sales at his request. His likeable personality and knowledge of Garrett trucks had made him a good salesperson earning a respectable commission.

Before Mr. Barton could start his search for a salesperson, he would have to receive approval from head office. From prior conversations with his superiors, he knew they were in favour of adding a salesperson, but he still had to submit a formal proposal outlining the specific details of the job and his reasons for asking for someone to fill it.

Exhibit 1
Garrett Truck Co. Ltd.
London Branch

Salesmen's Territories

—————— County Line

●●●●●●●● Territory
Boundary

Exhibit 2
Garrett Truck Co. Ltd.
London Branch Income Statement for the Years Ending September 30
(in 000's of dollars)

	1978		1979		1980	
Total sales		$2 865		$2 988		$5 541
Cost of sales		2 310		2 437		4 700
Gross margin		$ 555		$ 551		$ 841
Expenses		505		499		676
Profit (loss) before tax		$ 50		$ 52		$ 165
Breakdown of Total Sales, $ (Units)						
New trucks	(61)	$1 760	(47)	$1 635	(107)	$3 689
Used trucks	(54)	390	(42)	362	(64)	555
Total trucks	(115)	$2 150	(89)	$1 997	(171)	$4 244
Total parts		545		731		963[1]
Total labour		170		260		334[2]
TOTAL SALES		$2 865		$2 988		$5 541

[1]Margin on parts sales about 35%.
[2]Margin on labour about 50%.

Exhibit 3
Garrett Truck Co. Ltd.
London Branch

Sales Commission Payments

New Trucks

% Discount[1]	Rate of Commission
Under 19	5%
19-19.9	4.5
20-20.9	4
21-21.9	3.5
22-22.9	3
23-23.9	2.5
24-24.9	2
25-25.9	1.5
26-26.9	1
27 or higher	0.5

The average commission earned on new trucks in 1980 was 2.1%
Used Trucks — 2% on selling price

[1]Sale price on new trucks is quoted as a percentage discount from company-established list price.

Exhibit 4

Garrett Truck Co. Ltd.
Average Monthly Commissions

Current average sales and commissions for one salesperson in one month:

Unit sold: new	3
used	2
Sales dollars:	
new — 3 x $35 000 (avg.)	$105 000
used — 2 x $ 8 900 (avg.)	17 800
	$122 800
Commission earned:	
new — 105 000 x 2.1% (avg.)	$ 2 205
used — 17 800 x 2%	356
	$ 2 561
Monthly salary	400
Total monthly compensation	$ 2 961
Expenses paid to salesperson	$ 270
Total selling expenses to Branch	$ 3 231
Cost to sell — % of sales	2.6%

34

General Packaging Ltd.

In January 1984, General Packaging Ltd., a medium-size packaging and manufacturing firm located in St. Catharines, Ontario, purchased all the assets of R.B. Barnes, Ltd., a manufacturer and marketer of a wide range of horticultural dusts, sprays, and fertilizers for home gardeners. These were sold under the brand name Gro-Aid. (See Exhibit 1 for a partial list of products.)

For some time prior to January 1984, the management of General Packaging Ltd. had been searching for a line of consumer products which offered potential for growth and which would pick up some production/packaging capacity slack that occurred with their present line of products in the January to June period.

R.B. Barnes Ltd. had been established in 1979 by Mr. Roy Barnes and by 1983 all products manufactured by Barnes were marketed under the Gro-Aid brand name through six wholesalers, located in Ottawa, Kingston, Toronto, Hamilton, London, and Windsor. There was no contractual arrangement with these wholesalers but Barnes had given his line to only one wholesaler in any market. The wholesalers supplied approximately three hundred hardware stores, department stores and nursery outlets throughout southern Ontario. Sales had shown steady increases over the years (actual sales for 1982 and 1983 are outlined in Exhibit 2).

As a general rule, demand by retailers for the Gro-Aid line was highest during late winter and spring, declined in the late summer and was virtually nonexistent during the fall and early winter period. Mr. Barnes had devoted his full time to the company and two years previously had hired Mr. Robert C. Smith on a full-time basis. Casual labour was hired as required during the production period. Mr. Barnes devoted his time to selling activities and overseeing the general operations. Mr. Smith acted as production manager as well as handling incoming orders, billing and some general office work.

Mr. Barnes had leased manufacturing space in a building formerly occupied by a St. Catharines automobile dealer. The lease expired as of January 1, 1984 and could not be renewed. His difficulty in locating comparable low-cost space, the thoughts of relocating, and his declining health had prompted Mr. Barnes to contact a friend who was a vice-president of General Packaging Ltd. regarding the possible purchase of his company.

Under the terms of the purchase Mr. Barnes had contracted to work with General Packaging Ltd. for a period of six months. Mr. Smith had also been hired as an assistant production manager for the total plant, a position General Packaging Ltd. was attempting to fill at that time. Since the manufacturing of the Gro-Aid line was essentially a mixing and packaging operation comparable to other products handled by General Packaging Ltd., integration into the General Packaging Ltd. plant presented no problems.

Immediately following the purchase of R.B. Barnes Ltd., Mr. C.B. Kennedy was appointed product manager with responsibility for the Gro-Aid line. He was to operate as a profit centre with the budget outlined in Exhibit 3. Mr. Kennedy had been an assistant product manager with General Packaging for the past three years and was considered most capable. It was expected that he would work very closely with Mr. Barnes on marketing activities during the six months of Mr. Barnes's employment.

In the past Mr. Barnes had spent the major portion of his time doing missionary sales work, calling on his wholesalers and retailers. Any orders he received from retailers he would turn over to the nearest wholesaler for delivery and billing. For 1984 Mr. Kennedy intended to follow this approach.

Mr. Barnes attributed his past success to the high quality of his products and the fact that the Gro-Aid line was sufficiently broad to enable the retailer to offer customers a complete range of garden chemicals by purchasing only one line. Mr. Barnes was a chemical engineer and he personally had developed the formulations for the various Gro-Aid products. Retailers generally took a 40 percent markup on the suggested retail price of the product line while the wholesaler's margin averaged 20 percent of suggested retail. Although a number of other brands of garden chemicals were marketed throughout southern Ontario, Gro-Aid prices were competitive and no other manufacturer offered as wide a range of products.

Late in February 1984 Barnes and Kennedy learned that Bill Lockhart, one of the largest Toronto retail dealers, was no longer interested in carrying the Gro-Aid line. They discovered that the dealer had just been appointed the Ontario distributor of a Quebec-manufactured line of horticultural chemicals to be marketed under the brand name of Surgro.

Upon learning of this appointment, Barnes and Kennedy were able to determine from some of the other retail dealers that Lockhart had appointed three manufacturers' agents to promote the Surgro line to hardware stores, department stores, and nursery outlets throughout the province at dealer cost prices averaging 5 percent lower than those at which Barnes had traditionally sold Gro-Aid products. All wholesalers were to be offered the new line. Orders for ten cases or more could be placed directly by retailers with Lockhart and they would be billed at wholesaler prices. The Surgro line included only slightly fewer products than the Gro-Aid line.

Barnes and Kennedy learned that the company which manufactured Surgro planned to support the introduction of the line with a one-quarter-page newspaper advertisement in ten major markets in May, and would offer dealers an attractive wire display stand free with an initial $200 order.

Barnes had not felt it necessary or wise to invest in advertising Gro-Aid products, but during the past two years he had packed a simple combined display and price card into each case of products. Barnes found the dealers generally had not made extensive use of these since the products were usually stocked on shelves in the retail outlets.

In order to determine the quality of the new competitive lines, Kennedy decided to purchase and analyze samples of the Surgro products. Chemical analysis revealed that in all instances Surgro samples were inferior in quality to Gro-Aid products. On March 1, Kennedy sat down to examine all the information he had been able to gather about the new competitive development and to consider what, if any, adjustments in marketing strategy were required. In making his decision, Mr. Kennedy knew that he would have to consider the financial implications as well.

Exhibit 1
General Packaging Ltd.
Gro-Aid Product Line Types (Partial List)

	Size	Suggested Retail Price
Lawn Fertilizer	4 litre	$8.99
	750 ml	3.99
Plant & Shrub Fertilizer	4 litre	8.49
	750 ml	3.29
	250 ml	2.25
Rose Protector (Aphids)	750 ml	3.99
(Fungicide)	750 ml	3.59
	4 litre	13.35
Lawn Weed Killer	750 ml	4.29
	250 ml	2.99

Exhibit 2
General Packaging Ltd.
Profit & Loss Statements
Years Ending December 31, 1982 and 1983
For R.B. Barnes Ltd.

		1983		1982
Sales		$180 000		$144 000
Cost of goods sold		108 000[1]		90 100[2]
Gross margin		72 000		53 900
Operating expenses				
Mr. Barnes' salary	$14 000		$14 000	
Selling expenses	14 000		12 000	
Delivery expense	3 600		2 800	
Office expense	8 000	39 600	7 600	36 400
Net Profit before taxes		32 400		17 500
Income taxes		7 128		3 828
Net Profit after taxes		$25 272		$13 672

[1]Including $10 000 of Smith's salary.
[2]Including $4 000 of Smith's salary.

Exhibit 3
General Packaging Ltd.
Budget for the Gro-Aid Division, 1984

Sales		$240 000
Cost of goods sold		144 000[1]
Gross margin		$ 96 000
Operating expenses		
Mr. Kennedy's salary	$34 000	
Other selling expenses	14 000[2]	
Delivery expense	4 800	
Overhead allocation	12 000[3]	64 800
Budget Divisional Contribution		$ 31 200

[1]Transfer price of finished product from the manufacturing division to the Gro-Aid Division.

[2]Travelling expenses, etc. No charges for payments to Mr. Barnes were allocated to the Gro-Aid Division since for internal budgeting purposes they were considered as part of the original purchase price.

[3]Five percent of sales was allocated to all product divisions to cover administrative and other costs.

35
Kellmar Canada Inc.[1]

Kellmar Canada Inc. (Kellmar) was a multinational manufacturer and marketer of a number of heavily advertised lines of canned fruits and vegetables, hot and cold cereals, and pet foods, with 1982 Canadian sales of $100 000 000 and profits of $5 000 000. In November 1983, Kellmar's National Sales Manager, Frank Rivers, was preparing for a meeting with Bill Hawke, Regional Manager–Atlantic[2] to discuss Hawke's proposal to terminate their brokerage arrangement in Newfoundland and move to using salaried salespeople. The notion of moving to a direct sales operation in Newfoundland, similar to that utilized in the remainder of Canada, was not new. However, in the past the costs involved could not be justified by acceptable revenue increase projections.

O'Neil Brokerage Ltd. (O'Neil) had represented Kellmar in Newfoundland for over thirty years. Their principals were well known and well liked by the grocery trade in Newfoundland as a result of their continuing service and their historic coverage of the remote "outports." Bill Hawke (32), the Regional Manager, had been appointed in January 1982 after a seven-year successful track record in sales and sales supervision in Nova Scotia and New Brunswick. Prior to January 1982, Atlantic was an area reporting to the Quebec Region. It was now the smallest region, with seven sales representatives and a regional manager while other regions had fifteen to thirty sales representatives and one to three area managers reporting to a regional manager. Hawke was viewed by management as an upwardly mobile individual who clearly hoped to achieve success in his current assignment with a view to moving on to a bigger region or to a position at Head Office.

Newfoundland, with a population of 585 000 (See Exhibit 1), represented 2.4 percent of Canada's population and had historically been viewed as a "have-not" province. The economy was changing, however, and according to Statistics Canada was showing growth for 1980 on a number of dimensions as compared to some other provinces: disposable income was up 13.5 percent in Newfoundland compared to 10.1 percent for the Maritimes; jobs were up 7.5 percent versus 3.5 percent, retail trade was up 13.2 percent versus 11.1 percent and food sales were up 20.1 percent versus 15.3 percent.

In the report Bill Hawke had submitted, he pointed out that Kellmar's dollar volume in Newfoundland accounted for 17 percent of the combined volume for the other Maritime provinces, while the ratio for three other major food manufacturers who used their own sales force rather than brokers ranged from 19.5 percent to 51.3 percent (See Exhibit 2). Unfortunately market share data by brands or product lines were not currently available from the major reporting services, though they would be including Newfoundland in their reports starting in 1983. In Hawke's view there were

---

[1]All names of companies, products, and people have been disguised. Corporate financial data have been adjusted but relationships of data have been maintained.
[2]"Atlantic" includes the four provinces of New Brunswick, Nova Scotia, Prince Edward Island, and Newfoundland. "Maritimes" includes New Brunswick, Nova Scotia, and Prince Edward Island.

opportunities for growth by Kellmar in Newfoundland, as a number of Kellmar brands and sizes were not sold; and merchandising, shelf space, and shelf position for many Kellmar products were limited at the retail level. The major problem in Hawke's opinion was that while the broker maintained a sales force of seven people, Kellmar only received about 10 percent of their sales time and effort. The broker, who represented six major national manufacturers including Kellmar, as well as a few regional manufacturers, not surprisingly claimed that Kellmar received more effort than that. According to Hawke, however, O'Neil's salespeople had too many products to handle and were inclined to think of Kellmar as fourth or fifth on their list of priorities.

Bill Hawke had originally believed that Kellmar should have a sales supervisor based in St. John's and account representatives in St. John's and Grand Falls. Corner Brook would be covered from Cape Breton, as was done by a few other manufacturers, though this unfortunately involved considerable travel time and expense. In his formal proposal, he recommended that the company install a supervisory level representative in St. John's and account representatives in St. John's and Grand Falls with no support from Cape Breton. After applying Kellmar's sales call frequency decision model[1] which considered individual store volume and decision-making power at the store level, Hawke had calculated that 3.4 salespeople would be required to cover Newfoundland. He felt that a complement of 3 would still give sufficient coverage, as in his view there were a number of smaller volume direct accounts which should be buying from wholesalers and could receive less sales time. The total cost of the sales group of three would amount to about $100 000 (See Exhibit 3) and compared favourably with the previous year's brokerage commission of about $150 000.[2] With the added sales effort and greater control over the sales force, Hawke expected to increase sales from $2 100 000 to $2 500 000 in the next fiscal year, at an average contribution margin of 25 percent. Hawke proposed that, after formal termination of O'Neill's contract with six months' notice a letter be mailed out to all accounts (Exhibit 4). In the six months period preceding the actual termination Hawke proposed to recruit, train, and organize a sales team who would cover the territory for a number of months in conjunction with the broker's efforts. Sales for that perod would be credited to the broker's commission. Hawke stated that he did not expect O'Neil to be pleased with the decision, but that they would be cooperative until the end of the contract time in order to maximize commission income.

Although Frank Rivers shared Bill Hawke's interest in growth, he was concerned that Hawke had not calculated all the costs involved in the proposal. He anticipated that a number of headquarters costs could increase immediately, such as travel, national sales meetings, sales contests, etc. and that in the future there would be pressures for regional administrative and supervisory support. Nor was he convinced

---

[1] For each store weekly estimated sales volume, store control over shelving and space allocations, store control over displays and deal support, and store control over distribution were considered to determine maximum quarterly sales call frequency, which ranged from 0 to 6. Stores where salespeople could accomplish little because of low volume or because key decisions were made at the store headquarters received few calls.

[2] The $150 000 was composed of contracted sales commissions of $115 000 on Kellmar products shipped by Kellmar's Newfoundland warehouse and a supplement of $35 000 instituted in 1980 when Kellmar had increased its sales force size in Canada by 25 percent to improve effort and coverage at the retail level. They had increased the broker's commissions at that time to attain comparable coverage and effort increases. The broker had increased his sales complement from 6 to 7 as a result.

that the transition would flow that easily. The broker had shown steady sales increases for Kellmar over the years, and had dealt quickly and well with any and all issues that had arisen with retailers and wholesalers in the province. Frank still had in his files letters received from three major accounts some years ago when there were rumours that Kellmar would be replacing O'Neil with a direct sales force. The strongest one stated that "We are making plans to delete 50 percent of your goods from our inventory but hope you will change your mind." The other two were most supportive of O'Neil and clearly stated that they would be most unhappy with such a decision and would take some action. Six accounts out of fifty accounted for 65 percent of Kellmar's total dollar sales (ranging from a high of 15 percent to 6 percent) in Newfoundland. The support of those six accounts, only two of which were national accounts, was critical. If any of those key accounts chose to resist the changeover, it would create a host of problems, and Kellmar's sales could be seriously affected.

Exhibit 1
Newfoundland

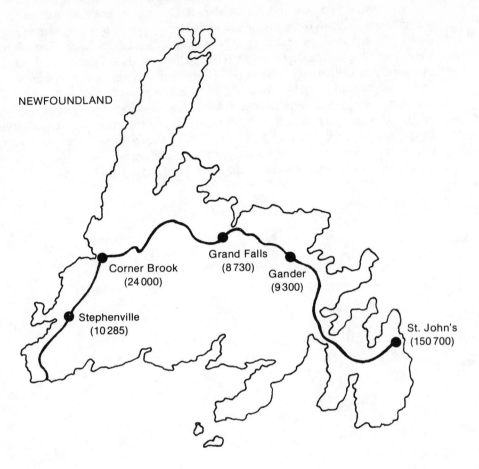

NEWFOUNDLAND

Corner Brook
(24 000)

Grand Falls
(8 730)

Gander
(9 300)

Stephenville
(10 285)

St. John's
(150 700)

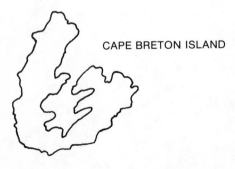

CAPE BRETON ISLAND

Exhibit 2

Analysis of Competitive Salaried Sales Force Deployment

Company A — 22.5 percent ratio Newfoundland to Maritimes Sales

1 District Manager, St. John's
2 Representatives, St. John's
1 Representative, Grand Falls
1 Representative, Corner Brook

Company B — 19.5 percent ratio Newfoundland to Maritime Sales

1 District Manager, St. John's
2 Representatives, St. John's
1 Representative, Corner Brook

Company C — 51.3 percent ratio Newfoundland to Maritimes Sales

1 Division Supervisor, St. John's
1 Representative, St. John's
1 Representative, Grand Falls
1 Representative, Corner Brook

Company D — 26 percent ratio Newfoundland to Maritimes Sales

1 District Manager, St. John's
1 Representative, St. John's
1 Representative, Grand Falls
Corner Brook covered from Cape Breton

Common Elements

A. Supervisory personnel in St. John's
B. Coverage in three district geographical areas — St. John's, Grand Falls, and Corner Brook.
C. All sales forces composed of at least four individuals.

Exhibit 3

Newfoundland Sales Force Feasibility Study as Submitted by Bill Hawke

In confirming the cost of establishing a Sales Group on the island, the following figures substantiate approximately $100 000.

The $100 000 is the actual outlay of expenses to sustain a three-person sales force for a year. This does not include the cost of an office or stenographic help, which at this point will not be required, nor does it include communications. There is also another factor of interest, the investment of three cars. In round figures, if we say each car is worth $10 000.00, we will have $30 000.00 invested at 17 percent, which is $5 100.00. I am not sure where this figures into the hard figures; however, it is certainly something one should keep in mind.

Salary

1	Supervisor Level Representative $486.00[1] per week x 52	= $25 272.00
2	Account Reps $375.00[1] per week x 52 (Salaries 90% Mid Point)	= 39 000.00
3	Car Expenses x $350.00[2] per month x 12	= 12 600.00
3	Car Depreciation x $150.00[2] per month x 12	= 5 400.00
3	Travel & Subsistence x $450.00[2] per month x 12	= 16 200.00
	Total	$98 472.00

[1]Includes benefit costs such as pension, insurance, etc. per the personnel department but this does not include any expenses included in the sales department expenses categories (sales meetings, awards, etc.).
[2]Same as used for budgeting purposes for Maritime Provinces salespeople.

Exhibit 4

Proposed Letter to All Newfoundland Accounts

The Kellmar Company of Canada Inc. is pleased to announce the establishment of its own Sales Force for Newfoundland, effective January 1, 1983.

O'Neil Brokerage Limited has represented Kellmar very well over the years and their efforts and accomplishments are appreciated. However, we believe that we can service our Newfoundland customers even more effectively with our own Sales Force selling Kellmar products exclusively.

It is our intention to hire only within Newfoundland to ensure that the Kellmar Sales Force is well experienced in your market place and that solid relationships continue with our valued customers.

Our sole intention in this move is to improve service to our customers and thereby fully realize the potential of the Newfoundland market. We look forward to servicing you in this new capacity; your Kellmar Sales Representative will call to meet you in the very near future.

Sincerely,

National Sales Manager

36
KeLy Fashions

Kerri Hampton and Lynda Reed, recent graduates of a prominent Ontario college's school of design, had formed KeLy Fashions, in Hamilton, Ontario, in September 1979, and were attempting to establish themselves as designers, manufacturers, and wholesalers in the Canadian women's fashion industry. After only twelve months of operation they felt they had made some progress with their product but were still learning the ropes about running their own business. Despite the hard work and frequent problems, both Kerri and Lynda were glad to be in business and on their own. They expressed their disappointment in their classmates who had followed the normal process of becoming established as fashion designers.

"The ones at the top of the class just did not pursue their careers. A few started in the industry, but we don't know how they're doing. Most graduate designers have to start at the bottom and work their way up. They might work for a manufacturer — sewing, cutting patterns, or just pinning. Eventually, after working for a while, they get more opportunity to show their work, and maybe one of the industry's designers will take them on as apprentices. We had been laid off from designing jobs with retail stores in this city, and since we didn't want to move to Toronto, we pooled our limited resources and our ideas to form KeLy."

WOMEN'S FASHION INDUSTRY

The total number of women's apparel manufacturing operations had remained reasonably constant throughout the 1970s. Although the number of factories had declined up to 1978, the use, and hence the number, of contractors had increased. Exhibit 1 provides information and definitions on the manufacturing industry from 1970 to 1978. Average sales growth had been 10.8 percent, but when the inflation rate for the clothing industry was considered, real growth averaged about 5 percent per year over the period. (Consumer price index and inflation rate statistics are included as Exhibit 2.) The number of factories and contractors was closely tied to the annual growth rates, which were expected to continue at the average rate into 1980.

Retail sales patterns and growth had a significant impact on the manufacturing industry. A proliferation of chain stores in the 1970s introduced mass merchandising and volume buying, and started the trend to manufacturing through contract work. Those factories and contractors able to get contracts survived. The exception to the rule appeared to be the independent manufacturer/retailer (or couturier) who sold made-to-order original or limited volume designs of their own creation, generally through small, personally owned boutiques.

Total retail sales growth of all women's apparel in Canada through department stores, chain stores, and independent retailers averaged 9.5 percent in 1979. Independent stores had the largest growth rate at 14.2 percent. Summary statistics, definitions, and information for the three types of retail operations are given in Exhibit 3. Chain and department stores were found almost exclusively in cities with populations greater than 50 000. Independent retailers tended to service smaller towns with a general merchandising approach, while independents in larger cities tried to cater to a specific clientele through narrowly defined or exclusive product lines. These independents in larger cities generally were classified as boutiques.

Fashion shows were held twice yearly in Toronto and Montreal. At these shows, retail store purchasing agents (buyers) viewed the work of fashion designers and purchased quantities of each design to be delivered to their warehouses or outlets. Department and chain stores, because of their volume buying, tended to concentrate on products offered by large fashion design companies which could guarantee the volume demanded. The smaller, independent buyers, purchasing in smaller volumes, paid higher per unit costs and often were unable to obtain more popular designs because the volume buying of the chains would effectively fill up the production capacity of manufacturers. (In some instances the department or chain store might even obtain exclusive rights to distribute for a couturier, but this practice was limited since it restricted the flexibility of the couturier and, subsequently, could affect growth potential.) One further problem facing the independent stores was that the independent buyer was often the manager of his or her own store. Many managers could not afford to spend two or three days at the trade shows leaving their stores short-staffed. Instead, manufacturers' agents visited the independent dealers at their stores. The agents would show samples and drawings to the retailers and take their orders. The agent would normally receive 7–10 percent commission on sales. Depending on the concentration of retail stores, the agent could probably visit three to six outlets in a day. Each customer required regular sales calls about once every three months.

The fashion designs were created by independent or in-house fashion designers who normally had a number of years of experience working for couture houses. There were many designers in Canada, but most worked only as designers, not as manufacturers. Most independent designers presented their designs for buyers and manufacturers at spring and fall fashion shows, then they turned their attention to the next season's line and to the trends that were developing in Paris, Rome, and New York. As a manufacturer, wholesaler, and designer, KeLy Fashions was one of only a few operations in Canada to integrate all three aspects of the fashion business.

THE WOMEN'S FASHION CONSUMER

Most retailers recognized two distinct, major consumer groups: the fad-conscious younger set, and the more conservative, over twenty-five group. The retailer focus for each group was quite different.

The retailers catering to the fad-conscious consumer tended to be more concerned with keeping up with the trends in clothing styles, and developing merchandising and display innovations. In 1979, this market was felt to be highly competitive, with a number of chain stores locked in a battle to increase market share through price cutting. Much of the advantage went to chain stores because they could buy in larger quantities and, hence, gain cost savings. Therefore, volume of sales was critical to profitability. The fad-conscious consumer was perceived to be more interested in the lower prices and the style of the product. Quality was not felt to be a priority since the clothing primarily went out of style by the next year.

The retailers of the more conservative designs held different views about their consumer. The general perception was that given the economic conditions of the 1970s, large, specialized wardrobes were too difficult to finance. Therefore, retailers began to see a demand for a mix-and-match type of product that would wear well over a period of time. Consumers such as businesswomen and secretaries seemed to be looking for styles that were less faddish and, hence, could be mixed with other garments in their wardrobe to provide a dual role rather than being used specifically for the office or for an evening out. In response to this trend, retailers concentrated on providing a quality product and knowledgeable salespeople who used their experience to help the customer coordinate colours and styles to suit existing wardrobes.

The retail market for the more conservative, mix-and-match consumer was not as fiercely competitive as the fad market. Sales were shared by department stores, several chains such as Irene Hill and Town and Country, and the independent retail stores.

Discussions with industry sources indicated that competition from home sewing was always present, and retailers felt that the quality of most manufactured clothing had to be consistently high as a selling feature. As well, prices had to be reasonable for the average woman to choose purchasing over home manufacture. Only a small number of exclusive couturiers, or boutiques carrying designer originals, could charge extreme prices and survive. With high quality and competitive prices necessary, the onus was on the manufacturer to ensure consistent quality control, which usually implied a full-time floor supervisor to check each product, and required volume production to provide economies of scale in purchasing material, and efficient usage of machine capacity and labour.

KeLy FASHIONS — THE FIRST YEAR OF OPERATION

Upon starting their business in September 1979, Kerri and Lynda began preparing for the 1980 spring and summer fashions since it was too late in the year to manufacture fall and winter styles. By studying European and other fashion magazines, and by applying their own ideas, they developed drawings of several lines of evening wear and dresses. From these drawings, they made patterns and then produced an original garment. After alterations and improvements, the patterns were set for the production of the product lines. Kerri and Lynda introduced their business and their spring and summer lines with a press release for southern Ontario newspapers (Exhibit 4). Kerri and Lynda used the same high-quality material that established designers used, though their low volume usually meant buying the leftovers after the big designers had purchased. On occasion, depleted stock made ordering or reordering of material impossible.

Since sales of their spring and summer lines would not materialize until several months after production was started, Kerri and Lynda also began producing lingerie and casual T-shirt dresses for local lingerie stores. The acceptance of these products had led to one lingerie store's in-store promotion for KeLy Fashions. As a result, KeLy continued to produce these products as well as their evening wear and dresses.

At the end of their first year of operation, sales had totalled approximately $30 000 in garments and $1500 in lingerie. The evening wear and dresses that KeLy sold, for an average of $75 per garment, were generally margined (mark-on) at the industry norm of 50 percent; hence, KeLy's garments retailed for $150 on average.

Kerri and Lynda had operated with a very low fixed overhead in their first year. Neither of the two had drawn any salary until the eighth month of operation, and much of their manufacturing had been done on their own machines. Kerri and Lynda did all of the sewing. Material costs were presently 35 percent of sales, and the commission paid to their sales agent was 10 percent. Fixed costs, totalling $11,000, included four months' salary ($3200) for Kerri and Lynda and $2400 in rent. On the balance sheet, equipment and furniture was listed at $4000 (cost) and was depreciated at a 20 percent rate.

Although no marketing research had been done, Kerri and Lynda felt they were producing for a twenty- to fifty-year-old age group, with slightly higher than average income. Their prices, slightly lower than those of other designers, seemed to be generating a mixed opinion from retailers. Some said that since the product was cheaper, it must be of poorer quality; while others said it was cheaper and better made, and therefore worth carrying. Still others would say that KeLy did not have a reputation, and hence, they were "still priced too high" or their "product did not have the profile" to suit the retailer's product line.

Kerri and Lynda had decided that a retail price of $90 to $160 per garment was satisfactory for the consumer. Some customers paid from $150 to $220 for fashions by established designers, but both partners felt they had yet to establish a saleable reputation. They had found, though, that being outside Toronto set them apart from the other designers, and hence, retailers seemed to remember the KeLy name because of the company's unique location. Although material shipping costs were higher, other costs, like rent, were lower. Overall, location was felt to be an advantage.

MARKETING

Both Kerri and Lynda felt that there was money to be made in the industry since, within reason, high prices could be charged. The partners generally priced their products based on what they felt the customer would pay at the retail level. For example, if they felt a particular design made with a certain material could be sold for $160, then they would discount the garment by the industry margin of 50 percent to arrive at their wholesale price of $80. The payment terms were 2/10 net 30, but most of their customers, being small independent stores, tended to extend payment to 60 or 90 days after receipt of the product. KeLy had incurred bad debt losses of $1000 over the first year. Although the use of factors[1] was a common practice in the industry, KeLy was too small to interest a factor in carrying their accounts.

Advertising was very limited because of the costs involved, so much of the promotion was done through direct sales contact. Prior to hiring their sales agent, Kerri had done the sales work. She had looked up the names and telephone numbers of the independent retail stores in the larger cities in Southwestern Ontario, then called each store to arrange a sales call. To an appointment, Kerri brought posters showing the

---

[1]Factor: A person who, or an institution which, for a fee, will insure collection of an account receivable within a specified period. If the debt is uncollected, the factor pays the amount owing to the client after the account is deemed uncollectible. In addition, about 50 percent of the clients in Canada use their "insured" receivables as collateral to gain required cash from the factor before the specified collection period ends. An additional interest charge is levied for this service.

prices, colours, and design drawings of their lines. These posters were prepared by a Toronto-based design artist who had graduated with Kerri and Lynda. Because of their personal relationship, they were able to get eight posters for $90, whereas the artist, who was well known in design circles, charged $90 per poster for other designers. As well as the posters, Kerri also took sample garments in a garment bag with the KeLy Fashion logo on the outside, a list of suggested retail prices and an order book. All garments had the KeLy Fashion label attached.

Advertising in the first year consisted of providing posters for retail outlets and some newspaper advertising. The posters, showing KeLy's designs, were generally hung in fitting rooms, though some retailers used them in window or in-store displays. The newspaper ads, which cost $75 for a 1½″ x 4″ spot in the fashion section of the local newspaper, showed a KeLy design with the heading "Fashions for weddings, graduations and proms — custom designing." The ads, run several times in late spring to bring in some business after the spring and summer line had been produced, were intended to clear some excess stock as well as fill up some idle manufacturing time before the fall and winter line. The posters and the ads had generated sales of about fifty garments, of which twelve had been custom-designed dresses. For this direct business, the price was set as wholesale price plus a mark-on of about 25 percent.

Other promotions had consisted of a fifteen-minute segment on a local television morning show and the inclusion of their product in local retailers' fashion shows. The television spot was a free interview conducted at KeLy's facility, showing their operation and fashions. The fashion shows were small, private showings by retailers for their clientele. As such, KeLy had no control over whether or not their garments were shown, though they knew of several shows in which their fashions had been included.

CONCLUSION

Both Kerri and Lynda had goals which they hoped to fulfill, starting with a substantial increase in sales. Within five years they hoped to be supervising a number of seamstresses, be members of the Canadian Designers Association (a guild of top designers), be able to pay themselves well, and be able to have their own design shows like other designers. Ultimately, both visualized business trips to New York and Paris, but first they wanted to get their business operating smoothly and "conquer the Canadian market." They realized this was going to require a lot of work and much more learning.

Current problems that they recognized related to selling their fashions and increasing their volume. Their sales agent, who carried two other non-competing lines of clothing in the Toronto area, was not pushing products. His philosophy was that the retailers would come to his studio if they were interested in designer fashions, but Kerri and Lynda wanted a more aggressive approach. As for growth, current facilities were restricted to a rented studio which was already getting crowded. In analyzing the possibility of doubling their sales volume for the next year, Kerri and Lynda found that their landlord would be willing to renovate their rented space to twice its size for an additional $150 per month, but there would be other costs. Two full-time seamstresses, who together could produce ten garments per day, would be necessary at $150 per week each. Increasing machine capacity would require an investment of $2500, and the partners felt they would like to pay themselves minimum salaries of $9000 for the year.

With all their ideas and learning, plus the hope of expansion, Kerri and Lynda believed they had the potential to grow, but they were still somewhat uncertain. They looked back at their first year and wondered if their approaches and policies had been correct. Looking at the future, they wondered how best to proceed to achieve growth. The idea of made-to-order garments initiated by customers' requests was a possibility, as was the possibility of expanding their product line to include knitwear, though this latter option required a substantial volume of business. Since the cost of equipment for knitwear was prohibitive, the only option for producing this line was the use of sub-contractors, who required a minimum guaranteed volume of one hundred garments per style. Kerri and Lynda felt the available options could be implemented; however, they were still uncertain about how to achieve their goals.

Exhibit 1

KeLy Fashions
Women's Apparel Manufacturing[1]

Year	Factories[2]		Contractors[3]		Total[4]		Annual Growth
	#	$(000)	#	$(000)	#	$(000)	of Total $ Sales (%)
1970	623	$ 512 804	252	$ 34 696	875	$ 547 500	—
1971	612	563 112	270	43 627	882	606 739	10.8
1972	598	607 101	287	51 608	885	658 709	8.6
1973	574	661 857	292	59 830	866	721 687	9.6
1974	586	745 710	313	69 850	899	815 560	13.0
1975	585	847 014	301	76 373	886	923 387	13.2
1976	566	913 509	277	86 958	843	1 000 467	8.3
1977	529	958 398	233	84 394	762	1 042 792	4.2
1978	575	1 119 684	315	119 965	890	1 239 649	18.9

[1]Source: Statistics Canada
[2]Factories are defined as manufacturing operations that control all facets of the manufacturing process (labour, equipment, material, etc.).
[3]Contractors are defined as operations which own only the material. All value added (labour, utilities, equipment, etc.) is arranged with outside sources (subcontracting).
[4]Total number of women's apparel manufacturing operations, and total sales $ taken as the total of factories plus contractors.

Exhibit 2

KeLy Fashions
Consumer Price Index[1] and Inflation Rates[2]

Year	All Items		Clothing[3]	
	CPI (Annual Avg.)	Inflation Rate (%)	CPI (Annual Avg.)	Inflation Rate (%)
1971	100.0	—	100.0	—
1972	104.8	4.8	102.6	2.6
1973	112.7	7.5	107.7	5.0
1974	125.0	10.9	118.0	9.6
1975	138.5	10.8	125.1	6.0
1976	148.9	7.5	132.0	5.5
1977	160.8	8.0	141.0	6.8
1978	175.2	9.0	146.4	3.8
1979	191.2	9.1	159.9	9.2

[1]Consumer Price Index (CPI): The index of price paid by urban wage-earning families as calculated by Statistics Canada. It is based on the actual retail prices of a wide variety of consumer goods and services collected in a number of cities across the country each month. The present index is calculated with reference to average prices of the base year 1971. Thus, when the index stands at 125, for example, it indicates that consumer prices, on average, have risen 25 percent since the base year.
[2]Annual inflation rates are calculated as the annual growth rates in the CPI.
[3]Clothing is defined as all men's and women's clothing, including imported products.

Exhibit 3

KeLy Fashions
Retail Statistics for Women's Apparel (1979)

Type of Outlet	Definition	Number in Canada	Sales ($000)[1]	% Of Total Sales	Growth 1978–79
Department Stores	Multi-product retail locations with women's apparel as only one of many lines	28 companies comprising about 700 stores	$ 768 175	35.4%	5%
Chain Stores	Businesses with four or more locations, but which concentrate in particular products (women's apparel in this instance)	30 to 35 companies of which 8–10 are national while the remainder are regional (Ontario, Quebec, etc.) or local (large cities)	742 923	34.3%	10%
Independents	Businesses dealing solely in women's apparel and having less than four locations	Based on statistical analysis, approximately one store per 3730 people (on average) in any given area	654 857	30.3%	14.2%
Totals			$2 165 955	100%	9.5%

[1]Dresses and evening wear made up 20%–25% of total women's apparel sales.

Exhibit 4

KeLy Fashions
Press Release — Spring 1980

KeLy Fashions is a newly created fashion manufacturer. Co-owner/designers of this exclusive cocktail and evening wear collection are Kerri Hampton and Lynda Reed, both graduates in design and fashion technique of Sheridan College, Oakville, Ontario.

Their new spring and summer collection is directed toward the distinctive woman. KeLy gives her a new look in fashion — soft, feminine, and conservative. Kerri and Lynda use delicate muted colours of cream, aqua, grey, pink, taupe, salmon, banana, and brighter tones of flamingo, emerald, yellow, and blue. These are the new colours for spring 1980.

The fabrics presented will be Nashigi crepe, polyester satin, silks, gauze, and sheers of 100% percent polyester, to ensure excellent wash and wear qualities. The silhouette is linear and simple, accenting the shoulders and waist.

The first collection of KeLy Fashions has been received by the fashion world with great enthusiasm. Their collection is being distributed by select shops throughout Ontario, and can be found in cities such as Toronto, Hamilton, Windsor, Sarnia, Chatham, St. Thomas, Kitchener, and London.

Fall and winter designs for 1980 are already in production and will be complete for showing in early 1980. KeLy Fashions' spring and summer collection is in the shops now.

37

Lambton Road Cash and Carry

Early in August 1980, Mr. Don Barlow, manager of Lambton Road Cash and Carry, a retail lumber and home improvement supply centre located in Sarnia, Ontario, learned that the Beaver Lumber Co. had acquired a property directly across Lambton Road from his location. Mr. Barlow also understood plans for the establishment of the Beaver outlet, which would focus on retail sales, were well advanced and construction was to begin soon. Beaver Lumber had operated in Sarnia for some time. Their main emphasis had been wholesaling (sales to tradespeople, contractors, industries, etc.) from a yard located in an older, industrialized section of Sarnia.

Lambton Road was a main thoroughfare in the northeast part of the city. Two nearby shopping malls built in the last year, whose stores were open from 10 00 to 22 00, guaranteed a reasonable flow of traffic past the Cash and Carry store.

The premises on Lambton Road were purchased in 1952 by the owners of Lambton Lumber and Builders Supply Ltd., a long-established company in the Sarnia area. Until early 1971, the Lambton Road location was used as a wholesale service yard. Prior to that time, all retail sales had been made through Lambton Lumber's predominantly wholesale yard, which was located on a main thoroughfare in an industrial area close to the downtown area.

In April 1971, the main emphasis of the Lambton Road store became retail business. It was felt the establishment of a separate, retail-oriented outlet, operating on a cash and carry basis, would relieve the main yard of the expensive and tedious process of filling, billing, and delivering many small orders from wholesale inventory. Prices on retail orders could be reduced since costs would be lowered, and the product line could be diversified and better merchandised in a retail-oriented outlet.

The city of Sarnia was located in Lambton County at the southern end of Lake Huron, directly across the St. Clair River from Port Huron, Michigan. Sarnia was one hundred kilometres west of London and one hundred kilometres northeast of the Windsor–Detroit area. The city's population in 1979 was about 85 000; Lambton County, including Sarnia, had a population of 120 000 in 1980. Due to the high concentration of petrochemical manufacturing in the area, the St. Clair basin was known as "Canada's Chemical Valley." In the Sarnia area there were three large oil refineries, a synthetic rubber plant, and a dozen allied chemical plants. In addition, two large plants manufactured auto parts. Many of the chemical and petrochemical plants called for continuous process manufacturing. As a result, three-shift operations were common, with shift changes usually at 08 00, 16 00, and 24 00. In other industries, the usual plant working hours were 08 00 to 16 30. Appendix 1 shows additional selected statistics on the Sarnia area.

The product line carried by the Lambton Road Cash and Carry outlet was very diverse. It included such items as household hardware, tools, bathroom fixtures, tile, and floor coverings as well as basic lumber products and building supplies. Sales at the Lambton Road store were close to $1 000 000 in 1979, gross margin was 28 percent, and net profits before taxes amounted to about $48 000.

The Lambton Road store was open six days a week, from 08 00 to 17 00, and was staffed by experienced personnel, most of whom were originally transferred from the downtown yard of Lambton Lumber. Home delivery of purchases was not encouraged but could be arranged on a fee basis.

Lambton Road Cash and Carry had used local radio stations as its main advertising medium on a regular basis. The table below shows the stations used, the programs currently sponsored, and the type of commercial message employed.

Station	Program	Time	Frequency	Type
CKJD	Newscast	08 00	Daily	60-second spot
CHOK	Sports	12 40	Daily	60-second spot
CHOK	Regular	10 00-12 00	Saturday	Remote

The Saturday morning program was broadcast from the Lambton Road location and had run for the past five years. The program featured music, interviews, and announcements of upcoming area events. Although the regular commercial time for this broadcast period was also sold to other sponsors, throughout the program the announcer stated where he was broadcasting from and often conducted interviews with store personnel and customers. At $100 per program, the Saturday morning time was considered by store personnel as a "good buy." In addition to regular radio advertising, Lambton Road Cash and Carry occasionally used a local daily newspaper, *The Sarnia Observer*, to announce special sales and promotions. The annual cost of newspaper advertising was approximately $750.

The company also participated in the Sarnia "Hi Neighbour" service. This service was designed to welcome new residents to Sarnia through personal visits by a hostess who gave general information about the city and presented gifts and samples from local businesses. Lambton Building Supply provided personalized key chains which were mailed to new arrivals after the visit of the hostess. Annual cost of this service was roughly $500 plus $300 for the key chains. Annual advertising in the telephone directory's yellow pages added $1 600 to the promotion budget.

Lambton Road Cash and Carry, through Lambton Lumber and Builders Supply Ltd., was a member of a federation of building material and supply dealers. In 1979 they had approximately 150 dealer-members throughout Canada and were organized to give members the advantages of centralized, high-volume buying.

The federation also provided promotional help through the publication of illustrated colour catalogues for distribution by member dealers to their customers. The standardized format of these full-colour, eighty-page catalogues allowed the dealers to purchase the catalogues each year at the low price of $.27 per copy. Exhibit 1 is a reproduction of the index page from a catalogue, showing the products offered by federation dealers. Twice a year the federation also published four-page "flyers" which described special bargains and cost dealers one cent each. Delivery costs for the catalogues and flyers totalled $3000 in 1979.

Soon after he heard of the planned Beaver outlet, Mr. Barlow attempted to learn more about their method of operation. In checking other centres, he found that Beaver stores often stayed open until 21 00 each weekday evening, and closed at 18 00 on Saturdays. Delivery services were available free of charge on virtually all purchases.

The Beaver Lumber chain had many member yards in Ontario and in the western provinces. The size of its membership meant that the Beaver outlet on Lambton Road could be expected to have buying power comparable to that enjoyed by Lambton Road Cash and Carry. In checking over a Beaver catalogue, Mr. Barlow found the products and prices offered were generally comparable to, and competitive with, those in their catalogue. Beaver Lumber's promotional program appeared to rely heavily on newspaper advertising.

April, May, and June had traditionally been the biggest selling months for the Lambton Road Cash and Carry, with December, January, and February relatively slow months. Sales fluctuated through the week, with Saturday by far the busiest day. Monday was usually the second biggest volume day of the week. Mr. Barlow also found the average weekday purchase in the Lambton Road store was $12, whereas the average purchase for generally comparable stores in the United States (the only data available) was $18 to $20. In studying his Saturday volume, Mr. Barlow found the average sale was $10.50, with 80 percent of the total day's sales made between 10 00 and 14 30.

Mr. Barlow felt the competition posed by the establishment of the new Beaver outlet warranted a thorough appraisal of his marketing approach. In addition, the other four lumber and building supply centres in Sarnia, though still wholesale-oriented, were continually becoming more aggressive in their efforts to develop retail volume. He was particularly concerned with the amount of money he should commit to advertising and promotion as well as the selection of advertising media and the timing and content of the advertising message. Very little information was available to help him, although he understood some dealers used 1.5 percent of gross sales as a rule of thumb to establish their promotional budgets. To aid him in his planning, Mr. Barlow assembled the cost and coverage data for Sarnia media as shown in Exhibit 2.

Exhibit 1
Lambton Road Cash and Carry
Your Index To Big Values in Building Materials

Exhibit 2
Lambton Road Cash and Carry
Sarnia Media

RADIO

	Station CHOK	Station CKJD
Broadcasting power	10 000 watts	10 000 watts
Time classifications	'AAA' 6 00 to 10 00	'AAA' 6 00 to 10 00
	Mon. to Fri.	Mon. to Fri.
	'AA" 10 00 to 15 00	'AA' 15 00 to 19 00
	15 00 to 19 00	Mon. to Fri.
	Mon. to Fri.	6 00 to 19 00
	7 00 to 19 00	Sat. and Sun.
	Sat. and Sun.	
	'A' 19 00 to 24 00	'A' 10 00 to 15 00
	Mon. to Sun.	'B' 19 00 to 24 00
		Mon. to Sun.

Rates:

	AAA	AA	A	AAA	AA	A
(approximate; 60 sec	$23.00	$18.00	$10.00	$20.00	$18.00	$16.00
no discounts 30 sec	18.00	14.00	8.00	18.00	16.00	14.00
shown)						

NEWSPAPERS

Newspapers	Circulation	Line Rate[1]
Sarnia Observer (Daily)	21 779	$0.31 (b/w)
Sarnia Gazette (Weekly)	12 500	0.25 (b/w)
London Free Press	N/A	1.35 (b/w)

[1]Approximate, no discounts shown.

Appendix 1
Industrial Survey of Canada's Chemical Valley

1. POPULATION

    Sarnia & District (1977) — 81 342   (1971) — 78 444
    Lambton County (1976) — 117 595
    Households in Sarnia (1975) — 25 775

2. RESIDENTIAL AND BUILDING — Home Ownership 65%

Housing (1978)

(a) Apartments:
    Availability   — Fair
    Type   — Wide range from ultramodern with pool to older homes.
    Rentals   — Modern two bedroom — $260 and up
                — Ultramodern two bedroom — $303 and up

    Houses:
    Availability   — for sale — good
                 — for rent — poor, $260 and up
    Average cost new 5-6 room — $60 000
    Average cost new exec. home — $70 000

3. RETAILING
   Stores in Metro Sarnia Area (1977)

8 Department stores	14	Hardware
11 Food (major)	64	Salons and barbers
23 Furniture and household appliances	15	Building material
14 Drugstores	109	Gas stations
	25	New car dealers
	27	Used car dealers
	22	Carpet, rugs and drapes

    Retail Sales (1976) — $222.9 million

4. TAXATION STATISTICS (1975)

Income Class	
Under 3 000	— 20.5%
$ 3 000 - 5 000	— 12.6%
$ 5 000 - 10 000	— 23.6%
$10 000 - 20 000	— 32.3%
Over $20 000	— 11.0%

38
Latimer Tool Co. Ltd.

In January 1985, Paul Desmarais, a dealer who had been selling the Latimer line of industrial tools in the Milltown area for about four years, approached Mr. A.W. May, general sales manager for the Latimer Tool Co., and requested that in the future he be considered as a territorial distributor and thus qualifying for an additional discount on his purchases from the Latimer Tool Co.

At the time of his request, the Latimer Tool Co. had distributorship arrangements with only two firms, both national distributors. Several executives in the Latimer Co. were opposed to granting any territorial distributorship, since this would, in effect, mean a complete change in the distribution policy of the company. However, it was recognized that the parent company in the U.S. had traditionally distributed its products through territorial distributors, and that this method of distribution had much to recommend it.

The Latimer Tool Co. was the largest Canadian manufacturer of cutting tools for metal working. These ranged in size from delicate watchmaking tools to large-scale cutting tools used by manufacturers of heavy industrial equipment such as large electrical generators and turbines.

It was the policy of Latimer to concentrate on maintaining high and uniform quality in its products. The company felt that long-lasting uniform tool wear enabled the user to produce a better, more consistent finish on manufactured goods.

The Latimer company was one of five major producers of cutting tools in Canada, and in 1985 had over one-third of the total Canadian market. Imports accounted for about 25 percent of total cutting tool sales in Canada, and of these imports 50 percent came from the United States while the rest were divided among England, Sweden, and Japan.

Latimer executives said that, in their experience, sales of cutting tools tended to follow industrial development closely. A wide range of industries used cutting tools in manufacturing their products, the total market from British Columbia to Newfoundland containing roughly 10 500 cutting tool users. The largest users were manufacturers of heavy apparatus, automobile parts manufacturers and other firms operating large machine shops.

Mr. May said that, from the customer's standpoint, the three most important elements in the sale of cutting tools are: (1) prompt service on the part of suppliers; (2) the quality of the products; and (3) the relationship of the seller with the buyer. He said that most cutting tool users maintained about a sixty-day inventory of their cutting tool requirements, although on standard tools where delivery could be obtained within a week, only a ten-day to two-week stock might be kept. Special items took from four to six weeks for delivery. Some larger companies like General Motors, the Steel Company of Canada, and the Ford Motor Co. of Canada made cutting tool purchases almost daily in order to maintain their inventory at minimum levels.

Mr. May felt the customer's purchasing agent was a very important factor in the sale of cutting tools, and it was Latimer policy that he be the first person contacted in the company. With the purchasing agent's permission, the Latimer salesperson would work down the line to shop superintendents, foremen, master mechanics, and tool room superintendents, pointing out the quality and reliability of Latimer cutting tools.

To ascertain their relative position in the industry, the Latimer Co. computed the percentage of Latimer sales to total cutting tool sales for Canada as reported by several trade and association journals. This percentage was called "normal." To break sales figures down further, executives established a potential for each industrial area, such as Milltown, by using salespeople's estimates, local trade directories, and Chamber of Commerce figures on industries and production.

Mr. May said one of the big problems facing the cutting tool industry was the lack of standards. In the Latimer Co. alone there were about four thousand standard items, varying in type of steel used, size of tool and shape of cutting edge. When three to five customers used the same type of cutting tool it was usually added to the list of standard items and a stock kept. More than half of the orders received by the Latimer Co. were filled from stock, but a large number were special-purpose tools for which no stock was kept.

In the general line of cutting tools, the company employed eight salespeople, whose main function was to give technical assistance to the distributor's salespeople, but who also attempted to find new business. Technical assistance generally involved specifying the proper cutting tool to use on any specific metal and type of material. Latimer salespeople were located in Hamilton, Windsor, Toronto (2), Montreal (2), Welland, and one in Calgary, whose territory was from the head of the lakes west. In providing technical assistance, the Latimer salesperson might accompany the distributor's salesperson on calls or try to find new customers for the Latimer Co. and the distributor.

Salespeople were compensated on a guarantee-and-incentive basis. A basic part of their salary was guaranteed, and the incentive was based one-half on the total company sales and one-half on the sales in each salesperson's own territory.

Typically, the salesperson was expected to make from four to five calls a day either on tool users or distributors. The sales manager believed that if the salespeople made more than this number of calls they were not doing their job properly. If a salesperson obtained an order from a new customer he or she was not in any circumstances to recommend one distributor over another.

In the Latimer Tool Co.'s terminology, a "dealer" was any outlet which bought direct from Latimer for resale, but which was not an authorized distributor of Latimer products. Mr. May said that distributors were expected to carry certain basic stocks, depending on the industries and area serviced, while dealers usually purchased infrequently and often on a customer's special order.

Dealers received a somewhat smaller discount on purchases than distributors. For example, on the typical tool the price list would be as follows:

List price	$18.40
Price to dealers	9.00
Price to distributors	8.00

A few large users of cutting tools purchased directly from Latimer. These accounts would be charged $12 in the case of the cutting tool described above. The pricing tables, as well as freight charges, were designed to encourage large purchases and thus discourage direct buying. Latimer would prepay freight on any purchase weighing over 50 kg, thus making small purchases uneconomical in most cases. The sales manager said he would prefer to sell only through distributors, but direct selling was continued because some large users preferred to purchase in that manner, and dealer sales were continued because they gave Latimer a substantial profit.

Competition in the cutting tool business came mainly from four Canadian companies. In all cases these companies sold through distributors, though one competitor made more use of dealers, since their product range included many items which would appeal more to the home market.

Since its founding in 1919, the Latimer Tool Co. had used Jackson-Dowling Ltd. as the sole national distributor for Latimer products. Jackson-Dowling handled a tremendous number of products in the industrial field, including a great deal of heavy machinery. They employed some 160 salespeople working out of 15 sales offices and warehouses located in Halifax, Saint John, Quebec City, Montreal, Ottawa, Toronto, Windsor, Thunder Bay, Winnipeg, Regina, Saskatoon, Calgary, Edmonton, Vancouver, and Victoria.

In 1975, a second national distributor was added, following a drop of approximately 7 percent in Latimer's total share of the industry sales. Executives believed that the dip was due in part to the fact that Jackson-Dowling was handling too many lines to give Latimer products the time and sales effort needed. The new distributor, Canatool Ltd., had only twenty lines, all noncompeting, and eighteen salespeople operating from sales offices and warehouses in Toronto and Montreal. When Canatool Ltd. was taken on, Latimer stressed that it was employed to solicit new business and not to take existing business away from Jackson-Dowling. However, Mr. May said this had not always been the case.

Mr. May said that Jackson-Dowling was unhappy at the addition of another distributor, but after he explained the situation to them they began working to recover sales lost to Canatool Ltd. In 1985, Jackson-Dowling was doing a greater volume in those areas of competition with the new distributor than before. Mr. May said competition like this was desirable because it increased the overall business for Latimer and "kept everyone on his toes." By 1984, Canatool had added new warehouses in Edmonton, Thunder Bay, and St. Thomas, Ontario, and a sales office in Hamilton. With the addition of each of these new outlets, Jackson-Dowling expressed dissatisfaction, but in each case Mr. May said he could show them that total Latimer sales increased after addition of the outlets. In 1984 the big bulk of sales were still made through Jackson-Dowling.

In 1981, neither of the Latimer Tool Co.'s national distributors had a warehouse located in Milltown, Quebec. Milltown was a medium-sized industrial city located in the centre of an area where, within a 96 km radius, close to four hundred industrial manufacturers were situated. These accounts were serviced by Jackson-Dowling through their Montreal warehouse, located 240 km from Milltown. The company's participation in this industrial area was only one-third normal, and in an attempt to improve on this showing Mr. May had for some time been trying to persuade Jackson-Dowling to build a warehouse in Milltown to service the area. He was convinced that the poor showing in Milltown was due in considerable part to the lack of any nearby source of supply for goods.

In 1981, Mr. Desmarais, owner of a local industrial supply house servicing the Milltown area, approached the Latimer Tool Co. and asked to handle the line as a distributor. Latimer executives rejected the request for a territorial distributorship. However, they did agree to accept the firm as a dealer with the understanding that the Latimer Tool Co. would provide the technical assistance through Latimer's salespeople. The Milltown supply house agreed to these terms.

This Milltown supply house had at that time two salespeople who called on the various industrial accounts in the area. Their lines covered virtually every major type of industrial hardware, and included grinding wheels, pumps, motors, materials-handling equipment, screws, nails, and hand tools, along with a wide variety of other items.

After a period of approximately four years, Latimer sales in the Milltown area had increased more than ten times. Virtually all of this increase had resulted from the efforts of the local supply house. According to participation or share of market figures of the Latimer Co., the Milltown area in 1985 was the most productive area in Canada in relation to its potential. The dealer had at this time four salespeople whom he had sent to the Latimer plant to receive training courses, and an office staff of eight people. He was servicing over three hundred accounts and purchases from Latimer amounted to $500 000 per year. The dealer carried a full line of standard Latimer products in stock, which meant he stocked an inventory valued at between $45 000 and $50 000. Eighty-five percent of the dealer's total sales were made by only ten lines that he carried, and Latimer products were one of those lines.

At this time, 1985, Mr. Desmarais again asked Mr. May for a distributor's discount for the following reasons: (1) he had increased Latimer's business in the area by over ten times in the past four years; (2) he was performing a warehousing and service function in the area comparable to a distributor's operations; (3) his salespeople were highly trained and, he said, serviced the area better than either of the national distributors; (4) he was now servicing over 75 percent of the accounts in the area; and (5) the company's total participation in this area was the highest in Canada.

The dealer pointed out that under a territorial distributorship his net profit would be twice that obtained under a dealer's discount. He would at the same time be able to extend more attractive bids to industrial users of competitive products. He claimed that, if given the extra margin, he would be able to increase his participation in the area to almost 90 percent.

Most of the Milltown dealer's success in promoting the line lay, Mr. May believed, in the fact that the dealer carried extensive stocks and was able to provide quick delivery and service where necessary. Local Milltown industrial firms therefore preferred to order locally for this reason, and because the dealer was part of their community. Latimer equipment was otherwise available from the two national distributors, whose nearest warehouses were located in Montreal. This usually meant a waiting period in filling orders by these distributors, whereas the local dealer filled the order the same day or in a maximum of four weeks if the desired product had to be produced to special order by the Latimer Co. Also, the dealer's qualified salespeople were able to carry out tests on certain products to the customer's specifications at any time they were desired. The national distributors had specialists who would have to be contacted by the company and a suitable time arranged to make the tests.

Mr. May felt that the Milltown dealer deserved a distributor's discount, but he realized that in granting such a discount he would be setting a precedent, in effect, by establishing a territorial distributor. Mr. May knew that the addition of a territorial distributor would endanger the company's relationships with the national distributors, and although Desmarais's volume was appreciated, it was significantly less than either of the national distributors. On the other hand, territorial distributorships seemed to be the best method of increasing sales in areas where the participation was low, though good local distributors were not always available. He was undecided as to what action he should take with regard to the Milltown dealer's request, particularly since continued refusal to grant the special discount might well mean loss of the dealer's business to a competitor.

39

McIntosh Filing Systems[1]

Herb Simpson had just finished a telephone conversation with the president of his largest customer, Office Supplies Limited, and he was angry. He had spoken to Jake Berry about a written request that Berry had sent him for a private label version of McIntosh's ten largest-selling sizes of general and specialized "Target" brand file folders.

Office Supplies Limited (OSL) had managed to secure private label names for more than forty big sellers in its nationwide operations from pens and pencils to staplers, tape, and standard office forms. Now, Jake was demanding that an equivalent quality line to Target brand file folders, which held almost 60 percent of the market, be manufactured under the OSL label. Herb's dismay was in part caused by the fact that this was the third time OSL had made such a demand.

On both previous occasions Herb had turned down the request, and OSL had continued to buy and actively support all of McIntosh's lines with excellent growth results. OSL bought almost 23 percent of Herb's total division file folder volume and Target brand top ten sellers represented about 43 percent of this volume.

Herb had spent his whole working life with McIntosh and he took personal affront at Jake's request because some twenty years earlier Herb had recommended Jake to OSL when Jake had graduated from university.

McIntosh Filing Systems was a division of STL. STL had acquired it when it was McIntosh Paper and Office Forms, a regional manufacturer of business forms on the verge of bankruptcy. STL made this business a success by moving it into the production of general and specialized file folders, labels, and markers for the office.

The chairman of STL from 1925 to 1960 was the legendary Harry Winston Prince, a former stock clerk who rose to become chairman after moving through the ranks to secretary-treasurer and then president. His personal stamp on the company included manufacturing quality, and the spending of R & D money to expand product lines and technologies. He had helped the company grow to more than $200 million at the time of his death in 1969. He retired in 1960 to be replaced by Jack McIntosh, the nephew of the former owner of McIntosh Paper. Jack McIntosh, an ex-World War II fighter pilot, aggressively pushed to diversify STL by acquiring two major companies in the health field: Burke Medical, a manufacturer of intravenous solutions; and Scanner Labs, a manufacturer of blood screening and test apparatus.

Thus by 1984, STL had achieved $1 billion in sales (15 000 products) and three divisions, namely STL Lubricants Division, McIntosh Filing Systems Division, and STL Health Care Division. To the list of four major technologies was added two more: Electronics and the Science of Body Fluids, and Blood Gas Exchange. It was rumoured that STL was on the brink of entering the electronic equipment market through the development of a new holographic imaging device with applications for supermarket checkouts, security identification markets, and on-line manufacturing inspection.

---

[1]All names have been disguised.

Herb knew the McIntosh policies on private label business because Harry Winston Prince's philosophy on this was well publicized. The late STL Chairman had allowed several plants to become dependent on sales of private label products for selected large companies. In the mid-1950s a competitor had underbid on two of the three contracts, which resulted in numerous layoffs and the temporary closing of two plants. From that time until his death in 1960, Prince had vigorously opposed any suggestions of private label manufacturing.

STL was a multinational multiproduct company headquartered in the United States. In Canada, McIntosh Filing was one of five strategic business units in the company. STL sales revenue in Canada in 1984 was $180 million, and McIntosh sales were $20 million, of which $10 million were file folders. McIntosh's business had grown rapidly, parallelling the growth in white-collar employment, and fed by a steady flow of new products. McIntosh now sold more than 200 types of file folders, 1000 types of file markers and labels, and a variety of indexing systems available in every size, colour, and type. No competitor could match McIntosh's scope in that end of the business. About 30 percent of McIntosh's file folder business was in specialized lines such as: over-sized blueprint and engineer drawings; adhesive-bearing files for storage of telexes and messages; rapid-read "see-through" files for medical markets; washable, greaseproof, and waterproof files for marine, oil field, and other hazardous environmental markets; and spring-loaded files for carry-on transport markets such as couriers and short haul truckers.

Competitors to McIntosh were mostly small regional paper converters, but excess capacity in the industry was substantial and these converters were always hungry for orders. To complicate matters, Herb faced the fact that some of these converters bought base stocks for custom folders and labels from McIntosh. Selling to converters made significant contribution to plant overheads.

Herb's distribution comprised ten regional stationery suppliers, OSL, and more than thirty-five local stationers who had both wholesale and retail operations. On average, the ten regional stationers each had about six branches, while the local stationers each had one wholesale outlet and three or four retail locations. The regional suppliers sold directly to large corporations and to some retailers. By contrast, OSL's main volume was essentially retail to small businesses and walk-in trade buying for personal use or emergency purchases for corporate use, with very few wholesale-type sales to large accounts.

Herb had real concern about the local stationers, who were seriously discussing the formation of buying groups in order to obtain discounts on volume from vendors, and thus compete more effectively with OSL's sixty retail stores and the big four regionals. None was nearly as sharp at marketing as OSL, which had carved a real name for itself in every major city in the country. Their outlets were modern and located in accessible downtown areas and a few major shopping malls. OSL's profits were the highest in the industry, its brands almost as well known as some key vendors', and its expansion plans aggressive. OSL was known to have approached a regional converter to buy it, but according to industry gossip, negotiations had broken down on price.

Herb was confident that McIntosh's brand names were well entrenched with the market, despite the fact that cash flow from McIntosh's operations had been put into new product work rather than into major advertising to users. McIntosh's profits were more than 38 percent before tax and Herb was very concerned that if OSL acquired a private label they would sell at a discount and possibly bring down all market prices. Across all lines of file folders, Herb averaged a 35 percent margin, but the high-volume sellers sought by OSL averaged only a 20 percent margin.

It was unclear to Herb whether OSL would continue to sell his Target brand line alongside OSL's private label folders, if OSL successfully concluded such a private label contract. OSL's history had been to sell branded and OSL private label side by side in most cases, especially if branded products such as writing pens had a high-quality, high-recognition name in the market.

Herb had always been intrigued by the idea of custom merchandising and pricing McIntosh's total line to certain specific target market segments. For example, Herb believed some large specific markets such as insurance companies might welcome a merchandise assortment of file folders, labels, and markers priced and packaged to meet their particular needs. He thought that this same type of idea was "theoretically" feasible for as many as 10 different commercial market segments representing probably 40 percent of McIntosh's total sales. According to the Office Products Association, 80 percent of file folder volume was purchased by the largest 20 percent of the end customers.

Herb knew that Jack McIntosh, the president, continued to look to him for outstanding performance. In fact, in the elevator that morning Jack had said, "Say, I just saw John Moxie's lab report on his Magnof file project, and I'm really excited. It looks like that could give a real boost to your profits, Herb." STL had just received patent approval on a new electronic security system for locking paper files. Herb had to get back to OSL's president by Friday of that week under threat that OSL would go private label with someone else if it wasn't McIntosh.

40

Mercury Insurance Company[1]

Connie Williams, Manager of the Mercury Insurance Company, had just received her printout of the company's auto insurance sales results for the first six months of 1980. What she read did not please her; the fact that premium income had climbed slightly was little consolation in view of the 13.4 percent overall decline in policies written to date in 1980 compared to the same period in 1979. Worse yet, the number of new policies had dropped 40.7 percent from 1979! These depressing statistics were clearly a result of her decision to raise the price of auto premiums 14.0 percent on March 1, 1980. Ms. Williams had three days to complete her semiannual report, which would be forwarded with the sales results to Mercury's parent company in the U.S. She wondered if she should point to the 1.2 percent increase in premium income over the six-month period and hold firm on her pricing policy. The other option was to reverse her earlier decision, which would, no doubt, please her sales manager and field staff.

INSURANCE: DEFINED

Insurance is big business in Canada today, as it is expected that companies operating in this country will write at least seven billion dollars worth of general insurance this year. The industry has come a long way, both in magnitude and complexity, since the first policy was written in 1604 — on Newfoundland fish cargo. However, the basic principle of insurance — sharing the losses of few among many — remains unchanged. The function of an insurance company, simply put, is to pool together and administer the premiums paid by individuals wishing to be insured against the risk of loss. Any of the so insured individuals actually suffering loss can then be reimbursed from the general fund.

The general types of risk which can be insured against are threefold:
1) risk of *personal* loss: such as death or disability however caused, or unemployment resulting from accident
2) risk of *property* loss: such as by theft, or damage due to accident
3) *liability* risks: where a person is obliged to pay for damage which another has sustained due to the first person's negligence; such negligence can occur in operation of a vehicle, maintenance of property, manufacture of products, or in a host of other circumstances. Liability insurance is referred to in the industry as "third party liability," with the insured individual being the first party, the insurance company the second party, and the individual who is claiming as a result of damages sustained being the third party.

AUTOMOBILE INSURANCE

Among the various types of property and casualty insurance, auto insurance has — in

---

[1]All names have been disguised.

recent years — been the largest sector, accounting for at least half of all premiums. Automobile coverage is available in the three risk groups set out above. Accident benefits and medical payments are provided for in the personal risk category, collision and comprehensive coverage fulfil the property risk, and third party liability for both bodily injury and property damage is available. The distinction between collision and comprehensive coverage is derived from the cause of damage; the former covers vehicle repairs resulting from a crash (with a deductible amount, or that part of the repair bill which the insured agrees to pay, between $50 and $250), while the latter reimburses repair bills for cars damaged in circumstances other than a crash (usually a basic $25 deductible).

Automobile insurance is compulsory in every province in Canada. In Ontario, this requirement came into effect on March 1, 1980, at which time it became illegal to operate a vehicle without at least $100 000 third party liability. The penalty for driving while uninsured is a fine of $500-$2500, suspension of license for up to one year, and possible impoundment of the vehicle — at owner's expense — for up to three months. Sources in the insurance industry indicate, however, that because the level of insurance among drivers had been high (greater than 95 percent), the passage of the new legislation did not result in a perceptible increase in premiums written.

PREMIUM PRICING

It is possible, with the use of past statistics, to predict the future likelihood and magnitude of loss due to any particular type of risk. Insurance companies determine their "pure premium" by utilizing such statistics, modified to reflect changing environmental trends, to calculate how much each person must be charged to cover the actual losses which are expected. The total premium, or amount actually paid by the consumer, is derived by adding expenses and profit to the pure premium. Underwriting is defined as assuming the risk, or agreeing to the risk by accepting the premium to cover the insured, and the underwriting profit margin goal is normally between $1\frac{1}{2}$ and $2\frac{1}{2}$ percent.

In order for an insurance company to operate successfully, it is necessary to insure a sufficient number of people so that the law of averages applies and the statistically predicted losses approximate the actual losses. In addition, a company seeks to spread its risk by insuring a wide variety of types and classes of risks, and by insuring over a wide geographic area. On occasion, companies have been "unlucky" and sustained losses much higher than predicted; this will often show up in higher premiums in the future. Even at the best of times, premium pricing is exceedingly difficult. As one insurance executive stated: "We are using data which is usually a year old to set prices for a year ahead to settle claims which often may not reach the courts for four or five years after the accident occurs." Losses are being dramatically affected by inflation and the rising cost of health care and car repair. In addition, over the past three years the courts have made some landmark decisions for unprecedented settlements in third party liability for bodily injury. Prior to these decisions, an award of $200 000 would have been considered very high; recently several settlements approaching a million dollars have been made.

Table 1
MERCURY INSURANCE COMPANY
Frequency and Magnitude of Claims for Selected Categories of Operators

	Claims per Hundred Cars in Urban Areas	Average Cost of Claim	Loss Cost*
• Pleasure drivers over 25 who don't drive to work.	6.00	$1,514	$ 90.84
• Cars owned or principally operated by single male drivers 16, 17, or 18 with less than one year's experience or a claim in the past 12 months.	36.31	$1,863	$676.45
• Cars owned or principally operated by single men 23 or 24 with less than one year's experience or a claim in the past year.	18.35	$2,183	$400.58
• Cars owned or principally operated by women 21 – 24 with less than one year's experience.	12.50	$1,663	$207.88
• Cars owned or principally operated by married men aged 21 – 24 with less than one year's experience.	16.53	$1,629	$269.27
• Pleasure drivers over 25 who drive to work.	7.45	$1,632	$121.58
• Occasional male drivers under age 25 with less than one year's experience.	4.62	$2,161	$ 99.84

Source: "A Buyer's Guide to Automobile Insurance," Insurance Bureau of Canada.

*Loss Cost: The amount required from each premium to pay just the liability losses of those cars involved in accidents.

AUTO PREMIUM PRICING

Risk categories in auto insurance are defined using a number of parameters familiar to any insured driver: age, sex, marital status, location of residence, driver education, proposed use of the vehicle, and so on. The risk categories are further modified by the number of years of accident-free driving, usually recorded from 0 to 5, logged by the operator. Statistically, the number and magnitude of claims varies markedly by risk category, as demonstrated in Table 1. The data presented in Table 1 substantiates the higher premiums charged to drivers in higher risk categories. The variation of premiums across categories makes it impossible to quote an "average" figure for car insurance and expect such a figure to be meaningful. The 14.0 percent premium increase which the Mercury Insurance Company applied was an average, resulting from specific increments of greater or lesser magnitude applied by category.

CONDITION OF THE INDUSTRY

The foregoing discussion of pricing has defined one of the potential methods by which insurance companies can profit. The amount by which premiums charged exceeds loss payouts and expenses is accrued to *underwriting profit*. The potential for earnings in this area is normally exceeded by profit earned in the second area; that of *investment income.* Insurance companies are required by law to hold adequate funds in reserve to meet expected claims, and the government specifies the acceptable investments (normally Canadian federal, provincial, or municipal securities, and some corporate bonds and preferred shares). The interest earned through management of premiums is known as investment income.

The major determinant of underwriting profit or loss is pricing, as the overall market for insurance has not increased substantively in recent years. The insurance industry is highly cyclical, and the variation in underwriting profit is illustrated in Exhibit 1. The preponderance of losses is not uncommon for the industry, which has suffered more "loss years" than profitable ones, for underwriting, since World War II. The most recent downward trend is continuing into 1980, and the industry expects that the 1974 losses will easily be exceeded. In fact, industry sources suggest that losses may well reach a record level of $800 million in 1980.

In February 1980, R. E. Bethell, Chairman of the Insurance Bureau of Canada, referred to the price cutting and mounting losses in the industry:

> During periods such as this, the question asked is: When will the industry return to its senses? The answer probably is "not soon." In fact, there are some indications that competition may be even more aggressive in the short term as capacity seeks out premium income just to become established.

In other words, many companies will continue to forsake underwriting profit in an attempt to secure market share.

The underwriting losses are not as dire as they appear on the surface, however. Until now, they have been easily alleviated by strong investment income. The 1979 industry underwriting loss of 185.7 million illustrated in Exhibit 1 was counteracted by investment income of $570 million. Recent years have been particularly fruitful as far as investment income is concerned, which offers a partial explanation of why many companies can justify aggressive price slashing.

THE CONSUMER BUYING DECISION

In light of the current pricing trends, it is perhaps not surprising that the March 1980 consumer attitude survey conducted by the Insurance Bureau of Canada showed a record 67 percent of car owners as satisfied that they are getting their money's worth out of their insurance dollar. Only 34 percent criticized price (compared to 44 percent in 1979), while a modest 15 percent felt that service could be better. Price appears to be one of three major influences leading the consumer to a choice of insurance company; the other two are the company itself and the agent.

The Company

Because the insurance industry is so closely regulated, the "product" or coverage offered does not vary significantly among companies. Occasionally, a direct or indirect experience with a company may lead the customer to avoid or patronize that company faithfully in the future. For example, some companies have a reputation for being slow and, often, uncooperative in making settlements. The company itself is likely to be the least important influence, however, mainly because of the way in which insurance is sold. Customers often deal through agents and obtain coverage without any direct involvement over the company which is chosen; they may not even *know* what company holds their policy.

The Agent

Approximately one third of insurance companies sell directly to the public, while a few other firms have exclusive agents working on their behalf. The most common arrangement, however, involves an independent agent who represents several companies — ranging from three to twenty — at the same time. This agent solicits customers, often striving to fulfil all of their insurance needs including life, auto, home, and business. The agent is the client's sole contact, and a strong customer loyalty often develops.

Agents are paid a commission by companies which they represent, and bonus schemes are often employed. Thus, their return is one factor which leads them to decide what company to place business with. Others are pricing, service, or special coverage which may be available. Finally, personal relationships and the efforts of the company representatives may play a part.

The Mercury Insurance Company operates through agents who are authorized to write normal policies on Mercury's behalf without its consent. The company also employs salespeople—three in Ontario—who visit the agents and market Mercury's services. The Mercury salespeople are salaried, with a bonus based on attaining a sales goal. They do not sell auto insurance directly to the end customer.

Pricing

In 1974, several American studies addressed the importance of pricing to the insurance consumer. A general conclusion was that the auto insurance buyer generally did not compare premiums, and was not price conscious. Approximately 80 percent of purchasers felt that premiums among companies would be the same or only somewhat different. Of the 45 percent of consumers who tried to compare prices, only half reported differences. Of the latter group, only half again bought from the company offering the lowest price. It was shown that the price difference had to be significant (a median of 18 percent lower) to prompt switching.

Data have shown that insurance prices do actually range for comparable coverage in a risk category. The Insurance Bureau of Canada states that prices can vary by about 20 percent. In the unsettled pricing situation of 1974, and again in 1980 as the underwriting loss situation is repeated, the differences can be even greater.

MERCURY INSURANCE COMPANY'S STRATEGY

Connie Williams's move to increase the price of automobile insurance in early 1980 was partly a result of policy set by her parent company. The strategy of the corporation as a whole was to earn an underwriting profit, and Mercury had been successful in doing so even in the face of 1979 industry losses. Ms. Williams explained the firm's pricing position with respect to the industry by suggesting that auto insurance prices could be seen on a continuum from 1 to 10, with the lowest prices represented by 1. In 1979, Mercury reduced its rates over 1978 and Ms. Williams estimated that this change placed them at a 3–4 on the scale. In other words, 30–40 percent of the companies in the industry charged comparable or lower prices than Mercury. When prices were raised in March of 1980, for the first time since 1976, she felt that the company moved into the 6–7 range. Exhibits 2(a) and (b) compare the operating results achieved at these two price levels.

Ms. Williams expressed surprise at the drop in policies following the price hike. When she made the initial decision, she had expected that other companies would not be far behind. In addition, the Mercury staff had explained the increase using material such as the insert shown in Exhibit 3. Finally, the company offered some attractive benefits to long-time customers; for example, the premium increment normally resulting from an accident was waived if the client had only one accident in five years.

Ms. Williams could not help but feel that the price increase had been a wise decision for the long term. Surely, she thought, Mercury would have a competitive advantage when other firms began their inevitable premium increases. Mercury would be able to boast a much lower increment, recapturing any lost market share. On the other hand, the six-month operating results before her reflected only four months of higher prices. Perhaps if she persisted in her policy over the next six months, premium dollars would show negative growth, just as total premiums sold had over this period. There was no doubt that her decision was not an easy one.

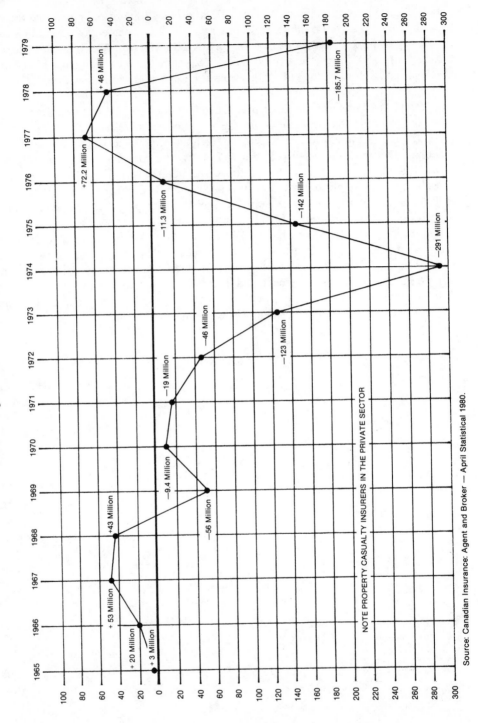

Exhibit 1
Mercury Insurance Company
Underwriting Profit & Loss Graph: 1965–79

NOTE PROPERTY CASUALTY INSURERS IN THE PRIVATE SECTOR

Source: Canadian Insurance: Agent and Broker — April Statistical 1980.

Exhibit 2 (a)
MERCURY INSURANCE COMPANY
Auto Insurance — Operating Results
1978 vs 1979

	1978	1979	% Change
New policies	3 120	7 251	132.4
Renewals	37 693	36 014	(4.5)
Total policies	40 813	43 265	6
Total premiums	$9 857 000	$9 983 000	1.2
Average policy price	242	231	(4.5)

Exhibit 2 (b)
MERCURY INSURANCE COMPANY
Auto Insurance — Canada
Operating Results
First Six Months 1979 vs 1980

	January – June Inclusive		
	1979	1980	% Change
New policies	3 554	2 107	(40.7)
Renewals	18 649	17 122	(8.2)
Total policies	22 203	19 229	(13.4)
Total premiums	$4 995 000	$5 055 000	1.2
Average policy price	225	263	16.9*

*The text refers to raising prices 14 percent in 1980 over 1979. The difference in the 1980 average policy price (263) and the 1979 *yearly* average (231) is 14 percent.

Exhibit 3
MERCURY INSURANCE COMPANY
Insert with Renewals, 1980

LABOUR — $21.00 PER HOUR!

Today that's becoming a familiar sign. And it's a situation we all have to face when we go to the garage for car repairs. Statistics show labour costs today ranging from $19.00 to $26.00 per hour and averaging a little over $21.00 per hour. That's a big jump from the $11.00 average back in 1974.

Unfortunately, inflation doesn't stop at one level. It moves in a circle creating a chain reaction, and auto insurance is right in its path. So, if you find your auto premium has increased, inflation may be the reason. That's right — almost every item which your insurance covers has increased in cost.

We know you don't like to pay more money and we certainly don't like to raise rates, but, from a consumer's standpoint we think you'll always be getting a bargain. Why? Because you're purchasing quality insurance backed by the professional services of an independent agent representing Mercury Insurance Company. He can take an impartial look at your coverage and help you get just the right protection.

Source: Company literature.

41

The Pinball Palace

> Everyone thinks that this is an easy, "quick buck" business but it's not. Look at that machine over there — it cost $4 000; that's 16 000 quarters before you see a dime of profit!

As he spoke, Rob Smeenk was counting some of those quarters into piles of four, making change for his customers who seemed anxious to help pay for the machine in question. Rob Smeenk was the owner of the Pinball Palace, a pinball and video game arcade located in downtown London, Ontario (population 300,000). In an industry saddled with a dubious reputation and characterized by the quick opening and closing of arcades, the Pinball Palace was an exception. By 1981, the firm was in its sixth year of operation and Smeenk felt that the business was well enough established to consider expansion. In late 1981, there were no arcades located on Dundas Street, downtown London's busiest shopping street. Smeenk was certain that he could run a profitable arcade on Dundas. He was wondering how best to go about the expansion and how this and future growth would affect his business. Smeenk knew that he was not the only arcade owner thinking of a downtown Dundas Street location so he felt under some pressure to act before someone else did.

ARCADES' REPUTATION

For years, pinball arcades had a reputation roughly on par with pool halls. Both types of establishments were seen as places where loitering young men engaged in anti-social behavior. If anything, pool halls had a slightly better reputation, since pool and billiards were games of skill with players from all classes of society. On the other hand, pinball was regarded as a game of chance like its cousin the "one-armed bandit" casino games, with no redeeming social value and strong ties to organized crime. Whether or not the industry had, in fact, been controlled by organized crime, and whether arcades were actually corrupters of youth or symptoms of deeper problems in society, were questions open to debate. The fact was that, deserved or not, pinball arcades had a very bad reputation, developed over decades.

THE PINBALL PALACE HISTORY

Robert Smeenk was born and raised in London, Ontario. Following graduation from university with an honours degree in Philosophy and History he moved to the Netherlands, where he played and coached semi-professional basketball for a year. One of the things that he noticed in Holland was that arcades were socially acceptable and were regarded as family entertainment centres. Smeenk studied the Dutch operations and had lengthy discussions with the arcade operators. He developed the opinion that a business of this sort could work in a Canadian setting.

Smeenk's return to Canada in 1975 coincided with a change in the law which would, once again, permit the operation of pinball arcades. For years previous, pinball machines were classified under the Criminal Code as games of chance. Before the change, the law would have viewed the operation of a pinball arcade in the same light as running a gambling casino. On January 1, 1976, Rob Smeenk opened the Pinball Wizard arcade on Hamilton Road in London, a few kilometres from the centre of the city.

From his discussions with the Dutch arcade owners, Smeenk had learned that a good location was essential to the success of an arcade. The Hamilton Road location had been chosen because it was near both an elementary and secondary school, and because that segment of Hamilton Road was something of a neighborhood shopping area. Initially, business was good, but as the novelty wore off, Smeenk realized that he had made a serious mistake. He learned that most of the high school students bussed to school each morning and bussed home right after school. The pedestrian shoppers seemed uninterested in playing pinball and the grade school students in this working-class neighborhood had little spending money. By the spring of 1976, Smeenk was working twelve- to sixteen-hour days running the arcade with daily revenues often as low as $20.

Mr. Smeenk was convinced that his concept was still viable and that only the location was wrong. In June 1976, the business moved downtown to a location on Richmond Street, a block and a half south of London's main intersection of Dundas and Richmond Streets. At the time of the move, the proprietorship became a limited company and the name was changed to the Pinball Palace. The downtown location was a great improvement over the Hamilton Road store. Even though he had gone further in debt to finance the move and to purchase additional machines for the larger store, Smeenk was confident enough to take a mortgage and purchase the Richmond Street premises in 1977.

When he opened on Richmond Street, Smeenk set out to run an arcade that would appeal to as many people as possible. The Pinball Palace was bright and clean. The floor was carpeted and chandeliers hung from the ceiling. A great effort was made to discourage undesirable patrons. Smeenk was always moving groups loitering outside his arcade. The customers were mostly teenaged males but it was not uncommon to see businessmen dressed in suits playing games beside high school students wearing blue jeans. In June 1981, *Today Magazine* rated the Pinball Palace the best arcade in Canada.

While the Pinball Palace was establishing itself, a competing arcade had opened downtown on Dundas Street three blocks away. In its few years of operation, the Dundas arcade confirmed local business and community leaders' fears of arcades. One local merchant explained,

> It was terrible! There was always a bunch of those punks hanging around the place. It hurt my business by making Dundas Street look slummy and God only knows what trouble those kids were up to.

As public opinion against arcades grew, local politicians set out to establish bylaws that would regulate those businesses. The draft bylaw proposed that arcades not be permitted near schools and that the hours of operation of arcades be severely limited. Smeenk fought the proposed bylaw because it was a threat to his business and because he felt that he had been unfairly grouped with those operators who had run questionable establishments. Smeenk was a strong believer in the free enterprise system. He regarded the bylaw as an unwarranted and unnecessary invasion of government into the world of commerce.

When finally passed, the bylaw was something of a compromise. Access to locations near schools was limited but arcades were permitted to be open during school hours, which the draft bylaw would not have allowed. The new bylaw required arcades to close at 11 p.m., which hurt the Pinball Palace's business — especially on weekends. Smeenk continued to fight the bylaw but realized that the threat of government intervention in the arcade industry was very real and would continue in the future.

VIDEO ARCADE GAMES

Without question, the biggest change in the arcade industry since the 1975 legalization had been the explosive growth of video arcade games. In 1972, a small California firm, Atari, developed an electronic tennis game. The game was called Pong. Pong was accepted as the common ancestor of all video games. In the late 1970s, the game Space Invaders established the arcade earning power of video games. One measure of the success of Space Invaders was that in Japan, where the game had been developed, Space Invaders had caused a nation-wide shortage of the coins required for the machine. In 1980, the success of the game Asteroids showed that other video games could generate substantial demand. Since that time, there had been great growth in the industry with even more sophisticated and complex games being developed.

Video games were free of the bad reputation that had followed pinball games. Instead of being related to "one-armed bandits," video games were a product of the computer age, spiced with a dash of Star Wars. Video games had gone a long way in legitimizing the arcade business and in attracting new customers. There were two major dangers developing in the video game industry. As consumers became more sophisticated and as more games came on the market each day, the arcade operator had to be careful to pick those games that would become hits and to avoid the expensive mistakes of buying unpopular games. As well, consumers could purchase home video games. In 1981, the home games lacked the sophistication of arcade games and were expensive — approximately $250 for the machine and $30–$50 for each game cartridge.

Many were of the opinion that arcades would suffer as, in time, the quality of home video would increase while prices would fall. Others felt that people would always enjoy going out to play arcade games and that home video could only help the arcades by increasing awareness and by attracting new players. By the fall of 1981, despite its name, the Pinball Palace had thirty video games and ten pinball machines. The video games accounted for approximately 90 percent of revenue. Daily revenue averaged between $200 and $400.

THE DUNDAS STREET EXPANSION

In thinking of expansion, Smeenk knew that an arcade in the two or three main blocks of Dundas Street could be run profitably. At that time, there were no downtown Dundas arcades but a few, including the Pinball Palace, were within three blocks.

Smeenk had heard rumours that one of his competitors was also investigating a move to Dundas Street. He was sure that others must also be interested. Again, there were rumours that Dundas Street property owners would not rent to an arcade. Smeenk reasoned that his track record, his membership in the Chamber of Commerce and the fact that he was a Director of the Board of Management of the London Downtown Improvement Area, might give him an advantage in convincing a landlord to co-operate. He knew that if he did open on Dundas, he would have to be extremely careful that his operation did not offend the local merchants. If space could be found, rent would be around $3 500 per month.

It had always been Smeenk's policy to own his machines, and with two locations he would be able to move machines between the stores, giving greater variety. However, the machines were expensive, costing between $2000 and $8000 each, with $4000 being an average price. An alternative was to have machines supplied by a route operator. As a rule, the operator owned and serviced the machines and split revenues equally with the arcade owner. Smeenk disliked the idea of losing control of the operation and questioned whether the route operators would always supply him with the best machines.

On the subject of machines Smeenk was thinking — should he continue with pinball and video machines or embrace the video trend totally? Other expenses for an arcade would involve wages, promotion, and utilities. The machines gave off such energy that there was no need to heat in winter but summertime air-conditioning was essential and expensive.

As he thought about expansion, Smeenk wondered about the long-term potential of the arcade industry. It had taken him six years to establish his one store — would each new store take that long? Was home video a threat or an ally? Was he riding the crest of a fad that would soon crash or had he got in on the ground floor of a long-term growth industry? Smeenk knew that he had to do something. He was too old to go back to basketball and too ambitious to stay running just one arcade. These thoughts and more went through his mind as Rob Smeenk sat down to plan his future.

42
The Slater Co. Ltd.

In 1973, Mr. William M. Slater organized The Slater Co. Ltd. and through it took over the sole ownership and operation of the assets of a small, nearly bankrupt manufacturer of a line of light air compression equipment which had been sold primarily for use in spray painting. After the takeover, Slater expanded this line to include small compressors which were used by service stations and garages to operate pneumatic tools and tire changers.

In July 1974, Slater was successful in obtaining the Canadian rights to distribute a U.S. line of spray guns and supplies. Subsequently, he developed a special "undercoating gun" to supplement the American line.

In mid-1975, the Tobin Co. of Chicago, Illinois, placed an advertisement in the *Financial Post* announcing that they were interested in appointing Canadian companies to manufacture and distribute their line of light welding equipment. Slater answered the advertisement and was awarded a five-year agreement under which he would manufacture and distribute the Tobin line in Ontario and Quebec on payment to Tobin of a 10 percent royalty on sales. He also agreed to purchase and install the $25 000 worth of equipment necessary to manufacture the products. Tobin supplied the necessary dies and designs. Sufficient manufacturing space was available in Slater's existing plant so no additional plant investment was required.

Prior to the Tobin agreement, Slater had employed one salesperson to call on garages, service stations, painting contractors, and light manufacturers in Ontario. In discussions with the Tobin Co., he agreed to add another salesperson and extend his sales coverage into the province of Quebec. As a result, one salesperson covered Ontario and the other covered Quebec, each carrying all the products Slater sold. Both salespeople were paid a flat salary.

Early in October 1980, Slater received notice from the Tobin Co. that they had decided to establish their own manufacturing facilities and marketing organization in Canada and did not intend to renew their licensing agreement which would expire on the following December 31. In their notice, Tobin offered to purchase all the inventory of finished goods and supplies of Tobin products which Slater might have on hand at the year end at 20 percent above his full factory cost. Slater was disappointed when he heard this news since, during the past five years, sales volume of the Tobin line had increased to the point where it was now contributing 40 percent of Slater's total sales revenue of $1 200 000.

In the process of determining the effect the loss of the Tobin business would have on his company, Slater noted that profits on the Tobin line had been extremely favourable, contributing approximately 55 percent of the 1980 gross profit.

Slater spent considerable time attempting to locate or develop a line to replace the Tobin business. He examined and discarded a number of products largely because potential volumes were too small, margins were too slim to permit profitable manufacture or because the products were not compatible with the existing Slater lines of air compression and spraying equipment.

Three possibilities did look promising, however, and, early in December, Slater sat down to give serious consideration to (1) undertaking the manufacture of his own line of light welding equipment, (2) entering into an agreement to distribute a line of electronic automotive engine-testing equipment which was manufactured in Japan, and (3) accepting an offer to act as a subcontractor, manufacturing components for a large local valve and plumbing supplies producer.

MANUFACTURING WELDING EQUIPMENT

Over the years, Slater had recommended to the Tobin Co. a number of improvements in their welding equipment line. The nature of the improvements suggested by Slater would permit adjustment of the torch flame to allow for welding of small parts more neatly and effectively. These improvements would increase the cost of the product about 35 percent. Tobin executives had repeatedly refused to permit their incorporation into the Tobin equipment line, believing that the required increase in the selling price would reduce the competitive effectiveness of the lines.

The two Slater salespeople had repeatedly mentioned requests from light manufacturers for such an improvement. Slater was confident the improved equipment could be developed and ready for the market in four months. Development costs were estimated at $25 000, largely for new designs and equipment.

If no improvements were made, direct material and labour costs to manufacture a Slater line very similar to the present Tobin line would run 5 percent above current costs (before royalty charges). This cost was felt to be the value of the dies and other assistance provided by Tobin. If the improvements were incorporated into certain models, manufacturing costs of these models only would be from 35 percent to 40 percent higher than for basic equipment.

DISTRIBUTING JAPANESE TESTING EQUIPMENT

Through the Department of Trade and Commerce listings, Slater had learned of a Japanese electronics manufacturer of high-quality automotive engine-testing equipment who was interested in obtaining distribution throughout Canada. A representative of the manufacturer expressed considerable interest in Slater's inquiries about the possibility of his company distributing the line in so far as Slater salespeople were already calling on a large number of potential customers for the equipment. The manufacturer's representative estimated the total Ontario and Quebec market for auto engine-testing equipment at approximately $6 million per year and suggested that Slater should be able to obtain 10 percent of this volume during the first year.

The Japanese product was comparable in quality to similar products being sold in Canada and would be priced to sell at prices 15 to 20 percent lower than similar equipment of the two large manufacturers located in Canada who currently dominated the market. As part of an agreement, Slater would have to stock a $50 000 inventory of the equipment and supplies, purchased on six-month terms for the original order, and sixty-day terms thereafter. Slater's markup on the product line would average 25 percent. Individual prices of equipment ranged in price to users from $200 to $5 000. A complete installation would be in the range of $8 000.

SUBCONTRACTING

In discussing the loss of the Tobin line with a friend of his, his friend told Slater that the company for which he was purchasing agent, Dundee Plumbing, a large valve and plumbing supplies manufacturer, had been unable to locate a satisfactory second source of supply for a line of machined components for one of its most important industrial valve products. The friend pointed out that the present supplier was located 480 km from the plant and, as purchasing agent, he was interested in obtaining a local supplier to manufacture a portion of the components and to provide emergency deliveries. Investigating further, Slater learned that the Dundee Co. purchased these components at prices which would permit Slater to earn a 15 percent manufacturing margin (before depreciation) on volumes over 5000 units per year. The purchasing agent estimated that Dundee's requirements from Slater would amount to approximately $750 000, or 25 000 units, in the best years, dropping to a minimum of $150 000, or 5000 units, in the poorest years. His 1981 estimate requirements from Slater was $400 000. As the components could not be manufactured on Slater's existing equipment, an $80 000 investment in new equipment would be required.

The company's balance sheet and profit and loss statement to their year end at September 30, 1980, are shown as Exhibits 1 and 2.

Exhibit 1
The Slater Co. Ltd.
Balance Sheet
as of September 30, 1980

ASSETS		LIABILITIES	
Cash	$ 51 000	Bank loan	$ 45 000
Accounts receivable	114 000	Accounts payable	54 000
Inventory			
Tobin equipment	36 000	Advances from	
Slater & other		shareholders	30 000
equipment	63 000	I.D.B. loan	60 000
	$264 000	TOTAL LIABILITIES	$189 000
		EQUITY	
Plant (net)	150 000	Capital stock	150 000
Equipment (net)	84 000	Surplus	159 000
		TOTAL LIABILITIES	
TOTAL ASSETS	498 000	AND NET WORTH	498 000

Exhibit 2
The Slater Co. Ltd.
Profit and Loss Statement
for Year Ended September 30, 1980

Sales			
Tobin equipment		$480 000	
Slater and other equipment		720 000	
			$1 200 000
Cost of goods manufactured			
Direct costs to manufacture			
Tobin equipment including 10% royalty		$300 000	
Slater & other equipment		555 000	
		$855 000	
Manufacturing overhead		45 000	
			900 000
Gross profit			$ 300 000
Operating expenses			
Selling expense		$ 84 000	
Transportation expense		24 000	
Office expense		36 000	
Executive salary		36 000	
Other expenses		9 000	
			$ 189 000
Net profit before taxes			$ 111 000

43

South Gables Golf and Country Club[1]

In May 1984, the Capital Planning Committee of the South Gables Golf and Country Club met to discuss a research report that they had just received. This report gave the results of a survey of the club membership on the issue of which capital projects the club should undertake this fiscal year. Members of the committee intended to use the report as a basis for selecting among alternative capital projects. A biographical description of the committee members is given in Appendix 1.

BACKGROUND TO THE STUDY

South Gables Golf and Country Club was a private club situated on the outskirts of Regina, Saskatchewan. The club was founded in 1936 as an eighteen-hole golf course and dining room.

In 1966, an additional nine holes were built, and in 1974 three outdoor tennis courts were built.

In the fall of 1983, the Capital Planning Committee had held a series of meetings where they had discussed possible projects requiring capital expenditures during 1984 and 1985.

From these meetings they identified five potential projects and the associated capital costs and operating costs per year. These projects were:

	Capital Cost	Operating Cost Per Year
(1) An additional nine golf holes complete with automatic watering system on existing lands.	$800 000	$90 000
(2) Swimming pool and club with lockers.	$160 000	$60 000
(3) Tennis clubhouse, court lighting, and bubble cover for winter.	$240 000	$40 000
(4) Three new tennis courts.	$ 41 000	$20 000
(5) Purchase of 150 acres of lands adjacent to club as a buffer against city expansion or for club expansion.	$600 000	$54 000

---

[1]All names and places have been disguised.

The committee decided to obtain the opinion of the membership on the five projects before reaching a decision. In December 1983, a research subcommittee was formed to undertake to obtain the views of the membership. It was the expressed intention of the whole committee to recommend the capital project or projects that the membership desired.

THE STUDY

The research subcommittee developed a questionnaire (see Appendix 2) designed to measure the preference of the membership for the five projects. In March 1984, this questionnaire was mailed to all senior and intermediate members of the club. Exhibit 1 shows the number of questionnaires mailed to each class of membership and the associated return rate. The report prepared by the research subcommittee consisted of a set of tables giving what the committee members thought were the main findings of the survey. These tables are presented in Exhibits 2 through Exhibit 5 as follows:

Exhibit	*Contents*
2	Project preference given financing knowledge
3	Projects favoured by type of membership
4	Projects favoured by projects favoured
5	Priority club should attach to projects

MAY 15, 1984 MEETING

All members of the Capital Planning Committee were present for the meeting held in the South Gables board room on May 15, 1984. Mr. John Watts, the committee chairman, opened the meeting by thanking the research subcommittee for their efforts. He also noted that the Board of Directors of the club had asked him to be prepared to make a recommendation concerning capital expenditures at the next board meeting. This meeting was to be held on May 21, 1984. Because of this time pressure, it would be necessary for the Capital Planning Committee to reach a decision at the May 15 meeting.

Exhibit 1
Questionnaire Returns By Class of Membership

	Number Mailed	Number Returned
Senior male (Club shareholders)	710	540
Senior female	650	402
Intermediate male (age 21 – 26)	205	110
Intermediate female (age 21 – 26)	75	32
TOTAL	1 640	1 084

Exhibit 2
Project Preference Given Financing Knowledge

			Projects		
	Golf	Swimming Pool	Tennis Club House	Tennis Courts	Land
Yes	32.5%	37.1%	32.9%	27.4%	23.7%
No	50.6%	59.6%	51.1%	53.6%	60.4%
No opinion	16.9%	3.3%	16.0%	10.0%	15.9%

*Respondents = 1084.

Exhibit 3
Project Preference by Type of Membership

			PROJECTS		
Membership Type	Golf	Swimming Pool	Tennis Club House	Tennis Courts	Land
Senior male	38.4*	21.2	20.1	15.6	36.4
Senior female	36.4	33.7	24.6	28.7	29.6
Intermediate male	31.2	46.5	39.7	38.2	21.4
Intermediate female	29.7	52.7	33.6	40.1	20.7

*Respondents = 1084.

*Row percentages add to more than 100% due to multiple responses.

Exhibit 4
Projects Favoured by Projects Favoured

	Golf	Swimming Pool	Tennis Club House	Tennis Courts	Land
Golf	100%	8.7	11.4	11.9	18.7
Swimming pool	24.7	100%	31.6	31.4	8.7
Tennis club house	11.6	18.9	100%	41.6	11.1
Tennis courts	13.7	21.4	33.9	100%	7.7
Land	18.5	4.9	12.1	13.6	100%

*Respondents = 1084.

*Cells give percent of respondents favouring row project who favoured column project.

Exhibit 5
Priority Club Should Attach to Projects

	High	Medium	Low	No Opinion
Additional nine holes	24.7	21.0	45.1	9.2
Swimming pool	28.5	18.7	45.9	6.9
Tennis clubhouse and lights	16.4	16.9	51.2	15.5
3 tennis courts	17.6	15.9	52.0	14.5
Lands	19.7	21.4	46.0	12.9

*Respondents = 1084. All numbers are percentages by row.

Appendix 1
Biographical Description of Capital Planning Committee Members

	Age	Family	Occupation	Club Activities
Mr. John B. Watts (Chairman)	62	Married 2 sons ages 29 and 27	President, Exeter Tool Company	Golf
Dr. L. Gary Johnston	45	Married, 1 daughter 20, 2 sons ages 17 and 12	Dentist	Golf, Tennis
Mr. Joseph R. Taylor	35	Married, 1 son age 7	Lawyer	Golf
Mr. Robert H. Robertson*	59	Married 3 daughters ages 32, 30, and 27	President, Robertson Advertising	Golf
Dr. Malcolm R. Richardson	42	Unmarried	Internal Medicine Specialist	Golf, Tennis
Mr. Kenneth L. Wecker*	69	Widower, 2 daughters, ages 42 and 38	Retired, Alpha Associates, Management Consultants	Golf
Dr. W. Lloyd Thains	53	Married, no children	General Practitioner	Golf
Mr. Bruce A. Frederick*	46	Married, 1 son age 16	Sales Manager, Beta Electronics	Golf

*Member research subcommittee

Appendix 2
Questionnaire

(1) *Class of Membership:*
Please indicate your membership class.
Senior male
Senior female
Intermediate male
Intermediate female

(2) *Junior members living at home:*
Ages of sons —
Ages of daughters —

(3) *Proposed Capital Projects*
Your Capital Planning Committee is presently evaluating a number of possible projects. As part of this evaluation we would like your opinion on the projects listed below:

	Capital Cost	Operating Cost Per Year
9-hole golf course with automatic watering system	$800 000	$90 000
Swimming pool and club house with lockers	$160 000	$60 000
Tennis clubhouse, court lighting and bubble cover for winter	$240 000	$40 000
Three new tennis courts	$ 42 000	$20 000
Purchase of land adjacent (150 acres) to the 16th and 17th holes	$600 000	$54 000

(A) What is *your* interest in these projects?

	High	*Medium*	*Low*
Additional 9 holes			
Swimming pool			
Tennis clubhouse & lights			
3 tennis courts			
Lands			

(B) What priority should the club attach to each of these projects?

	High	*Medium*	*Low*
Additional 9 holes			
Swimming pool			
Tennis clubhouse & lights			
3 tennis courts			
Lands			

(4) *Financing*

Your committee has expressed above the capital and operating costs for each project. Below we have stated these costs in terms of the effect these projects will have on the fees of senior members. Would you be in favour of proceeding with the following projects?

Annual fee increase to senior member

	To finance construction over 10 years	Operating costs	Total	In Favour Yes	No
Additional 9 holes	$58	$60	$118		
Swimming pool	$12	$ 4	$ 16		
Tennis clubhouse & lights	$18	$30	$ 48		
3 tennis courts	$ 4	$14	$ 18		
Lands	$44	$40	$ 84		

44

The Stratford Shakespearean Festival
Foundation of Canada

In February 1984, April Martin, Director of Marketing at the Stratford Festival, looked at the headline of the newspaper clipping sent to her: "I'd give you a seat, but the empty ones are all full." The headline, not about Stratford, struck April as interesting because she had been exploring a new approach to advertising for the Festival, a television campaign. This approach was intended to help fill the Festival's 3 779 seats each night over a twenty-three-week season from mid-May to the end of October.

THE STRATFORD FESTIVAL

April joined the Stratford Festival in 1983, at the close of the thirty-first season. With a budget of $14 million, the Festival was the largest performing arts institution in Canada and the only classical repertory theatre in North America. The Festival annually drew an audience of more than 500 000, which resulted in box office receipts that typically averaged about 70 percent of revenue. Attendance had peaked in 1978 at 557 991 and since had dropped to 505 973 in 1983. Approximately 30 percent of its audience visited from the United States and a further 30 percent were from Toronto (150 km from Stratford). Fifty thousand of the audience members were students from both Canada and the United States. A 1982 survey suggested that 80 percent of the audience was fairly evenly distributed between 21 to 64 years of age, 11 percent were 65 and older and the balance were under 20 years of age.

The 1984 season plans called for 477 performances of thirteen productions presented in repertory on three stages. Four Shakespeare plays and a Moliere would be performed in the 2 262-seat Festival Theatre. In the Avon Theatre, three Gilbert & Sullivans would be presented in the summer and followed in the Shoulder Season (Labour Day to October 27) with plays by Terence Rattigan and Tennessee Williams. At the Third Stage, a small theatre seating 410 on three sides of the stage, the Young Company, a group of professional actors receiving training in classical theatre, would present two Shakespeares, and the senior members of the Festival Company would present *Waiting For Godot*. Four concerts and six lectures were interspersed through the season at the Festival Theatre.

Tickets prices ranged from $6.50 to $27.50 with an average of $17.87. Prices depended upon play, time of week, and seat location.

THE CITY

The Stratford Festival was located on the banks of the Avon River in Stratford, Ontario, a small town equidistant between London and Kitchener–Waterloo. Stratford's residents numbered around 27 000. The tourist industry resulting from the operation of the Festival was an economic boom for the city each year, supporting the local merchants and a number of exclusive restaurants and inns. The city enhanced the

"Stratford Experience" with miles of groomed parkland along the Avon River, presenting a low-key tourist destination.

THE MARKETING PROGRAM

April had initiated the usual campaign for the upcoming season, beginning with a direct mail brochure sent to all 1983 ticket purchasers and Foundation members. The brochure was also distributed with an accompanying poster to tourist information booths and stores in southwestern Ontario and the northern border States. Print advertising was purchased to correspond to the opening of the box office, the beginning of the preview performances and the official opening of the season. Advertising space was purchased in Toronto, Hamilton, Kitchener, Stratford, London, and Detroit. Support in the print media was received from the Ministry of Tourism which placed ads in American papers and magazines which featured the Festival prominently. Radio advertising was purchased on six stations, covering a 300-km radius around Stratford. In addition, contra deals[1] were made with radio stations across southwestern Ontario, in Montreal, Ottawa, Detroit, and Buffalo. April had not yet decided whether to continue a practice begun only two years before of producing a second direct mail piece mid-season to bolster typically low Shoulder Season sales.

In addition to this program, April and the Marketing Committee of the Festival's Board of Governors agreed that the Festival should follow Broadway's lead of marketing theatre on television. The Festival's advertising agency was asked to submit a proposal for a $100 000 television campaign, funds the Marketing Committee had approved in addition to the original marketing/public relations budget of $1.7 million ($650 000 for marketing).

As April reviewed the agency's proposal for a single thirty-second spot, she found herself increasingly uncomfortable with it. They had suggested scenes from several Stratford plays with a voice-over opening the commercial "The play's the thing" and closing with "Come to the Stratford Festival." The disconcerting part of the proposal was the price tag of the production of this thirty-second piece — $60 000.

April felt she needed a splashy commercial that would grab a young, educated, thirty- to forty-year-old audience, an affluent group who probably only have enough time to watch the news programs at the end of the day. In thirty seconds she wanted to give them a taste of the spectacle of the Festival with a commercial that was so packed with intriguing characters from the plays that people would watch it closely.

The commercial was intended to be supported by print and radio advertising containing information on this year's plays and tickets. April thought of the commercial as a dripping tap that, through its persistence, would keep Stratford on people's minds. But she believed that to effect the dripping tap strategy she would require a substantial budget for airtime, not just $40 000. April's original broadcast plan was to spend about $60 000 for forty slots a week for four weeks around the Festival's opening in June. She had asked the Marketing Committee to approve further funds to allow her to air the commercial twenty times a week for an additional two weeks and was awaiting their reply.

April wondered what action to take on the proposed television campaign.

---

[1]Contra deals involved providing radio stations with tickets to give away in return for the publicity provided.

45
Tony's Restaurant

Mr. Tony Dupas was going over the plans for his new restaurant. Up until six months previously, he had operated a snack bar concession in a large office building in Toronto but had recently sold the fixtures and goodwill for a very good price, which had enabled him to lease the restaurant site in a new shopping centre in a growing western Canadian city.

He had just visited the manager of the centre where he was establishing his new restaurant. The centre was not yet completed but the manager had taken him on a tour of the buildings. When they had looked around the supermarket, Mr. Dupas had noticed a counter being installed. When he asked the manager about it, he had been told it was a snack bar which the supermarket planned to operate during regular store hours. The manager told him the snack bar was designed to handle fifteen people at a time, and would serve sandwiches, doughnuts, drinks, and so on. There were no stools as the expectation was that customers would stand or they could sit in the interior of the mall.

Mr. Dupas was a little disturbed as he had hoped that he would have the only restaurant facility in the centre. He had planned to feature snacks and light lunches in the front of his restaurant and to serve full meals in a separate dining room in the back. Mr. Dupas had counted on the lunch and snack trade from both shoppers and the centre employees to contribute substantially to his fixed costs and he was worried that this trade would go to the snack bar in the supermarket. "After all," he told his wife, "those big fellows can operate this as a convenience to their customers. They don't have to cover overhead, their regular merchandise will do that. They can price their food just to cover out-of-pocket costs, but if I do that, I'll be bankrupt."

At this point, Mr. Dupas started to reconsider his plans.

The centre was located in a new and growing suburb of a city of 300 000 people. In general, it was a middle-income area with most of the houses ranging between $60 000 and $100 000, though a few went as high as $150 000. The centre itself contained some twenty stores, including a larger supermarket, a small department store, a major drugstore, two chain shoe stores, three women's clothing stores, two banks, and assorted specialty shops selling books, men's clothing, and so on. Adjacent to the centre was a small office building which the shopping centre developers had built. It contained the offices of two contractors, an architect, two consulting engineers, three doctors, and a dentist. In all, Mr. Dupas estimated that some forty to fifty people worked there, and he had been told that an addition was planned to furnish space for a branch office of an insurance company plus a small sales office for a large machinery manufacturer. He had heard that this would probably mean that another ten to fifteen people would be working there. Two blocks from the centre a new district high school had just opened and the centre manager had told him some 1500 students would be enrolled there in the next two years.

Generally, Mr. Dupas was delighted with the centre. The manager of the centre had organized a merchants' association and Mr. Dupas was impressed by the people operating the various stores who would be his associates. At the charter meeting of the association, plans had been laid for a grand opening in three months' time and it had been agreed that dinner meetings should be held once a month in Mr. Dupas's restaurant. The manager of the bank where he now had his account, which was operating from temporary facilities near the centre, had also asked Mr. Dupas if he would be interested in joining a chapter of a service club which was being organized for the area.

Mr. Dupas knew he had to make the final decision on the layout of his restaurant within the next week. Time was running short if he was to be ready for the grand opening. As he thought about the problem, he decided there were two major alternatives. First, he could open the whole area up and have one large dining room. His kitchen and storage room could be at the rear of the area and could be serviced through a door to the exterior wall of the centre, or he could have an open kitchen arrangement in the centre of the area, but with sufficient space on one side to permit people to move readily from the front to the rear of the restaurant. This would give the appearance of two rooms. (See Exhibit 1.) Since his space was adjacent to one of the centre's entrances, he had two doors, one of which would be used only if he were open when the rest of the centre was closed.

The other decision which concerned Mr. Dupas was whether he should put in a counter with stools. He felt this would cater to people who wanted a quick snack and, in particular, to the high school crowd. On the other hand, he believed that such counters tended to conflict with the normal restaurant business. They were generally noisy and gave the impression of short-order cooking rather than carefully planned, well-prepared meals.

These were the essential problems concerning Tony Dupas, and he was well aware that he must make his decision very quickly or he would miss the opening of the centre.

Exhibit 1
Tony's Restaurant
Alternative Layouts for Restaurant

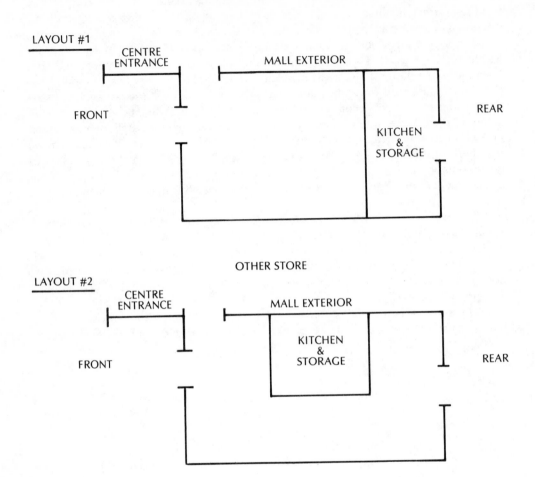

SECTION VII
An Introduction to Production/Operations Management

One of the key determinants of a company's success lies in the ability of its people to *produce* goods and *operate* services efficiently and effectively. This production/operations ability is important for not only mining, pulp and paper, and automobile companies, as well as a whole host of other manufacturing concerns, but also financial and educational institutions, health care delivery systems, and fast food service operations. In fact, managing any organized activity — whether preparing a family meal, coaching an NHL team, staging a disco/rock concert or running a national airline — involves production/operations principles.

There are four fundamental aspects common to all organizations producing goods and services that we believe will help you to develop an effective operating point of view and to develop decision-making skills applicable to a wide number of operating contexts. These four aspects are:

1. The purpose of production/operations and the basic components involved;
2. The key tasks that production/operations managers must manage well in order for their respective organizations to do well;
3. The basic types of production/operations processes and their management requirements;
4. The basic tools for diagnosing production/operations problems.

1. THE PRODUCTION/OPERATIONS PURPOSE AND BASIC COMPONENTS

Function

A common model for the production/operations function is the input–transformation–output diagram shown in Figure 1. That is, goods or services, purchased from a variety of suppliers, are changed in some manner and then distributed and sold to a variety of customers.

Figure 1
A Production/Operations Model

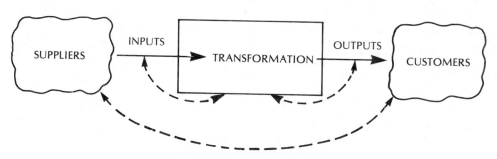

One of the first points to note in using such a model is that the outputs from one organization are often the inputs for another and vice versa. For example, consider Stelco, The Darnell Caster Company and The Canadian Linen Supply Company; three firms significantly different in the goods and services produced, yet, strangely enough, related. A portion of Stelco's plate and bar steel output may be purchased by Darnell. In turn, Darnell, using certain processes, equipment, and labour, transforms this steel along with other materials into the housings for their rubber-wheeled casters. Canadian Linen Supply may purchase a quantity of Darnell's casters for installation on materials-handling equipment. Canadian Linen uses the dollies, carts, and trailers to move linens and towels through their cleaning (i.e., transformation) process. Furthermore, it may well be that Stelco contracts the services of Canadian Linen to provide clean towels for Stelco employees. In this example, we might say Darnell is a Stelco "customer" in the sense that Darnell makes a further transformation on the purchased steel. We might say, however, that Canadian Linen is a "consumer" of Darnell's product in the sense of being the end user and not providing any further transformation to the purchased product. The application of this transformation model, therefore, is to be considered relative to a specific organization.

A second point to note is that the production/operations function is viewed as providing the link between the suppliers of goods and services and the customers of the transformed goods or services. For example, the production/operations function of a bank is essentially to pay depositors interest for putting money into savings accounts or bank notes and in turn to charge borrowers a higher interest for loaning the money. The basic assumption underlying the model is that the value added or provided to the purchased goods and services during transformation is desired and paid for by the various customers. Otherwise the organization does not survive.

A third idea with respect to this model (Figure 1) concerns the solid and dotted lines. The solid lines depict the flow and movement of goods and services. The broken lines depict the flow of information through the organization. It is the flow and interpretation of this information which allows management to determine how well the firm is doing.

The fourth and most important point to emphasize from this model is the transformation itself. It is the heart of production/operations; where the action is. The key message in the following material will stress the notion that the production/operations management function is to "make things happen" in changing inputs into outputs.

Components

Transformation normally involves different pieces of equipment, a number of people with a range of skills and an inventory or stockpile of goods to help smooth out the whole operation. Thus equipment, people, and inventory are the elements we shall refer to as the basic components of the transformation phase in ongoing production/operations systems. (See Figure 2).

Figure 2
Transformation
Basic Components

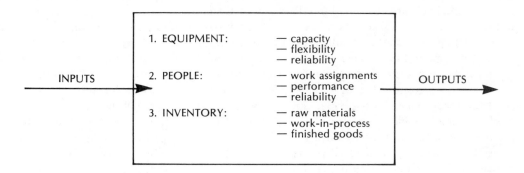

Equipment

Three important aspects of equipment are capacity, flexibility, and reliability. Equipment capacity in some cases is a measure of size; for example, the capacity of a beer-brewing kettle might be 7000 L. In other cases, equipment capacity is a measure of the rate of output or the number of units per period of time; for example, the capacity of a bottle-capper might be forty bottles per minute. Capacity is normally discussed in terms of theoretical or designed capacity and operating or actual capacity. *Theoretical capacity* is what the equipment manufacturer designed and built the unit to be or to do. *Operating capacity* is what happens when the equipment is in actual use. Thus, one measure of equipment efficiency is the ratio of operating to theoretical capacity. For example, if the bottle-capper's theoretical capacity was forty bottles per minute and the operating capacity was measured at thirty-five bottles per minute, the machine would be 87.5 percent efficient. *Equipment flexibility* refers to the ease with which equipment can be modified to perform a range of jobs. Thus, general purpose equipment has high flexibility and special purpose equipment has low flexibility. *Equipment reliability* refers to the probability that the equipment will perform as designed. Increasing down-time and maintenance costs may indicate a possible decrease in equipment reliability.

People

The people component of the transformation brings the psychological concepts and theories discussed earlier in the human resources chapter face to face with specific work assignments, performance assessment, and the reliability of human behaviour required in product and service transformations. There are two aspects of assigning work which are important for operations managers to consider. First, production/operations managers need to know the kinds of work and work sequences required to produce products and services. For example, what is the best way to make a hamburger at McDonald's? How would a manager make sure that an employee makes such a hamburger correctly? Job design and methods and task analysis techniques are tools to help ensure efficient and effective transformation processes. Second, production/operations managers need to know the kinds of behavioural skills and numbers of people required for the various jobs. Recruitment and hiring decisions, training and development and manpower-scheduling techniques are useful in the proper matching of people and jobs. Once people and jobs come together, production/operations managers are responsible for measuring the quantity and quality of the output. A part of the measurement will be machine productivity, and a part will be assessing and reinforcing behavioural performance. Standards, production rates, and quality levels are some of the measuring tools. Incentives and other compensation schemes can be useful reinforcers when required performance levels are achieved. A key factor in maintaining a smooth link between work assignments and performance is the reliability of the work force. High turnover and absenteeism are signs of low reliability and, in all likelihood, low performance.

Inventory

Inventory may be defined as anything purchased or acquired for the purpose of transforming it for resale *or* assisting in the transformation of saleable goods and services. As such, we can talk about an inventory of people, an inventory of plant and equipment or an inventory of light bulbs. For our purposes, however, we will restrict our discussion of inventory to include only the purchased materials (i.e., inputs) that are directly transformed into saleable outputs. There are three basic "kinds of inventory". *Raw materials inventory* is a stockpile of materials accumulated before any transformation is initiated. *Work-in-process inventory* is a stockpile of materials accumulated during transformation. This work-in-process inventory is really the partially completed units that are flowing through the operation. *Finished goods inventory* is a stockpile of materials accumulated after transformation is completed but before being sold to a customer. One of the "purposes" for having inventories is to help smooth out the flow of materials through the transformation. *Buffer* and *decouple* are words used to describe the purpose of inventory in allowing successive steps in a transformation process to be completed independently. How much inventory and what kind should an organization have? Nobody has a complete answer for this question. Marketing may want a lot primarily in finished goods in order to give quick delivery. Finance probably would prefer not to have any, and if necessary only a little, in raw materials in order to minimize the money tied up. Production ideally wants just the right amount of each kind in order to safeguard against unreliable suppliers, to separate or decouple parts of the transformation, and to handle customers' rush orders. Further to the question of how much inventory to hold is knowing the cost to carry and the cost not to carry (see Appendix A).

This brief discussion on the function and basic components of production/operations gives us a framework around which to discuss the key tasks for management.

2. THE PRODUCTION/OPERATIONS TASK[1]

The production/operations task refers to what an organization must do to ensure that the product is manufactured or the service performed in a manner that meets the needs of the customer and therefore allows the organization to realize its overall objectives. For example, in manufacturing automobiles, the production task includes transforming steel into shaped pieces, then assembling these pieces into automobiles that meet the style, price, and safety requirements of customers. Similarly, in a service organization such as a railroad, the production task includes transporting passengers and freight from one place to another as quickly as possible without endangering the safety of either in the process. More specifically, the production task in all organizations is to deliver the right product (or service), at the right price, in the right place, at the right time, and in the right quantity. To understand this task, the "environment" of the production manager must be considered.

First, marketing is the liaison between production and the firm's customers. Marketing should help translate customers' needs and wishes into sales volume forecasts, product features, delivery schedules, and so on. Marketing should also be geared to sell what the operating system can produce. Second, personnel is the liaison between production and its sources of employees. Personnel should help to locate, train, keep records, and so on. And third, finance is the liaison between production and the company treasury. Finance should help production make investment decisions and measure the costs incurred in the production process. Finance should also be prepared to provide the funds necessary to support effective production systems. The production manager needs to deal with these sometimes conflicting aspects of his or her internal environment. In addition, he/she also must keep up with technological developments (changes in equipment and new ways of making things), material developments (such as shortages) and competitive developments (such as changes in industry capacity). This task is easier said than done.

One way to help specify the production/operations task is to return to one of the messages in the marketing section. As noted there, the customer is the one who really determines what product or service we should provide. Five customer needs that have implications for the task of production/operations management can be identified. These are (1) quality and function; (2) quantity; (3) price; (4) delivery; and (5) service and continuity.

Quality and Function

If you were buying a car, you would want to be sure that the quality was acceptable. You would not want it to fall apart after one year's use. Most people are familiar with this concept of quality. At the same time, there is a function requirement. You want your car to perform under a variety of conditions. Actually, that is the most important aspect of all. The function the product can provide must match the function the

---

[1]This section is partly based on an unpublished note prepared by Professor Michiel R. Leenders of the School of Business Administration, The University of Western Ontario, London, Canada.

customer wants performed. At the same time, the quality must be such that the function will be performed reliably. The words *function* and *quality* are often used to mean the same thing. We will make the distinction that design of the product will determine its function. Manufacturing from design will affect quality. For example, the installation of a faulty headlight will result in a poor-quality finished product. Failure of a car to negotiate a tight turn may well be the result of a poor design, even though the quality is perfect because the finished product matches the design exactly. Under this definition, a high-quality manufacturer may well be in trouble if the product does not match market need. The buggy-whip manufacturer has disappeared not because of lack of quality but because of lack of functional need. The Ford Edsel did not fail because it fell apart in use, but because the customer demanded a different design to perform a different function: an inexpensive compact to give economy transportation.

Quantity

Quantity is an easily understood demand. The customer wants a sufficient number to satisfy his or her needs. If a rich father-in-law wanted to give microwave ovens for Christmas presents to his six daughters-in-law, he would not be happy if he could only buy one or two. Similarly, a railroad must ensure that enough space is available for all passengers and freight. Too few locomotives or cars would lead to a loss of business to other forms of transport. However, too many locomotives or cars implies that the railroad will incur higher costs than necessary.

Price

Price is also a fairly simple idea in the customer context. Most customers have limited income and are able or willing to spend only certain amounts on specified products. For example, in most parts of the United States and Canada, a snowmobile may be considered a luxury item subject to the appropriate consumer views regarding the price of such articles. Its popularity would be severely limited if the price were greater than the price of a new automobile. And again, with a railroad, the price charged for freight service must be comparable to that of competing transportation services such as truck or air. If the railroad prices are too high, shippers will switch to alternative services.

Delivery

Delivery simply means the customer wants a product or service by a certain time. It is no good delivering snowmobiles in May or Christmas cards in February or drugs after a death.

Service and Continuity

Service and continuity are somewhat more difficult to define. They include assurance that if the product does not function well, adjustments may be expected, as well as replacement of poor-quality parts. They may include financial arrangements, checkups, availability of parts, labour, and advice, and also assurance that the manufacturer will be alive for the life of the product. No one was too keen on buying Studebakers once the company had announced its intention to discontinue making cars.

Why is all this attention focused on marketing in a production chapter? Simply because production must supply goods and services that satisfy specific customer needs. The viability of the enterprise depends on how well this job is done. Of course, a well-managed production function will not automatically guarantee corporate success. The financial and marketing and human relations functions must also be in good shape and well coordinated within the total company. However, it is extremely difficult to have a successful company with a poorly managed production operation. Because of this, and since production costs usually average from 50 to 70 percent of selling price, and production employs most of the personnel in the firm, it warrants key attention. The customer needs must be used to provide the objectives toward which production management should be organized. These objectives are set in most cases jointly with the marketing group in cooperation with the financial managers.

Quality and function come through the new product development group. The design must be functional and the manufacturing process must result in the same finished product as the design specifies. Thus, throughout the production process, targets are set and measurements taken to make sure that quality requirements are met.

Customer quantity needs are translated sometimes by marketing alone, and sometimes jointly by production and marketing, into quantities of products which must be produced. The problem is always one of matching quantity produced to quantity demanded in the market. Both overages and underages may result in losses.

The customer price need is translated into a manufacturing cost target, which, if exceeded, will reduce company profits or, if improved on, will increase profits. Thus, production/operations management is highly cost oriented and elaborate cost-measuring and control systems are set up to ensure profitable operation.

The customer delivery need is translated into a time objective for production. Each product must be completed by a certain time. This requires scheduling and continual monitoring of where everything is in the total operation. Information must be available on what is late and why, what is ahead of schedule and what plans can be made to expedite the items that are behind.

The service and continuity need is translated similarly to the price need. Many service aspects have quality and function, quantity, cost, and delivery implications and can, therefore, be considered as part of these objectives. It is also necessary, however, to manage the production function to assure continuity. It is not good enough to meet the first four targets dead on. The process must be repeatable and improvable. Production/operations must be managed in harmony with overall company policies and objectives. There is a need to plan for the long term. It is not good enough to do everything well today. It must also be done well tomorrow.

The role of the production/operations manager is to accomplish these tasks as efficiently and effectively as possible.

- Efficiency refers to the extent to which the desired objective is achieved with a minimum of cost, effort, and waste — that is, doing things "right."

- Effectiveness refers to the extent to which an objective is realized. That is, doing the "right" thing.

For example, in the railroad business, efficiency can be described as carrying goods to a destination using as little fuel, labour, and equipment as possible. Effectiveness is delivering all goods to the designated place at the designated time, and, moreover, remaining flexible to changes in future demand. Therefore, it is possible for a railroad to be efficient but not effective (low cost, but late and unreliable), effective but not efficient, or neither. The ideal, of course, is to be both effective and efficient, but these two goals often conflict. The relative importance of efficiency and effectiveness depends on the organization and its major objectives and required tasks. For instance, in medical care the importance of effectiveness is much greater than efficiency, and consequently medical costs tend to be high.

3. THE PRODUCTION/OPERATIONS PROCESS TYPES AND MANAGEMENT IMPLICATIONS

You have undoubtedly seen several different kinds of production processes ranging from large assembly plants to a McDonald's outlet to a physiotherapy ward in a hospital. What is the best way to transform inputs into outputs in order to perform the production/operations tasks best? One of the very first considerations is the degree of flexibility or specialization required in the production facility. This degree of flexibility is determined in part by (a) market volume (both at the moment and in the future) and (b) product standardization. Depending on the size of the volume required and the extent to which the product is standardized, we may select a process somewhere along a spectrum:

Continuous Process

When a market is large with relatively certain present and future demand expectations, and when the product variation is small, the production process will generally be most efficient and effective if it is very specialized (and thus not flexible). This kind of process is referred to as *continuous process* and is exemplified by oil refineries, chemical plants and assembly line manufacturing. The characteristics of continuous processes are:

1. A limited variety of output,
2. The movement of each production through the same sequence of operations,
3. No designation of the products of the process to a particular customer,
4. Special purpose facilities and equipment — that is, the operations or machines have low flexibility and cannot easily be changed to perform different tasks.
5. Low to semiskilled labour.

Since all the units of production normally go through the entire sequence of operations in an identical order, the critical element to be managed is the smoothness of the flow-through. A break in production at one point could cause the entire line to be idle. The first thing to be done, then, is to ensure that the rate of movement of a unit of production through each step in the sequence is even. This is normally referred to as *line-balancing* and ensures the absence of bottlenecks. To give you an idea of a bottleneck, suppose three people were washing dishes: one washing, one drying, and one putting away. If the person drying is slower than everyone else, the whole system will be bottlenecked at the drying stage: the washer will run out of places to put wet dishes and the one putting them away will be waiting for something to do. In order to determine the degree of balance a basic technique called *process analysis* is very useful. We will talk about process analysis in our next major section along with a second technique, useful in production/operations management, called *trade-off analysis*. But first we will review the other two major process types — job shop and project.

Job Shop Process

A job shop process is more appropriate when the market is, relatively speaking, somewhat smaller, or has a less certain future or if there is a large variety of products. This type of process is characterized by:

1. The potential for an extensive product line.
2. A variable routine of jobs — not all units of production go through every operation.
3. Production for individual customers.
4. General purpose facilities and equipment — that is, the operations or machines have high flexibility and are easily transformed to perform different tasks. Examples are machine shops, auto service centres, hospitals or beauty parlours.
5. Semi- to high-skilled labour.

Job shop processes are more product- and customer-oriented than continuous processes. With a wide variety of potential products, no one set sequence of operations usually exists. This means that purchasing, inventory planning, manpower planning, and scheduling cannot be established in isolation from specific customer orders. The incoming order is the trigger for all of these activities to begin interacting. For example, custom manufacturers or automobile repair facilities are job shops which are entirely customer bound, in that every unit of production is at all times associated with a particular customer. However, the individual orders are generally not highly complex and there will be similarities over different jobs. Tuning an engine, for example, is not a process that has to be redesigned in its entirety for each car brought in to a service station. On the other hand, some job shops do not appear to be so strictly customer bound and have certain similarities to continuous flow in that some of the demand for the many different products can be forecasted. For example, in a restaurant which offers five standard dinners and a number of à la carte items, the kitchen is a job shop. However, the cook does not always have to wait for customer orders before starting. If Irish stew is on the menu, the cook may prepare a quantity in advance based on forecasted demand. Hence, the word *batching* appears in brackets on the process spectrum.

Given customer-determined quantity, quality, and design objectives, the main task will be to optimize the trade-off between minimizing delivery time to customers and maintaining a low-cost operation through high facilities utilization and low in-process inventory. The production/operations manager's problem is to juggle the conflicting objectives of the system. In order to minimize delivery time, it would seem best to process each order through each operation (or job station) as soon as it appeared. This policy, unfortunately, would entail the need for extensive production facilities in order to handle periods of peak demand. These facilities would then stand idle at periods of lower demand, and unnecessarily increase cost. However, if capacity is designed for the average load, periods of heavy demand will result in backlogs of jobs at different job stations. These jobs must then be scheduled. To complicate this problem, since different jobs will require different operations and in varying sequences, a scheduling decision for any given station should include consideration of all the jobs in the shop, their process requirements, and the current backlog at all job stations. There are some useful, though certainly imperfect scheduling rules. First come, first served is one example, and it is applied rigorously in banks where various employees in different departments service a variety of customers with myriad demands. Another rule of thumb gives precedence to the job with the shortest process time. Automobile repair garages use a judicious mix of the two rules.

Quite another problem arises in managing a job shop when we again try to minimize delivery time to customers. One of the characteristics of a job shop is that it utilizes general purpose rather than specialized facilities. Thus, a job station needs to be adjusted differently for each custom job. The set-up time is nonproductive and hence is costly. Costs can be minimized through better facilities utilization if jobs are "batched" into groups with similar characteristics. A printing press, for example, needs to be adjusted for paper size, thickness, and ink colour. It would be preferable, then, to do all printing jobs of one type at the same time and eliminate as many changeovers as possible. Naturally, this can greatly magnify the scheduling problem.

On the other hand, the cost of maximizing facilities usage is not just the inconvenience to the customer of longer delivery time. The longer a given job is part of the operation, the larger the investment in work-in-process inventory. For the company producing industrial boilers, it is obvious that the longer the time between the purchase of steel and the sale of a completed boiler, the larger the financial cost to the company. Similarly, in an auto repair shop, the longer it takes to complete a task, the greater the investment of the garage owner (bills for replacement parts and mechanics' wages must be paid independently of when the customer pays his bill). For those job shops with raw materials inventory and finished goods inventory, poor forecasting of demand (and hence of materials requirements) will also unnecessarily increase costs.

The most difficult task for the manager of a job shop, however, is not the decision at a given moment of the optimum "batch size" job station schedule, or size or mix of inventory. Rather, management must watch for changes over time in customer demands along the five basic needs. As these demands change, the manager must be prepared to adapt the existing process. Consider, for example, an automobile repair shop doing a variety of jobs. Over the years it becomes known for reliable, fast muffler repairs. At the same time the manager might find that the mix of services demanded has changed, so that the shop is now faced with a high proportion of muffler repairs and requests for this service come in on a steady basis. The quantity of these jobs has increased, the expected delivery time is probably shorter than for most jobs, and inefficiencies of scheduling these jobs around larger jobs might well be increasing overall cost. Adjusting the operation from a straight-forward custom-type job shop to one where at least muffler repairs are done with a more continuous-type job shop flow may well be important to future profitability.

Project Process

For those instances when the market for a product is very small (possibly for only one customer, on one occasion), or when the product is very complex and/or unique, a project approach to production will be most efficient and effective. Here economies of scale and specialization do not apply. The organization is normally "product-dedicated," with the job characteristically stationary, and production resources brought to it. Examples are space vehicles, bridges, repair of large machinery, and air rescue missions.

In some ways, a project resembles a job shop handling a special custom order. It obtains its unique character from the size and complexity of the job. Here the key component in cost is the investment in materials and human resources. Thus, early completion of a project is of as much interest to the producer as it is to the customer. The main task, then, is normally to minimize overall completion time, and, thus minimizing investment in the components of the project by ensuring they are not produced before they are required. Scheduling the various parts of the project is usually the critical task; to ensure that each component is ready exactly when required (and thus that its component parts or raw materials are made or ordered at the appropriate time). The Willowbrook Castle case illustrates a useful technique called *critical path method* (CPM) in managing project-type processes.

We must emphasize that these three major types of production processes are points on a spectrum. You may often encounter difficulties in trying to describe a particular production system as one form rather than another because it is a mixed type. These three major classifications are useful, however, because:

1. They emphasize the importance of selecting a process in accordance with the production tasks to be performed, and
2. They represent very different kinds of production processes each of which has certain critical characteristics that must be managed carefully.

In order to manage a production/operations system we need to do more than just select the general type of process we will use. Here are some additional decisions you might face in managing production systems. The first four items in the list are examples of the day-to-day focus of an operating manager. The remaining items are examples of the initial design issues or structural focus in operating contexts.

- Purchasing. Infrequent big orders or frequent little orders? (What purchasing and inventory policies do you have for your grocery items? Why?)

- Maintenance. When needed or preventative? (When would you change the light bulbs in a large factory?
- Scheduling. Which jobs get priority — first in, shortest, emergency, etc.? How far ahead do you plan? (How would you schedule an automobile repair garage?)
- Subcontracting. Do it yourself or hire someone else? (Suppose you had limited funds but wanted to put in a backyard swimming pool. What jobs would you subcontract to someone else?)
- Location. Near source of supply or new customers? (Why are Stelco and Dofasco in Hamilton?)
- Layout. By machine groups, by production steps, etc.? (How would you lay out the kitchen of a McDonald's restaurant?)
- Equipment. Rent or buy, specialized or general purpose, etc.? (What equipment decisions would you make if you were starting a landscaping and gardening service?)
- Job Design. Specialization; rotation; etc.? (Would you make cars on an assembly line where every worker repeatedly performs a small task — like General Motors — or would you use teams of workers who do major portions of cars together not on an assembly line — like Volvo?)
- Research and Development. Do your own or buy someone else's? (Why does Imperial Oil have such a large Research and Development Department?)

All of these decisions must be made with appropriate consideration of the production tasks and the internal and external environment of the production/operations group. Many choices may be constrained by available company resources while others will be constrained by the type of output desired. In the clothing industry, for example, a large producer of off-the-rack ladies' wear would probably use a form of continuous process implying specialized machinery and relatively unskilled labour. An entirely different production strategy would be followed by a small producer of custom clothing where design and quality are of paramount importance and volume is low. In this case, mechanization would be low and the people hired would have to be fairly skilled. In countries where labour is expensive, the initial investment in equipment may be very high. Alternatively, in Hong Kong, the production of clothing is labour intensive because the cost of skilled craftspeople is low.

Some of these decisions represent long-term commitments (such as location) others are medium-term (such as equipment investment), and yet others are short-term (such as purchasing policies). When making longer-term decisions in particular, we must bear in mind both the current circumstances and our anticipation of future developments. Changing major decisions such as plant location and layout of primary machinery is always expensive and disruptive, sometimes to the point where it cannot be done without jeopardizing the future of the firm.

4. TWO BASIC PRODUCTION/OPERATIONS ANALYSIS TOOLS — PROCESS ANALYSIS AND TRADE-OFF ANALYSIS

Process Analysis

A key objective in managing production/operations processes is to ensure that the rate of movement of a unit of production through the process proceeds as scheduled. In continuous processes this normally means even or level production. In order to determine whether or not the process is balanced, one must perform a process analysis. This analysis tool is fundamental to the management of all production/operations systems and typically proceeds as follows:

1. A list is made of all the steps in the proper sequence from the start to the finish of the transformation of the inputs to the outputs. The list should include movement, storage, inspection, and the specific operations performed on the product.
2. The flow of material through the sequence of steps is traced using a diagram sketch and the standard notation shown in Figure 3.
3. The capacity or rate of production is determined for each specific operation using a common unit of measurement appropriate to the process under consideration.
4. The demand level or the rate of output required from the production process is determined. This level is often the forecasted or known customer demand.
5. Each operation in the process is analyzed to ensure that the processing method and sequence is appropriate and that the operations are reasonably balanced.
6. If the process is out of balance, that is, bottlenecked or idle, the appropriate decision(s) is (are) made to get the process back in balance.

As an example of a process analysis, consider the following simplified dishwashing operation in the patients' dietary services department of a large hospital. For illustrative purposes, we will assume that: (a) washing personnel work an eight-hour shift with a half-hour for lunch and two fifteen-minute breaks; (b) the hospital has 361 treatment beds which on average are 97 percent occupied; (c) the supply of dishes is sufficient to service one day's demand; (d) each patient receives an average of six dishes per meal excluding cutlery; and (e) each machine wash and dry cycle, including loading, takes one hour. Figure 4 lists the processing steps, diagrams the flow of dishes through the washing operation and indicates the operating capacities of the four specific operations.

The question is, is the washing operation balanced with sufficient capacity to satisfy the dietary demand for clean dishes? We need to determine two things before answering this question. The first is to calculate the capacity of each specific operation using a common unit of measurement. Taking dishes per day as our unit and the seven hours of working time, the capacities of the four operations in sequence are 8400, 6300, 6300 and 7350 dishes per day. The second thing is to calculate the required demand. At 6 dishes per meal and 350 patients on average, dietary will need 6300 clean dishes per day.

It is obvious that the washing operation has just sufficient capacity to handle the average demand. That is, we might say the operation is effective. It is equally obvious that the washing operation is not balanced. That is, we might say the operation is not efficient. There is significantly more capacity available on operations one and four than is necessary. This means that the personnel working on these operations will have idle time. Achieving a perfectly balanced system is not always possible, nor in some instances desirable. But if you were the supervisor of this operation, you might consider having a closer look at the issue of idle labour in this process. A useful tool in this investigation is a trade-off analysis.

Figure 3
Process Analysis Notation

SYMBOL	INDICATES	EVENT
——→	=	MOVEMENT
△	=	STORAGE
□	=	INSPECTION
○	=	OPERATION
D	=	DELAY
- - - -→	=	INFORMATION

Trade-Off Analysis

A trade-off analysis is a management tool that helps to answer the question "Is there a better way?" Like process analysis, trade-off analysis involves a logical step-by-step sequence.

Applying the logic will not guarantee managerial success, but failure to do so often means managerial disaster. The sequence of steps is as follows:

1. Keep looking for possible trade-off situations. This statement is really a fundamental statement of sound managerial practice.
2. List the various alternatives that management can take.
3. Specify the costs or disadvantages of each alternative. This step should list all the qualitative as well as the quantitative disadvantages.
4. Specify the savings or advantages of each alternative. This step should list all the qualitative as well as the quantitative advantages.
5. Try to translate to a common unit as many of the disadvantages and advantages as possible. Money is most often used as the common unit, though output units and processing rates are sometimes used. This step is very often difficult since in many instances determining a dollar equivalent to a qualitative benefit such as better customer service is not always possible.
6. Decide on the course of action that results in the largest net gain. This step necessarily involves sound managerial judgment since some of the costs and savings from steps four and five will remain as qualitative statements.

We can return now to our dishwashing example to illustrate some of the logic of trade-off analysis. You will recall that our process analysis determined some idle labour time on two of the four operations. The question before us now is, is there a better way to process the dirty dishes? Can we make the process more efficient and still be effective in meeting the dietary need for 6300 clean dishes per day? When you recog-

Figure 4
Simplified Dishwashing Process Analysis

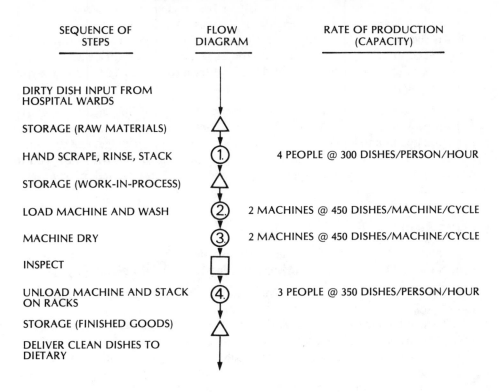

SEQUENCE OF STEPS	FLOW DIAGRAM	RATE OF PRODUCTION (CAPACITY)
DIRTY DISH INPUT FROM HOSPITAL WARDS		
STORAGE (RAW MATERIALS)		
HAND SCRAPE, RINSE, STACK	①	4 PEOPLE @ 300 DISHES/PERSON/HOUR
STORAGE (WORK-IN-PROCESS)		
LOAD MACHINE AND WASH	②	2 MACHINES @ 450 DISHES/MACHINE/CYCLE
MACHINE DRY	③	2 MACHINES @ 450 DISHES/MACHINE/CYCLE
INSPECT		
UNLOAD MACHINE AND STACK ON RACKS	④	3 PEOPLE @ 350 DISHES/PERSON/HOUR
STORAGE (FINISHED GOODS)		
DELIVER CLEAN DISHES TO DIETARY		

nize that the output in this example determines the input, (i.e., 6300 clean dishes return as 6300 dirty dishes), there is no need to maintain excessive idle labour time.

Two of the many alternatives to "trade-off" are: (a) do nothing, and (b) remove one person from operation one, reassign the work loads of the three remaining people on operation one plus the three people on operation four so that both operations are performed on a rotating basis, and use varying inventory levels to allow operations one and two to be performed independently of operation four and dietary demand.

The basic cost of alternative (a) or, in effect, the saving of alternative (b) is the yearly wage of one person. Assume this amounts to $7800. If you feel that by keeping an "extra" person on operation one you gain flexibility to handle absenteeism, turn-over/hiring problems, labour fatigue as well as avoiding possible labour unrest with a layoff and work reassignment, then your decision in this case would be to do nothing. Otherwise you would decide in favour of alternative (b) or possibly continue your investigation into other trade-offs.

The complexities and challenges of managing the continuous process in our limited example are increased substantially when you consider questions like the following:

- What are the purchasing policies for new dishes to compensate for pilferage and breakage?
- What do you do if one of the washer/dryers breaks down?
- How do you handle a sudden increase or decrease in demand?
- What is the best way to schedule the pick-up of dirty dishes from the wards?
- Is too much money tied up in carrying too large an inventory of dishes?
- Should you purchase a new high speed washer/dryer to replace the two twenty-year existing units?

We maintain that if you have a good understanding of how a process works through process analysis and if you can carefully construct a trade-off analysis you will be in a good position to make effective production/operations management decisions. There are a number of production problems in Appendix B that will allow you to practise using these analysis tools and to develop your production/operations management skills.

CONCLUSION

The purpose of this chapter has been to broaden your knowledge of production/operations situations by discussing four basic aspects of operating systems:

1. The input-transformation-output process and the basic components of equipment, labour and inventory.
2. The key production/operations management tasks of quality and function, quantity, price, delivery and service, and continuity.
3. The basic types of processes (continuous, job shop, and project) and their management requirements.
4. The two basic tools of process analysis and trade-off analysis.

The difficulty and complexity of production/operations problems vary. We believe you can make a start in dealing with these complexities and accepting these challenges with an understanding of these four aspects.

Appendix A
The Cost of Inventory

Any decision to hold or not to hold inventory must be made with the understanding that there are associated costs.

THE COST OF HAVING INVENTORY

A decision to hold inventory involves not only the cost of the items themselves but the cost of several other factors.

Financing. A company must pay for the money invested in inventory through either debt or equity. A lender charges a firm a rate of interest for the use of their money. Likewise an investor expects a return on the money invested in a firm in the form of dividends. Equity financing is often more expensive than debt financing since the risk to an investor is higher than that to a lender. Financing inventory or the cost of capital invested in inventory normally accounts for the largest component of inventory carrying costs.

Obsolescence. There may be some risk that the inventory will lose its value during the time it is held. Novelty and seasonal items such as toys or Christmas trees can have a high obsolescence cost resulting in a partial or a complete loss of the investment.

Damage. There are costs associated with inventory damaged through improper handling, weather, vermin, or spoilage of perishable goods such as food.

Rent, Utilities, and Insurance. These are costs associated with maintaining the storage facilities and are often accounted for in the inventory carrying cost since the storage facility could have been used for some other purpose.

These and other costs can combine to be a substantial expense. Some methods used to calculate the cost of carrying inventory are:

i) Only the financing charges might be considered. For example, if the firm's borrowing rate at the bank is 12 percent per year, then the cost of carrying inventory would be 12 percent of the average inventory value held over the year. Since a number of other costs may be incurred, only using the financial charges can significantly understate the actual carrying expense.

ii) A firm may calculate specific costs based on their particular situation. For example, if the costs of financing (Cf), obsolescence (Co), damage (Cd), rent (Cr), utilities (Cu), insurance (Ci), and other miscellaneous items (Cm) are determined then the carrying cost would be:

Inventory Carrying Cost = Average Annual Inventory Value × (Cf+Co+Cd+Cr+Cu+Ci+Cm)

Calculating the data and making the necessary management judgments on the various costs is both time-consuming and difficult.

iii) Some firms simply use a "rule-of-thumb" approach. For example, over time a firm has experienced that the cost of carrying inventory has been 25 percent, and they simply use 25 percent as the future charge for carrying inventory. Firms should note, however, that a good "rule-of-thumb" for one firm may not be such a good "rule-of-thumb" for another firm.

This carrying cost is assigned only when analyzing alternative strategies which involve holding inventory. It is not specifically presented on an income statement as it would be spread out through many of the other accounts (Interest Expense, Cost of Goods Sold, etc.).

THE COST OF NOT HAVING INVENTORY

A decision not to have inventory may result in shortages or production stoppages. For example, a firm may decide not to maintain a raw materials inventory, relying instead on the promised delivery dates of various suppliers. If the promised deliveries do not materialize, then the facilities, equipment and labour force may become idle. The firm would then incur a cost for not having inventory available.

Likewise a firm may decide not to carry a finished goods inventory. A shortage of finished goods may result in a backorder, in which the customer waits until the item is available or by a lost sale. Backorders incur additional costs for shipping, invoicing, machine start-up, and notifying the customer. Lost sales result in lost profit opportunities and possible future loss of revenues as customers cease buying from the firm. Whenever a business makes a decision that results in the loss of potential sales revenue it has incurred an opportunity cost. This cost is often the most serious cost of not having inventory.

In the final analysis, the only reason to carry inventory is that the cost of doing so is less than the cost of not doing so.

Appendix B[1]
Production Problems

The following production problems are designed to give practice in using the concepts, language, and tasks of production as outlined earlier in the introductory note. These problems will help you understand and work with the notions of demand, capacity, balance, inventory cost, trade-off analysis, process analysis, and quantitative and qualitative judgments.

As a starting point, consider the following checklist of questions and issues for addressing production problems. Knowing the right questions to ask leads to more immediate and effective analysis.

1. What aspect of the input-transformation-output model am I dealing with? If input is the issue then the questions are what is needed, when is it needed, how much is needed, where does it come from, what is the cost for the quality required. If transformation is the issue then the questions are: what is the best process to use in producing the product or service, what equipment is required and how it is working, what inventory is required and where, are enough (too many) people available and are they performing as required? If output is the issue then the questions are: what quantity is required, what quality is required, when is it required, and how much does it cost?

---

[1]Based on an unpublished note prepared by Chris Graham and Richard Mimick, School of Business Administration, The University of Western Ontario, London, Ontario, Canada, 1983.

2. What is the demand? Is demand expressed in units or dollars? What time period is involved? For example, if the annual demand for home computers is $10 000 000 with an average selling price of $2 500 and an average 250 working days per year, we know that average home computer demand per day is 160 units or $40 000. You must make sure demand levels are connected to the same units as used for the production output.

3. What is the rate of production output? Production output is usually stated in units per unit of time and is normally referred to by one of two terms: theoretical, or operating rate of output. The theoretical rate (designed rate) is the output that would be expected from a process, machine, or person under ideal conditions over long periods of time. Such factors as work breaks, equipment down-time, and process bottlenecks prevent most facilities from achieving theoretical output rates. The operating rate is the output that is expected under actual conditions. The operating rate is generally less than the theoretical rate. Comparing the operating rate to the theoretical rate gives a measure of the efficiency of the production operation.

4. Is the output less than, equal to, or more than the demand? If the output is less than the demand then the questions are: can demand be changed by backordering, and can the output be increased by changing the efficiency and effectiveness of the process, changing or adding equipment, urging people to work harder through various incentives, working overtime, adding more people, subcontracting the work? If the output is equal to demand then there may be questions of how to reduce costs and increase efficiency through more effective material scheduling, process and equipment management, and labour force management. If the output is greater than the demand then the questions are: can demand be increased through advertising and promotion, can the output be stored, can the output be reduced through fewer hours of work, layoffs, having some idle time?

5. Before getting involved in too much detail, make sure in analyzing each situation that you know the specific problem and objectives of the decision maker.

Sentsun Stereo

Fred Dirkin, foreman of the frame building division for Sentsun Stereo, had recently been criticized by the general manager about some idle workers. These were workers who installed heat sinks (an electrical part) into a metal frame. The frames were produced by nine frame assemblers. Eventually, after many more components were added, these frames became stereos. Upon investigation Fred found that the fifteen heat sink installers were often idle. In comparison the frame assemblers had little idle time. The hourly requirement from the frame building division was 500 frames. Fred knew that an experienced frame assembler could normally produce 60 frames an hour. Installing a heat sink was more complex and on the average took 1 minute and 15 seconds. Fred wanted to measure the efficiency of the heat sink and metal frame operations as well as ensuring that people were busy before the general manager made his next tour through the plant.

Tanner Bike

Demand for Tanner Bikes had grown rapidly in recent years, and a demand for 60 000 bikes was forecast for next year. During the past year, the gear division could not keep up with the demand and the company had to have the gears assembled by an outside firm at a cost of $2.35/assembly above Tanner's normal labour cost. The gear division was currently producing 24 units per hour. Due to some quality problems with the externally-sourced units, Tanner management wanted to supply demand from inside the plant.

The gear division had three work stations under the supervision of Kathy Wright. At the first station the workers took a wheel hub from a parts bin and threaded a freewheeling gear to the hub. Once completed the hub and freewheeler were put on a conveyor belt. The workers at the second station added the bearing races, bearings, and axles to the hubs. These workers often complained that the conveyor moved too fast and, in fact, some of the hubs reached station three incomplete. These hubs had to be taken back to station two to have the work finished. At station three the workers tightened the assembly to the proper specifications and then checked it for alignment. Once completed, the gear assemblies were placed on racks and moved to the next department. These racks were moved once a day.

Ten people worked in the gear division: three workers at station one, four at station two, and the rest at the third station. From her own experience Kathy knew that a freewheel worker could work on 12 units an hour and that the third station could produce 27 gear assemblies an hour. The Tanner workers earned $8.00 an hour with time and a half for overtime, to a maximum of 8 hours per week. The factory operated 40 hours/week and produced 50 weeks during the year with a two-week break in the summer for vacations and maintenance. Tanner's management had requested that Kathy make recommendations on how to increase production. She wanted to calculate the present observed capacities of each station and analyze the costs and savings associated with each of her recommendations.

Accufine Drillpress

Accufine Drillpress was considering expanding its automatic precision drilling operation because of a large increase in demand. Accufine charged its customers $30/hour for the service. Except for setting up the controls, placing the part in a jig, and removing it after drilling, the process was automatic. A recent time study showed the following information regarding the operation:

i) Machine capacity was one unit/minute

ii) The operator spent an average of 20 seconds on each unit that was drilled.

Accufine officials were suprised to find that the cost of this type of equipment had doubled since they had purchased the original machine. The precision driller now cost $109 000, which included a $3 000 installation charge. Maintenance on the present machine totalled $2 000/year and electricity cost $1.00/hour. Any new equipment would incur similar expenses. With operator wages costing $15.00/hour and a 6 000-hour lifespan on these machines, the company was not sure if it should expand.

Mr. James Simpson

Mr. James Simpson sold a line of industrial solvents. Since James had no technical background he had the solvents mixed and packaged by independent processors. To date this arrangement had worked very well. Recently, however, the Mixpure processing company had notified James that its ordering procedure would change. Now James would have to order one of his major products, Clean Machine, at the beginning of each month and would receive it at the end of that month. Mixpure would still charge James $291 per 100 litres for mixing, packaging, and shipping Clean Machine.

Tech-Chem, a competitor of Mixpure, had approached James with a counter-offer. Tech-Chem's offer meant that James could order on the Monday of one week with delivery on the following Monday. Tech-Chem also charged a higher price of $315 per 100 litres.

Clean Machine accounted for $273 000 in annual sales. It sold for $5.25/litre and was in steady demand year round.

James's accountant had just completed the financial statements and informed James that his cost of carrying inventory was 23 percent per annum. James wanted to decide whether to stay with Mixpure or accept the Tech-Chem offer.

A&D Truck Parts

John Richardson, the purchasing agent at A&D Truck Parts, had just received the production schedule for the upcoming week. Looking over the expected production, the parts requirements, and the present inventory levels, he wondered how much of each part should be ordered.

Production Schedule

	Product A	Product B	Product C
Volume	50 units	32 units	87 units

Parts Requirement	Part 1	Part 2	Part 3
Product A	2	3	0
Product B	4	0	3
Product C	2	1	4

Explanation: To make one unit of Product A there are two units of Part 1 needed, three units of Part 2 required and no units of Part 3 necessary.

Present Inventory

	On Hand	Safety Level*
Part 1	44 units	10 units
Part 2	28	5
Part 3	18	20

*Safety level is the amount of parts inventory that A&D liked to keep available to prevent stock-outs.

46

Bankruptcy (R)

Bob Wilcox had just been assigned the new job of production manager — games and toys for the Exemplar Manufacturing Co. Previously, Bob had worked as a foreman in another division of Exemplar for seven years. Exemplar had several well-established product lines and was beginning to diversify into new areas. Bob's superior, the general production manager, asked him to work with the new products manager on the latest product, code-named *Bankruptcy*. *Bankruptcy* was a new adult game that marketing seemed to think would be an immense success, competing with board games such as *Diplomacy* and *Monopoly*. Bob would be responsible for designing and controlling the manufacture of *Bankruptcy*.

An Exemplar staff member, John Duncan, informed Bob that the basic tasks to be performed were assembling components purchased from other manufacturers. In repeated attempts John was able to assemble completed versions of *Bankruptcy* in fifteen minutes. He also found that if three workers performed only two assembly operations each, instead of all six, each operation could be completed in half the time shown below. Thus, while one person working alone could produce thirty-two games a day, a team of three people working together could produce 192 games of *Bankruptcy* per day. The assembly operations could be performed in any order. The time required and material costs of the various components for each operation were given to Bob as follows:

| Assembly Operation | Time Required | | Material Cost |
	For One Person Working Alone	For a Three-Person Team	
A	1 minute	½ minute	$ .50
B	4 minutes	2 minutes	1.25
C	2 minutes	1 minute	.25
D	2 minutes	1 minute	.50
E	3 minutes	1½ minutes	2.50
F	3 minutes	1½ minutes	5.00
	15 minutes	7½ minutes	$10.00

All materials could usually be obtained within one week of being ordered. On occasion, materials could take up to two weeks to be delivered. The vice-president of finance recently had sent around a memo to managers asking that all inventories be kept at minimum sizes since costs for the company had risen substantially. He asked to be informed of all investment needs exceeding $10 000.

A good supply of semiskilled personnel was available in the community. The starting rate at Exemplar was $3 per hour (including benefits): normal hours were 07 30 to 16 00, with thirty minutes for lunch. Thus, each worker was paid an average of $24 per day. Considering that on average there were twenty working days in a month, this worked out to $480 per month. Bob was told he could hire as many workers as he thought he needed and pay them on whatever basis he wished so long as he did not exceed the plant average of $4.50 per hour regular time for semiskilled labour. Overtime, if used, was calculated at time and a half.

Bob was allotted space in the plant of 20 m x 5 m and told he could arrange his operations as he saw fit. The department would be charged $24/m² per year for the entire space allotted. Additional space required beyond the 100 m² was also available, but would be charged to his operation at $36 per square metre per year. The raw materials inventory (at $10 per unit) and finished goods inventory (valued at material cost plus labour cost) required roughly the same amount of cubic space. As the boxes were fairly bulky, he could store the equivalent of sixty units of *Bankruptcy* on each square metre of floor space, assuming he piled them as high as possible. John Duncan told Bob he figured they would need 50 m² for assembly operations including tables, work stations, lockers, etc. Other fixed manufacturing overhead costs associated with *Bankruptcy* were estimated to be $2060 per month.

The new products manager told Bob that the marketing department forecasted a demand of 3600 units per month for at least the first year. This could vary from 3000 to 4000 in any given month. He also stressed that as *Bankruptcy* was basically an impulse purchase, stock-outs were considered very costly and said he would be after Bob to avoid such situations. The intended selling price was $12 per unit. Marketing fixed costs (mostly for packaging design, advertising, and point of purchase displays) were estimated at $20 000.

Bob was also told that one of his suppliers, Hutchison Ltd., had sent in a quotation of $11 per completed unit to produce the year's requirements of *Bankruptcy* for Exemplar. Their quality was not considered as good as Exemplar's, but they said they were prepared to provide units on any schedule desired. Unfortunately, they added, the delivery time could vary from one to four weeks depending on how busy they were.

47

Canadian Cards Ltd. (R)

Mr. Paul Haskins, general manager of Canadian Cards Ltd., sat back after reading the company's operating statement for July 1980. The statement showed that the company was still not realizing the profit forecast for its counter line of cards and invitations. Although sales for the year to date were in line with the 1980 sales forecast, and prices had remained firm in spite of increasing competition, the line was producing little profit. Mr. Haskins realized that he had to take action to improve performance in this product area. However, he was not sure whether his problems lay with the work force, the inventory, the flow of materials, or the nature of the whole production system for the counter line.

RECENT COMPANY HISTORY

Although originally foreign owned, the company had been bought in 1968 by three Canadians who were determined that the firm would remain Canadian owned and grow into a printing industry leader. From its plant in Peterborough the company shipped cards and invitations to a chain of two hundred retail dealers all over Canada. Prior to 1978 all sales were of custom-printed, personalized stationery, but in 1978 a new line was introduced of eighteen standard items to be sold over the counter by the retail dealers. Sales of the counter line currently accounted for about 15 percent of the firm's total annual sales of $4 800 000.

CUSTOM STATIONERY PRODUCTS

The major product line marketed by Canadian Cards Ltd. was personalized wedding, Christmas, and anniversary cards and invitations. There were over three hundred items in this line. Retail dealers displayed a catalogue of all the designs available from Canadian Cards Ltd. Customers ordered cards and invitations from the retailer, and left with the retailer the personal message to be printed on the card or invitation. Most orders were for between twenty and one hundred cards of any one item. The retail store forwarded the order to Canadian Cards Ltd. for printing and delivery within seventy-two hours. The company was proud of its order turnaround, which was the fastest of any Canadian firm.

In the Peterborough factory the operations performed to fill a customer order were:

1. Receive order and establish delivery date.
2. Make out work order, and note on card design and customer's message.
2. Set type for printing customer's message.
4. Select card from raw material's stock.
5. Print the message on the cards.
6. Inspect and count (done by pressman).
7. Box and address for dispatch.

The layout of the Peterborough plant is shown in Exhibit 1. The custom stationery product line occupied most of the space in the plant. Raw material stocks of cards were purchased from stationery suppliers and stored on shelves next to the printing presses. Supervision in the plant was the responsibility of Mr. Jessel, the plant manager, and his two foremen, one for day shifts and one for nights. These two foremen were responsible for all operations in the plant. The factory management had never set standards of performance for the personalized stationery printing operations since Mr. Jessel felt that each order could be unique, and the printers themselves were skilled and took great pride in their own work.

THE COUNTER LINE BUSINESS

In 1978, Mr. Knowles, the sales director, saw an opportunity for the firm to expand its product line. Young people appeared to want cards and invitations that had space provided for writing in messages and invitations, rather than going to the expense of custom printing. Mr. Knowles decided that the company should market a line of eighteen standard items for weddings, Christmas parties, and birthday parties that the retail sales outlets could stock and sell over the counter. He called the line of standard items the "counter line."

Mr. Haskins decided to install a small production line in the Peterborough plant to produce these items. For the first time the company cut and printed its own cards from blank stock. The new line was installed at the end of the factory opposite the main offices. The management of the line was still handled by Mr. Jessel and his two foremen, but a pressman and six new women were hired to operate the line. The average hourly wage rate for the women was $3.92; the pressman could earn up to three times as much.

The procedure for printing and packaging the cards was as follows:

1. An order was initiated when the retail dealer noticed that his counter line stocks needed replenishing. He sent an order to Canadian Cards stating the items required and the expected delivery. An average order consisted of four counter line items, each for two boxes. A box of counter cards contained either twelve or twenty cards, and cost the retailer on average $8.20.
2. The Peterborough sales office noted the required order delivery and made up a work order for the items on the order. This work order was then filed under delivery date.
3. Each day orders were issued to the factory on the basis of delivery date.
4. The work order travelled first to the cutter. The cutter selected the bank card stock from the shelves and cut it to the required size and quantity.
5. From the cutter the items passed to the printer. Each set-up took approximately half an hour, but varied somewhat depending on the complexity of the colours and the type. The printer then ran each order individually and passed the printed cards through to the counting station. Exhibit 2 shows the work sheet for the printer for the week of July 14, 1980.
6. At the counting station the operator folded the cards and counted them into piles of twelve or twenty. They were then placed on trays and passed to the packaging machine.

7. At the packaging station the cards were placed between two parallel sheets of plastic film. This film was then automatically heat-sealed and cut. The packages dropped into a box behind the machine. A typical work sheet for the packager is shown in Exhibit 3.

8. It was the job of the woman operating the heading machine to pick up the boxes of packages from the packaging station and carry them to her own machine. On the heading machine a paper label was attached to the top of the package which identified the type of card and the number in the package.

9. From the heading station the cards were carried to the dispatch section, where they were neatly boxed and prepared for shipping.

Initially, the operators experienced some difficulty in making the machines on the line operate correctly. The maintenance man was unfamiliar with the new machines and took longer than normal to repair breakdowns. The women were unfamiliar with the process of setting the machines up for new package sizes and the packaged cards frequently had to be torn apart and repackaged. However, after several months these problems appeared to be well under control.

After the line had been operating for a year it became apparent to Mr. Jessel that it did not perform to capacity. Retailers complained that their orders were delivered late and they were losing sales due to stock-outs. The foreman reported to Mr. Jessel that the packaging and heading machines were operating at only half their rated capacity. Mr. Jessel and Mr. Haskins discussed the problem and agreed that the time to set up for customer orders was consuming much potential operating time. Mr. Haskins approached Mr. Knowles to see if customers would order in larger quantities, and therefore cut down on the number of orders. Mr. Knowles told Mr. Haskins that the retailers were highly adverse to holding more stock of the counter line.

At the end of 1979, Mr. Haskins instituted a second shift on the counter line in an attempt to cut down on the order backlog. Production from this new shift was very slow and he received several complaints from retailers of shortages in the packets of cards. Often there were twenty envelopes and only eighteen cards in a package.

Mr. Haskins realized that to increase the profitability of the line some action would have to be taken to increase output without increasing costs. Several courses of action appeared to be available. One was to put full-time supervision on the line in an attempt to increase the rate of work and reduce the counting errors. Alternatively, he could ask Mr. Jessel to study ways of speeding up delivery of customers' orders, though he was not clear how this could be done. Nevertheless, he thought that a study of the counter line business might indicate ways of improving the line's operations.

Exhibit 1
Canadian Cards Limited
Peterborough Factory Layout

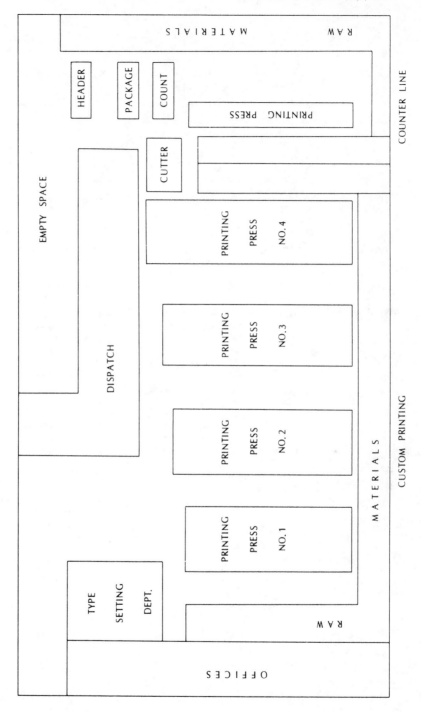

Exhibit 2
Canadian Cards Ltd.
Work Sheet

Press No. 5 — Counter Line — Morning Shift
Week Beginning Monday July 14, 1980

	Order No.	Quantity	Item No.	Time on	Time off	Comments
Mon. 14	80/1225	1300 cards	CL17	08 00	08 50	Part Lot
	80/1361	2880 cards	CL10	09 30	10 50	
	80/1281	1750 cards	CL4	11 30	12 20	
	80/1311	2880 cards	CL16	13 25	15 00	
	80/1312	400 cards	CL12	15 45	16 00	Part Lot
Tues 15	80/1410	1750 cards	CL10	08 40	09 35	
	80/1375	2800 cards	CL11	10 00	11 30	
	80/1376	1750 cards	CL1	12 05	14 15	
	80/1380	2050 cards	CL15	15 00	16 00	Part Lot
Wed. 16	80/1292	2150 cards	CL8	08 00	09 15	Part Lot
	80/1327	1750 cards	CL10	09 40	10 40	
	80/1355	1950 cards	CL1	11 05	12 00	
	80/1356	1750 cards	CL16	13 00	14 15	
	80/1420	2880 cards	CL2	14 35	16 00	
Thur. 17	80/1409	300 cards	CL5	08 00	08 15	Part Lot
	80/1412	1000 cards	CL7	08 35	09 20	*Rush* Part-Order
	80/1346	1750 cards	CL4	09 50	10 45	
	80/1342	2900 cards	CL9	11 15	12 25	
	80/1414	2900 cards	CL12	13 20	15 00	
	80/1400	1400 cards	CL13	15 20	16 00	Part Lot
Fri. 18	80/1390	2900 cards	CL16	08 15	10 10	
	80/1391	800 cards	CL10	10 30	11 00	*Rush* Part-Order
	80/1436	1750 cards	CL3	11 15	12 15	
	80/1323	1750 cards	CL7	13 10	14 00	
	80/1324	1000 cards	CL1	14 15	14 45	*Rush* Part-Order
	80/1350	1750 cards	CL2	15 10	16 00	

12 30-13 00 Lunch
Time on is start-up time

Exhibit 3
Canadian Cards Ltd.
Work Sheet

Packager — Counter Line — Morning Shift
Week Beginning Monday July 14, 1980

	Order No.	Quantity	Item No.	Time on	Time off
Mon. 14	80/1250	144 pkg.	CL10	10 10	10 40
	80/1241	144 pkg.	CL6	11 00	11 15
	80/1266	144 pkg.	CL2	11 25	11 50
	80/1267	288 pkg.	CL17	12 00	01 20
	80/1270	144 pkg.	CL18	13 40	14 00
	IDLE	—	—	14 00	16 00
Tues. 15	80/1325	288 pkg.	CL17	08 00	09 00
	IDLE	—	—	09 00	10 20
	80/1306	144 pkg.	CL4	10 20	10 45
	80/1311	144 pkg.	CL16	10 55	11 20
	80/1312	144 pkg.	CL12	11 30	11 45
	80/1313	288 pkg.	CL4	12 00	01 10
	80/1281	133 pkg.	CL4	13 10	13 30
	80/1410	144 pkg.	CL10	13 45	14 10
	IDLE	—	—	14 10	16 00
Wed. 16	MAINTENANCE	—	—	08 00	10 30
	80/1380	288 pkg.	CL15	10 40	11 40
	80/1381	288 pkg.	CL16	11 50	01 20
	80/1375	144 pkg.	CL11	13 35	14 00
	80/1376	144 pkg.	CL1	14 10	14 25
	80/1377	288 pkg.	CL6	14 35	15 25
	80/1378	144 pkg.	CL7	15 30	16 00
Thurs. 17	80/1327	144 pkg.	CL10	08 05	08 25
	IDLE	—	—	08 25	09 00
	80/1292	144 pkg.	CL8	09 05	09 20
	80/1355	144 pkg.	CL1	09 35	10 00

Exhibit 4
Canadian Cards Ltd.
Organization Chart

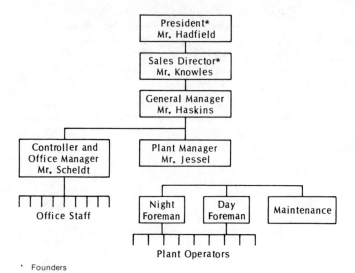

* Founders

48

Fine Footwear Limited (R)

In May 1982, Rob Gianni and Joe Perella, co-owners of Fine Footwear Limited, a women's shoe manufacturer located in Toronto, Ontario, were deciding whether or not to increase production in the coming months. If production was increased, they wondered what effect this would have on the production process, the equipment, and the labour force. They also wanted to maintain the quality of their product. In addition, an exclusive women's store had approached Fine Footwear with an offer to purchase high fashion designer shoes. Mr. Perella, Fine Footwear's shoe designer, was excited by the opportunities this contract presented.

COMPANY BACKGROUND

The company began in November 1980 when Joe Perella, a shoe designer, and Rob Gianni, a shoe producer, decided to leave the shoe company where they worked and fulfill their dream of owning their own company. Mr. Perella recalled their beginnings: "We decided we wanted to have the facilities ready before we approached potential buyers, so after checking about fifty locations, we finally rented a building. At that stage, we had no buyers or orders for our shoes—just a lot of confidence." Financial assistance was obtained through the Federal Business Development Bank and a chartered bank. Twenty-one machines costing a total of $105 000 (Exhibit 1) were ordered, and sales agents were contacted.

Production began after one worker was employed. Together the three set out to learn how to use the machines. One thousand pairs of shoes were produced in the first six weeks. In the second and third months, production increased to 2 000 and 3 000 pairs of shoes per month as more workers were hired. As demand grew, production increased until the current monthly level of 12 000 pairs of shoes was reached in April, 1982. Sales of over 40 000 pairs of shoes for the year ending December 31, 1981, exceeded $700 000.

THE PRODUCT

Fine Footwear Ltd. produced women's dress shoes made of a synthetic material. The company currently sold about ten different styles of closed-toed shoes in various colours. The average pair of shoes had a retail selling price of approximately $40. This was considered in the low price range for women's shoes.

DESIGNING AND MARKETING

Since shoes were a clothing accessory, shoe styles closely followed the trends in the clothing industry, and the company was required to produce new styles. In order to stay abreast of rapidly changing styles, Mr. Perella attended trade shows in Europe and followed many trade journals. Mr. Perella noted: "A shoe designer should also be a marketer — he must know what is selling." Accordingly, Mr. Perella had close contact with his two sales agents, one who sold in Ontario, and the other in Quebec. The agents did not work exclusively for Fine Footwear Ltd., but received a selling commission of 10 percent on manufacturer's sales.

The company's trade customers consisted of five chain stores. One of the chains was a very large Canadian retailer which accounted for over half of Fine Footwear's sales. Most chains carried Fine Footwear's shoes under a private brand name, though one large chain also carried a line of Fine Footwear shoes. Sales were fairly steady throughout the year. Orders usually ranged from 500 to 3 000 pairs with an average order size of 1 500 pairs. Most orders consisted of three different styles of shoes. Some chains ordered regularly each month, some ordered only twice a year, while others ordered at various times throughout the year. It usually took three months from the placing of an order until delivery, but orders could be completed faster if required. A few customers in the past had been upset when the shoes that they ordered were out of style by the time they were delivered. According to Mr. Perella, shoppers looked for a quality product in popular styles to fit their needs at an affordable price.

LABOUR

The workforce consisted of thirty-three non-unionized factory employees (mostly female) and one part-time bookkeeper. Keeping employees was sometimes difficult, as some workers would last only one day. New workers started wherever a vacancy occurred in the production process. The highest turnover of new employees occurred on the lasting conveyor line which was also the most complex job. Workers without previous shoemaking experience were usually not able to acquire the skills quickly enough to satisfy Mr. Gianni. Yet it was difficult to find experienced workers and expensive to hire them. The hourly wage rate varied from $3.65 to $8.00 (averaging $6.00) depending on the task and the worker's experience. The company was currently operating on a single-shift basis of 45 hours per week. Most employees worked this shift from 0730 to 1700 (5 p.m.) Monday to Friday with half-hour lunches and two ten-minute breaks.[1] Some employees also worked overtime (at one and a half times the regular pay) by working a half day on Saturdays or by working from 0700 to 1800 (6 p.m.) on some days, as required. Some firms in the industry used full-time second shifts at a wage premium of 25 percent over day wages. At present there were no bonus incentives. Most employees could perform several jobs and were frequently required to do so because of absenteeism. As a result workers would have to stop working at one station to help with orders at other stations.

INVENTORY AND SCHEDULING

Once an order was placed by one of the chain stores, materials were ordered, usually from the United States, Italy, or Germany, and arrived four to ten weeks later. Only the most basic raw material (such as soles and heel material) inventories were kept in stock in order to keep the inventory as low as possible. Work-in-process inventory could be found throughout the plant at various stages of assembly (see Exhibit 2). In fact, it seemed like most of the available floor space in the occupied portion of the plant was taken up with either machinery or work-in-process inventory. Most of this inventory

---

[1]Workers were paid for the two ten-minute breaks but not for the half hour of lunch. This is standard industry practice.

was located on trays which could be wheeled from operation to operation stacked on a cart (which held about fifty pairs of shoes) or was moved around on a conveyor during the lasting operation. (A last was a plastic form in the shape of a foot.) Finished goods (which were shipped F.O.B. factory)[1] were held until the customer arranged for delivery.

After all of the raw materials had arrived for the order, Mr. Gianni arranged the production scheduling and tried to balance the line if any bottlenecks developed by moving workers from one area to another. From past experience he was able to determine approximately how long an order would take to complete, and this information was used to arrange a production schedule. With ten different styles being currently offered and the range of colours available, there were often many orders being worked on at the same time. For example, eleven different orders were currently in various stages of production throughout the factory. From the time work actually started on an order of shoes to the time they were completed, a month usually went by, though a rush order could be completed in one week.

PRODUCTION PROCESS

Fine Footwear Ltd. produced only women's dress shoes. (The manufacturing of men's shoes, running shoes, and other types of shoes required a completely different production process.) The process for this particular type of women's dress shoe involved cutting, preparation, soling and heeling, lasting, and finishing. A one page/one copy production order was made up by Mr. Gianni (see Exhibit 3).

Shoes were made of two distinct parts. The sole and the upper were produced separately and then attached at the lasting operation.

1. Cutting

Two people were involved in the cutting operation, each working on a cutting machine. The machines acted like "cookie-cutters" and each could cut material for about 250 pairs of shoes per day. Soles, lining, and any extra material to be placed on the shoes (such as tassels) were cut from a large sheet of material. The soles were cut to resemble the shape of a footprint, while the lining was cut into the shape of a thick "V." About forty to fifty soles could be cut from a typical piece of material. If the shapes were cut too far apart (as sometimes occurred) wastage resulted. After cutting, the soles were taken to the soling area, and the lining and tassels were moved to the preparation area. The production order accompanied the lining and tassels.

2. Preparation

About twelve people worked on various machines in the preparation area. A thin piece of reinforcement material was attached to the lining. This was pressed together, then this flat piece was bent (or "closed") into the shape of a shoe with no bottom. This was called an "upper." After the upper was folded on the folding machine, the size and lot number were stamped on each upper. Over a two-day period, this area could produce 1500 pairs of uppers. Additional reinforcements were attached inside the toe, then the reinforcements and lining were stitched together on one of the four sewing machines.

---

[1] Buyer must pay transportation charges from the factory.

Any extra material was trimmed and the uppers were sized and placed in containers, ready to be brought to the lasting area. The production order was taped to one of the containers.

3. Soling and Heeling

In the soling area the shoes were first trimmed around the edges by a trimming machine, then sprayed with black paint and left to dry on a rack. Next the soles were "split" (formed to the shape of the shoe) and cemented with glue. Finally the soles were put in a bin and carried to the press (in the lasting area).

In the heeling area, glue was placed on the top of the heels (which were either cut in the factory or bought pre-cut) and these heels were placed in a rack and taken to the press. With the existing equipment and labour the soling and heeling area could produce, at most, 520 pairs of soles and heels each day.

4. Lasting

It was in the lasting area that the upper, the sole, and the heel became a shoe. The lasting operation consisted of nine operations, each with a machine and an operator. The shoes went through the lasting operation in pairs. Each operation, except the drying oven, took on average one minute for each pair of shoes (this included move time). Both machine and worker needed the full minute to complete the operation. The lasting operation produced 60 pairs of shoes per work hour. One area where things did not always go as planned was the operation where the heel and sole were attached to the upper. Sometimes the workers could not find the right bins of heels or racks of soles, even though the production order was with the uppers. At other times the soles and heels had not even been produced yet, or they were still in the soling and heeling area of the plant.

To start, an insole (the inside bottom of the shoe) was stapled onto a last (a plastic form in the shape of a foot). The insoles were purchased from an outside supplier. The company owned about 550 pairs of lasts, each pair costing about $24. Next, a counter (the inner material located at the back of the shoe) was placed in latex glue and cemented to the insole. Nails from a nailing machine were then placed along the edge of the insole and more glue was applied. The upper was then placed over the last and was nailed onto the insole. Cement and filler were added to ensure a good bond between the upper and insole. Shoes were then placed in a slowly rotating oven (it could hold 36 pairs at a time) for fifteen minutes in order to dry and shape the shoes. Next the heel and the outer sole were placed in a small heating element (in order to reactivate the cement) and then pressed onto the insole. The last was taken out of the shoe and the final nails were placed in the heel. The shoes were then placed on a cart and wheeled to the finishing area. One worker was responsible for moving the lasts from the end of the line to the beginning of the process.

5. Finishing

In the finishing area, one person placed a sock lining inside the shoe and performed the final cutting and stapling. Two others then cleaned the shoes, removing any excess glue, and touched them up with colour, if needed. The shoes were taken to a table for final inspection, placed in boxes, hand stamped with the size, colour, and customer number, closed and placed in the shipping area. See Exhibit 4 for a job breakdown of the workers. The finishing area could handle 2,750 pairs of shoes in a five-day period.

FUTURE OUTLOOK

Mr. Gianni and Mr. Perella felt that with next year's forecasted growth in demand from existing chain store customers a production level of between 700 and 800 pairs of shoes a day could be warranted; however they were concerned with becoming too dependent on any one customer. Mr. Perella was interested in the order for high fashion shoes. These shoes would retail at a price level that was significantly higher than Fine Footwear's current product. It could mean up to 20 orders for exclusive designs a month with 50 pairs of shoes to each order. Material costs would be substantially higher than their current shoes. Labour costs would also increase due to the higher quality that this product would demand. In addition designs would change each month to meet the demands of high fashion. Mr. Perella wanted to try some new designs that were not suitable for their current market.

With only two-thirds of the 960 square metres of floor space currently being used, they felt they had room to expand. However, they realized they might eventually have to add another shift or move to a new location. If daily production was increased to 700 or 800 pairs of shoes, new employees might have to be hired and other production changes could also be required. See Exhibit 5 for cost breakdowns. The owners were concerned with the effect that an increase in production would have on the quality of their product. Having quickly developed a successful and profitable organization, Mr. Gianni and Mr. Perella were wondering how to proceed.

Exhibit 1
Fine Footwear Limited (R)

Equipment Costs

2 cutting machines @ $13 280 each		$26 560
Lining, pressing & bending machine		6 500
Folding machine		6 860
4 sewing machines @ 1 120 each		4 480
Trimming machine		10 490
Splitting machine		11 500
Heel cutter		3 700
Stapler	$ 2 300	
Cement applicator	4 800	
Nailing machine	1 750	
Cement applicator	4 800	
Nailing machine	1 750	
Fill machine	980	
Oven	11 420	
Press	3 967	
Nailing machine	1 750	
	33 517	
Stapler		1 393
		$105 000

Exhibit 2
Fine Footwear Limited (R)

Plant Layout

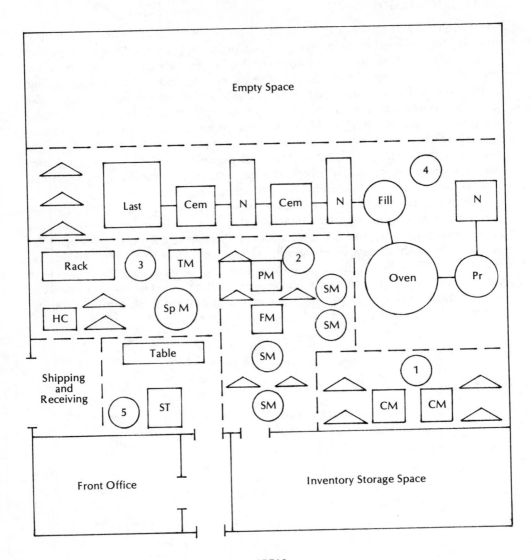

AREAS

① CUTTING AREA
② PREPARATION AREA
③ SOLING AND HEELING AREA
④ LASTING AREA
⑤ FINISHING AREA

Exhibit 2 (Cont'd)
Fine Footwear Limited (R)

Plant Layout

MACHINE KEY

CM	*CUTTING MACHINES*
PM	*LINING, PRESSING, BENDING MACHINE*
FM	*FOLDING MACHINE*
SM	*SEWING MACHINES*
TM	*TRIMMING MACHINES*
Sp M	*SPLITTING MACHINE*
HC	*HEEL CUTTER*
Last	*LASTING AND STAPLER*
Cem	*CEMENT APPLICATOR*
N	*NAILING MACHINE*
Fill	*FILL MACHINE*
Oven	*ROTATING OVEN*
Pr	*PRESS*
Table	*FINISHING TABLE*
ST	*STAPLER AND INSPECTION TABLE*
△	*WORK IN PROCESS INVENTORY*

Exhibit 3
Fine Footwear Limited (R)

Production Order

N? 6491

STYLE NO. 45201

CUSTOMER

DATE July 1/82

COLOUR BLACK CALF. SOCK STAMP

DESCRIPTION GREY Lining.

SIZE	5	–	6	–	7	–	8	–	9	–	10	TOTAL
PAIRS	1		1	2	3	3	3	2	2		1	18.

LAST 452. SOLE BLACK. HEEL 491 D.

Exhibit 4
Fine Footwear Limited (R)

Job Breakdown

Operation

Cutting	2 workers
Preparation	12 workers
Soles and Heeling	2 workers on soles
	2 workers on heels
Lasting	1 worker on lasts
	9 workers on machines
Finishing	1 worker on socks
	2 workers on cleaning
Shipping/Receiving Inventory	1 worker
Boxing/Stapling	1 worker
TOTAL	33 workers

Exhibit 5
Fine Footwear Limited (R)

Cost Sheet

Labour	$ 3.65–$8.00/hour ($6.00 Average)
Material	$10.15 per pair on average

Monthly Costs:

Maintenance, cleaning, repairs	$ 480
Factory rent	3 600
Heat, light, power	1 200
Bookkeeper	500
Management salaries (Gianni, Perella)	4 280
Travel expenses	2 500
Interest charges	1 313
Depreciation expenses (10-year life)	875
Total Monthly Costs	$14 748

49
Fish Forwarders

A. THE SITUATION

Fish Forwarders supplies fresh shrimp to a variety of customers in the New Orleans area. It places orders for cases of shrimp from fleet representatives at the beginning of each week to meet a demand from its customers at the middle of the week. The shrimp are subsequently delivered to Fish Forwarders and then, at the end of the week, to its customers.

Both the weekly supply of, and demand for, shrimp are uncertain. The *supply* may vary as much as 10 percent from the amount ordered, and, by contract, Fish Forwarders must purchase this supply. Fish Forwarders has determined that the probability of this variation is as follows:

- 10 percent from amount ordered: 30 percent of the time
  0 percent from amount ordered: 50 percent of the time
+ 10 percent from amount ordered: 20 percent of the time

Similarly, the *demand* for shrimp varies as follows:

  600 cases: 5 percent of the time
  700 cases: 15 percent of the time
  800 cases: 60 percent of the time
  900 cases: 15 percent of the time
1000 cases: 5 percent of the time

A case of shrimp costs Fish Forwarders $30 and it sells for $50. Any shrimp not sold at the end of the week are sold to a cat food company at $4 per case. Fish Forwarders may, if it chooses, order the shrimp "flash-frozen" by the supplier at dockside, but this raises the cost of a case by $4, and hence costs Fish Forwarders $34 per case. Flash freezing enables Fish Forwarders to maintain an inventory of shrimp, but it costs $2 per case per week to store the shrimp at a local icehouse. The customers are indifferent to whether they get regular or flash-frozen shrimp. Fish Forwarders figures that its shortage cost is equal to its markup; that is, each case demanded but not available costs the company $50 – $30, or $20.

B. OBJECTIVES

To manage inventory and purchasing policies to make the maximum possible gain.

Reprinted with permission from Chase and Aquilano, *Production and Operations Management*, Revised Edition (Homewood, Ill.: Richard D. Irwin, Inc., 1977).

C. PROCEDURE FOR IN-CLASS EXERCISE

This exercise will be conducted in class. *Prior to class*, you are expected to study this situation and formulate some decision rules to maximize your gain. The instructor, using a random procedure, will tell you what supply you received and what demand you faced each week. There will be short pauses "each week" during the exercise, but you should be prepared to make reasonably quick decisions. You will have to decide how many cases to order of regular shrimp and flash-frozen shrimp each week and enter orders and results in Exhibit 1. The order quantity of each may be any amount. Assume that there is *no opening inventory* of flash-frozen shrimp.

Steps in the exercise:

1. Decide on the order amount of regular shrimp and/or flash-frozen shrimp and enter the figures in column 3 of Exhibit 1.
2. The instructor then will tell you what variation there was in the supply received. The same variation applies to both regular and frozen shrimp orders. For example, if you ordered 1000 regular and 100 frozen, and were told the variation was –10 percent, you would receive 900 regular and 90 frozen shrimps. You enter the amount received in column 4 of Exhibit 1.
3. Add the amount of flash-frozen shrimp in inventory, if any (as shown in column 2), to the quantity of regular and frozen shrimp just received and enter the total in column 5. This shows how much is available for sale that week.
4. The instructor will then tell you what the demand for shrimp was that week. Enter this amount in column 6.
5. Determine the amount sold. This will be the minimum of column 5 (amount available) or column 6 (amount demanded). Enter this quantity in column 7.
6. Determine the excess. The amount of excess is simply that quantity remaining, if any, after demand for a given week is filled. Always assume that regular shrimp are sold before frozen shrimp.
7. Determine shortages (unfulfilled demand). This is the amount demand exceeds quantity available for sale each week and it occurs only when demand is greater than sales (column 6 greater than column 7). Since all customers use the shrimp within the week in which they are delivered, back orders are not relevant. Enter the amount of shortages in column 9.
8. After repeating this procedure for the specified number of weeks, determine your economic gain using Exhibit 2 as a guide.

Exhibit 1
Fish Forwarders
Worksheet

(1)	(2)	(3) Orders Placed		(4) Order Received		(5) Available For Sale		(6)	(7)	(8) Excess		(9)
Week	Flash Frozen Inventory	Regular	Flash Frozen	Regular	Flash Frozen	Regular	(Col.2 + Col.4) Flash Frozen	Demand	Sales (Min. of Col.5 and Col.6)	Regular	Flash Frozen	Shortages (If Col.6 Exceeds Col.5)
1												
2												
3												
4												
5												
6												
7												
8												
9												
10												
Total												

Exhibit 2
Fish Forwarders
Economic Gain

Revenues

1. From sales: _____ cases (Col. 7) × $50   = $_____

2. From sales: _____ cases (Col. 8, Reg.) × $4   = $_____
   (to cat food)

3. Total   (1 + 2) $_____

Costs

4. Regular purchases: _____ cases (Col. 4, reg.) × $30   = $_____

5. Frozen purchases: _____ cases (Col. 4 froz.) × $34   = $_____

6. Holding frozen
   shrimp in
   inventory: _____ cases (Col. 8, froz.) × $2   = $_____

7. Total   (4 + 5 + 6)

8. Net profit   (3 – 8) $_____

9. Less: Economic loss
         from shortages: _____ cases (Col. 9) × $20   = $_____

10. Net economic gain   *(8 – 9) $_____

50

Haitian Rebar Co. (A)(R)

In January 1980, five months after the start of a melt shop at Haitian Rebar, Mr. John Duncan, plant manager, received a request from Mr. Lord, melt shop superintendent, to purchase two additional ladles.

COMPANY BACKGROUND

In 1976, Mr. Lawrence Murray and two friends studied the feasibility of producing reinforcing steel in Port-au-Prince, Haiti. Haiti, population six million, covered one-third of the island of Hispaniola; the Dominican Republic occupied the remainder. Following independence from France in 1804, the Haitians fought a longer and bitter struggle for political stability and economic independence. Haiti had developed its major industries of coffee, sugar, cotton, and citrus products. In 1952 a Canadian and an American firm established mining companies for copper and bauxite which by 1976 employed 1200 workers. Mr. Murray, a thirty-year resident of Haiti, had worked in the Canadian company since 1953. Construction of homes and office buildings increased significantly and by 1976 this industry employed about 12 000 workers. Mr. Murray had followed this economic and industrial development closely and believed there was a market for locally produced construction steel. Consequently, early in 1974 the three friends founded the Haitian Rebar Company and hired an American expert to design a plant. Reinforcing steel was to be produced from scrap, converted in an electric furnace, and formed in a rolling mill.

In 1978 the company obtained from the government the right to operate as a monopoly. As soon as the local company became productive, the government agreed to cut off all construction steel imports and all scrap steel exports.

Plant construction was started in 1978 and completed in August 1979. The electric furnace cost $500 000 and the rolling mill $2 400 000.[1] The immediate objective was to produce quality steel for sale on the local market by January 1980.

Mr. Murray and his partners had decided on the following policies before operations were begun. All scrap deliveries from local and country vendors would be accepted on a sliding price scale depending on grading and preparation time. Minimum price per ton[2] would be $10 and the maximum $30. On the selling side the company established a minimum order quantity of 200 tons, and promised a three-month delivery on all shipments of not less than 20 tons. Terms were cash with order, with discounts on orders over 500 and 1000 tons. Six bar sizes were to be produced. These fell into three distinct ranges: 1 in.[3] and $\frac{7}{8}$ in.; $\frac{3}{4}$ in. and $\frac{5}{8}$ in.; $\frac{1}{2}$ in. and $\frac{3}{8}$ in. The selling price for one ton of 1-inch bars was set at $220.

The recruitment and training of labour and staff were difficult, because no similar industry existed on the island. As a first step, Mr. Murray hired three experi-

---

[1] All figures shown in this case are in U.S. dollars.
[2] 1 ton = 907.2 kilograms.
[3] 1 inch = 2.54 centimetres.

enced steel makers from the United States and Canada: a plant manager, a melt shop superintendent, and a rolling mill superintendent. Mr. Murray and his management team then met to discuss hiring and training criteria for the foremen and work force. They reviewed a number of applications and passed the final selections to a doctor and a psychiatrist. Emphasis was not placed on any prior industrial experience but on literacy, past work records (attendance and job changes), and the expressed willingness and ability of the applicants to work. The company started with a skeleton force of fifty nonunion labourers. A crew of fifteen men started immediately on scrap preparation. Another fifteen concentrated on melt shop start-up while the remainder were assigned to the rolling mill and essential services. The wage scale was slightly above the industry average for Port-au-Prince. Wages for unskilled work averaged $.80 per hour and for skilled work $1.20 per hour. The skeleton crew started during the equipment installation phase in the plant in order to learn about the machinery and how it operated. Just before plant completion, management and workers held discussions and seminars on steel making and practised job duties and responsibilities using simulated runs on the equipment.

PROCESS START-UP

The first stage of the manufacturing process involved scrap steel preparation, furnace refining and pouring ingots. The second stage involved ingot reheating and mill rolling. The company planned to start up regular production in two steps: the melt shop first, followed four months later by the rolling mill. Before full-scale rolling could be started the melt shop had to build up an inventory of in-process ingots and the melt could only operate on a restricted hourly basis. The furnace required large amounts of electricity (approximately 575 kWh/ton), and the Haitian government restricted the company's use of the furnace to 22 30 to 6 30 Monday–Friday and on weekends from 6 30 Saturday to 6 30 Monday.[1] Government officials promised that a new electrical substation would be built by early 1981, which would allow the company potential twenty-four-hour operation, seven days a week.

Rebar produced the first ingots from the melt shop in August 1979. Management planned to operate initially on a one-shift basis. The scrap preparation crew worked eight hours a day, five days a week, and the melt shop crew worked eight hours for four nights and ten hours on Saturday and Sunday.

In the first few months the rolling mill worked eight hours a day, five days a week on experimental runs on all sizes except the ⅜ in. bar.

MELT SHOP PROCESS

The melt shop process involved four distinct operations: scrap preparation, refining, ladling and pouring of ingots (Exhibit 1).

Scrap preparation was divided into sorting and sizing. Sorting included separating the cast iron and high carbon content steels from the better grades of scrap. Sizing was required to bring pieces down to manageable proportions. This normally meant

---

[1] As of 1980, Haiti was not yet using the 24-hour clock.

cutting into 3-ft[1] lengths. The size and the quality of the scrap caused variations in the size of charging loads and melting times in the furnace. A large electric magnet operating from an overhead crane loaded the scrap into the three charging buckets. Each charging bucket weighed 7 tons, could carry 5000 lbs[2] of scrap and was designed with a false bottom for top charging the furnace (Exhibit 2).

Refining took place in a direct arc electric furnace. The furnace occupied half of a concrete pit 30 ft. by 15 ft. by 6 ft. Its mounting allowed tilting to 35° for tapping[3] and 15° in the opposite direction for adding refining agents and drawing off slag. The roof swung away during charging. Three carbon electrodes arced with the metal and melted the scrap (Exhibit 3). Total time per heat including charging, refining, and tapping depended primarily on the ability of the metal to conduct the heat through the furnace and ranged from about two to five hours. Loads were charged successively; after the first had melted, the second was added and the third load followed the same way. The electrodes required about twenty minutes to enter the bath with each charge accompanied by tremendous noise as arcing took place. While refining took place, carbon, manganese, silicon, chromium, and limestone were added and metallurgical analyses made.

When the heat reached the required temperature (2900° F)[4] and composition, a second overhead crane placed a ladle in the pit beside the furnace ready for tapping. The crane then placed the full ladle in the travelling pouring cradle on the teeming[5] line. The cradle (Exhibit 4) was a square metal structure, open both top and bottom and mounted on four railway wheels. This supported the ladle as each mould along the line was teemed using the top pouring method (Exhibit 5). The overhead crane removed the red-hot ingots from the moulds and placed them in piles. After an hour's cooling a fork lift truck carried them to the ingot storage yard in the back of the plant (Exhibit 6).

Exhibit 7 summarizes melting equipment and labour.

LADLING OPERATION

The laid-down cost of the three ladles at Rebar was $20 000. Each ladle weighed 5 tons and could hold 16 tons of molten steel. The circular cross section, tapering inward from top to bottom, was lined with a double layer of firebrick called refractory (Exhibit 8). The inner refractory lining protected the steel shell, and the outer lining expanded on contact with the melt to form tight joints during pouring. The pouring nozzle was a graphite rod inside a refractory sheath. The pouring lever moved the rod up and down, allowing the molten metal to flow through the pouring refractory into the mould.

At the start of each heat the crane operator put a ladle under the preheater. Each ladle required two to three hours of open flame preheating to reach a temperature close to 2900° F. Twenty minutes before the refining process ended, the crane operator positioned the preheated ladle in the pouring cradle where two operators inserted the preheated pouring nozzle. Placing the nozzle was a key operation in the melt shop. If the nozzle-operating mechanism was not well lubricated with graphite and did not

---

[1] 1 foot = .3048 metres.
[2] 1 pound = .4536 kilograms
[3] Tapping is the process of pouring molten steel from the furnace to a ladle.
[4] 2900° F = 1594° C.
[5] Teeming is the process of pouring molten steel from the ladle into ingot moulds.

move freely, there was a high probability that the nozzle would freeze up during teeming. The crane operator then lowered the ladle into the pit beside the furnace. All personnel cleared the area as the furnace operators started rotating the furnace to tap the molten steel. The crane operator next placed the ladle back in the pouring cradle, unhooked and swung over to place another ladle at the preheater.

Total teeming time normally was fifty minutes. The crane operator removed the empty ladle from the cradle, dumped the remaining skull[1] into a skull pot and finally placed the ladle in the reconditioning area. Two of the cradle operators then burned out the pouring refractory and nozzle using an oxygen flame. Total time, starting with preheating through nozzle burnout normally required four hours (Exhibit 9). The ladle cooled for the next four hours before a mason started chipping away the remnants of steel and refractory around the pouring hole (Exhibit 10). He then put in new firebricks so that the pouring refractory and nozzle could be installed after preheating. At the start of Rebar melting shop operations, the mason required three to four hours to replace the pouring refractory. However, as he became familiar with the repair work, he reduced his time to the present industry average of one and one-half hours, though occasionally it might take up to two and one-half hours if the ladle was in rough shape.

Normally one of the ladle operators performed the repair and masonry work but every member of the pouring crew could do this work. In North America, masons usually worked on ladles within two hours after nozzle burnout. Mr. Lord had tried to persuade his men to start masonry work sooner, but they all claimed the ladle was much too hot to work on any earlier.

Material costs for pouring refractory repairs ranged from $50 to $70. Ladle operators became skilled in noticing when the outer refractory lining was deteriorating and informed the melt shop superintendent. Mr. Lord then scheduled a major ladle overhaul (after twenty to twenty-five heats).

Good refractory outer lining was important in protecting the thin inner lining. In extreme cases, the melt could burn through the inner lining to the steel skull and make the ladle nonrepairable. The mason required from eight to sixteen hours to overhaul the complete lining. Material costs for major refractory repairs ranged between $1000 and $1200.

On January 11, 1980, three weeks after the melt shop started two-shift operations (Exhibit 12), Mr. Duncan received a request from Mr. Lord to purchase two new ladles. Mr. Lord said that ladle delays were becoming more frequent as a result of increased furnace efficiency and an increased number of heats per week. He had already installed portable fans to assist in cooling the ladles and still the masons complained about the intense heat. He said that furnace capacity might be limited if no further ladles were purchased.

Mr. Duncan wanted to review the melt shop records (Exhibit 11) before acting on Mr. Lord's request. He expected thirty heats per week by June 1980, using the same two shifts. He knew that Mr. Murray and his partners were concerned about the amount of money already invested in the mill. Additional requests for funds would, therefore, have to be carefully substantiated. Moreover, he was not sure himself whether the melt shop superintendent had a legitimate case.

---

[1]Skull represents unusable steel. This loss is caused by oxidation in the ladle during the pouring operation. When the nozzle operator sees a bright orange colour, he knows the pour has ended. The remaining melt is skull.

Exhibit 1
Haitian Rebar Co. (A) (R)
Plant Layout

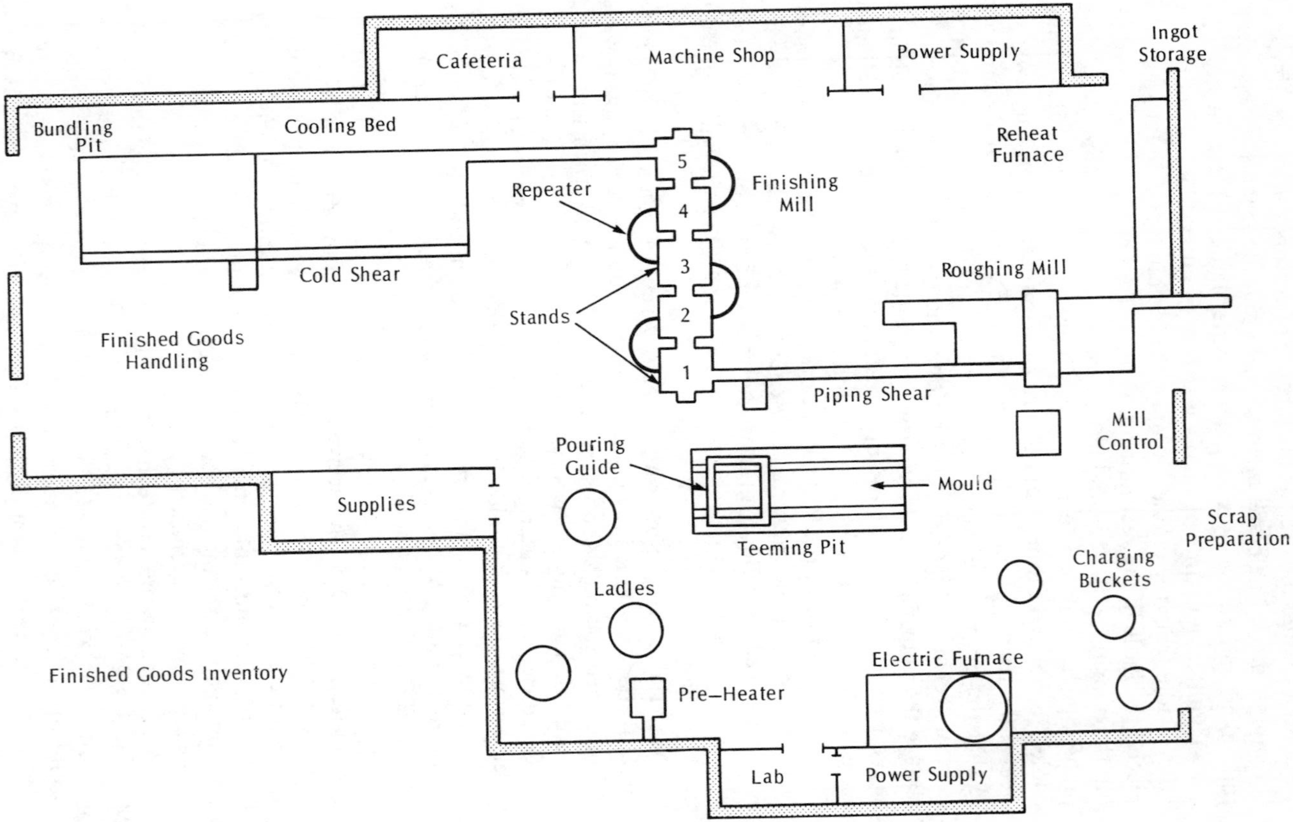

Exhibit 2
Haitian Rebar Co. (A) (R)
Melt Shop View Showing Scrap
Piles and Charging Bucket

Exhibit 3
Haitian Rebar Co. (A) (R)
Diagram of Arcing Principle in an Electric Furnace

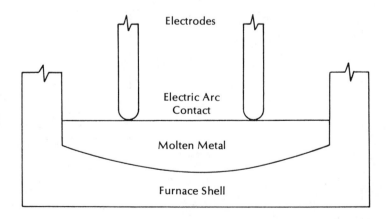

Exhibit 4
Haitian Rebar Co. (A) (R)
Travelling Pouring Cradle and
Mould Line

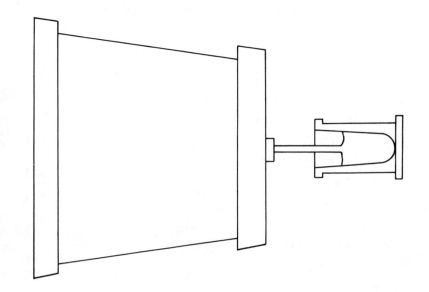

Exhibit 5
Haitian Rebar Co. (A) (R)
Teeming Top Pouring Method

Exhibit 6
Haitian Rebar Co. (A) (R)
Ingot Storage

Exhibit 7
Haitian Rebar Co. (A) (R)
Melt Shop Equipment and Labour Summary

Operation	Equipment	Labour Job Function	Number S = skilled U = unskilled
Prepare scrap	Cutting torches	Sort scrap	10 U
		Cut scrap	5 U
Charging	3 charging buckets Crane	Operate crane	1 S
		Assist crane operator	1 U
Refining	Electric furnace	Operate furnace	2 S
Ladling	3 ladles Crane	Operate 2nd crane	1 S
		Assist crane operator	1 U
Pouring	Pouring cradle Moulds	Teem moulds, insert hooks, prepare moulds and loosen ingots	6 S
Miscellaneous	Fork lift truck	Operate lift truck	1 S
		Prepare hooks	1 U

Exhibit 8
Haitian Rebar Co. (A) (R)
Ladle Construction

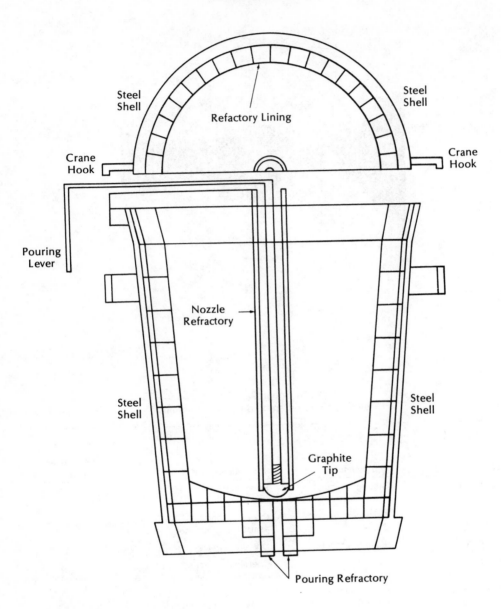

Exhibit 9
Haitian Rebar Co. (A) (R)
Ladling Operations and Times

Operation	Time (minutes)
1. Preheat ladle	120-180
2. Move ladle to cradle and insert nozzle	20-30
3. Move ladle to furnace pit, tap and place back in cradle	20
4. Teem ladle	50
5. Move ladle to reconditioning area, burn out nozzle and pouring refractory	20-30
6. Ladle cooling	240
7. Ladle reconditioning	90-150

Exhibit 10
Haitian Rebar Co. (A) (R)
Ladle Ready for Reconditioning Showing
Broken Pouring Nozzle Refractory

Exhibit 11
Haitian Rebar Co. (A)(R)
Weekly Melt Shop Record — Starting August 20, 1979

Week No.	Total heats	Ladle No.	Times Used	Charging Weight (lbs)	Melt Time Hrs	Mins	Teeming Weight (lbs)[1] (Ingots Poured × 275)	Total Ingots Poured	Skull and Other Melt Shop Losses (lbs)	Comments
1	7	1	2	156 900	25	35	144 100	524	12 800	Electrical delay 165 min.
		2	2							
		3	3							
2	9	1	3	210 800	28	30	196 075	713	14 725	
		2	3							
		3	3							
3	12	1	4	285 000	37	15	272 255	990	12 745	
		2	4							
		3	4							
4	11	1	4	265 000	32	55	250 350	914	14 650	
		2	4							
		3	3							
5	12	1	3	301 000	37	35	284 859	1034	16 150	
		2	5							
		3	4							
6	13	1	5	352 000	41	40	321 000	1168	30 800	
		2	4							
		3	4							
7	12	1	3	336 000	40	10	296 450	1078	39 550	Pouring refractory froze — lost 1/3 of one heat.
		2	5							
		3	4							
8	12	1	6	327 000	41	00	301 950	1098	25 050	Defective coil 180 min, broken electrode 30 min., pouring refractory froze.
		2	3							
		3	3							

									Notes
9	16	1	5	421 500	41	00	398 200	1408	34 550	
		2	6							
		3	5							
10	13	1	4	352 800	36	30	328 900	1196	23 900	Mechanical and electrode delays 120 min.
		2	5							
		3	4							
11	14	1	5	381 400	31	10	351 725	1279	30 675	Lost one day's production — area power failure.
		2	5							
		3	4							
12	15	1	4	406 600	37	50	376 475	1369	32 125	
		2	6							
		3	5							
13	14	1	4	374 800	35	10	330 000	1200	41 800	Ladle delay 75 min Furnace roof cave-in.
		2	5							
		3	5							
14	14	1	4	379 450	39	55	338 250	1230	41 200	Nozzle freeze-up lost 1/3 of one heat.
		2	5							
		3	5							
15	10	1	3	279 400	24	35	264 275	961	15 125	Ladle delays 150 min Bad furnace and ladle bottom.
		2	3							
		3	4							
16	18	1	8	534 200	51	00	500 500	1820	33 700	Crane delay 15 min First full week operating two shifts.
		2	8							
		3	2							
17	21	1	7	619 050	59	35	572 275	2081	46 875	Broken water jacket delay 240 min. crane delay 10 min. electrode delay 30 min.
		2	7							
		3	7							
18	15	1	5	452 900	47	50	404 250	1470	48 650	Ladle delays 75 min. Ladle not heated — 60 min. delay Crane repair delay 60 min.
		2	6							
		3	4							

[1]One ingot weighs 275 pounds.

Exhibit 12
Haitian Rebar Co. (A) (R)
Melt Shop Two Shift Schedule

Day	Production Hours	Shift One	Shift Two
Monday	8	22 30-06 30	
Tuesday	8	22 30-06 30	
Wednesday	8		22 30-06 30
Thursday	8	Clean-up	22 30-06 30
Friday	8		22 30-06 30
Saturday	24	06 30-18 30	18 30-06 30
Sunday	24	06 30-18 30	18 30-06 30
Total	88	40	48

51

Haitian Rebar Co. (B)(R)

In January 1980, Mr. John Duncan, plant manager, was considering a request to extend the mould line in the melt shop. This followed an earlier request for more ladles [see Haitian Rebar Company (A)(R)]. Three weeks after melt shop operations had begun in August 1979, Mr. Duncan had extended the mould line 20 feet[1] with good results. This time, the request from the melt shop superintendent seemed to be similar to the earlier situation. Mr. Duncan wondered, therefore, if the same criteria could again be applied.

MOULDS

Moulds were used to shape the ingots. Each mould weighed 400 lbs[2] and cost $250 (Exhibit 1). Ingot weight was 275 lbs. Before a pour, two men, with the help of the overhead crane, straightened out the moulds so they were lined into three parallel rows between the railway tracks of the pouring line. The foundation of the pouring line (teeming pit) consisted of concrete covered by a 2-in. layer of sand. Two rails carried the travelling pouring cradle (Exhibit 1). The cradle was constructed so that its top carriage carrying the ladle could move sideways.

Six operators worked on the pouring line. A group of three men teemed. One positioned the cradle so that the pouring nozzle lined up with each mould. One operated the nozzle lever and the third one inserted a handle bent from a $\frac{1}{2}$-in.[3] reinforcing rod in each molten ingot. At the start of each pour the lever operator opened the graphite nozzle slightly. A slow initial pour formed a protective pad at the bottom of the mould. A quick pour filled the mould, followed by another slow pour to top off. Pouring time ranged from twenty to twenty-five seconds per mould.

The pouring crew started in the middle of the line and poured centre moulds for half the length. This gave maximum protection to the operators. They then travelled along one complete outside row and this finished one pour of 100 ingots (Exhibit 1).

The remaining crew of three men removed the ingots from the moulds. After a dozen moulds had been teemed, two men began to loosen the ingots. They levered with heavy steel bars stuck under the handle in the ingot. The last pouring crew member helped the crane operator lift the loose ingots out of the moulds. The crane carried a steel bar with eight hooks chained to it. The worker inserted one hook into each ingot handle and the crane moved eight red-hot ingots to the cooling area. After all the ingots were removed, all moulds that had fallen were set up again, but not necessarily in a straight row. Three men using the empty cradle swabbed the inside of each mould with a graphite wash to prevent sticking on the next pour. Should the men have trouble loosening an ingot after several tries with the steel bar, they sprayed the mould with water and tried again. If this did not work, the ingot was considered a "sticker." The

---

[1]1 foot = .3048 metres.
[2]1 pound = .4536 kilograms.
[3]1 inch = 2.54 centimetres.

crane moved all stickers to the scrap preparation area, where it bounced them onto a steel platform. If this still did not loosen the ingot, both ingot and mould were considered scrap. If this did remove the ingot, the mould was inspected and either considered scrap or reusable. If the latter, it was marked with an *X* and placed at the far end of the teeming pit. The pouring crew kept a close eye on all sticker moulds. If sticking became too frequent the mould was sent to scrap. A mould of reasonable quality should last at least four months and might go for a year. A number of variables affected the life of a mould. During line set-up the mould had to be set vertically or the molten metal would splash and burn the shell. Burning led to small deformations (pits) in the mould, which increased the probability of sticking. The nozzle operator could burn the bottom if he started each pour too fast. The nozzle had to be well lubricated and positioned so that accurate flow control was possible. During the teeming operations, moulds reached a temperature of 1000° F[1] and after ingot removal required three hours to cool. Shell expansion and ingot loosening seemed to be optimal if the pour was started with the mould at room temperature.

POURING LINE START-UP

The teeming operation at Rebar was started with 240 moulds, 100 in inventory and 140 on the pouring line. Right from the beginning in August 1979, more than seventy ingots were teemed from each furnace heat. Thus every second heat some of the moulds were reused. Operators had difficulty preparing the line because of the intense heat, the number of moulds that had fallen and the number of sticker moulds that had to be replaced. After operating for two weeks, Mr. Duncan (on Mr. Lord's request), extended the pouring foundation 20 ft at a cost of $240 per ft. The teeming pit now had space for 203 moulds and could handle two heats before reusing any one mould. The pouring crew was now less rushed than before and the sticker rate immediately fell to 3.9 percent. During the next three months the melt shop crew generally became more proficient at their tasks. The sticker rate, however, did not drop, and on February 7, 1980, Mr. Lord requested a further extension to the pit sufficient to hold another 100 moulds. Mr. Lord indicated that stickers were starting to increase again and he felt the moulds were overworked.

Mr. Duncan knew that although space was tight another 40 ft could be added to the line. He was also aware that during the first five months the company had put more than 400 new moulds into service. He had difficulty assessing the cause of the high sticker rate (industry average was less than 1 percent per heat).[2] The melt shop now operated two shifts (see the preceding Haitian Rebar (A)(R) case, Exhibit 12) with an expected output of thirty heats per week by June 1980.

Mr. Duncan did not know how to answer Mr. Lord's request, because lately he had been primarily concerned with rolling mill operations. He was generally pleased with the melt shop start-up (see the preceding Haitian Rebar (A)(R) case, Exhibit 11), and he knew Mr. Lord had done an excellent job in improving the productivity of the electric furnace.

---

[1] 1000° F = 538° C.

[2] The company did not keep records of sticker frequency. The teeming crew recalled roughly how many stickers they had on each pour and they were the source for the figures and trends mentioned in this case.

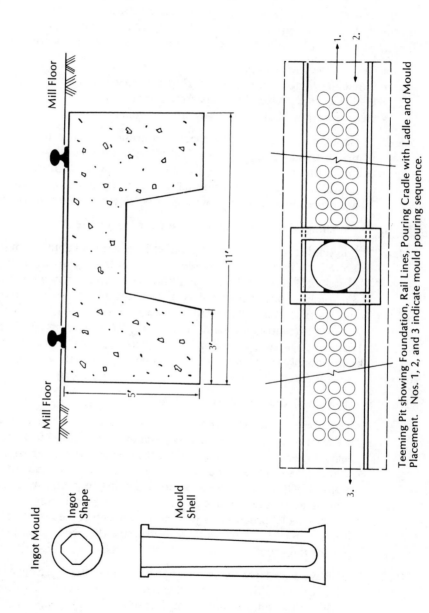

Exhibit 1
Haitian Rebar Company (B)(R)
Pouring Pit Foundation

Teeming Pit showing Foundation, Rail Lines, Pouring Cradle with Ladle and Mould Placement. Nos. 1, 2, and 3 indicate mould pouring sequence.

52
Howdy Toy Company

At the end of one of the weekly production meetings that were held every Friday morning, Alex Howdy, president of the Howdy Toy Company, asked four of his foremen to stay behind to solve a special problem. The four men were:

- Norm Jones, Machining Department foreman
- Domenic Paino, Woodworking Department foreman
- Dick Swenson, Assembly Department foreman
- George Ferano, Painting Department foreman

Alex: Gentlemen, I've called a special meeting with you because one of our products is in trouble. It's known as The Good Ship Howdy and it is running into a pricing problem from our main competitor's Jolly Roger. It is well named too, because they pirated the design from our Good Ship Howdy and are proceeding to sink us with a broadside of cutthroat pricing.

Norm: (laughing) Aye, aye, captain. We get the message.

Alex: All kidding aside, men, this product is in serious trouble. I'm sure that you are all familiar with the model that I am talking about. If not, there is a sketch of it in front of you [see Exhibit 1]. This has never been a particularly high-volume line because it is high-priced but it was profitable. We have always made it out of the best hardwood and painted it well. It normally sold to our distributors for $3.00 but the Jolly Roger is selling for $2.50. Our sales people tell us that if we can cut our price to $1.75, we can probably double and possibly triple our present volume. I would, however, like to keep our quality reasonably high.

Dom: How many did we turn out last year?

Alex: According to the sales records, we sold about 4 000. I feel that if we can get the price down to $1.75, we can probably sell about 12 000 units in the next year. If we can sell that many, we will have to speed up our assembly process. Frankly, I think the manufacturing technique was designed to make a maximum of 500 units a year. If volume is going to go up, we shall have to get some mass production methods into the shop to handle them.

I've had a process analysis sheet drawn up of the system that we use now [see Exhibit 2]. Dom, would you describe the production process in your part of the shop?

Dom: Well, we use a knot-free, kiln-dried hardwood plank, 7.5 cm wide and 2.5 cm thick for the hulls. Naturally, this is expensive material because it is the top-of-the-line wood. We use a template to outline the shape of the hulls on the plank and then cut them out individually on a band-saw. These are sent to a belt sander where the saw marks are smoothed off the sides. The hulls then go to the paint shop. The cabins are cut out the same way except we use 4 cm plank instead of 7.5 cm plank. They also have the sides sanded. The funnels are angle cut on a rotary saw, using a stop, tumbled and sent to the paint shop. The mats are cut to the necessary length from a 6 mm dowel in large batches and sent to the assembly area. We get the hulls back to drill the hole for the mast after they have been sprayed.

Alex: What happens in the paint shop, George?

George: We put them on our spray racks, move them into the spray booth and spray them blue. The cabins are sprayed white and the funnels are done in red. They are a real problem because the spray makes them roll around a lot. We waste a lot of time with the funnels. We also have to spray about 20 percent more of them than the hulls and cabins because so many get split in the assembly operations. After the parts are dry, we inspect them and send the hulls back to have the mast holes drilled while the rest of the parts go to the assembly department.

Norm: Why don't you drill the mast hole first?

George: Because they fill up with paint.

Alex: What happens in the assembly department. Dick?

Dick: The first worker takes the parts off the paint racks, runs the cabins over a glue wheel, puts them in place and drives a nail to hold it until the glue dries. The nail goes under the funnel so it won't show. This worker pushes it to the next position where worker number two puts a dab of glue on the bottom of the funnel and carefully drives a very fine nail down through the funnel. Often it splits, so that's why we have extra made up. Worker number two then puts a dab of glue on the mast and sticks it into the mast hole. At the next position, worker number three soaks the decals that say "Good Ship Howdy," and applies them to both sides of the bow. They are then racked to dry for four hours, inspected and put into boxes. The boxes are packed twenty-four to a cardboard crate and sent to finished goods inventory.

Alex: Is any protective spray put over the decals?

Dick: No. We used to do that but it meant an extra step in the process so we dropped it. We really should put it back in because the first time the kid puts the boat into the bathtub, the decals wash off.

Alex: I didn't know that processes like this existed anymore. I feel pretty certain that we should be able to reduce our costs a lot. I had Henry Wolfe draw up some approximate costs of materials, labour, and overhead on this line to give you some idea where our money is being spent (see Exhibit 3). For the rest of the meeting, I would like some ideas from you on how we can get The Good Ship Howdy back into a competitive position.

Dom: Can we change the design of the ship a little?

Alex: Sure! The ship isn't meant to be a work of art but I'd like to keep it looking approximately like a boat with the same red, white, and blue colouring. Within these limitations, we can do anything.

Exhibit 1
Howdy Toy Company
Plan and Side View of the Good Ship Howdy

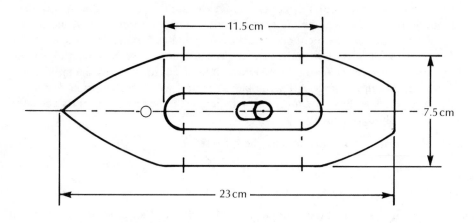

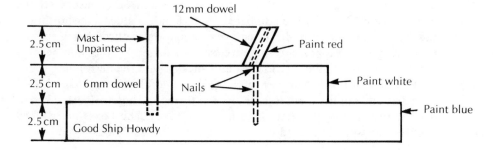

MATERIALS REQUIRED

1 — Hardwood plank 23 cm × 7.5 cm × 2.5 cm

1 — Hardwood plank 11.5 cm × 4 cm × 2.5 cm

1 — Twelve-millimetre diameter dowelling

1 — Six-millimetre diameter dowelling

2 — Finishing nails: — 1-3 cm in length
                            — 1-4 cm in length

Exhibit 2
Howdy Toy Company
Process Analysis Sheet

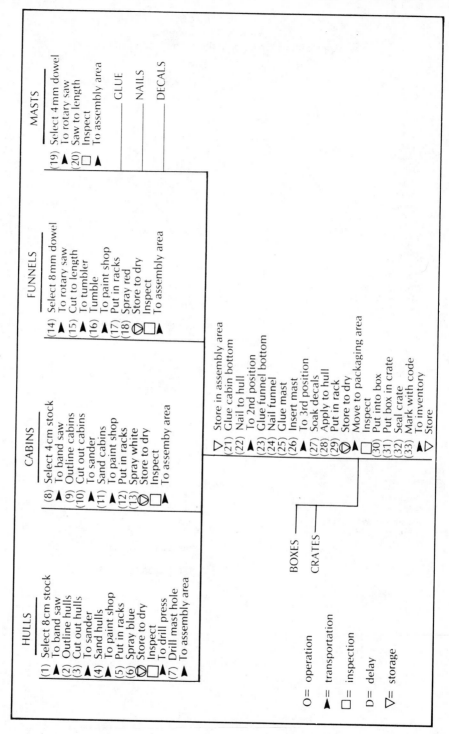

HULLS

(1) Select 8 cm stock
(2) To band saw
(3) Outline hulls
(4) Cut out hulls
 To sander
(5) Sand hulls
 To paint shop
(6) Put in racks
 Spray blue
 Store to dry
(7) Inspect
 To drill press
 Drill mast hole
 To assembly area

CABINS

(8) Select 4 cm stock
(9) To band saw
(10) Outline cabins
 Cut out cabins
(11) To sander
 Sand cabins
(12) To paint shop
 Put in racks
(13) Spray white
 Store to dry
 Inspect
 To assembly area

FUNNELS

(14) Select 8 mm dowel
(15) To rotary saw
 Cut to length
(16) To tumbler
 Tumble
(17) To paint shop
 Put in racks
(18) Spray red
 Store to dry
 Inspect
 To assembly area

MASTS

(19) Select 4 mm dowel
 To rotary saw
(20) Saw to length
 Inspect
 To assembly area

GLUE

NAILS

DECALS

(21) Store in assembly area
(22) Glue cabin bottom
 Nail to hull
(23) To 2nd position
 Glue funnel bottom
(24) Nail funnel
(25) Glue mast
(26) Insert mast
(27) To 3rd position
 Soak decals
(28) Apply to hull
(29) Put in rack
 Store to dry
 Move to packaging area
(30) Inspect
 Put into box
(31) Put box in crate
(32) Seal crate
(33) Mark with code
 To inventory
 Store

BOXES

CRATES

O = operation
▲ = transportation
□ = inspection
D = delay
▽ = storage

Exhibit 3
Howdy Toy Company
Approximate Costs of Making The Good Ship Howdy

	Average Cost per Boat
	cents per unit
Materials	
Hulls	12.5
Cabins	7.5
Funnels	2.0
Masts	0.5
Nails	0.5
Decals	3.5
Packaging — boxes	6.0
— shipping cartons	2.5
Subtotal Materials	35.0
Labour Costs	
Work on hulls	35.0
Work on cabins	30.0
Work on funnels	10.0
Work on masts	5.0
Subtotal Woodworking	80.0
Painting of hulls	15.0
Painting cabins	15.0
Painting funnels	15.0
Subtotal Painting	45.0
Assembly — 1st position	20.0
— 2nd position	22.5
— 3rd position	12.5
Subtotal Assembly	55.0
Other Costs	
Inspection	10.0
Packaging	10.0
Overhead and burden	47.5
Profit	17.5
Subtotal Other Costs	85.0
TOTAL COSTS OF PRODUCT	300.0

53
Ned Tom Industries Ltd.

In early May 1975, Tom Dany, one of the two owners of Ned Tom Industries (NTI), was reviewing the progress of his company since its start-up three months before. During these three months the product line had changed drastically from what had been anticipated. This change caused modifications in the workers and skills needed, inventory, design, and plant size. Both the owners and workers felt space in the plant was now inadequate. Consequently, plans were being discussed for expanding the size of the plant. Before anything was finalized, Mr. Dany wanted to assess his operation's capacity to establish whether or not an addition was actually needed.

COMPANY BACKGROUND

In early February 1975, Ned Tom Industries was ready to manufacture CSA[1] Approved homes and doublewides[2]; NHA[3] housing units; and office trailers, industrial additions, mobile home porches, and accessories. The company was developed, owned, and managed by Ned Himic and Tom Dany.

Ned Himic was thirty-seven years old, an accountant, and had ten years' extensive managerial experience in the mobile home industry, including positions as plant controller, general manager, and vice-president.

Tom Dany's experience in the mobile home industry covered a five-year period during which he held the positions of purchasing manager, sales manager, and general manager. Mr. Dany was thirty years old. Out of a common ambition to own their own business they teamed together to form NTI in 1974.

PERSONNEL

Tom and Ned owned Ned Tom equally. Both agreed to share equally the management responsibility of the company. Ned Himic would be responsible for the financial control and Tom Dany the operational aspects; however, they would both constantly be helping each other. They would also share the marketing responsibilities, which consisted of telephoning potential buyers and mailing out informative literature outlining NTI's entrance into the market and the services available.

Shortly after developing the initial plans for Ned Tom, a designer was found whose responsibility was to develop feasible drawings of interior and exterior specifications to meet the customers' requirements. The designer, Bill Verbah, had four years' related experience in the mobile home industry. Ned Himic commented, "The designer is extremely critical to an operation such as ours. He's got to be able to take the custo-

---

[1]Canadian Standards Association (CSA.) — sets *minimum* safety standards for electrical wiring, insulation, connections, etc.
[2]Doublewide mobile units refer to joining two 3.6 m x 9 m trailers, for example, to produce one 7.2 m x 9 m unit.
[3]National Housing Association (NHA) — sets minimum standards for housing loans available to low-income persons.

mer's idea and lay it out on paper in such a way so that we can build it, the customer can use it, and we're both happy about the cost."

Four hourly paid employees were also hired in January 1975, and these men all had previous mobile home experience. Each man had a special skill yet was also expected to be able to help out at jobs other than his own. Their respective skills were in welding, carpentry, metal and electrical work, and finishing (interior trim work). These men had all been junior foremen in their previous jobs and had been in charge of from four to six workers each. The hourly pay for these men was $4.50, an average industry wage in the area. A bonus system was also developed whereby the workers would share in a percentage of the net profits.

LOCATION

A plant was leased in an industrial zone on the outskirts of Cambridge, Ontario, which was directly serviced by CNR and CPR railways plus a secondary highway directly traversing the Highway 401 — Ontario's major expressway.

Cambridge was part of Metropolitan Kitchener (Kitchener, Waterloo, Cambridge, and smaller towns) with a population just over a quarter-million. The area had experienced a 16 percent growth in population from 1971 to 1976. Retail sales totalled $773 million (on a per capita basis, 5 percent above national average), and personal disposable income totalled $1553 million, (on a per capita basis, 5 percent above national average). Also, the plant site was one hundred kilometers from Metropolitan Hamilton (one million people). Since both Hamilton and Kitchener were experiencing growth in residential and industrial segments, Tom Dany assumed most sales would be generated close by.

THE MARKET

In relating to the future of relocatable structures, Tom Dany commented, "The need to provide Canadian people and business with economical building alternatives is one of the most pressing problems facing the Canadian economy today. Increasing land costs, lengthy, weather-hampered, on-site construction operations and the high price of money have combined to drive the price of conventional construction beyond the reach of a vast number of potential customers.

"The mobile home segment, for example, endeavours to provide a housing alternative for that segment of society which can't afford conventional housing. The same philosophy holds true when you consider the needs of industry."

The sales objective for 1975 was to produce and market approximately 56 units, 1.9 percent of the 3000-unit market available in their marketing area.

Sale of mobile homes and doublewides would be on a wholesale basis to dealers, park owners, and housing developers.

Office trailers and industrial units would be sold through the dealer organization and on a direct basis to contractors and industrial concerns, while porches and accessories would also be marketed through the dealer organization and to park operators. Sales responsibility rested with both Ned and Tom — whoever initiated the sale.

To date, NTI has received an open order for fifteen to twenty homes for delivery sometime in 1975 from a park operator who purchased between fifty and seventy units per year. This order represented NTI's first production task, and had been obtained through friendship with the client over the years when he had done business with Ned Himic's former employers.

Ontario had over 125 dealers actively engaged in the retail of mobile homes. The principals of NTI personally knew fifty-eight of these dealers through previous business relationships and had some knowledge of many of the others. It was hoped that NTI's experience in this market would enable them to sell products to these dealers.

FINANCE

With an initial investment of $67 500 (Exhibit 1), Ned and Tom started operations in February 1975. They projected their sales and profits (Exhibit 2) based on data obtained from their former employers and on an initial seizure in their first year of 1.9 percent of the total market for housing units, mobile homes, office trailers, industrial units and accessories.

Both managers were firm in their commitment to "keep the overhead down" since their start-up capital was limited. Consequently, a plant was leased rather than purchased, and supplies and equipment were to be kept at minimum levels. Ned Himic noted, "We'll have to watch every penny in our first year in order to meet our commitments to our creditors."

PRODUCTION

The first orders produced by NTI were 3.6 m x 9 m standard mobile units to be used as retail sales offices by a local housing developer. They had been ordered because the developer did not want to tie up his homes as offices and when the project was completed they could be easily relocated. However, after these first standard units were completed it became apparent that the market wanted specially designed and equipped custom units. Orders and inquiries were increasing for customized structures, examples of which can be seen in Exhibit 3.

Tom Dany commented, "These first units made were put together by everyone — we all pitched in. We wanted to get the feel of building our own products, plus we had to give advice to the new men to insure that the units were quality products. When the custom orders started coming in we also had a lot to do with the units' construction. Ned and myself pitched in whenever we could. The trouble is that with this type of custom business, sometimes you'll need special additions to the standard unit, like extra structural reinforcements, plumbing, electronic equipment, custom furnishings." Adding to their problems was the limited amount of plant space, which severely restricted inventory levels. Ned Himic had wanted at least one inventory turn per month and hoped for a maximum of eighteen per year. But with custom orders, many special parts were needed, and since the individual mobile units varied it was considered impractical to purchase quantity lots of special appliances, wire, wood, lighting fixtures, etc. These were bought on an "as needed" basis and often they did not arrive by the time they were needed for assembly. The trailer was then either finished and the parts installed later, or the trailer was moved outside until the item arrived. It was then pulled back inside and completed. This presented many problems especially if other units had to be moved and rescheduled as a result of this delay. Some moves had taken all the men one full day to complete. Bulk items (lumber, steel, aluminum) were bought in the best uncut or lot quantities available and then processed to NTI's specific needs in the plant.

"Ned and I will hear of special deals and go pick up around $500 to $800 worth of the stuff and hope we have a place to store it. We've saved up to 20 percent in raw material costs by buying in lot sizes," said Tom Dany.

Metal and roofing came from London, 105 km away; lumber from Kitchener, 24 km away; windows and doors from Quebec, 640 km away.

Delivery time was dependent upon the size of the unit, its complexity, and the amount of prescheduled work. The two owners hoped to promise a maximum time of six weeks for their largest 3.6 m x 18 m unit, with a price range of from $6500 to over $20 000, depending on its complexity. However, since each unit usually required different assembly procedures due to its "custom" nature, delivery of the first units was expected to take up to fifteen weeks. Due to the high cost of start-up and added to the fact that 45 percent of the payment for each unit was made only upon delivery of the finished product, delays caused serious cash-flow problems for NTI. The initial 55 percent of the payments were paid in two instalments; 35 percent upon receipt of the order and 20 percent after two weeks.

When a price quote was given to a potential customer, it was based on a total of material plus labour plus overhead plus a 35 percent profit margin on top of this total. However, the partners agreed that their profits were being eroded by the delays and high cost of labour, which at times was being inefficiently utilized. Table 1 outlines the value added toward total unit cost at each major stage of the assembly process for a 3.6 m x 9 m unit.

Table 1

	Material	*Labour*
Frame and running gear (axles and tires)	20%	15%
Floor, decking and walls	40%	40%
Metal	25%	20%
Finishing and electrical	15%	25%

To break even, the owners felt they had to sell thirty-six 3.6 m x 9 m units at an average price of $10 000 and had projected a volume of fifty-six units for their first year (Exhibit 2). Ned felt that these projections might have to be altered since they had only produced ten units in their first two and a half months for a sales revenue of approximately $87 000.

Difficulties were also encountered when it came to estimating labour time requirements, and construction techniques required for these custom units. The designer took the specifications over the phone and developed his blueprints from the data given.

The process flow from the time a potential customer phoned to the time the unit was ready for shipping is outlined in Exhibit 5. When an assembly problem arose, all the workers would get together to discuss the optimum solution. This type of delay was very common and could last up to a full day. Several experiences were related of having to reconstruct parts of trailers that had been inappropriately built.

Both owners were very concerned that their products had to be of superior quality, and would go to "any expense" to ensure that the unit was "top notch from head to toe." Ned Himic further clarified this reasoning: "We have to make sales, and since word of mouth advertising is so important in this industry, we can't afford to let our units leave the plant if they have any flaws. We've discovered that only in the U.S.A. can you get our type of service, but with U.S. freight and import costs, we'll soon be getting more orders than we can handle."

DILEMMA

It was felt that in order to capitalize on the new potential market additional production space would be needed. NTI's landlord offered to build an addition to the plant (Exhibit 4) which would triple capacity up to a potential sales volume of $1.2 million dollars. The new addition would permit a larger wood-working area essential for custom orders requiring on-the-spot modifications. There would also be more room for inventory and office space. The addition could be started the following month, in June, and should be completed by mid-December 1975. It was estimated that this addition would increase their fixed costs by 20 percent per year.

Ned sized up their dilemma: "We both think the market's growing and now is the time to grow with it. But we've got to do something about our production system so we can get the most out of it!"

Exhibit 1
Ned Tom Industries Ltd.
Manufacturing Plant
Financial Feasibility

Pro forma financial information is highlighted as follows:

APPLICATION OF CASH	
Machinery and equipment	$ 22 500
Operational requirements	45 000
	$ 67 500

SOURCE OF CASH	
Mortgage on machinery and equipment	$ 22 500
Short-term borrowings secured by current assets	22 500
Shareholders' investment	22 500
	$ 67 500

Short-term borrowings will not be required as the shareholders' investment will be sufficient to sustain operations.
It is assumed that a loan will be obtained to finance the purchase of machinery and equipment. The mortgage is assumed to be on a five-year term with equal monthly instalments commencing in the fourth month of operations. Interest is at 13.5 percent and payable monthly.

Exhibit 2
Ned Tom Industries Ltd.
Pro Forma Profit and Loss Statement
for the First Three Years Ending December 31
(000's)

	Year 1	Year 2	Year 3
Sales (based on an average selling price of $10 000)	$ 563	$ 675	$ 720
Sales incentives	6	7	7
Net sales	$ 557	$ 668	$ 713
Variable costs:			
Material	$ 349	$ 419	$ 446
Labour	62	76	83
Manufacturing	16	20	22
Service	5	5	6
Selling	4	5	5
Total variable costs	436	525	562
Contribution	$ 121	$ 143	$ 151
Fixed costs:			
Manufacturing	$ 45	$ 46	$ 48
Administrative	20	19	19
Selling	15	16	16
Total fixed costs	80	81	83
Net profit before tax	$ 41	$ 62	$ 68
Federal income tax	17	26	29
Net profit after tax	$ 24	$ 36	$ 39

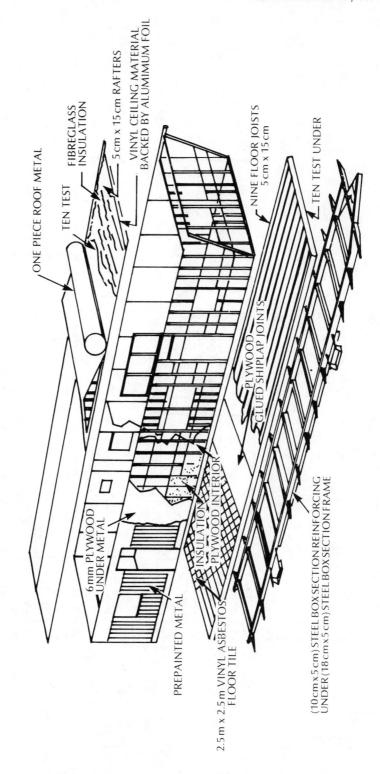

Exhibit 3
Ned Tom Industries Limited
Product Samples

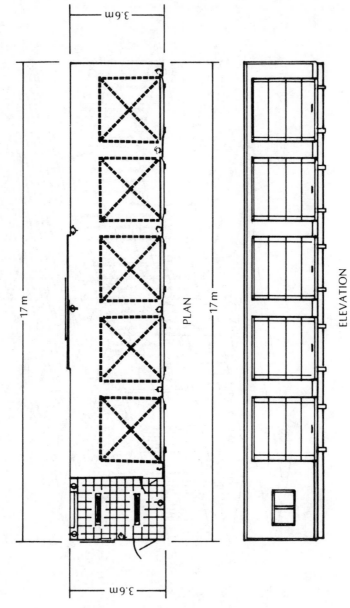

Exhibit 3 (continued)
Ned Tom Industries Limited
Product Samples

3.6 m

17 m

PLAN

17 m

3.6 m

ELEVATION

RELOCATABLE FREIGHT TERMINAL

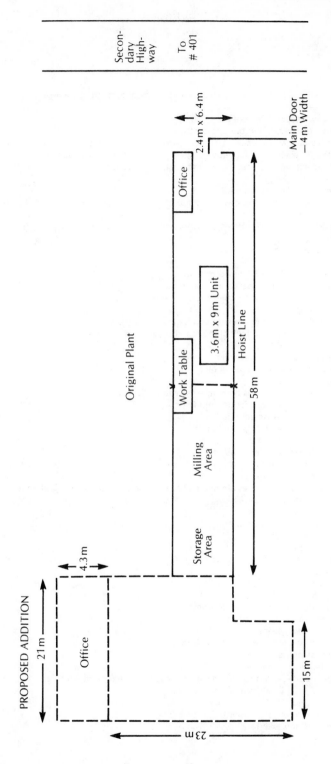

Exhibit 4
Ned Tom Industries Limited
Plant Layout

Exhibit 5
Ned Tom Industries Ltd.

Process Flow
(assumption: $10 000 unit)

Preassembly

1. Order phoned in — details taken (dimensions needed and special equipment required)
   — Tom or Ned.
2. Rough drawing developed from details — Tom.
3. Costing, delivery quotation, and price to customer
   — suppliers are contacted for price of special items and delivery time available
   — delivery date for customer is set depending on his need or parts availability
   — price is bid depending on competition, unit cost and complexity
   — Ned.
4. Order accepted and supplies ordered.
5. Frame, floor plan and electrical drawings completed.
   — Bill.
6. Finalize and iron out potential problems in coordinating unit's assembly.
   — Tom, Ned, and Bill.
7. Production specs taken to Tom or Ned.

Assembly (times are for a simple 3.6 m x 9 m unit)[1]

1. (a) Weld frame — steel is cut, welded and painted
          — usually one man unless steel beams too long to handle.
          — approx. 8 hrs.
   (b) Start floor and roof truss (main supports for floor and roof)
          — cut from stock lumber in mill, glued together, and insulation added
          — one man, approx. 8 hrs.
   (c) Start floor partitions and side walls
          — cut from stock in mill and assembled
          — one man, approx. 8 hrs.
2. Join floor to frame — floor has been assembled upside down
          — drop frame onto floor
          — fasten together
          — flip right side up
          — 1 man, 2 hrs.
3. (a) Add subfloor and floor (deck and tile)
          — tile, wood, carpet (whatever required) is attached to plywood floor frame covering
          — 1 man, 16 hrs., or 2 men, 8 hrs.
   (b) Start ceiling — ceiling frame cut in mill and assembled so as to be ready when walls finished
          — insulation added
          — 2 men, 16 hrs.
4. Plumbing if needed — 1 man, 15 hrs.
5. (a) Set sidewalls and partitions
          — sidewalls hoisted into unit
          — partitions usually small enough to carry
          — add insulation
          — 2 men, 16 hrs. (total, 32 hours)
   (b) Finish plumbing — 1 man, 7 hrs.
6. Set ceiling — ceiling is hoisted onto frame
          — nailed and strapped down
          — 1 man, 4 hrs.
7. Strap and join unit together — 1 man, 4 hrs.
8. Start electrical wiring — 1 man, 24 hrs.
9. Finish insulation — 1 man, 4 hrs.
10. Exterior metal added — put flake-board or plywood to frame for strength and for backing for metal
          — aluminum screwed on
          — 1 man, 16 hrs.
11. (a) Install galvanized roof (if needed) — 1 man, 8 hrs.
    (b) Install windows and exterior doors — 1 man, 6 hrs.

12. Trim and finish interior and electrical wiring
   — loose ends tidied up
   — interior doors, cupboards, lighting, etc.
   — 2 men, 72 hrs. (total, 144 hours).
13. Clean up and test electrical — 1 man, 4 hrs.
14. Final inspection (CSA approval) and shipment
   — Ned, Tom and Bill, 1 hr.

[1]The woodworking required for each unit was being done throughout the assembly process — 1 man, 50 hrs.

54

The Residence Admissions Office

In late May 1983, Ms. Anna Chou, the recently appointed Manager of Residence Admissions at The University of Western Ontario in London, Canada, was faced with an onerous task. With a record 9 507 first-year residence applications, it was Ms. Chou's responsibility to determine the number of guaranteed residence offers to be made in order to fill the 1 502 available first-year beds.

THE UNIVERSITY OF WESTERN ONTARIO

The University of Western Ontario was situated on spacious grounds in London, Ontario. In 1982, there were 16 180 full-time students attending the University, of which 4 189 were in their first year. During the fall and winter a further 5 360 students enrolled in part-time studies. About 24 percent of the full-time students were natives of London. Most of the remainder came from within a 300-km radius.

SENATE COMMITTEE ON STUDENT HOUSING (SCOSH)

The University Senate was responsible for academic decisions within the University. Joint policy decisions on financial matters were often made by the Senate and the University Board of Governors. SCOSH was a Senate standing committee with representatives from administration, faculty, and student groups. The committee studied residence issues and made policy recommendations to the Senate.

Since a guarantee of residence accommodation was a major influence on a high school student's choice of which university to attend, SCOSH had developed precise admissions policies. Some admissions policies for first-year students included:

a) Approximately 65 percent of total residence accommodation available was to be set aside for first-year students.

b) To be eligible for residence accommodation, a student must have completed an application for residence and received an offer for full-time academic admission. Note that all applicants, regardless of whether Western was first, second, or third choice, should be given equal opportunity for residence.

c) All major University scholarship students, regardless of whether they had applied for residence, were offered accommodation.

d) Offers of accommodation were determined by a lottery system. The assigned lottery numbers were used to make guaranteed residence offers and to upgrade conditional offers to guaranteed offers.

e) The number of offers made were within established quotas. Those quotas included 706 first-year places in women's residences and 796 for first-year men.

f) All Ontario Scholars or their academic equivalents received guaranteed offers of residence if they had completed a residence application form before the lottery date.

g) Early offers of accommodation were made on a first come, first served basis, to a maximum of 100 first year students from outside Ontario, who had been granted early academic admission to the University.

THE RESIDENCE ADMISSIONS OFFICE

The Residence Admissions Office was operated by Anna Chou, four full-time clerks, and two part-time clerks.

It was Ms. Chou's responsibility to ensure the efficient admission of eligible students to the University residences, and to keep the residences filled during the year. Office activities included the timely preparation of all documents and records. Assistance was also provided to students, faculty, and departments (by phone, interview, or correspondence) regarding residence information, application forms, and any personal requests.

THE ADMISSIONS PROCESS

Students interested in applying to an Ontario university were required to complete the Ontario Universities Application Form and send it to the Ontario University Application Centre in Guelph, Ontario. This form allowed students to give their preference rankings for three Ontario universities. Space was also provided for students to indicate their interest in residence information. This application information was accumulated and periodically sent to each university.

Initial mailing of first-year residence applications and information began in March 1983 and continued until the last week of May, one week before the first-year lottery. Concurrently, early offers of residence accommodation were made to a maximum of 100 out-of-province applicants who had been given early academic admission by the Office of the Registrar.

In the initial first-year lottery, eligible first-year students were each randomly assigned lottery numbers. The lottery numbers determined whether an applicant received a guaranteed offer. Conditional offers were given to those who were not given guaranteed residence offers, and were considered for upgrading to Guaranteed Status to fill vacancies. In the summer of 1982 there were 26 men and 22 women upgraded to guaranteed offers from conditional offers, in order to fill the vacancies.

THE MANAGER'S DILEMMA

As Ms. Chou scrutinized the 9 507 applications, she wondered about the constraints SCOSH policies placed on the offering process. The early out-of-province offers made and accepted amounted to 100, split evenly between men and women. The University was also making 152 guaranteed offers to major scholars, for whom she did not know the sex breakdown or whether an application to residence had been made.

Ms. Chou noted that the University Information Department had batched all applicants according to sex, Ontario Scholar status and Western's rank as a university choice, as shown in Exhibit 1. Ms. Chou knew that all Ontario Scholar applicants must be offered residence, and aside from the sex breakdown was not sure of any other uses of the information. In her file labelled "The Offering Process," Ms. Chou found historical residence admissions acceptance rate statistics (Exhibit 2), but was not sure whether the information was outdated or still useful. She also wondered what had caused the differences between the 1980 and 1982 acceptance rates.

With the lottery just one week away, and 9 507 first-year residence application cards in the filing cabinet, Ms. Chou leaned back in her chair and contemplated the number of guaranteed residence offers to make in order to fill the 1 502 available beds.

Exhibit 1
The Residence Admissions Office

1983 Western Residence Applicants

	Male		Female	
	Ontario Scholar	Non-Ontario Scholar	Ontario Scholar	Non-Ontario Scholar
Western 1st choice	271	1 324	426	1 455
Western 2nd choice	352	1 219	501	1 308
Western 3rd choice	351	1 020	381	899
	974	3 563	1 308	3 662

Exhibit 2
The Residence Admissions Office

Guaranteed Residence Offer Acceptance Rates

		Male		Female	
		Ontario Scholar	Non-Ontario Scholar	Ontario Scholar	Non-Ontario Scholar
Western 1st choice	1980	.7377*	.7044	.6818	.6563
	1981	.7372	.6344	.6390	.6471
	1982	.7048	.6972	.6905	.6173
Western 2nd choice	1980	.2614	.3149	.2706	.2721
	1981	.2051	.3741	.2102	.3041
	1982	.2926	.2515	.4224	.4489
Western 3rd choice	1980	.1172	.1654	.1066	.1113
	1981	.1343	.2468	.1009	.1250
	1982	.1425	.1732	.2921	.2975

*In 1980, the male Ontario Scholars who had Western as their first choice, accepted a Guaranteed Residence Offer 73.77% of the time. Conversely, 26.23% of the students in that category declined the offer.

55

Willowbrook Castle

"Jim, as general supervisor on this home, you ought to be able to supply me with some badly needed information. I must know not only the expected completion date, but also the times when I can get mortgage draws from my trust company. It is imperative I have a plan because my financing will depend upon exact timing. Otherwise, I will not be able to build this house."

The request was made by Mr. Charles Talbot, the prospective owner of a new home to be constructed on a good out-of-town property site. He was speaking to Jim Fraser, who would be responsible for the home construction, though he would not be directly responsible for the hiring of the subcontractors.

Mr. Talbot also informed Jim Fraser that timing was critical because the Talbots' apartment lease would expire in 108 days. Mr. Talbot would have legal possession of the site in ten days which, according to him, meant the home had to be constructed in seventy *working days* after that.

Jim had recently heard about the Critical Path Method (CPM) of scheduling projects such as house construction. This method promised to provide a clear visual aid in determining (1) which jobs or activities (sequenced in their direct technological order) were "critical" in their effect on total project time, and (2) how best to schedule resources devoted to the project in order to meet a target date at minimum cost. (See the Appendix for additional information on CPM.) With this in mind, Mr. Talbot's letter from the mortgage company (Exhibit 1) and a list of the activities that were involved in building the Talbot home, Jim decided to prepare a CPM chart for the project. He hoped it would help him answer Mr. Talbot's questions.

Exhibit 1
Willowbrook Castle

Reliable Trust Co.
395 Main Street
Littleton, Ontario

Mr. Charles Talbot
725 West Avenue
Littleton, Ontario

Dear Mr. Talbot:

This will confirm that a first mortgage at current rates will be granted to you on the proposed new home to be constructed on Lot 18, Concession 10, Township of Frontenac.

Mortgage draws will be as follows:

First Draw	—1/3 total (approx.). When house is framed.
Second Draw	—1/3 (approx.). When drywall and plastering are completed.
Final Draw	—Remainder. When home is declared completed and hydro inspected for living.

Although mortgage draw times vary slightly with different trust companies, we have found these stated times to be mutually acceptable to most of our clients. Inspection will be completed at the above specified times at the owner's request. Final mortgage paper will be closed upon final inspection and completion.

Yours very truly,

Jason Hogg
Mortgage Manager

JH:jm

Exhibit 2
Construction of Willowbrook Castle

Job Name	Description	Immediate Predecessors	Time (Days)
A	Prepare site	—	2
B	Excavate site	A	1
C	Form and pour footings	B	1
D	Pour concrete foundation	C	5
E	Lay sewer tile	B	1
F	Pour basement and garage floors	E	3
G	Backfill	D, F	1
H	Framing and rough roof	G	9
I	Rough in plumbing and vacuum system	H	3
J	Rough in wiring	H	2
K	Rough in heating	H	2
L	Shingling	H	3
M	Install windows	H	1
N	Bricklaying — interior and exterior	H	4
O	Finish roofing	L, N	2
P	Insulating	I, J, K	3
Q	Lathing and plastering	P, M, N	17
R	Finish wiring and plumbing	Q	8
S	Finish flooring	R	4
T	Trimming	S	14
U	Interior painting and varnishing	T	4
V	Install kitchen equipment	U	1
W	Install light fixtures	U	2
X	Finish exterior	O	6
Y	Finish walks, driveway, and landscaping	X	3

Appendix
Willowbrook Castle

A. BRIEF INTRODUCTION TO THE CRITICAL PATH METHOD

The management of projects includes project design, scheduling, material and manpower planning, and control (e.g., completing the project on time and within budget). Increasingly complex and costly projects have taxed management abilities and have led to a variety of helpful management techniques. These techniques, differing in specifics and names, all have some common characteristics: (a) a recognition that a project can be divided into a set of identifiable independent jobs or tasks or activities; (b) a recognition that a project consists of a sequence of these tasks where some jobs must be started before others and some jobs may be performed simultaneously with others; (c) an attempt to portray the project components, in sequence, graphically, with estimates of completion time for each task indicated; and (d) an attempt to determine how long the entire project may take, what trade-offs are involved (e.g., time to change completion time or project cost). Some of the names for these techniques are PERT (Program Evaluation and Review Technique). CPM (Critical Path Method), CPS (Critical Path Scheduling), and PEP (Program Evaluation Procedure). In order to use any of these techniques, first one must master the basic tool of analysis, the network diagram.

1. *The Network Diagram*

A network diagram begins with the separation of a project into independent tasks or activities, estimation of the time required to complete each task, and determination of the technological sequence of the tasks. There are two network diagram procedures: "Activity-on Node Diagram" (AON) and "Arrow Diagram." An Arrow Diagram is the more common approach, but can become very difficult to work with. Therefore, this note will concentrate on the AON method.[1]

Suppose the project being diagrammed was the construction of the patio. From past experience (or perhaps consultation with expert advisors), one might determine the following table:

Job Name (Activity)	Description	Immediate Predecessor	Time Estimate (Minutes)
a	Prepare site	—	60
b	Level ground	a	90
c	Prepare concrete forms	a	60
d	Install concrete forms	c	30
e	Pour concrete	d	60
f	Level concrete and let set	e	480
g	Install lighting	b	45
h	Install barbecue	b	60
i	Complete landscaping	f, g, h	60

Given this hypothetical example, one may construct a diagram wherein the jobs are presented by circles (hence the name "node") and precedence relationships represented by arrows. Identification of jobs and the time required for each is shown in the circles. In addition, a "start" and a "finish" circle are included. The AON diagram for this example is on the opposite page.

2. *Determination of the Critical Path*

The "critical path" is the longest sequence of connected activities through the network diagram. Its length determines the time required to complete the project. The critical path can be identified by determining the length of every possible path from start to finish. If the diagram is complex this becomes an immense job so mathematical techniques have been devised to determine the critical path. In simple diagrams, it is usually easiest to find the critical path by working through each path. The longest of these is the critical path. The point is simple: to shorten the time to complete a project one must shorten the critical path or, put differently, to affect the completion date of a project, one must affect the length of the critical path (e.g., reducing the duration of jobs not on the critical path will not shorten the duration of the project).

Returning to the patio example, the following paths are apparent.

Path	Time
a, b, g, i	255
a, b, h, i	270
a, c, d, e, f, i	750 Critical Path

---

[1]The complication referred to with Arrow Diagramming is the requirement in some situations of "dummy arrows." For more information, see Wiest and Levy, *A Management Guide to PERT, CPM* (Prentice-Hall, 1969).

Patio Project
Willowbrook Castle

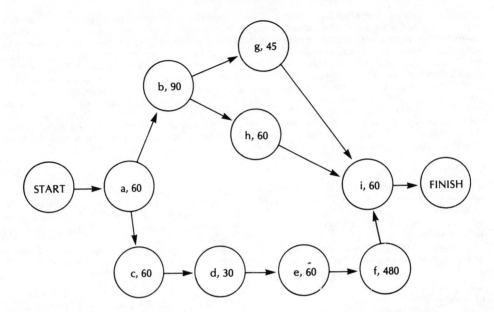

To build the patio in less time, one must shorten the path a, c, d, e, f, i. Also, if the activities on path a, c, d, e, f, i are allowed to exceed the 750 minutes planned, it will take longer to complete the patio. However, activities on the other two paths could be allowed to more than triple in duration before one of those paths becomes critical instead. For example, if installing the barbeque (h) took fourteen hours (840 minutes), then path a, b, h, i becomes the critical path (1050 minutes).

56
Worldwide Pulp and Paper Ltd.

It was November 1, 1983, and Mike Garfield, new plant manager of the West Coast Division of Worldwide Pulp and Paper Limited (WPPL), had just received an extremely disturbing telephone call from his superior located at the company's head office. Apparently, the head office staff had received several complaints from customers supplied by the West Coast Division. These complaints concerned inferior product quality and increasingly late deliveries. Given only two weeks in which to investigate and report back to his superior, Mike Garfield wondered what specifically could be done to quickly improve the overall operating efficiency and effectiveness of the plant.

The West Coast Division

The West Coast Division was a manufacturing operation involved in the processing of cut timber (wood) and the production of various paper products. The company's sales and marketing effort was carried out through the head office. Sales orders received by the head office were transmitted via a sophisticated computer communications network to the most "appropriate" plant. Two factors were considered in determining the appropriate plant for the order. Firstly, proximity to the customer was important. The closest plant to the customer was often selected in an attempt to minimize the high transportation costs associated with the industry. Secondly, and most importantly, most plants were designed to produce only a small range of paper products. Therefore, depending on the type of product ordered, only certain plants were capable of manufacturing product to meet the customer's specific requirements.

The West Coast Division plant was a fully integrated operation, in that it produced and processed all of the wood pulp (raw material) it required for its manufacturing of paper products. In the simplest terms, the plant or mill was designed to accept cut timber (wood) at one end of the plant, and to ship large rolls or "logs" of paper out of the other end. These large rolls of paper were then transferred to the customer's plant for final processing into finished paper products. A more detailed description of the production process appears later.

The Consumer

Although an endless number and variety of paper products were sold at the retail level, the West Coast Division plant supplied companies that produced or used paper products for two basic uses.
1) Approximately 90–95 percent of the plant's production was newsprint, used primarily in the production of daily newspapers. End consumers of this product (newspaper readers) thought little of the actual newsprint unless it was of unusually high or low quality. Only reasonable quality was expected. The newspaper chains,

however, were characterized by the marketing staff as extremely price-conscious and very concerned about delivery schedules.

Recent financial analysis received by Mike Garfield indicated that between 95 and 98 percent of the West Coast Division's net profit after tax resulted from sales to this segment.

2) The remaining 5–10 percent of the plant's production was for use as specialty writing paper products. This paper was to be high quality and was produced to widely varying customer specifications. Sales to this segment had begun only two years ago. The marketing staff had identified the specialty writing paper products segment as a small but poorly serviced market "niche" or segment. The marketing staff believed that *any* sales, however small, would be a bonus to add to the larger newsprint sales.

End consumers for these paper products tended to buy infrequently in small quantities. These consumers were willing to pay a premium price for image or status qualities such as unique sizes, shapes, colours, and textures.

Financial records indicated that only 2–5 percent of net profit after tax resulted from sales to these customers.

Mike Garfield recalled that although the West Coast Division plant was originally designed primarily for the production of high volume, low-to-medium quality newsprint, machine adjustments could be made to enable the equipment to produce a range of product types. However, this often resulted in shorter, more costly production runs as a result of significantly increased machine downtime.

THE PRODUCTION PROCESS

The production process was quite complex at the West Coast plant, but could be simplified into three key components: wood processing, pulp production, and paper production. The total investment in plant and equipment was approximately $350 million. (See Exhibit 1 for details.)

Wood Processing

The entire production process began with the receiving of wood logs. Upon receipt, these logs were weighed and sorted by tree species (e.g., spruce, pine, hemlock) and stored separately in an area known as the woodyard. As needed, specific log species were floated in water passageways to two de-barking machines. In the de-barking machines, the tree bark was removed by tumbling the logs against one another vigorously in long de-barking drums.

Once de-barked, the logs were moved to a "chipper" machine. Within several seconds, a large de-barked log was reduced to a pile of wood chips or fragments. The wood chips were then stored in large silos (storage bins). Once again, there were separate silos for different tree species. Separate storage of wood chip species permitted the controlled mixing of chips into precise combinations or "recipes" required for the particular paper products being produced.

The entire wood processing component of the production process could provide 70 tons of wood chips per hour. Wood processing operated 24 hours per day, 365 days per year.

Pulp Production

Pulp, the key raw material for the production of paper, was produced using a complicated chemical process known as the Kraft process. Two tons of wood chips were required to produce one ton of pulp. Basically, the Kraft process worked by dissolving the lignin or "glue" that bonds wood fibres together. This "ungluing" was accomplished in two tall pressure-cookers known as digesters, by cooking the wood chips in a chemical solution of caustic soda and sodium sulphide.

Upon leaving the digesters, the digested chips entered a machine known as a blow tank. The blow tank was maintained at a significantly lower pressure than the digesters. This pressure difference caused the wood fibres to "blow apart" as lignin, the bonding glue, was no longer present in the wood fibres. The resulting wood fibre pulp was cleaned and bleached to remove unwanted impurities that might later affect the quality of the paper. The refined pulp remained in temporary storage where chemical additives could be mixed in to further prepare the pulp for paper production.

The pulp production facilities were capable of converting as much as 800 000 tons of wood chips into about 400 000 tons of pulp per year.

Paper Production

The two paper-making machines in the West Coast plant were extremely large and involved an investment of about $75 million each. Each paper-making machine could be used to convert up to 225 000 tons of pulp into 225 000 tons of paper per year. (One ton of pulp can be converted into approximately one ton of paper). Contribution per ton of paper was estimated by the finance department to be $12.00.

A paper-making machine had a wet end (where the diluted wood fibre pulp entered the process), and a dry end (where the completed paper was wound into very large rolls or logs of paper). Paper orders of a similar nature were run at the same time to minimize the machine set-up time. Except for this set-up down-time, the paper-making machines ran as close to 24 hours per day as possible.

The paper-making process was very complex and required the monitoring of many variables such as temperature, chemical content, and machine speed. In total, approximately 75 technical measurements had to be made every 30 minutes. Currently, about 50 of these measurements were made automatically by computerized process controls. These controls constantly adjusted the machine settings based upon "correct" values as predetermined by the production engineers. The remaining 25 measurements were made by a team of 8 inspection employees. There was a team for each of the three shifts. These workers, all members of the Canadian Paperworkers Union, earned an average of $9.85 per hour.

Mike Garfield recalled a report prepared by the Director of Computer Services that indicated a computer program was available that could enhance the present system so that all 75 measurements could be computer controlled. The report cited increased accuracy and labour savings as the major benefits of such an acquisition. The program would cost $450 000. To Mike, it seemed to be worthwhile, but he wondered why his predecessor hadn't authorized the expenditure.

If machine capacity was at the root of the complaints, Mike knew that a report recently prepared by the production engineers would be most helpful. The report included cost estimates for increasing capacity at various points in the production process. Excerpts of the report appear as Exhibit 2.

The Complaints

To better understand the source and cause of the recent complaints, Mike held a meeting with the Chief Production Supervisor, Charlie Robertson. When asked about his understanding of the situation, Charlie responded, "It's not my fault! It's those bastards in Sales/Marketing that keep sending me those stupid, small fancy orders... I don't want them! Never used to get them. My guys are constantly shutting down to make machine adjustments . . . by the time the order is completely through the process, we're just beginning to figure the proper settings! . . . About those late deliveries, what do you expect? If we keep accepting those special orders, the newsprint just has to wait its turn! Really, Mike, it's *your* problem."

With demand for newsprint expected to increase from 300 000 tons of paper in 1983 to 350 000 tons in 1984, Mike knew the current complaints might be a sign of worse days ahead. As plant manager, Mike knew he was ultimately responsible for the efficiency and profitability of his plant. With this in mind, he set out to prepare his report to his superior at head office.

Exhibit 1
Worldwide Pulp and Paper Ltd.
Plant and Equipment Investment
(in millions of dollars)

Paper-making machines (2)	$150
Digesters (2)	62
Chipper machine	22
Blow tank	20
De-barking machines (2)	16
Storage silos	14
Log weighing/sorting equipment	11
Miscellaneous plant/equipment	55
TOTAL	$350

Exhibit 2
Worldwide Pulp and Paper Ltd.
Capacity Enhancement Cost Study Results

1. Wood Processing

. . . $125 000 per increased production of 100 000 tons of wood chips per year

That is, to increase wood chip production by 100 000 tons per year, WPPL must spend approximately $125 000

2. Pulp Production

. . . $200 000 per increased production of 1 000 tons of wood fibre pulp

3. Paper Production

. . . $7 500 000 per increased production of 25 000 tons of paper

SECTION VIII
An Introduction to General Management

General management decision making requires the coordination of all aspects of business into an integrated management program. In other words, general managers are concerned with strategy formulation and strategy implementation. This means a continual assessment of what business to be in and how one will do business both in general and very specific terms. The previous chapters on the functional areas of business — finance, marketing, production and human resources — are essential for undertaking general management problems. The general manager must relate financial issues to a proposed marketing program, changes in techniques in production to human resources implications, and so on.

PART 1: THE GENERAL MANAGER

The meaning of general management varies by circumstances. In a small one-person business, the chief decision maker has to be an all-round general manager capable of longer-term planning as well as daily "fire fighting" since there is no specialized staff to delegate these responsibilities to. In larger firms, the general management tasks are essentially the same, though a little more complicated. However, there are usually several people who share the general management workload. Even the titles used to describe the individuals responsible for general management vary from company to company: president; managing director; vice-president, administration; and so on. In this chapter the title General Manager will refer to an individual who has overall responsibility for a business or major unit of business.

What are the responsibilities of a general manager? Usually they include the following:

1. Long-term planning for new products, production/operation processes, new markets, financial flexibility, and organizational changes.
2. Finding and training competent subordinates. The general manager's goal would be to delegate as much responsibility and authority as possible to subordinates in finance, marketing, production, and human resources in order to be free for the major decisions concerning the overall company.
3. Coordination. The general manager's goal would be to ensure that the various activities of the company reinforce one another, rather than work at cross-purposes. The general manager would act as a liaison, ensuring that coordination is sought and achieved among the various functional areas of the business.
4. Decision making. The general manager will make decisions that subordinates cannot make, either because of disagreements or because they lack a sufficiently broad perspective on the issues that need to be considered.

In short, the general manager must understand all functional areas of business and be especially competent in human resources management. As one can see, the general manager is concerned with strategic decision making (longer-term directions for the business) and operational decision making (shorter-term specific actions to accomplish shorter-term goals). The general manager delegates, coordinates, and facilitates decisions to the extent possible, and where necessary makes the "big" decisions affecting company welfare. To perform this demanding role adequately, the general manager must be able to appraise the company and its environment thoroughly and objectively.

PART 2: COMPANY PERFORMANCE ANALYSIS

A general manager's major concern is improving the overall performance of the company. To do so, he or she must understand what objectives are being sought, what strengths and weaknesses characterize the company, and what options there are for improvement given the operating circumstances.

Objectives

Company goals or objectives are essential, both as a guide for activities in all functional areas of the business and as criteria for evaluation. Objectives must be specific enough to provide useful guidelines for planning and act as benchmarks for performance. Objectives that are too general, such as "to make a profit," do not give much help in planning ways to achieve performance. A more specific objective, such as, "to achieve a 10 percent return on investment after tax next year in the original equipment radial tire market," generally is more helpful.

Sometimes difficulties are encountered in identifying what objectives have been established for a particular company, particularly in smaller companies where the owner's personal aims become intertwined with business objectives. In general, there are two common causes of apparent lack of objectives: (a) the objectives simply have not been established or (b) the objectives exist but have not been communicated clearly.

It is often necessary to consider trade-offs among objectives. Often, it is only possible to achieve one objective at the expense of another. For example, one management consultant identified the following trade-offs:

1. Short-term profits versus long-term growth.
2. Profit margins versus competitive position.
3. Penetration of existing markets versus development of new markets.
4. Related versus unrelated new opportunities as a source of long-term growth.

In undertaking case analysis, if you are having trouble evaluating or formulating objectives in a particular situation, we suggest you ask yourself, "What is most important to this company? What are they trying to accomplish?" Choose your answer as the major objective. If after further consideration of the situation you feel you can add to the statement of objectives, come back to this step and do so. The important thing is not to get hung up at this stage of the analysis.

Performance Evaluation

Analyzing corporate performance can be difficult because there are so many dimensions that can be examined and often there is not enough information or time to do a thorough job. In these circumstances, we suggest you begin with a "big picture" approach, gradually becoming more specific as circumstances warrant it. Here are three questions you might ask yourself:

1. How well has the company done in terms of resources it had to work with? Resources include the people, finance, marketing, and production resources available to the firm.
2. How well has the company done in terms of the market opportunities it had? Market opportunities refer to the size of the market, the company's position vis-à-vis competition, environmental trends, etc.
3. How well has the company done in terms of its overall objectives? Objectives usually include profitability, return on investment, market share, new product introductions, etc.

Generally speaking, we are interested in assessing how well the company is performing on financial measures (such as profit), marketing measures (such as market share), production measures (such as capacity utilization), and human resources measures (such as employee turnover). These measures, and there are many, can be compared to objectives, to how well the company has performed in the past, to how well competitors are performing, or to estimates of potential. To interpret performance meaning fully, we must understand what the company has (its capabilities), what the company is trying to do (its objectives), and what circumstances the company faces (its environment). In short, we do an internal and external analysis of the company.

Internal Assessment

When we assess the various activities of the firm we must evaluate the strengths and weaknesses in each functional area. We are interested in determining why performance in each aspect of the company was as good as it was and why it wasn't better. We must decide whether less than satisfactory performance was the result of incorrect strategy, the result of incorrect execution, or the result of incorrect strategy and incorrect execution. Each section of this book was designed to enable you to do this. For example:

1. In Finance we discussed management of a company's cash position, analysis of past and projected financial performance, and sources of additional funds.
2. In Marketing we tried to understand and to predict the response of consumers and competitors to changes in a company's product, price, distribution, and communications policies.
3. In Production/Operations Management we examined the various processes a company may use to produce goods and services and the techniques a company may use to improve its production efficiency and effectiveness.
4. In Human Resources we discussed ways to understand individuals, groups and organizations in order to accomplish tasks through the efforts of other people.

As general manager, you should look at each of these aspects of the overall company in order to determine:

1. Company strengths. What can the company do and, especially, what can the company do particularly well? (What is its "distinctive competence"?)
2. Company weaknesses. What aspects of the company need to be strengthened in order to improve company performance?

These strengths and weaknesses are best identified by comparing what a company has or does with what is particularly required to succeed in the business being examined (i.e., "key success factors" in the industry). The prudent general manager attempts to build on strengths and overcome weaknesses.

External Assessment

External assessments refers to the assessment of an industry. The purpose of the assessment is to identify opportunities and risks in the industry; plus the internal factors, under the control of management, that are required for success.

In the Marketing chapter, we outlined ways to analyze customer demand characteristics and ways to analyze the nature of competitors seeking the patronage of your target market. By using those techniques, you should be able to arrive at an assessment of (a) what market opportunities exist (e.g., size and growth rate of a market), (b) what investments and risks are associated with pursuing those opportunities (e.g., strength of competition), and (c) what key success factors are involved in bettering competitive efforts to gain consumer acceptance and make a profit (e.g., the key success factor in door-to-door cosmetic marketing is a very large, highly motivated sales force, and the key success factor in a price competitive, basic commodity industry is being a low-cost producer).

Similarly, we discussed in the marketing chapter how to examine environmental trends of importance. Until recently, most business decisions could be satisfactorily made with scant attention to the "environment of business." However, the fast-paced major changes in the political, legal, economic, social, and technical features (P.E.S.T.) of our society can no longer be neglected. Such changes have created and destroyed major industries remarkably quickly by offering new opportunities and imposing severe constraints. Thus, astute general managers now monitor or scan the environment in order to identify and react to changes of importance to their companies.

PART III: DEVELOPMENT OF ALTERNATIVES

The general manager has six fundamental alternatives or stratagems.

1. Penetration. In stratagem one, the general manager improves the efficiency and effectiveness of resources devoted to the marketing and the production/operations for current products in order to increase the market penetration in current markets and increase profitability. For example, this might entail convincing current customers to use more of the company's product or to use it more frequently.
2. New market development. In stratagem two, the general manager develops new markets for current products. New markets may involve expanded sales territories

and developing marketing and production/operation plans to appeal to new market segments.

3. New product developments. In stratagem three, the general manager proposes the development of new products to serve current markets. In the performance evaluation, the general manager may have identified market segments currently poorly served by the enterprise's competitors' products.

4. Diversification. In stratagem four, the general manager proposes the development of new products for new markets.

5. Integration. In stratagem five, the general manager may integrate forward (closer to the final customer) by developing or acquiring distribution outlets or integrate backward (closer to supply sources) by developing or acquiring suppliers of materials or parts.

6. Concentration. The above five stratagems focus on growth. There may come a time when an enterprise is attempting to offer too many products and services across too many markets. Under these circumstances, the general manager will focus on concentration of effort to areas which offer the greatest chance of success and profitability. Stratagem six, concentration, involves the redeployment of resources within the company to current products and services. If there are excess resources that cannot be used profitably within the enterprise, disposal of portions of the business usually is appropriate.

Each of these broad alternatives can then be further defined. For example, if we are marketing milk and we opt for market penetration, how are we going to get our existing customer to drink more? Perhaps we might try an overall strategy of suggesting more occasions when milk drinking is appropriate or perhaps we find new uses for milk such as in cooking.

As you generate and evaluate different strategic options, you will probably notice that there are differences in the skills and resources required to implement these strategies. Also, there are probably differences in the degree of risk associated with these options and differences in the expected payoff to the company. These differences are what make strategy formulation difficult and interesting.

Valuation

For acquisitions, integration, and concentration, overall company valuation is important. If owners wish to sell their enterprise, they need to know what their selling price should be. Investors look at the potential earnings of the firm to maximize their returns on their stocks. There are three basic ways to evaluate a company's value: "capitalization of earnings," "net book value," and "economic appraisal." One or all of these methods can be used in valuing a business. No one method is the best in all circumstances. (A detailed discussion of valuation is beyond the scope of this text.)

1. The capitalization of earnings method uses a price/earnings multiple to be applied against expected earnings. Price/earnings multiples observed for the common stocks in the same industry on public stock exchanges can form the base for estimating an appropriate multiple. The multiple is affected by growth expectations (the higher the growth rate, the higher the multiple), by risk (the higher the risk the lower the

multiple) and by the debt proportion (the higher proportion debt is of the total capital structure, the lower the multiple).

2. Net book value involves simply subtracting the total liabilities from the total assets to arrive at "book value." This method does not account for the prevailing market value of the firm's assets, nor for intangible asset investment. As an improvement of this method, analysts subtract intangible assets from total assets, before deducting liabilities.

3. A third way to evaluate a company's worth involves economic appraisals. Appraisals are often done by a city or municipality for tax reasons. Lenders often favour this method over book value. For example, land may appear on the books at $54,000. A real estate company may determine through an appraisal, however, that the market value of this land at the time of appraisal was $200,000. Appraisals may be based on replacement value or liquidation value. Consider a machine for filling bottles. To buy a new one to perform the same function may cost us $15,000, but if the current machine was sold (especially if buyers knew we were anxious to be rid of it) only $2000 might be received. In other words, the economic value placed on a firm's assets depends largely on the reason for valuation and the circumstances of the firm. Assets are nearly always worth more if the firm is considered an ongoing business than if it is about to be liquidated. To arrive at net economic value of the equity, liabilities are deducted from the sum of the asset appraisals.

The determination of appropriate strategic alternatives should take advantage of company strengths and avoid weaknesses. In other words, we must be concerned with "external consistency" (fit of the strategy with the environment) and "internal consistency" (fit of the strategy with various aspects of the firm).

One very useful way to assess an idea for change is to compare the projected results of that change with the projected results without that change. In other words, we suggest you project the firm's performance first under a "no change" scenario then compare that with the "change" scenarios. Once you have settled upon a major direction for your company, your job as general manager becomes one of ensuring that detailed plans for finance, marketing, production, and human resources are prepared and implemented in accordance with the overall strategy of the firm.

PART IV: ALTERNATIVE IMPLEMENTATION

Obviously, to be of any use, the general manager's action plan must be specific enough to enable him/her or his/her peers or subordinates to carry out the strategy in accordance with the plan's intentions. Such a plan should clearly specify:

1. What to do
2. When to do it
3. Who has the responsibility and authority to do it
4. How results will be measured
5. How results will be regarded in terms of compensation or promotion, and so forth

A good situation analysis and a good analysis of strategic alternatives will enable you to formulate an action plan relatively easily because the action should practically "drop out" of your analysis. Remember, as a general manager it is your responsibility to see that the functional area plans (finance, marketing, production/operations, and human resources) fit together into an integrated whole, constituting your overall corporate action plan. Exhibit 1 is a summary of this chapter.

A good test of whether you have thought it through sufficiently is to try to persuade a skeptical person that your plan of action makes sense. As a general manager, you should be able to explain both *what to do specifically* and *why it is worth doing.*

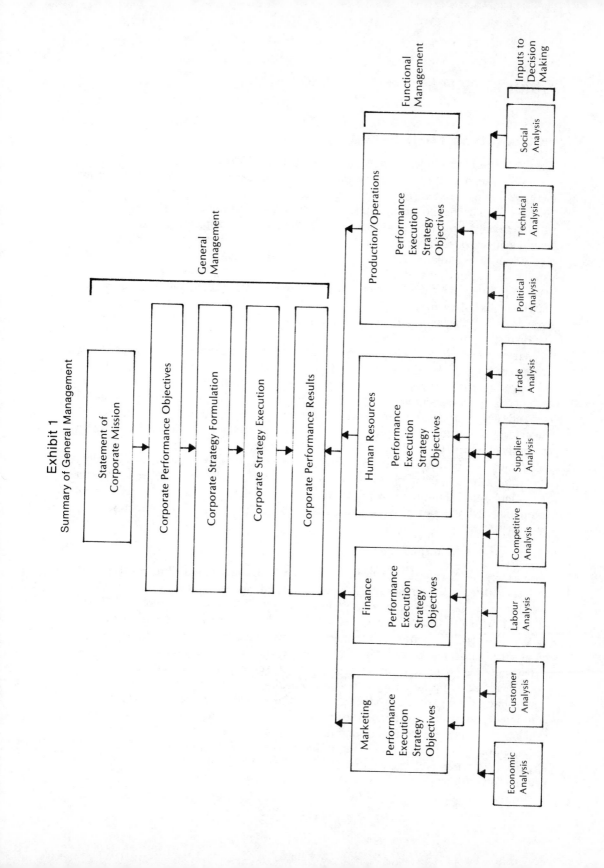

Exhibit 1
Summary of General Management

57

Arthur Kelly Printing Company Limited (A)

THE CANADIAN COMMERCIAL PRINTING INDUSTRY

The Commercial printing industry is composed of establishments primarily engaged in the production of custom manufactured printed items using a wide variety of printing methods and processes. Printed products include print advertising, labels, books and business forms. The industry is highly service-oriented with well-developed relationships between manufacturer and customer. The commercial printing industry is not heavily concentrated; instead, it is characterized by a large number of small establishments. With an estimated 2300 establishments across Canada in 1980, there are more companies in printing and allied industries than there are in any other sector. The average printing plant in Canada employs twenty people and has shipments of about $600 000. Sixty-five percent of the companies in the industry have fewer than ten employees, and the largest single plant employs nearly 1100 people. Exhibit 1 presents a statistical profile of the industry.

Growth in the industry is relatively stable, not growing dramatically in prosperous times and being insulated from economic downturns by the customer's perceived need for more advertising in periods of falling sales levels. Industry analysts suggest that the commercial printing industry will experience a 1–2 percent real increase in annual demand for the foreseeable future. Such a forecast is supported by at least two factors: the growth of the computer industry and computer-associated business forms, which currently comprise about $600 million of total industry sales, and the growth of print advertising within the business sector. The forecast is tempered by the vulnerability of the industry's market place to erosion from at least two main sources: current customers establishing their own internal printing facilities, and the advancement of competing technologies, such as word processors and high-quality photocopiers.

Management Within the Industry

As a general rule, only the larger firms in the industry are managed by professionals with specialized management skills. In the small and medium-sized plants, virtually all decisions are made by one or two people who are either owner-operators or entrepreneurs with production and direct selling backgrounds but little experience and expertise in other functions such as marketing, financial control, and systems development. The industry is relatively labour-intensive. In 1975, wages represented almost 42 percent of the manufacturing costs or close to seven percentage points above the average for all manufacturing industries. Finishing operations tend to be the most labour intensive step of the production process as a result of the concentrated effort of equipment suppliers to automate the preparation and printing steps. The industry has ranked in the top quarter of all manufacturing wage rates in Canada. In 1980, the average hourly wage in the printing industry was $9.02 compared to $8.76 for the aggregate of manufacturing sectors. This reflects the high skill requirements of many printing operations.

The Markets

The market for printed products is segmented along product categories, conventionally defined within the industry as: commercial and advertising printing; publications; labels; securities/cheques; books; business forms; instant printing; and other financial printing. The nature of a company's competitive strategy is dependent upon the product market that it serves, and firms that serve many markets must emphasize different services to different types of customers.

The majority of customers are small, placing orders intermittently for a variety of printed products. In most cases, their needs are unique and since the value of individual orders is small, servicing the individual client needs is a prime determinant of success in obtaining repeat business. Consequently, the typical printing firm tends to service only its local market and generate orders through personal contact with customers. The company that establishes a particular market niche, appropriately matching equipment and customer is often the one that obtains the most profitable market share.

The quality of the finished product, the printer's ability to, and flexibility in, meeting the customer's delivery schedule, cooperation and an ability to handle sudden problems are the discriminating factors used by customers. Printers lose accounts because of a lack of reliability, low quality reproduction, excessive price and a lack of subsequent follow-up on the part of the printer.

It is important to note that regardless of the market niche, most firms must provide their customers with a full line of services, whether they are produced in-house or subcontracted, for the particular product offered. These services include: artwork and design, camera work, typesetting, platemaking, press and bindery.

The Production Process

The production process in the commercial printing industry is essentially batching/jobshop and can be separated into three basic steps:

a) Preparation, which includes: separation, the arrangement of information by hand, typewriter or typesetting machines; colour separation; and platemaking, the production of printing plates containing information and illustrations to be produced by mechanical, photomechanical, and electromechanical means.
b) Printing, which involves the reproduction of the images contained on the plates onto paper or other substances. One- to four-colour work could be printed either by running the job through a multi-colour press, or by sending the job through a one-colour press the appropriate number of times, and changing the ink and washing the printer plates each time.
c) Finishing, which includes such operations as folding, cutting, collating, and binding.

Currently, industry presses are operating well below their capacity. Industry statistics showed total equipment usage in the 71–80 percent of one-shift capacity range; thus, there remains significant opportunity to expand printing output and productivity with existing resources. Additionally, there appears to be equal opportunity to increase profitability, as on the whole, the industry reports a chargeable time to available staffed equipment of only 71 percent.

Supplies for the commercial printing industry can be categorized into three major groups: paper, ink, and other (chemicals, films, plates, etc.).

The industry's paper requirements are predominantly satisfied by four major suppliers: Abitibi-Price, Domtar, Eddy, and to a much lesser extent, Rolland Paper. These companies supply about 90 percent of the industry's needs. Smaller industry suppliers include Great Lakes, Fraser, and Island Paper. A small percentage of the industry's paper requirements are imported and consists of specialty papers not produced in Canada. Only the largest printing companies buy paper directly from the mills; the rest of the industry purchases its paper requirements from paper dealerships which are usually owned by the mills. Independent mills do exist, however. The small printing operation is in a relatively stronger position vis-à-vis the ink industry than the paper industry in obtaining the most favourable prices because the ink market is very competitive with a large number of firms.

The Selling Process

The key to successful market penetration for the commercial printer is an ability to create a need on the customers' behalf by using salespeople, who serve as the contact with the end users to ensure steady demand.

There are essentially three types of printing buyers:

a) The casual buyer. This individual has a prime responsibility other than buying print and is therefore not familiar with the graphic arts processes and products. The buyer perceives his needs as simply to get a printing job done.

b) The professional purchasing agent. This individual fulfills all the purchasing needs of a company and therefore strives to obtain the best value for that company. He may or may not have some knowledge of the printing industry; however, he is aware of the appropriate purchasing questions associated with the buying process.

c) The professional print buyer. This individual is a skilled print buyer, familiar with the graphic arts industry and involved with print buying on a daily basis. Over time, he has developed an acute understanding of the industry and is aware of current activities, trends, and developments. This individual works in promotion firms and specializes in print advertising.

Given the wide variation in printing buyers' knowledge of the industry and their requirements, the selling process for the commercial printing industry is also appropriately differentiated.

The professional buyers and purchasing agents specify their needs to the print salesperson whose major responsibility is then to advise the buyers of ways to reduce costs and to offer his/her knowledge of new techniques in printing for achieving requirements more effectively and efficiently.

Casual buyers, however, constitute the majority of buyers in Canada. Because of their unfamiliarity with the industry, these buyers require a different selling process by the printing company. A firm has a printing need and contacts or is contacted by a commercial printing sales rep. The sales rep attempts to educate the buyer about what type of print is available and which type would most appropriately satisfy the buyer's needs. In so doing, the sales rep actually creates a need for a certain product through the selling process. The main goal of the sales rep is to develop a client relationship to ensure repeat business. Once such a relationship is established, clients then become part of a regular sales cycle. The ultimate goal of the sales rep is to become part of the buyer firm's planning process and in doing so, become aware of future requirements, thus enabling him/her to develop the means to best service the firm on a continuing basis.

Competition

The Canadian commercial printing industry has traditionally been and remains today a domestic industry in both ownership and market. Artificial protections in the form of trade tariffs have existed in Canada for many years, but a worldwide movement towards freer trade has resulted in a 40 percent decline in the tariff on imported printed products over the last eight years. Thus, as imports increasingly find their way into the Canadian markets, Canadian printers will have to augment their efforts to penetrate foreign markets over the longer term in order to continue to enjoy their present growth levels.

Given the large number of small competing firms in the industry, competition is intense, and service offerings are the prime requisite for success. The four largest companies account for 24 percent of shipments and the fifty largest firms, or 2 percent of the industry's firms, are responsible for 50 percent of industry output. Eighty-five percent of the industry's shipments and employment occur in the large metropolitan areas of Ontario and Quebec. However, printing plants are located in virtually every population centre in Canada, and, while a slow trend toward rationalization has emerged in recent years, the development of multiplant organizations is not yet significant in the industry.

The industry as a whole and, to a varying extent, individual markets, are subject to indirect competition in a number of forms. In-plant or private printing operations have an important impact upon the commercial printer's market place. With word processing and high-speed photocopy reproduction technologies, many nonprinting organizations are tempted to expand their printing departments. Additionally, even where there is no threat of in-plant operations, almost all trade publications on the office of the future stress the need to minimize the use and handling of textual materials. Such a trend is being supported by the emergence of low-cost word- and information-processing systems.

Government Involvement in the Industry

Changes in postal rates, regulations, and mail disruptions have a significant influence on the industry, since close to one-quarter of total shipments are ultimately distributed through the postal system. For example, Canadian shipments of greeting cards increased every year from 1968 to 1974 except in 1969 and 1972, reflecting higher first class mail rates which took effect on November 1, 1968, and June 1, 1972. Similar experiences can be expected with the nearly doubling of the first class mail rates on January 1, 1982. In the last few years, the federal government and the governments of Alberta, British Columbia, Ontario, and Quebec have moved on several fronts to promote the growth of book and periodical publishing in Canada in order to reduce foreign cultural influence. Commercial printers in Canada have and will continue to benefit from the strengthening of the publishing sector. It is estimated that about half the industry's shipments consist of products which are protected by the Canadian Copyright Law. The present law came into effect in 1924 and no major revisions have since been made. Consequently, the law does not take into account new technologies and the illegal photocopying which has, to some extent, reduced sales of certain classes of books and periodicals.

There is little evidence to suggest that the trend toward greater government involvement in the business process will be reversed or even slowed in the future. Consequently, a wide variety of issues are arising and will continue to arise at both the federal and provincial levels, which will have an impact on the industry. Higher taxes, postal rate increases, and costly compliance requirements in the safety and pollution control field are examples of adverse government action that is costly and reduces the competitive viability of the industry. However, it is also noted that export promotion, incentives to industry, government purchasing from the private sector and regulative changes in support of industry positions will serve to reduce the severity of these adverse government actions.

Summary

The large, mature, commercial printing industry in Canada is likely to remain in a stable state for the future. Current state of the art reveals that different levels of technologically advanced equipment are being used to differentiate competing firms. Extensive research and development activities by machinery and equipment suppliers, in an area such as laser printing, will continue to produce technological developments for firms to be more competitive in their existing and potential markets.

Exhibit 1
The Canadian Commercial Printing Industry
A Statistical Profile

Year[1]	Number of Commercial Printing Establishments	Number of Employees	Salaries and Wages (000's)	Selling Value of Shipments (000's)
1976	1978	43 353	$ 529 373	$ 1 465 026
1977	1908	42 498	575 781	1 585 184
1978	2171	45 658	664 470	1 883 485
1979[2]	2250	48 000		2 173 200
1980[2]	2300	53 000		2 570 900

Year[3]	Sales per Employee	Paper Costs (% of Sales)	Factory Payroll (% of Sales)	Administrative Expenses (% of Sales)	Selling Expenses (% of Sales)	Profit Before Taxes (%)	Collection Period of Receivables	Return on Investment (%)
1976/77	$34 746	23.07	30.41	9.75	8.22	7.87	70.2 days	4.13
1977/78	38 406	22.91	28.43	9.89	8.22	5.14	66.7	8.02
1978/79	41 672	22.93	28.59	9.58	7.93	5.98	67.3	9.32
1979/80	48 516	23.31	27.69	8.86	7.58	7.12	69.4	10.67
1980/81	52 550	24.19	26.66	9.47	7.78	6.12	67.8	10.31

NOTES:
[1]Statistics Canada Catalogue 36-203 Annual Printing, Publishing and Allied Industries 1979
[2]MacLean-Hunter Research Bureau estimates
[3]1980/1981 Canadian Ratios for Profit Planning, Graphic Arts Industries Association Operating Ratios for all firms reporting.

58

Arthur Kelly Printing Company Limited (B)

In early September 1981, Mr. John Dempsey, President of the Hamilton-based Arthur Kelly Printing Company was assessing whether he should request that the Board of Directors of the Investex Holding Company approve a $165,000 expenditure for a Miller four-colour offset press. Mr. Dempsey considered the new press to be a potential vehicle for increasing sales in the Hamilton market. Increasing sales was a prime concern for Mr. Dempsey since he was expected to present a three-year growth plan to the Investex Holding Company, the parent of Arthur Kelly, by the end of the month.

COMPANY HISTORY

Arthur Kelly Printing Limited was founded in April 1933 by Arthur Kelly, who served as president and salesman, with his wife as secretary-treasurer and manager. Between 1933 and 1973, the company grew steadily and established its reputation in the Hamilton market. Arthur Kelly concentrated on selected large accounts such as Dare Foods Ltd, Allen Candy, and the Hamilton Board of Education — accounts the company still has today.

By 1974, Arthur Kelly had lost interest in the company and decided to sell. His two sons, both graduates of medicine, had established their own practices and were not interested in continuing the family business. Dan Molloy, then a recent graduate MBA from the University of Western Ontario, purchased the company with available personal funds. Molloy felt that Arthur Kelly Printing had good potential to increase its share of the fragmented Hamilton market. Although the company's $250,000 sales level was declining, the company appeared relatively "healthy," supported by the few "gilt-edged," established accounts that had been its mainstay for many years. Plant and equipment consisted of two offset and four letterpress machines. The staff of seven included two older, part-time salesmen who handled the established accounts. The work was standard: single colour, mechanical, medium volume, and with an emphasis on prompt service.

Shortly after the purchase, Molloy hired John Dempsey to become the company's chief salesman and assume responsibility for increasing the company's sales. Discovering that customer needs were largely for two-colour work, Molloy purchased new and better equipment and hired additional support staff, while Dempsey continued to increase sales. The company strategy at that time was to remain in the two-colour, mechanical market in Hamilton, with medium volume, but with above-average quality.

In 1977, Dempsey purchased half of the company from Molloy and assumed full operation responsibility. Initially, Dempsey concentrated on three areas: strengthening the skills of the existing staff; purchasing larger, two-colour offset machines to handle larger paper and producing higher quality products; and improving the folding and binding functions of the production process.

In the fall of 1979, Arthur Kelly became an operating division of Investex Incorporated, a holding company formed by Molloy, Dempsey, and a small group of investors. Molloy assumed the presidency of Investex Incorporated while Dempsey became President of Arthur Kelly. Both Molloy and Dempsey had one seat of the six seats on the Investex Board of Directors. Investex owned three small businesses.

Together, Dempsey and Molloy desired to develop management systems for Arthur Kelly that would provide the necessary infrastructure for the future employment of a professional manager and maximize the value of the company as an ongoing enterprise, if it was sold in the future. Molloy felt that the future success of Investex would depend on the proper blend of established, lower-risk enterprises, such as Arthur Kelly, to generate funds in support of the propagation of new, higher-risk ventures. Dempsey believed that Arthur Kelly should operate as profitably as possible while achieving an appropriate balance between quality of working life considerations and employee productivity. To successfully achieve these objectives, Molloy and Dempsey targeted a sales level of two million dollars by August 1983, while continuing to attract and develop employees of the highest possible skill level and management potential.

ARTHUR KELLY IN THE HAMILTON MARKET

The Hamilton market was a microcosm of the Canadian commercial printing industry and could be segmented along conventional industry lines. The city's seventy-eight firms operated in every segment of the market from short-run insta-print production (low quality), to long-run four-colour production (high quality). A survey of the operating dimensions of nine representative firms is outlined in Exhibit 1.

The 1981 market for commercial printed products in Hamilton was approximately $50 million and growing at 2 percent per year. Given the relatively low barriers to entry, there were characteristically a large number of market entries and exits within a year. Furthermore, the market for printed products was not confined to Hamilton proper. Hamilton printers serviced more than the Hamilton market and the Hamilton market was also serviced by non-Hamilton printers.

Equipment purchases were often an indicator of competition in various segments. Single-colour and two-colour offset were often traded between firms and in the past few months, four large forty-inch, four-colour presses were purchased by companies in the Hamilton area.

ARTHUR KELLY SERVICES

Arthur Kelly competed in a market that demanded every printed product between insta-print and four-colour process long-run work. Its product line included: stationery, booklets, and advertising printing; books, forms, tags and labels; posters, folders, pamphlets, brochures; presentation folders, numbering, embossing, die cutting, and foil stamping; all printed in one, two, or four colours.

Commercial printing made up 20–30 percent of the company's business, advertising 30–40 percent, labels 10 percent, books, publications and annual reports 10 percent, business forms 10 percent and other printing including tags, menus, and coasters 10 percent.

While the company provided a full line of services, it subcontracted all artwork and typesetting demanded by clients. In 1980 the company subcontracted $51 000 worth of typesetting and $36 000 in artwork and design. In-house services included camera work, colour separation, platemaking, printing, and binding. Forty to 50 percent of all sales required some typesetting and 60 percent of all sales required some bindery.

Arthur Kelly served a broad base of customers in the Hamilton area. The company's largest customer was Farm Business Consultants, which represented 6 percent of 1980-1981 sales. The top ten of 700 customers comprised 32 percent of sales; the top 39 customers constituted 59 percent of total sales. In fiscal 1980-1981, Arthur Kelly spent $1218 on advertising. Most of this expense was for the company's advertisement in the Yellow Pages Directory.

In 1981, company sales were $1 302 012 with earnings before tax of $109 836 or 8.4 percent of sales. The company had twenty employees who worked a nine-and-one-half-hour per day (one shift), four-day week. Total assets were $439 021 including machinery and equipment of $225 169. These and other relevant operating statistics are detailed in Exhibits 2 and 3.

HUMAN RESOURCES

Of the company's twenty employees, two were management, nonproduction personnel, three were salespeople, twelve were skilled production employees, and three were related support staff. The company emphasized the quality of employee work life with such features as a compressed four-day work week, a management stock participation plan, company-wide performance bonuses, increased individual responsibility and competitive wages.

There are no written descriptions for each full-time position nor was there a formal, annual, staff-performance appraisal system based on job description duties. Salaries were negotiated individually between the general manager and the employee while benefits (including vacation), the ten statutory holidays, and overtime rates were uniformly applied company-wide. There were no formal training programs; however, when the need arose to upgrade employee skills, the company was prepared to subsidize the cost of training.

MARKETING

Sales Staff

The sales team at Arthur Kelly consisted of the sales manager, Ben Sherk, two full-time salesmen, Mark Becker and Mark Vigna, a part-time salesman, Daryl McDonell, and John Dempsey. The salesmen had a variety of backgrounds; some had had experience in the industry, others had not.

The company did not formally divide the Hamilton market into sales territories, but rather, each salesman was responsible for a group of customers — a client list. Each salesman serviced his client list and made "cold calls" to provide the company with a steady flow of new business. In general, the salesmen did not seek business with very small companies whose printing needs were limited to short, unprofitable, time-consuming runs.

Given the company's growth over the past few years and the resulting increased administrative activities, John Dempsey's selling time had declined considerably. However, during fiscal 1980–1981, John still serviced about 120 clients, which accounted for almost 24 percent of sales.

Ben Sherk serviced about 80 clients. These clients contributed a total of 30 percent to Arthur Kelly 1980–1981 sales, while ten of them accounted for almost 23 percent of company sales. Ben had ten years' experience in the printing industry and as he was Arthur Kelly's top salesman, Ben's clients tended to be the professional print buyers. Ben's responsibilities as sales manager included recruiting salesmen, setting both company and individual sales targets, and making a month-end sales evaluation for each salesman. Ben was also responsible for attending to 20 to 30 federal government tenders[1] that become available every Wednesday in the lobby of the federal government building on James Street. The tenders were usually for printing orders in the range of $500–$1800. After a cost estimate was completed and checked, with Dempsey, the company submitted a bid. Arthur Kelly was successful in about one in ten bids.

Mark Becker had worked for Arthur Kelly for two years and had no previous experience in the industry. Mark serviced about 80 clients who were generally casual buyers or purchasing agents. Mark was responsible for 15 percent of company sales, or $191 000 in 1980–1981.

Mark Vigna was the most recent addition to the sales force and served some 40 clients, a client list he assumed from a previous salesman. The only part-time salesman, Daryl McDonell, had been with Arthur Kelly for twenty-five years and concentrated on three large and twelve smaller accounts which in 1980–1981 contributed $70 000 to sales.

House sales were those accounts that came in off the street and were not generally associated with any one salesman. There were 145 different such accounts contributing just over 4 percent of sales in 1980–1981.

Order-Taking Process

Salesmen were responsible for soliciting and processing orders from customers. From their conversations with the clients, the salesmen had to estimate a price for each individual order. If the job was routine, the price could be found on a standard price list derived from historical costs. If the job was a repeat order, relevant historical information was located from the customers' file and was then used as a guide to pricing current work. Once an estimate was complete and verified by the Sales Manager or the President (in the case of estimates over $800), it was documented and returned to the customer. On confirmation of the job, the information moved into the production process and became the responsibility of the plant foreman.

---

[1]The Supplies and Services Department of Canada did not have in-house printing facilities in Hamilton. All local Federal Government printing orders were made available to the established commercial printing company that bid the lowest price.

PRODUCTION

Salesman orders received by production personnel were accompanied by a specification sheet that described the order, and generally included a price quotation already made by the salesman. Quotations required the salesman to assign the job to a specific press and the production manager only reassigned the job, due to capacity constraints, and only after giving consideration to the quality, quantity, and actual size of the printed material. A description of printing machinery and capacities is given in Exhibit 4.

Arthur Kelly received three types of orders: camera-ready jobs, new jobs, and repeat orders. A new docket was created for each order with the following information recorded: name of the customer, docket number, date, delivery and billing address, and a description of the order. The order was then recorded in the Docket Book which kept a running log of all dockets used.

Camera-Ready Work

All camera-ready work[1] was attached to a docket and placed on the production table. Each morning and afternoon, the production manager gave a list of all jobs and an explanation of the job specifications to the preparation staff. The preparation staff laid out all jobs to be photographed in an effort to minimize film wastage. The negative was developed and dried and colours were separated for each job individually. The colour negatives were placed on a light table and attached to a masking sheet to ensure that the work was in the proper position for the press. The plate for the job was created from the masking sheet. Once completed, the plate was attached to the docket and forwarded to the Production Manager. The Production Manager then placed the docket and the plate, by delivery date, in the box for the appropriate machine. The entire process from making the negative to plate-making averaged about one-half hour.

New Orders

Although Arthur Kelly did not have the layout equipment or personnel required to design printed products, the company still accepted orders from the idea stage through to the printing stage. To handle these specific needs, the company subcontracted the layout and design work to an appropriate design house. Requests for high-quality artwork were sent to Promotional Communications Ltd., Taylor Design Associates, or Christoph Composition, while orders requiring quick turnaround and low cost were sent to A and B Designs. In 1980 the company subcontracted $36 000 in artwork and design. Once the artwork was received, the order was processed as camera-ready work.

Repeat Orders

Old dockets were retrieved from the docket room for all repeat orders. (It was company policy to keep all dockets for a minimum of three years.) A new docket was completed and the customer file and old plate were retrieved. The plate was attached to the docket and the production manager placed the docket and the plate in a

---

[1]Camera-ready work is completely laid out artwork that is ready for photography, colour separation, and platemaking.

box by machine and delivery date order. Costs of repeat orders were significantly lower since the camera work and platemaking was not necessary.

Production Scheduling and Monitoring

Every day, the pressmen would retrieve the plates and the dockets from the production manager's station. The work was then arranged according to colour and size. The pressmen began with the smaller sheet sizes and worked up to the larger sizes in order to reduce setup and "breakdown" time of the machinery. Lighter colours were run before darker ones to reduce the washup time for the plates and to ensure the trueness of the current colour. A press was set up by inserting the plate, applying the ink and adjusting it for the sheet size. The appropriate paper (size, colour, quality, quantity) was inserted onto the press and one or two sheets of paper are run to adjust the press positioning. During the entire run, pressmen continuously examined copies coming off the press. Once the number of impressions were run (including 5 percent "overs" for expensive jobs and 10 percent "overs" for most other jobs), the printed sheets and the docket were stacked on skids near the next operation. Follow-up operations included cutting, perforating, collating, stitching, binding, numbering, packing, and shipping. Such operations were listed on the docket and checked off as completed. Each job going through the plant repeatedly received the attention of the production manager. Every night, prior to quitting time, he would make a list of the work in the preparation area, the jobs on each press and their delivery dates. Every morning and afternoon, the President, the Plant Foreman and the Production Manager would meet to review the list of work and to expedite the orders to the various machines. This procedure was designed to monitor all jobs while ensuring minimal press down-time and prompt delivery dates.

THE CURRENT SITUATION

"This company is on the threshold of some tremendous growth areas, and I'm not sure which way to move," sighed John Dempsey, thinking ahead to the board meeting. "There must be more work in the Hamilton market but how do I get it? The half-billion dollar Toronto market is only thirty minutes away, and I sure would like some of that action. The only costs I can see of entering that market are the salesman's salary and benefits of $20 000 and miscellaneous expenses of $5000 to $7000 per year. My concern is whether one salesman can generate enough sales to cover these costs just by making cold calls. There are hundreds of printers in and around the Toronto area!

"Another alternative is to enter the market of four-colour work. To do four-colour work we could purchase Miller four-colour offset press but this would require board approval. The press would cost $165 000, and the company would also have to hire a skilled operator at $18 000 per year. Sales would have to be generated from the quality conscious consumer, and the normal Investex payback period of five years should be met." Historical costs from industry reports indicated a gross margin excluding labour costs of 56 percent for a four-colour printing press.

Dempsey also considered an expansion of services in preparation and finishing operations. "Improvements in the processes personnel and machinery in these areas will allow Arthur Kelly to complete a printing job in-house from the idea phase through production and finishing." "I'll just have to get the sales force to drum up the business, but how much?" "A good layout designer usually averages $20 000 per year salary and Graphic Arts Industry Association statistics value layout equipment at a minimum $15 000, and material costs 22 percent of sales." A further concern was the quality of the work. Dempsey wondered whether one designer could singularly form an art department, "Additional fixed costs would certainly be controlled by hiring only one designer, but can I expect one person to generate all the imagination and creativity to produce good quality work? Contracting the layout service to other printers on an 'as needed' basis might make this venture viable, but will they deal with us? Similarly we could also look at contracting out our finishing operations such as folding, collating, stitching, and binding to the undercapitalized small printers, but is it profitable?"

With these alternatives in mind, Dempsey began to plan his recommendations to the Investex Board of Directors. Dempsey realized that all new programs and requests for capital funds would need a demonstration of financial feasibility before board approval would be considered.

Exhibit 1
Arthur Kelly Printing Limited
Nine Hamilton Market Printing Firms

Company Name	Number of Employees	Estimated Sales (000's)	Specialty Products	Customer Remarks
1. Arthur Kelly	20 (3-4 Salespeople)	$1 300	Two-colour brochures and booklets	• good turnaround 3-4 days • excellent prices • not a high quality printer • aggressive salesforce calls every 2 weeks
2. Rieger Printing	25	$1 800	Multi-colour work	• best quality printer in Hamilton • 2-3 weeks turnaround
3. Turner Press	35 (4-5 Salespeople)	$1 839	Multi-colour work	• good quality work • 2-3 weeks turnaround • medium to high prices • sales force calls every 3 weeks
4. Prestige Printing House	25 (3-4 Salespeople)	$2 500	Multi-colour work	• excellent turnaround (1-1½ weeks) for multi-colour work • 7-day turnaround on 2-colour work • growing company, quality improving, prices becoming competitive
5. The Printing House	12	$ 63	Two-colour brochures and booklets	• 7-day turnaround
6. Steel City	13	$ 68		
7. Sterling Print-All	9	$ 47	Two-colour work	• 2 weeks turnaround
8. Davidson Henderson	35	$1 840	Multi-colour Single-colour	• Kitchener production facilities • 2 weeks turnaround • Salesman calls every 1-1½ weeks
9. L and H Litho Arts	30	$1 580	2 or 3 colour work	• Brantford production facilities • 2 weeks turnaround • Salesman calls every 2 weeks

Exhibit 2
Arthur Kelly Printing Limited
Income Statement
Years Ended August 31

	August 31, 1980	August 31, 1981
Net sales	$ 777 342	$1 302 012
Factory cost of product materials used	$ 329 051	$ 556 088
Total factory payroll	166 415	259 139
Total fixed expenses	74 489	95 422
Total factory cost	569 955	910 649
Gross profit	$ 207 387	$ 391 363
Administrative expenses	79 647	125 765
Selling expenses	77 719	104 268
Income before interest and management fee	$ 50 021	$ 161 330
Interest expense	21 815	26 575
Management fee (Investex)	11 893	24 919
Net income before tax	$ 16 313	$ 109 836

Exhibit 3
Arthur Kelly Printing Limited
Balance Sheet
As at August 31, 1981

	August 31, 1981
CURRENT ASSETS	
Cash	$ 0
Accounts and notes receivable	235 364
Less allowance for doubtful accounts	5 417
Net receivables	229 947
Inventories	20 706
Prepaid	3 948
Total current assets	$ 254 601
FIXED ASSETS	
Machinery and equipment	$ 225 169
Type and metal	3 514
Office furniture and fixtures	16 389
Leaseholds	48 312
Subtotal	$ 293 384
Less accumulated depreciation	108 964
Net fixed assets	184 420
Total assets	$ 439 021
CURRENT LIABILITIES	
Due to bank — Overdraft	$ 27 038
— On demand	67 708
Accounts payable and accrued charges	160 128
Taxes payable	23 967
Current portion of long term debt	8 667
Total current liabilities	$ 287 508
Deferred income taxes	14 625
Long term debt	15 880
Total liabilities	$ 318 013
Equity	121 008
Total liabilities and equity	$ 439 021

Exhibit 4
Arthur Kelly Printing Limited
Description of the Printing Presses

Name	Make-Ready Time (Minutes)	Capacity Impressions/Hour Theoretical/Actual	Estimate Idle time	Contribution Percent*	Remarks
Multi-Offset	15-30	10 000/4 000	0%	66%	• one page per impression • letterheads, business cards, envelopes, etc.
Multi Two-Colour	30	10 000/4 000	50%	52%	• two pages per impression • 2-colour — letterheads, envelopes, etc. • good quality, fast
Hamada	30	8 000/3 750	10%	21%	• two pages per impression • for orders larger than 15,000
Heidelberg Kora	30	5 500/4 000	25%	44%	• four pages per impression • highest quality printing machine made
Solna	30	8 000/4 000	25%	56%	• four pages per impression • for orders larger than 4,000 • fastest machine • high quality work
Heidelberg Cylinder "Letter Press"	30	2 500/2 000	90%	N/A	• four pages per impression • print, score, number, perforate
Heidelberg 10 x 15 Letter Press	15	3 500/2 000	0%	N/A	• one page per impression • print, score, number, perforate • handles overspill from one colour multi

*Contribution percent was calculated by dividing material costs and variable overhead for each machine by the sales made from work performed on the machine.

59
Coffees of the World

Coffees of the World was a specialty store selling teas, coffees, and coffee-making accessories, started by Tim Snelgrove and his partner, Peter Lockie, in September 1975 in a small store in a London, Ontario, shopping plaza. The plaza was located on a main road in a district that combined single-family housing with a developed high-rise apartment area. The new business developed from a project Snelgrove had worked on during his MBA program. The project indicated that the venture could be successful. The operation appeared particularly attractive to the partners because only a minimum amount of capital was required, and only a part-time management commitment was needed. The personal financial resources of the partners were limited, as was their time: both were embarking on their professional careers.

By March 1976, Coffees of the World was considering expansion into the Toronto market because the London location had proven successful. Snelgrove and Lockie were considering three expansion alternatives: (1) leasing mall retail locations, one at a time; (2) acquiring the firm The Coffee Blender Inc., an existing chain of specialty coffee stores; or (3) franchising the Coffees of the World name and operation.

TEA AND COFFEE MARKET

Tea and coffee are two of Canada's popular beverages, with 64 percent of the population being coffee drinkers and 53 percent tea drinkers, as opposed to only 41 percent for juices and 31 percent for soft drinks. Per capita consumption of coffee had increased slightly from 1.91 to 1.99 lbs.[1] per person during the period 1960 to 1970. The thirty-to-forty-year age group drank 47 percent more cups per day than all the others, and as the "baby boom" population entered this age group it was expected to have an upward effect on consumption.

In 1970 the coffee market was split in half between instant and regular coffee. Twenty-eight percent of Canadian homes served both types of coffee. There was substantial growth in the use of domestic coffee makers such as "Mr. Coffee." It had been suggested that, with the rapidly increasing price of coffee, once the consumer was paying over $2.50 per pound of coffee, he or she would take the time and trouble to make it properly.

In 1975 the world's coffee production was low. This was expected to send the price of coffee soaring. In fact, rapidly increasing prices had been the case during the year.

Good-quality, fresh-roasted coffee was available through a small number of coffee specialty stores and gourmet shops. Supermarkets generally offered only low-quality blends; supermarket prices were as much as 50 percent lower than specialty shops; coffee was considered and used as a traffic builder. Rather than a blend, specialty shops featured a variety of specific growths, such as Colombian and Mocca Java. Because the shelf life of roasted coffee was only a few weeks, storing large inventories of coffee was not practical.

---

[1] 1 lb. = 0.454 kg.

OPERATIONS

Peter Lockie was already located in Toronto. In early 1976, he had acquired a partnership interest in a small legal practice after being called to the bar. Tim Snelgrove was completing the final year of his MBA program in London. Tim was married and had a young family. Upon graduation, he was planning to return to an executive position in the management consulting firm he had left when he entered the MBA program. A major objective of the partners was to be able to pursue their individual careers while still running the Coffees of the World business in their spare time. All of their assets were pledged to support loans used to finance both Coffees of the World and their career development. Each had an equal number of shares in the company.

The Coffees of the World shop in London was $400 over budgeted sales for the first five months of operation and was expected to make the first year's sales forecast of $74 000. At the fiscal year end of January 31, 1976, a small profit of $1296 was realized after all start-up items, as shown in Exhibit 1. Exhibit 2 presents the balance sheet after the first five months of operation. The store was run by a manageress who hired and scheduled staff, bought merchandise as needed and prepared a weekly sales and cash reconciliation. Part-time help was used for evenings and weekends. The manageress was paid $5 per hour; all other help earned $3 per hour. Merchandise was bought from a number of Toronto suppliers on thirty-day terms. Initially, inventory turned over twelve times a year and all sales were cash so that there were no credit collection problems. Gross margins were 40 percent on coffee, tea and accessories and 50 percent on giftware. Recent quantity purchases of giftware had increased the margins on some items to as high as 75 percent. The store started selling its own brand of tea and tea bags with margins over 60 percent. Similar improvements in margins could be obtained for increased coffee purchases.

OPPORTUNITIES FOR EXPANSION

Lease Mall Locations

Tim Snelgrove was considering expanding into two leased locations in Toronto suburbs. At this time there were no locations for lease in the popular high-traffic Toronto malls, and no additional mall locations were being built. The two mall locations under consideration were eleven and twenty-two kilometres from downtown Toronto and located in single-family residential areas.

Negotiations were under way for the two store locations, and Snelgrove expected the mall rent would be similar to that paid in the London location of $11.10/m² for a 39 m² store, or 7 percent of gross sales, whichever was higher.

The Coffee Blender Inc.

In February 1976, The Coffee Blender Inc. was listed for sale with a Toronto real estate broker for $85 000. Exhibits 3 and 4 were the financial statements given to Mr. Snelgrove by the owners, Mr. and Mrs. Winstone. The Coffee Blender Inc. was Toronto's largest retailer of roasted coffee with three mall retail outlets and a Don Mills warehouse. The St. Clair and Yonge Street stores had sales of $112 000 each and the Don

Mills store had sales of $49 000 for total sales of $273 000 in 1975. All of the store locations were in high rental areas. Sales had grown at the annual compound rate of 22 percent. The firm sold only a limited amount of high-margin giftware and coffee accessories, and coffee sales accounted for over 70 percent of the store volume. In contrast, Coffees of the World sold 30 percent coffee and 70 percent accessories. Despite the fast growth in sales and the high volume of sales, operations were only marginally profitable in 1974. In 1975, a small loss was incurred, as shown in Exhibit 3: Mr. Winstone had prematurely joined the business full time. Consequently, the firm had higher fixed costs for the $15 000 salary of Mr. Winstone. Also contributing to the low profitability was the Bloor Street store which, after opening in 1973 at an expenditure of $15 000 in fixed assets, experienced a slow growth in sales volume. The store was just becoming profitable on a monthly basis. Snelgrove felt an offer equal to the book value of the assets of The Coffee Blender Inc. would be accepted, though he was uncertain of what offer, if any, he should make.

Franchising

Tim Snelgrove had been approached about franchising the Coffees of the World concept for a location in Richmond Hill, thirty-two kilometres north of Toronto, and later, by a different party, for a franchise in Calgary, Alberta. If any agreement was to be made, Tim Snelgrove thought the deal should be structured as follows:

1. The franchise would pay $1000 plus 5 percent of gross sales annually for the use of the sign, merchandise bags, and Coffees of the World logo;
2. A $95 per month rental charge would be levied for the coffee-grinding machine, weigh scale, and cash register; and
3. The franchise would be required to buy all his/her merchandise from Coffees of the World, noncoffee items at a 10 percent discount from normal wholesale prices and coffee at 5 percent below normal wholesale prices.[1]

As protection, Coffees of the World would agree to buy back the franchise after two years of operation if the franchisee was not satisfied. The repurchase price would be $2000, plus inventory at cost and any leasehold improvements, but not including any losses incurred. Tim Snelgrove believed that the best way to design a franchise agreement would be "to make the franchise work so well that the franchisee doesn't want out of the agreement." He knew each franchise had to be successful to attract new ones.

---

[1]The resultant costs as a percentage of retail price would be

	Coffee Items		Non-Coffee Items	
	Normal	New Franchise	Normal	New Franchise
Retail price	1.00	1.00	1.00	1.00
Wholesale price	.60	.55	.50	.40
Coffees of the World cost				
—no increase in purchases	.60		.50	
—increase in purchases		.40		.25

Exhibit 1
Coffees of the World Inc.
Statement of Income and Retained Earnings
for the Five Months Ending January 31, 1976

Revenue		
Sales recorded	$37 485	
Less: provincial sales tax collected	1 011	
Net sales		$36 474
Cost of goods sold:		
Purchases	$27 227	
Less: closing inventory	5 178	
Cost of goods sold		22 049
Gross margin		$14 425
Expenses		
Wages	$ 5 613	
Rent	1 885	
Utilities and maintenance	146	
Cash short	56	
Cash register rental	320	
Bank service charges and interest	198	
Miscellaneous store expenses	54	
Packaging	685	
Advertising	746	
Freight in	367	
Telephone	376	
Insurance	177	
Organization expense	541	
Administrative expense	1 273	
Depreciation and amortization	260	
Total expenses		12 697
Net operating profit		$ 1 728
Provision for income taxes		432
Net earnings		
and retained earnings, January 31, 1976		$ 1 296

Prepared by T. Snelgrove.

Exhibit 2
Coffees of the World Inc.
Balance Sheet
as of January 31, 1976

ASSETS

Current Assets
Cash	$4 245	
Merchandise inventory at cost	5 178	
		$ 9 423

Fixed Assets:
Store equipment	$ 992	
Store fixtures	1 355	
Lease improvements	780	
	$3 127	
Less: accumulated depreciation	260	2 867
TOTAL ASSETS		$12 290

LIABILITIES

Current Liabilities
Bank loan payable	$3 000	
Accounts payable	4 053	
Payroll deductions payable	148	
Rent payable	442	
Accrued expenses	146	
Accrued income tax	432	
Total current liabilities		$ 8 221

SHAREHOLDERS' LOANS AND EQUITY
Shareholders' loans[1]	2 769	
Capital issued and fully paid	4	
Retained earnings	1 296	
Total equity		4 069
TOTAL LIABILITIES AND EQUITY		$12 290

[1]Shareholder loan is subordinated to the bank.

Prepared by T. Snelgrove.

Exhibit 3
The Coffee Blender Inc.
Statement of Operations and Retained Earnings
for the Year Ended May 31, 1975
(with comparative figures for 1974)

	1975	1974
Revenue	$273 148	$213 572
	—	—
Cost of sales		
Inventory — opening	$ 5 250	$ 6 331
Purchases	169 655	131 415
	$174 905	$137 746
Less: inventory — closing	5 664	5 250
Cost of sales	169 241	132 496
Gross profit	$103 907	$ 81 076
	—	—
Direct expenses		
Wages	$ 54 009	$ 35 279
Canada pension	688	549
Unemployment insurance	692	401
Total wages and salaries	$ 55 389	$ 36 229
Advertising	2 592	1 035
Chargex costs	596	—
Store maintenance and expense	986	1 619
Store rent	23 673	19 496
Telephone	656	670
Hydro	836	691
Business taxes	604	432
Workmen's compensation	373	154
Bad debts	23	8
Depreciation — equipment	742	927
— leasehold improvements	3 598	3 598
	90 068	64 859
Contribution to profit	$ 13 839	$ 16 217
Other operating expenses		
Warehouse expenses	$ 3 513	$ 1 416
General and administrative expenses	10 516	12 092
	14 029	13 508
Profit (loss) for year, before provision for income taxes	(190)	2 709
Provision for income taxes	—	731
Net profit (loss) for year	$ (190)	$ 1 978
Retained earnings — beginning of year	11 269	9 291
Retained earnings — end of year	$ 11 079	$ 11 269

Exhibit 4
The Coffee Blender Inc.
Balance Sheet as of May 1, 1975

	1975	1974
ASSETS		
Current Assets		
Cash	$ 2 817	$ 7 719
Inventory — valued at lower of cost or market prices	13 248	12 113
Prepaid expenses	—	84
Corporation income tax receivable	770	1 389
Total current assets	$16 835	$21 305
Fixed assets:		
Furniture, cost	$ 7 668	$ 7 010
Automobile, cost	5 684	2 935
Leasehold improvements, cost	17 989	17 989
	$31 341	$27 934
Less: accumulated depreciation	13 440	8 481
Total fixed assets	17 901	19 453
Other assets, at cost:		
Incorporation expense	$ 537	$ 537
Goodwill	20 000	20 000
Utility deposits	110	200
Total other assets	20 647	20 737
TOTAL ASSETS	$55 383	$61 495
LIABILITIES		
Current Liabilities		
Demand loan — bank	$11 000	$15 000
Accounts payable and accrued expenses	17 144	22 356
Employees withholding taxes and sales tax	1 105	808
Note payable — G.M.A.C.	1 493	—
Total current liabilities	$30 742	$38 164
Shareholders' loans	13 557	12 057
SHAREHOLDERS' EQUITY		
Capital		
Authorized:		
30 000 — 6% noncumulative, redeemable (at par) preference shares with a par value of $1 each. Issued, none.		
4 000 common shares without par value, not to be issued for a consideration exceeding $4 000.		
Issued and fully paid:		
5 common shares	$ 5	$ 5
Retained earnings	11 079	11 269
Total equity	11 084	11 274
TOTAL LIABILITIES AND EQUITY	$55 383	$61 495

60
Extra Valu Stores[1]

As he hung up the phone, Doug Jones, southwestern area manager of Extra Valu Stores, cursed his misfortune. The last thing he wanted on Friday afternoon was to have to drive for two hours to check out consumer complaints about a store closing. Thirty minutes earlier the company president, Mr. Rogers, had received a telegram from a group of customers who patronized one of the two Trimball, Ontario, stores that were being closed. Apparently the group felt that their neighbourhood store should remain open. Mr. Rogers had passed the problem on to him and asked for a report by Monday morning. A call to the Trimball store manager suggested that the telegram was merely the "tip of the iceberg." The store was located across the road from a neighbourhood "action" organization and the manager expected problems. Doug decided to visit Trimball.

COMPANY POLICY

As he drove, Doug reviewed the rationale behind the decision to close the two Extra Valu Stores in Trimball, both of which he believed were still marginally profitable. During the last five years the company had been phasing out its older, smaller stores. Food retailing was highly competitive and small free-standing stores were not as profitable as large stores in mall locations. Over the past five years Extra Valu had closed forty small old stores (one-fifth of the total number in operation) and replaced them with units which were on average more than three times as large (i.e., 2300 m² to 2800 m² of gross floor area versus 550 m² to 750 m²). Moving to a new store was nearly always more attractive than incurring the high cost of renovation of old facilities, especially when renovations did not provide more selling space. As a result, about 30 percent of the company's present retail capacity had come on stream in the last five years. This program of conversion to big modern outlets had improved the company's efficiency, in turn allowing it to offer better prices and generate more store traffic without a proportional increase in store personnel.

Table 1

	1974	1969	' Change	' Change Corrected for Inflation
Sales per sq ft (0.093 m²) of store space (weekly)	$ 4.90	$2.70	+81%	+16%
Sales per employee (weekly)*	$1 317	$783	+68%	+17%

*Using the ratio of two part-time employees equal to one full-time employee.

---

[1]All names and places have been disguised.

Since the labour cost and the store upkeep cost were the company's two major operating expense categories (using approximately 12 percent and 3 percent of every sales dollar respectively), this improvement in personnel and facility utilization was critical to profitability.

The move to larger retail outlets had also allowed the company to enrich its merchandise assortment by expanding into more profitable product departments — convenience and frozen foods, delicatessens, in-store bakeries, snack bars, and so forth.

In addition, Extra Valu had set up a few prototype stores in the 3700 m² to 4500 m² size range which devoted about 30 percent of their floor area to the display and sale of non-food items such as sewing supplies, hobby items, inexpensive children's apparel and other more traditional products (health and beauty aids, home cleaning products, tobacco, and so on). These products represented inexpensive, routine purchases which an increasingly affluent society seemed to want for one-stop shopping convenience. Exhibit 1 shows the store layout for a 3200 m² "superstore" in Trimball.

Doug recalled a recent report from the company's planning department which illustrated the potential impact on profitability that this expanded product mix could have. They estimated that (a) 20 percent of a new superstore's volume was done in non-food items (versus 10 percent historically); and (b) gross profit margins on non-food items would average 30 percent of sales (versus 17 percent on food products).

Table 2

	Store Type	
	Small Size	*New*
Food	.90 X 17% = 15.3%	.80 X 17% = 13.6%
Non-food	.10 X 30% = 3.0%	.20 X 30% = 6.0%
Gross profit margin	18.3%	19.6%

This improvement in gross profit margin was very important considering that Extra Valu currently earned only about 1.5 percent on sales (before income tax) after all operating charges. Doug's performance was evaluated on the profitability of his area so he was pleased when he could replace small stores with the more profitable superstores.

Extra Valu's policy was very successful. During the past five years their market share had risen 5 percent, much of it at the expense of independent food merchants whose existence was founded on non-price factors such as personalized service, delivery, and convenient location.

THE SITUATION IN TRIMBALL

Doug reached Trimball by 19 00 and visited the store on Hudson Street first. Large red window banners announced that it would close in one week and offered 10 percent off all store merchandise. There was no sign of any protest in or around the store. A few elderly ladies from the nearby senior citizens' building browsed through the discounted merchandise. The manager told him that he had not been approached by any organized groups, though a city alderman had been around seeking information and some individual senior citizens had complained. This scene was in direct contrast to the situation he found at the Farnham Road store. About thirty picketers marched in a circle in front of the store carrying signs protesting the closing.

Finding a parking spot in the tiny lot proved difficult; however, Doug was not in a hurry to enter the store. He was careful to wait in his car until the television crew from the local station had finished filming. As he walked up to the entrance two elderly women approached him and identified themselves as working for the Farnham Road Council (FRC). One asked him if he would like to sign their petition (Exhibit 2), while the other offered him a form letter (Exhibit 3). The women told him that other FRC workers were canvassing the neighbourhood getting signatures on the petition and distributing form letters. They hoped to have several thousand names by Monday morning. Doug refused politely, then entered the store. Because the store was small, there were few high margin products for sale (Exhibit 1). Weak lighting and a wooden floor did not project the same image of Extra Valu that the larger modern stores did.

Doug was puzzled by the intense consumer reaction. The banners that announced the closing had gone up only the previous afternoon. In a little over twenty-four hours the citizens had organized this protest. They could not have had advance notice because not even the store manager had known in advance. Prior to any knowledge of consumer reaction, Doug had approved the offer of some free merchandise to customers (Exhibit 4) if they went to another Extra Valu store in town. He had no information on the extent to which customers had used this offer or how they felt about it.

Doug as eager to learn as much as he could about the group that sponsored the Farnham Road protest, the people it represented and their reasons for protesting. He decided to make some enquiries about the neighbourhood and solicited the store manager's help.

THE FARNHAM ROAD AREA

The area, which had a population of 9500, was in an older part of Trimball. The problems of this particular neighbourhood were typical of the central section of the city. Family incomes were lower, averaging $8000 compared with the city average of $10 700. Tenant/landlord problems were common and juvenile delinquency was higher per capita than in other neighbourhoods in Trimball. There were a large number of family crisis situations.

THE COUNCIL

The Farnham Road Council was an unofficial voluntary organization which met monthly in an area school. There was no charge for membership. All those who lived in the Farnham Road area were considered to be members. The executive, which was elected yearly at a public meeting, considered their role to be one of helping people to help themselves. Whenever an area resident wanted to discuss local problems he or she contacted the executive and the problem was put on the council's agenda, which was published in the council newspaper. Other interested individuals attended the meeting to meet people with similar concerns. The executive helped these interest groups form subcommittees which were responsible for their particular concerns. The executive were residents who had dealt with the various levels of government and could serve as resource persons for subcommittees.

When area residents wanted a crosswalk installed on a busy street the council helped them prepare a petition and write a successful brief to the city. Similarly, another subcommittee convinced the city to designate some undeveloped city property as a park. The council's most recent success was getting a neighbourhood improvement grant. The store manager showed Doug the FRC monthly newspaper, which had a circulation of 6500 copies. It had a front page article which asked for suggestions from the citizens on how to spend $500 000 that the government had decided to allocate to the Farnham Road area, one of two in Trimball that had qualified for grants under the Neighbourhood Improvement Program. The manager explained that the city hoped the money would help prevent further deterioration of the neighbourhood.

While the manager had been helpful, Doug wanted to get a first-hand impression of the neighbourhood and set out for the FRC meeting place in the White Library and Resource Centre, which was a short walk down the street. Wandering through the small cement block building Doug noticed offices for a full-time social worker as well as offices for a part-time public health nurse, a child management counsellor and a family benefits worker. He was intrigued by posters throughout the building publicizing various programs and activities for both children and adults. One poster reminded residents to save their Extra Valu Store cash register tapes. The poster had a photo of the new kitchenette for the volunteer nursery that Extra Valu had sent in exchange for $251 000-worth of register tapes.

Doug stopped a moment to watch a group of residents who were setting up paintings for a show of the works of amateur artists from the Farnham Road area. The residents were talking about the good coverage the protest had received in the evening paper.

Doug left the White Centre but bought a newspaper before heading back to Valleyville. He quickly found the article which explained the citizens' protests. The major problem seemed to be the high proportion of senior citizens in the area. The apparent organizer, Elizabeth Chambers, remarked that the old people shopped two or three times a week because they could not carry heavy loads very far. Miss Chambers claimed that once the Extra Valu store was closed, the seniors would have to take the bus to the next nearest supermarket — a ride which she said would be expensive for those living on pensions and impossible for those with severe arthritis. Mr. Jones noticed that Miss Chambers did not mention the numerous small variety stores in the immediate vicinity but only referred to the supermarkets. Miss Chambers also said:

"We can appreciate the profit pinch but food supply is more than a matter of profit making. It is an essential service. Even if the store is a marginal operation, or losing a bit, we think it should stay open for humanitarian reasons. Surely a conglomerate like Extra Valu can support the odd weak link in its strong chain. . . . We are not asking it to lose money. In fact, we are not certain it is losing money. If service was cut to essentials and prices were reasonable, then we would be very happy. . . . There were a lot of good independents around here when this Extra Valu store opened twenty-five years ago, but they could not compete and went out of business. Extra Valu comes in, gets the dollar, then slips away leaving us high and dry."

As he drove back to Valleyville, he wondered what coverage was given in the local television late evening news. He suspected it would not be very favourable to the company.

MONDAY MORNING

On Monday morning Doug phoned both Trimball store managers to learn the latest developments before talking with Mr. Rogers. The Hudson Street store manager said that there had been no organized protest at his store, though some residents of the nearby city-run senior citizens apartment had complained individually to him. Apparently, they had contacted their aldermen in the hope that the city would intercede on their behalf. The Hudson Street manager was unable to identify any area organizations that were strongly protesting the closing.

The manager of the Farnham Road store said that the article in Friday's paper was run again at the top of an inside section in Saturday's newspaper. The protest had received radio news coverage as well as coverage on the city's most popular open-line radio show. Senior citizens had phoned to complain publicly that they were unable to travel on buses to shop because of arthritis and that taxis were too expensive. Other people phoned to complain that they would not even be able to buy bread and milk in the neighbourhood once Extra Valu closed. Everyone seemed angry with Extra Valu.

As Doug sat mulling over the problem, a phone call from Mr. Rogers interrupted his thoughts. Mr. Rogers had received three hundred protest letters in the morning mail and although most of them were form letters he wanted Doug to hear one particularly well-written letter (Exhibit 5). He asked Doug about his progress in coming to a decision. Before hanging up he reminded Doug that he needed a decision that morning because he was receiving but not taking calls from Trimball aldermen and radio stations who wanted to know what Extra Valu was going to do.

Exhibit 1
Extra Valu Stores

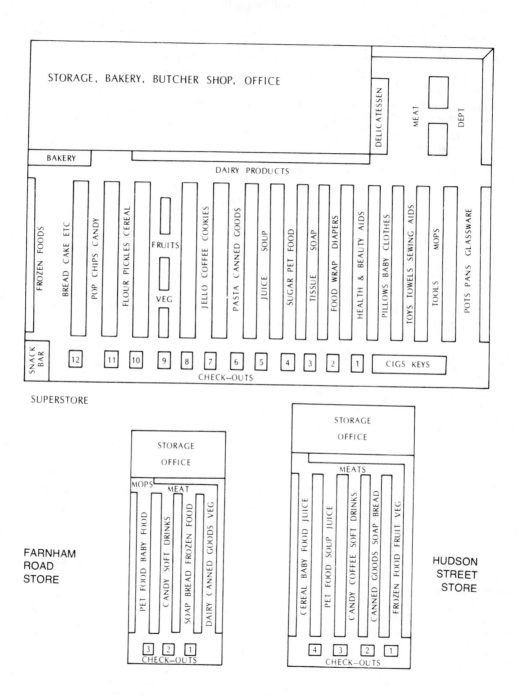

Exhibit 2
Extra Valu Stores
Petition Form

We, the undersigned, are opposed to the decision to close the Extra Valu store at Bayview and Farnham Road in Trimball. The store, which is centrally located, has served our neighbourhood for years, so that many people especially Senior Citizens (which number one in ten) have become dependent on it.

The issue is *SERVICE* to neighbourhood residents, especially our Senior Citizens, from a *LONGTIME NEIGHBOUR*, Extra Valu.

We feel strongly in our desire to have the store remain open or, as a last resort, stay open until another store can move in, thus meeting the needs of the neighbourhood.

Petition sponsored by our
FARNHAM ROAD COUNCIL

Name	Address	Phone Number
1		
2		
3		
4		
5		
6		
7		
8		
9		
10		
11		
12		
13		

Exhibit 3
Extra Valu Stores Protest Form Letter
Extra Valu Is Proud to Serve You!

Is Extra Valu Serving Us?

After years of being a part of your Farnham Road area neighbourhood, they are closing down their store! Is Extra Valu being a good neighbour of our Farnham Road area by moving out?

Who Shops at this Store?

A lot of neighbourhood people make this store their store. Senior citizens of the Farnham Road area (numbering one in ten), who have no means of transportation, are dependent on this store because of its proximity. *Where else will the seniors go?* For others, this store is a time- and money-saving convenience.

Where Will the People Shop?

Since Shoppers' World at Beach & Farnham road closed down a year and a half ago, and if Extra Valu now closes, the nearest stores will be: Floyds' at Hudson and Beach, Shoppers' World in the Bentley Plaza and Dollar Stretcher at Bayview and Highbury, which are at the very fringe of our Farnham Road neighbourhood. Extra Valu is right in the middle of our neighbourhood.

YOU'RE AHEAD AT EXTRA VALU!   BIG DISCOUNT PRICES!
If Extra Valu leaves *who* will   Does this mean Big Discount
be ahead?   service too?

If you are opposed to this store closing and would like the decision reconsidered, please mail in the coupon below.

This flyer is sponsored by our
FARNHAM ROAD COUNCIL

Mr. R. Rogers, President
Extra Valu
217 Seashore
Valleyville

Dear Mr. Rogers:

I/we strongly protest the closing of the Farnham Road and Bayview Extra Valu store in Trimball and urge you to reconsider in light of the service to area residents and our long association with you as our neighbour.

Name _____

Address _____

Telephone No. _____

Exhibit 4
Extra Valu Stores
Offer to Customers

September 23, 1976

Dear Customer:

We sincerely regret to announce the closing of our branch at 500 Farnham Road, Trimball, at 6:00 P.M., Saturday, October 2.

Our appreciation is extended for your past patronage at this location, which has served the area for many years.

Our closest stores are at 1001 Farnham Road and 1350 Hudson Street East, both with ample parking facilities, and 172 River Street at Duke Road featuring a Customer Delivery Service at a nominal charge.

Your patronage is invited to any of these locations, and, as a token of our regret in closing 500 Farnham Road, this letter will be accepted by cashiers at the above stores for a free pound of our freshly ground Extrafine coffee, with assorted purchases totalling $5 and over.

EXTRA VALU MEANS TOP QUALITY AT LOW PRICES

Exhibit 5
Extra Valu Stores
A Protest Letter

September 25, 1976

Mr. R. Rogers, President
Extra Valu
217 Seashore
Valleyville

Dear Mr. Rogers:

I am again contacting you with respect to the scheduled October 2 closing of the Extra Valu store at 500 Farnham Road, Trimball.

Specifically, I draw your attention to the enclosed letter which is being distributed to your customers. This letter does *not* state why our neighbourhood Extra Valu is being closed.

We would suspect that insufficient profit is the reason, but again we really do not know what "insufficient" means. Is the store breaking even or is its profit margin too low in comparison to what you expect of your stores?

We have "heard" that profit is not the main reason for closing this store. Rather it is that the interior of the store does not fit Extra Valu's image. We would assume that if this is the case, the profit outlook for this particular store will not be sufficient to merit renovations.

We realize that, as a private corporation, we cannot force you to share with your customers the reason why you are closing our neighbourhood food store.

We can only appeal to the twenty-five years that Farnham Roaders have patronized this Extra Valu Store. That is a lot of years at being neighbours.

We acknowledge that there could indeed be a valid reason for closing this store. Could we not expect of Extra Valu the same closing policy Shoppers' World came forward with last year here in Trimball when they were planning to close their McMaster Road store? Shoppers' World gave a verbal promise not to close the store until such time that arrangements could be made for another food store to service that particular neighbourhood.

Could I again reiterate the invitation to Extra Valu to meet with area residents Wednesday, September 29, 7:30 P.M. at the White Library, 550 Farnham Road. This meeting will afford you or your representative a chance to hear first-hand our deep concerns at having our only neighbourhood food store removed from our area. Also it will provide us with an opportunity to hear first-hand Extra Valu's reason for closing.

Could I kindly ask you, Mr. Rogers, to get back to me (1-653-433-1010) as soon as possible with a reply to our invitation? I thank you for dealing with this matter.

Respectfully yours,

Elizabeth Chambers
Farnham Road Council

61
Flyte Craft

For almost eight years Charles Williamson had produced power boats ranging in size from 3.5 m to 5.5 m. During that period Flyte Craft had grown from a one-man operation producing custom units to a company with a well-developed line producing in excess of forty boats a year and retailing a large variety of hardware supplies through their factory-store outlet. However, during the years 1972 and 1973 sales volumes had been static (forty-three and forty-one units respectively) dropping to twenty-nine units in 1974. Williamson felt that major changes had to be made if the company was to return to an acceptable growth pattern. Fiscal 1974 resulted in an unexpected loss of almost $12 000, accentuating Williamson's problem.

THE BOATING INDUSTRY

The pleasure boating industry in North America had undergone dramatic change since World War II. Rapid growth, material changes, increased power options and new hull designs combined to increase the product offerings now available in the market place. Shorter work weeks, increased leisure, longer vacations, earlier retirement and rising income levels provided the fuel for dramatic industry growth. Individual manufacturers, however, did not benefit uniformly from the boom. Overproduction and tight money coupled with increased need for capital investment and marketing skills caused substantial industry restructuring. The trend to bigness continued, evidenced by the fact that 60 percent of the market was dominated by ten companies. Only the producers of the larger luxury boats were somewhat immune to the fluctuations in industry operations (Exhibit 1).

There were several explanations behind the dramatic change in industry structure. Among these was a shift in materials (Exhibit 2). By 1968 the use of wood in power boats had all but disappeared. Aluminum and fibreglass made up the bulk of material used, with aluminum predominant in hulls under 4.5 m and plastic dominating the medium craft over that size. Together these materials accounted for 85 percent of all boats made. Canoes were the only major item where wood products remained dominant. Change in materials caused changes in technology. Metal fabrication techniques permitted capital investment and volume output in the smaller pleasure craft. Fibreglass technology, geared to low investment, flexibility of application, and design variety, permitted the entry of many new producers into the industry in the late 1950s and early 1960s. These characteristics prompted new entries seeking growth and profit and resulted in overproduction, inferior products, high inventories, and price cutting. Profits plunged, and the marginal producers disappeared. *Allied Boating Canada* reported that "of the list of 150 producers in 1959, only 50 were still in business by 1968." By 1968 some price stabilization had taken place. Smaller manufacturers had concentrated in specialized lines. Some manufacturers had closed down their Canadian operations, while others had greatly expanded.

DESIGN DEVELOPMENTS

Since 1945, the sleek, fast, deep-*V* hull design dominated the powerboat industry. Its ability to handle the rough water at relatively high speeds with moderate power demands made the design popular with powerboat enthusiasts. Recently, however, the "gull wing" design had appeared, offering stability and easy riding. Although this hull sacrificed rough water performance, the introduction of increased power packages had offset these disadvantages.

THE POWERBOAT CONSUMER

While over 70 percent of all boaters were between the ages of twenty-five and fifty-four (Exhibit 3), there was a growing trend toward younger buyers. Although participation increased with income levels, middle- and lower-income buyers were having a growing impact on boat sales (Exhibit 4). Many purchasers began with an initial purchase of used equipment then traded up to new equipment as incomes increased. In general, consumer studies indicated that buyers were more interested in quality and design than price. The average buyer began with a four-metre fibreglass or aluminum runabout costing approximately $2000 complete with trailer and outboard motor. Recent surveys indicated that most buyers were dissatisfied within two years and there was a constant upward movement to more space, power, and luxury.

Competition was keen. Good representation was at a premium, and advertising, promotion, and selling were growing in professional presentation. Over the past decade the boating industry adopted a similar marketing approach to that of the auto industry. Boats were sold on appearance; purchasers were swayed by luxury, trim and interior appointments, colour, and options, often to the exclusion of the technical and handling characteristics or hull designs.

The consumer had been conditioned by the automobile industry to expect discounts off list price. Thus in the peak selling season (March through July) 10 percent discounts were normal, while in the off season (August to December) 15 percent discounts were common.

Trade-ins were common in the industry. As a result, dealers became involved in a business complicated by inventories, service, and selling that was unknown in the late 1950s and early 1960s. Such activities involved increased credit lines and the addition of the mechanical skills necessary to perform complicated service procedures on sophisticated power packages. The increase in options, the growth in variations within the lines of individual manufacturers, and the broad range of power equipment added substantially to the dealer investment necessary to satisfy growing customer demands.

DISTRIBUTION

Almost 20 000 dealers served the North American boating consumer. These ranged from large specialized boat stores, department stores, and boat yards to the small hardware stores that carried boats as a sideline. To reach these dealers, manufacturers typically used one or more of four alternatives:

1. Manufacturers' representatives who established a force of wholesale distributors and dealers — for a fixed percentage of wholesale volume;
2. Wholesale distributors, which made use of the distributors' sales organization and often had national distribution available to the manufacturer of products with wide consumer appeal;
3. Smaller wholesalers for regional coverage;
4. In-house sales force that went directly to the retailer.

Some smaller manufacturers handled sales directly to the consumer, selling from the factory or factory outlets.

Most manufacturers bypassed wholesale channels and sold directly to retailers. Factory salespeople, familiar with local markets, provided the retailer with advertising, display, and promotional help. And since good dealers were crucial, boatmakers provided financial help in the form of credit and inventory support to insure that the dealer maintained a complete stock for effective selling.

Dealers, faced with a proliferation of models in the lines of major manufacturers, began to rationalize their product policies. This often had the effect of eliminating the products of small manufacturers who offered limited product lines, and who seldom had much marketing support for the retailer.

The average dealer gained revenue from three sources: new equipment, 60 percent; used equipment, 20 percent; service and repairs, 20 percent.

Typically, the dealer received discounts of 20 to 25 percent on inboards and sailboats, 30 percent on outboard boats and trailers, 32 percent on outboard motors and 35 to 40 percent on boating accessories. Often there was a further variation in these discounts based on volumes, time of purchases, and boat sizes. For luxury boats, the discounts were approximately half those of standard units. In most regions the dealer's buying decision was made in late fall. Orders were confirmed between January and March, and dealer sales materialized between April and July.

To finance their boat inventories dealers arranged floor plan loans with their local bankers. This type of plan covered up to 90 percent of stock purchase price. The dealer covered the remainder plus freight, insurance, and handling charges. These plans guaranteed immediate cash for the builder, allowed the dealer some financial flexibility and insured adequate stock for display and sale.

EXPORTS AND IMPORTS

In 1966, the U.S.–Canada balance of trade in the boating industry was about even. By 1970 Canada was exporting at twice the level of U.S. imports (Exhibit 5). Two major factors kept U.S. boats out of Canada: a 17.5 percent most favoured nation tariff and the devalued Canadian dollar. The latter had been erased and Tariff Board Notice R-182 would soon remove the former. Canadian advantages, such as lower labour costs, immigrant skills, and strong competitive performances were major factors in exporting successes to date. However, lower material costs, greater efficiencies due to longer runs, and a strong marketing effort by large and diversified U.S. firms raised serious questions about future trends. In the area of specialized designs and production, Canadian producers had a potentially bright future, though effective marketing to these selective segments was a limiting factor.

FUTURE TRENDS

Although expenditures for recreational boating will increase they will take a declining share of total recreational spending. The major reason for this is that boating is an expensive activity and it competes for the consumer dollar with many less expensive outdoor recreational activities.

Purchases of boats will increase as a percentage of total boating expenditures, due in part to the increase in size of boats, plus the switch to costlier hull materials. Expenditures for repair and maintenance will decline as a percentage of total, since the hull materials now being used are easier to maintain and less likely to need extensive repairs.

Sales of inboard/outdrive boats, houseboats and sailboats will also experience rapid growth. Shipments of inboard/outdrive engines will have the largest growth of all propulsion systems.

Aluminum has been the dominant hull material for recreational boats. However, reinforced plastics have been gaining rapidly, and by 1978, 65 percent of boat shipments will have reinforced plastic hulls. Wood hulls will continue to lose market share while thermoform plastics will find increasing application as a hull material, especially for smaller boats.

Acquisitions and mergers in the industry are expected to accelerate as both leisure-time companies (e.g., AMF, Bangor Punta, Browning Arms, Brunswick Corp., Conroy Inc., and Fugia Industries) and large diversified companies (e.g., Ashland Oil, Beatrice Foods, Chrysler Corp., North American Rockwell and Whittacker Corp.) continue to acquire smaller boat producers. After the industry shakeout eight to ten large companies will dominate recreational boating markets. The most successful companies are expected to be large firms involved mainly in producing and marketing leisure time products and services. Their presence should give the industry greater stability and offer dealers more support in terms of inventory credit and advertising.

Outside of totally new design concepts, improvements for the near future will be refinements to significantly increase quality and performance. Greater use will be made of the design freedom offered by fibreglass (e.g., modular unitized interiors instead of built-in joiner work). And there will be increasing servicing demands as glass hulls age, though these requirements will vary from historical repair work.[1]

Although the boating boom was expected to continue, many industry participants doubted that the 1970s would duplicate the market growth which characterized the past decade. Increased affluence and leisure time as demand factors were expected to be supplemented by a growing replacement and second-boat market, so that boating was expected to get a fair, but declining, share of the 78-billion-dollar recreational market projected in North America by 1978.

THE COMPETITION

Within the region serviced by Flyte Craft there were numerous boat retailers. No official figures covering sales could be found for the region bordered on the west by Belleville and on the east by Brockville. The whole area was an important tourist region and it abounded with cottages, summer homes and private and public camp-

---

[1]*Allied Boating Canada Report* 1972.

grounds. With Lake Ontario, the St. Lawrence River, and many smaller lakes in the region, it was a boaters' paradise.

Charles Williamson, the president and general manager of Flyte Craft, had some information on boat sales and competition in the region but it was general. As he commented:

"It was only recently, in fact this year when our sales started to skid, that we paid much attention to the competition. In fact, we always felt our product appealed to a unique market. Few of our customers were first-time purchasers. We always believed that the buyer had to know a lot about boats before Flyte Craft could sell. Now we are not so sure. In fact, I suspect that few first-time buyers ever heard of us and it is only after they get into boating that they see our wares. Because we can make minor adjustments, customizing, I guess you'd call it, our buyers tend to come looking for combinations they can't get elsewhere. But, of course, first-time buyers lack the skills to do this and as a result they don't see our product or service, given its higher per metre price, as a competitive option. Our major competitors? I guess in this area the big sellers are Starcraft, OMC (Outboard Marine Corporation), and Chrysler. They have a number of dealers, wide product lines, a lot of promotion and big names.

"As I say, we really never thought of them as competition but I can certainly see how many buyers find it extremely difficult to see any difference between our product and theirs. We price about the same but they are big marketers — we've never considered that approach. It was only when I heard from some of the local dealers in the Kingston area that their sales had held up well in 1974 that this whole competition thing began to bother me — we're looking at it now but frankly, as a small company I'm not sure what we can do about it."

FLYTE CRAFT BOATS LTD.

Charles Williamson had produced powerboats under the Flyte Craft name for almost eight years. Located in the Kingston, Ontario, area, Flyte Craft had grown from a part-time boat service and accessory business into a manufacturer and seller of powerboats and related equipment. With the boat-manufacturing boom, Williamson had expanded the retail outlet which sold his boats. Exhibit 6 shows Flyte Craft's sales along with the sales of other equipment and accessories. Typically, about 50 to 60 percent of sales were gained through selling Flyte Craft while the balance came from those items that Williamson sold as a retailer. Flyte Craft had only the one outlet and all boats were sold directly, without the use of salespeople, agents, or distributors.

FLYTE CRAFT HISTORY

Williamson had lived most of his life in the Kingston area, a region noted for tourist and boating activities. He acquired a small boating supply firm from his father. He had originally intended to sell the shop and property; however, late in 1966 he had lost his job in a temporary layoff. During this period, Williamson decided to build a 5.5 m wooden powerboat that he had been planning for some time. Before he was able to complete the boat he sold it and began building a second. He never did return to his job. With the help of one full-time employee and some part-time assistance he completed and sold thirteen units in 1967. Early in 1968, Williamson had several requests for fibreglass boats. These, coupled with a dwindling demand for his wooden boats, prompted him to expand his facilities and move into the production of fibreglass powerboats. In 1968, he began to sell snowmobiles and broaden his line of accessories. These sidelines were to aid immeasurably in keeping the business afloat for the two years it took to get his boat operations up over break-even. Since 1969, unit sales, revenue, and profits had increased consistently until 1973. In 1974, Flyte Craft experienced a wide range of problems. Unit prices were not increased to cover increases in unit costs and the volume of sales in both boats and the other lines had declined, resulting in a net loss of $11 247 for the year. It was in this setting that Charles Williamson was reappraising Flyte Craft's future direction.

"The loss came as a complete surprise. Oh, we knew that sales were off but we also knew that 1974 revenues would exceed those of 1971 and in that year Flyte Craft's profits exceeded $8000. It's only now since the loss became evident that I've begun to worry about where this business is going. Always before we just made and sold boats and accessories and, as you can see, except for 1968 (changeover from wood to fibreglass) and 1974, the bottom line always came up right. We've never spent a lot of time managing the details, everyone around here knows his job and I've always assumed if each of us did our jobs we could avoid this type of thing."

FLYTE CRAFT ORGANIZATION

Flyte Craft, with only eleven employees, never had developed an organization chart. Exhibit 7 gives an idea of the way company responsibilities were divided. Williamson filled both the president's role and that of production manager with most of his time spent on the latter. One of the store employees, William Carrier, had originally worked in the shop with Williamson but following an accident several years before he had returned to handle retail sales for the firm. He continued to fill his position, though he now had help to maintain the store hours which had been extended to include nights and weekends during the peak seasons.

In production two individuals acted as department lead hands. Pierre Tremblay supervised the hull-layup operations while Monty Phillips, a cabinetmaker by trade, supervised the finishing operations.

MARKETING

Unlike many boat manufacturers, Flyte Craft had no agency, wholesalers, or dealers. All of the company's boats were sold directly to the consumer through the company's own retail operations. In-store displays of two or three units were maintained to allow the prospective buyer a view of available models. About 50 percent of sales were made from floor or inventory units with the balance classified as custom built.[1] The company offered twenty- to thirty-day delivery on these special units with immediate delivery on inventory items.

---

[1]Colour, trim, power, etc., to fit customer specification.

Advertising for new and used boats was limited to classified placements in the newspapers of Kingston, Belleville, Brockville, and Napanee. In addition, the company occasionally displayed boats and boating accessories in recreational equipment shows. Williamson was convinced that word of mouth created most sales; that, and former customers coming back to upgrade.

Flyte Craft had not gone to the trouble of designing brochures, though specification sheets with sketches had been mimeographed. These were available to prospective customers who visited the shop. There were also assorted photographs of boats that could be viewed at the store to show colour combinations and trim arrangements.

PRODUCTION

Wooden moulds, capable of producing 1000 hulls, started the process. These moulds, one for each size in the line (four), formed the base for the combinations of polyester and fibreglass cloth which constituted the hull (three to six layers of fibreglass). The first layer was carefully rolled to remove bubbles and insure a smooth hull surface. Additional layers of fibreglass were added for strength, with the transom and the keel reinforced to withstand the stresses of motor operations. Subsequently, the floor and ski rack were added to the hull before the boat was "blown" from the mould. The hulls were then moved to the assembly areas on dollies where the "glass" was trimmed, vinyl floor installed, front and rear sections of the hulls painted, moulded deck outfitted with hardware, deck installed, gunnel mould placed, leatherette dashboard and panels installed, steering gear and controls placed and windshield, and trim installed. These operations varied somewhat where inboard or inboard/outboard power was involved. The plant layout is shown in Exhibit 8.

Inventory of marine hardware, supplies, and manufacturing materials was stored in an area at the rear of the plant. No formal records were kept to monitor supplies. The lead hands from both assembly and hull layup kept an eye on these materials and advised Williamson when it was time to reorder. Special items were ordered when the sale was made, and installed as the boat reached the finishing stages. Orders for store inventory were handled by Carrier.

The factory operated on a forty-hour week, though the practice during busy periods was to work more than forty hours, accumulating this time for additional vacation during the slack summer months.

CONTROL

While the regular financial accounting duties were handled by the bookkeeper, Gary Robbins, little in the way of internal control was used to make operating decisions. Hours (direct and indirect), materials, and supplies were not assigned to a specific hull so that costs could be calculated only on an average basis from purchase order data and payrolls. Some attempt had been made to install a piecework system, but Williamson and his bookkeeper could never find time to keep up to date with the records required. Accumulating or even relating labour inputs to a particular job was complicated by a production process that constantly shifted workers from job to job — responding to urgency. During slack periods production workers shifted to maintenance jobs and repair work, and, once again, no records were kept to identify this work and its cost.

The "books," as they were currently kept, consisted of a general journal, accounts payable ledger, accounts receivable ledger, payroll ledger, and journal of purchases and expenses. The books were drawn together at year end by a small accounting firm which prepared the annual statement. The bookkeeper prepared a monthly operating statement which indicated sales, expenses, and estimated profit; however, since inventories and work in process were not valued, such statements constantly over- or understated the actual situation. Some additional records were kept in conjunction with tax, unemployment insurance, and pension requirements but these were for government use and provided no management data for Flyte Craft.

FINANCIAL

From its inception almost eight years before, Flyte Craft had suffered from undercapitalization. The equity base was made up of common stock (10 percent), preferred stock (25 percent) and retained earnings (65 percent). The company relied heavily on debt financing and used a combination of personal loans from friends and relatives as well as bank loans for both the working capital (factory) and floor plan (retail operations) needs. The loans were secured by plant, equipment, and inventory with much of the debt being short term. The issue of broadening the equity base had never been discussed, though Mr. Williamson speculated that it might become an issue when the local bank manager saw his latest statement. He was aware that debt financing had permitted the business to survive and grow but it was becoming increasingly evident that his use of short-term funds for capital expenditures had put the company in a position where working capital was strained to the limit. The financial statements are shown in Exhibits 9 and 10.

The seasonal nature of the boat business forced the cash requirement to peak over the production season between February and June. In recent years, Williamson had tended to hold off producing for inventory, but this had put an upper limit on Flyte Craft's output. Inventory reductions through preseason and postseason sales (10 to 15 percent reduction) had helped the cash flow but reduced profits.

Store operations were integrated into company financial statements with no specific attention paid to retail profitability. The sale of winter recreation equipment had provided a contraseasonal line to keep the store open and some part of the work force productively employed. However, in the past two years a slackening in the demand for snowmobiles in particular had prompted large discounts in order to reduce inventories and free capital for boat operations. Repair and warranty work, accessory sales, and used boat sales made a substantial contribution to Flyte Craft's operations, though Williamson was not sure all of these different facets of the business were profitable.

THE CURRENT SITUATION

"We are at a turning point in Flyte Craft and I'm really not sure which way to move. We are in a lot of different businesses here and I seem to be in a position of either cutting back drastically so I can manage this thing effectively or expanding to the point where I can afford to add the equipment and people I need to insure profitable operations. I seem to be trapped either way. Cutting back to maintain the informal atmosphere that we have grown up with is certainly consistent with my personal objectives.

"But I'm convinced that it would just be a matter of time until the technology and the competition would pass us by, perhaps forcing Flyte Craft to get out of boat production. I have to trade that off against the enjoyment I get out of designing and building boats — going back to just retailing someone else's boats doesn't hold much interest either.

"A couple of months ago I spoke briefly to a government consultant who visited us as the result of a loan request we submitted to one of the government agencies. After spending some time here he was convinced that either we broaden our product line so we could get a larger share of our local market or get involved with a distribution system that would open much broader markets to our limited product line. Either way there are major implications for almost everything we do. I know we lack the management skills, financing, control, and marketing. Vaguely, I know what has to be done but I'm sure the bank manager will want a detailed plan that looks at the various ways Flyte Craft might develop and, frankly, I'm not really sure how to go about this task. We build a good boat; for the price and class, it's among the best available but the more I talk to various people about what happens next to Flyte Craft, the more I feel I will have to move away from my primary interests as a boat designer and builder and concentrate on management. On the other hand, I don't exactly relish the role of standing behind the counter taking orders for somebody else's boat."

Exhibit 1
Flyte Craft
Boat Shipments by Category

	1961	1963	1965	1967	1969
Unit Shipments					
Canoes	5163	4959	8260	9540	12389
Rowboats	2463	3951	2810	8845	8778
Sailboats	438	1810	6631	2561	2748
Outboards					
Aluminum	7591	10781	12540	15775	22772
Plastic	7057	7856	10141	11840	17422
Wood	4857	4832	2789	1099	599
Commercial	505	615	754	399	488
Cruisers & yachts	—	—	183	652	818
$000's Shipments					
Canoes	$ 597	$ 671	$1042	$1229	$ 1565
Rowboats	241	482	320	1305	1514
Sailboats	451	2218	3885	5251	8642
Outboards					
Aluminum	1675	2456	2626	3332	4593
Plastic	3910	5055	6289	7550	12027
Wood	2085	2324	1708	908	250
Commercial	3030	4501	2815	3355	4258
Cruisers & yachts	—	—	2321	4548	6726

Exhibit 2
Flyte Craft
Boats in Use by Material

Material	1963	1968	1973	1978 (projected)
Aluminum	22.3%	28.6%	33.0%	36.0%
Reinforced Plastic	19.4	31.3	40.0	46.0
Steel	2.7	2.6	2.0	2.0
Wood	50.7	34.7	22.0	12.0
Other	4.9	2.8	3.0	4.0

Exhibit 3
Flyte Craft
Age Distribution of Boating Participants

Age	North American Population	North American Boating Participants
Under 25	46.4%	10.5%
25-34	12.1	21.2
35-44	11.5	25.7
45-54	11.4	23.7
55-64	9.0	13.9
Over 65	9.6	5.0
	100.0%	100.0%

Exhibit 4
Flyte Craft
Income Distribution of Boating Participants (U.S.)

Household Income	Total	Boating Participants
Under $2 000	12.6%	2.0%
$2 000-$3 999	13.9	7.9
$4 000-$5 999	14.2	12.1
$6 000-$7 999	15.9	14.1
$8 000-$9 999	13.5	17.5
$10 000-$14 999	19.4	19.5
Over $15 000	10.5	26.9

Exhibit 5
Flyte Craft
Canadian Exports — Pleasure Craft U.S.

Year	$000's
1966	$ 3 400
1967	4 400
1968	7 300
1969	10 700
1970	11 000

Exhibit 6[1]
Flyte Craft
Flyte Craft Sales

Year	Sales Units	Boat Dollars	Other Equipment[2]	Total Sales	Profit (Loss)
1967	13	37 570	31 240	68 610	$ 2 120
1968	8	24 960	47 920	72 880	(4 680)
1969	21	68 040	81 600	149 640	4 489
1970	31	112 220	96 470	208 690	6 678
1971	35	138 985	105 980	244 965	8 328
1972	43	179 310	121 240	300 550	(2 322)
1973	41	178 824	146 312	325 136	13 005
1974	29	129 630	128 610	258 240	(11 247)

[1]Flyte Craft's books were audited in 1973. The auditors at that time also reviewed (and changed) the statements for the years 1967 on.

[2]Includes outboard motors, parts, boating equipment, snowmobiles, etc.

Exhibit 7
Flyte Craft Organization

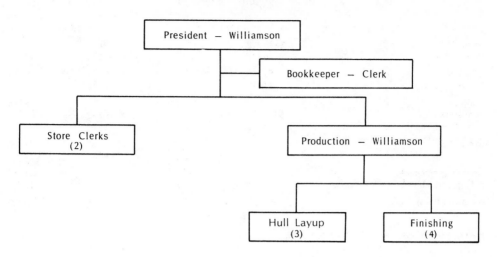

Exhibit 8
Layout — Flyte Craft Plant

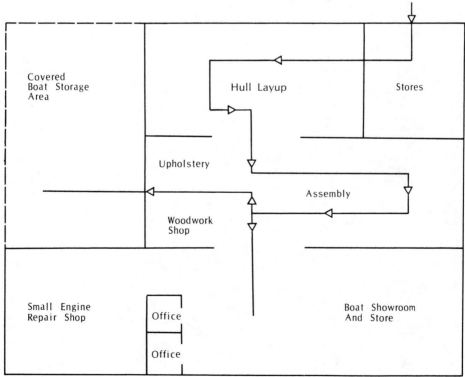

Exhibit 9
Flyte Craft
Profit and Loss Statements

	1973		1974	
Sales retail[1]	$146 312		$128 610	
Cost of goods	98 029		90 035	
Gross profit	$ 48 283		$ 38 575	
Direct expenses	31 279		32 590	
Contribution		$17 004		$ 5 985
Boat sales	$178 824		$129 630	
Cost of goods sold	141 343		112 778	
Gross profit		37 481		16 852
		$54 485		$22 837
Operating expenses		24 970		21 464
Selling and administrative expenses		16 510		12 620
Net profit (loss)		$13 005		$(11 247)

[1]Excludes sale of boats manufactured by Flyte Craft.

Exhibit 10
Flyte Craft
Balance Sheet

	1973		1974	
ASSETS — CURRENT				
Cash		$ 720		$ 659
Accounts receivable (net)		7 210		6 140
Due—Finance Co.		590		620
Inventories				
Materials	$14 710		$16 420	
Work in process	9 974		10 274	
Finished goods — boats	11 460		13 260	
— parts and motors	15 590	51 734	14 420	54 374
Prepaid and other		1 978		2 095
TOTAL CURRENT ASSETS		$ 62 232		$ 63 888
ASSETS — FIXED				
Land		14 290		14 290
Buildings	$54 790		$54 790	
Less: depreciation	21 916	32 874	24 655	30 135
Machinery and equipment	$31 724		$37 620	
Less: depreciation	18 710	13 014	21 165	16 455
Furniture and fixtures	$ 2 174		$ 2 490	
Less: depreciation	1 570	604	1 760	730
Other equipment	$ 7 129		$ 7 129	
Less: depreciation	3 610	3 519	4 410	2 719
Jigs, patterns, and moulds		35 460		35 460
Other assets		9 710		7 071
TOTAL ASSETS		$171 703		$170 748
LIABILITIES — CURRENT				
Accounts payable		$ 10 390		$ 13 970
Accrued expenses		5 610		6 170
Employees' tax and pension		705		812
Federal and provincial taxes		7 470		8 271
Notes — short term		19 110		20 270
Customer deposits		4 082		5 724
		$ 47 367		$ 55 217
LIABILITIES — LONG TERM				
Notes payable		$ 18 320		$ 21 700
Bank loan		14 910		16 316
Mortgages		31 844		29 500
		$ 65 074		$ 67 516
CAPITAL				
Preferred stock		12 000		12 000
Common stock		5 000		5 000
Retained earnings		42 262		31 015
TOTAL LIABILITIES AND CAPITAL		$171 703		$170 748

62

Kettle Creek Canvas Company

Melanie Stevens leaned back in her chair. It was May 1980. Melanie and her partner Jim Sorenti had several critical decisions to make regarding the future of their business, the Kettle Creek Canvas Company. Located in Port Stanley, Ontario, the firm manufactured and retailed brightly coloured canvas[1] garments and accessories.

The business had enjoyed enthusiastic consumer reaction in its first year, and as a result the partners had been approached by various persons regarding possible franchising and partnership agreements.

The partners were uncertain as to what method of expansion they should pursue and how it should be financed.

BACKGROUND

At the age of sixteen Melanie left school to begin working and travelling. She worked for bakeries, movie theatres, and various retail stores in and around the Port Stanley area but found them all uninteresting.

Melanie's interest was sparked, however, when one day a friend dropped by to show her a bed comforter she had purchased in Kitchener. Melanie knew the approximate materials cost of the comforter and was surprised at its high markup. Consequently, she began sewing comforters and selling them to friends and later to shops in the Port Stanley area.

Eventually, Melanie's work room (her apartment) became overly cramped with materials and she decided to rent some inexpensive space. The space she located happened to be near the Port Stanley docks and as a result she began to receive requests from sailors for all types of custom bags and garments. As the number of requests grew, Melanie began to see a large potential for her business and decided to open the Kettle Creek Canvas Company in Port Stanley.

In May 1979, Kettle Creek opened its doors with a labour force of one (Melanie) producing a limited number of canvas goods. Consumer response was favourable, and within four weeks the number of back orders necessitated a step-up in production.

Since the floor space was limited, cottage industry[2] was the quickest method of increasing the production. By September of 1979, sales had reached $15 000. Port Stanley is a summer tourist area. Therefore, a decision where to market for the fall and winter season had to be made. The London outlet was opened in November 1979 and achieved sales of $70 000 during its first six months. The store is illustrated in Exhibit 3.

Kettle Creek's first year's wholesale sales had been modest, but above budget at approximately $69 000 (See Exhibits 4, 5, and 6). With demand increasing rapidly,

---

[1] A closely woven cotton cloth available in several weights suitable for a wide variety of applications including clothing, rugs, and upholstery. Exhibit 1 illustrates the information attached by a tag to each canvas product, while Exhibit 2 illustrates the range of products.

[2] Precut garment pieces were picked up by local housewives who would sew them together in their own homes, thereby reducing the demand for floor space in Melanie's store.

Melanie's partner Jim estimated that with two more outlets, retail sales could exceed $600 000 in year two.

MARKETING

Melanie's designs were simple yet attractive. The bright solid colours were different and appealing to both men and women. The partners had very little additional information regarding their consumers. Prior to the opening of the London store, they hired a marketing consultant to estimate Kettle Creek's likely future sales volumes. He soon gave up, saying that because of the odd product mix, the firm could not be compared to any data on existing consumer or store groupings. The consultant did state that he had never seen products, or a product mix, quite like Kettle Creek's.

Melanie anticipated, however, that within the next year or two several larger manufacturers might begin to market their versions of the "simple" style.

PRODUCTION

Production of the garments was straightforward. Melanie simply ordered the canvas from the stock of a Toronto-based wholesaler. The canvas was laid out and cut in the cutting room. The individual pieces of a garment were matched and tagged with the name and size of the item. The pieces were then picked up by one of twenty-five local housewives who took them home and sewed them at her convenience. When the batch was completed the sewer returned the articles to be checked for quality. If the garments passed, an invoice from the sewer to Kettle Creek was filled out and paid on the spot.

Melanie and Jim were pleased with this arrangement and felt they could support $2 000 000 in retail sales without any changes. Good sewers seemed to be in ample supply. However at certain times of the year, the partners did have difficulty in maintaining a sufficient level of sewers. This occurred at canning time and just prior to Christmas, when a good number of the sewers were busy with family responsibilities. It had been suggested to Jim and Melanie that they consider opening their own sewing facilities. This would entail renting space, purchasing machinery and hiring sewers on an hourly basis. The partners were unsure of how their sewers would react to this plan. They had collected the information they felt necessary, however, they had not analyzed it. A three-year lease for factory space close to Kettle Creek's Port Stanley location could be obtained for $3.00 per square ft/yr (Exhibit 7). Melanie estimated heat, light, power, and other general factory overhead to be $200 per month.

She felt each sewer would require approximately 80 square feet of workspace. In addition, a general office for the foreman would be required as well as washrooms and an employee lunchroom. The partners estimated this additional space requirement at 300 square feet. A supervisor could be hired for $1200 per month while sewers would expect $4.00 per hour. Melanie estimated the average[1] number of garments produced per sewer per week would be 70 to 80 and the average retail[2] price of the garments she approximated at $25.00. Currently, the sewing machines were purchased by the

---

[1]Average figures were considered representative.
[2]Retail price = 2 x wholesale price = 4 x variable cost.
  Variable cost = 50% labour + 50% material.

sewers. However, the partners felt Kettle Creek would have to purchase the machines under the new proposal. The machines were available for $600 each.

THE FUTURE

Jim and Melanie felt they had hit upon a potential moneymaker but they realized it could be easily copied. They were anxious to fully exploit the situation while they had the upper hand. Melanie suggested that they might even be able to sell the firm in a few years and move on to something completely different.

The partners had narrowed the expansion options to:

1) Manufacture and Wholesale Only

They felt that this was a viable alternative. It would certainly cause less strain on their limited resources. They were concerned about control of how and where the products would be sold. Also the partners were not sure how important it was to establish the Kettle Creek name.

It was Melanie's feeling that her products became "lost" when displayed next to other types of casual clothes. She felt that if they wholesaled, the retailer would have to be encouraged to display Kettle Creek products in a separate display section. Ms. Stevens was concerned that, if sales were not up to a particular customer's expectations, that the line, rather than merchandising technique would be blamed. Melanie was unsure of how, or whether, this could be controlled.

2) Additional Retail Outlets

This alternative actually takes at least three forms:

a) More company-owned stores
b) Partnerships
c) Franchised outlets

Melanie estimated retail sales for the first full year in London to be $160 000 and for a downtown Toronto store $225 000. The cost of leasehold improvements for new stores were estimated at $10 000 each. Annual rent, wages, and miscellaneous expenses were projected to be $35 000 and $75 000 in London and Toronto respectively. The partners also felt a Vancouver location could be opened with costs and sales equivalent to Toronto's.

Melanie felt a one-time $20 000 set-up fee to a franchisee would be fair. The franchisee would then pay Kettle Creek $1 per year for the use of the name and would be required to purchase its merchandise from Melanie's firm.

Recently a well-to-do couple had also approached the partners, with the idea of a partnership. These new partners were prepared to pay Jim and Melanie $40 000 for 49 percent of the equity of a proposed new store in Toronto. The new partners would then manage and staff the new store. After speaking with the interested party, Melanie and Jim decided to drive down Yonge Street before heading back to London. Coincidently, a perfect location was available for lease in downtown Toronto! As they left the city, the two partners felt a sense of urgency.

To complicate matters even further, buyers from both Simpson's and Eaton's had approached Melanie to quote on volumes of clothing that were beyond her present capacity.

CONCLUSION

Melanie and Jim realized their decisions regarding expansion would be critical to the success of the business. They also realized that competition was growing and Kettle Creek would have to act quickly.

Exhibit 1
Kettle Creek Canvas Company

Port Stanley is a small fishing village situated where Kettle Creek meets Lake Erie.

All our garments and bags are handmade in homes in and around the village. We use 100% cotton canvas and duck woven in Canada. The colours are vat-dyed to insure colour fastness and we are proud of the high standard of quality our team puts into each garment and bag.

If however, our quality does not measure up to your expectations, return for repair, replacement, refund or credit.

If you are in our area drop by to see the home base, you'll love the village.

Washing Instructions:

To keep your canvas looking great for years, turn garments inside out and machine wash in cold water. Hang to dry or tumble dry on low setting. Coats should be drycleaned.

Turn bags inside out, put in a pillowcase and wash on gentle cycle. Hang to dry. Smaller bags should be stuffed with paper to avoid wrinkles. Don't use spot cleaners around tag since the dyes in the leather will run. The colour will not run but will "wear in." If this is not desirable, dryclean to maintain bright colours longest.

Thanks for your interest in "Kettle Creek."

Exhibit 2
Kettle Creek Products — Design Sketches

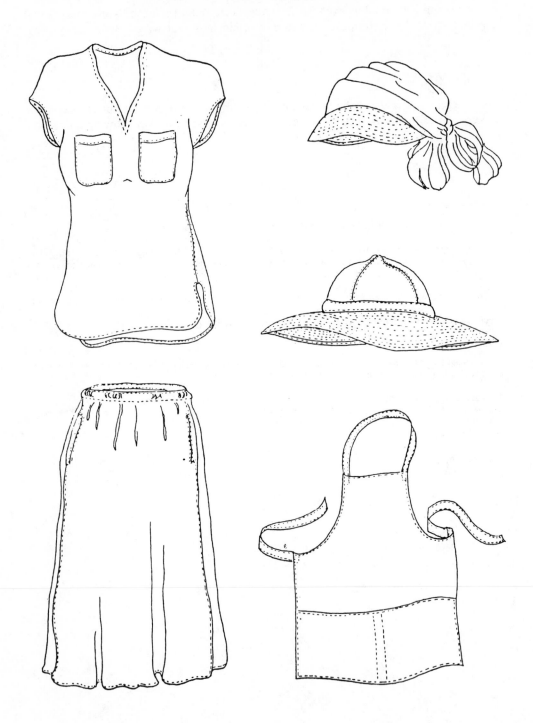

Exhibit 2 (cont'd)

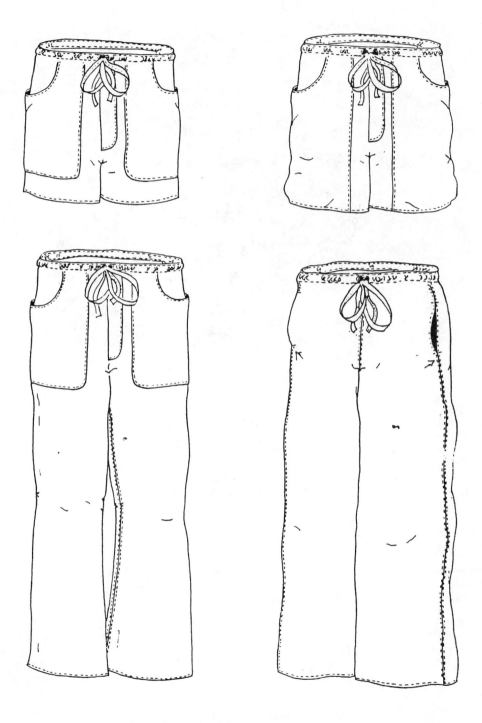

Exhibit 3
Kettle Creek Canvas Company
Illustration of London Store

Exhibit 4
Kettle Creek Canvas Company
(Wholesale Division)

Statement of Income
For the Year Ended April 30, 1980

Sales		69 000
Cost of goods sold		35 000
Gross profit		$33 500
Less: expenses		
Rent	$ 8 500	
Officers' salaries	14 300	
Office wages	10 000	
Other	2 500	
[1] Start-up expenses	10 000	45 300
EARNINGS (loss) for the period		($11 800)

[1]Non-recurring start-up expenses.

Exhibit 5
Kettle Creek Canvas Company

Balance Sheet
April 30, 1980

ASSETS

Current:

Cash	$ 100
Accounts receivable	11 100
Notes receivable[1]	700
Inventory	54 000
	$65 900

Fixed:

Machinery (net)	$ 3 400
Leasehold improvement (net)	3 000
	6 400

Other:

Note receivable	4 100

TOTAL ASSETS:	$76 400

LIABILITIES AND PROPRIETORY CAPITAL

Current:

Bank — Overdraft	$ 7 300
— Demand loan	24 100
Accounts payable	47 900
	$79 300

Proprietors capital (deficiency)	(2 900)

TOTAL LIABILITIES AND PROPRIETORS CAPITAL	$76 400

[1]Advance to shareholders.

Exhibit 6
Kettle Creek Canvas Company
(Retail Division)

Statement of Income
For the Year Ended April 30, 1980

	London (six months of operation)	Port Stanley (three months of operation)
Sales	$70 000	$20 000
Cost of goods sold	35 000	10 000
Gross profit	$35 000	$10 000
Less: operating expenses		
Rent	8 000	0
Wages	9 800	3 000
Leasehold improvements[1]	5 600	3 600
Earnings (loss)	$11 600	$ 3 400
Income tax	2 900	850
Net earnings (loss)	$ 8 700	$ 2 550

[1]Expenses completely in first year.

Exhibit 7
Kettle Creek Canvas Company

R.E. Dolan Realty Limited
Port Stanley, Ontario

October 19, 1981

Ms. Melanie Stevens
Kettle Creek Canvas Company
First Street
Port Stanley, Ontario

Dear Melanie:

Just a note to confirm our telephone conversation today. Mr. N. Loder, of Loder Developments, is willing to rent you any or all units of his new industrial mall (minimum space 1000 square feet per unit) in Port Stanley at a rate of $3.00 per square foot on a three year lease.

He is quite anxious to rent to you since you indicated that you might want two, three, or even four thousand square feet. This would be to his advantage since he would not have to put up dividing walls between a number of smaller tenants.

Further, he indicated that since he is embarking on a large housing development northeast of London, he would be willing to sign a lease at $2.75 per square foot on a five-year basis.

There is no doubt that he sees your firm as a desirable tenant causing less wear and tear on the premises. Considering that rental rates go up on renewal, I suggest that you go with the five-year lease.

Sincerely,

R.E. Dolan
RED:hh

63

Mill Lake YWCA (A)

In October of 1979, Helen Franklin, Executive Director of the Mill Lake YWCA, a volunteer organization, was pondering what recommendations she would make to the Board of Directors regarding the future direction of the Food Services branch. For the past three years, the service had either made small profits or incurred net losses which had to be subsidized from capital allocations and donations to the organization.

HISTORY OF THE MILL LAKE YWCA

The Mill Lake YWCA was founded in 1902, as a local chapter of the Young Women's Christian Association (YWCA). The philosophy of the YWCA stated that it was a volunteer organization of, by, and for women. It was part of a world-wide Christian membership movement which provided services and programs to the community.

At the outset, the Mill Lake YWCA's activities ranged from classes in sewing, English, French, Latin, and commercial subjects, to girls' club work, traveller's aid, and an unemployment bureau for girls and women.

During World War I, the YWCA conducted first-aid and home nursing courses. During the 1918 influenza epidemic, the association ran distribution and diet kitchen services.

The current building, which housed meeting rooms, a gym, a residence and a food service cafeteria, was opened in 1930. At that time, the membership raised the funds to both purchase the land and erect the building. When the building was opened, only $5000 of the original mortgage remained outstanding. The commitment and energy of these early members seemed to set a precedent for the future membership.

Over the years, the needs of the women in the community had evolved into some rather complex and challenging areas. In response, the Mill Lake YWCA had developed newer and more appropriate programs. During World War II, the YWCA focused on the following programs: physical fitness for school children and women in industry; rural recreation; and "Living After Victory." During 1945, the "Youth Movement" gained momentum, with emphasis on a Teen Canteen program and leadership courses for teens. In the 1970s, counselling both the financial and the emotional needs of the community became an important aspect of the YWCA's services.

MILL LAKE

Mill Lake was an old established railway town, with a population of 27 000. It was located about halfway between a university city of 250 000 and a small, older resort town. Many of Mill Lake's citizens were blue-collar workers, employed in one of the heavy industries which were located in the town. Many others worked at a nearby car manufacturing plant, which employed 1500 assembly workers.

The city was a very picturesque one, with many large, gracious, older homes in the areas close to downtown. There was, reportedly, a large group of elderly people, per capita, who were socially influential in the city. New suburban areas, with homes in the $40 000 to $60 000 range, seemed to be blossoming everywhere.

PROGRAMS AND SERVICES

The Mill Lake YWCA felt that one of its most important functions was to provide an emergency housing unit. Opened in 1976, this rented home was maintained, by the members, as a shelter for women in a crisis situation, who found it necessary to vacate their homes, at any hour of the night or day. Volunteer duty officers and, very often, the executive director of the YWCA, aided the new admissions to the emergency home in emotional areas, as well as giving them assistance to register for government financial and counselling aids. Since its inception in 1976, over 80 women and 150 children had used the emergency house. The average length of stay at the home was sixteen days, though residents could use the facility for a maximum of six weeks. The community of Mill Lake felt that the emergency house was an extremely important service in the community, and were pleased to give their financial support to the YWCA because of this service.

General programs were offered on a fee-for-enrolment basis. These programs ranged from preschool gymnastics to belly-dancing and tennis instruction.

In 1977, a Youth and Community Program was established which successfully involved hundreds of children in dances, floor hockey leagues, Saturday games days, volleyball, arts and crafts, and a leadership training program. An after-school program for core area children ran for one hour three times a week. There was no charge for this program in which the children could take part in arts and crafts or recreational activities. In the summer, special day camps and activities were organized for these same children.

The YWCA operated a twenty-six-bed residence for women. Staff were on the premises twenty-four hours a day, working closely with the residents and the agencies in the community; so the women residents were aware of the various social, religious, and employment resources within the community.

The Consumer Debt Counselling Service of the YWCA opened in 1976. One day, each week, a professional debt counsellor assisted people in the community, who were experiencing critical financial problems. Since the service opened, 147 people had benefited from this program.

In 1977, the YWCA opened a "Fitness Centre," which was furnished with modern exercise equipment and provided an opportunity for members to exercise on their own or with supervision. This facility housed a modern whirlpool and sauna. Adult members paid approximately $100 for a yearly membership to the Fitness Centre.

The YWCA provided services and accommodations to many groups and organizations within the community. Some service clubs used the building as their meeting place. Despite the fact that it was a yearly battle to seek funds for additions and improvements to various operations and programs, the Mill Lake YWCA was proud of the fact that its doors were always open to the community.

MANAGEMENT

In 1976, after many years of valuable membership in the YWCA, during which time she served on many committees including the Food Service Committee, Mrs. Helen Franklin was appointed to the position of Executive Director of Mill Lake YWCA. As a paid staff member, she was directly responsible to a board of twenty-four directors. The directors were volunteer women from the community, who were elected for a two-year term of office by the general members of the YWCA. The board relied heavily on information and advice from the executive director about the day-to-day operations and planning of the YWCA. Mrs. Franklin prepared monthly budgets for presentation to the board. There were approximately forty other paid staff members, who reported directly to the executive director. Of these, twelve people, including four kitchen staff, were employed on a full-time basis.

The Board of Directors made all of the policy decisions for the local YWCA, and had complete authority for the allocation and the use of funds. Board members chaired the various committees of the YWCA membership. There were committees for programs, for emergency housing, for food services, for investment purposes, for leadership development and for public relations. These committees reported directly to the board for approval of their future plans and directions. Bingos were held by the board members every Wednesday evening, and teen dances were sponsored every second week. These activities were meant to generate funds for the YWCA's operations.

FOOD SERVICES HISTORY

The dining-room was built when the building was erected in 1930. Its purpose, at that time, was mainly to provide a restaurant service to the community, in an effort to generate funds for the YWCA. Another goal of the food service was to make nutritious, low-cost meals available to that segment of the community on fixed and low incomes, while still making a profit. The same price was charged to all customers.

Since the YWCA pays no taxes, nor does it have to cover capital costs from revenue, it has considerable advantage in terms of pricing. These advantages enable the YWCA to achieve its goal of low-cost meals.

The early successes of the food services may be attributed to the lack of other food establishments in Mill Lake, at that time. The Mill Lake YWCA was located one-half block from the main downtown section of the city. This location was ideal for servicing the luncheon requirements of various business and professional people, retailers, and their employees who were located downtown.

As late as 1969, the food services was a very profitable operation. In that year, the service opened daily at 6:30 a.m. and closed at 8:00 p.m. Four women staffed the kitchen during these hours, six days a week, for a weekly salary of $50.00. Unfortunately, one of the staff members died on the job, and shortly after that, because of difficulties in finding a suitable replacement, things began to go downhill.

In 1974, the YWCA members held a capital campaign to raise $129 000, in order to update and renovate the existing building. In three months, the members raised $145 000 from major firms and foundations. Forty thousand dollars was allocated to the food services. With this money, the members purchased new equipment, including steam tables, dishwashers, chairs, paintings, and drapes. The dining-room was closed for three months in 1975 in order to complete the renovations.

When the dining-room reopened with the same staff, the same style, and the same philosophy of service, it was a dismal failure. During the time of the renovations, alternative restaurants had opened in the city. Members believed that a popular hamburg chain and several new pizza parlour entries to the community had captured, and kept, a lot of the YWCA's former customers. On top of these problems, a key kitchen-staff member took an extended leave because of illness and nervous problems.

In 1975, because of the loss of the key staff member, the food service was closed daily at 2:00 p.m. The dining-room was reopened in the evenings, by request only, for special events. In the same year, the YWCA suffered a $24 000 deficit in operating revenues. The executive director, who failed to provide budgets to the board, and who was rumoured to have a drinking and memory problem, was fired in 1975.

When Mrs. Franklin was hired in January of 1976, one of her first duties was to fire the food services supervisor, who was unable to account for his food inventory purchases within the kitchen. She also formally set the hours of operation to be 6:30 a.m. to 2:00 p.m.

THE COMPETITION

Many restaurants and take-out services were located in downtown Mill Lake. These establishments offered a wide variety of foods, varying from pizza to fresh fish. Some restaurants offered a wide variety of foods within their own menu. Four such establishments were located within a four-block radius of the YWCA. None of the YWCA's competitors had a high-priced image, nor did they have any distinct advantage in terms of atmosphere, reputation, or quality of food. Most were open from 9:00 a.m. to midnight.

Because of the liquor licensing, some food outlets may have offered an advantage over the YWCA's menu. Otherwise, most of the competitive restaurants in Mill Lake were closer to the YWCA's target market, and more visible, by virtue of their location, on the main street of Mill Lake.

Three newer fast-food outlets which catered to "family" dining were located together nearer the industrial segment of the city, about one mile from the YWCA, at the opposite end of the main street. These establishments were advertised nationally on television. One in particular, campaigned heavily for breakfast trade.

FOOD SERVICES 1979

The dining-room was bright and clean. It was decorated with yellow arborite tables and gold-cushioned chrome chairs, offset by mauve drapes and multi-coloured carpeting. Windows were plentiful, and the dining-room had its own outside entrance. The service was run in cafeteria style. Patrons travelled the length of the steam table to make their selections, then carried their trays to a table, if one was available. Seating capacity was about 35 persons. Fortunately, the dining-room opened onto a large meeting room with several large boardroom style tables and chairs. When it was available, this meeting room was opened to the cafeteria clients, in order to handle the overflow. There were about twenty chairs arranged around a boardroom table in this room.

Often, various groups and organizations held their luncheon meetings in the YWCA cafeteria. These groups travelled through the cafeteria line with the other daily clients, and then took their trays to either the adjacent meeting room, or another room upstairs. No charge was solicited from these groups for the meeting rooms.

A survey of the cafeteria customers was conducted in the spring of 1979. It indicated that the patrons enjoyed the "home-like" menu, the friendly staff and the atmosphere. Results of this survey are shown in Exhibit 2.

One main course was offered each day, In addition, customers could choose soups, juices, small salads, sandwiches and pastry desserts. The YWCA cafeteria was famous in Mill Lake for its delicious pastries. Pies could be purchased, by special order, by anyone in the community. A small amount of catering was done in the evenings for special groups or events.

Mrs. Franklin was extremely proud of the high-quality ingredients in the cafeteria meals. Although the range of menu was limited, the main course was changed daily, and consisted of the highest quality and freshest ingredients. The chief kitchen worker planned the daily menu on the basis of the availability of raw materials, the seasonality of various foods, and her expertise in preparation. Mrs. Franklin's only concern regarding the food preparation was that there seemed to be no way to keep account of the costs of the various menu items. She expected variations in costs of purchases due to the seasonality of fresh produce and the other variances inherent in grocery purchases. Despite Mrs. Franklin's careful attention to costs, she believed that she was disadvantaged due to small volume purchases. Nevertheless, she believed that some control over the ingredients of the various menu items would help her to appropriately price the cafeteria's products.

Most customers used the facility during the lunch hour (12:00 a.m. to 2:00 p.m.). Although it was open for the breakfast trade, the cafeteria served only about five or six people per day at these hours. On any one day, customers could be found behind the steam table, or in the kitchen, making their own sandwiches, or looking for an item that was not on the menu. The kitchen worker who served the hot meals was inclined toward giving larger pieces of meat to customers who (in her estimation) looked particularly thin. She inquired about everyone's health and generally added to the "home-like" atmosphere.

The executive director indicated that 15 000 meals, including meal tickets and transient meals (see Exhibit 1) were sold by the kitchen yearly. The majority of these sales were to employees and business people from downtown Mill Lake.

THE FOOD SERVICES COMMITTEE

In an effort to revive the profitability of the dining-room, the committee for food services had conducted a survey of its customers (Exhibit 2), and had solicited some estimates for cosmetic changes to the service.

A local decorator had submitted a bid of $3000 to revamp the dining-room and the adjacent meeting room with some wicker accessories, tables, and chairs.

The survey had indicated that about 20 to 25 percent of the patrons would purchase liquor with their meals if it were available. It was estimated that $4000 would be required, to build washroom facilities close to the dining-room. It would be necessary to install these facilities before the government would authorize a liquor license. Otherwise, the facility met all government standards.

If wine and beer were sold, their prices to the cafeteria client would be $1.25 and $.90 respectively. The gross margin on the wine and beer sales would be 50 percent.

A restaurant consultant from a nearby college was asked to visit the Mill Lake YWCA to make some suggestions for improvements. The consultant's recommendations and her suggested sample menu are shown in Exhibit 3.

Mrs. Franklin estimated that, in any event, one additional staff member should be hired for the kitchen, in order to relieve the already overwhelming workload.

A salad bar facility could be installed for $2000. Various other small items, such as new glasses and cutlery, could be purchased for approximately $1500.

About $12 000 was available, from capital funds in 1980, for the food services. This money would come from the same sources of funds that the YWCA had traditionally used.

Contemplating the situation, Mrs. Franklin wondered if they had lost sight of the organization's goals.

"We're a 'Y', not McDonald's. If there are people in Mill Lake who need subsidized meals, then it's a soup kitchen we should be running. Or perhaps it would be best just to close the food operation and channel our energies into those programs we do so well. One concern with closing, though, is what would we do with the kitchen facilities?"

FUNDING

Through bequests and endowments from the estates of Mill Lake citizens, the YWCA had acquired a surplus of $120 000 of principal funds during the 1970s. Many of the donors had eaten regularly at the food services. Many of the members believed that this contact with the YWCA food services had been the motivating force behind the donors' decisions to will monies to the YWCA.

The $120 000 of capital from the bequests was invested and generated about $10 000 or $12 000 of interest yearly. The current board had decided that the $120 000 would remain intact, to be invested in perpetuity. The yearly interest could be used only for capital acquisitions, like renovations to the YWCA building (including Food Services), or the emergency housing unit. In 1979, the YWCA had applied for, and received, $29 000 from the United Way for operating expenses. In addition, the trustees of a local foundation had given the YWCA $5200. Of this money, $4000 was to be used for food services.

THE DECISION

Mrs. Franklin was faced with the decision of what she should recommend to the Board of Directors to revive the profitability of the food services. She knew the Board believed that the dining-room should generate much-needed operating funds which could be used to subsidize other programs and services. She felt the results of the survey suggested several possible courses, but she was not sure which ones, if any, would be viable. Mrs. Franklin also believed that the food services could realize a greater volume of trade if some advertising was done, but she was not sure what form this would take or how much should be spent. One of the senior board members had reservations about the advisability of introducing wine and beer into the dining-room services.

Mrs. Franklin was asked, by the board, to submit final proposals for changes to the Food Services, its operations and its philosophy, at the November meeting. The board, on the advice of Mrs. Franklin, wished to implement any new strategies early in 1980.

Exhibit 1
Mill Lake YWCA (A)
Income Statements of Food Services
for Years Ended December 31, 1975–1979

	1979	1978	1977	1976	1975
Meal tickets[1]	$ 1400	$ 3319	$ 5140	$ 1785	$ 2299
Transient meals[2]	38399	34860	32040	24612	21119
Catering[3]	5194	5406	6643	5386	4218
Total Sales	$44993	$43585	$43823	$31783	$27636
Plus: restricted contribution					1103
Less: food purchases	20130	19574	17383	11134	11726
Gross profit	$24863	$24011	$26440	$20649	$17013
Other Expenses					
Wages & salaries	$20047	$21402	$20623	$15415	$15246
Employment benefits	929	1056	825	655	506
Office expenses	206	248	211	172	155
Building general expenses	1120	984	859	599	532
Utilities[4]	2145	1920	1922	1556	1314
Gas	302	285	236	166	154
Equipment	223	450	545	566	267
Advertising	—	90	88	133	166
Miscellaneous	14	14	5	5	—
Total expenses	24986	26449	25314	19267	18340
Net funds available (required)	($123)	($2438)	$ 1126	$ 1382	($ 1327)

[1]Meal tickets were sold to residents in the YWCA.
[2]Meals sold to the general public.
[3]Catering to special events.
[4]Allocated as a percent of total charges to the entire building.

Exhibit 2
Mill Lake YWCA (A)

DINING ROOM SURVEY RESULTS

The following are the compiled results of the Food Services Questionnaire.

There were a total of 226 questionnaires given out during the week of April 30 to May 4. Many people did not answer all of the questions; therefore the totals are sometimes less than 226.

Question 1. How often do you come to eat?

a) infrequently	78 (35%)
b) monthly	23 (10%)
c) weekly	77 (35%)
d) Monday–Friday	39 (18%)
e) other	4 (2%)

Question 2. How long have you been coming?

a) over a year	198 (88%)
b) less than a year	28 (12%)

Question 3. How did you find out?

a) advertising	9 (4%)
b) word-of-mouth	170 (77%)
c) other	41 (19%)

(these could be classified as word-of-mouth)

Question 4. Why do you come here?

a) prices	115 (23%)
b) food	174 (35%)
c) service	114 (23%)
d) location	140 (28%)
e) atmosphere	81 (16%)
f) other	12 (2%)

(most of these could be service and location)

Question 5. How do you find the prices?

a) low	9 (4%)
b) reasonable	194 (92%)
c) high	8 (4%)

Question 6. What do you most frequently choose to eat?

a) hot meal	96 (21%)
b) soup	86 (19%)
c) sandwich	72 (16%)
d) salad plate	84 (19%)
e) hot dog	24 (5%)
f) dessert	85 (19%)

Question 7. What do you least likely choose?

a) hot meal	68 (33%)
b) soup	17 (8%)
c) sandwich	14 (7%)
d) salad plate	21 (10%)
e) hot dog	60 (29%)
f) dessert	27 (13%)

Question 8. Which of the following items would you choose if menu were to change?

a) open-face sandwich	67 (12%)
b) smoked meat sandwiches	22 (4%)
c) crusty roll rye bread sandwiches	113 (21%)
d) salad bar	162 (30%)
e) egg and cheese dishes	74 (13%)
f) crepes	15 (3%)
g) french fries	44 (8%)
h) hamburgers	52 (9%)

Question 9. Do you usually eat dessert?

yes	111 (51%)
no	105 (49%)

Question 10. Would you buy beer or wine with lunch?

yes	45 (21%)
no	170 (79%)

Exhibit 2 (continued)

Question 11. Would you patronize a "take-out" service?

yes	97 (47%)
no	111 (53%)

Question 12. Would you use the dining-room if it were open at other times?

yes	105 (49%)
no	109 (51%)

Question 13. Would you prefer service other than cafeteria?

yes	17 (8%)
no	190 (92%)

Question 14. Do you know about the catering at the YWCA?

yes	153 (72%)
no	60 (28%)

Question 15. Would you use the catering service?

yes	129 (65%)
no	70 (35%)

Question 16.

Comment on what you like about our dining-room, how it could be improved.

There were many favourable responses to this question. We have categorized verbatim responses under "What They Like' and "Suggestions for Change".

What They Like

— the ladies in charge could not be more helpful or kinder (10)
— ladies very careful — nothing is too much trouble
— best in Mill Lake
— everything fine. Food is superb!
— waitresses are so clean looking, pleasant and obliging
— best food I ever ate

— don't know why I don't come here every day!
— we live in Chatham and prefer to eat here when possible
— secret to pie pastry, I seldom go anywhere else
— quality of food is first rate
— food super — staff great — only complaint is I can't use sauna (male postal worker)
— I won't come back if you change it (!)

Suggestions for Change

— more diet foods
— sandwich fillings skimpy
— no smoking area in dining room
— open Thursday and Friday evenings
— more advertising (4)
— separate salads and sandwiches from hot meals
— floater to serve second cup of coffee
— tablecloths and nicer decor
— bumsteads
— re-allocate empty (3) tray cart somewhere else
— put trays and silverware at other end of line-up
— have fresh fruit
— music
— "topless waitresses"
— show "soup of day" on menu

— post next day's menu
— box take-out lunches
— skim milk
— leave green room free at lunch time
— erect a height extension to reduce draft at entrance
— serve earlier than 11:30 a.m.
— more cooks in kitchen
— not so much packaged jams, jellies, sugars — takes away from "home style"
— not well known to, a) people who shop nearby, b) general public, c) male population
— build a porch to eliminate 10 X 10 entrance — more space

Exhibit 3
Mill Lake YWCA (A)
Restaurant Consultant's Recommendations

November 9, 1979.

Dear Mrs. Franklin:

After our meeting on Tuesday, I discussed your situation with my colleague, Mat Morrow. We talked at great length and the following is the result of our conversation.

I have listed what I feel to be your major areas of concern: 1) renovating costs of establishing dining area. 2) additional labour costs involved. 3) adapting existing staff to handle extra load. 4) operation of dining room as a dinner outlet. Other areas of concern are access to dining area, traffic flow, and a connection between yourself and the labour market.

In the case of setting up your dining room, acquiring prices, examining different cosmetic features, chinaware, cutlery, stemware, etc, I believe you have already contacted someone to handle this for you. If you have not, may I suggest that you contact one of the following agencies: R. Foods, Restaurant Equipment and Supply Co., or Western Ontario Food Equipment. All three are listed in the directory. Explain to these people what you would like to see and they will be able to supply you with the costs of equipment suitable to your needs. They will also provide blueprints (which you will be needing), included in their fee as part of the contract. They will help you to decide how to solve your traffic flow problems as well as gaining easy access to the area.

Your existing kitchen staff should be able to adapt to the new facilities, if the menu that you now present in the cafeteria could be incorporated into the new menu. For example, I would suggest starting off by featuring a set lunch, such as roast beef in the dining room, then leftover beef could be used for salads or sandwiches the following day in the cafeteria. Doing so would eliminiate the risk of a large food cost percentage, and save on hiring new people, as I am sure your current staff could handle such preparations. If the volume of the restaurant were to grow immensely, the problem would not exist, as income would justify hiring additional staff.

Of course the hiring of waitresses or waiters is essential to your dining room. Shaw College in Toronto offers a fifteen-week course through Canada Manpower, training people to become competent dining-room service personnel. It might be possible to hire these people upon graduation.

To operate the room as a dinner outlet separate from the cafeteria, hire one competent cook. You should be able to hire someone at approximately $4.50 per hour. Devise a simple yet attractive menu using items that can be prepared to order until business establishes a pattern. If this person is not able to handle such a menu, I might be able to assist you at a nominal fee.

If you require further help, a professional consultant will range from $250 to $450 per day. If you are interested in hiring a consultant, may I suggest calling Barry Bird, the coordinator of the Hotel/Restaurant Management Program at Shaw College. He will refer you to someone who can be of use to you.

Sincerely,

B. E. Fin

Exhibit 3 (continued)

Sample Menu

Item	**Comments**
Appetizers:	
Soup du Jour	French onion, cream of tomato, etc., whatever is being served in the cafeteria.
Artichoke Hearts Vinaigrette	Very little spoilage or waste.
Fresh Fruit Cocktail	Very simple to prepare and can be used in cafeteria.
Individual Caesar Salad	Easy to assemble, elegant.
Main Course:	
Roast top Sirloin au Jus	Easy to prepare, meat can be used following day.
Shish-Kebob à la Y.W.C.A.	Again easy to prepare and would use same type of beef as roast sirloin.
Pork Chops Avesnoise	Beautiful method of preparing chops — topped with a mixture of cream, cheese, and dijon mustard.
Breast of Chicken Cordon Bleu	Boneless breast of chicken stuffed with ham and cheese.
Reuben Sandwich	Rye bread with corned beef, sauerkraut, and Swiss cheese.
Monte Cristo Sandwich	Three-decker with ham and cheese and dijon mustard, dipped in egg and fried.

Main courses served with fresh seasonal vegetable and potato.

Desserts:

Corresponding to cafeteria

Lemon Meringue Pie
Banana Cream Pie
Apple Pie
Peach Melba — Half a peach on top of a scoop of ice cream with melba sauce.

Fresh pot of coffee or tea.

Exhibit 4
Mill Lake YWCA
Vertical Analysis

	1979	1978	1977	1976	1975
	(%)	(%)	(%)	(%)	(%)
Meal tickets	3.2	7.6	11.7	5.6	8.3
Transient meals	85.3	80	73	77.4	76.4
Catering	11.4	12.4	15.2	17	15.2
Total sales	100	100	100	100	100
Restricted contribution	—	—	—	—	4
Food purchases	44.7	44.9	39.7	35	42.4
Gross profit	55.3	55.1	60.3	65	57.6
Other Expenses					
Wages & salaries	44.6	49.1	47.0	48.5	55.2
Employment benefits	2.1	2.4	1.9	2.1	1.8
Office expenses	0.5	0.6	0.5	0.5	0.6
Building general expenses	2.5	2.3	2.0	1.9	1.9
Utilities	4.8	4.4	4.4	4.9	4.8
Gas	0.7	0.7	0.5	0.5	0.6
Equipment	0.5	1.0	1.2	1.8	1.0
Advertising	—	0.2	0.2	0.4	0.6
Miscellaneous	—	—	—	—	—
Total expenses	55.5	60.6	57.7	60.6	66.4
Net funds available (required)	(0.2)	(5.5)	2.6	4.4	(4.8)

Growth Ratios	1978–79	1977–78	1976–77	1975–76	
Sales					
Meal tickets	(57.8)	(35)	188	(22.3)	
Transient meals	10.1	8.8	30	16.5	
Catering	(3.9)	(18.6)	23.3	27.6	
Liquidity					
*Age of receivables	1	1	1	2	2
Age of payables	29	30	33	31	28
Age of inventory	7	5	6	8	7

*Note: All sales, except catering, were on a cash basis. Detail may not add to total because of rounding.

64

The Old Bridge Inn

One day in October 1981 Tim Agnew, fourth-year business student at the University of Western Ontario, approached his friend and fellow classmate Tom Bauer with a problem. The Inn which Tim's mother owned and operated in Young's Point, Ontario, had encountered financial difficulties. Cash reserves had dwindled to zero. Creditors, including the federal government, had threatened to place a lien on the premises if payments were not met. At the same time Mrs. Agnew had just taken ill, and was unable to deal properly with the situation. As a result, Tim decided to leave school in order to run the business. He wondered if Tom might have any suggestions as to how the Inn's operations should be managed.

On the first weekend in November Tom set out from London for Young's Point, which is located 20 kilometres northeast of the city of Peterborough (see Exhibit 1). While the initial drive along Highway 401 was rather uninteresting, the scenery soon improved as Tom turned north onto Highway 115 outside Port Hope. After a 45-minute drive Tom saw a weather-beaten sign indicating that his destination was near. Almost before he realized it, Tom drove through Young's Point and found himself in the country again. There was no sign of the Inn. Remembering Tim's description of the Inn as lying beside the Trent–Severn canal system, Tom retraced his route. Near the point where the highway crossed the Otonabee River he saw, buried among a myriad of nameplates, a tiny sign for the Old Bridge Inn. Following the sign to the end of a short, dead-end road Tom found himself in front of a large two-storey red-brick building. On the roof of the building stood a relatively small, simple sign stating: Old Bridge Inn.

Tom pulled his car into the empty parking lot adjacent to the building, got out, and approached the front door. The curtains were drawn and inside there appeared to be no sign of life. Tom pulled on the door and found, much to his surprise, that it was open. He walked in, his eyes trying to accustom themselves to the darkness. "Good afternoon, can I help you?" a voice asked from the back. It belonged to Mary, the 21-year-old cook. After explaining the purpose of his visit Tom was shown upstairs, where he found Tim.

HISTORY OF THE INN

Tim provided Tom with a brief background of the Inn. The main support beam dated back to 1887. The Inn had originally been built as a general store/roadhouse at the junction of the Otonabee River and the old Highway 28. Its clientele was composed mainly of loggers and raftsmen. Initially business flourished, but as Highway 28 was expanded and moved 50 metres to the west in 1940 business dropped off. The original bridge beside which the Inn stands is now closed to vehicular traffic and open only to pedestrians.

With the decline in business the Inn fell into a state of disrepair. It changed ownership several times, being used exclusively as a private residence. In 1955 the Inn was bought by Mr. Russ Brooks. He obtained a liquor license, hired a honky-tonk piano player, and turned the Inn into a local drinking establishment. Tim summed up the Inn's previous reputation as being a "booze-it-up joint." Although ownership of the Inn changed hands four times within the Brooks family, its operations remained essentially unchanged. Throughout this period the Inn had a record of consistent, though minimal, earnings losses.

AGNEW FAMILY INVOLVEMENT

In August of 1980 the Old Bridge Inn was purchased by Mrs. Annabelle Agnew. Mrs. Agnew, a widow for ten years, had been left a sizeable inheritance by her late husband. With her sons no longer living at home, Mrs. Agnew decided that she wished to try her hand at running a business. While visiting a real estate agent one day in her hometown of Toronto she saw a picture of the Inn, and immediately fell in love with it. Although she had no previous experience in the restaurant business, Mrs. Agnew had taken several Cordon Bleu cooking courses. She decided that the Inn presented a perfect opportunity to combine business with her love of cooking. As a result, a purchase agreement was drawn up in which ownership was transferred to Mrs. Agnew at a "distress price" of $75 000. A further $15 000 was invested to restore the Inn to its current condition.

DIFFICULTIES FACING THE INN

Although Mrs. Agnew had been able to increase gross sales from $10 000 to over $90 000, the Inn was still faced with financial difficulties (see Exhibit 2). The Inn had narrowly succeeded in paying off its overdue accounts, and its cash reserves were now nonexistent (see Exhibit 3). Mrs. Agnew was hoping to find a new buyer for the Inn, but sale of the Inn before the turn of the new year seemed highly unlikely. In order for the Inn to survive that long a positive cash flow was badly needed. The cash flow problem was aggravated by the fact that most of the Inn's revenues were generated by tourists during the summer season (see Exhibits 4 and 5).

While cash flow was the Inn's most pressing concern, profitability in the past had been hurt by a high level of operating expenses. Tim had taken several steps to reduce these expenses. Cost of food sold had been reduced drastically by arranging for weekly delivery from a large Ontario meat processing firm rather than buying at retail from a local supermarket. Renegotiation of the Inn's first mortgage at 14 percent through a Small Business Development Bond from a chartered bank would save an additional $2 450 annually. Tim also felt that the Inn's wage expenses were too high, though he was unsure how they might be reduced.

THE INN'S UPSTAIRS

Having explained the history of the Inn and the current difficulties facing it, Tim decided to give Tom a tour of the premises. They started off by viewing the second floor. This level consisted of two unattached sections, each accessible via its own staircase (see Exhibit 6). The larger section consisted of eight single rooms and two bathrooms. Five of the eight rooms were currently inhabited by Mrs. Agnew, Tim, and their great dane Abraham. The remaining three rooms were used to store various articles.

The smaller upstairs section, consisting of four rooms and a bathroom, was available for rent on a nightly basis. Each room was simply furnished, and contained a mirror and washbasin. Three of the four rooms held double beds, while the fourth held two single beds. The nightly charge per room was $18. Income derived from the rental of rooms accounted for almost all that listed under "Other Revenue" in the operating statements.

KITCHEN OPERATIONS

The next stop on the tour was the kitchen (see Exhibit 7). The kitchen area had been built onto the Inn in 1955. A long wood-topped counter ran down the middle of the kitchen, making maneuvering rather cumbersome. One side of the kitchen was lined with a counter containing a household dishwasher; three sinks; two ovens, one with six ranges, the other with a heating plate; a microwave oven; and a deep freezer. The other wall of the kitchen was occupied by three large old refrigerators, and shelves containing numerous memorabilia from the Agnew family past.

An outline of typical operations was obtained through discussion with Mary, the cook. The initial part of the day was spent on the preparation of food items prior to cooking. Such preparation was carried out on an ongoing basis from 10:00 a.m. until early evening. It was interrupted frequently as customer orders for meals were received.

Further discussion revealed the existence of several recurring problems which had been encountered in the past. A major concern was the limited cooking capacity. The two stove/ovens combined were only able to heat a maximum of twelve plates at any given time. The microwave oven presented an even greater bottleneck. It was only able to accommodate five individual servings of vegetables. Cycle time for the microwave was approximately three minutes, compared to five minutes for the oven. During banquets or the peak summer period, when up to seventy people might be eating dinner at the same time, this lack of capacity became a definite problem. Maintaining enough clean dishes and glasses to serve customers also became a problem during busy periods, since the household dishwasher had a cycle time of 45 minutes. To help alleviate this problem a student was sometimes hired to wash dishes by hand.

Another problem mentioned was the lack of space in the kitchen. In the summer the kitchen was often staffed with five people: Mrs. Agnew acting as head cook, Mary as assistant cook, two kitchen helpers, and a dishwasher. In addition, waitresses would constantly walk in and out of the kitchen to place/pick up orders. As a result it was "near impossible to make it from one end of the kitchen to the other without knocking someone or something over."

THE DINING AREA

The scene which he had just heard described contrasted sharply with the calm Tom found as he entered the dining area. Although it was 6:00 pm on a Saturday evening, there were only four couples in both dining rooms. Tom sat down at the polished wood bar and ordered a drink from the bartender Karen. He chuckled to himself as he tried to picture what a group of fishermen in hip-waders would look like amidst the dark oak beams, Tiffany lamps, and spotless silverware. Apparently, hobby fishermen frequently walked over to the Inn from the nearby locks during the summer months, but few actually stayed for a drink or a meal after looking in the door.

A piano standing in one corner of the front dining room caught Tom's attention and he enquired if it was ever used. Karen replied that during the summer the Inn had a policy of providing live entertainment every Friday and Saturday evening. A singer/songwriter from the Peterborough musicians union was usually hired at a cost of $150 per weekend. Most of the performers played middle-of-the-road pop, though the Inn's most popular performers had been a country and western duet. Advertisements in the local newspapers and radio were used to notify the public of upcoming entertainers.

Through further discussion with Karen, Tom discovered that the low turnout was a common occurrence in the off-season. In fact the Inn often closed its doors early due to a lack of customers. The Inn's mainstay patrons during the winter season fell into three groups: young couples, families, and senior citizens. Of these, the latter group seemed to represent the only steady repeat customers. Most customers lived outside a 10 km radius from the Inn. When asked why this was so Karen conceded that the Inn had earned a bad reputation among the local populace. Most disliked the high-class image which the Inn conveyed. Comments such as: "The prices are too high," "I can't relax here," "Why don't you get rid of this silver and get some brighter tablecloths!" were typical of the local sentiment.

In addition, there were unflattering comments about the level of service, especially during the summer. One local banquet group was so upset by the slow service that its members had vowed never to return to the Inn. Word of such incidents spread quickly throughout the community, and as a result Karen felt that the Inn would have to work hard in order to regain the confidence and business of the local population.

By this time Tom was getting rather hungry, and as a result, Tim's offer of a complimentary meal was gratefully accepted. While glancing over the handwritten menu (see Exhibit 8) and wine list, Tom mentioned the several points which Karen had raised previously. Tim agreed that the Inn did not have a strong local draw. He felt that its current operations were targeted at the middle and upper income groups living in the Peterborough area (see Exhibit 9). The problem of poor service was probably the combined result of limited cooking capacity and inexperienced waitresses. Hiring waitresses with the desired level of experience from the local labour pool had proven to be difficult in the past.

With the arrival of the meal the conversation broke off. Tom had ordered the soup of the day to start off his meal. The first spoonful of piping hot broth convinced him that the soup was definitely home-made. The main course turned out to be as pleasant a surprise as the appetizer. The seafood creole was warm, the vegetables crisp, and the potatoes plentiful. With the mention of dessert Tom started to eye his waistline. However, within no time at all he found himself ordering a second serving of a freshly baked pumpkin pie.

As Tim and Tom contemplated the day's progress over a second complimentary bottle of wine, their thoughts were interrupted by a vocal uprising from the side dining room. A table of four middle-aged customers was demanding that the waitress bring over Mrs. Agnew and the dog Abraham. Tim walked over to the table and explained that Mrs. Agnew was sick and upstairs lying in bed. However the group persisted with their demand until Tim grudgingly went upstairs to call his mother and the dog. Upon Tim's return Tom eagerly inquired as to the nature of the problem. "No problem at all," replied Tim, "It's just a bunch of my mother's friends who get upset if they don't see her and the dog whenever they come here."

THE PATIO

With the completion of the bottle of wine Tim and Tom got up to finish their tour of the Inn. All that remained was the patio. Although it was dark outside floodlights helped to illuminate the patio area. The patio was a recent addition to the Inn, having been set up by Tim the previous summer. Cedar tables and benches had been handbuilt by a local craftsman. The maximum number of customers allowed on the patio under the liquor license was 66 people.

During the summer the patio had been open every day from noon until 11:00 p.m. A portable bar had been set up outside. An additional bartender had been hired to take orders and serve both food and drinks. Four large vats filled with ice served to keep the drinks cold. A self-serve barbeque was set up for customers wishing to grill hamburgers, etc. Other items could be ordered via the bartender from the kitchen. These items were typically similar to those offered on the luncheon menu. No full course meals were offered outside. A small speaker system hooked into the main system indoors broadcast music or live performances from inside when they occurred.

Although the patio had been moderately successful, Tim felt that the Inn had not taken full advantage of the potential which it offered. Tim thought that most of the people using the patio were customers who were waiting for an empty table inside so that they could eat a full dinner. Tim also thought that the live entertainment offered on weekends in the front dining room served to draw customers from the patio to inside. As a result, the level of patio sales usually dropped abruptly after 9:00 p.m.

Having completed the rather lengthy tour of the Inn, Tim suggested that Tom might want to take a look at the operations of the Chemong Lodge. The Lodge was an operation similar to the Inn located 14 km away in Bridgenorth. En route to Bridgenorth the two decided to stop off at the Commercial Hotel, the local watering hole. The Commercial was typical of most small-town bars — loud, crowded, and unpretentious, with entertainment provided by a guitar player dressed in cowboy attire. After a lively discussion with Fred, an elderly regular who also frequented the Inn, Tom and Tim continued on their way.

The Chemong Lodge was an interconnected network of log cabins built by its owner, with approximately twice the seating capacity of the Old Bridge Inn. Items offered on the menu were typically of the surf-'n'-turf variety, with entrees priced about $2 higher than the Inn's. At the time of the visit the Lodge was slightly over one quarter full. Most of the customers were well-dressed couples in their late twenties or early thirties. By eavesdropping on various conversations Tim and Tom established that most of the customers were from Peterborough. After several more drinks Tom decided that it might be wise to drive back to the Inn.

The next day Tom enquired about the Inn's advertising policy. Tim retrieved copies of newspaper advertisements which had been placed in the Peterborough Examiner and the local Kawartha Sun (see Exhibit 10 for examples). Tom was unable to determine the exact frequency with which advertisements were placed as the Inn did not have a formal expenditure control system. He estimated that a daily listing in the Peterborough Examiner at a cost of $42 and a weekly listing in the Kawartha Sun at a cost of $35 was representative of the Inn's summer advertising expenditures. During the off-season advertising dropped off substantially.

The Inn also placed occasional thirty-second spots on the local AM and FM radio stations (see Exhibit 11). Mrs. Agnew would phone the radio station to inform them of various events she wanted publicized. The announcer would then write a commercial and read it on the air without further consultation. Due to the ad hoc nature of the Inn's radio advertising, Tim felt it was largely unsuccessful in delivering an accurate picture of the Inn to potential customers. In addition to its local radio advertisements, the Inn had also received free publicity through a highly complimentary review broadcast throughout Ontario on CBC radio (see Exhibit 12).

Tim was concerned that the Inn was not getting the maximum return from its advertising expenditures. He was unsure whether the frequency of advertising was optimal, especially the heavy weighting in the summer. On the whole, he suspected that the Inn advertised with about the same frequency as its competitors. Tim also wondered if the ads were conveying the right message to his customers and potential customers. He believed the Inn had a fairly widespread reputation for the quality of its food. However, he worried that many people who had heard of the Inn did not know where it was located. In order to help Tom formulate an advertising strategy, Tim had collected some information about the local media as shown in Exhibit 13.

Before Tom left, Tim reiterated what he felt to be the Inn's most pressing problems. First among these was cash flow. Tim had initially thought that closing the Inn's doors during the winter would be a possible solution. However, in order to sell the Inn he felt the onus would be on him to prove to a potential buyer that it was a viable ongoing business concern. Short-term funds of up to $5000 could likely be obtained from a local bank to implement operational changes, provided that all expenditures were accounted for in advance. A plan to improve the long-term profitability of the Inn was also important, since Tim figured that there was only a 50 percent chance that the Inn would be sold before the following summer.

As Tom was about to leave, Tim gave him a letter he had received on Friday by registered mail, reproduced here as Exhibit 14. Tim felt that the tone of the second paragraph served to bring into focus the urgency of the situation currently facing the Inn and its operations. "Let me know very soon what you think I should do," continued Tim, "because time is running out."

Exhibit 1
The Old Bridge Inn Near "E"

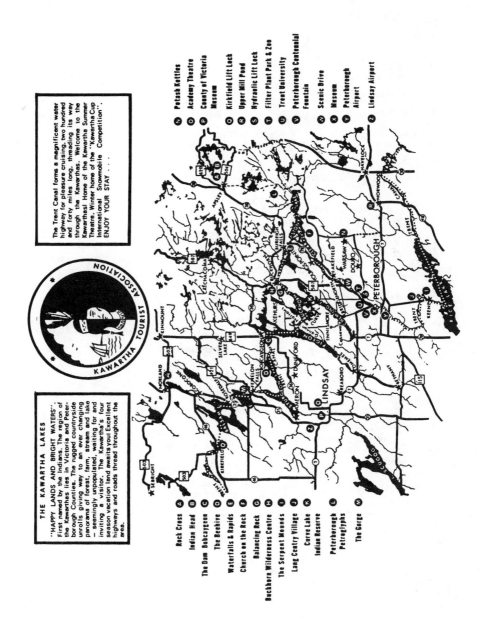

THE KAWARTHA LAKES

"HAPPY LANDS AND BRIGHT WATERS". First named by the Indians. The region of the Kawarthas lies in Victoria and Peterborough Counties. The rugged countryside unrolls giving way to an ever changing panorama of forest, farm, stream and lake — seemingly unpopulated, waiting for and inviting a visitor. The Kawartha's four season vacation land awaits your Excellent highways and roads thread throughout the area.

The Trent Canal forms a magnificent water highway for pleasure cruising, two hundred and forty miles long, threading its way through the Kawarthas. Welcome to the Kawarthas! Home of the Kawartha Summer Theatre. Winter home of the "Kawartha Cup International Snowmobile Competition". ENJOY YOUR STAY . . . .

KAWARTHA TOURIST ASSOCIATION

- Ⓐ Rock Cross
- Ⓑ Indian Head
- Ⓒ The Dam Bobcaygeon
- Ⓓ The Beehive
- Ⓔ Waterfalls & Rapids
- Ⓕ Church on the Rock
- Ⓖ Balancing Rock
- Ⓗ Buckhorn Wilderness Centre
- Ⓘ The Serpent Mounds
- Ⓙ Lang Century Village
- Ⓚ Curve Lake Indian Reserve
- Ⓛ Peterborough Petroglyphs
- Ⓜ The Gorge

- Ⓝ Potash Kettles
- Ⓞ Academy Theatre
- Ⓟ County of Victoria Museum
- Ⓠ Kirkfield Lift Lock
- Ⓡ Upper Mill Pond
- Ⓢ Hydraulic Lift Lock
- Ⓣ Filter Plant Park & Zoo
- Ⓤ Trent University
- Ⓥ Peterborough Centennial Fountain
- Ⓦ Scenic Drive
- Ⓧ Museum
- Ⓨ Peterborough Airport
- Ⓩ Lindsay Airport

Exhibit 2
The Old Bridge Inn
Income Statement
For the Year Ended October 15, 1981

REVENUES

Food sales	$62 995		
Cost of food	19 821	(31%)	$43 174
Beverage sales	$29 665		
Cost of beverages	10 369	(35%)	19 296
Other revenue			2 108
Gross margin			$64 578

EXPENSES

Telephone	$ 695		
Utilities	5 512		
Services	3 396	(3.5%)	
Advertising	4 272		
Office supplies	592		
Kitchen & bar supplies	1 588	(1.6%)	
Entertainment	5 497		
Wages	41 763	(44%)	
Insurance	1 273		
Depreciation	4 220		
Taxes	789		
Interest	8 343		77 940
Profit/(Loss)			($13 362)

Exhibit 3
The Old Bridge Inn
Balance Sheet
(October 15, 1981)

ASSETS

Cash		$ 0
Inventory: Food		1 900
Beverage		2 000
Bar/Dining Supplies		400
Office Supplies		500
Building —	$44 459	
less: Depreciation	2 046	42 413
Equipment —	12 353	
less: Depreciation	2 174	10 179
Land		35 000
TOTAL		$92 392

LIABILITIES

Accounts payable	$ 9 912
First mortgage	42 000
Second mortgage	8 000
	$59 912

EQUITY

Agnew	$32 480
	$92 392

Exhibit 4
The Old Bridge Inn
Income Statement
For the 6 Months Ended April 15, 1981

REVENUES		
Food sales	$11 869	
Cost of food	5 478	$ 6 391
Beverage sales	6 723	
Cost of beverages	2 484	4 239
Gross margin		$10 630
EXPENSES		
Telephone	$ 484	
Utilities	3 227	
Services	1 616	
Advertising	1 602	
Office supplies	342	
Kitchen & bar supplies	1 382	
Entertainment	1 630	
Wages	12 656	
Depreciation	4 220	
Interest	2 181	29 340
Profit/(Loss)		($18 710)

Exhibit 5
The Old Bridge Inn
Income Statement
For the 6 Months Ended October 15, 1981

REVENUES		
Food Sales	$51 126	
Cost of food	14 343	$36 783
Beverage sales	$22 942	
Cost of beverages	7 885	15 057
Other revenue		2 108
Gross margin		$53 948
EXPENSES		
Telephone	$ 211	
Utilities	2 285	
Services	1 780	
Advertising	2 670	
Office supplies	250	
Kitchen & bar supplies	206	
Entertainment	3 867	
Wages	29 107	
Insurance	1 273	
Taxes	789	
Interest	6 162	$48 600
Profit/(Loss)		$ 5 348

Exhibit 6
Second Floor Plan

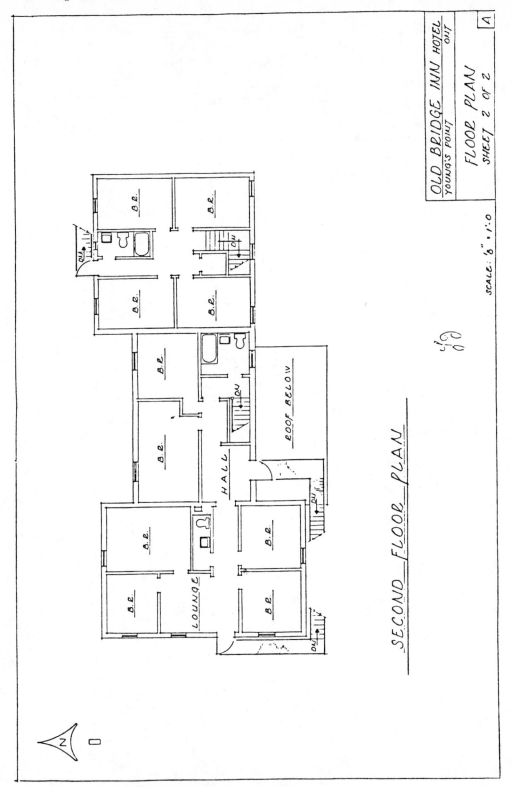

SECOND FLOOR PLAN

Exhibit 7
First Floor Plan

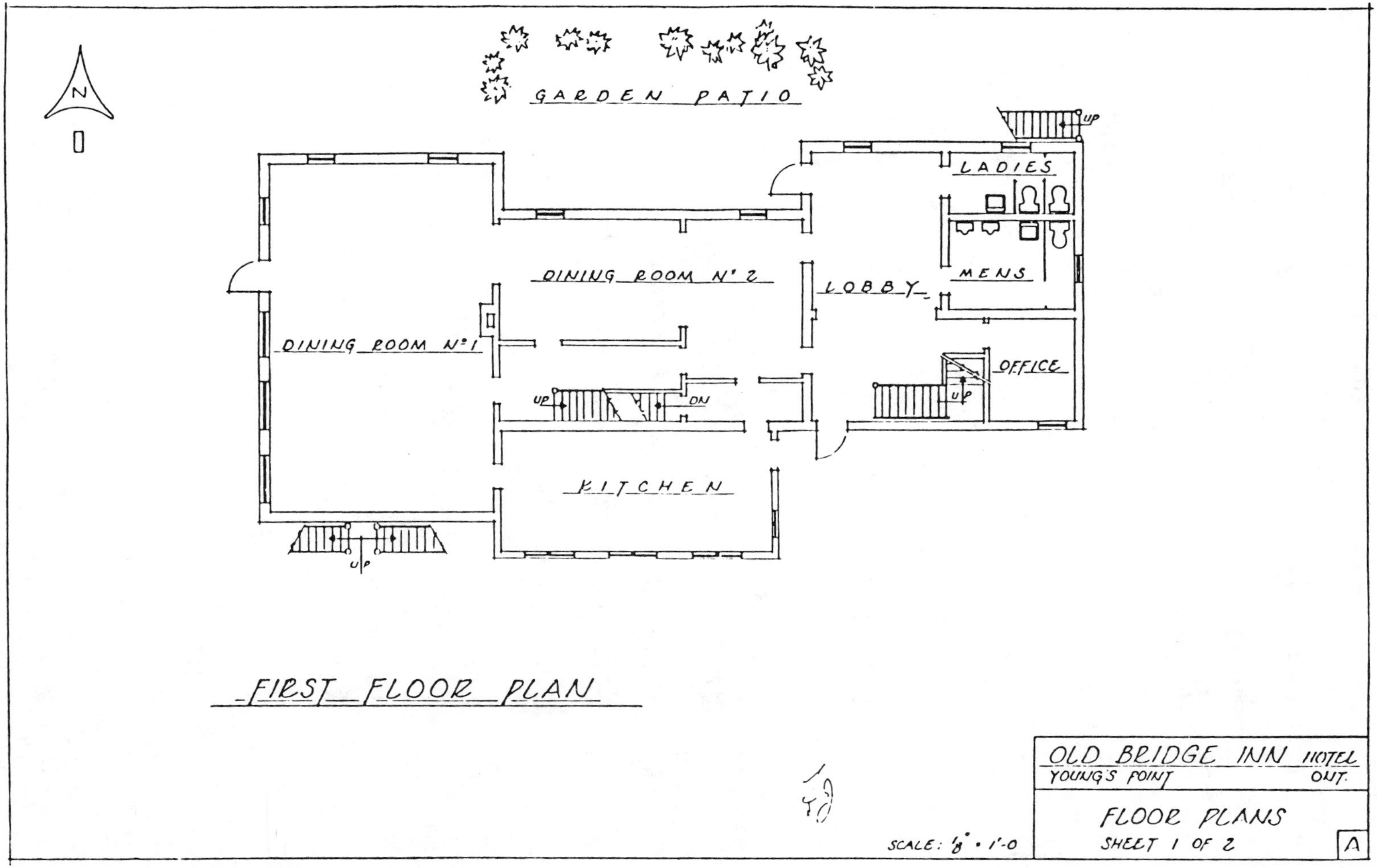

FIRST FLOOR PLAN

GARDEN PATIO

DINING ROOM Nº 2

DINING ROOM Nº 1

LOBBY

LADIES

MENS

OFFICE

KITCHEN

UP

DN

OLD BRIDGE INN HOTEL
YOUNGS POINT
OUT.

FLOOR PLANS
SHEET 1 OF 2

A

SCALE: ⅛" · 1'·0

Exhibit 8

THE OLD BRIDGE INN

Young's Point, Ontario
(705) 652-3661

Menu

Roast Beef.	$ 10.50
Peter's Seafood Pot.	$ 9.25
Lobster, Shrimp & Crab in a creamy Sherry sauce.	
Barbecued Ribs	$ 8.95
Sirloin Steak	$ 9.50

above served with Homemade Vegetable soup or tossed Salad & Parsley Potato.

choice of creamed carrots, onions, Ratatouille or cauliflower & broccoli in a cheese/wine sauce.

Desserts

Pumpkin Pie	$ 1.50
Raisin Pie	$ 1.50
Tipsy Trifle	$ 1.75
Coffee, Tea or Milk	.40

Exhibit 9
Census Agglomeration of Peterborough

Market: 34% above national average

Retail sales, 1979	$280 000 000
% Canadian total	0.37
Per capita	$4265

Income: 7% above national average

Personal disposable income, 1979	$505 800 000
% Canadian total	0.30
Per capita	$7706

Current Growth Rate: 2% per decade

Population, June 1, 1979	65 600
% Canadian total	0.28
% Change, '76-'79	+0.47

POPULATION:

1976 Census:

Total	65 290
Male	31 450
Female	33 840

Age groups:	Male	Female
0-4	2250	2,120
5-9	2410	2400
10-14	3050	2910
15-19	3310	3355
20-24	3185	3095
25-34	4620	4565
35-44	3320	3410
45-54	3485	4005
55-64	3025	3565
65-69	1135	1425
70+	1670	3000

FAMILIES

	1976
No.	16 965
Aver. no. per family	3.3

LEVEL OF SCHOOLING

	1976 Census	% Total
Population, 15 yrs. +	50 210	100
Less than gr. 5	880	2
Grades 5-8	9 010	18
Grades 9-10	10 845	22
Grades 11-13	14 340	29
Post-secondary, non-university	7 740	15
University only	4 390	9
University & post-secondary, non-university	3 015	6

Note — Level of Schooling refers to the highest grade or year completed by the person. Those currently enrolled reported their present grade or year.

EMPLOYMENT
(1961=100)

	Peterborough	Canada
1974	140.8	142.8
1975	147.6	141.1
1976	140.6	144.1
1977	132.5	144.3
1978	136.0	146.5

HOMES BUILT

	1978	1977	1976
No.	605	781	*883

*For 1971 area

HOUSEHOLDS

	1976
No.	21 620
Aver. no. per household	2.9

HOUSING

	1976 Census	% Total
Occupied dwellings no.	21 620	100
Owned	14 320	66
Rented	7 300	34
Type of dwelling:		
Single detached	14 385	67
Double	665	3
Row	750	3
Apartment	4 335	20
Duplex	1 395	6
Mobile	10	...

MOTHER TONGUE

	1976 Census	% Total
English	61 755	94.6
French	530	0.8

RACIAL ORIGIN

	1976 Census	% Total
British	53 545	84.2
French	2 635	4.2
German	1 905	3.0
Italian	1 180	1.9
Netherlands	1 420	2.2
Polish	470	0.7
Scandinavian	385	0.6
Ukrainian	200	0.3
Other	1 835	2.9

MANUFACTURING INDUSTRIES

	1976
Plants	70
Employees	9 825

	-$000-
Salaries, wages	136 187
Mfg. materials cost	173 163
Mfg. shipments, value	374 768
Total value added	219 227

BANKING

Branches, no. (1979)	*19
Cheques cashed:	-$000-
1978	3 395 659
1974	2 072 940

*For city of Peterborough only.

HOUSEHOLD FACILITIES

	1971 Census No.	% Total
Occupied dwellings	18 770	100.0
Dwellings with:		
Refrigerator	18 730	99.8
Home freezer	5 920	31.5
Television	18 290	97.4
Automobile	15 345	81.7
Furnace heating	15 720	83.7
Fuel:		
Oil	13 270	70.7
Electricity	1 655	8.8
Coal	60	0.3
Gas	3 650	19.4

Exhibit 9 (cont'd)

RETAIL TRADE

1971 Census

Total sales, $000		133 569
Stores, no.		457
Year-end inventory, $000		15 481
Employees, no.		2 614
Payroll, total, $000		14 045

By kind of business group:	Stores No.	Sales $000
Food	74	33 934
Groceries, confectionery & sundries	14	1 105
Grocery	17	2 186
Combination*	22	28 955
Meat markets	5	702
General merchandise	18	21 352
Department	3	14 364
General merchandise	4	3 526
Variety	9	+
Automotive	125	37 212
New motor vehicle dealers	15	22 317
Tire, battery, etc.	5	+
Home & auto supply	2	+
Service stations	55	6 831
Garages	10	730
Paint & body shops	16	1 280
Apparel & accessories	59	9 112
Men's & boys clothing	15	1 790
Women's & misses'	15	1 446
Family clothing	4	3 029
Family shoe	14	+
Hardware & home furnishings	55	10 211
Hardware	7	977
Furniture	5	756
Furniture, TV, radio, appliance, etc.	13	6 374
Other stores	126	21 746
Pharmacies	12	2 738
Liquor	4	5 331
Jewellery	12	1 314
Sporting goods	13	1 157

+Confidential.
*Grocery stores with fresh meat.

TAXATION STATISTICS

Income class:	1977	% of Total
Under $2 500	6 893	16.0
$2 500-5 000	7 229	16.8
5 000-7 500	6 220	14.5
7 500-10 000	4 327	10.1
10 000-12 500	4 105	9.5
12 500-15 000	4 274	9.9
15 000-20 000	6 292	14.6
20 000-25 000	1 620	3.8

TAXATION STATISTICS (cont'd)

25 000-30 000	1 109	2.6
30 000 & over	952	2.2
Total returns, no.	43 021	100.0
Total Inc., $000	434 460	...
Average income, $	10 099	...
Total tax, $000	60 997	...
Average tax, $	2 276	...

LABOUR FORCE

	1976 Census	
	Male	Female
In labor force	18 025	11 845
Participation rate	75.8	44.8
15-24 yrs	4 525	3 830
25-44	7 390	4 510
45-64	5 670	3 230
65+	445	270
Employed	16 860	10 485
Unemployed	1 165	1 355
Unemployment rate	6.5	11.4
Married females in labor force	...	7 305
Participation rate	...	45.3

RELIGION

	1971 Census	% Total
Protestant	36 055	62.0
Roman Catholic	15 300	26.3

NOTE — For the city of Peterborough only.

BUILDING PERMITS

	1978	1977	1976
		-$000-	
Value	15 001	22 225	32 742

NOTE — For city of Peterborough only.

EARNINGS

		Av. weekly earnings $
	Peterborough	Canada
1974	183.61	178.09
1975	205.08	203.34
1976	225.25	228.03
1977	239.18	249.95
1978	250.22	265.37

NEWSPAPERS

Newspaper, daily: 1979
Examiner (Thomson)

Circulation, total	23 712
city	15 388
outside	8 324

Newspaper, weekly:

Review	29 700

RADIO STATIONS

CHEX, 10 000 watts.
CKPT, 10 000 watts.
CFMP-FM, 31 400 watts.
CKQM-FM, 50 000 watts.

TELEVISION STATION

CHEX-TV, Video, 163 000 watts ERP.

PORT HOPE

POPULATION

1976 census

Total		9 785
Male		4 720
Female		5 065

Age groups:	Male	Female
0-4	425	380
5-9	400	360
10-14	425	435
15-19	415	420
20-24	420	415
25-34	745	720
35-44	475	460
45-54	500	555
55-64	450	540
65-69	180	235
70+	285	555

FAMILIES

	1976
No.	2 590
Aver. no. per family	3.2

MOTHER TONGUE

	1976 Census	% Total
English	9 265	94.7
French	100	1.0
Netherlandic & Flemish	110	1.1

HOUSEHOLDS

	1976
No.	3 317
Aver. no. per household	2.9

HOUSING

	1976 Census	% Total
Occupied dwellings, no.	3 320	100
Owned	2 245	68
Rented	1 075	32
Type of Dwelling:		
Single detached	2 110	64
Double	230	7
Row	135	4
Apartment	715	22
Duplex	110	3
Mobile	...	...

EARNINGS — Av. weekly earnings $

	Port Hope	Canada
1974	172.54	178.09
1975	199.22	203.34
1976	222.99	228.03
1977	245.28	249.95
1978	263.32	265.37

BUILDING PERMITS

	1978	1977	1976
	-$000-		
Value	10 963	2 174	1 706

EMPLOYMENT

(1961=100)	Port Hope	Canada
1974	189.3	142.8
1975	180.5	141.1
1976	183.5	144.4
1977	189.1	144.3
1978	188.7	146.5

LEVEL OF SCHOOLING

	1976 Census	% Total
Population, 15 yrs. +	7 370	100
Less than gr. 5	190	3
Grades 5-8	1 305	18
Grades 9-10	1 780	24
Grades 11-13	2 165	29
Post-secondary, non-university	1 025	14
University only	545	7
University & post-secondary, non-university	360	5

NOTE — Level of Schooling refers to the highest grade or year completed by the person. Those currently enrolled reported their present grade or year.

Exhibit 10
Sample Ads

THE OLD BRIDGE INN

Now Under New Management   Licensed Under The L.L.B.O.

Our patio is now open.
Enjoy a hamburger while
overlooking beautiful Lock 27

ENTERTAINMENT
FRIDAY & SATURDAY EVENINGS

Reserve Now **652-3661** *Young's Point*

Summer 1981

THE OLD BRIDGE INN

Now Under New Management   Licensed Under The L.L.B.O.

YOU OUGHT TO BE
ON THE OTONABEE
FOR FINE COUNTRY DINING

FRIDAY EVENING ENTERTAINMENT
RALPH FRASER

Reserve Now **652-3661** *Young's Point*

Summer 1981

THE OLD BRIDGE INN

Now Under New Management   Licensed Under The L.L.B.O.

Our patio is now open.
Enjoy a hamburger while
overlooking beautiful Lock 27

ENTERTAINMENT
FRIDAY & SATURDAY EVENINGS

Reserve Now **652-3661** *Young's Point*

Kawartha Sun
September 3, 1981

Call For
Reservations Now

652-3661

for your

THANKSGIVING DINNER

Open daily from 12 noon to 1:00 a.m. for
daily luncheon and dinner menus.
Licensed under the LLBO.

THE **OLD BRIDGE INN** HOTEL

ownership and management
of the Agnew family.

Young's Point

Peterborough Examiner
October 1981

Exhibit 11
Sample Radio Commercial

Media Music 908/2/3.

Where Katchewanooka and Clear Lake Waters join, under the settler-trodden wooden bridge, stands the OLD BRIDGE INN. This Hallowe'en, enjoy the fun of an old-fashioned Box Lunch Social — just a dollar and a half per couple, with proceeds going to UNICEF. The ladies will prepare an attractive Box Lunch to be auctioned to the eager beaux at 6:30 p.m. Book now for your Christmas or New Year's party — and remember the Hallowe'en Box Lunch Social — at the OLD BRIDGE INN, just off Highway 28 at Young's Point.

Exhibit 12
CBC Commentary
Young's Point — The Old Bridge Inn

For Ontario Morning. — CBC

I think we have here at Young's Point what is probably the finest Inn in the province. I know there are others at Caledon East, Huntsville, Elora, Acton, Bayfield, Niagara-on-the-Lake, Jackson's Point, and possibly Deep River which, according to the Ontario Morning correspondent seems to have everything — but the *Old Bridge Inn* is surely the most beautifully situated. A two storey turn-of-the-century house of warm and solid red brick. It stands guard over the Old Wooden Bridge which fords the Otonabee River and gives access to the locks of the Trent Canal and keeps a constant eye on the thundering waters of the Dam. The old bridge is closed to cars and so it is a walker's dream and an Oasis to those seeking peace, away from the world of the traffic that passes out of hearing on to the Kawarthas and Buckhorn Lakes. The Village of Young's Point cleverly hides under the new bridge comfortably enfolding its 300 or so regular residents. Not everybody here sounds like me but their ancestors all came from where this voice first sounded in Ireland in a house between the River Barrow and the Royal Canal in County Kildare. This Meeting of the Waters is Canada's version of that famous Vale of Avoca, not far from Dublin, that inspired Thomas Moore to write his immortal song *The Meeting of the Waters!*

> There is not in this wide world a valley so sweet
> As that vale in whose bosom the bright waters meet

> the poem ends:

> Sweet vale of Avoca, how calm could I rest
> In thy bosom of shade, with the friends I love best
> Where the storms that we feel in this cold world should cease
> And our hearts, like thy waters, be mingled in peace.

So it is at Young's Point as I say to myself with Shakespeare's Falstaff: "Shall I not take mine ease in mine Inn?" If *location* is an essential of the good Inn so indeed is the Innkeeper, and let me tell you our Innkeeper Annabelle is as refreshing as the sight and sound of the waters alongside her Inn. She inherits a fine tradition following on the genial original Russ Brooks, now in retirement and on guard over the other end of that wooden bridge in the original family residence and the original post office, which in turn faces today's post office where despite the charm of Mrs. Jack Young, Winnie and Dorothy, the world intrudes in the mail as we all pick up there with the inevitable bill from Sears, Simpsons or Eaton's. After location and an Innkeeper I suppose the atmosphere of an Inn is the third element of the trinity of graces an Inn should possess. What I call Annabelle soup is always homemade although called by more accurate names from day to day or Jour to Jour. The food is always homely but imaginative and lends to your whiskey or wine a distinction it might not otherwise have. There are some rooms should you require to take your ease overnight.

An Inn is a serious matter and I wish there were more to act as an oasis and haven as we travel our long lonely roads.

As Dr. Johnson said in March of 1776, "There is nothing which has yet been contrived by man by which so much happiness is produced as by a good tavern or Inn." Anyway I wonder does your community boast an Inn that has that Trinity of Graces, each separate, none greater than the other, of LOCATION, INNKEEPER, BILL OF FARE? If you'll excuse me I'll get up from my chair and go down to the Inn and test out what G. K. Chesterton said in his *Song Against the Grocers*.

> God made the wicked grocer
> For a mystery and a sign
> That men might shun the awful shop
> And go to Inns to dine
> The righteous minds of Innkeepers
> Induce them now and then
> To crack a bottle with a friend

Exhibit 13
Local Media Information — 1981

A) RADIO

1. CHEX — AM

60 SECOND SPOTS	1x	156x	312x
Class "AAA"	29.20	21.80	18.75
Class "AA"	19.95	18.15	14.50
Class "A"	17.20	14.50	12.10
Class "B"	14.60	12.10	9.70

30 seconds — 75% of 60 second rate

CHEX-AM TIME CLASSIFICATIONS

CLASS "AAA"	(Rotation) 6:00 a.m.-10:00 a.m. Monday to Saturday
CLASS "AA"	(Rotation) 10:00 a.m.-3:00 p.m. Monday to Saturday Select hours Sunday
CLASS "A"	(Rotation) 3:00 p.m.-6:30 p.m. Monday to Saturday
CLASS "B"	(Rotation) 6:30 p.m.-Midnight 5:00 a.m.-6:00 a.m. Monday to Saturday

REMOTE BROADCAST $95.00 per hour plus lines and location costs

TAGS on National Announcements $5.75

ALL NIGHT RADIO Midnight to 6:00 a.m. Rates on Request

SATURATION CONTRACTS

150 x 60 seconds
. . . . 15.95   30 seconds 13.45
300 x 60 seconds
. . . . 13.95   30 seconds 11.45
500 x 60 seconds
. . . . 13.30   30 seconds 10.90
750 x 60 seconds
. . . . 12.70   30 seconds 10.35
1000 x 60 seconds
. . . . 12.10   30 seconds 9.70

25% of spots in total to be aired each 3 months

NEWS & SPORTS-5 MIN.	1x	156x	312x
Class "AAA"	37.50	24.20	20.60
Class "AA"	35.10	20.60	18.15
Class "A"	32.60	18.15	16.00
Class "B'	30.25	15.70	13.30

10 minutes – 40% additional

TOTAL AUDIENCE PLAN

10%-AAA   40%-AA   30%-A   20%-B

	10x	20x	30x
60 SECONDS	193.05	358.60	499.95
	19.30	17.93	16.66
30 SECONDS	166.65	292.82	399.30
	16.66	14.64	13.31

GENERAL INFORMATION

Contracts are subject to cancellation by either party by a 30 day advance written notice.

Cancelled or interrupted contracts are subject to short rate.

Advertisers who reduce or interrupt their schedule must begin a new contract for discount purposes.

Accounts are due and payable in Canadian funds when rendered.

Exhibit 13 (Cont'd)

2. CFMP — FM

CFMP — STEREO — FM — 101.5

ANNOUNCEMENTS		ONE	104	156	312
CLASS AAA	60 Seconds	18.00	13.00	12.00	11.00
6:00 a.m.-12:00 Noon	30 Seconds	15.00	10.00	9.00	8.00
Monday-Friday					
CLASS AA					
12:00 Noon-6:00 p.m.	60 Seconds	16.00	11.00	10.00	9.00
Monday-Friday	30 Seconds	13.00	8.00	7.00	6.00
Saturday & Sunday					
CLASS A	60 Seconds	14.00	9.00	8.00	7.00
6:00 p.m.-Sign-Off	30 Seconds	11.00	6.00	5.00	4.00
Monday-Friday					
NEWS & SPORTS			AAA	AA	A
(5 Minutes)					
	3x Weekly		16.00	14.00	12.00
(10 Minutes 40%					
Additional)	6x Weekly		12.00	10.00	8.00
SATURATION PACKAGES		10x	20x	30x	50x
Best available times	60 Seconds	13.50	13.00	12.50	12.00
to be used within					
2 weeks	30 Seconds	10.50	10.00	9.50	9.0
SATURATION CONTRACTS		300x	500x	750x	1000x
	60 Seconds	10.50	10.00	9.50	9.00
(to be used in					
12 Months)	30 Seconds	7.50	7.00	6.50	6.00

SPECIAL FEATURE & PROGRAM RATES ON REQUEST

Card No. 5 Effective September 1, 1981

Exhibit 13 (Cont'd)

B. NEWSPAPER (1981 Data)

1. KAWARTHA SUN

   Circulation: 20 000 in the Kawarthas and Lakeshore Districts.

Full Page: 31¢/line		($416.64)
1/2 Page & Up: 32¢/line	OR	$4.48/column inch
1/4 Page – 1/2 Page: 33¢/line	OR	$4.62/column inch
1/8 Page – 1/4 Page: 34¢/line	OR	$4.76/column inch
1/16 Page – 1/8 Page: 35¢/line	OR	$4.90/column inch
Transient Rate: 37¢/line	OR	$5.18/column inch
Feature Rate: 37¢/line	OR	$5.18/column inch

2. PETERBOROUGH EXAMINER

   Circulation: 23 391 (1979)

   Full Page: 46¢/line   ($1275.00)
   All sizes at flat rate of 46¢/line
   Format: 9 columns x 308 lines each
   Position charge: 15% extra
   Colour (min. size 600 lines): 1 Col. + $165; 2 col. + $245.

Exhibit 14

Ontario	Ministry of Revenue	Retail Sales Tax Branch	208 Dundas St. East Belleville, Ontario K8N 1E3

(613) 962-9108
Zenith 71820

REGISTERED MAIL

Refer to: D. E. Graham
V.P. #47289651

November 4, 1981

The Old Bridge Inn
Youngs Point, Ontario
K0L 3G0

Attention: <u>Mr. Agnew</u>

Dear Sir:

We would like to thank you for the two cheques in
the amount of $2,500.00 and $2,875.80 to clear your
outstanding tax liability of $5,375.80. Your proposal
to pay your outstanding tax liability is accepted
on the conditions that your current return is filed on
or before the due date and your cheques are honoured
when presented for payment.

If the above conditions are not kept we will have
no alternative but to take whatever legal action that
we deem necessary to collect without further notification
to you.

Interest will continue to accrue at 12 per cent per
annum on the unpaid balance.

Yours very truly,

T. O'Sullivan

Acting District
Compliance Supervisor.

TOS:jb

65

Rebel Fire Apparatus Ltd.

THE FIRE EQUIPMENT INDUSTRY

The products of the fire equipment industry included fire trucks, hoses, fire extinguishers, sprinkler systems and component parts such as nozzles, valves, siamese,[1] and couplings. Firms in this industry usually specialized in a particular line of products (such as trucks) and no firm produced a complete line in any product.

Certain minimum standards must be met by all fire equipment products before they can be placed in public buildings. These requirements ensure that the public will be protected from faulty emergency equipment that could result in unnecessary property damage and personal harm. Recommended standards used in drawing up provisions for the regional fire prevention codes were prepared by several government agencies, national technical societies, and trade associations.

Fire prevention codes varied throughout the different regions of Canada. At present, there were over twelve regional screw thread patterns in existence in Canada, and although some attempts had been made to standardize threads, a conversion to a single national thread was nearly impossible due to the expense of such a conversion. Companies required a thorough knowledge of regional standards if national distribution of their products was to be achieved.

Because of the large number of different nozzle sizes and the many different regional threads used on them, mass production of fire prevention equipment was nearly impossible. Consequently, each order had to be produced separately. This characteristic of the fire equipment industry explained why several small firms had been able to carve out a niche for themselves in a very competitive situation.

The markets in the fire equipment industry were broken into four major areas — construction, fire equipment, industrial fire protection and special equipment.

The construction segment required basic equipment for installation in new buildings. This equipment must conform to building and fire prevention codes. The major proportion of products was used in hose cabinets which were installed in public buildings at the time of construction. Products included hose racks, valves, hoses, nozzles and extinguishers. Products for this market segment were produced and sold in large quantity compared to products for other market segments. Product design did not vary significantly with the producer. The major problem in the construction segment was to ensure that the right threads were being used on orders that went to various regions of the country. Price was the major consideration when selling these products. Rapid delivery was much less important.

Although fire equipment must be installed when a factory is constructed, additional equipment may be required because of the nature of the business conducted in the factory. The additional equipment falls under the segment termed industrial fire protection. The equipment was more sophisticated than the equipment installed by the contractor. For example, if the company had a computer, carbon dioxide equipment

---

[1]Y-shaped outlets used on apartment and commercial buildings for water supply.

was required at the site. Larger nozzles of more complex design were required in the industrial segment. Due to the limited market and product complexity, prices were higher than in the construction segment.

The fire department market segment required highly sophisticated equipment. Fire departments must have equipment designed for use in fighting many different classes of fires. Also, each piece of equipment must have technical qualities that enable it to perform its function in the best possible manner. The producer of this equipment must be competent in technical product design, have research for new products, and have facilities for testing each piece of equipment sold. Because a fire department cannot afford to be without a piece of equipment for any length of time, delivery was the prime consideration in this market segment. Price was not as important, because a fire department expected to pay a premium for the quality set down on its specifications.

Products in the special equipment segment were generally unique ones requiring a large amount of work. They were produced in small numbers and were very expensive. These products came about as a result of the user's needs and designer/producer's skill in meeting those needs. In many cases, the manufacturer worked on the cost-plus basis. (The producer accumulated all costs associated with the job and added a profit margin to this cost figure when the job was completed.)

MANUFACTURING COMPANIES

Most of the firms in the Canadian fire equipment industry were subsidiaries of large American firms. Among the more prominent companies were Elkart, Wilson and Cousins, Fyr-Fyter, and Akron. Most of these companies imported partially completed products from parent firms in the United States and finished them in their Canadian plants. Nearly every firm produced products for the construction segment and each specialized in another line in a different segment of the market. The product range in this industry was so broad that even the bigger firms did not produce a complete line.

Product distribution in this industry took place in two ways. Some of the large manufacturers had their own sales force and distribution system, though most manufacturers also supplied a separate distributor-warehousing network.

Most distributors handled competing products from many companies. Independent distributors did not like to handle products of companies who sold directly, and went to great lengths to obtain products from the smaller companies who used independent distributors exclusively. In addition, most distributors handled products for the safety equipment industry such as plastic coats, goggles, and safety clothing. Prominent national distributors included such companies as Dyer and Miller, Safety Supply, Canadian Electric Box and Stamping Ltd., Wilson and Cousins, and National Fire Hose.

FOREIGN COMPETITION

Foreign competition in Canada was limited in most market segments where delivery was important. Canadian buyers purchased few foreign products because of the difficulty in getting repair parts from the foreign manufacturers. However, Canadian distributors did buy some items from American manufacturers. These items consisted of certain replacement parts which Canadian manufacturers had stopped making and certain specialty items which were either not produced in Canada or cost three or four times as much to purchase in Canada.

FUTURE OF THE FIRE EQUIPMENT INDUSTRY

The fire department, special equipment and industrial protection segments had grown in proportion to the overall population increase. Equipment in these segments had become more sophisticated as demands became more complex.

Growth in the construction segment depended on economic conditions. It followed the cyclical patterns of the construction industry and in the long run increased as the demand for housing increased.

As far as new products were concerned, a trend toward the use of plastics was growing. Many of the initial problems confronted by plastic manufacturers had been remedied and major companies such as Wilson and Cousins and Akron had begun to sell plastic nozzles. As the cost of brass continued to increase, plastic probably would occupy an even greater portion of the market.

THE COMPANY — REBEL FIRE APPARATUS LTD.

Rebel Fire Apparatus was a Hamilton-based manufacturer of brass components employed in fire fighting equipment. Its product line, which was continually expanding, included nozzles, valves, siamese, and adapters. The company machined and assembled a limited line of fire equipment apparatus and sold it through distributors nationwide as well as in regions of the United States.

Don Steen, the owner of the company, had worked for eighteen years with Wilson and Cousins, producers of a wide line of fire fighting apparatus. In 1966, at the age of thirty-eight, Mr. Steen decided to resign from his job as plant manager and establish his own company. With virtually no general management experience but with an excellent knowledge of the products and the industry, Mr. Steen personally began to machine and sell fog nozzles to a number of fire equipment dealers.

Mr. Steen had an aptitude for improving old products and designing new ones. Because his products were of high quality and advanced design and priced competitively, Mr. Steen's reputation as a manufacturer grew. Sales rose steadily (Exhibit 1) from $50 000 in 1967, the first full year of operation, to a projected $300 000 in 1970. Mr. Steen predicted that the present sales level would double within three years. (The company's balance sheets for 1967–69 are presented in Exhibit 2.)

With orders constantly increasing, few problems existed in obtaining higher sales, but Mr. Steen became alarmed at the backlog of orders. Fewer deadlines were being met each week. Mr. Steen felt the company was getting too large for him personally to continue supervising each area. The problem of preparing Rebel Fire Apparatus for future growth needed attention but Mr. Steen had less and less time to think about it.

MARKETING

Rebel competed mostly in the construction segment of the fire apparatus market. By promising fast delivery and underselling the competition by 10 percent Rebel had been able to gain a large portion of the market. In addition, Mr. Steen felt his personal contact with distributors had been a big reason for repeat business.

Rebel used independent distributors exclusively to market its products. It did not sell directly to jobbers or employ any salespeople of its own. As a result, Rebel's distributors had been very loyal. Rebel had a limited number of customers and in 1969 five major purchasers accounted for almost 75 percent of Rebel sales (Exhibit 3).

PRODUCTS

The three main products produced by Rebel were fog nozzles, siamese, and adapters. A comparative analysis of sales by product for the months of December 1968 and November 1969 is given in Exhibit 4.

Nozzles used in fire fighting are similar to the common garden hose nozzle except that they can be subjected to very high water pressures. Prices range from ten dollars per unit for a small basic nozzle to five hundred dollars per unit for more sophisticated nozzles. The company's major line was the 2.5 cm nozzle. Mr. Steen estimated that he held a 50 percent share of an 18 000-unit total market for this size nozzle.

Siamese are *Y*-shaped fire hydrants attached to the outside of buildings. The annual total market for siamese was approximately 65 000 a year, of which Rebel held approximately 80 percent.

Adapters are brass couplings which enable two pieces of equipment with different thread sizes to be joined. Mr. Steen estimated the market to be 40 000 annually and noted that Rebel sold almost 60 percent of Canadian needs.

FOUNDRY

Initially, Rebel purchased all its castings from an outside foundry, but due to slow delivery and poor service the arrangement was not successful. In September 1968, Mr. Steen acquired the bankrupt Jeffery Foundry with a loss to carry forward of $29 000[1] which could be applied to the profits of the company over the next five years. Mr. Steen retained 100 percent ownership of the foundry himself and it remained a separate legal entity from Rebel Fire Apparatus.

Rebel purchased the materials needed for the foundry; Jeffery Foundry then formed castings from the material owned by Rebel and charged $1.20 per kilogram for the service. This transfer price (somewhat above the market price for casting services) allowed the foundry to generate a profit to be used against the $29 000-loss carry forward and still left Rebel competitive in its product pricing. The capacity of the foundry was approximately 8200/kg of castings per month, though it was at present

---

[1] Under the tax laws, a loss suffered by a company in any year could be used to offset an equal amount of profit generated by that company within a five-year period following the loss. By taking advantage of this loss carry forward, a company paid lower taxes than it otherwise would.

producing only 5500 kg per month. Mr. Steen felt the capacity of the foundry could be doubled if an additional man was hired and equipment costing approximately $4000 was purchased.

The foundry cast only for Rebel and did not accept outside orders. Mr. Steen felt he had enough to do without having to handle potential foundry sales to outside companies. The former owners continued to manage it. Mr. Steen had very little contact with the foundry except for the few minutes each morning when he picked up the day's castings for the machine shop. There were no time clocks, expense reports or budgets used in the foundry. As long as it produced the castings needed for the machine shop, Mr. Steen raised few questions.

PERSONNEL

When Mr. Steen started his company, he persuaded six experienced employees to join him at Rebel. As an incentive, Mr. Steen gave each of these six men a financial interest in the company. As a result, the workers were a very task-oriented group whose goal was building a new company. It was not uncommon for the men to work overtime at regular rates if there was a large backlog of orders to be completed. Payments for overtime were figured into the Christmas bonus that each man received.

There was no formal organization chart in the company but Bill Turner, who looked after expediting and shipping, assumed responsibility for the shop when Mr. Steen was absent. At one time, Mr. Steen had been ill for two weeks and Bill managed the company excellently. Remal Biggs was considered the head machinist, and he had little trouble supervising the other machinists and training new help. Remal had a thorough knowledge of all the company products and knew exactly how much time was required to machine each item.

COMPETITION

Rebel's two largest competitors were Wilson and Cousins, a subsidiary of Purex, and Coulter Brass. Wilson and Cousins was a very large company with substantial financial resources. It offered a very wide range of products and had its own distributors which sold only Wilson and Cousin's products. It accounted for about $200 000 of sales in the fire apparatus market and this represented only 12 percent of Wilson and Cousins's total yearly sales. The remaining products sold were purchased from outside suppliers. As this company placed more emphasis on becoming a distributor, Mr. Steen felt that his company had a good chance of becoming a supplier of the brass components needed by Wilson and Cousins.

Coulter Brass was the other major competitor for Rebel. Coulter Brass's sales were smaller than Rebel's and since they were having problems meeting the prices offered by other companies their sales were expected to decrease in the future.

Akron Manufacturing, an American firm, had a subsidiary operation in Aylmer, Ontario. They produced mostly for the fire department segment of the market and as such were only limited competitors of Rebel. This market segment required high quality and technical expertise on the part of competing firms. Akron had a highly regarded research and development department as well as a staff of trained engineers.

Mr. Steen felt, however, that the fire department segment offered some opportunities that could be serviced profitably by Rebel.

ORDER PROCESS

The majority of orders were received by phone from the distributor, who preferred to speak to Mr. Steen personally. Usually Mr. Steen quoted a price when the order was phoned in but if it was a custom order he called the customer back within a few hours once he had determined a price. For most orders, a customer was promised delivery in a week or ten days although Mr. Steen realized he might not be able to meet it.

A phone order was first recorded on any scrap piece of paper that happened to be lying near the phone and then placed in a file folder. Customers usually followed up a phone order with a letter or purchase order and upon receipt of the confirmation, the piece of paper was removed from the file and replaced by the order itself. These orders were batched together and constituted a file of back orders.

When the castings were available from the foundry, Bill Turner checked the back order file and made a list of all the parts that had to be machined before the order could be completed. This information was verbally relayed to the head machinist, who added it to the products that had to be machined during the rest of the week.

There were no written schedules used by the machinists and output was dependent upon what castings were available and the number of rush orders that popped up. Often Mr. Steen took a rush order without considering what work was already in the plant at the time. Shuffling jobs to accommodate rush orders had resulted in missed delivery dates for the remaining backlog of orders. On one occasion, the assembly of 150 fog nozzles was held up because one part had been forgotten, though all the other parts were completed.

At all times, there was a considerable amount of work in process. Components and castings waiting for further work were stacked on the floor in the vicinity of the machines.

COSTING

Very little costing was done by Mr. Steen but he sometimes referred to costing data salvaged from his previous employer. Although these data were outdated, Mr. Steen adjusted for increases due to higher wages and slightly better machine efficiency. He considered casting a time-consuming and expensive undertaking since every machinist worked at a different rate, and each "performed according to how he felt on any particular day."

As a rule of thumb, he established the cost of a finished product at twice the material cost. If his competitors sold below this estimate cost, he often chose not to manufacture the product. Normally his price was slightly below his competitors'.

When asked by the casewriter whether this method would yield a profit for all product lines, Mr. Steen replied, "Some people have told me ways of determining costs and profits. They all involve too much paperwork and time. I have yet to hear a method which is easier than mine. All I have to do is figure the cost I pay for materials and anything above that is profit because all my overhead and wages are fixed. If I pay $10 for a casting from the foundry, I can sell it for $11 and make a dollar profit." After a moment's pause, he added, "Although since I hired the last couple of employees, I don't think my profits have been as high as they were."

FINANCE

The majority of funds for Rebel Fire Apparatus Ltd. came from a bank loan and a loan from the Industrial Development Bank (I.D.B.). The bank loan was callable and was secured by assignment of accounts receivable. The I.D.B. had imposed restrictions on further capital expansion and required, among other things, that quarterly statements be submitted to them.

The growth increase had placed continual pressure on the company's working capital position (Exhibit 2). Mr. Steen had tried to combat this problem by offering a discount for prompt payment and selling only to relatively quick-paying distributors. Fortunately, the company had been operating at capacity, which permitted Rebel to be somewhat selective in the orders it accepted. (Exhibit 5 presents some selected ratios.)

CONCLUSION

As Mr. Steen reviewed his operation, he knew that there were problems needing immediate attention if the company were to develop its full potential. He was unsure about which problems should receive priority and what could be done to alleviate them. He felt any changes should leave the organization in a flexible position to meet changing demands and greater future growth. Mr. Steen stated, "I want to be the only manufacturer of fire equipment in Canada," and he was aware that some of the decisions he was going to make shortly would play an important role in deciding whether he would meet this objective.

Exhibit 1
Rebel Fire Apparatus Ltd.
Income Statements 1967–1969

	Seven Months May 31, 1967	Year Ended May 31, 1968	Year Ended May 31, 1969
Sales	$37 230	$101 608	$151 278
Cost of goods sold	25 979	79 084	119 185
Gross profit	$11 251	$ 22 524	$ 32 093
General and administration expenses	8 775	17 032	24 165
Profit	$ 2 476	$ 5 492	$ 7 928
Other income		584	765
Profit on sale of fixed assets		234	
Income before tax	2 476	6 310	8 693
Income tax	NA	1 380	2 011
Net income	$ NA	$ 4 930	$ 6 682

Exhibit 2
Rebel Fire Apparatus Ltd.
Summary of Balance Sheets 1967–1969

	Year Ending May 31, 1967	Year Ending May 31, 1968	Year Ending May 31, 1969
ASSETS			
Current assets:			
Cash	$ 673	$ 687	$ 1 437
Accounts receivable	4 191	12 650	14 617
Inventory	6 395	5 530	9 305
Prepaid insurance	204	426	567
Total current assets	$11 463	$19 293	$25 926
Fixed assets:			
Machinery and equipment	$12 756	$32 185	$43 169
Less: depreciation	2 143	8 211	15 645
Net	10 613	23 974	27 524
Incorporation expense		535	535
Goodwill	10 336	10 336	10 336
TOTAL ASSETS	$32 412	$54 138	$64 321
LIABILITIES			
Current liabilities:			
Bank loan	$ 1 900	$ 7 000	$ 6 000
Accounts payable	5 747	7 225	12 671
Tax payable	223	697	1 863
Current portion L.T.D.		7 179	6 885
Total current liabilities	$ 7 870	$22 101	$27 419
Long-term liabilities			
I.D.B.		$ 7 600	$ 6 400
Note — truck		2 064	885
Note — non-interest	4 542	3 242	2 042
Long-term liabilities	$ 4 542	$12 906	$ 9 327
Less: current portion		7 179	6 885
Total long-term liabilities	4 542	5 727	2 442
Deferred income tax		1 380	2 848
TOTAL LIABILITIES	$12 412	$29 208	$32 709
EQUITY			
Capital stock issued:			
1 900 preference shares	$19 000	$19 000	$19 000
103 common shares	1 000	1 000	1 000
Retained earnings		4 930	11 612
	20 000	24 930	31 612
TOTAL LIABILITIES AND EQUITY	$32 412	$54 138	$64 321

Exhibit 3
Rebel Fire Apparatus Ltd.
Rebel Customer Purchases

Rebel Customers Purchasing	Number of Customers
More than $25 000 annually	3
Between 15 000-$25 000	2
Between $5 000-$15 000	3
Under $5 000	20

Exhibit 4
Rebel Fire Apparatus Ltd.
Sales by Product

	December 1968	November 1969
Fog nozzles (all sizes)	$ 6 840.00	$ 8 756.00
Siamese	3 115.00	4 740.00
Brass couplings	2 122.00	4 506.80
Miscellaneous products[1]	863.00	1 273.20
Total monthly sales	$12 940.00	$19 276.00

[1]Includes some special products and custom orders.

Exhibit 5
Rebel Fire Apparatus Ltd.
Ratio Calculations

	1967[1]	1968	1969
PROFITABILITY			
Return on investment (R.O.I.)	12.3%	22%	23.6%
Net profit %	—	5%	4.4%
Gross profit %	30%	22%	21%
LIQUIDITY			
Current ratio	1.4	.87	.9
Working capital	$3 593	($2 808)	($1 493)
Age of receivables	24 days	45 days	35 days
Age of payables	46 days	33 days	38 days
Age of inventory	52 days	25 days	28 days
STABILITY			
Net worth to total assets	62%	46%	49%
Debt to equity	17%	28%	16%
GROWTH			
Sales growth		+172%	+49%
Profit growth		—	+35%
Asset growth		+67%	+18%
Equity growth		+25%	+27%

[1]7 months; used 210 days

66

Stillwell Ice Cream Ltd.

Early in 1971, Mr. Jack Thompson and Mr. Neil Dudley decided to pool their resources and buy a business with apparent growth potential. Neil Dudley was fifty-two years old. He had spent most of his life developing and expanding a small restaurant which he sold for considerable gain in 1966. He had been semiretired since that time. Mr. Dudley found that retirement did not fit his "get-up-and-go" personality and consequently he was eager to get back into business. Jack Thompson, thirty-six years old and a close neighbour of Mr. Dudley, had started as a salesman for a large ice cream producer following his graduation from university and in 1971 became sales manager. Among the several businesses Mr. Dudley and Mr. Thompson had looked at was a local ice cream plant that seemed particularly inviting.

Stillwell Ice Cream Ltd. was the largest ice cream producer in Simcoe County. It was owned by two elderly partners, John Cole and Earl Stillwell, who had spent their entire lives building up the company. Since both men were approaching seventy years of age and neither of their families showed any interest in running the business, they were receptive to the idea of selling and retiring. Mr. Thompson and Mr. Dudley decided to spend the next four weeks looking into the ice cream industry in general before making any firm purchase plans. In particular, they were concerned with the current operating problems facing Stillwell Ice Cream Ltd., as well as the problems that they might face in expanding the business. Finally, there was a price question. Messrs. Thompson and Dudley realized that they had to come up with an offer that would be acceptable to the present owners as well as one which would provide an adequate return on their investment.

THE ICE CREAM INDUSTRY

Ice cream was first produced in the United States and soon after gained worldwide popularity. This popularity was evident in Ontario where, in 1970, ice cream production reached a new peak of 88 million litres. Market forecasts predicted that this figure would be exceeded in 1971 and 1972.

Before 1940, there were hundreds of locally owned ice cream producers. These plants served their own city or town and the surrounding rural area. The townspeople were loyal to their local producer and appeared more concerned with supporting a member of the community than buying ice cream at the lowest price. After 1940, larger ice cream manufacturers began to take over the market by producing and advertising a good-quality ice cream at prices lower than the local plants were offering. As the price of ingredients, labour, and overhead began to climb, the small local producers found their operations becoming unprofitable. Consolidation in the ice cream industry began with the big companies purchasing many of the smaller plants.

Ice cream production in Ontario was divided among four large firms with several plant operations and eighty-five regional one-plant operations. The four major producers were: Silverwood, Sealtest (Dominion Dairies Ltd.), Borden, and Neilsen. Ice cream plant concentration could be broken into the following regions:

Toronto	18 plants
Central (Belleville-Orillia)	16 plants (Stillwell)
Eastern (Ottawa-Kingston)	17 plants
Northern	18 plants
Southwest	36 plants

There was downward pressure on the selling price of ice cream. Ice cream which sold at $.89 per two litres in 1960–65 was regularly featured at $.69 and $.79 in 1970. Costs of production were climbing for small ice cream producers and mass production seemed necessary to stay competitive. The larger companies were still purchasing the smaller operations and using them as distribution rather than production centres. (During the next ten years, it was expected that consolidation and merger would play an even greater role as the two major concerns which shared 80 percent of the market worked to improve their positions.)

In the past, ice cream companies had placed refrigerated dispensers in outlets that handled their products as an incentive for dealers to sell their brand of ice cream. Almost any small store that handled a producer's ice cream would receive an ice cream case. In more recent years, companies which handled large numbers of small store accounts had been forced to take a critical look at this practice, although little action resulted.

With the cost of refrigerated cases as high as $1000 and repair costs up, many companies no longer supplied freezers to dealers who sold under 1600 litres per year. The average cost of stopping a truck to service an account was estimated at approximately $8 and many of the larger companies had been forced to place the minimum sale level per stop at $25.

A drastic shift in the sales of package products like ice cream from the corner store to the chain store had taken place in the past several years. The introduction of the $.69 two-litre packages by the supermarkets had disastrous results for the corner store since it often could not meet the chain store price on ice cream. In many instances there were drastic reductions in sales. Furthermore, the major share of ice cream sales by corner stores was now in the less profitable novelty items such as popsicles and drumsticks.

To ensure a minimum quality of ice cream, the Food and Drug Regulations prescribed the ingredients for marketable ice cream. Specified minimum amounts of solids, milk fat, stabilizer, and bacteria were required in any sample. The quality of ice cream was determined by the amount of butterfat in the product as well as the overrun.[1] Butterfat gave ice cream the cream texture. Lower-quality ice cream (low butterfat concentration) tended to taste and feel more "icy."

Winter temperatures were not conducive to ice cream sales. As a result, production in July was three times that of January. Because the shelf life of ice cream was, at most, five months (three months for a high-quality product) and because refrigerated space was extremely expensive to build and maintain, ice cream was not stockpiled.

---

[1]When a quantity was placed in an ice cream machine, the machine forced air into the mix while freezing it. The increase in volume of the mix due to air was called overrun.

Consequently, heavy production demands had to be met in the summer, while the winter months afforded a more leisurely production pace.

Studies by the Ice Cream Institute indicated that the average shopper was generally unaware of the ingredients of ice cream and therefore unable to make a sound judgment on its quality. This inability to discriminate quality forced the buyer to rely on the appearance of the package and the price of the ice cream to determine the quality of the product. Most people assumed that high quality and high price were synonymous.

There had been a great growth in substitutes for ice cream such as mousse, mellorine, ice milk, and sherbet. The cost of equipment to produce these products was high and often one producer would buy a machine and then supply all the companies in the industry with the new substitute. The appearance of these products had sensitized the price of ice cream to the price of substitutes. The use of substitutes was expected to grow in the future, and price competition from other desserts and snack goods would likely become more intense.

STILLWELL ICE CREAM LTD.

Stillwell Ice Cream Ltd. grew out of a small family-owned dairy operation near Barrie, Ontario, which began in 1876. In 1902, the operation was moved to its existing location three kilometres from the city. The business was expanded to include the manufacture and sale of butter. Although the company produced ice cream as early as 1920, it was not until 1946, after the purchase of a semi-automatic ice cream maker, that the ice cream sales began to flourish.

During the previous five years sales growth had levelled off while material, operation, and selling costs continued to climb (Exhibit 1).

Stillwell Ice Cream Ltd. had produced its own line of top-quality ice cream for over half a century. In central Simcoe County the name Stillwell was almost a household word. Many customers demanded Stillwell ice cream by name. It was not uncommon for people who lived outside of Stillwell's distribution area to make special trips to purchase Stillwell ice cream. Many retailers who handled other brands also stocked Stillwell ice cream for those who demanded it. One dealer suggested that many customers would seek out Stillwell ice cream rather than buy the store brand.

Stillwell ice cream had a 12 percent butterfat content, which made it one of the highest-quality ice creams on the market. A comparable ice cream, as regards quality, was Silverwood "Deluxe" which had an 11 percent butterfat rating. Stillwell felt that the high quality of the product resulted in customer acceptance and loyalty. Stillwell ice cream sold generally for $1.05 per two litres but it varied from $.99 to $1.10. Silverwood "Deluxe" sold for $1.15 to $1.19 per two litres. Silverwood had a lower-quality second line of ice cream, "Medigold," which sold at approximately the same price as Stillwell ice cream. Stillwell sold its ice cream to dealers for $.85 plus a $.05 per two-litre freezer charge, while Silverwood sold "Deluxe" to the dealer for $.99 and "Medigold" for $.95 per two litres.

In 1970 ingredients for a litre of ice cream cost Stillwell $.19 and the package cost $.01. The direct labour and overhead amounted to $.035 and $.02 respectively while the fixed overhead was $.015 per litre. The administrative and selling expenses were $.05, and $.15 per litre respectively.

THE ICE CREAM PLANT

Earl Stillwell, a hard worker who knew the production of ice cream well, was in charge of the ice cream plant. As plant manager, he was responsible for general management, production, and sales, Although John Cole knew the operation within the plant, he had assumed the role of a silent partner. He had put a large amount of capital into Stillwell Ice Cream and was always consulted before any major decisions concerning the business were made. Mr. Cole had many other activities aside from the ice cream business which demanded his time and attention. One of his major interests was photography and he was in constant demand for weddings and special occasions.

In addition to Mr. Stillwell the plant employed a bookkeeper, four production men, and two driver-salesmen. The four production employees, with the exception of the youngest man (fifty-one), had an average age of sixty-eight and an average length of service with the company of forty-three years. Relations within the plant were excellent and everyone was on a first-name basis. After many years on the job together, the men had developed strong friendships and it was not uncommon for them and their wives to get together socially.

Stillwell paid its production men relatively low wages and had no pension or insurance plans. It considered the low wages one of the big factors in its ability to stay competitive and profitable. Although one of the oldest workers had given notice that he intended to retire in the fall, Earl Stillwell felt that the remaining workers would not retire in the near future because they did not have sufficient savings. As Mr. Stillwell stated, "They need the income from the plant to supplement their government pensions."

The two driver-salesmen were young and had been with the company for only two years. They were paid a small salary plus commission which made their total wages comparable to other driver-salesmen doing a similar job.

PRODUCTION

The production of ice cream at Stillwell was mainly a manual operation. There was very little automatic equipment and a man was needed at each step of the process. The making of the ice cream mix was the first step in the production of a final product. A man measured out specific quantities of milk, milk solids, glucose, emulsifier, and stabilizer and placed them in a pasteurizer where the mixture was steam heated to remove all bacteria. Once the temperature reached 65°C the fluid was piped to a homogenizer where the solids were broken down to create a smooth uniform product. The batch, consisting of 900 litres, was then poured into 35-litre milk cans which were manually transported to a cool storage room where the mixture sat for a minimum of sixteen hours but no longer than two weeks. Stillwell used two pasteurizers for this process. The pasteurizing equipment, old and inefficient, required a man in constant attendance to see that the mixture did not overheat.

The pasteurized formula, along with required flavouring, nuts, fruits, etc., was poured into the ice cream machine by an operator. The operator then poured the ice cream manually into two-litre cardboard containers. (The machine required approximately thirty minutes before production could begin. Thereafter, the operation was continuous until a change in flavour took place.) He placed the filled container on a table near the machine where a second worker sealed the open end and placed the containers on hardening racks in a cold storage room (at $-23°C$) for a minimum of four hours. The ice cream machine produced at a rate of 410 litres per hour but the production was limited by the capacity of the hardening room. It held 1250 litres of ice cream. At peak production during the summer some ice cream was taken from the racks before four hours. The quality of the product was lowered as a result.

The only way to increase the capacity of the hardening facilities was to increase the size of the freezers. It was estimated that the cost of increasing Stillwell's hardening capacity to 2300 litres every four hours was between $5000 and $6000.

In the winter, ice cream was produced four days a week for six hours a day. During the summer when demand exceeded production capabilities, the plant atmosphere was hectic. Scheduled production increased to ten hours a day for a six-day week.

Vanilla and butterscotch ripple flavours made up 50 percent of the sales. This proportion was quite stable throughout the year. The demand for other flavours was also fairly constant. The production employees simply checked the cooler to see what ice cream the salesmen had taken. They then replenished the stock.

MARKETING

The Stillwell distributors were generally small stores in small towns. In 1969, 30 percent of Stillwell's ice cream sales came from within Barrie, while the other 70 percent came from a variety of 145 accounts spread in a forty-eight-kilometre radius around Barrie. The majority of Stillwell sales were made to general food stores and dairy bars, but other accounts consisted of restaurants, service stations, golf clubs, resorts, hotels, and chain stores. These accounts ranged in size from 70 to 30 000 litres per year.

Stillwell employed two driver-salesmen to distribute ice cream. It was the driver-salesman's responsibility to stock his own refrigerated truck and to see that his customers did not run out of flavours. Each salesman followed a weekly route; one man covered Barrie and local accounts while the other man covered the remaining accounts. In Collingwood, Ontario, about sixty kilometres away, Northern Dairy distributed Stillwell Ice Cream to local merchants.

It was Stillwell's policy to supply refrigerated cabinets to accounts if they did not have their own and if they were able to attain a volume of five hundred litres per year. If the cabinets were supplied, the wholesale price per two litres was increased by $.05 to make the final wholesale price $.90 per two litres. An analysis of the accounts showed that this policy was not tightly enforced because at least fifty accounts with cabinets did not meet the required minimum. Management explained the exceptions as long-time accounts. "The cabinets are very old and thus do not really mean a loss to Stillwell."

The seasonal nature of the ice cream market had been a constant concern to Stillwell. The amount of ice cream sold in the summer months of May to August almost equalled the amount sold in the remaining eight months. The problem was slightly more peaked for Stillwell than for the rest of the industry, which sold approximately 45 percent of the total year's production during the four summer months. The maximum shelf life for high-quality ice cream was three months. If it sat for a longer period it began to change, losing its smooth and creamy texture and becoming granular.

Stillwell supplied many outlets in the summer resort areas surrounding Barrie, including the area of Wasaga Beach. Many of these accounts were strictly four-month summer operations. An analysis of Stillwell's accounts showed that only 4.15 percent of their total annual sales were to these four-month summer accounts. This analysis further showed that the major factor causing the fluctuating sales for Stillwell was consumption habits.

Earl Stillwell quickly admitted that the company was not market oriented. He credited its success to their high-quality reputation and the company's long history in Simcoe County. "If anything, our problem has been producing enough ice cream to meet the demand rather than trying to find a buyer once the ice cream is produced," Mr. Stillwell stated. On another occasion Mr. Stillwell said, "Hell, John and I know we could be making lots more money if we wanted to invest the capital needed to increase our volume and to spend the time necessary to take advantage of the growth in our market area. But why should we bother when the company is making us a comfortable living now and when we are going to retire shortly?"

This philosophy of letting the customer come to Stillwell was evident in the amount of advertising done by the company. In the past, Stillwell spent very little money to advertise its products. The small advertising budget was held at 1 percent of sales. The advertising mix consisted mostly of radio spots over a local radio station and a full-page ad in a Barrie newspaper during June. In addition, Stillwell bought a half-page advertisement in a local monthly advertising booklet. Stillwell seldom made an effort to push any type of specials or to concentrate on any one product for a period of time. The advertisements were geared more toward the name Stillwell than toward a particular product.

Unlike the competition who ran specials and discounted their prices to the dealers, Stillwell seldom cut its price. If the dealer wanted to use a Stillwell product as a drawing card the dealer had to take a drop in margin him or herself. Competition in this respect was very tough with some ice cream companies often featuring their products below cost.

FUTURE PROSPECTS

As Mr. Dudley and Mr. Thompson became more acquainted with Stillwell and the ice cream industry, they began to discuss several alternatives which might aid the expansion of ice cream sales.

They considered the possibility of adding a second line of lower-quality ice cream that could be marketed under a different brand name. The line would be aimed at the market where price, not quality, was the major purchase factor. Mr. Thompson felt there could be a market of approximately 70 000 litres for this second line of ice cream. It was his feeling that the production cost of a litre of this ice cream would be approximately the same in all aspects as the high-quality line, with the ingredient cost the only exception. Mr. Thompson felt that the ingredient cost could be trimmed to approximately $.175 per litre. With Stillwell "Supreme" holding approximately 50 percent of the present market in central Simcoe County the men wondered how much the lower-quality line would cannibalize their present line. They also wondered what effect the lower-quality line might have on the quality reputation Stillwell had built over the years. The second alternative was to build the sales of Stillwell ice cream outside the existing market area and concentrate on the more populated areas around Toronto, one hundred kilometres away. To do this Stillwell would have to buy more trucks to deliver ice cream to these areas or establish a relationship with a distributor who would receive a commission on sales. Messrs. Thompson and Dudley realized that the name "Stillwell' was not known outside their current market area and that great amounts of money would have to be spent to advertise their product.

As the men discussed these proposals they were concerned with the effects of such changes on present customers as well as on the plant itself. They would not want to hurt the present relationship that the company held with its old customers but, at the same time, they were not sure that it was good business to stand still. They also were concerned about the changes that would have to be made in the plant to meet the increased production and wondered if it could be undertaken without too many complications.

Exhibit 1
Stillwell Ice Cream Ltd.
Summary of earnings

	1970		1969		1968	
Sales[1]						
Bulk ice cream		$159 037		$140 106		$131 297
Ice cream specialties		16 940		15 597		12 169
Butter		156 780		151 657		156 964
Total sales		$332 757		$307 360		$300 430
Cost of goods						
Ingredients	$233 996		$218 945		$215 833	
Other costs	28 160		23 400		20 440	
Total cost of goods		262 156		242 345		236 273
Gross profit		$ 70 601		$ 65 015		$ 64 157
Admin. expense	$ 23 760		$ 20 280		$ 18 250	
Selling expense	47 520		40 560		36 500	
Total expenses		71 280		60 840		54 750
Net profit (loss)		(679)		$ 4 175		$ 9 407
Tax		—		840		1 880
Net profit after tax		$ (679)		$ 3 335		$ 7 527

[1] Both butter and ice cream specialties were purchased from other manufacturers. Butter was purchased at dealer list less $0.02 per 500 g (dealer list $0.62 per 500 g). Ice cream specialties were purchased at dealer list less 10 percent.

Exhibit 2
Stillwell Ice Cream Ltd.
Summary of Balance Sheets

	1970	1969	1968
Current assets	$ 59 653	$ 54 926	$ 53 271
Mortgage receivable	3 100	3 500	3 800
Fixed assets (net)	72 010	75 200	65 735
Total assets	$134 763	$133 626	$122 806
Current liabilities	$ 36 500	$ 34 684	$ 27 199
Capital stock	80 000	80 000	80 000
Retained earnings	18 263	18 942	15 607
	$134 763	$133 626	$122 806

Exhibit 3
Stillwell Ice Cream Ltd.
Size of Accounts

	(Annual Volume in Litres)			
	Under 500	500-3100	3100-6750	Over 6750
Barrie	5	12	4	3
Outside Barrie	43	78	16	8

Exhibit 4
Stillwell Ice Cream Ltd.
Percentage Breakdown of Sales

	1965	1966	1967	1968
May–August	48%	49%	49%	47%
September–April	52	51	51	53
Total	100	100	100	100

67

Superior Belt Limited

Mr. David Grant formed Superior Belt Limited in 1958 to produce belts for the Montreal cut-up trade.[1] In December of 1972, Mr. Grant and his son Howard decided to manufacture and distribute belts directly to retail outlets. However, by the end of 1974, rapid growth and new customers had introduced new problems and the Grants were trying to devise a strategy which would increase sales and profits for 1975.

Despite a Grade 8 education, Mr. Grant, Sr., always made a small but reasonable profit on about $300 000 of sales. In 1968, Mr. Grant's oldest son entered the business. Howard, twenty-five and an engineer, agreed to a salary, car, and life insurance on the condition that he would manage the business. Mr. Grant, Sr., was approaching sixty years of age and he was more than pleased to have Howard take over the company.

At the end of 1972, sales of belted dresses and suits had reached an all-time low. It was then that the Grants decided to produce for the retail market as well. Although this was a more volatile fashion market, the Grants felt that they could design readily acceptable products. In addition, they had developed a sales force of thirty-five company salesmen and sales agents across Canada.

Following the 1972 decision, Superior's designs in the "stand alone" belts were prolific and well accepted. In two years the Grants had designed seventy-five to one hundred new belts in six styles and ten colours in vinyl, elastic, suede, and leather. By the end of 1974, Superior Belt had achieved sales of $2 000 000 at manufacturer's prices and was one of the top six belt manufacturers in Canada.

The Superior organization was expanded to forty-five production employees, a foreman, fifteen shippers, a head shipper, a bookkeeper and a general sales manager. Mr. Grant, Sr., was primarily concerned with the day-to-day operations and he and Howard between them made most of the decisions. Company personnel were instructed on what to do on an hourly basis and there were few written documents.

PRODUCTION

Superior Belt occupied an old four-storey brick building in the heart of downtown Montreal. Prior to the end of 1973, the production facilities had been quite adequate for producing 400 000 belts per year but with about 660 000 belts produced in 1974, the facilities were near capacity for one shift with the current number of employees.

The Grants believed that as many as 12 000 belts a day could be produced by increasing the number of production employees to seventy-five and working two shifts. Costs were dependent upon lots and style. Production was much easier if the daily orders were for a few style groupings rather than for small orders of many styles. There were different manufacturing processes based on the type of material used. For example, belts using synthetic materials were glued, while leather belts were stitched.

Most of the operations were quite simple and it was relatively easy for an entre-

---

[1] The cut-up trade was also called the wholesaling trade. Clothing manufacturers placed orders for belts to be appended to dresses, suits, and coats.

preneur to acquire the equipment for a belt-manufacturing business. Most of the Superior Belt machinery was very old and somewhat given to temperamental periods.

Production employees, half of whom were women, were unionized. It took a day to train a new female employee for one machine. Male employees were rotated from one operation to another as part of a long-term program. Within seven months to a year, a new man would know all the operations and would therefore increase in value to the company by being able to take over anywhere. The turnover of female employees was much higher than for male employees; most of the female employees quit in favour of other jobs. Superior's wages compared favourably with wages paid by other companies in the area.

Raw materials including synthetics, suede, and buckles were ordered two to three months in advance from suppliers in the United States. Leather was the only raw material purchased in Canada. Because the company was small compared to other manufacturers, suppliers gave Superior a low priority in terms of shipping dates. Furthermore, suppliers always tried to pressure Superior into paying as soon as Superior received the goods.

Every day Mr. Grant, Sr., the foreman and the head shipper made notes concerning receipt of goods, work in process, finished goods, and shipping. There was no one available to keep records of inventory or production costs. Periodic style changes were introduced as the year progressed and at any one time there were over 40 000 assorted belts in finished goods inventory. By the end of 1973, inventory at cost was valued at about $289 000.

FINANCE

In 1973 Superior Belt had earned $109 758 before tax on sales of $1 157 495, as shown in Exhibit 1. The cost of goods sold is detailed in Exhibit 2, while the selling and administrative expenses are listed in Exhibit 3. The financial statements for 1974 would not be available until early February of 1975.

Because of a tight cash situation, Superior Belt always factored[1] its accounts receivable. The factoring arrangement made Superior liable for any bad debt losses suffered by the factor. Occasionally, during periods of peak need, Superior was allowed to borrow money from the factor on a secured basis. Exhibit 4 shows the balance sheet at the end of 1973.

MARKETING

The Grants estimated the belt market in Canada to be $40 million at retail prices but 20 percent of this demand was supplied by imports. Retail markups usually were at least 50 percent of the retail selling price.

Howard Grant believed that everybody was a potential customer for Superior belts. He thought that customers looked first for a store, then a particular style, and

---

[1]Factoring is the practice of selling receivables to a finance company. The sale may be with or without full recourse, depending on the arrangement negotiated. Superior sold its receivables for 98.5 percent of their face value and paid an interest charge of 1 percent over bank rate on the money so obtained, until the factor actually collected the debt from the customer.

finally for prices. There were five types of outlets for belts. These were department, general merchandise, men's clothing, women's clothing, and family clothing stores. Of Superior's 1800 accounts, 5 were independent department stores, 25 were chain stores, 1000 were men's wear stores, 200 were women's wear stores and 570 were general merchandise stores.

Department stores and men's and women's stores bought 70 percent of Superior's retail volume. Chain stores such as K Mart, Woolco, Steadmans, and Towers sold the largest volume. An order from one central chain store buyer provided immediate distribution across Canada. Exhibit 5 shows data on 1973 Canadian belt sales by type of outlet with specific information on chain and independent stores.

Howard Grant made the following comments about distribution: "Generally a retail buyer is looking for profits when deciding on lines to handle. That is, the best margin with the best volume in addition to delivery. As a result our approach varies with the type of outlet.

"In the powerful, high-volume chain stores, typically only one or two belt brands will be represented. As a result, competition is fierce. This means that some of our competitors will use any method, including pay-offs, and I'm not just talking about colour television sets. For example, we had this new woman buyer who wanted to buy from us on a simple product superiority basis. We were talking of an initial order of maybe 1200 dozen belts. When the order didn't materialize I phoned her and asked her what had happened. Her reply was that her boss had made 'prior commitments.' That's typical in this business."

Howard Grant priced his merchandise at whatever he felt the retail outlet would support. He felt that the ideal gross margin, based on total cost, was 30 percent. However, since he did not know what total costs were, he could not be sure that his gross margin was in fact 30 percent. Retail prices varied quite substantially. For example, a particular belt could be priced at three to four dollars in a general merchandise store, five to six dollars in a department store and six to eight dollars in a men's wear store. There was constant pressure on profits as raw material costs rose while competition forced prices downward.

All members of the sales force were paid 10 percent commission on sales. Eight company salesmen were located in Quebec. The other provinces were served by twenty-seven sales agents who handled clothing lines but not competing belt lines. There were eighteen sales agents in the West, eight in Ontario, and one in the Maritimes.

Each agent set his own call pattern. Five key members of the sales force regularly fed competitive and customer information back to Howard Grant, Jr., while the remainder reported only their monthly gross sales of belts. Howard saw his Montreal man twice a week and was in daily telephone contact with his Calgary agent and Ontario salesman. As soon as Superior received the orders, commissions were mailed to the sales agents. A monthly sales list was assembled to show sales by province and salesman. Typically, there was a period of three days between receipt of an order and the shipment of goods. Retailers usually paid their bills about two months after receipt of goods.

Howard Grant explained: "Beyond general yearly changes which are fixed to fashion changes, we change one style here about every ten days. We have to do this blind. That is, we hear rumours or we are given suggestions from industry associates, suppliers, and employees. If we think it will sell, we produce it and distribute it. As a result, we turned over 50 percent of our styles last year. This gave us a definite styling advantage."

In 1973, Superior had spent $14 000 on advertising in the national trade magazine *Elan* during the peak spring and fall buying seasons. In 1974 the company spent $20 000 in total on *Elan* and a trade show in New York City. As further promotion, dealers were offered a free belt rack if they ordered more than twenty-five belts at any time. Each belt rack cost about $20.

COMPETITION

Until 1973, there were only two companies manufacturing belts for sale to the retail market in Canada. Both were located in Montreal. Canada Belt Company Limited sold belts and women's accessories, while Arrow Manufacturing Limited sold belts only. The Grants believed that Canada Belt and Arrow had shared 80 percent of the retail belt market prior to 1973.

During 1973, retail sales of belts soared and twenty competitors entered the market. A fight ensued for the twenty key department stores and three thousand major outlets across Canada. According to the Grants, Canada Belt and Arrow reacted by selling belts on consignment, something that the smaller manufacturers could not afford. Howard Grant estimated that Canada Belt and Arrow belt sales at retail during 1974 were about $8 million and $7 million respectively.

SITUATION DECEMBER 1974

Howard Grant explained. "The company's objective is to make money. Maybe I'd sell it but only with sales and profits substantially higher. I'd like to move to a bigger building or meanwhile become more sophisticated business-wise, but I have run into some problems.

"The first is that some of my customers are grumbling about the elastic, the buckles and some of the leathers in my belts. What gets me is that they want the belts for nothing at the same time.

"The second is that we had exclusive rights to market a feather-edged belt early in 1974. We imported it from Indonesia. It was strictly top quality — sold in better men's and women's stores for $10. It was a good deal — we paid $18 a dozen for them landed in Montreal and sold them for $30 a dozen. I was ordering two thousand belts a month. Well, this was fine for a couple of months until a Boston firm bought the Indonesia firm. Without warning one hundred thousand similar belts were dumped into the Montreal area. I lost $75 000 on that little fiasco.

"The third thing was that I decided to try and tap the $300 million U.S. market. I had a deal with International Outlook Limited, a company which sold sunglasses in the United States. International Outlook was willing to add the Superior line exclusively beginning in July 1974. I was expecting U.S. sales of over $1.5 million for 1973. We sent them samples of our product so that they could choose the particular styles. Well, they copied our styles and set up their own manufacturing plant.

"The last thing is that during 1974 our sales went up to $2 000 000, our inventory to $300 000 and our receivables to $228 000; we are now in debt to the factors and the banks for about $537 000. They're all making noises about repayment. Our suppliers are threatening to put us on C.O.D. Our cash balance is zero. Our financial statements will not be ready for two months, given the state of our records. I do not know what is happening; we made no capital investments in 1974."

Exhibit 1
Superior Belt Limited
Statement of Earnings
for the Years Ended December 31, 1972 and 1973

	1973	1972
Sales	$1 157 495	$438 765
Cost of goods sold	738 175	$285 146
Gross profit	$419 320	$153 619
Operating expenses		
Selling	$165 405	$ 51 985
Administrative	144 157	67 031
	309 562	119 016
Earnings from operations	$109 758	$ 34 603
Provision for income taxes	45 645	8 644
Earnings before extraordinary item	$ 64 113	$ 25 959
Extraordinary item		
Loss on investments	(14 528)	(13 901)
Net earnings for the year	$ 49 585	$ 12 058

Exhibit 2
Superior Belt Limited
Schedule of Cost of Goods Sold
for the Years Ended December 31, 1972 and 1973

	1973	1972
Inventories, beginning of year	$ 45 018	$ 11 848
Purchases	737 918	186 654
Wages	167 477	91 941
Travelling and buying	4 878	—
	$ 955 291	$290 443
MANUFACTURING EXPENSES		
Rent	11 920	6 775
Insurance	4 028	2 320
Blocks and dies	7 703	2 637
Employees' wage levies	7 602	3 192
Health and vacation fund	10 642	8 087
Maintenance and repairs	873	3 540
Factory	10 847	3 172
Light and power	2 656	2 594
Depreciation — machinery	12 630	4 917
Depreciation — leasehold improvements	3 295	2 487
	$1 027 487	$330 164
Inventories, end of year	289 312	45 018
COST OF GOODS SOLD	$ 738 175	$285 146

Exhibit 3
Superior Belt Limited
Schedule of Expenses
for the Years Ended December 31, 1972 and 1973

	1973	1972
SELLING		
Commissions	$ 83 584	$24 609
Automotive	7 887	6 610
Selling and travelling	27 182	9 025
Advertising	14 563	1 031
Express and cartage	14 498	2 983
Shipping supplies	15 517	2 674
Depreciation — automotive	2 433	3 475
(Gain) loss on disposal of equipment	(259)	1 578
	$165 405	$51 985
ADMINISTRATIVE		
Management salaries	$ 30 220	$17 525
Office salaries	31 614	21 918
Office costs	9 365	3 281
Telephone and telegraph	9 017	5 621
Professional fees	6 916	3 605
Miscellaneous	2 241	3 038
Donations	830	140
Bad debts	7 565	5 495
Discounts allowed	10 874	2 781
Interests and bank charges	13 353	2 560
Depreciation — furniture and fixtures	3 403	1 067
Factory charges	18 759	—
	$144 157	$67 031

Exhibit 4
Superior Belt Limited
Balance Sheet
as at December 31, 1972 and 1973

A S S E T S

	1973	1972
CURRENT ASSETS		
Cash	$ 100	$ —
Accounts receivable — assigned to factor		
(after allowance for doubtful accounts)	334 449	136 191
Inventories, valued at the lower of cost		
and net realizable value	289 312	45 018
Loans receivable	1 620	806
Loans receivable — shareholders	5 931	—
Prepaid expenses	1 419	1 626
	$632 831	$183 641
EQUIPMENT — at cost		
Machinery	$113 635	$ 70 413
Furniture and fixtures	26 093	13 347
Automotive	11 585	11 585
Leasehold improvements	21 004	10 526
	$172 317	$105 871
Less: accumulated depreciation	90 097	68 595
Net equipment	82 220	37 276
TOTAL ASSETS	$715 051	$220 917

L I A B I L I T I E S

	1973	1972
CURRENT LIABILITIES		
Bank indebtedness	$ 89 527	$ 14 592
Loan payable — factor (secured)	205 959	—
Accounts payable and accrued liabilities	256 183	126 819
Income taxes payable	45 645	8 848
Liens payable — current portion	1 842	2 506
	$599 156	$152 765
Liens payable on equipment	2 512	5 018
Less: current portion	1 842	2 506
	670	2 512
TOTAL LIABILITIES	$599 826	$155 277

S H A R E H O L D E R S ' E Q U I T Y

	1973	1972
CAPITAL STOCK		
Authorized		
250 Preferred 5% noncumulative, redeemable		
shares, par value $100 each		
150 Common shares, par value $100 each		
Issued and fully paid		
200 Preferred shares	$ 20 000	$ 20 000
50 Common shares	5 000	5 000
Retained earnings	90 225	40 640
TOTAL EQUITY	115 225	65 640
TOTAL LIABILITIES AND EQUITY	$715 051	$220 917

Exhibit 5
Superior Belt Limited
Selected Data on Belt Manufacturing and Sale, 1973
Canadian Domestic Belt Production

	No. In Dozens	Value in $(000's)
1970	349 283	4094
1971	492 144	7599
1972	637 635	9296
1973	437 967	8089

Canadian Chain Store Retail Data, 1973

	No. of Organizations	No. of Stores
Department	36	531
General merchandise	20	1273
Men's clothing	36	465
Women's clothing	77	1269
Family clothing	38	584

Percentage Distribution of Chain Store Sales
(all Merchandise Categories) by Type, Location, and Size of Chains

By Type of Operations:	No.	Sales
Local chains	26.5%	4.6%
Provincial chains	41.4%	29.7%
National Chains	32.1%	65.7%
By Province:		
Ontario	45.0%	4.6%
Quebec	21.7%	20.4%
British Columbia	10.6%	12.4%
Alberta	7.8%	8.0%
By No. of Stores Operated:		
4-9	58.9%	9.4%
10-49	31.8%	18.3%
50-99	5.3%	11.4%
100+	4.0%	60.9%

68

The Used Book Store

In May 1981 Tim Leishman, Vice President Operations of the University Student Council, University of Western Ontario, was concerned about problems emerging from the student-operated Used Book store. Enrolment at the University was about 16,000 full-time students including nearly 4,000 freshmen. Tim knew that any changes to the present operation would have to be in effect before the start of the new academic year in early September.

THE USED BOOK STORE

The idea that students could save a considerable amount of money by buying used rather than new books was not a new one. For a number of years the Circle K club had operated a second-hand book sale at the beginning of the academic year on the University campus. During the late seventies, however, rapid increases in book prices had generated a demand for second-hand books as the difference between the cost of new and second-hand books became substantial. In 1979, anticipating a demand which would overwhelm the resources of the Circle K club, the University Student Council appointed a Used Book Store Commissioner who took over the job from the Circle K club.

As a student-run operation, the Used Book Store was charged with the responsibility to at least break even. Revenues in excess of costs were returned to the University Student Council. The purpose of the Used Book Store was not to make a profit but to provide a service to students. In this regard there were two groups of students to whom "service" was being provided: those who were selling books and those who were buying. In Tim Leishman's words, "there always has been, and always will be, an active trade in used books. Our job in providing the Used Book Store service is to make that transaction easier for students."

In 1979 and 1980 the Used Book Store operated more or less as it always had, though with large increases in the number of buyers and sellers. After the 1980 operation had closed down the verdict was that the service had operated at maximum capacity. There had been frequent long line-ups, storage space had barely been adequate, and the manual information system used to keep track of the transactions was too time-consuming.

As a service to students the Used Book Store had strong support. Many students felt that the service should be expanded to Summer School classes, Intersession classes, to the Winter semester in January, and maybe even to operate on a full-time basis.

THE EXISTING USED BOOK STORE OPERATION

Under the existing system a student who had books to sell would take them into the University Student Council Offices at the beginning of summer. A record would be made of the name of the student, the price to be charged (fixed by the student), the course for which the book was being used, and the name of the book. Books collected in this manner were stored wherever there was available space. The receiving operation was staffed by the full-time employees of the Student Council. It was Tim's opinion that these extra duties did not adversely affect the performance of the administrative staff nor did they resent the extra effort that was required. Continually increasing demand would, however, create problems.

After the Used Book Sale had taken place in early September, students who had deposited books could collect their money if the book had been sold less a commission of 12 percent.

PROBLEMS

The most obvious problem during the operation of the Used Book Store sale was that enormous line-ups developed. The space available, the Tower Room, was about 600 square feet and contained very large boardroom tables. The room filled up easily and there was considerable browsing as buyers weighed the various qualities and prices of books, considered which of their textbooks they would buy second-hand, located the books for their courses, and then completed the transaction record so that the student who had brought that book in could be compensated.

Because the University was in full operation during early September when the book sale was held, the possibility of easily obtaining more space was remote. In addition, more space would mean increased costs which would be reflected in increased commission charges. Similarly, any increase in staff to speed the recording of transactions would have the same effect.

Adequate space during the operation of the sale was not the only kind of space problem. Storing thousands of volumes prior to the sale was a continual headache. There was no organized catalogue of inventory, neither was there any designated space reserved for book storage. It was a question of cramming oddly sized boxes of books, identified in a variety of ways, by course, by title, etc., wherever there was some space. Because storage space and the Tower Room were in different locations on campus, moving book stocks was a problem. Both Tim Leishman and the Used Book Store Commissioner had investigated the possibility of securing storage space more conveniently located to the Tower Room. There was not, however, any storage space available.

The almost completely open acceptance policy on books for the sale also posed some difficulties for the Used Book Store. Although the intention was to accept course books only, this policy was applied very loosely. A great variety of reference and fiction books, for example, not on any course reading list were accepted and sold in the sale. A large number were not sold.

Textbook changes were difficult to handle for the Used Book Store, even in high-enrolment courses where the reading list was very predictable. New editions rendered the previous year's textbook useless. The Used Book Store had in the past accepted, stored, and in some cases sold the wrong edition in September before finding out about changes. In an effort to combat this particular problem, Tim Leishman had contacted Mr. Mason, the University Bookstore Manager, so that the Used Bookstore could be alerted when new reading lists were compiled during the summer for courses starting in September. Mr. Mason's response was that the Used Book Store was a useful facility to have on campus and that he would be pleased to help wherever possible. The present book ordering system, however, could not easily be modified to yield the information that the Used Book Store needed. It seemed to Tim that the most effective solution to the problem of textbook changes was to try to get course instructors to notify the Used Book Store when changes were made.

Many courses, however, had low enrolments, the content of course reading lists changed yearly, and the face value of the books were low. This meant that a large proportion of the books sorted prior to the Book Sale were low priced, not relevant for next year's courses, occupied a lot of storage and sale space, and were in a condition such that even though priced less than a new copy, the absolute difference was small enough that students bought their own.

Tim tried to evaluate the expansion alternatives of operating full-time all year round and extending service to other times of the year. Tim knew that without changes increased demand would overwhelm the current operation. Yet he was unsure as to what changes he should initiate with the Used Book Store Commissioner and in what direction the Used Book Store should be moving.

69

Wayfarer Products Ltd.

"From the first time I saw Graplin tent stakes, I was certain that they had potential," said Mr. Tom Kendall in the fall of 1971. "And although our last year has not been a very successful one financially, nothing has occurred to change my belief in the future of the product."

Mr. Tom Kendall was president of Wayfarer Products Ltd., a firm which he had incorporated in 1970 to manufacture and market a patented tent peg called Graplin. The patent for the product was held by the South African designer. Wayfarer had an agreement with him for the manufacture and sale of Graplin tent stakes in North America.

During Wayfarer's first year of operations, the company lost over $13 000 on sales of $4800. While sales for the current year were up substantially, Mr. Kendall predicted that even greater losses would result in 1972.

THE CAMPING EQUIPMENT INDUSTRY — THE TENT STAKE MARKET

During the previous twenty years, the camping equipment industry had undergone dramatic expansion. Although the available statistics of camping growth were general, substantial evidence existed to document the market's growth. Exhibit 1 shows the number of overnight stays by campers in the U.S. National Park System for 1950 through 1968, while Exhibit 2 presents similar information for the State Park System. Exhibit 3 presents data on tent sales in Canada.

Although the figures in these exhibits do not show either primary or secondary tent stake sales, general industry growth was apparent. Best estimates in 1967 placed tent stake sales in North America at thirty-three million units (twenty-two million original equipment and eleven million replacement stakes). While increasing trailer and pick-up camper sales during the latter half of the 1960s slowed the growth of tent stake sales, the more recent emphasis on hiking equipment and the use of auxiliary shelters gave new impetus to tent stake prospects. Standard and Poor's industry survey, *Amusement*, described the U.S. camping market as follows: "The camping market is currently one of the most dynamic in American business." The survey projected 1969 consumer purchases of tents at $83 400 000 in the U.S., up from $60 500 000 in 1964.

The major tent manufacturers in North America were located in the U.S. with four companies reportedly supplying 35 percent of the new tent market. Original equipment manufacturers looked for several features in the tent stakes they purchased: quality, appearance, safety, cost, and producer stability, with cost and stability of supply ranking as the key factors.

In the secondary market the individual camper was influenced by appearance and the word of other campers. They looked for durability and safety but seemed reluctant to pay an excessive premium for these features. The purchases were seasonal, often spur of the moment, and usually with little product loyalty. Wholesale purchases were made between January and June and retail purchases between February and August. Original equipment purchases remained relatively stable year round.

Small firms in the business of equipment rental purchased tent stakes in large quantities. Other uses included anchors for mobile and prefabricated homes, military uses, and farm uses such as temporary grain storage under tarpaulins. Potential uses for Graplins included tension structures covering swimming pools, tennis courts, and skating rinks, as well as portable garages. Many of these applications required larger stakes than those used for ordinary tents.

Government influenced several factors key to tent stake sales, including the development of new camp grounds, grants for the development of new products, government and military purchases, currency exchange rates, tariffs, and export and market development assistance. These were all factors influencing the operations of a small company competing in the North American market.

Three broad product types competed for the tent stake market — wood, metal, and plastic — each with distinct price and performance characteristics. While some of the major tent manufacturers owned captive operations which produced their own pegs, most purchased their stake requirements from specialty producers. The specialty producers were material oriented and usually sold a number of products made from the same material and using the same basic process. For example, producers of wood stakes also made pallets, specialized shelving, and cabinets, while those producing lightweight metal pegs used the same production equipment to fabricate automotive parts, components for the appliance industry, and miscellaneous metal products for households and industry. Few of Wayfarer's competitors were dependent on the production of tent stakes for a large portion of their business.

WAYFARER PRODUCTS LTD. — THE COMPANY

Wayfarer was incorporated early in 1970 to produce and market a revolutionary new tent stake known as the Graplin. The product was developed in the late 1950s in South Africa[1] and had attained a market share of over 70 percent in that country. The inventor, a Mr. Calhoun, anxious to have the product introduced into the North American market, contacted the Department of Industry in Ottawa and listed it for Canadian licence in 1966.

At that time, Mr. Kendall was employed by Niagara Steel Products. Part of his job responsibility was the identification and development of new products for Niagara. He noticed the information on Graplin in a Department of Industry publication advertisement and followed up on this lead. In 1969, after two years of correspondence and a visit by Mr. Calhoun, Niagara obtained a licence to produce and market Graplins in North American. Niagara, in turn, had reached an agreement with Canadian Coleman whereby that firm would have exclusive rights to service the Canadian replacement market until mid-1972. In return, Coleman agreed to purchase a minimum of 300 000 Graplins prior to that date. Niagara produced the 300 000 Graplins immediately. Part of this production run was shipped to Coleman. The rest was inventoried for future delivery.

---

[1]The product had been tested and ued by the military and this market had been extremely important in the initial development of the product.

A short time later, Niagara encountered major operating problems and, in an effort to curtail increasing costs, product and market development of all new products, including Graplin, was discontinued. This change in plan by Niagara abrogated the company's agreement with Mr. Calhoun.

Mr. Kendall, who had great faith in the potential of Graplin, contacted Mr. Calhoun about obtaining the North American licence. Mr. Calhoun was enthusiastic and in a short time the two men reached an agreement that resulted in the formation of Wayfarer Products by Mr. Kendall. Mr. Calhoun provided major financing for the new firm. Mr. Kendall, however, retained control.

Canadian Coleman retained the exclusive rights to the Canadian replacement market until mid-1972. Wayfarer Products would supply any Graplins required beyond the 300 000 in Canadian Coleman's original agreement. Aside from this, the firm had the exclusive rights to the manufacture and sale of Graplins in North America.

At its inception, Mr. Kendall had no well-defined objectives for the firm. It was his belief that he should be seeking to replace competitive products, though he was aware that this was likely to take considerable time. Both Mr. Kendall and Mr. Calhoun agreed that maintenance of their ownership position was important.

Several months after the new company was formed, Mr. Kendall resigned from his job at Niagara Steel Products. At the same time he purchased substantial production equipment including dies and fixtures for Graplin from Niagara Steel Products.

THE PRODUCT

The patent protecting Graplin covered the design and the principle upon which it worked. The Graplin worked on a very simple principle whereby the tension at the hook was transferred through the resilient shoulder to the entire length of the shank in such a manner that the shank seeks a firmer hold when under strain rather than pulling over. This feature, coupled with its unique surface arm that "gives" to compensate for shrinking guy ropes or buffeting winds, insured that once erected the tent needed no further attention (Exhibit 4).

The Graplin was easy to insert and remove. Its ground level profile was safe against tripping, and the "give" feature was effective under a variety of weather conditions. The product, which could be made in a variety of sizes, was currently offered only in the 22.5 cm size.[1] Since this was by far the most popular tent peg, Wayfarer had not purchased tools to mass produce other sizes.

PRODUCTION

Graplins were made from high-carbon, high-tensile steel. Stelco was the only Canadian supplier of the steel and because custom production of many sizes of steel rods was required, Stelco had a 45 tonne minimum order size for each diameter of steel rod. For a 22.5 cm Graplin, the minimum steel order was the equivalent of 65 000 stakes

The steel rod was purchased in lengths adequate for producing two Graplins. The

---

[1]Mr. Kendall estimated that 65 to 70 percent of the tent stake market could be served with the 22.5 cm Graplin.

material was delivered to Brantford Stampers where it was cut in two. The cut, made at a 45° angle, provided a sharp point which permitted easy insertion into the ground. These blanks were than shipped to Wayfarer's facilities, located in rented space at the rear of Patrick's Iron Works in Hespeler, Ontario.

The Wayfarer process was centred around a 40 tonne Toledo horn press with dies and fixtures for producing the Graplin. The process also included a heat-treating unit. The precut blanks were fed into an air-activated feed chute, three at a time. From here the blanks were placed into a forming die that gave the Graplin its shape. As the press ram rose, the formed blanks were ejected onto a slanted rail which allowed the blanks to slide into a gas-fired furnace. This process added strength and resilience to the elbow of the Graplin, permitting it to regain its original shape after it had been under stress. The heat-treated pieces dropped off the end of the heat-treating unit into a work in process rack holding approximately 160 units.

The formed parts were rustproofed and painted before removal to the packing area. The parts were removed from the in-process racks six at a time, taped in bundles of six and placed in boxes, two bundles to each. The display boxes were placed in a carton and then palletized for storage.[1]

Since the equipment was not operating at capacity, Mr. Kendall did not schedule the plant operations nor did he feel it necessary to develop any complex system for inventory control.

MARKETING

Due to some delay in the start of production, Mr. Kendall was unable to begin selling the Graplin stake until early 1971 and, as a result, missed the major sales of the 1971 camping season. Mr. Kendall's current attention was focused on obtaining distribution throughout the United States in the replacement market. In Canada, Coleman had included the item in their catalogue and had advertised the product extensively, though they did not require all Coleman dealers to carry it. By late 1971, Wayfarer had received only a few small orders from Coleman.

In the United States, Mr. Kendall was working to establish three types of distribution: (1) direct selling to tent manufacturers; (2) direct selling to distributors; and (3) the use of manufacturers' representatives. The latter two serviced the replacement market through dealers. Mr. Kendall felt that manufacturers' representatives would provide the best coverage since they had to live on commission. In addition, because the Graplin was a radically different product, selling it required direct and frequent contact with the dealers.

1. Pricing

Sales to the tent manufacturers in both Canada and the United States were difficult because of price. Prior to 1970, some of the largest producers had switched to plastic from wood and had paid a premium for the new product. However, since Mr. Kendall's original study of the market in 1970, prices in plastic stakes had dropped over

---

[1]Subsequently the rustproofing operation was eliminated by using galvanized stock.

40 percent. Tent manufacturers in the U.S. had looked at the Graplin but felt that the added cost of this product in the tent pack would make the total product noncompetitive. The addition of Graplin would not, in the opinion of most, influence many consumers to select their product.

Price was also an important factor in the replacement market. Exhibit 5 shows the pricing structure in this market. Many retailers believed that customers were unwilling to pay a premium price for tent stakes and planned their inventory accordingly. Retail margins for all stakes varied between 40 and 50 percent. Wayfarer had recently quoted Coleman a price of 5.5 cents per stake. Coleman, in turn, sold to dealers at $1.50 per dozen and the retail price varied between $2.66 and $2.99 per dozen.

Tariffs and shipping charges associated with selling into the United States market from Canada amounted to from 17 to 20 percent of Wayfarer's selling price. Mr. Kendall felt that U.S. facilities might be required if a major market breakthrough was achieved. However, he was reluctant to invest further in facilities until the product gained a degree of market acceptance.

2. Advertising

Because the Graplin was radically different from competitive products, Mr. Kendall believed that the consumer had to be convinced that the product would work and that it was worth the premium price. At the same time, he was reluctant to spend his limited funds on consumer advertising. As an alternative, he was working on the development of word of mouth communication to develop consumer knowledge and interest in the product. In this respect, he visited campgrounds and handed out samples, provided samples to the Boy Scouts and other camping groups, and did some dealer-oriented advertising in the trade sporting publications.

In an effort to demonstrate the Graplin, Mr. Kendall had promoted it at such events as the International Plowing Matches, the National Hikers and Campers Association, and various camping and sporting goods shows. While such exposure had not yet resulted in significant sales, Mr. Kendall felt that it was important in the long-run development of the product.

ACCOUNTING AND FINANCE

Mr. Kendall summed up the finance and accounting aspect of Wayfarer as "an area I know very little about." However, since pricing was important, Mr. Kendall had attempted to develop realistic costs, but the lack of good information made accurate costing difficult. The information in Exhibits 6 and 7 was used in his calculations.

Mr. Kendall had been approached by the stamping company with a subcontract that involved $1 000 per year space rental plus $4.75 per hour for labour. Mr. Kendall currently paid $2.75 per hour for labour but, unlike the subcontract arrangement, his current labour cost was not totally variable. Manufacture of some of the large-size pegs used on various structures was currently subcontracted.

Wayfarer had no cost system, and its accounting procedures were set up by the auditors. The most recent statements, as prepared by the auditors, appear as Exhibits 8, 9, and 10.

WAYFARER MANAGEMENT

After one year as an incorporated company, Wayfarer consisted basically of Mr. Kendall. And while he contemplated hiring a part-time bookkeeper-secretary to facilitate his absence from the office, no other additions seemed necessary. In the plant there were two part-time employees, but even here substantial sales increases were required to justify permanent employment for the workers.

Mr. Kendall's chief concern and interest lay in the area of marketing. He was aware that major improvements in production in terms of both capacity and cost reduction could be effected, but until sales were increased, any internal improvements would only add to his unutilized capacity. Financing the inception and growth of Wayfarer was also singled out as a potential problem, but thus far Mr. Kendall had not given it much attention. He personally felt that a ten percent return on his investment was more than adequate and both he and his principal in South Africa were more interested in penetrating the North American camping equipment market with a product they believed was a substantial improvement over anything else available. On the subject of ownership, Mr. Kendall felt that both he and Mr. Calhoun preferred to maintain control until the potential of Wayfarer could be more realistically appraised. Certainly, any future outside investors would not get controlling interest in the company if Mr. Kendall could help it, though this stance would be reconsidered if the owners felt that such outside involvement was the only way to success. A number of vital issues faced Mr. Kendall. How could Wayfarer break into the original equipment and replacement markets? What overall strategy had the highest probability of success? Should the company consider contracting out production of the Graplin in both the U.S. and Canada to save on shipping costs and get around the tariffs involved in shipping into the U.S. market? Should he be volume pricing to get an order from one of the major original equipment producers or should his concentration be on the replacement market where prices seemed somewhat less important? Should he be concerned about the company's ability to finance the period of market development, and did the various alternatives facing the company make any significant difference to the probability of Wayfarer's success?

The major concern was summed up when Mr. Kendall stated that he and Wayfarer could last for some time if the approach to the market was low key and evolutionary. In this situation, almost all of his costs could be kept variable. However, he was unsure about the ultimate impact of such an approach in a rapidly growing market. Even the product patent raised some questions. Neither he nor Mr. Calhoun was completely sure that it would stand up in a court of law and both were certain that they wanted no part of a long, high-cost court battle to protect the patent. This led Mr. Kendall to his second option, which involved quick penetration of the market at a reasonable price. This, he felt, would remove the possibility of other producers jumping on the bandwagon.

"I also am aware," said Mr. Kendall, "that Wayfarer, small as it is, has numerous options aside from Graplin. We could be developing other products for the camping market, for example, though I don't really see that I will have time for this kind of activity until Graplin is off the ground and running. At the same time, perhaps I should be exploring some of these choices in greater depth than I have to date, because some of them may have important implications for the company and my own future."

Exhibit 1
Wayfarer Products Ltd.
Overnight Stays by Campers in U.S. National Park System

Year Ending June 30	*Camping Nights*
1950	2 231 000
1955	3 275 000
1960	4 846 000
1965	8 085 000
1966	9 000 000
1967	9 314 000
1968	10 967 000

Source: Statistical Abstract of the United States, 1969.

Exhibit 2
Wayfarer Products Ltd.
Overnight Stays by Campers in U.S. State Park System (000's)

	1950	1955	1959	1960	1961	1962	1967
Total overnight visits	6 079	11 057	17 994	20 569	22 999	24 050	36 244
Organized camps overnight stays	1 480	1 697	2 096	2 235	2 206	2 249	2 055
Tent and trailer overnight stays	3 377	7 650	13 734	16 217	18 563	18 753	31 839

Source: Statistical Abstract of the United States, 1969.

Exhibit 3
Wayfarer Products Ltd.
Tents Manufactured and Shipped in Canada

	1962		1964		1966		1968		1970	
	Quantity	Value $000's	Quantity	Value $000's	Quantity	Value $000's	Quantity	Value $000's	Quantity	Value $000's
Regular tourist	55 044	1 372	36 043	1 276	54 420	1 710	76 747	2 195	NA	1 233
Cottage or cabin style	21 129	1 067	32 300	1 750	21 426	991	25 330	1 025	NA	1 269
Standard wall	4 163	188	5 677	309	8 333	295	NA	NA	NA	NA
Trailer tents	NA	NA	NA	NA	NA	NA	NA	2 124	NA	2 419
Hiker or children's play tent	NA	NA	NA	NA	NA	NA	15 707	192	NA	237
Other domestic	13 970	601	25 665	934	22 666	1 101	18 914	640	NA	842

Source: Dominion Bureau of Statistics, *Canvas Products Industry*, Catalogue No. 34-202.

Exhibit 4
Wayfarer Products Ltd.

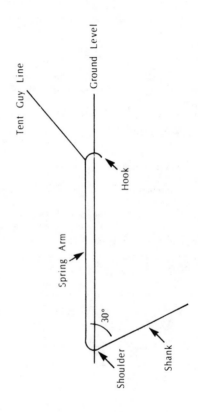

Exhibit 5
Wayfarer Products Ltd.
1971 Canadian Prices for Tent Stakes

Type of Stake[1]	Factory Selling Price of 1000[2]	Wholesale Selling Price Dozen	Retail Selling Price Dozen
Wayfarer	60.00	1.49	2.98
Wood	34.00	.60	1.19
Metal — Light sheet	21.00	.36	.69
— Die cast	55.00	.85	1.99
Plastic — Lightweight	32.00	.56	1.09
— Heavyweight	50.00	.80	1.79

[1]These were approximate prices for stakes competitive with the 22.5 cm Graplin.
[2]While the factory selling price could be reduced on extremely large orders, the prices shown are approximately what the original equipment producers were paying for tent stake supplies.

Exhibit 6
Wayfarer Products Ltd.
Labour Productivity Data

	Hours Per 1000 Pieces	Capacity
Forming	.670	1 500 units/hour
Heat treating	.670	1 500 units/hour
Packing	1.735	2 000 units/hour
Storage and material handling (no estimate)		

Exhibit 7
Wayfarer Products Ltd.
Material Cost per 1 000 Pieces (Model 9190A — 22.5 cm Graplin)

Steel galvanized	$20.00	
Point of sale, display box	6.50	
Carton	.84	
Pallets	1.00	
Polyethylene	.06	
Strapping	.25	
TOTAL		$28.65
Indirect items:		
Cut and clean	$ 2.50	
Propane gas	1.00	3.50
TOTAL		$32.15

Exhibit 8
Wayfarer Products Ltd.
Balance Sheet as of May 31, 1971

ASSETS — CURRENT		
Cash	$ 5 830	
Accounts receivable — trade	2 253	
Sales tax refundable	193	
Inventory	2 050	
Prepaid expenses	50	$10 376
ASSETS — FIXED		
Plant and equipment	$12 253	
Dies (at cost)	1 066	
Automobile (at cost)	3 325	
Office equipment	686	
	$17 330	
Less: accumulated depreciation	4 262	13 068
OTHER ASSETS AT COST		
Incorporation	$ 655	
Trademark	203	858
TOTAL		$24 302
LIABILITIES — CURRENT		
Accounts payable	$ 2 902	
Royalties payable	104	
Advances from shareholders	4 350	$ 7 356
EQUITY		
Preference stock (27 953 issued)	$27 953	
Common stock (4000 shares)	1 998	
	$29 951	
Operating deficit	(13 005)	16 946
TOTAL LIABILITIES AND EQUITY		$24 302

Exhibit 9
Wayfarer Products Ltd.
Statement of Earnings for the Year Ending May 31, 1971

Sales		$ 4 806
Cost of sales		
Inventory (beginning)	$ —	
Purchases	5 084	
Inventory	2 050	3 034
Gross profit		$ 1 772
Expenses		
Salary[1]	$2 000	
Bank charges	10	
Legal fees	1 241	
Automobile expenses	1 554	
Telephone	541	
Freight	555	
Office expenses	564	
Promotion and display	2 717	
Sales commission	40	
Travel	1 311	
Postage	200	
Repairs and maintenance	148	
Life insurance	359	
Royalties	104	
Depreciation	4 262	15 606
Operating loss		($13 834)
Miscellaneous income		829
Net loss for the period		($13 005)

[1]Mr. Kendall's wife had a full-time job and this enabled him to draw a minimum salary from the firm.

Exhibit 10
Wayfarer Products Ltd.

ANCHOR YOUR TENT WITH

the Patented

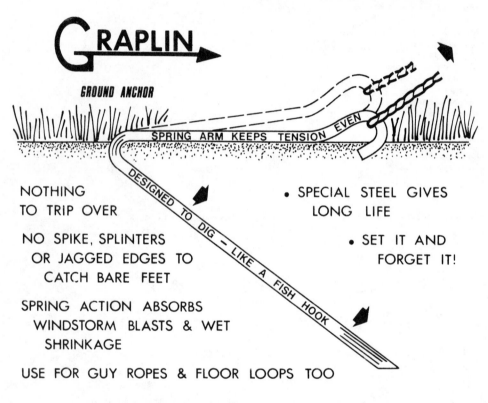

G RAPLIN

GROUND ANCHOR

SPRING ARM KEEPS TENSION EVEN

DESIGNED TO DIG – LIKE A FISH HOOK

NOTHING
TO TRIP OVER

NO SPIKE, SPLINTERS
OR JAGGED EDGES TO
CATCH BARE FEET

SPRING ACTION ABSORBS
WINDSTORM BLASTS & WET
SHRINKAGE

USE FOR GUY ROPES & FLOOR LOOPS TOO

• SPECIAL STEEL GIVES
LONG LIFE

• SET IT AND
FORGET IT!

HOLDS AFTER STRAIGHT STAKES HAVE QUIT

WAYFARER

CAMPING PRODUCTS LTD.

Exhibit 11
Wayfarer Products Ltd.

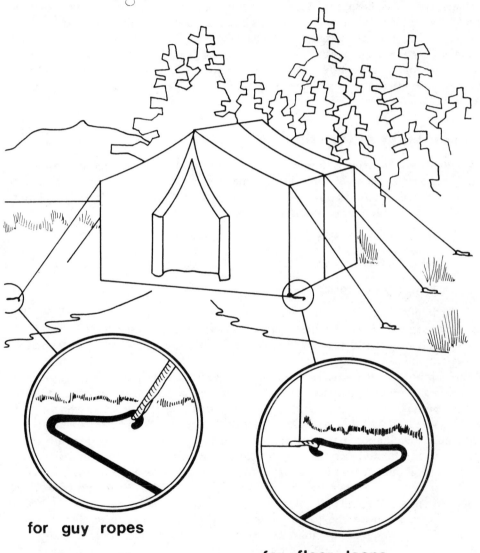

this is how it works

for guy ropes

for floor loops

SECTION IX

An Introduction to Business Decision Making
in a Broader Context

All too many people believe that nonbusiness organizations cannot benefit from an application of business decision-making skills and experiences. On the contrary, time and again charities, hospitals, churches, museums, and so on have discovered that the ideas discussed in previous sections of this book can be used to their advantage. However, it should be emphasized that decision making in nonprofit and nonbusiness organizations is not entirely the same as in business organizations. The purpose here is to outline some of these differences and similarities. A number of nonprofit and non-business case situations to challenge you are found in the previous sections. (See, for example, cases 18, 44, 54, 63, and 68.)

PERFORMANCE EVALUATION

One of the most notable differences between business profit-oriented organizations and other organizations is found in the objectives of the organization. Most profit-oriented organizations are obviously seeking profit and growth. Nonprofit and non-business organizations have other objectives such as:

> An art museum: "to collect, preserve and present contemporary art"
> A church: "to serve God"
> A blood donor clinic: "to meet the blood and blood-related needs of local hospitals"
> A political campaign group: "to get John elected"
> A charity: "to raise $100 000"

The implication of these different objectives is that performance evaluation will be against unusual — to the business person — objectives. Nonetheless, the exercise of setting goals and objectives to guide activities and later against which to assess performance remains as valid as for a profit-oriented organization assessing its performance.

In a profit-oriented organization, the management and shareholders are the principal assessors of performance. Of course employees, customers, suppliers, and others also have a stake in the organization's performance and thus have performance expectations as well. In a nonbusiness or nonprofit organization, frequently we can think of performance evaluation in two ways: (a) how well did the organization do in attracting the resources it needed (fund raising, etc.) and (b) how well did the organization do in using or allocating the resources it had (efficiency and effectiveness of activities, etc.). These questions arise when the organization is thought of as between two external groups: donors and clients, as shown in the diagram in Figure 1.

Actually, of course, the donor group and the client group may consist of several groups. For example, donors may be local government, business organizations, private individuals, etc. Not only will the organization be assessing its performance in terms of how well it obtained and used resources, but also its donors and clients will be assessing its activities. It is on this basis that one charity gets more money than another or one museum gets more audience than another. These kinds of organizations thus compete with one another in a different kind of market place, with different kinds of accountability for performance.

Figure 1
Conceptual Diagram of a Nonbusiness Organization

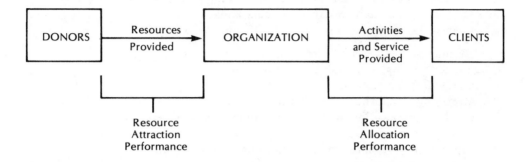

FINANCIAL MANAGEMENT

Nonprofit and nonbusiness organizations are similar to profit-oriented organizations in their need to manage money. The abilities and systems of people faced with this task in nonprofit and nonbusiness organizations are widely varying — some are extremely sophisticated (such as major hospitals) and others are extremely crude (such as some community groups). The concepts of accounting and financial statement preparation discussed earlier apply, though naturally the names of some of the accounts vary and the income statement typically looks more like a cash-flow statement. The goal of financial management of a nonprofit enterprise will be directed to gaining maximum benefits rather than profits for cash used.

Because nonprofit and nonbusiness organizations generally operate close to or below break-even, financial management is often highly related to fund-raising. Skills in obtaining grants from governments and so on may explain an individual's title as "treasurer" more than his or her ability to look after the financial records.

HUMAN RESOURCES MANAGEMENT

One finds the same entire range of human resources and industrial relations problems in nonprofit and nonbusiness organizations as in profit-oriented organizations. If anything, the range of problems found is broader. The Red Cross may be wondering how to attract volunteers, the Big Brother organization how to attract and keep Big Brothers, and a community group wrestling with the question of who's in charge of what, while a hospital worries about a threatened walkout by some of its employees. Frequently, the two most difficult human resources questions in medium-sized and small nonprofit and nonbusiness organizations are (a) how to motivate when money is not available, and (b) who should make what decisions.

MARKETING MANAGEMENT

Profit-oriented organizations seek and serve customers; nonprofit and nonbusiness organizations seek and serve clients. The former does market analysis and the latter audience analysis. Yet, fundamentally, all the principles and techniques discussed in the marketing section apply. This difference in jargon is more than just habit. Many nonprofit and nonbusiness individuals distrust and dislike the words and notions of marketing, advertising, selling, promoting, and so on. Interestingly, these marketing notions when properly translated and applied to nonprofit and nonbusiness organizations have resulted in many instances in remarkable improvements in organizational performance. The translation is not that difficult; for example:

consumer analysis → audience analysis
product offering → service, idea, benefits offering
price → fee, charge, cost to client
advertising → information provided
distribution →location, network, or people providing benefits
salespeople → volunteers
competition → reasons why audience might not respond
market share → proportion of potential clients reached

In other words, there is great potential for the use of marketing concepts and techniques in these organizations.

PRODUCTION/OPERATIONS MANAGEMENT

In most instances, the raison d'être of a nonprofit or nonbusiness organization is to take money and human resources provided and transform those resources into needed and wanted services, ideas, and activities. Accordingly, P/OM concepts and techniques are exceedingly useful to management. For example: university administrators can use scheduling techniques in the assignment of custodial services to various buildings and facilities as well as in deriving class and time schedules based on student demand and faculty staffing constraints. A Boy Scout Apple Day director can use layout, inventory, and other principles in his planning. A Goodwill director can use batch process concepts in deciding how to handle inflows of used clothing and household items. P/OM understanding often spells the difference between being able to provide the services desired given limited resources and not being able to do so.

GENERAL MANAGEMENT

All of the above suggests that nonprofit and nonbusiness organizations also need to be managed. Strategies can and should be developed to attract and use resources, objectives set and used to assess performance, and, above all, decision choices carefully analyzed to ensure the viability and success of the organization. Many organizations we have examined would benefit greatly from an improved understanding of concepts such as "distinctive competence" so that they might focus their efforts more meaningfully. Managing a nonprofit or a nonbusiness organization can be just as challenging and just as rewarding as a profit-oriented organization. A nonprofit manager once commented on this by saying, "It is more difficult to get someone to give a dollar than to spend a dollar."